45,00
90€

JEWISH MYSTICISM

GARLAND REFERENCE LIBRARY
OF SOCIAL SCIENCE
(VOL. 210)

JEWISH MYSTICISM
An Annotated Bibliography on the Kabbalah in English

Sheila A. Spector

GARLAND PUBLISHING, INC. • NEW YORK & LONDON
1984

© 1984 Sheila A. Spector
All rights reserved

Library of Congress Cataloging in Publication Data
Spector, Sheila A., 1946–
Jewish mysticism.

(Garland reference library of social science ;
vol. 210)
Includes indexes.
1. Cabala—Bibliography.   2. Mysticism—Judaism—
Bibliography.   3. Hasidism—Bibliography.
I. Title.   II. Series: Garland reference
library of social science ; v. 210.
Z6371.C2S67   1984 [BM526]   016.2961'6   83-48224
ISBN 0-8240-9042-X (alk. paper)

Printed on acid-free, 250-year-life paper
Manufactured in the United States of America

לחיים וברכה

CONTENTS

Introduction	xi
A. *Festschriften* and Other Analyzed Collections	3
B. General Reference Works	
Bibliographies	19
Encyclopedias and Dictionaries	21
Histories	27
C. Introductory Surveys	
Primary Sources	45
Secondary Sources	51
D. Topics in Jewish Mysticism	
Critical Approaches	67
Magic	
Primary Sources	68
Secondary Sources	70
Messianism	
Primary Source	74
Secondary Sources	74
God and Creation	80
Emanations and the Concept of the *Sefirot*	82
The Problem of Evil	83
Man and His Soul	85
Torah	87
The Mystic Way	
Primary Source	89
Secondary Sources	89

Myth and Symbol	94
Prophecy and Apocalyptic	98
Psychology	99

The History of Kabbalah

E. Antecedents
- Primary Sources — 109
- Secondary Sources — 114

F. Merkabah Mysticism and Jewish Gnosticism
- Primary Sources — 131
- Secondary Sources — 135

G. Medieval Ḥasidism
- Primary Sources — 151
- Secondary Sources — 152

H. The Crystallization of the Kabbalah
- Primary Sources — 159
- Secondary Sources — 161

I. The Zohar
- Primary Sources — 170
- Secondary Sources — 173

J. Isaac Luria and His School
- Primary Sources — 177
- Secondary Sources — 178

K. Sabbateanism and Mystical Heresy
- Primary Sources — 186
- Secondary Sources — 187

L. Ḥasidism
- Primary Sources — 197
- Secondary Sources — 213

M. The Latest Phase
    Primary Sources   255
    Secondary Sources   258

N. Major Scholars
    Leo Baeck   293
    Martin Buber   294
    Abraham Joshua Heschel   304
    Gershom G. Scholem   305

O. Non-Jewish Kabbalah
    Primary Sources   309
    Secondary Sources   313

Index
    Primary Materials   359
    Authors   367
    Subjects   386

INTRODUCTION

Traditionally, an air of secrecy has surrounded Jewish mysticism. According to the ancient sages, only one in four was capable of assimilating this "dangerous knowledge," the other three running the risk of apostasy, madness or even death.[1] But one danger which the sages did not foresee, one which resulted directly from their attempts to keep Kabbalah secret, was the transmission of inaccurate or erroneous information. Before the advent of the printing press, it was relatively easy to keep this knowledge secret. Few Jews recorded their visions, and those who did could feel secure that these mystical testimonies would only be transmitted to the adept, those worthy of exploring this knowledge.[2] However, mass production of texts, along with an awakened interest in Hebrew among Christians, made it difficult to protect the secret knowledge. In addition, apostates eager to ingratiate themselves with their new co-religionists frequently reported the "absurdities" of Kabbalah in order to slander the Jews. Consequently, throughout history, a number of contradictory, conflicting, sometimes ridiculous, accounts of Kabbalah have been printed, and because until this century, the Jews themselves refrained from writing about what many, like Abram Sachar, considered a "perversion" (B65), it was virtually impossible to tell which accounts, if any, represented the true mysticism of the Jews.

To further complicate the matter, Christian occultists adopted aspects of Kabbalah for their own mystical systems.[3] While originally, these borrowings remained relatively close to their Jewish prototypes, in time, the Christian versions developed in their own directions, often to the point that their Jewish origins are unrecognizable, except that they retain the name "Kabbalah." And eventually, believing the word Kabbalah (or "Cabala," "Qabalah," etc.) to be a generic label for the knowledge or rites of any kind of secret society, occultists began to call works having nothing at all to do with Kabbalism—either Jewish or Christian—Kabbalah, so that texts wholly unrelated to our topic represented the mysticism of the Jews to the popular mind.

The history of English Kabbalah reflects just this confusion. It was not until almost two hundred years after the first book purportedly dealing with Kabbalah (Cornelius Agrippa's *Three Books of Occult Philosophy*, 1651 [01]), was published in English that a Jew, Morris J. Raphall, wrote on the subject in English, and his article, "Cabbala" (C21), is only a brief, eight-page survey of the history of Kabbalah and the doctrine of the *Sefirot*. Another century was to elapse before Gershom G. Scholem wrote his *Major Trends in Jewish Mysticism* (C45), the ground-breaking study which finally provided historically accurate information about Jewish mysticism for the English reader. However, in the period between Agrippa and Scholem, the presses did not remain still. English Kabbalah has a long and rich history of publications purporting to deal with Jewish mysticism. The only problem is that before those published in this century, none relied on Jewish sources, and authorial intention not withstanding, none accurately reflects the mysticism of the Jews. Instead, English literature developed its own tradition of Kabbalah, a kind of Christianized Jewish mysticism which was erroneously attributed to the Jews. For this reason, a bibliography of the Kabbalah in English does *not* reflect Jewish mysticism per se, but rather, that which Englishmen believed Kabbalah to be, a field best approached both from the perspective of the history of Jewish mysticism, and the development of Christian Kabbalah.

Etymologically, the word Kabbalah derives from the Hebrew *kabel*, "to receive," signifying the traditional knowledge of the Jews. According to legend, at Creation God endowed Adam with immense stores of knowledge which, as a result of the Fall, our first father lost. Then, in order to console Adam for his loss, the Godhead sent the angel Raziel down to instruct man on the ways by which he could be redeemed. Adam passed the knowledge on to Seth who, in turn, delivered it to Enos, on through Enoch, Noah, Abraham, Isaac, Jacob, Moses, and David and Solomon, considered to be the wisest of men. But because of his sins, Solomon lost much of this knowledge, and from then on, as the hidden truths were delivered to Jehoiakim, Malachi, Ezra, and so on, the information was gradually diminished so that we have received only a small portion of the teachings of Raziel.

Actually, the development of Kabbalism is far different.[4] While technically, the word Kabbalah refers to the movement of Jewish mysticism begun around the twelfth century in Provence, it is frequently generalized to denote the entire history of Jewish mysticism, though we are uncertain of its origins. Historically, the existence of mystical societies has only been traced back to the time of the Second Temple, but in part as a result of

Introduction   *xiii*

information gleaned from the Dead Sea Scrolls, scholars are now investigating the possibility that the mystical strain can be found throughout Jewish history, biblical as well as post-biblical. Even though the apocalyptic and prophecy are not necessarily mystical, some of these biblical and apocryphal treatises evince antecedents of the mysticism which was to appear during the time of Christ. Consequently, the line of demarcation between Christianity and Jewish mysticism is being reexamined from the perspective that Christianity began not as a separate movement but as one of the many Jewish sects prevalent at the time.

The earliest form of Jewish mysticism, labeled by Scholem "Merkabah Mysticism and Jewish Gnosticism," lasted roughly from the first century B.C. to the tenth A.D., a period long enough to witness a flowering—during which time mystics produced *The Greater and Lesser Heikhalot,* and ultimate degeneration—as seen in the *Alphabet of Rabbi Akiba* and *The Midrash of the Ten Martyrs.* If at its height, Merkabah mysticism was a secret school of Gnosis which required high moral qualifications of its initiates, at its lowest, it deteriorated into pure magic and moral criticism of others.

The earliest phase, *Merkabah Mysticism* (contemplation of Ezekiel's chariot), is represented by the *Heikhalot* literature which describes the ascent—paradoxically termed as a descent—of the Throne of Glory through the seven heavens, the purpose of which is to perceive Supernal Man, the One seated on the Throne (see F48, F83). Supernal Man himself became the object of contemplation, the *Shi'ur Komah* providing great detail about "the measure of the body" (F27). In addition to *ma'aseh merkabah,* mystics of this period also contemplated *ma'aseh bereshit,* Creation, producing the *Sefer Yetzirah* (Book of Creation), one of the most popular kabbalistic texts (F2, F4, F5, F9, F12, F25). A brief work of less than two thousand words in its longer version, the *Sefer Yetzirah* (author and date of composition unknown) explains cosmology and cosmogony in terms of the thirty-two paths of wisdom, and the twenty-two letters of the Hebrew alphabet, said to be the basis of Creation. The last part of this period is characterized by an interest in angelology and theurgy. In addition, *gilgul,* transmigration of souls, became an established part of Jewish mysticism, as did Gematria, numerological practices used to discover mystical meanings of the Sacred Names.

This period was followed by the Ḥasidic movements, primarily in Germany and Egypt, which lasted roughly from 1150 to 1250. Influenced variously by early *Merkabah* mysticism, Neo-Platonism, and occultism (derived from both earlier Jewish magic and the ancient German belief in demons and witches), as well as Islamic Sufis and Christian ascetics, the Ḥasidim advocated a pietistic society rather than an apocalyptic vision, that is, a religious community which participated in an immanent relationship with the Godhead, as opposed to a future ideal state. The most influential text of the period, Baḥya ibn Paquda's *Ḥovot ha-Levavot* ("Duties of the Heart," c. 1080, translated into Hebrew 1161, [G1, G2, G8]), while not generally considered mystical, was used by German Ḥasidim "as an instructional manual of Jewish pietism which culminated in mystical intent" (C65). Though not directly influenced by the Ḥasidism of Europe, a similar movement of Ḥasidut developed in Egypt, particularly in the literature of Abraham b. Moses b. Maimon (d. 1237). In France and Germany, the Ḥasidei Ashkenaz were most influenced by the *Sefer Ḥasidim* of Judah b. Samuel he-Ḥasid (d. 1217, [G4, G6, G7]), who delineated the ethical aspects of medieval Ḥasidism.

The twelfth century marks the beginning of the mystical movement of Provence, the crystallization of Kabbalism, with the appearance of the *Sefer ha-Bahir* (c. 1150–1200 [H9]), a pseudepigraphical work which infuses Gnostic ideas onto the merkabah tradition. While the *Bahir* incorporates the teachings of a number of earlier mystics, it is distinct in that it presents a new idea of contemplation, not on the letters of the alphabet, a characteristic of Abulafian mysticism, but on the *Sefirot,* emanations of the Godhead through which He was to have effected Creation; and it accepts as self-explanatory the theory of *Gilgul,* transmigration of the soul, despite the opposition of Jewish philosophers. The Jewish community itself fostered an upsurge of mystical endeavor, and for the first time in Jewish history, men such as Isaac the Blind (d. c. 1235) devoted their lives to mysticism.

From France, the movement spread to Spain where Naḥmanides (c. 1194–1270) gave it the respectability which it might not otherwise have gained. As a combination of theosophic-gnostic and neoplatonic-philosophical elements, thirteenth-century Jewish mysticism was characterized by the competition between the two elements with, for example, Isaac ibn Latif (c. 1210–c. 1280) being considered half kabbalist, half philosopher. Abraham Abulafia (1240–after 1292), another representative of the philosophical-mystical tradition, is most known for his prophetic mysticism, believing his system to be a continuation of Maimonides' *Guide for the Perplexed*.

As the new Kabbalah spread from Provence to Spain, mysticism became even more popular, kabbalistic texts finding an even greater audience. Then, sometime between 1280 and 1286, Moses b. Shem Tov de Leon

Introduction

compiled what was to become the cornerstone of kabbalistic literature, the *Zohar* (I6, I15). Pseudepigraphically attributed to Simeon b. Yoḥai, a second-century rabbi (F63), the *Zohar* is an amorphous aggregate of exegesis and mystical speculation based on the Pentateuch, the Song of Songs, Ruth and Lamentations. The appearance of the *Zohar* served to popularize Kabbalah even more, and through the fourteenth century, Jewish mysticism flourished, until the expulsion from Spain in 1492.

After the expulsion, the character of Jewish mysticism changed drastically, as messianism became a crucial consideration. Because the dissolution of what had been a flourishing culture came so rapidly, many mystics equated this holocaust with the messianic wars which were to precede the return to Jerusalem, and the focus of speculation shifted from Creation to Apocalypse. Many of the exiled mystics moved to Safed in Palestine, where an extremely vibrant kabbalistic community, under the leadership of Moses Cordovero (1522–1570, [J4]) and his pupil Isaac Luria (1534–1572 [J5, J6]) developed radically new theories which, in turn, became the basis of most kabbalistic movements to the present.

In the seventeenth century, Jewish apocalypticism, in conjunction with Christian Millenarianism, made the appropriate background for the appearance of Shabbetai Zevi, the mystical messiah (K41). Proclaiming his divinity in 1666, the Christian year of the Apocalypse, Shabbetai Zevi, along with his prophet Nathan of Gaza, exploited tenets of Lurianic Kabbalah to persuade the Jews to abrogate the law which the false messiah claimed to supersede. Later that year, Shabbetai Zevi declined the Turkish Sultan Mehmed IV's offer of martyrdom, preferring, instead, to convert to Islam, taking with him a number of "believers" who accepted Nathan's identification of the apostasy with the messiah's antinomian descent into Hell. Shabbetai Zevi was followed in the next century by Jacob Frank (1726–1791 [K45]), yet another false messiah, who himself converted to Christianity in 1759.

Because of these upheavals in the Jewish community, the tenor of kabbalistic studies changed. Unlike the enthusiastic speculators of the Safed school, seventeenth-century kabbalists who remained outside the Shabbatean movement became very conservative. Pretending that the Shabbatean corruption of Kabbalah had never occurred, they limited popular access to Jewish esotericism, trying to reestablish its historical position as an elitist pursuit. In spite of their efforts, however, a popular form of mysticism did emerge in the eighteenth century, Ḥasidism, under the leadership of Israel b. Eliezer, the Ba'al Shem Tov. Ḥasidism opposed the sophistry of the rabbinate to postulate a simple and natural relationship with God.

The origin and early history of Hasidism, the form of Jewish mysticism most represented in this bibliography, are unclear. According to Joseph Dan (L74), it is difficult to date the origin of Hasidism because while 1736 marks the first public appearance of the Ba'al Shem Tov, we have little information about his theology. The Besht was succeeded in 1760 by Rabbi Dov Baer, the Maggid of Mezherich, about whom we have more information (L33), but the movement did not reach its characteristic form until the Maggid's death (1772), when his disciples established their own courts to produce the "multi-centered movement" which reflects today's Hasidism. In this form, each Zaddik became the spiritual leader of his own congregation (L155). When Hasidism reached this point, it encountered strong opposition from the rabbinic authorities who not only feared competition, but also, Dan suggests, suspected that the movement might become a new form of Shabbateanism.

Contrary to popular belief, the earliest literary form of Hasidism is not the story, but the sermon, "the 'Hasidic story' [being] to a great extent a twentieth-century fantasy created by writers who overemphasized a literary form that they found more satisfying than the movement's authentic literature. If we are to achieve a true perspective on early Hasidic teachings, we must leave these distorted modern outpourings behind" (L74). In the early sermon literature, Hasidim incorporated mystical doctrines and terminology in their interpretations of traditional texts. The first narratives, *Shivhey Ha-Besht* (L42), and the *Stories* of Rabbi Nachman of Bratslav (L21, L59), were published in 1815, the next collection appearing in 1863.

Another problem associated with the movement is the distinction between Hasidism and Neo-Hasidism. According to Rivka Shatz-Uffenheimer (B40), the term derives from Samuel Joseph ish Horowitz who, in 1909, characterized the early Hasidism as a disorganized movement, the Besht as a charlatan, and the "neo-Hasidic" work of Martin Buber and Micha Josef Berdyczewski as the attempt to impose on Hasidism "ethical values and a positive popular force, in particular in the Hasidic 'joy,' which they interpreted as a protest against the dejection produced by the conditions of the Diaspora." In contrast, later scholars have been defining Neo-Hasidism sociologically, as the accommodations made by the movement for existence in the modern world. In addition to Hasidism—or Neo-Hasidism—modern mysticism has been influenced by Zionism, the literal "return from exile," the foremost twentieth-century mystic being Abraham Isaac Kook.

Introduction xvii

This history of Jewish mysticism bears little relation to what many English readers—even today—believe Kabbalah to be. In order to comprehend the development of "English" Kabbalah, it is necessary to survey briefly the history of Anglo-Jewry.[5] While the Jewish community in England dates back to the time of the Romans, it never developed to the point that it would foster mystical pursuits.[6] As did the other countries of Western Europe, England expelled its Jews in the Middle Ages, and until the last half of the nineteenth century, when English Jews were emancipated, the community was never secure enough to produce the kind of educational environment in which Jews traditionally studied Kabbalah. Until the nineteenth century, the Rabbinate was imported from the Continent, the English community being unable to provide its own spiritual leaders; and Anglo-Jewry itself was most noted for its lack of Jewish education.[7] Through the eighteenth century, only two English Jews were said to be versed in Kabbalah. The first, Samuel Jacob Hayyim Falk (c. 1710–1782), was most likely a Shabbatean who dabbled in the occult (K11, K12, K14). And the second, Jacob Hart, wrote his kabbalistic treatises in Hebrew and published them under his Hebrew name, Eliakim ben Abraham, on the Continent, presumably for lack of a local audience.[8] Only towards the end of the last century did English Jews begin writing on kabbalistic matters.

Understandably, America lagged even further behind than England. In Colonial times, Jews, like everyone else, were too busy establishing settlements to study Kabbalah. While there were synagogues in the colonies, the number of worshippers was small, so the religious structure could not have been very strong. Up to 1880, German-Jewish immigrants dominated American Jewry, introducing Reform Judaism, a liberalized view of religion which fostered a relaxed attitude towards the Law and introduced English into its shortened services. As a result, American Jews grew less interested in Jewish learning than in secular, believing they needed no more than a rudimentary background in Hebrew. After 1880, Eastern European immigrants came, bringing with them their stricter views of the Law and introducing the traditional Hebrew education and strong sense of community characteristic of American Jewry today. Until this century, the only Americans credited with a knowledge of Kabbalah were Christians, Judah Monis (an apostate), and Ezra Stiles.

Only a quick glance at this bibliography is necessary to indicate that while the Jews were silent on the subject, Christians were not. Ever since Pico della Mirandola (1463–1494) declared that "no science can better convince us of the divinity of Jesus Christ than magic and the Kabbalah,"[9] Christians have used Kabbalah to demonstrate the truth of Christianity and, later, to persuade Jews of that truth. Johannes Reuchlin (1455–1522), the Christian Hebraist, published the first two books on the subject written by a non-Jew: *De Verbo Mirifico* (1494) and *De Arte Cabalistica* (1517 [O15]). And under the aegis of Cardinal Edigio da Viterbo (1465–1532), who himself wrote several treatises, a number of works were translated into Latin, as Christians became more and more interested in kabbalistic speculation.

In 1531, Cornelius Agrippa initiated what was to become the popular notion of Kabbalah—numerology and witchcraft. In his *De Occulta Philosophia,* Agrippa gives credit to Kabbalah, primarily the use of Gematria, for the basis of his magic, and from then on, despite the fact that the Jews always discouraged practical Kabbalah, which they stringently limited to "white magic," Christians associated Kabbalah with black magic, and many denounced the Jews for pursuits that, in fact, were characteristic of Christian mages. The practical Kabbalah of Agrippa became the basis of a number of Christian secret societies, such as the Rosicrucians in the seventeenth century, Freemasons in the eighteenth, and Theosophists in the nineteenth. In all cases, these occultists appropriated elements of Jewish mysticism, taking them out of their original contexts so that even though kabbalistic aspects, especially the *Sefirotic* Tree, appear in these works, they are used to denote different things.

In addition to the occultists, in the seventeenth century, a group of Christians interested in unifying all peoples, that is, Catholics, Protestant, and Jews, into a single universal religion became interested in Kabbalah, at first to justify Christianity, but ultimately, to persuade Jews to convert. Under the auspices of Christian Knorr von Rosenroth (d. 1689), son of a Protestant minister, several Christian kabbalists compiled the *Kabbala Denudata* (2 vols; Sulzbach, 1677–84), the major Latin compendium of kabbalistic literature. Containing *Sefer ha-Gilgulim,* supposedly from the writings of Luria, as well as other Jewish material, such as Moses Cordovero's *Pardes Rimmonim,* the *Denudata* made Kabbalah available for the first time to a mass Christian audience. However, the work is flawed, for in the attempt to render the Hebrew originals as accurately as possible, translators sometimes became obscure; but also, the work has a decidedly philo-Semitic bias, including only those aspects of Jewish mysticism which agree with Christianity.[10] From its publication until this century, von Rosenroth's *Kabbala Denudata* has been the major source of information about Kabbalah available to those who cannot read the material in the original. Hence, it has spawned generations of inaccurate treatises on the mysticism of the Jews.

The history of English Kabbalah reflects just this inaccuracy, for until Scholem's *Major Trends* was translated into English, there were virtually no reliable studies of the field, and it is only in the past few decades that we have begun to get accurate translations of texts. Therefore, when considering English Kabbalah, we literally have to consider the source, for not only were most of the works written by people with no access to originals, but, actually, most are derivative texts, being either translations of works written in other languages or studies based on translations.

The earliest Englishmen to deal with Kabbalah were Christians who wrote in Latin, so their works are beyond the purview of this bibliography. While the sixteenth-century Englishman John Dee was supposed to have been steeped in Kabbalah, his few English works do not reflect this knowledge. In the seventeenth century, the Cambridge Platonists, like Henry Ainsworth and Ralph Cudworth, used kabbalistic commentary to support or annotate other theological systems so that their work is not, strictly speaking, kabbalistic. The first major work called "Cabbalistic" is Henry More's *Conjectura Cabbalistica* (O2), but the Cambridge Platonist not only knew little Hebrew but boasted that he did not rely on Jewish mysticism at all— "That though I call this Interpretation of mine Cabbala, yet I must confesse I received it neither from Man nor Angel"—and in the *Conjectura*, he is decidedly scornful of the Jews.

During this period, the Rosicrucians were using Kabbalah to develop their theosophy of the Rosy Cross, and the works of men like Thomas Vaughan and Robert Fludd are replete with kabbalistic concepts and diagrams, but very little has to do with Jewish mysticism. Fludd does include a chapter on Kabbalah in his *Mosaicall Philosophy* (O3), but, again, the material is subordinated to his greater theosophical system.

The first Christian kabbalist whose work was reproduced in English was Franciscus Mercurius van Helmont, a Dutch theosophist who contributed greatly to the *Denudata*. Not only did he translate several of the treatises into Latin, including Luria's, but his *Adumbratio Kabbalae Christianae* was appended to the second edition of the compendium.[11] Van Helmont stayed in England for ten years, during which time he served as physician to Lady Anne Conway, the center of a large intellectual circle (see O80). Van Helmont taught Kabbalah to Lady Conway, and her *Principles of the Most Ancient and Modern Philosophy* (O7), which he had published on the Continent, evinces a strong kabbalistic influence. But while Lady Conway and her friends were influenced by van Helmont, others were not, including Henry More. By the end of the seventeenth century, the only kabbalistic works available in English were by van Helmont (O4–O6, O8). All others were admixtures of occultism which in no way reflected Jewish mysticism but were still used to define the mystical pursuits of the Jews.

As in the seventeenth century, in the eighteenth, all works dealing with Kabbalah were by Christians, not Jews. However, in contrast to the previous century, in the eighteenth, most Christians were interested in Kabbalism as an historical curiosity rather than esoteric knowledge, and in most cases, they used studies of Kabbalah to prove larger points about the Jews, occasionally sympathetic, though usually anti-Semitic. The century opened with the publication of Tho. Taylor's translation of Jacques Basnage's *History of the Jews* (1708 [B43]). A mammoth compilation of information intended to complete Josephus's *Antiquities of the Jews,* Basnage's is credited as being the first modern history of the Jews, by Jew or non-Jew. In addition to sporadic references to Kabbalah throughout the work, Basnage includes a long chapter on the "Particulars of the Cabbala" (pp. 184–256), concerning such topics as the *Zohar, Merkabah* mysticism, Gematria, the *Sefirot,* and the history of Kabbalah. Although the Frenchman is usually considered to be a relatively objective historian, his attitude towards Kabbalah is somewhat derisive, understandable given the fact that he had to rely on Latin sources, especially the *Denudata,* since he could not read Hebrew. Therefore, what he reports to be the mysticism of the Jews is, in fact, the Christianized version used for evangelical purposes. Of course, Basnage is even-handed in his treatment, deriding the Christian kabbalists as much as the Jewish.

Because of its breadth, Basnage's *History* became the major resource for information about the Jews. Thomas Lewis (B44) used Basnage for his six-page recension of the pseudepigraphical history of Kabbalah, kabbalistic explication of Scripture, and practical Kabbalah; and William Enfield (B47) based his hostile and inaccurate account of Kabbalah on the same source. Not interested in the Jews at all, Thomas Maurice (B48) used Basnage to demonstrate the Indian origins of Kabbalah; and John Allen (B50) concludes that Jewish beliefs in general are "an awful delusion," in part because of Maurice's renditon of Kabbalah.

The one eighteenth-century study not based on Christian sources is John Peter Stehelin's *Traditions of the Jews* (B45), a softened version of *Das Entdeckte des Judenthums,* by Johann Eisenmenger, a German who, distressed in his youth to find what he considered large numbers of Christians converting to

Judaism, spent nineteen years studying Jewish sources in an attempt to refute the appeal of Judaism. His flagrantly anti-Semitic work so enraged the Jewish community of Frankfort that the emperor forbade the book's publication, though the king of Prussia did permit a second edition to be published in 1711. Stehelin took a philo-Semitic approach to Eisenmenger's work. Toning down the polemics, he gently tried to persuade the Jews that "Articles of your Faith, if rightly explain'd, contain the true Doctrine of Christ, and may be subscrib'd by us Christians ourselves." In his chapter on Kabbalah, Stehelin deals primarily with Gematria.

But if the English reader cannot use this bibliography as a gauge of Jewish mysticism per se, he can learn from it the attitudes towards Kabbalah of the largest Jewish community in the Diaspora. From the historical perspective, the bibliography reflects Christian attitudes towards both Jews and their mystical practices; and contemporarily, it indicates the interests of English-speaking Jews towards the mystical strain found throughout their history. And equally important, the bibliography is essential for comparative studies. Since, when viewed outside the realm of Judaica, the greatest impact of Kabbalah has been in its influence on other forms of mysticism, the bibliography is useful for studies of kabbalistic elements found in the works of the Rosicrucians, Freemasons and Theosophists, Milton, Blake, and Yeats. The bibliography provides access to the sources available to English readers from the seventeenth century on, as well as the studies which have already been written on the subject.

The turning point in kabbalistic studies was the publication of Gershom Scholem's *Major Trends* in 1941. Since then scholarship has become more objective and accurate and has covered a broader range of topics. Before 1940, however, English Kabbalah was both limited and distorted, reflecting the historical milieux which produced it. But if earlier studies cannot be relied upon for information about Jewish mysticism, they are invaluable both as a record of critical attitudes towards Kabbalism and as sources for those of earlier centuries who were influenced by Kabbalah. Therefore, in compiling this bibliography, I have cited for the earlier periods every reference I could find, regardless of length or accuracy, down to brief, one-paragraph entries in dictionaries and encyclopedias. But as scholarship became more reliable, I became more selective, including for the modern period only those items which, broadly speaking, contribute to the field and which bear a recognizable resemblance to what we now know Kabbalah to be. Even so, there are entries which some will undoubtedly feel do not rightly belong in a bibliography of Jewish mysticism. However, no one has yet derived a viable definition of mysticism itself, much less distinguished absolutely between mystical and non-mystical prophecy, messianism, or apocalyptic, for example. Therefore, I felt it wiser to err on the side of inclusion than exclusion, and have included some material which, while only remotely related to Jewish mysticism, still generally contributes to kabbalistic studies.

Because Kabbalism is a relatively new field, there exists no single critical stance for evaluating the material. While Scholem and his successors have established the basis for scholarship, neither their approaches nor their conclusions have been universally accepted. Therefore, a critical bibliography would be misleading, for not only would it ignore the four-hundred-year history of Kabbalah in English, but it would imply a universality of opinion which simply does not yet exist. Therefore, *Jewish Mysticism: An Annotated Bibliography on the Kabbalah in English* is not a critical bibliography. Rather than annotating the material contained within this bibliography from the perspective of either Scholem or his critics, I have attempted to let the authors speak for themselves, wherever possible using their own words to indicate the material contained within the works cited. And the authors themselves indicate their own biases, whether anti-Semitic or philo-Semitic, whether Christian occultist or Jewish mystic, whether traditionalist or revisionist. In this way, the reader can judge for himself the development of kabbalistic studies in English.

Needless to say, any bibliography covering a four-hundred-year span contains a great deal of amorphous material; and this bibliography is no exception. Therefore, the organization of *Jewish Mysticism* is somewhat complex. I have divided the material into six major chapters: General Reference Works; Introductory Surveys; Topics in Jewish Mysticism; The History of Kabbalah; Major Scholars; and Non-Jewish Kabbalah. The first two chapters, General Reference Works and Introductory Surveys, are self-explanatory, the one containing entries on bibliographies, encyclopedias and dictionaries, and chapters from history text books, and the other, introductory studies which survey either the basic doctrines and/or history of Kabbalism. The third chapter, Topics in Jewish Mysticism, contains generic material which is not limited to any particular historical period or figure, but which focuses on concepts spanning the breadth of Kabbalah. While most of these topics can be found in Scholem's *Kabbalah* (C65), some, like Critical Approaches, Magic, and Psychology, reflect the particular interests of English readers, so they are given less prominence in Scholem's study.

Chapter Four, The History of Kabbalah, is organized to correspond roughly with the chapters of Scholem's *Major Trends,* though scholarship

Introduction xxiii

since 1941 has necessitated some modifications. Preceding the section corresponding to Scholem's lecture on "Merkabah Mysticism and Jewish Gnosticism," I have included a section on Antecedents for material dealing with mysticism in the biblical and post-biblical periods, including the Dead Sea Scrolls; I have expanded the focus of Scholem's lecture on "Hasidism in Medieval Germany" to include all medieval Ḥasidism, Egyptian as well as German; and similarly, I have broadened the section on "Abraham Abulafia and the Doctrine of Prophetic Kabbalism" to embrace all materials pertinent to "The Crystallization of Kabbalah," which began in Provence and then spread through southern Europe, and beyond. And finally, I have divided Scholem's last lecture, "Hasidism: The Latest Phase," in two, distinguishing between Ḥasidism, and Neo-Ḥasidism (defined roughly as the adaptation of Ḥasidism for the modern world), post-Ḥasidic trends, and contemporary approaches to mysticism.

The last two chapters reflect the concerns of English Kabbalah more than Kabbalism in general. Chapter Five, Major Scholars, focuses on the critical debate which has arisen since Kabbalah became established as a respectable scholarly pursuit, isolating the material dealing with the approaches taken by the major scholars whose work is available in English: Leo Baeck, Martin Buber, Abraham Joshua Heschel, and Gershom G. Scholem. And finally, Chapter Six deals with Non-Jewish Kabbalah, manifestations of Kabbalism in areas outside the specific boundaries of Jewish mysticism.

In each chapter, the primary sources, where they exist, have been listed before the secondary. Also, in order to reflect the development of attitudes towards Kabbalah and to facilitate influence studies, all entries have been placed in chronological order. Thus, from reading the annotations, the reader can discern the attitudes prevalent during a given historical period, as well as locate those sources most influential on specific writers who relied on English materials. While I have tried to organize the material as clearly as possible, there are still some anomalies. A few entries simply do not fit into any of the categories, and others belong in more than one. Consequently, I have been forced to make a few relatively arbitrary decisions, placing some entries into chapters which they only generally resemble and choosing between two equally suitable sections for others. Therefore, the reader is encouraged to make frequent use of the three-part Index. The first section, Primary Materials, lists the titles and authors of kabbalistic works found in this bibliography. The Author index contains the authors, editors, and translators of secondary materials, as well as individuals to whom *Festschriften* are dedicated; and the Subject index deals with the subjects covered.

While the bibliography is intended to be as useful as possible to as many readers as possible, it still has certain limitations. First, only published materials have been included. While there do exist manuscripts, letters, theses, and dissertations which deal with Kabbalah, they have been omitted from this bibliography. Also, because of the range of materials consulted, book reviews have been excluded. And finally, with the exception of folktales, the bibliography contains only non-fictional primary and secondary sources. Folktales, especially those of the Ḥasidim, are included, of course, because they are considered by believers to be true, and because in many cases, they constitute the best primary sources available.

A final word on the limitations of this bibliography: All bibliographers hope to provide as comprehensive a resource of their fields as possible, but, as they work, they must face certain realities about their projects. So, too, with this bibliographer. Kabbalism is not only a newly established field but one which, given its unusual development, has historically been maligned by scholars who felt it lacked the stature of established academic endeavors. As a result, there are few research tools available to the bibliographer. The only full-length bibliography is Scholem's *Bibliographia Kabbalistica* (B3), compiled in 1927, which, as the first attempt to organize this diffuse material, is incomplete, especially its English entries. While general bibliographies, such as Issachar Joel's *Index of Articles on Jewish Studies,* contain sections on Kabbalism as well as on specific topics, such as Messianism and Ḥasidism, they are not comprehensive, being limited both by their definitions of Kabbalah and by the journals which they index. Therefore, while I have included everything which I have found on the subject, using the broadest possible definition of Kabbalah, there are undoubtedly sources which I have overlooked. In addition, in order to make the bibliography as up to date as possible, I have included materials through 1983, even though those bibliographies indexing 1983, and in some cases 1982—or even 1981—were not yet published when this bibliography was printed. The reader should be aware that there are omissions, especially for the last few years. Finally, because of technical limitations, I have been unable to reproduce all of the diacritical marks used in the Hebrew, Aramaic, and Arabic titles, and have used apostrophes where necessary to indicate their positions.

That the bibliography is at all comprehensive is largely due to the help I have received in its compilation. I wish first to thank the Library of Congress for granting me the use of its study facilities and for locating the mass of materials required for the compilation of this source book. I wish also to thank the staff of the Jewish Division of the New York Public Library for

Introduction

facilitating my use of their collection. In addition, librarians of the McKeldin and R. Lee Hornbake Libraries of the University of Maryland, the Van Pelt Library of the University of Pennsylvania, Library of the Jewish Theological Seminary of America, Mendel Gottesman Library of Hebraica-Judaica of Yeshiva University, Stern College Library, Jung Foundation Library, the Beinecke Rare Book and Manuscript Library of Yale University, the Harry Elkins Widener Memorial Library of Harvard University, the Milton S. Eisenhower Library of the Johns Hopkins University, the Library of the Peabody Conservatory of Baltimore, as well as Suzanne Coonley of the Comparative Literature Centre, Dartmouth College, Henry Suzuki of the Weiser Book Store, New York, and Chris Popenoe of the Yes! Incorporated Bookstore, Washington, D.C., have all contributed to the completion of this bibliography.

A number of individuals have also been most generous in helping me. Stanley J. Spector granted me full use of his personal library, and Miriam Simon and Benjamin Simon both sacrificed beautiful summer weather for time in the library. Joseph A. Wittreich, Jr., of the University of Maryland, has kindly advised me on all aspects of the bibliography. John Howard, also of the University of Maryland, provided the initial impetus for the project as well as continual advice on its execution. And Steven T. Katz, of Dartmouth College, helped clarify some references for me. Most of all, I thank Kathryn F. Hilt, of Bernard Baruch College, whose faith, encouragement and assistance have led to its completion. The strengths of the bibliography are due to all those who have helped me during its compilation; its weaknesses are mine.

NOTES

1. Talmud Ḥag 14b contains the oft-cited parable about the four who "entered the 'Garden,'" only one of whom, Rabbi Akiba, "departed unhurt."

2. See Louis Jacobs' *Jewish Mystical Testimonies* (C12) for texts of extant mystical testimonies.

3. Little scholarship on Christian Kabbalah is available in English. Our best sources are Joseph Blau's *The Christian Interpretation of the Cabala in the Renaissance* (O98) and Gershom G. Scholem's section on "The Christian Kabbalah" in *Kabbalah* (C65). In French, see: François Secret's *Les Kabbalistes chrétiens de la Reniassance* (O125), and *Kabbalistes Chrétiens* (A107), which contains a French translation of Scholem's "Zur Geschichte der Anfänge des christlichen Kabbala," originally published in

Essays ... Leo Baeck (1954), pp. 158–93. And in German, see Ernst Benz's *Die Christliche Kabbala: Ein Stiefkind der Theologie* (Zürich: Rhein-Verlag, 1958). In "Milton and the *Conjectura Cabbalistica*," R.J. Zwi Werblowsky provides a cogent analysis of the distinctions between Jewish and Christian Kabbalah (O109).

4. This summary relies primarily on Scholem's surveys in C45 and C65.

5. This discussion is based primarily on Cecil Roth's *History of the Jews in England*, 3rd ed. (Oxford: Clarendon Press, 1964).

6. According to Scholem (C45), only after a community reaches its third stage of development, that is, after religion has become established to the point that it causes man to experience a gap between himself and his Creator, does the phenomenon of mysticism occur.

7. See Todd M. Endelman's *The Jews in Georgian England, 1714–1830: Tradition and Change in a Liberal Society* (Philadelphia: Jewish Publication Society of America, 1979), for a detailed discussion of the history of Jewish education in England.

8. It is interesting to note that in his *History,* Roth refers to these as "scientific brochures of high interest."

9. As cited by Scholem, C65.

10. A deceptive phrase, philo-Semitism refers to the Christian belief that if shown the light in a reasonable fashion, Jews will of their own free will convert to Christianity. The philo-Semitic bent of the *Denudata* is made explicit in the correspondence between von Rosenroth and Henry More, included in the *Denudate* (part 2, pp. 176–77), the latter advising the former to affirm "nothing for true, but what the Christian as well as the Jew is agreed in," the former finding the suggestion "not only useful, but necessary."

11. Although not available in English, there is a French translation by Gilly de Givry (Paris: Bibliothèque Chacornac, 1899).

JEWISH MYSTICISM

A. *FESTSCHRIFTEN* AND OTHER ANALYZED COLLECTIONS

Included in this section are all anthologies containing material dealing with Kabbalism. The numbers following each entry refer to the specific articles found in the collection, and the citation for each article refers back to the specific anthology in which it is contained.

A1 Schechter, S. *Studies in Judaism.* First Series. New York and London: Macmillan & Co., 1896. Philadelphia: Jewish Publication Society of America, 1911. Rpt. Freeport, New York: Books for Library Press, 1972.

   L80, L81.

A2 Frisch, Ephraim, ed. *Hebrew Union College Annual.* Cincinnati: Hebrew Union College, 1904.

   L83.

A3 *Jews' College Jubilee Volume.* London: Luzac & Co., 1906.

   G12.

A4 Harper, Robert Francis, Francis Brown, and George Foot Moore, eds. *Old Testament and Semitic Studies in Memory of William Rainey Harper.* 2 vols. Chicago: University of Chicago Press, 1908.

   F32.

A5 Schechter, S. *Studies in Judaism.* Second Series. Philadelphia: Jewish Publication Society of America, 1908.

   J11, L85.

A6 Simon, Leon, ed. *Aspects of the Hebrew Genius: A Volume of Essays on Jewish Literature and Thought.* London: George Routledge & Sons, Limited, New York: Bloch Publishing Co., 1910.

   C33.

A7   *Studies in Jewish Literature Issued in Honor of Professor Kaufmann Kohler ... on the Occasion of His Seventieth Birthday.* Berlin: Georg Reimer, 1913. Rpt. New York: Arno Press, 1979.

D103, J12.

A8   Hirsch, Samuel Abraham. *The Cabbalists and Other Essays.* London: W. Heinemann, 1922. Rpt. Port Washington: Kennikat Press, 1970.

C31.

A9   *A Symposium on Eschatology by Members of the Society of Biblical Literature and Exegesis.* New Haven: Yale University Press, 1923.

E46.

A10 Hertz, J.H. *The Jews at the Close of the Bible Age.* London: Jews' College, 1924.

E47.

A11 Schechter, S. *Studies in Judaism.* Third Series. Philadelphia: Jewish Publication Society of America, 1924.

G14.

A12 Gaster, Moses. *Studies and Texts in Folklore, Magic, Medieval Romance, Hebrew Apocrypha and Samaritan Archaeology.* 3 vols. London: Maggs Bros., 1925-28. Rpt. New York: Ktav Publishing House, 1971.

D10, E23-E25, F13, I25.

A13 Philipson, David, ed. *Hebrew Union College Jubilee Volume (1875-1925).* Cincinnati: Hebrew Union College, 1925. Rpt. New York: Ktav Publishing House, Inc., 1968.

O67.

A14 Adler, Cyrus, and Aaron Ember, eds. *Oriental Studies Published in Commemoration of the Fortieth Anniversary 1883-1923 of Paul Haupt as Director of the Oriental Seminary of the Johns Hopkins University, Baltimore, Md.* Baltimore: Johns Hopkins Press, and Leipzig: J.C. Hinrichs'sche Buchhandlung, 1926.

E49.

A15 Bevan, Edwyn R., and Charles Singer, eds. *The Legacy of Israel.* Oxford: Clarendon Press, 1927.

O75.

A16 Ginzberg, Louis. *Students, Scholars and Saints*. Philadelphia: Jewish Publication Society of America, 1928. Rpt. New York: Meridian Books, 1958.

L97.

A17 Spiegel, Shalom. *Hebrew Reborn*. New York: Macmillan Company, 1930. Rpt. Cleveland: World Pub. Co., 1957, 1962.

J13, L102.

A18 Schechter, Abraham I. *Lectures on Jewish Liturgy*. Philadelphia: Jewish Publication Society of America, 1933.

D104.

A19 Hooke, S.H. *The Labyrinth: Further Studies in the Relation Between Myth and Ritual in the Ancient World*. London: Society for Promoting Christian Knowledge, 1935.

E52.

A20 Regensberg, Chaim David, ed. *Gibeath Saul: Essays Contributed in Honor of Rabbi Saul Silber*. Chicago, 1935.

K19.

A21 Hertz, J.H. *Sermons, Addresses and Studies*. 3 vols. London: Soncino Press, 1938.

C44, E54.

A22 Poupko, Bernard Aaron, ed. *Eidenu: Memorial Publication in Honor of Rabbi Dr. Bernard Revel, Late President of the Rabbi Isaac Elchanan Theological Seminary and Yeshiva College*. New York: Issued by the Students of The Rabbi Isaac Elchanan Theological Seminary, 1942.

L109.

A23 Rosenthal, Erwin I.J., ed. *Saadya Studies*. Manchester: Manchester University Press, 1943.

D92.

A24 Schwartz, Leo W., ed. *Memoirs of My People through a Thousand Years*. New York: Farrar and Rinehart, 1943. Rpt. New York: Schocken Books, 1963.

H1, L11, N5

A25 Epstein, Isidore, Ephraim Levine, and Cecil Roth, eds. *Essays, in Honor of the Very Rev. Dr. J.H. Hertz.* London: Edward Goldston, 1944?

   F42.

A26 Baron Salo W., ed. *The Jewish People Past and Present.* 4 vols. New York: Central Yiddish Culture Organization, 1946.

   C49, D43, D44

A27 Buber, Martin. *Mamre: Essays in Religion.* Trans. Greta Horte. Melbourne: Melbourne University Press, and London: Oxford University Press, 1946.

   L110, L111

A28 Baeck, Leo. *The Pharisees and Other Essays.* New York: Schocken Books Inc., 1947, 1966.

   F45.

A29 Buber, Martin. *Hasidism.* New York: Philosophical Library, 1948.

   K20, L113-L119.

A30 Löwinger, Samuel, and Joseph Somogyi, eds. *Ignace Goldziher Memorial Volume.* 2 vols. Budapest and Jerusalem, 1948-58.

   K22.

A31 Finkelstein, Louis, ed. *The Jews: Their History, Culture, and Religion.* 4 vols. Philadelphia: Jewish Publication Society of America, 1949. 2nd ed. 2 vols. New York: Harper, 1955; 3rd ed. 1960. 4th ed. 3 vols. New York: Schocken Books, 1970-71.

   C50.

A32 Schnur, Harry C. *Mystic Rebels.* New York: Beechhurst Press, 1949. Rpt. Freeport, New York: Books for Libraries Press, 1971.

   K23.

A33 Greenberg, Hayim. *The Inner Eye: Selected Essays.* Ed. Shlomo Katz. New York: Jewish Frontier Association, Inc., 1953-64.

   K25.

A34 *The Joshua Starr Memorial Volume: Studies in History and Philology.* Jewish Social Studies, Publications No. 5. New York: Conference on Jewish Relations, 1953.

K24.

A35 Jung, Leo, ed. *Jewish Leaders (1750-1940).* New York: Bloch, 1953.

L126.

A36 Soltes, Mordecai, ed. *Jews in the Arts and Sciences.* Jewish Academy of Arts & Sciences, Jubilee Volume. New York: Herald Square Press, 1954.

D149.

A37 Ginzberg, Louis. *On Jewish Law and Lore.* Philadelphia: Jewish Publication Society of America, 1955. Rpt. Cleveland: World Pub. Co., 1962; New York: Atheneum, 1970.

C53, D93.

A38 Mattuck, Israel I., intro. *Aspects of Progressive Jewish Thought.* New York: Farrar, Straus and Young, 1955.

D107.

A39 Aland, Kurt, and F.L. Cross, eds. *Studia Patristica.* Volume I: Papers Presented to the Second International Conference on Patristic Studies Held at Christ Church, Oxford, 1955. Berlin: Akademie-Verlag, 1957.

H22.

A40 Altman, Alexander, ed. *Between East and West: Essays Dedicated to the Memory of Bela Horovitz.* London: East and West Library, 1958.

M33.

A41 Buber, Martin. *Hasidism and Modern Man.* Trans. Maurice Friedman. New York: Horizon Press, 1958.

Volume I of *Hasidism and the Way of Man.* Volume II, A47. Contents: L25, L135-L137, M34, N9.

A42 Schechter, Solomon. *Studies in Judaism: Essays on Persons, Concepts, and Movements of Thought in Jewish Tradition.* New York: Meridian Books, 1958. Rpt. New York: Atheneum, 1970.

J20, L138-L140.

A43 Blau, Joseph L., ed. *Essays on Jewish Life and Thought, Presented in Honor of Salo Wittmayer Baron.* New York: Columbia University Press, 1959.

D49.

A44 Novek, Simon, ed. *Great Jewish Personalities in Ancient and Medieval Times.* New York: B'nai B'rith Department of Adult Jewish Education, and Farrar, Straus and Cudahy, 1959.

L144.

A45 Rexroth, Kenneth. *Bird in the Bush: Obvious Essays.* New York: New Directions, 1959. Rpt. Freeport, New York: Books for Libraries Press, 1970.

N10.

A46 Berk, Fred, ed. *The Jewish Dance: An Anthology of Articles.* New York: Exposition Press, 1960.

L157.

A47 Buber, Martin. *The Origin and Meaning of Hasidism.* Trans. M. Friedman. New York: Horizon Press, 1960. New York: Harper & Row, 1966.

Volume II of *Hasidism and the Way of Man.* Volume I, A41. Contents: K27, L146-L153.

A48 Kaufmann, Walter, ed. *Religion from Tolstoy to Camus.* New York: Harper & Brothers, Publishers, 1961.

L167.

A49 Rexroth, Kenneth. *Assays.* New York: New Directions Paperbook, 1961.

C56.

A50 Ben-Horin, Meir, Bernard D. Weinryb, and Solomon Zeitlin, eds. *Studies and Essays in Honor of Abraham A. Neuman, President, Dropsie College for Hebrew and Cognate Learning, Philadelphia.* Leiden: E.J. Brill for the Dropsie College, Philadelphia, 1962.

E67.

A51 Kasher, Menahem M., Norman Lamm, and Leonard Rosenfeld, eds. *The Leo Jung Jubilee Volume: Essays in His Honor on the*

Festschriften 9

Occasion of His Seventieth Birthday. New York: Jewish Center, 1962.

F51.

A52 Roth, Cecil. *Essays and Portraits in Anglo-Jewish History*. Philadelphia: Jewish Publication Society of America, 1962.

K32.

A53 Altmann, Alexander, ed. *Biblical and Other Studies*. Philip W. Lown Institute of Advanced Judaic Studies, Brandeis University, Studies and Texts, Volume I. Cambridge: Harvard University Press, 1963.

F54, H27.

A54 Frank, Joseph, Helmut Minkowski, and Ernest J. Sternglass, eds. *Horizons of a Philosopher: Essays in Honor of David Baumgardt*. Leiden: E.J. Brill, 1963.

N14.

A55 Novek, Simon, ed. *Contemporary Jewish Thought: A Reader*. B'nai B'rith Great Books Series, Vol. 4. B'nai B'rith Department of Adult Education, 1963.

L174, M3.

A56 Novek, Simon, ed. *Great Jewish Thinkers of the Twentieth Century*. B'nai B'rith Great Book Series. B'nai B'rith Department of Adult Jewish Education, 1963.

M52, N15.

A57 Silver, Daniel Jeremy, ed. *In the Time of Harvest: Essays in Honor of Abba Hillel Silver on the Occasion of His 70th Birthday*. New York: Macmillan Company, and London: Collier-Macmillan Ltd., 1963.

D50, K3, L176.

A58 Jacob, Walter, Frederick C. Schwartz, and Vigdor W. Kavaler, eds. *Essays in Honor of Solomon B. Freehof*. Pittsburgh: Rodef Shalom Congregation, 1964.

D111.

A59 Scholem, Gershom G. *On the Kabbalah and Its Symbolism*. Trans. Ralph Manheim. New York: Schocken Books, 1965.

D28, D94, D112, D136, D137.

A60 Loewe, Raphael, ed. *Studies in Rationalism, Judaism and Universalism in Memory of Leon Roth*. New York: Humanities Press, 1966.

D86.

A61 Podhoretz, Norman, ed. *The Commentary Reader: Two Decades of Articles and Stories*. New York: Atheneum, 1966.

N17.

A62 Rosenthal, Judah, ed. *Meyer Waxman Jubilee Volume, On the Occasion of His Seventy-Fifth Birthday*. Jerusalem and Tel Aviv: College of Jewish Studies Press, Chicago, and Mordecai Newman Publishing House Ltd., 1966.

F57.

A63 Roth, Cecil, Gen. Ed. *The Dark Ages: Jews in Christian Europe 711-1096*. Volume II of *The World History of the Jewish People*. Second Series, Medieval Period. New Brunswick, New Jersey: Rutgers University Press, 1966.

F58.

A64 Shulvass, Moses A., ed. *Perspectives in Jewish Learning*. 2 vols. Chicago: College of Jewish Studies Press, 1966.

H29.

A65 Altmann, Alexander, ed. *Jewish Medieval and Renaissance Studies*. Philip W. Lown Institute of Advanced Judaic Studies, Brandeis University, Studies and Texts: Volume IV. Cambridge: Harvard University Press, 1967.

G24, H31, H32.

A66 Schilpp, Paul Arthur, and Maurice Friedman, eds. *The Philosophy of Martin Buber*. LaSalle, Ill.: Open Court, and London: Cambridge University Press, 1967.

N19, N20, N22, N24.

A67 Urbach, Ephraim E., R.J. Zwi Werblowsky, and Ch. Wirszubski, eds. *Studies in Mysticism and Religion Presented to Gershom G. Scholem on His Seventieth Birthday, by Pupils, Colleagues and Friends*. Jerusalem: Magnes Press, Hebrew University, 1967.

H30, L181, O131. At the end of the Hebrew section is a bibliography of the Published Writings of Gershom G. Scholem.

Festschriften

A68 Fackenheim, Emil L. *Quest for Past and Future: Essays in Jewish Theology.* Bloomington and London: Indiana University Press, 1968.

L185.

A69 Neusner, Jacob, ed. *Religions in Antiquity: Essays in Memory of Erwin Ramsdell Goodenough.* Studies in the History of Religions (Supplements to *Numen*), XIV. Leiden: E.J. Brill, 1968.

E73.

A70 *Timeless Documents of the Soul.* Studies from the C.G. Jung Institute, Zurich. Evanston: Northwestern University Press, 1968.

L186.

A71 Altmann, Alexander. *Studies in Religious Philosophy and Mysticism.* London: Routledge & Kegan Paul Ltd., Ithaca: Cornell University Press, 1969.

D68, D97, G27, H33-H36.

A72 Kitagawa, Joseph M., and Charles H. Long, eds. *Myths and Symbols: Studies in Honor of Mircea Eliade.* Chicago and London: University of Chicago Press, 1969.

D80.

A73 Rosenfeld, Alvin H., ed. *William Blake: Essays for S. Foster Damon.* Providence: Brown University Press, 1969.

O133.

A74 Cohen, Arthur A., ed. *Arguments and Doctrines: A Reader of Jewish Thinking in the Aftermath of the Holocaust.* New York, Evanston and London: Harper & Row, Publishers, 1970.

D99.

A75 Goldin, Judah, ed. *The Jewish Expression.* New York: Bantom Books, Inc., 1970. Rpt. New Haven: Yale University Press, 1976.

C59, J24, N30.

A76 Werblowsky, R.J. Zwi, and C. Jouco Bleeker, eds. *Types of Redemption: Contributions to the Theme of the Study-Conference Held at Jerusalem 14th to 19th July 1968.* Studies in the History of Religions (Supplements to *Numen*), XVIII. Leiden: E.J. Brill, 1970.

E74, F64, L198.

A77   Ben-Sasson, H.H., and S. Ettinger, eds. *Jewish Society Through the Ages*. Originally published as a special number of the *Journal of World History*. Eds. Guy S. Metraux and Francois Crouzet. New York: Schocken Books, 1971.

D55, L201.

A78   Berlin, Charles, ed. *Studies in Jewish Bibliography, History and Literature in Honor of I. Edward Kiev*. New York: Ktav Publishing House, 1971.

L200.

A79   Heinemann, Joseph, and Dov Noy, eds. *Scripta Hierosolymitana*. Vol. XXII: *Studies in Aggadah and Folk Literature*. Jerusalem: Magnes Press, Hebrew University, 1971.

G29.

A80   Passow, Isidore David, and Samuel Tobias Lachs, eds. *Gratz College Anniversary Volume*. Philadelphia: Gratz College, 1971.

F67.

A81   Scholem, Gershom. *The Messianic Idea in Judaism, and Other Essays on Jewish Spirituality*. New York: Schocken Books, 1971.

D33, D53, D54, D100, D115, D139, K5, K36, K37, K39, L203, L204, N31.

A82   *Ex Orbe Religionum: Studia Geo Widengren Oblata*. 2 vols. Leiden: E.J. Brill, 1972.

E77.

A83   Neusner, Jacob, ed. *The Study of Judaism: Bibliographical Essays*. New York: Anti-Defamation League of B'nai B'rith by Ktav Publishing House, Inc., 1972.

B9.

A84   Gordis, Robert, and Ruth B. Waxman, eds. *Faith and Reason: Essays in Judaism*. New York: Ktav Publishing House, Inc., 1973.

M93.

A85   Sharpe, Eric J., and John R. Hinnells, eds. *Man and His Salvation: Studies in Memory of S.G.F. Brandon*. Manchester: Manchester University Press, 1973.

L218.

A86 Efros, Israel Isaac. *Studies in Medieval Jewish Philosophy*. New York and London: Columbia University Press, 1974.

H38.

A87 Lamm, Norman, ed. *The Good Society: Jewish Ethics in Action*. New York: Viking Press, 1974.

H5.

A88 *Mélanges d'Histoire des Religions offerts à Henri-Charles Puech*. Paris: Presses Universitaires de France, 1974.

F75.

A89 Neusner, Jacob, ed. *Understanding Rabbinic Judaism, from Talmudic to Modern Times*. New York: Ktav Publishing House, 1974.

C62, C64, G8, L220.

A90 Newman, Charles, and Mary Kinzie, eds. *Prose for Borges*. A TriQuarterly Book. Evanston: Northwestern University Press, 1974.

O152.

A91 Unnik, W.C. van, ed. *La Littérature Juive entre Tenach et Mischna: Quelques Problemes*. Leiden: E.J. Brill, 1974.

E80.

A92 Fishbane, Michael A., and Paul R. Flohr, eds. *Texts and Responses: Studies Presented to Nahum N. Glatzer on the Occasion of His Seventieth Birthday by His Students*. Leiden: E.J. Brill, 1975.

I31, L230.

A93 Király, Bela K., ed. *Tolerance and Movements of Religious Dissent in Eastern Europe*. East European Monographs, No. XIII. Boulder: East European Quarterly, distributed by New York and London: Columbia University Press, 1975.

K42, L233, L236.

A94 Mayne, Seymour, ed. *The A.M. Klein Symposium*. Ottawa: University of Ottawa Press, 1975.

L229.

A95 *Bibliographical Essays in Medieval Jewish Studies.* The Study of Judaism, Volume II. New York: Published for the Anti-Defamation League of B'nai B'rith by Ktav Publishing House, Inc., 1976.

Volume II of A83. See B12.

A96 Cross, Frank Moore, Werner E. Lemke, and Patrick D. Miller, Jr., eds. *Magnalia Dei: The Mighty Acts of God: Essays on the Bible and Archaeology in Memory of G. Ernest Wright.* Garden City, New York: Doubleday, 1976.

E86, E93.

A97 Nickelsburg, George W.E., Jr., ed. *Studies on the Testament of Abraham.* Society of Biblical Literature Septuagint and Cognate Studies, Number 6. Missoula, Mont.: Scholars Press for the Society of Biblical Literature, 1976.

E87-E89, E91, E92.

A98 Scholem, Gershom G. *On Jews and Judaism in Crisis: Selected Essays.* Ed. Werner J. Dannhauser. New York: Schocken Books, 1976.

M114, N36.

A99 Alter, Robert. *Defenses of the Imagination: Jewish Writers and Modern Historical Crisis.* Philadelphia: Jewish Publication Society of America, 1977.

N61.

A100 Lavender, Abraham D., ed. *A Coat of Many Colors: Jewish Subcommunities in the United States.* Contributions in Family Studies, Number 1. Westport, Conn. and London: Greenwood Press, 1977.

M122, M124-M126.

A101 Shinan, Avigdor, ed. *Proceedings of the Sixth World Congress of Jewish Studies, Held at The Hebrew University of Jerusalem, 13-19 August 1973, under the Auspices of The Israel Academy of Sciences and Humanities.* Jerusalem: World Union of Jewish Studies, 1977.

F79, G31, O180.

A102 Arendt, Hannah. *The Jew as Pariah: Jewish Identity and Politics in the Modern Age.* Ed. Ron H. Feldman. New York: Grover Press, Inc., 1978.

D58.

Festschriften

A103 Chiel, Arthur A., ed. *Perspectives on Jews and Judaism: Essays in Honor of Wolfe Kilman.* New York: Fabbinical Assembly, 1978.

L244, L245, L249, L253.

A104 Heifetz, Harold, ed. *Zen and Hasidism: The Similarities between Two Spiritual Disciplines.* Wheaton, Ill., Madras and London: Theosophical Publishing House, 1978.

D119, D120, L232, L243, L248, L251, L254, M10.

A105 Katz, Steven T., ed. *Mysticism and Philosophical Analysis.* New York: Oxford University Press, 1978.

D2.

A106 Bulka, Reuven P., ed. *Mystics and Medics: A Comparison of Mystical and Psychotherapeutic Encounters.* New York: Human Sciences Press, 1979.

D171-D176, L261.

A107 *Kabbalistes Chrétiens.* Cahiers de l'Hermétisme. Paris: Albin Michel, 1979.

O191.

A108 Katsh, Abraham I., and Leon Nemoy, eds. *Essays on the Occasion of the Seventieth Anniversary of the Dropsie University (1909-1979).* Philadelphia: The Dropsie University, 1979.

L260.

A109 Stein, Siegfried, and Raphael Loewe, eds. *Studies in Jewish Religious and Intellectual History Presented to Alexander Altmann on the Occasion of His Seventieth Birthday.* Published in Association with The Institute of Jewish Studies, London, by University, Alabama: University of Alabama Press, 1979.

F81, J33, L259, M142.

A110 Belmaker, Robert H., and H.M. van Praag, eds. *Mania: An Evolving Concept.* New York: Spectrum Publications, 1980.

K47.

A111 Nahon, Gérard, and Charles Touati, eds. *Hommage à Georges Vajda: Études d'histoire et de pensée juives.* Louvain: Editions Peeters, 1980.

G34, H41.

A112 Stern, J.P., ed. *The World of Franz Kafka*. New York: Holt, Rinehart and Winston, 1980.

M153.

A113 Talmage, Frank, ed. *Studies in Jewish Folklore: Proceedings of a Regional Conference of the Association for Jewish Studies Held at the Spertus College of Judaica, Chicago, May 1-3, 1977*. Conference Coordinator Dov Noy. Cambridge, Mass.: Association for Jewish Studies, 1980.

L265.

A114 Yardeni, Myriam, ed. *Les Juifs dans l'histoire de France: Premier Collaque International de Haïfa*. Institut d'Histoire et de Civilisation francaises de l'Universite de Haïfa. Leiden: E.J. Brill, 1980.

H43.

A115 Berger, Peter L., ed. *The Other Side of God: A Polarity in World Religions*. Garden City, New York: Doubleday, 1981.

L273.

A116 Jospe, Raphael, and Stanley M. Wagner, eds. *Great Schisms in Jewish History*. New York: Center for Judaic Studies, Denver, and Ktav Publishing House, Inc., 1981.

E100, L272.

A117 Dan, Joseph, and Frank Talmage, eds. *Studies in Jewish Mysticism: Proceedings of the Regional Conference Held at the University of California, Los Angeles and McGill University in April, 1978*. Cambridge, Mass.: Association for Jewish Studies, 1982.

C76, D123, D126, F87-F90, G37, H45, H46, L278.

A118 Ostow, Mortimer, ed. *Judaism and Psychoanalysis*. New York: Ktav Publishing House, Inc., 1982.

K49.

A119 Reinharz, Jehuda, and Daniel Swetschinski, eds. *Mystics, Philosophers and Politicians: Essays in Jewish Intellectual History in Honor of Alexander Altmann*. Duke Monographs in Medieval and Renaissance Studies Number 5. Durham, North Carolina: Duke University Press, 1982.

E101, J39, L279.

Festschriften

A120 Katz, Steven T., ed. *Mysticism and Religious Traditions.* New York: Oxford University Press, 1983.

   D4.

A121 Katz, Steven T., ed. *Post Holocaust Dialogues: Critical Studies in Modern Jewish Thought.* New York and London: New York University Press, 1983.

   N48.

A122 Rouner, Leroy S., ed. *Foundation of Ethics.* Boston University Studies in Philosophy and Religion, Volume Four. Notre Dame and London: University of Notre Dame Press, 1983.

   D5.

A123 Wandycz, Damian S., ed. *Studies in Polish Civilization: Selected Papers Presented at the First Congress of the Polish Institute of Arts & Sciences in America, November, 25, 26, 27, 1966 in New York.* New York: Institute on East Central Europe, Columbia University, and The Polish Institute of Arts & Sciences in America, n.d.

   K51.

B. GENERAL REFERENCE WORKS

Included in this chapter are the basic tools of research: Bibliographies, Encyclopedias and Dictionaries, and Histories which contain sections on Jewish mysticism.

Bibliographies

B1 Neubauer, Adolf. *Catalogue of the Hebrew Manuscripts in the Bodleian Library and in the College Libraries of Oxford.* Oxford: University Press, 1886.

Kabbalah, col. 537-641, and passim.

B2 Neubauer, Adolf, comp. *Catalogue of the Hebrew Manuscripts in the Jews' College, London.* Oxford: University Press, 1886.

Mystic Literature and Kabbalah, pp. 22-37.

B3 Scholem, Gerhard. *Bibliographia Kabbalistica: Verzeichnis der gedruckten die jüdische Mystik (Gnosis, Kabbala, Sabbatianismus, Frankismus, Chassidismus) behandeln den Bücher und Aufsätze von Reuchlin bis zur Gegenwort.* Mit einem Anhang: Bibliographie des Zohar und Seiner Kommentare. 2 vols. Leipzig: Drugulin, 1927; 2nd ed. Berlin: Schocken, 1933.

Only available full-length bibliography of Jewish mysticism; in German, but with some English entries.

B4 Schwarzschild, Steven S. "Survey of Current Theological Literature." *Judaism*, 9(1960), 269-76.

Study of "the growing influence and effectiveness of Hasidic Judaism in this country. Hasidism is being transmitted to and implanted in American Jews in two forms: one which, though adjusted to different circumstances, stands in direct line of succession to its traditional mode; the other, in a new Westernized form."

B5 Schachter, Zalman M. "Some Recent Mystical Literature: The Dimension of Devoutness in Jewish Mysticism." *Judaism*, 11(1962), 271-82.

Review of recent mystical literature, including sections on Kabbalah and Hasidism.

B6 Jacobs, Louis. "Current Theological Literature: Mysticism." *Judaism*, 16(1967), 475-81.

Survey of contemporary interest in mysticism, both Jewish and Christian.

B7 Jacobs, Louis. "Current Theological Literature--Hasidism." *Judaism*, 18(1969), 337-42.

Review article on recent publications on Hasidism.

B8 Jacobs, Louis. "Current Theological Literature--Time and Eternity." *Judaism*, 18(1969), 458-63.

Discusses literature which contrasts the "two views in medieval Jewish thought on the relationship between time and eternity. The philosophers tend to distinguish between God's time and the succession of years, days, hours and minutes that we call time, while the Kabbalists tend to think of God as outside time altogether."

B9 Rothschild, Fritz, and Seymour Siegel. "Modern Jewish Thought." In A83. Pp. 113-84.

"The following essay attempts to provide bibliographical information on modern Jewish thought.... works which were written since the second half of the eighteenth century." Section on Hasidism, pp. 128-32.

B10 Fitzmyer, Joseph A. *The Dead Sea Scrolls: Major Publications and Tools for Study.* Sources for Biblical Study, 8. Missoula, Mont.: Society of Biblical Literature and Scholars Press, 1975.

In an effort to sort out all this material [Dead Sea Scrolls], to explain the various sigla used for it, to indicate the places of publication of the Sead Sea Scroll material made available to date, to explain the contents of the texts and to introduce the student to various tools of study, this compilation has been made.

B11 Popenoe, Cris. *Books for Inner Development: The Yes! Guide.* Washington, D.C.: Yes! Inc., distributed by New York: Random House, 1976; rev. ed. 1979.

Index guide to the books sold at Yes! Bookshop, an occult bookstore in Washington, D.C., including section on Jewish mysticism.

B12 Wijnhoven, Jochanan H.A. "Medieval Jewish Mysticism." In A95. II.267-330.

"The literature on mysticism in the biblical period and in contemporary times will be dealt with only briefly in this essay. The principal focus will be on developments from late antiquity until the nineteenth century." The bibliography is divided into: General Studies, Chronological Treatment of Periods, Trends, and Personalities in Jewish Mysticism, and Borderline Areas of Mysticism. The Epilogue deals with Contemporary Jewish Mysticism. Following the bibliographical essay is an alphabetical list of sources, not necessarily in English.

B13 Moonan, Willard. *Martin Buber and his Critics: An Annotated Bibliography of Writings in English through 1978.* Garland Reference Library of the Humanities, Vol. 161. New York and London: Garland Publishing, Inc., 1981.

"The purpose of the present work is to bring together in a systematic arrangement all significant material by and about Buber published in English through 1978."

B14 Faierstein, Morris M. "Hasidana Americana: A Survey of American Literature on Hasidism." *Conservative Judaism*, 35, 3(Spring 1982), 66-74.

"In this survey we will consider literature of Hasidism which has been produced in the United States since 1945, limiting the discussion to scholarly works and translations. Buber's translations of hasidic tales will be considered because, though not originally produced in the United States, these translations have had an enormous impact on the American Jewish community."

Encyclopedias and Dictionaries

B15 Chambers, Ephraim. *Cyclopedia: or an Universal Dictionary of Arts and Sciences; Containing an Explication of the Terms, and an Account of the Things Signified Thereby, in the Several Arts, both Liberal and Mechanical; and the Several Sciences, Human and Divine.* 2 vols. London, 1728. 2nd ed. London, 1738; 3rd ed. Dublin, 1740; 4th ed. London, 1741; 5th ed. London, 1741; 6th ed. London, 1750; 7th ed. London, 1751. Supplemented and improved by Abraham Rees. 5 vols. London, 1778-88; 1786-89. Revised by Rees. 39 vols. London, 1819.

Contains entries on Cabbala, Cabbalists, Gematria and Notaricon.

B16 Calmet, Augustin. *An Historical, Critical, Chronological and Etymological Dictionary of the Holy Bible.* Trans. Samuel D'Oyly and John Colson. 3 vols. London, 1732.

Rev. ed. *Calmet's Great Dictionary of the Holy Bible: Historical, Critical, Geographical, and Etymological.* Ed. C. Taylor. 3 vols. London: C. Taylor, 1797-1801.

Brief entry, Cabala, focuses primarily on Gematria; but the *Dictionary* contains kabbalistic doctrines throughout.

B17 Adams, Hannah. *An Alphabetical Compendium of the Various Sects which have Appeared in the World.* Boston, 1784. Rev. ed. *A Dictionary of all Religions and Religious Denominations, Jewish, Heathen, Mahometan and Christian.* London, 1815.

"The design of [the dictionary] is not to convey an idea of all religious principles being equally true, or safe, to those who imbibe them; but to exhibit the multiplied speculations of the human mind in as just and impartial a manner as possible." In the brief entry on Cabbalists, Adams notes "that nothing can be conceived more silly or extravagant than these mysteries, which are therefore held in contempt by the more intelligent part of the Jewish Nation."

B18 *Encyclopaedia Parthensis; or Universal Dictionary of Knowledge, Collected from every Source; and Intended to Supersede the Use of All other English Books of Reference.* Perth: C. Mitchel and Co., 1806?; 2nd ed. and Supplement, Edinburgh: J. Brown, 1816.

Brief one-page entry on Cabbala, "A mysterious kind of science, pretended to have been delivered by revelation to the ancient Jews, and transmitted by oral tradition to those of our times." Includes a section on Artificial Cabbala, which discusses Gematria, Notaricon and Temurah, and distinguishes between Jewish and occult uses of Kabbalah. Also contains a brief discussion of Cabbalists.

B19 Hook, Walter Farquhar. *A Church Dictionary.* Rev. 4th ed. London: J.G.F. & J. Rivington, 1844; 14th ed. London, 1887.

Discussions of Caballa and Cabbalistics, devoted to Oral Law, and Artificial Cabbala-- Gematria, Notaricon and Temurah: "Most of the heretics, in the primitive Christian Church, fell into the vain conceits of the Cabbala; particularly the Gnostics, Valentinians, and Basilidians." In the paragraph on "Cabbalists," Hooks discusses "Simon, the son of Joachai,... The first Cabbalistical author that we know of."

B20 Kitto, John. *A Cyclopaedia of Biblical Literature.* 2 vols. Edinburgh: A. and C. Black, 1845; New York: M.H. Newman, Cincinnati: W.H. Moore & Co., 1846. Abridged ed. Edinburgh: A. and C. Black, 1852. 3rd ed. greatly enlarged and improved, ed. William Lindsay Alexander. Edinburgh: A. & C. Black, 1862-66.

Article on Kabbalah written by Christian D. Ginsburg; discusses: The Name and its Signification; The Fundamental Doctrines of the Kabbalah; Origin, date, and design of the Kabbalah, and its relation to Platonic and Neo-Platonic philosophy; and Literature.

B21 *The English Cyclopaedia: A New Dictionary of Universal Knowledge.* Conducted by Charles Knight. 25 vols. London: Bradbury and Evans, 1854-72. Synoptical Index, London: Bradbury and Evans, 1862.

Contains brief survey of scholarship, primarily seventeenth-century Christian, about Kabbalah; "Arts and Sciences," vol. 2, col. 488-89.

B22 Ripley, George, and Charles A. Dann, eds. *The New American Cyclopaedia: A Popular Dictionary of General Knowledge.* 16 vols. New York: D. Appleton and Company, 1863. New ed. under title *The American Cyclopaedia: A Popular Dictionary of General Knowledge.* 16 vols. New York: D. Appleton and Company, 1873-76. 2nd ed., 1879. With *A General and Analytical Index to the American Cyclopaedia.* T.J. Conant, ed. New York: D. Appleton and Company, 1878.

Brief introductory entry on "Cabala" (III.521-22), covering etymology, major texts (*Sefer Yetzirah* and Zohar), and basic ideas (*En Sof*, *Sefirot*, pre-existence of souls and Gematria).

B23 McClintock, John, and James Strong. *Cyclopaedia of Biblical, Theological and Ecclestiastical Literature.* 10 vols. New York: Harper, 1867-86; suppl. 1884-87. Rpt. Grand Rapids, Mich.: Baker Book House, 1968; New York: Arno Press, 1969.

"The aim of the work is to furnish a book of reference on all the topics of the science of Theology, in its widest sense, under one alphabet." The article Cabala (II.1-6), "chiefly compiled from Kitto's *Cyclopaedia* [B20] and Herzog's *Real-Encyklopadie*," covers: The Name; Original Documents; Fundamental Doctrines--Nature of the Deity, Development of the Deity, Forms of this Development, Process of the Divine Development, Psychology; Origin, Date, Design, and Relations of the Cabala; and Later Processes of Cabalism.

B24 *The Encyclopaedia Britannica: A Dictionary of Arts, Sciences and General Literature.* 9th ed. 35 vols. Edinburgh and London: Adam and Charles Black, 1875-1889.

Contains an article on Kabbalah by Christian D. Ginsburg (XIII.810-14), which covers the cardinal doctrines of the Sefirot, the four souls and worlds, Christian Kabbalah, and includes a brief bibliography.

B25 Smith, William, and Henry Wace, eds. *A Dictionary of Christian Biography, Literature, Sects and Doctrines, Being A*

Continuation of "The Dictionary of the Bible." 4 vols. London: John Murray, Boston: Little, Brown, and Company, 1877-87.

For this work "designed to furnish, in the form of a Biographical Dictionary, a complete collection of materials for the History of the Christian Church from the time of the Apostles to the Age of Charlemagne, in every branch of this great subject except that of Christian Antiquities," Christian D. Ginsburg updated the article he wrote for Kitto's *Cyclopaedia* (B20).

B26 Baldwin, James Mark, ed. *Dictionary of Philosophy and Psychology; Including Many of the Principal Conceptions of Ethics, Logic, Aesthetics, Philosophy of Religion, Mental Pathology, Anthropology, Biology, Neurology, Physiology, Economics, Political and Social Philosophy, Philology, Physical Science, and Education; and Giving a Terminology in English, French, German, and Italian.* 3 vol. London and New York: Macmillan, 1901-5. New ed. 4 vols. New York: Macmillan, 1910-11. Rpt. New York: Peter Smith, 1925, 1940, 1949.

In accord with the "moderate task" of the dictionary, "to understand the meanings which our terms have, and to render them by clear definitions," the one-page entry Cabala provides only a brief introduction to the doctrines and texts of Kabbalah, primarily the *Sepher Yetzirah* and the *Zohar*.

B27 *The Jewish Encyclopedia: A Descriptive Record of the History, Religion, Literature, and Customs of the Jewish People from the Earliest Times to the Present Day.* Eds. Cyrus Adler and Isidore Singer. 12 vols. New York and London: Funk & Wagnalls, 1901-6; new ed. 1925.

Standard English reference work on Judaica through the first half of the century; contains several articles on Kabbalah, including a general article, Cabala, and Book Yezirah, both by Louis Ginzberg, Zohar, by Isaac Broyde, Pseudo-Messiahs, by H.G. Friedman, and Angelology, by Kaufmann Kohler.

B28 Hastings, James, ed. *Encyclopaedia of Religion and Ethics.* 13 vols. Edinburgh: T. & T. Clark, and New York: C. Scribner's Sons, 1908-26.

Entry on Kabbalah, by H. Loewe, discusses History, Chief theories and doctrines of Kabbalah, and The Chief Kabbalists and their works, and is followed by a brief bibliography. M. Gaster's article on The Zohar covers the Problem of Origin, and History and Influence. In addition, throughout the *Encyclopaedia* there are references to Kabbalah as it relates to other topics.

Encyclopedias and Dictionaries

B29 Mathews, Shailer, and Gerald Birney Smith. *Dictionary of Religion and Ethics*. London: Waverley Book Company, Ltd., and New York: Macmillan Company, 1921. Rpt. Detroit: Gale Research Company, 1973.

Contains very superficial entry on Kabbala by Gotthard Deutsch.

B30 De Haas, Jacob, ed. *The Encyclopedia of Jewish Knowledge, in One Volume*. New York: Behrman's Jewish Book House, 1934, 1938.

Contains brief, introductory articles on Cabala and the Zohar, as well as most of the major figures of the Jewish mystical movement.

B31 *The Universal Jewish Encyclopedia ... an Authoritative and Popular Presentation of Jews and Judaism since the Earliest Times*. Ed. Isaac Landman. 10 vols. New York: Universal Jewish Encyclopedia, Inc., 1939-43. *A Reading Guide and Index*. Comp. Simon Cohen. New York: Universal Jewish Encyclopedia, Inc., 1944.

Jacob S. Minkin's article Cabala (II.614-20), is divided into three main parts: Introduction (Name and Origin); History (Esoteric Speculation in the Bible and Talmud, Mystic Literature of the Gaonic Period, Spread of Kabbalah from the Ninth Century On, Mystic Groups in Central and Western Europe, The Zohar, The Safed School of Mysticism, Cabala in Poland, and The Influence of Cabala on Jewish Life); and Doctrines (God and the World, Man and His Soul, The Hidden Meanings in the Bible, The Conquest of Evil). In Zohar (X.670-71), Ernst Muller lists the parts of the *Zohar*, and briefly discusses authorship, language and major teachings. The *Reading Guide and Index* lists all articles dealing with Jewish mysticism (p. 34).

B32 Ferm, Vergilius, ed. *An Encyclopedia of Religion*. New York: Philosophical Library, 1945.

A "desk-size ready reference work in this vast field," containing several concise entries relating to Jewish mysticism, especially Kabbalah, Zohar and Chasidism.

B33 Gaynor, Frank, ed. *Dictionary of Mysticism*. New York: Philosophical Library,, 1953; London: Wildwood House, 1974.

Dictionary of mystical terminology, including most of Kabbalah's.

B34 *The Standard Jewish Encyclopedia*. Editor-in-chief, Cecil Roth. Jerusalem: Massadah Pub. Co., 1958; Garden City, New York: Doubleday, 1959. Rev. ed. 1962; new rev. ed. 1966.

4th ed., under title *The New Standard Jewish Encyclopedia*, Jerusalem and New York, 1970; and London: W.H. Allen, 1975. 5th ed. 1977.

"... intended basically as a work of contemporary reference"; contains several concise articles related to Kabbalism and major kabbalistic figures.

B35 *The New Jewish Encyclopedia.* Ed. David Bridger, in Association with Samuel Wolk. New York: Berman House, Inc., 1962.

Consists of "a single-volume, handy guide for all those who would like to have the basic and precise information about Judaism ready at hand." Superficial entries on Kabbalah and Zohar.

B36 *Encyclopaedia Britannica: A New Survey of Universal Knowledge.* 14th ed. 24 vols. Chicago: Encyclopaedia Britannica, 1964.

Contains articles on various aspects of Kabbalah written by Alexander Altmann.

B37 *The Encyclopedia of the Jewish Religion.* Eds. R.J. Zwi Werblowsky, and Geoffrey Wigoder. New York: Holt, Rinehart & Winston, Jerusalem: Massada--P.E.C. Press, 1965; and London: Phoenix House, 1967.

An "encyclopedia of Jewish religion, providing the interested layman with concise, accurate, and non-technical information on Jewish belief and practices, religious movements and doctrines, as well as the names and concepts that have played a role in Jewish religious history"; contains entries on the major concepts and figures of Jewish mysticism.

B38 *The Encyclopedia of Philosophy.* Editor-in-chief Paul Edwards. 8 vols. New York: Macmillan Company and The Free Press, and London: Collier-Macmillan Limited, 1967.

"The present encyclopedia is intended ... to cover the whole of philosophy as well as many of the points of contact between philosophy and other disciplines." In the article Cabala (II.1-3), Joseph L. Blau discusses Major Doctrine (Creation, Revelation, Redemption) and Historical Expressions. Blau includes a brief bibliography.

B39 *Man, Myth, and Magic: An Illustrated Encyclopedia of the Supernatural.* Ed. Richard Cavendish. 24 vols. New York: Marshall Cavendish Corp., and London: BPC Publishing, 1970.

The entry Cabala (III.381-387), written by R.J. Zwi Werblowsky, discusses Creation and Splendour, The Abyss of Nothingness, The Ten Sefiroth, The Four Worlds, The Sacred

Marriage, The Breaking of the Vessels, and The Christian Cabala. The *Encyclopedia* also contains a brief entry on Cabala and Modern Magic.

B40 *Encyclopaedia Judaica.* 16 vols. Jerusalem: Keter Publishing House, 1971.

Contains entries on most concepts and figures associated with Jewish mysticism, including extensive articles on Kabbalism and the Zohar by Scholem, and discussions of Hasidism by Avraham Rubenstein, Louis Jacobs and Rifkah Schatz-Uffenheimer. Scholem's articles have been compiled in C65.

B41 *The New Encyclopaedia Britannica.* 15th ed. 30 vols. London, Chicago, etc.: Encyclopaedia Britannica, Inc., 1974.

Contains an article on Jewish Mysticism by G. Vajda (X.182-91), discussing: The Nature and Characteristics (The Judaic Context, Three Types of Jewish Mysticism); Main Lines of Development; and Jewish Mysticism Today. In addition, there are a number of references to Kabbalah in related articles.

B42 Ferguson, John. *An Illustrated Encyclopedia of Mysticism and the Mystery Religions.* London: Thames & Hudson, 1976; and New York: Seabury Press, 1977.

Contains several articles dealing with Jewish mysticism, including Adam Kadmon, Hasidism, Kabbalah, Sefer Yesira, Sefiroth, and Zohar.

Histories

B43 Basnage, Jacques. *The History of the Jews, from Jesus Christ to The Present Time: Containing Their Antiquities, Their Religion, Their Rites, The Dispersion of the Ten Tribes in the East and the Persecutions this Nation has Suffer'd in the West. Being a Supplement and Continuation of The History of Josephus.* Trans. Tho. Taylor. London, 1708.

The first modern history of the Jews, containing the first extensive treatment of Kabbalah in English, though based on Latin sources: "Some perhaps may think, that we are too large upon the Cabalists, whose mystical Science is not discover'd without Difficulty, and seems useless. But not to examine at present, whether it be proper to expose the Vanity of their Speculations, three Things have made this discussion necessary to us. *1st.* The Gnosticks and Hereticks of the second century, had a great Affinity with the Cabalists, from whom they borrow'd their *Emanations*, *Aeons* and barbarous Names.... *2dly*. Besides, 'tis almost a general Prejudice among the Learned, that the Heathens have taken their Cabala and Tradition from the Jews; and that the Religion of the latter hath been receiv'd by the others,... This very Prejudice hath engag'd us to run up as high as the Original Source of the Cabala among the Egyptians, to unfold the Principles of Philosophers, and to shew that they did not agree with the Jews, but in notions common to Mankind; and that the Rabbins have been rather their Disciples, than Masters." Most of Book III is devoted to "the Particulars of the Cabbala" (pp. 184-256).

B44 Lewis, Thomas. *Origines Hebraeae: The Antiquities of the Hebrew Republick ... Design'd as an Explanation of Every Branch of the Levitical Law, and of All the Ceremonies and Usages of the Hebrews, both Civil and Sacred.* 4 vols. London, 1724-25. New ed. Oxford: University Press, 1835.

Attempts "to explain with Learning and Judgment the Antiquities of so renowned a Part of Mankind as the *Republick of the Hebrews*" because it "admirably serves the Interest of Christianity itself; insomuch that to attempt after Knowledge in the Doctrine and Discipline of the Gospel, without searching into the Customs and Ceremonies of the Law, is a preposterous Persuit, and must end in Ignorance and Disappointment." Vol. IV, chapter 29, The Cabala (pp. 164-69), briefly surveys the mythological history of Kabbalah, and then distinguishes "three Sorts ... a Mystical, Allegorical, or Analogical Explication of Passages of Scripture ... a sort of Magic or Necromancy" and Gematria.

B45 Stehelin, John Peter. *The Traditions of the Jews, with the Expositions and Doctrines of the Rabbins. Contain'd in the Talmud and Other Rabbinical Writing.* 2 vols. London, 1732-34; 1742-43.

Though based on Johann Andreas Eisenmenger's *Entdecktes Judenthum* (Judaism Unmasked), Stehelin's *Traditions of the Jews* is distinct from its original since "Dr. Eisenmenger's Scope was different from mine; his was to ridicule the Traditions of the Jews, mine is to explain them" because "Articles of your Faith, if rightly explain'd, contain the true Doctrine of Christ, and may be subscrib'd by us Christians ourselves." Pages 142-66 of the second volume are devoted to "the Cabala, a famous Art among that People, by which the Adepti therein pretend to reach the Knowledge of all Mysteries, and to accomplish very wonderful Matters, which are not to be effected by the Laws or Powers of Nature." The section contains a brief introduction to Kabbalah in general, and Christian Kabbalah in particular, the kinds of Kabbalah, mythical origin of the subject, and a detailed explanation of the values and meanings of the letters of the Hebrew alphabet.

B46 Burnet, Thomas. *Doctrina antiqua de rerum originibus; or, An Inquiry into the Doctrine of the Philosophers of All Nations, Concerning the Original of the World.* Trans. Mr. Mead and Mr. Foxton. London, 1736.

"But besides these most antient Matters, we have interwoven a Sort of philosophical History, not universal, but so far as relates to Doctrines, and those chiefly which regard the Original of Things; observing moreover, the Genius of each Nation or sect, and their Method of philosophising, whether Vulgar or Mystical, Accurate or Fabulous." In Chapter 7, Of the Hebrews and the Cabala (pp. 56-90), Burnet explains "That the Jews were the most trifling of all the Barbarians, and that they were the only People who had never found out any Thing useful for Life." Therefore, "the Jewish Cabala is but a Dream without an Interpreter,... and whatsoever it has been formerly, at present, it is like Salt which has lost its Savour, it is therefore good for nothing but to be thrown away." Using the *Kabbala Denudata* as his primary source, Burnet derides kabbalistic theories of Numerology, the *Sefirot*, Cosmology, basic tenets of Lurianic Kabbalah, the Zohar, Creation and Apocalypse.

B47 Enfield, William. *The History of Philosophy from the Earliest Periods: Drawn up from Brucker's Historia Critica Philosophiae.* 2 vols. London, 1791; Dublin, 1792; London, 1819; London, 1837; London, 1839; London, 1879.

"I could not render my country men better service than by taking upon my self to become ... their reader; and determined to undertake the task of communicating to them, in their vernacular tongue, the *substance*" of Brucker's Latin *History of Philosophy.* In Book IV, The Philosophy of the Jews, Enfield explains Kabbalah as the "mystical interpretation of the law, [which] was brought over from Egypt to Palestine by Simeon Shetach.... The traditionary mystical wisdom, called the Cabbala, which after the destruction of the Jewish state was studied and taught with great industry. The most famous Cabbalists were Akibha, the author of the book *Jezirah*, and Simeon Jochaides, who wrote the book *Sohar*. A disciple of the former was Simeon Ben Jochai;... "

B48 Maurice, Thomas. *Indian Antiquities: or, Dissertations, Relative to the Ancient Geographical Divisions, the Pure System of Primeval Theology, the Grand Code of Civil Laws, the Original Form of Government, the Widely-Extended Commerce, and the Various and Profound Literature, of Hindostan: Compared, throughout, with the Religion, Laws, Government, and Literature, of Persia, Egypt, and Greece. The Whole Intended as Introductory to, and Illustrative of, the History of Hindostan, upon a Comprehensive Scale.* 7 vols. London, 1793-1806; 1800-12.

In Volume IV, In Which the Hebrew Trinity and the Oriental Triads of Deity are Extensively Investigated, Maurice devotes pages 166-210 to Kabbalah, discussing: the oral transmission of doctrine; major kabbalistic texts (the Zohar and *Sefer Yetzirah*); the *Sefirot* as they relate to Mithratic and Eleusynian Mysteries; and the names of God and numerology, as resembling Hinduism. Relies heavily on Basnage (B43) for information about Kabbalah.

B49 Adams, Hannah. *The History of the Jews from the Destruction of Jerusalem to the Nineteenth Century*. 2 vols. Boston, 1812; London, 1818.

"The design of this work, including the introduction, is to give a brief sketch of their situation, after their return from the Babylonian captivity, to the nineteenth century." The last section of Chapter III (I.119-26), devoted to Kabbalah as discussed by Basnage (B43) and Enfield (B47), briefly covers the origin of kabbalistic doctrine, the Zohar and *Sefer Yetzirah*.

B50 Allen, John. *Modern Judaism: or, A Brief Account of the Opinions, Traditions, Rites, and Ceremonies, of the Jews in Modern Times*. London, 1816, 1830.

"A firm believer in Christianity himself, the Author cannot but contemplate Modern Judaism as an awful delusion,... he has studied to be impartial; neither to extenuate nor exaggerate, but to describe things as they are." Chapter 5, The Cabbala (pp. 65-94), covers: The Term explained; Two kinds, Theoretical and Practical; The latter a mere System of magical Superstition; The Theoretical Cabbala subdivided into two Species: Symbolical and Literal; Some Account of each; and Different Opinions of the Value and Use of the Cabbalah. For information, Allen relies on Brucker (English trans. B47) and Maurice (B48).

B51 Milman, Henry Hart. *The History of the Jews, from the Earliest Period down to Modern Times*. Murray's Family Library. London, 1829-30; New York, 1841. Rev. ed. London, 1863; New York, 1864.

A relatively comprehensive history of the Jews; devotes part of Chapter 27 to false messiahs—Sabbatai Zevi and Jacob Frank. In the revised edition, Milman also includes Chapter 30, Survey of Influence of the Jews on Philosophy, Poetry, History, &c., containing discussions of Kabbalah based on A. Franck (C39): a comparison of Kabbalah and Zendavesta, an analysis of Kabbalah's attitude towards marriage, and an introduction to the adepts of Kabbalah.

B52 Finn, James. *Sephardim; or, The History of the Jews in Spain and Portugal*. London, 1841.

Contains a brief introduction to Kabbalah: definition, pseudepigraphical history, and discussion of the three basic types--Theoretical, Aenigmatical and Practical (pp. 241-47).

B53 Costa, Isaac da. *Israel and the Gentiles: Contributions to the History of the Jews from the Earliest Times to the Present Day.* Trans. Mary J. Kennedy. London, 1850.

"The sketch of Jewish history presented here in these pages, and viewed in the light of Christian truth, may perhaps appear as foolishness, and an offence to my brethren concerning the flesh; but in taking up the book, they will find, nevertheless, that still bears the impress of its author's Israelitish origin." (Translator's note) Da Costa discusses Sabbathai Zevi, the False Messiah (pp. 475-84), and Sabbathaism as influenced by Kabbalah and leading up to Chasidism (pp. 506-45).

B54 Etheridge, John Wesley. *Jerusalem and Tiberias; Sora and Cordova, a Survey of the Religious and Scholastic Learning of the Jews; Designed as an Introduction to the Study of Hebrew Literature.* London: Longman, Brown, Green, and Longmans, 1856.

A study of Hebrew literature intended to open the lines of communication between Jews and Christians; divides Hebrew literature into seven "Orders": 1. In the New Hebrew of the Soferite and Mishnaic Time; 2. In Aramaic; 3. The Mixed or Talmudic dialect; 4. Arabic; 5. Arabized Hebrew; 6. The purer Hebrew of the Renaissance; and 7. Works written in the several languages of Europe. Beginning Order 7 is Kabalists (pp. 293-362), a discussion of the major doctrines and texts of Jewish mysticism, concluding that "its material was deduced out of the theosophic dogmas of Zoroaster, not, indeed, as a servile copy, but as a modification adapted, so far as the Jews could make it, to the theology of Moses and the prophets."

B55 Steinschneider, Moritz. *Jewish Literature from the Eighth to the Eighteenth Century, with an Introduction on Talmud and Midrash: A Historical Essay.* London: Longman, Brown, Green, Longman, & Roberts, 1857. Rpt. New York: Hermon Press, 1965, 1970; Hildesheim: Gg. Olms, 1967.

An expansion and English translation of an article written for Ersch and Gruber's *Encyclopaedia*; contains a survey of Jewish writings as literature. The thirteenth section of Period II, Mysteries and Kabbala (pp. 104-15), is an attempt to trace the historical development of the transformation of the older mysteries (Period I, section 5: Haggada) "into Kabbala first in Europe, and subsequently in the East," beginning with Isaac the Blind, "Father of the Kabbala," twelfth century through the fifteenth.

B56 Ueberweg, Frederich. *A History of Philosophy from Thales to the Present Time*. Trans. George S. Morris. 2 vols. London: Hodder, and New York: C. Scribner and Company, 1872-74. Rpt. Freeport, New York: Books for Libraries Press, 1972.

Section 97, The Philosophy of the Jews in the Middle Ages (I.417-28), considers medieval Jewish philosophy as "Partly the Cabala and partly the transformed doctrine of Plato and Aristotle." Contains an extensive bibliography.

B57 Graetz, Heinrich Hirsch. *History of the Jews*. Trans. Bella Lowy. 6 vols. Philadelphia: Jewish Publication Society of America, 1891-98.

"This translation ... is not a mere excerpt of my 'Geschichte der Juden' ... but a condensed reproduction of the entire eleven volumes. But the foot-notes have been omitted, so as to render the present work less voluminous for the general reader." Graetz discusses mysticism in several places: The Maimunist Controversy and the Rise of the Kabbala (Vol. III, ch. 16, pp. 522-62); Cultivation of the Kabbala, and Proscription of Science (Vol. IV, ch. 1, pp. 1-45); The Kabbala and Messianic Fanaticism. the Marranos and the Inquisition (Vol. IV, ch. 15, pp. 477-528); Spinoza and Sabbatai Zevi (Vol. V, ch. 4, pp. 86-167); and The New Chassidism (Vol. V, ch. 9, pp. 374-94). In addition, there are smaller sections on various kabbalistic topics.

B58 Abrahams, I. *A Short History of Jewish Literature*. London, 1906. Chapter 17.

Unavailable for annotating.

B59 Baskerville, Beatrice C. *The Polish Jew: His Social and Economic Value*. New York: Macmillan Company, 1906.

The "result of eight years' residence in the country"; writen "both for the sake of the pauper aliens themselves and for that of the peoples among whom they eventually settle." Part II, chapter 3, Frank and his Followers (pp. 261-81), focuses on the effects of Jacob Frank on the Polish Jewish community.

B60 Dubnow, Semen M. *History of the Jews in Russia and Poland, from the Earliest Times until the Present Day*. Trans. I. Friedlaender. 3 vols. Philadelphia: Jewish Publication Society of America, 1916-20. Rpt. New York: Ktav Publishing House, 1975.

Contains several chapters on mysticism: Secular Science, Philosophy, Cabala, and Apologetics (I.131-38), focusing on Kabbalah as "an Orthodox counter-philosophy" in Poland; and chapter 6 of the first volume (pp. 188-241) explores the effects of mystical literature, the Sabbatian Movement, the Frankist Sect, Hasidism and Israel Baal-Shem Tob, Hasidic Propaganda, and Tzadikism, on Polish Jewry.

B61 Graetz, Heinrich Hirsch. *Popular History of the Jews.* Trans. A.B. Rhine. 6 vols. New York: Hebrew Publishing Company, 1919.

Amplified translation of Graetz's three-volume *Volkstümliche Geschichte der Juden* (1888). Sections devoted to mysticism are: The Prevalence of Fanaticism and of the Cabala: 1270-1306 (Vol. III, pt. ii, ch. 9, pp. 370-420); The Activity of the Maranos and the Cabalistic-Messianic Fancies: 1530-1548 (Vol. IV, pt. iii, ch. 2, pp. 325-65); and Spinoza and Sabbathai Zebi (Vol. V, pt. i, ch. 5, pp. 136-82). There are also brief references to mysticism throughout the work.

B62 Oesterley, William O.E., and George H. Box. *A Short Survey of the Literature of Rabbinical and Mediaeval Judaism.* London and New York: Macmillan, 1920. Rpt. New York: Burt Franklin, 1973.

Contains an outline of The Mystical Literature (pt. iv, ch. 3, pp. 235-54), much of which is based on articles from the *Jewish Encyclopedia* (B27), Christian Ginzburg's *Kabbalah* (C25), and A. Franck's *La Kabbale* (English translation, C39). Includes discussions of texts (*Sepher Yetzirah, Zohar, Shi'ur Komah, Sepher Raziel,* and *Hekaloth* literature and the Bahir), major figures (Aaron ben Samuel ha-Nasi, Solomon ibn Gebirol, Isaac the Blind, Azriel, Moses de Leon, Isaac Luria), and Chasidism.

B63 Webster, Nesta H. *Secret Societies and Subversive Movements.* London: Boswell Printing & Publishing Co. Ltd., 1924. Rpt. New York: E.P. Dutton & Co., 1955.

"The object of the present book is [to trace] the course of revolutionary ideas through secret societies from the earliest times, indicating the role of the Jews only where it is to be clearly detected, but not seeking to implicate them where good evidence is not forthcoming." Chapter 8, The Jewish Cabalists (pp. 177-95), explains that "throughout the Middle Ages it is as sorcerers and usurers that [Jews] incur the reproaches of the Christian world, and it is still in the same role, under the more modern terms of magicians and loanmongers, that we detect their presense behind the scenes of revolution from the seventeenth century onward." Webster discusses Manasseh ben Israel, Sabbatai Zevi, the Ba'al Shem Tov, Joel ben Uri Heilprin, Jacob Frank, Martines Pasqually and Hayyim Samuel Jacob Falk.

B64 Dubnow, Semen M. *An Outline of Jewish History.* 3 vols. New York: Max N. Maisel, 1925.

In this condensed translation of Dubnow's longer *History of the Jews* (B85), basic information on Kabbalah can be found in the third volume: The Cabal and the Zohar (pp.114-18); The Jews in Turkey and Palestine Up to the Decline of Sabbathism (1492-1750), with sections on The Cabala--Ari (pp. 184-88), Sabbatai Zevi (pp. 188-92); and The Messianic Movement and Its Fall (p. 193). Dubnov also includes sections on Sabbathians and Frankists (pp. 260-67), Israel Besht and Hassidism (pp. 286-91), and The Struggle Between the Rabbis and the Hassidim (pp. 291-97).

B65 Sachar, Abram Leon. *A History of the Jews*. New York: Alfred A. Knopf, 1930; 2nd ed. 1940; 3rd ed. 1948; 4th ed. 1953; 5th ed. 1965.

The first section of Chapter 18, Degeneration, is devoted to "the perversions of the Cabala ... a blind faith in false Messiahs" (pp. 233-36). Sachar deals primarily with *Sefer Yetzirah*, the Bahir and the Zohar. In the fifth section of Degeneration, he discusses Shabbathai and his Successors (pp. 242-45); and the first two sections of Chapter 20, The End of the Jewish Middle Ages, focus on the Baal Shem Tob (pp. 264-66), and Elijah, The Vilna Gaon (pp. 266-67).

B66 Waxman, Meyer. *A History of Jewish Literature*. 5 vols. South Brunswick, New York and London: Thomas Yoseloff, 1933, 1960.

"The purpose of this history is to make accessible to the large lay intelligent public the results of Jewish scholarship and reserch in the various branches of Jewish literature, carried on during the last century; to coordinate and correlate the scattered facts and the numerous data, so as to present a complete picture of the productivity of the Jewish genius during the ages." In the section on The Kabbala (Vol. II, ch. 7, pp. 337-421), Waxman provides an Introduction to German types of Kabbala, Speculative Kabbala and Symbolism; and sections on the Teachings of the Kabbala (The Theory of the Sephiroth, The Four worlds, Creation and Man); and The Literature of the Kabbala: General features, Early Kabbalistic works, The Zohar, The character of the Zohar, Kabbalistic literature of the fourteenth and fifteenth centuries, Later Kabbalistic literature, Moses Cordovero, Isaac Luria Ashkenazi (the Ari), and Post-Lurianic literature. He also includes sections on early mysticism (Vol. I, ch. 12, pp. 372-93), and Hassidism (Vol. III, ch. 1, pp. 18-51).

B67 Saurat, Denis. *A History of Religions*. London: Jonathan Cape, 1934.

Chapter 6, Israel, contains a section on The Cabala (pp. 183-92), discussing "the Cabala [as] a system of optimistic pantheism," dealing with God, The Sexual Law, Wrath and Reincarnation.

Histories

B68 Baron, Salo Wittmayer. *A Social and Religious History of the Jews*. 3 vols. New York: Columbia University Press, 1937.

The shorter, three-volume version of Baron's *Social and Religious History of the Jews* (see B71), includes little information specifically about mysticism. The major exception, the section on Hasidism (II.153-62), describes the growth of the movement as "the rebellion of the half-illiterate rural Jew against the supremacy of the learned urban Jew."

B69 Agus, Jacob B. *Modern Philosophies of Judaism: A Study of Recent Jewish Philosophers of Religion*. New York: Behrman's Jewish Book House, 1941.

"The purpose of this book is to expound the basic ideas of modern Jewish religious thought. We do not attempt to discuss all the problems of Jewish theology which occupy the attention of modern rabbis.... Our main interest is in the conception of God and in His relation to man." Agus includes an "extended treatment of Buber's writings" because "Buber's mysticism and lifelong spiritual development is of a most interesting type, and, we venture to add, typically Jewish. Since the life of the spirit cannot be departmentalized, it is necessary to discuss Buber's youthful literary vagaries and his public activities along with his distinctly mystical works" (Ch. 4, Martin Buber, pp. 213-79).

B70 Greenberg, Louis. *The Jews in Russia: The Struggle of Emancipation*. 2 vols. New Haven: Yale University Press, 1944-51; rpt. 1965. Rpt. New York: Schocken Books, 1976.

"This book deals with the rise and development of the movement for civic rights carried on by Russian Jewry during the second half of the nineteenth century." In Chapter 5, The Cultural and Moral Status of Russian Jewry (pp. 68-72), Greenberg explores the thesis that "The importance which *Hassidism* attached to the emotional aspects of Judaism as opposed to the intellectual was an expression of the revolt of the masses against the aristocracy and autocracy of the learned class."

B71 Baron, Salo Wittmayer. *A Social and Religious History of the Jews*. 17 vols. 2nd ed., rev. and enlarged. New York: Columbia University Press, 1957.

Expanded version of B68, containing an expanded treatment of mysticism. Volume V, chapter 25, covers Messianism and Sectarian Trends: Apocalyptic-Aggadic Messianism; Poetic and Exigetical Derivations; Messianic Rationales; Messianic and Sectarian Movements; Samaritanism; Newer Divisions; National Upsurge, Military and Ideological Commotions; Reappearance of Pseudo-Messiahs; and Unity within Diversity. Volume VIII, chapter 33, Magic and Mysticism, discusses: the Homiletical-

Mystical Heritage; Works of Creation and of the Chariot; Attitude toward Law and History; Mixed Reception; Book of the Bright Light; Provençal Conventicles; German Hasidism; and Occult Byways.

B72 Bouyer, Louis. *The Meaning of Sacred Scripture.* Trans. Mary Perkins Ryan. Notre Dame [Ind.] University. Liturgical Studies, Vol. 5. Notre Dame: University of Notre Dame Press, and London: Dartons, Longman & Todd, 1958.

Text of twenty-four lectures delivered by Father Bouyer; explores "the purpose of divine revelation, as evidenced in all the books of the Bible." Chapter 13, Is There a Jewish Mysticism (pp. 135-48), refutes the notion "that mysticism and the Jewish religion are terms exclusive of one another"; and Chapter 14, Moses and Elias in Jewish Mysticism (pp. 149-55), isolates these "two prophetic personalities as having a unique significance."

B73 Agus, Jacob B. *The Evolution of Jewish Thought from Biblical Times to the Opening of the Modern Era.* Ram's Horn Books. London and New York: Abelard-Schuman 1959.

About "the unfolding of Jewish thought from its beginnings in antiquity to the modern period." Contains two chapters dealing with mysticism: Chapter 9, The Qabbalah (pp. 276-90), considers the Nature of Qabbalistic literature and its authority; Qabbalah as the attempt to justify naive faith against the challenge of rationalism; Tension between the personalistic thinking of Judaism and the mechanistic logic of Aristotle; Principles of polarity and continuity in Qabbalah; Reasons for the Commandments; and the Cosmic status of the Jewish people. And Chapter 11, Hasidism (pp. 315-70), includes references to Sabbatai Zevi and Jacob Frank as precursors to the mystical piety of the Baal Shem Tov.

B74 Epstein, Isidore. *Judaism: A Historical Presentation.* Harmondsworth, Middlesex and Baltimore: Penguin Books, 1959; rpt. 1960, 1964, 1966, and 1968.

" ... essentially concerned with Judaism as a religious and a distinctive way of life which it seeks to present against a background of 4,000 years of Jewish history from Bible times to the establishment of the modern State of Israel in our own days." Chapter 19, Jewish Mysticism: The *Kabbalah* (pp. 223-51), provides a brief historical survey and basic introduction to the major tenets of Jewish mysticism.

B75 Baer, Yitzhak. *A History of the Jews in Christian Spain.* Trans. Louis Schoffman. 2 vols. Philadelphia: Jewish Publication Society of America, 1961.

Chapter 6, Mysticism and Social Reform (I.243-305): "The same thirteenth century, marked by social tension, also witnessed the growth of interest in mysticism. The cabalistic movement contributed decisively to the shaping of Jewish history. It is worthwhile for the historian, therefore, to trace the roots of this movement in its native soil in terms of the conditions prevailing at the time of its emergence. For the cabalists were not absorbed solely in mystical thought; they also opened a vigorous attack against the dominant courtier class and participated actively in the efforts to raise the level of religious and moral life.... we will attempt in the following pages to relate this great metaphysical movement to its physical background."

B76 Bergmann, Samuel Hugo. *Faith and Reason: An Introduction to Modern Jewish Thought*. Trans. Alfred Jospe. The Hillel Little Books, Vol. 5. Washington: B'nai B'rith Hillel Foundations, 1961. Rpt. New York: Schocken Books, 1963.

" ... concentrates on an analysis of the two major issues which he considers of paramount importance for the Jew in our time: How does the thinker resolve the tension between faith and reason, and how does he answer the question whether there still is a distinctively or uniquely Jewish way to God?" (Translator's note) In exploring these questions, Bergman includes sections on Martin Buber (pp. 81-97), and Rav Kook (pp. 121-41).

B77 Katz, Jacob. *Tradition and Crisis: Jewish Society at the End of the Middle Ages*. New York: Free Press of Glencoe, Inc., 1961. Rpt. New York: Schocken Books, 1971.

"We propose to describe, in terms of a socio-historical analysis, traditional Jewish society in the stage prior to its dissolution, i.e., from the sixteenth to the second half of the eighteenth century. This dissolution itself, the transition to Hasidism in eastern Europe and to Enlightenment and Emancipation in the West, forms the epilogue to our subject." Chapter 22 focuses on The Transition to Hasidism (pp. 231-44).

B78 Blau, Joseph L. *The Story of Jewish Philosophy*. New York: Random House, 1962. Rpt. New York: Ktav Publishing House, 1971.

"This book is not written for philosophers or for scholars in the Jewish field, though I hope that even these may find in it something to arouse or to hold their interest. It is written as part of a larger program,... to make the age-old tradition of the Jewish people available to modern men and women in a language that they can understand and an idiom that is not strange or obscure." Chapter 4, From Gnosticism to Kabbala (pp. 89-121), covers: Jewish Gnostics; Mysticism of the Throne; The Mystery of Creation; Beginnings of the Kabbala; The Pious of Germany; Mystical Speculation in Provence and Spain; Abraham ben Samuel Abulafia; Joseph ben

Abraham Gikatilia; The Book of Splendor; The Ideas of the Book of Splendor; and Moses Cordovero, Systematizer."

B79 Cahn, Zvi. *The Philosophy of Judaism: The Development of Jewish Thought throughout the Ages, the Bible, the Talmud, the Jewish Philosophers, and the Cabala, until the Present Time.* New York: Macmillan Company, 1962.

Intention is "to provide answers for some of the layman's basic questions on the origin and development of the ideas and ideals that make up Judaism." Chapter 11, The Messianic Ideal (pp. 207-17), discusses: The Beginning; The Messiah of the Pharisees; The Hezekiah Group; The Qualities of the Messiah; The New Views; Ideology of the Gnostics; The Beginning of Christianity; and The Jewish View as of Today. In addition, throughout the book are other topics related to mysticism: The View of the Mystics concerning the ideology of reward and punishment; Paradise and Gehenna; The Ideology of the Resurrection of the Dead; The Beginnings of the Cabala; and The "Golden Age" of Spain, which includes The Discovery of the Zohar.

B80 Dimont, Max I. *Jews, God and History.* New York: Simon and Schuster, 1962.

Purpose is to present "a popular history of this amazing people, written without bowing to orthodoxy or pandering to anti-intellectualism." Chapter 22, Kabala and Kinnanhorra (pp. 271-86), which identifies Kabbalah as the sum of "the spirit of Jewish Middle Ages," contains a brief survey of Kabbalah as it relates to Jewish history, touching on the major texts and figures of both Jewish and Christian Kabbalah.

B81 Spencer, Sidney. *Mysticism in World Religion.* South Brunswick and New York: A.S. Barnes and Co., 1963.

In order "to present an account of the various types of mystical religion in a single volume ... the present work has been written." Chapter 6, Hebrew and Jewish Mysticism (pp. 170-211), discusses first, Mysticism in the Old Testament, and then, Jewish Mysticism, specifically: Early Jewish Mysticism; Medieval Hasidism; Abulafia and Prophetic Kabbalism; The "Zohar" and Speculative Kabbalism; The School of Isaac Luria and Messianic Kabbalism; Sabbatianism, a Mystical Heresy; and Modern Hasidism.

B82 Kadushin, Max. *Worship and Ethics: A Study in Rabbinic Judaism.* Evanston, Ill.: Northwestern University Press, 1964.

"The aim of this book is to describe how Halakah [the rabbinic law], working with the value concepts of the folk as a whole, enables the individual to achieve a religious experience." Chapter 7, Worship as Normal Mysticism (pp. 163-98), is divided into four sections: From *Gilluy Shekinah* to Normal Mysticism; Interrelation of Worship and Ethics; What Normal Mysticism is Not; and *Kawwanah*.

B83 Borchsenius, Poul. *The History of the Jews*. 5 vols. New York: Simon and Schuster, 1965.

Very basic history of the Jews, containing very basic introduction to The Cabbala (Vol. II, ch. 9, pp. 137-57); Safed (Vol. III, ch. 4, pp. 67-82); and Hasidism (Vol. II, ch. 12, pp. 204-12).

B84 Rabinowicz, Harry M. *The Legacy of Polish Jewry: A History of Polish Jews in the Inter-War Years, 1919-1939*. New York and London: T. Yoseloff, 1965.

"This work relates the story of Polish Jewry during these fateful inter-war years, outlining basic trends and sketching a general picture of the Polish scene." Chapter 8, The Fires of Chassidism (pp. 126-47), focuses on the growing power of the Chassidic movement during the inter-war years.

B85 Dubnow, Semen M. *History of the Jews*. Trans. Moshe Spiegel. 5 vols. South Brunswick, New Jersey, New York and London: Thomas Yoseloff, 1967.

"This is a universal history of the Jewish people in that it fully corresponds to the contents and the scope of this extraordinary part of the history of mankind." See: Vol. II, ch. 61, Apocrypha and Apocalypse (I.692-701); Vol. II, ch. 97, Philo of Alexandria, (I.828-37); Vol. III, ch. 71, The Religious Philosophy of Saadyah Gaon, the Rationalists and the Mystics (II.412-20); Vol. IV, ch. 40, Moralists and Mystics (II.715-20); Vol. V, ch. 18, Mystical Theosophy, Kabbalists and Messiah-Seekers (III.123-28); Vol. V, ch. 19, The Zohar (III.129-33); Vol. V, ch. 26, Anti-Rationalism, Mysticism, and Martyrology (III.167-71); Vol. VI, ch. 7, The Mystic [sic] of Safed: Cordovero and Ari (III.503-9); Vol. VI, ch. 8, Practical Kabbala, Its Influence in Life and Literature (III.509-16); Vol. VI, ch. 18, Rabbinism and Mysticism (III.581-86); Vol. VI, ch. 49, Theology, Kabbala, Apologia, Popular Literature (III.810-21); Vol. VII, chs. 4-8, on Sabbatai Zevi (IV.45-81); Vol. VII, ch. 22, Kabbalists and Sectarians; The Secret Shabbetaians (IV.167-71); Vol. VII, ch. 52, Spiritual Split, The Apostate Frankists (IV.378-94); Vol. VII, chs. 53-54, on Hasidism (IV.394-409); Vol. VIII, ch. 51, The Hassidic-Mithnagged Schism and the Intervention of the Government (IV.742-47); Vol. VIII, ch. 52, The Rabbinate and the Triumphant Hasidism (IV.747-53).

B86 Kertzer, Morris N. *Today's American Jew*. New York, Toronto, London and Sydney: McGraw-Hill Book Company, 1967.

This "profile of the American Jew" considers the questions: "In what way are Jews different because they happen to live in the United States? In what way is America different because of its Jews?" Chapter 12, The Hasidim (pp. 158-72), is a basic introduction to Hasidism in America.

B87 Eban, Abba. *My People: The Story of the Jews*. New York: Behrman House, Inc., and Random House, Inc., and Toronto: Random House of Canada Limited, 1968.

"This is not only or mainly a record of the uncommon events which compose my people's story. It is largely a personal reflection on these events and a particular response to their origins and echoes." In Chapter 14, Mysticism and Messianism (pp. 231-45), Eban briefly discusses False Messiahs, Hasidism, and The Nature of Messianism.

B88 Gersh, Harry. *The Sacred Books of the Jews*. New York: Stein and Day, 1968.

"The books discussed in this volume ... were chosen because they were and are read wherever Jews are permitted to function as Jews, because they changed the ways in which Jews thought, expressed themselves, and reacted, and because they were important to the much wider world in which Jews lived." Chapter 13, Mysticism: The *Kabbalah* and the *Zohar* (pp. 197-213), traces the development of Kabbalah as it "served two major purposes: it elevated prayer, the mystic union of man with God, to a central position in Judaism, when formal Talmudic study tended to de-emphasize it; and it moved Jews away from the dead end of Aristotelianism. But in doing so, Kabbalah also gave to Judaism--particularly to Chasidism--a burden of magic and superstition that was foreign to its ethical-rationalistic base."

B89 Katsaros, Thomas, and Nathaniel Kaplan. *The Western Mystical Tradition: An Intellectual History of Western Civilization*. New Haven: College & University Press, 1969.

"This work sets in historical perspective the Western mystical tradition from its early Greek beginnings to the present day and points out its relevance to twentieth-century man. Intellectual currents are examined for their streams of mystical thought, inherent in the founding of all major religions and many philosophical and psychological systems." The chapter on The Cabalah (pp. 268-84), which relies heavily on Franck (C39) and Müller (C48), includes material on *Sefer Yetzirah*, the Zohar, the *Sefirot*, the souls and Abraham ben Samuel Abulafia.

B90 Bridges, Hal. *American Mysticism: From William James to Zen*. New York: Harper & Row, 1970. Rpt. Lakemont, Georgia: CSA Press, 1977.

Specifies Abraham Joshua Heschel as exemplifying one of the three varieties of American mysticism as it developed from the Judeo-Christian tradition (pp. 60-65).

B91 Neusner, Jacob. *A History of the Jews in Babylonia.* Post-Biblica, V. Later Sasanian Times. Leiden: E.J. Brill, 1970.

"This book ... is no exhaustive history of Babylonian Jewry and Judaism, but at best an effort to promote the understanding of a few basic problems of Talmudic historiography and religion." Chapter 6, Other Jews, Other Magicians (pp. 217-43), "review[s] the chief exempla of magical bowls apparently written by or for Jews (or both) and then consider[s] their implications for the study of the history of Judaism." As a supplement to Chapter 6, Baruch A. Levine studies The Language of the Magical Bowls (in the Appendix, pp. 343-73), as part of "a large body of literature produced in late antiquity and in the Medieval period dealing with the acquisition of mystical knowledge and its utilization either in theurgic or mystical activities."

B92 Mahler, Raphael. *A History of Modern Jewry, 1780-1815.* New York: Schocken Books, and London: Valentine, Mitchell, 1971.

"*A History of Modern Jewry, 1780-1815* presented here for the reader is the first, self contained part of a projected multi-volume history. It begins in the middle of the eighteenth century and includes the period of enlightened absolutism, the French Revolution and the Napoleonic Wars, down to the Congress of Vienna, 1815." Chapter 12, The Rise of Hassidism and its Flowering (pp. 430-535), an analysis of "The abundant creative force accumulated by the teeming and seething masses of eastern European Jewry [which] erupted for the first time in its full splendour with the Hassidic movement," has three parts: A. Social and National Background of the Hassidic Movement; B. The Age of Growth and of Controversy; and C. Efflorescence and Expansion (a. Hassidism in Lithuania and White Russia, b. Hassidism in the Ukraine and Galicia, and c. The Beginnings of Hasidism in Poland).

B93 Zinberg, Israel. *A History of Jewish Literature.* Trans. Bernard Martin. 12 vols. Cleveland and London: Press of Case Western Reserve University, 1972.

Zinberg "is concerned not only with belletristic writings produced by Jewish authors in the European period of Jewish history, but with a tremendous variety of other types of literature.... Hence, it would not be much of an exaggeration to say that his *History of Jewish Literature* in fact comes close to being a history of Jewish thought and culture in the thousand-year period with which it deals." (Editor's note)

Volume III, pt. iv, is devoted to The Struggle of Mysticism and Tradition against Philosophical Rationalism; and Vol. IX, pt. x, to Hasidism and Enlightenment (1780-1820). In addition, Vol. IV, pt. v, Italian Jewry in the Renaissance Era, contains a section on Jewish Mysticism and the Italian Humanists (ch. 2, pp. 25-36).

B94 Silberschlag, Eisig. *From Renaissance to Renaissance.* Part I. *Hebrew Literature from 1492-1970.* New York: Ktav Publishing House, Inc., 1973.

"The fifteen chapters of the present volume have surveyed movements and personalities in Hebrew literature from 1492 to recent times." Chapter 1, Humanism and Mysticism: 1492-1750, discusses the Mysticism of Safed (pp. 45-56). And Chapter 6 considers Interpretations and Reinterpretations of Hasidism (pp. 119-34).

B95 Weinryb, Bernard D. *The Jews of Poland: A Social and Economic History of the Jewish Community in Poland from 1100 to 1800.* Philadelphia: Jewish Publication Society of America, 1973.

"The author has ... attempted to capture the social situation of each period, to convey some idea of how it must have felt to live at that time. He has attempted to understand actions and attitudes from within, from the position of the various actors and groups in this life drama of coexistence." Chapter 10, Messianism: The Sabbatai Zevi Upheaval and Its Impact (pp. 206-35), is a review of the general background of the Sabbatian movement; Chapter 11, Messianism's Aftereffect--Jacob Frank and Frankism (pp. 237-61), discusses the impact of Frankism on Poland; and Chapter 12, Hassidim and Hassidism (pp. 262-303), describes "Hassidism's development of a separate though parallel existence with official Judaism. Thus it was strong enough to withstand the pressures of organized Jewry when they came, while Frankism was nipped in the bud by these pressures."

B96 *A History of Judaism.* Vol. 1: Silver, Daniel Jeremy. *From Abraham to Maimonides.* Vol. 2: Martin, Bernard. *Europe and the New World.* New York: Basic Books, Inc., 1974.

"These volumes are an attempt to give an historical account of Judaism ... we have written to provide Jews with self-understanding and to suggest to others the contributions of Judaism to the creative development of world civilization." In Volume II, chapter 2, Jewish Mysticism: The Kabbalah (pp. 33-53), Martin provides an historical survey of the development of Kabbalah from its antecedents in the ninth century to the present. And in chapter 7, Hasidism (pp. 168-88), he discusses Hasidism as "the last major manifestation of medievalism and the first important manifestation of modernism in the Jewish world."

B97 Ben-Sasson, H.H., ed. *A History of the Jewish People.* Cambridge: Harvard University Press, 1976.

Includes sections on: The Apocalypse, pp. 289-290; Rationalistics and Mystics, pp. 538-42; The Doctrines of Hasidei Ashkenaz, pp. 545-53; Kabbalists as Spokesmen for the Opposition During the Fourteenth and Fifteenth Centuries, pp. 614-17; Divinity, Existence and Exile in the Doctrine of Safed, pp. 695-701; The Messianic Leadership, pp. 701-3; The Messianic Movement of Shabbetai Zevi, 1665-6, pp. 703-7; Mystical Ferment: Jacob Frank and His Sect, pp. 767-68; The Ba'al Shem Tov and the Beginnings of Hasidism, pp. 768-770; The Crystalization of the Hasidic Movement: The Maggid of Mezhirech and His Disciples, pp. 770-72; The Struggle against Hasidism: The Gaon of Vilna, pp. 772-74; Hasidism and the Autonomous Institutions of East European Jewry, pp. 774-76; and Traditionalists in the East: Hasidism, the Lithuanian Yeshivot and the Musar Movement, pp. 842-44.

B98 Parrinder, Geoffrey. *Mysticism in the World's Religions.* London: Sheldon Press, 1976.

"The purpose of this book is to introduce the great religions in their mystical expressions." Part III, Mystical Theism, contains a section on Cabbalism and Hasidism (pp. 116-20), which discusses the Jewish attitude towards "The unity of God and the world."

B99 Kedourie, Elie, ed. *The Jewish World: History and Culture of the Jewish People.* New York: Harry N. Abrams, Inc., Publishers, 1979.

Chapter 12 contains a brief survey of Jewish Mysticism by R.J. Zwi Werblowsky (pp. 217-23), which covers: The Prophetic Mission, The Period of the Second Temple, Mysticism and the Talmud, The Middle Ages, Maimonides, ha-Levi and Bahya, The Mysterious World of the Kabbalah, and the Later Kabbalah.

B100 Seltzer, Robert M. *Jewish People, Jewish Thought: The Jewish Experience in History.* New York: Macmillan Publishing Co., Inc., and London: Collier Macmillan Publishers, 1980.

"In this work, I have attempted to survey the Jewish historical landscape and orient the reader to its main features, opening up for him access to the rich scholarly literature on Jewish history, theology, philosophy, mysticism, and social thought that has been produced in the last century and a half." Chapter 9, Medieval Jewish Mysticism and Kabbalah (pp. 419-50), discusses Kabbalah as "both a symptom and a response to an age in which the limited openness of Western society to Jewry was shrinking. The Kabbalah was a withdrawal, for the purposes of reinvigoration, into Judaism alone." Seltzer also includes sections on The

Lurianic Kabbalah (pp. 462-67), Shabbatai Zevi (pp. 467-74), and Hasidism (pp. 485-96).

B101 Williams, Jay G. *Judaism*. A Quest Book. Wheaton, Ill., Madras, India and London: Theosophical Publishing House, 1980.

"The purpose of this volume is simple; it is to introduce the interested reader to the major men and movements of the history of the Jews." Williams includes brief sections on The Mystical Tradition (pp. 57-60), and the Zohar (pp. 89-93), as well as references to Safed (pp. 110-11), Shabbetai Zevi (pp. 112-13), and Hasidism (pp. 122-24).

C. INTRODUCTORY SURVEYS

Primary Sources

C1 Hershon, Paul Isaac, trans. *A Talmudic Miscellany: A Thousand and One Extracts from The Talmud, The Midrashim and The Kabbalah*. London: Trubner & Co., 1880. "Selections from the Kabbalah," pp. 317-43.

"The practical Kabbalah is a branch of the theoretical, and treats of the practical use of the mysterious names of God and of angels. By uttering properly the ... Shem-hammephorash, *i.e.*, the ineffable name of Jehovah, or the names of certain angels, or by the mere repetition of certain Scripture texts, miracles and wonders were and still are performed in the Jewish world. Specimens of this will be found in the following pages, and also in other parts of this work."

C2 *Hebraic Literature: Translations from The Talmud, Midrashim and Kabbala*. Intro. Michael H. Harris. Washington and London: M. Walter Dunne, Publisher, and New York: Tudor Book Co., 1901; 1936, 1939, 1941, 1944. "The Kabbalah," pp. 265-88.

Anthology of brief selections; contains an introduction to "The Symbolical Kabbalah--Gematria," and "The Real Kabbalah--Theoretical and Practical," and short passages taken from various kabbalistic texts.

C3 Gewurz, Elias. *Beautiful Thoughts of the Ancient Hebrews*. New York: Bloch Publishing Company, 1924.

"There are great treasures to be found among the pages of the vast volumes of the Talmud, the Midrash and the Kabbalah. Their parables, allegories, proverbs and legends are among the finest examples of wit and wisdom in the world's literature.... In the present volume, I have given a few specimens of these precious gems of poetical prose."

C4 Schwarz, Leo W., ed. *The Jewish Caravan: Great Stories of Twenty-Five Centuries*. New York: Holt, Rinehart and Winston, 1935; rev. and enlarged ed. 1965.

Contains "a selection of stories and narratives written by Jewish writers who felt the need of expressing themselves as

Jews and of recording and interpreting Jewish life not only for the cultivated few but, perhaps primarily, for the people, and it is arranged to mirror the social and cultural growth of the Jewish people." Contains many mystical stories, and a section on "The World of Hasidism" (pp. 373-405).

C5 Marcus, Jacob R. *The Jew in the Medieval World: A Source Book: 315-1791*. Philadelphia: Jewish Publication Society of America, 1938. Rpt. New York: Atheneum, 1969.

"This source book attempts to reflect the life of the medieval Jew as seen through the eyes of contemporaries. The documents and historical narratives given here have been selected with the view of allowing the actors and witnesses of events--that is, the historical facts--to speak for themselves." The section, Jewish Sects, Mystics, and Messiahs (pp. 225-283), contains: The Messiah in Crete, about 321; The Medieval Jewish Kingdom of the Chazars, 740-1259; Anan and the Rise of Karaism, about 760; Aaron the Mystic, of Bagdad, about 870; Practical Cabala, about 900-1400; David Alroy, False Messiah, about 1146-1147; David Reubeni and Solomon Molko, 1524-1532; Isaac Luria, the Cabalist, 1534-1572; Shabbethai Zebi, False Messiah, 1666; The Rise of the *Hasidim*, about 1735-1740; An attack on the *Hasidim*, 1786; and The Frankists, 1755-1817.

C6 Ben Zion, Raphael. *The Way of the Faithful: An Anthology of Jewish Mysticism*. Los Angeles, 1945. Rpt. New York: The Judaica Press, Inc., 1981.

"There is no attempt here at 'scholarly' translation,... I have used no manuscripts, nor have I dabbled in criticism. The texts used as the bases for these translations are the ordinary printed editions of these works which one can find strewn around the benches of any Palestinian or European Yeshivah. My aim has been consistently to transmit the *spirit* of the work, even at the occasional sacrifice of scientific precision." The texts are: "The Speech of Elijah" (Maamar Patah Eliyahu), from Tikune Zohar, 13th century; "The Palm Tree of Deborah" (Tomer Deborah), R. Moses Cordovero, 16th century; "The Portal of Unity and Faith" (Shaar Hayihut Vehaemunah), R. Shneur Zalman of Ladi, 18th century; and "The Soul of Life" (Nefesh Hahayim), R. Hayim of Volozhin, 19th century. These translations of entire texts are prefaced by very brief introductions, and there are notes at the end of the volume.

C7 Raskin, Saul. *Kabbalah in Word and Image. With the Book of Creation and from the Zohar*. New York: Academy Photo Offset, Inc., 1952.

"And what is my task? It is to *show* the Kabbalah. For the first time in its long history, to present it in images, in drawings, comment on it pictorially." Raskin begins with three versions of the *Sefer Yetzirah*--Hebrew, Yiddish and English (based on the Westcott and Stenring translations [F5, F12]), and follows with illustrated discussions of Rabbi Akiba ben Joseph, Pardes, Abraham ben Samuel Abulafia, The Zohar--Its Author and Teaching, Isaac Luria--Ashkenazi, and selections from the Zohar.

C8 Glatzer, Nahum, ed. *The Judaic Tradition*. Boston: Beacon Press, 1969. Issued originally as three separate volumes: Pt. 1. *The Rest is Commentary*, 1961; Pt. 2. *Faith and Knowledge*, 1963; and Pt. 3. *The Dynamics of Emancipation*, 1965.

"This source book attempts to present significant examples from the vast and manifold post-Biblical Jewish literature in the various parts of the world." Chapters 9 and 10 of the second part, Faith and Knowledge, are devoted to mysticism. In Chapter 9, The Ways of the Mystics (pp. 419-440), Glatzer includes selections from the Zohar, Abraham Abulafia, Solomon ibn Adret, Solomon Shloemel ben Hayyim Meinstrl, and Moses Cordovero. Chapter 10, The Ways of the Hasidim, (pp. 441-458), provides Hasidic accounts of the Baal Shem Tov, teachings of Mendel of Kotzk, preparation for the Day of Atonement, a selection from the writing of Abraham Kalisker, and the Hasidic teaching about death.

C9 Jacobs, Louis. *Jewish Ethics, Philosophy and Mysticism*. Chain of Tradition Series. New York: Behrman, 1969.

An anthology of thinkers of the Jewish Middle Ages; divided into three parts: Jewish Ethics, Jewish Philosophy and Jewish Mysticism. The section on mysticism (pp. 111-68), contains a brief introduction to and selections from: *Tikkuné Zohar*, *Zohar*, Moses Cordovero, Hayyim Vital, Elijah de Vidas, Eliezer Azikri, Israel Horowitz, *Shomer Emunim*, Alexander Süsskind, *Sefer Baal Shem Tov*, and Rabbi Abraham Isaac Kook.

C10 Kravitz, Nathaniel. *3,000 Years of Hebrew Literature: From the Earliest Time through the 20th Century*. Chicago: Swallow Press, Inc., 1972.

Anthology of Hebrew literature containing a brief chapter on Cabala (pp. 340-368), "the queerest collection of various ideas, expressions of the soul, wonderful teachings, prayers of great inspiration, visions of Paradise and of worlds beyond, descriptions of angels and Seraphim, Messianic predictions, magic numbers, and combinations of the numerical values of words and divine names." Includes brief selections from: *Sefer Ha-Bahir*, Abraham ben Solomon Abulafia, Moses de Leon, *Sefer Zohar*, Cabala Center at Safed, David Re'ubeni and Solomon Molko, Joseph Caro, Moses Alshech, Solomon Alkabiz, Moses Cordovero, Isaac Luria Ashkenazi, Hayyim Vital Calabrese and Isaac ben Moses Najara.

C11 Bin Gorion, Micha Joseph. *Mimekor Yisrael: Classical Jewish Folktales*. Trans. I.M. Lask. Ed. Emanuel Bin Gorion. 3 vols. Bloomington and London: Indiana University Press, 1976.

Compendium of Jewish folktales intended to display the Jewish national character; divided into four books: National Tales, Religious Tales, Folktales, and Oriental Tales. Book II, section 2, contains Stories from the *Zohar* (II.709-39), and Section 4, Kabbalists and Hasidim (II.828-1031.)

C12 Jacobs, Louis. *Jewish Mystical Testimonies*. Jerusalem: Keter Publishing House, 1976; New York: Schocken Books, 1977.

"The aim of this book is to present a number of mystical texts, in translation, taken from the earliest period in Jewish mysticism, that of the Bible, and extending down to the twentieth century. Each text is prefaced by an introduction and is followed by a comment which seeks to elucidate the text. Wherever possible, however, the text have been allowed to speak for themselves." Includes twenty-one mystical testimonies: "Ezekiel's Vision of the Heavenly Throne," "The Four Who Entered the King's Orchard," "The Riders of the Chariot and Those Who Entered the Heavenly Halls" "Maimonides On Being With God," "The Mystical Piety of Rabbi Eleazar of Worms," "The Prophetic Mysticism of Abraham Abulafia," "Responsa from Heaven," "The Zohar on the High Priest's Ecstasy," "The Visions and Mystical Meditations of Abraham of Granada," "The Communications of the Heavenly Mentor to Rabbi Joseph Karo," "The Visions of Rabbi Hayyim Vital," "The *Maggid* of Rabbi Moses Hayyim Luzzatto," "The Mystical Epistle of the Ba'al Shem Tov," "The Mystical Meditations of Shalom Sharabi and the Kabbalists of Bet El," "The Mystical Experiences of the Gaon of Vilna," "The Prayer Meditations of Alexander Susskind of Grodno," "Two Epistles in Praise of the Hasidic *Zaddikim*," "The Mystical Accounts of Kalonymus Kalman Epstein of Cracow," "The *Tract on Ecstasy* by Dov Baer of Lubavich," "The Secret Diary of Rabbi Isaac Eizik of Komarno," and Aaron Roth's essay "Agitation of the Soul."

C13 Meltzer, David, ed. *The Secret Garden: An Anthology on the Kabbalah*. A Continuum Book. New York: Seabury Press, 1976.

"This collection of Kabbalistic texts in translation, concluding with a group of texts from the Sabbatian movement of the seventeenth century, should be regarded only as a source book, an attempt to approach the written element of the Kabbalah. It is in no way comprehensive or definitive." In addition to selections from "Baraita on the Work of Creation," "Shiur Qoma," "Sefer Yetsirah" and "Book Bahir," Meltzer includes portions of the writings of Solomon Ibn Gabirol,

Eleazer of Worms, Abraham ben Samuel Abulafia, Moses de Leon, Shalom Buzaglo, Isaac Luria, Hayyim Vital, Moses Cordovero, Abraham ben Mordecai Galante, Elijah de Vidas, Isaiah Horowitz, Abraham ha-Yakhini, Shabbati Zevi and Jacob Tausk of Prague.

C14 Neugroschel, Joachim, trans. *Yenne Velt: The Great Works of Jewish Fantasy and Occult.* New York: Stonehill Publishing Company, 1976.

"Ranging from the bizarre and the visionary to the scathingly satirical, here are thirty-one short stories and novelettes of *yenne velt*--the other world--by such gifted writers as Rabbi Nakhman, whose work influenced Franz Kafka, and Y.L. Peretz, whose writings are considered among the finest in Yiddish literature. Some of these tales reveal the strong influences of rationalism and traditionalism, while others approach messianic revelation. All are richly imaginative, and each makes a unique contribution to the small body of occult and fantastic literature than [sic] can truly be considered classic."

C15 Wright, Wayne, ed. *The Chicken Prince and Other Old Tales of Cabala, Collected from Various Traditional Sources.* El Cerrito, Calif.: Rhinoceros Press, 1977.

On the highest level of understanding, *Sod*, the "inner understanding ... transcends the capabilities and applications of logical forms and verbal languages. The understanding of sod is integral and gestalt." In this brief collection, Wright presents nine traditional kabbalistic legends, not to be analyzed, but experienced: "The Imperfect Lamp," "The Wheel of Fortune," "The Book of Adam," "The Marriage of Sampson," "The Hidden Zaddik," "The Name of the Road," "The Chicken Prince," "The Poor Man's Song," and "The Death of King David."

C16 Blumenthal, David R. *Understanding Jewish Mysticism: A Source Reader.* Vol. I. *The Merkabah Tradition and the Zoharic Tradition.* The Library of Judaic Learning, Vol. II. New York: Ktav Publishing House, Inc., 1978.

"The purpose of this book is threefold: first, to present in translation some of the major texts of the Jewish mystical tradition; second, to help the concerned reader reach an understanding of these texts without having to cope with overly learned footnotes; and third, to deal with some general questions about the nature of Jewish mysticism." Includes: portions of Genesis, *Sefer Yetsira*, "Ezekiel's Vision," *Pirkei Heikhalot*, the *Zohar*, and a Lurianic meditation. Each selection is preceded by an introduction, and many are followed by concluding remarks. Volume 2, C20.

C17 Rothenberg, Jerome, ed. *A Big Jewish Book: Poems & Other Visions of the Jews from Tribal Times to Present.* Garden City, New York: Anchor Press, Doubleday, 1978.

The Big Jewish Book is "itself an act of *poesis:* the creation--from all conceivable sources & attempts at definition--of 'a big Jewish book,' a composition & collage that would project my vision of the Jewish mysteries. That intention has determined the structure of the book as a whole. In brief, then, my first decision as to structure was to stress idea over author, or, by a non-chronological arrangement, to play up the relationship between older work & very contemporary developments in poetry, particularly those practiced in the U.S. over the past few decades.... The model for the present gathering is in fact the 'big Jewish book' par excellence, the *Bible:* an anthology ... whose common name in Hebrew ... is an acronym based on its three traditional divisions: *Torah* (or 'Law'), *Neviim* (or 'Prophets'), & *Khtuvim* (or 'Writings'). With this in mind I worked out a similar three-part structure into Ways, Visions, & Writings, & a movement from myth to history to language & poetics *per se.*"

C18 Patai, Raphael. *Gates to the Old City: A Book of Jewish Legends.* New York: Avon, 1980.

"This anthology is intended to serve as a guide and an introduction to the vast storehouses of the Agada (legend) literature accumulated by the Jews in the course of three thousand years. It contains selections from the seven major genres of Jewish literature that are, among other things, repositories of legends: the Bible, the Apocrypha, the Talmud, the Midrash, the Kabbala, folklore, and Hasidism. The background notes which precede each of these parts give essential information about the genre." Chapter 5, Kabbala (pp. 419-511), contains: Of Body and Soul, The Mysteries of Eden, Death and Punishment, Mysterious Worlds, The Matronit, The Legend of Lilith, Mysteries in History, Sages and Saints, and Of Safed Kabbalists. Chapter 7, Hasidism (pp. 669-747), includes: "About the Ba'al Shem Tov," "R. Leib Sarah's," "R. Yitzhaq, the 'Seer' of Lublin," "R. Nahman of Bratzlav" and "Other Tzaddiqim."

C19 Bokser, Ben Zion. *The Jewish Mystical Tradition.* New York: Pilgrim Press, 1981.

"The material offered in this volume offers representative selections from the most significant writings of the Jewish mystics from the earliest times to our own day." After a general introduction, Bokser presents selections from the Bible, the Talmud, mystical Midrashim, *Sefer Yezirah,* Bahya ibn Paquda, Moses Maimonides, *Sefer haBahir, Sefer Ḥasidim,* Abraham Abulafia, Joseph Gikatilla, the *Zohar,* Moses Cordovero, Isaac Luria, Hayyim Vital, Judah Loew of Prague, Moses

Introductory Surveys 51

Hayyim Luzzato, and Kabbalists and Liturgists. Hasidic writers include Israel Ba'al Shem Tov, the Maggid of Mezhirech, Menahem Nahum of Chernobyl, Menahem Mendel of Vitebsk, Shneur Zalman of Lyady, Mordecai of Chernobyl, Nahman of Bratslav, Zadok haKohen of Lublin; and latter-day mystics include Hayyim of Volozhin and Abraham Isaac Kook. "The introductory chapter characterizes the general nature of mysticism, and the distinctiveness of its Jewish component. Each of the figures whose writings are quoted is introduced briefly, in the context of his times, with an assessment of his general philosophy. The texts quoted are also introduced briefly, with an indication of their general nature, and the circumstances of their original publication."

C20 Blumenthal, David R. *Understanding Jewish Mysticism: A Source Reader.* Vol. II. *The Philosophic-Mystical Tradition and The Hasidic Tradition.* The Library of Judaic Learning, Vol. IV. New York: Ktav Publishing House, Inc., 1982. Part II of C16.

"This book, which is a sequel to *Understanding Jewish Mysticism*, Volume I, continues the task of presenting original texts in translation from the Jewish mystical tradition. Unit I presents texts from the philosophic mystical tradition and deals with such questions as: Where did philosophy and religious experience meet and overlap in medieval Judaism? What was the motivating force, the heartbeat, of Jewish philosophy? And, what is the relationship between the mind and the holy? Unit II presents texts from the Hasidic tradition and deals with such questions as: What is the relationship between mystical ecstasy and the folk-story? What are the various types of mysticalecstasy within Hasidism? And, how did the holy embody itself in a mass movement, in the Hasidic community? With the setting-forth of these two traditions, the presentation of the sources for the study of Jewish mysticism is, to my mind, complete." Unit I: The Philosophic-Mystical Tradition (General Introduction, The Maimonidean Paradigm, A Yemenite Synthesis, The Abulafian Transformation, General Conclusion); Unit II: The Hasidic Tradition (General Introduction, The Hasidic Story, The Hasidic Prayer-Life, The Zaddik and His Community, General Conclusion); Retrospect and Prospect (Looking Backward, Some Conclusions, Looking Forward, The Future of Jewish Spirituality).

Secondary Sources

C21 Raphall, Morris J. "Cabbala." *Hebrew Review and Magazine of Rabbinical Literature.* 1(1834-35), 17-21, 33-34, 49-50.

Basic introduction to Kabbalah, focusing on history and the *Sefirot*.

C22 Anon. "The Kabbalah, and Recent Investigations in Jewish Mysticism." *Eclectic Review*, n.s. 11(1856), 141-57.

Summary review of John Oxlee, *The Christian Doctrines of the Trinity and Incarnation, Considered and Maintained on the Principles of Judaism* (3 vols.; London, 1850), Adolph Franck, *Die Kabbalah, oder die Religions-Philosophie der Hebräer* (English trans., C39), D.H. Joël, *Die Religious-Philosophie des Sohar*, and S. Munk, *Philosophie und Philosophische Schriftsteller der Juden*, to determine "the intrinsic interest attaching to the study of the Kabbalah.... If the reader will follow us for a little, we hope to convince him of its importance."

C23 Rosenberg, D. *Explication of an Engraving Called the Origin of the Rites and Worship of the Hebrews; Together with Remarks on Creation, and a Brief Account of Some Observances and Their Symbolical Signification.* Trans. Max Woolf. New York: Printed at the Office of the "Jewish Messenger," 1859.

"By treating of the moving causes that led to the Law of Moses, and by means of an Engraving, representing the Origin of the Rites and Worship of the Hebrews, we trust to accomplish the work we have undertaken," to investigate the root of Judaism from the perspective of Kabbalism. In the Appendix, Max Woolf discusses The Twenty-Two Letters of the Hebrew Alphabet.

C24 Anon. "Kabbalism." *Christian Remembrancer, A Quarterly Review*, 43(1862), 345-84.

Summary of Adolphe Francke's *La Kabbale, ou La Philosophie Religieuse des Hébreux* (English trans. C39) and *Etudes Orientales*, intended "to trace the various developments of Kabbalistic philosophy through its different stages, from its earliest appearance to its present phase: we are quite aware that the sketch we have given is a very imperfect one, but this is entirely owing to the great mass of materials collected around us in our investigations, the difficulty being on all occasions to make a proper selection: for while on the one side the subject is often abstruse, and requires explanations and illustrations; on the other, we could only have given those explanations at the expense of more important matters. The subject has never, as far as we know, been treated as a whole, nor its connexion with modern philosophy and theology, nor its influence on modern thought adequately considered. A work treating the subject in this manner would be of great value at the present day, and would be of considerable assistance to the student of philosophy."

C25 Ginsburg, Christian D. *The Kabbalah: Its Doctrines, Development and Literature.* Proceedings of the Literary and Philosophical Society of Liverpool, No. 19(1863), Appendix. Rpt. London: Longman, Green, Longman, Roberts, & Green, 1866. Rpt. London: George Routledge & Sons Ltd., 1925. Rpt. with *The Essenes, Their History and Doctrine*, London: Routledge & Kegan Paul 1955; New York: Barnes & Noble, 1956; New York: Weiser, 1972.

Originally presented because with the exception of three "defective descriptions ... no Treatise exists in English on this esoteric doctrine"; and written because of "the enquiries which have lately been made for a Manual to the Kabbalah." Ginsburg's intention being to provide "a guide for those who wish to be initiated into the mysteries of this theosophy, I have aimed to be as elementary as possible in this Essay, and have, therefore, frequently explained allusions to points in Jewish history and literature with which the more advanced scholar is perfectly familiar, but which are unknown to tyros in these departments." The essay is divided into three major parts: I. The Meaning of the Kabbalah; II. The Books; and III. The Schools.

C26 Heckethorn, Charles William. *The Secret Societies of All Ages and Countries: Embracing the Mysteries of Ancient India, China, Japan, Egypt, Mexico, Peru, Greece, and Scandinavia, the Cabbalists, Early Christians, Heretics, Assassins, Thugs, Templars, The Vehm and Inquisition, Mystics, Rosicrucians, Illuminati, Freemasons, Skopzi, Camorristi, Carbonari, Nihilists and Other Sects*. 2 vols. London: R. Bentley and Son, 1875. New and rev. ed. London: G. Redway, and New York: New Amsterdam Book Company, 1897. Rpt. New Hyde Park, New York: University Books, 1965.

"But the rule I have followed in adopting societies as 'secret' was to include in my collection all such as had or have 'secret rites and ceremonies' kept from the outer world, though the existence of the society itself be no secret at all." The first section of Book II, Emanationists, is devoted to The Cabbala (I.83-88), covering: Origin, Date of Cabbala, The Book of the Creation, Different Kinds of Cabbala, Visions of Ezekiel, The Creation out of Nothing, and Revival of Cabbalistic Doctrines.

C27 Gaster, M. *The Origin of the Kabbala*. Reports of the Lady Judith Montefiore College. London: Wertheimer, 1893-4. Pp. 15-28. Rpt. New York: Gordon Press, 1976.

Unavailable for annotating.

C28 Binion, Samuel A. "The 'Wonders' of the Kabbalah." *Metaphysical Magazine*, 1(1895), 289-301. Rpt. New York: Metaphysical Pub. Co., 1905.

Describes "That system of theosophy called Kabbalah [which] has had its rise and its progress; but now it is in its third stage which all things, even theories, are subject to--decadence. Whether, Phoenix-like, a new system will arise from its ashes, or it will be entirely shelved and forgotten, is difficult to tell."

C29 Binion, Samuel A. "The Kabbalah." In *Library of the World's Best Literature, Ancient and Modern.* Ed. Charles Dudley Warner. New York: R.S. Peale and J.A. Hill, 1896-97, 1902, 1917. XV.8425-42. Rpt. Metuchen, New Jersey: Mini-Print Corp., 1972.

"My subject divides itself into two branches: first, the Theoretical Kabbalah, an esoteric theosophy; and second, the Practical Kabbalahs, the various treatises on which comprise the great majority of the books belonging to the subject: and I will try to state broadly what the Kabbalah is, and indicate its various stages and the uses made of it."

C30 Waite, Arthur Edward. *The Doctrine and Literature of the Kabalah.* London: Theosophical Publishing Society, 1902.

"A comprehensive account of the Kabalah, in the main bibliographical and historical, but seeking to establish its connections with other forms of occult philosophy and to determine its influence and importance from more than one standpoint, is the design of the present work, in which special regard has been also paid to the limitations and requirements of English readers." The eight sections of the book are devoted to: I. Post-Christian Literature of the Jews; II. The Doctrinal Content of the Kabalah; III. Source and Authority of the Kabbalah; IV. The Written Word of Kabalism: First Period; V. The Written Word of Kabalism: Second Period; VI. The Written Word of Kabalism: Third Period; VII. Some Christian Students of the Kabalah; and VIII. The Kabalah and Other Channels of Esoteric Tradition.

C31 Hirsch, S.A. "Jewish Mystics--An Appreciation." *Jewish Quarterly Review,* o.s. 20(1908), 50-73. Rpt. in his A8.

Considers two problems: "There is, first, the question whether the term 'The Rise of the Cabbala,' frequently used in Jewish literature to denote the period commencing with the twelfth century, is not somewhat ill-chosen; and, secondly, whether the judgment passed on the mediaeval Cabbalists by several Jewish writers on Jewish history is not altogether erroneous."

C32 Pick, Bernhard. "The Cabala." *Open Court,* 24(1910), 143-63.

Basic introduction to Kabbalah, including sections on Name and Origin of the Cabala, and History of the Development of the Cabala in the Pre-Zohar Period.

C33 Sperling, H. "Jewish Mysticism." In A6. Pp. 145-76.

Survey of Jewish mysticism from the perspective that "In the early days, when the nation is still plastic, as in the time of the Prophets, mysticism appears at its purest. Subsequently, after the crystallisation of a number of national and religious customs, mysticism appears in the shape of an attempt to pierce through these customs and to use them as symbols for the higher truths sought, as it was in the Middle Ages. In the attempt to interpret Holy Writ mystically, grammar may be atrociously handled, logic outraged, philosophy perverted;... Mysticism has its charms as well as its dangers."

C34 Pick, Bernhard. "The Cabala and Its Influence on Judaism and Christianity." *Open Court*, 25(1911), 321-42. Sel. rpt. O56, p. 16.

Sequel to C32 and I22; discusses: The Most Important Doctrines of the Cabala (En Soph, Creation, The Realm of Evil, The Messiah, Man, Psychology, The scripture--Gematria, Notarikon, Temurah), Effects of the Cabala within Judaism, and The Cabala in its Relation to Christianity.

C35 Abelson, J. "Jewish Mysticism." *Quest*, 4(1913), 707-31.

"From all these scrappy and haphazard bits of information that I have pieced together in this paper one or two considerations emerge which are vital to a correct understanding and a just estimate of our subject. It is noticeable that Jewish mystical literature, no matter of what age, always finds a place for the Bible.... The result has been this: that mystical speculation among Jews kept its devotees admirably free from the dangers of pantheism."

C36 Abelson, Joshua. *Jewish Mysticism: An Introduction to the Kabbalah*. London, 1913. Rpt. New York: Hermes Press, 1969, 1981.

"... a bird's-eye view of the salient features in Jewish mysticism rather than a solid presentation of the subject as a whole." In the Introduction, Abelson discusses the numerous misconceptions which have developed around Kabbalah; the study has eight chapters: I. Some Early Elements: Essenism; II. The Merkabah (Chariot) Mysticism; III. Philo: Metatron: Wisdom; IV. Kingdom of Heaven: Fellowship: Shechinah; V. The Book "Yetsirah"; VI. Some General Features of the "Zohar" Mysticism; VII. The Ten Sefirot; and VIII. The Soul.

C37 Pick, Bernhard. *The Cabala: Its Influence on Judaism and Christianity*. La Salle, Ill.: Open Court, 1913; rpt. 1974.

Writes because "As far as we are aware, nothing has been pubished [on Kabbalah] in English since 1865." Covers: I.

Name and Origin of The Cabala; II. The Development of the Cabala in the Pre-Zohar Period; III. The Book of Zohar or Splendor; IV. The Cabala in the Post-Zohar period; V. The Most Important Doctrines of the Cabala; and VI. The Cabala in Relation to Judaism and Christianity.

C38 Hertz, J.H. "Jewish Mysticism: An Historical Survey." *Hibbert Journal*, 14(1916), 784-98.

"We have passed in review only the mountain-peaks in the realm of Jewish mysticism. Enough, however, has been said to show that to ignore Cabala--whether it be its ethico-religious or its metaphysical or human side--is to leave unexplored larger portions of the map of Jewish life and thought; that to remain ignorant of Jewish mysticism is largely to fail to grasp one of the distinctive sides of the Jewish genius and one of the greatest driving-forces in Jewish history."

C39 Franck, Adolphe. *The Kabbalah, or the Religious Philosophy of the Hebrews*. Trans. I. Sossnitz. New York: The Kabbalah Publishing Company, 1926; rpt. New York: Arno Press, 1973. Rpt. of short version without notes, New Hyde Park, New York: University Books, 1967.

Aim is to provide "an exact idea and to find the place which [Kabbalah] really holds among works of intelligence." After an introduction focusing on the position of Kabbalah among other products of the mind, Franck explores: I. The Antiquity of the Kabbalah; The Kabbalistic Books; Authenticity of the Sefer Yetzirah; Authenticity of the Zohar; II. The Doctrine Contained in the Kabbalistic Books; Analysis of the Zohar; III. Systems which offer some resemblance to the Kabbalah; The Philosophy of Plato, The Alexandrian School; The Doctrine of Philo; Christianity; and the Religion of the Chaldeans and Persians. The Appendix contains bibliographic notices on editions, elements and translations of the *Zohar*.

C40 Godbey, J.E. "The Jewish Cabala." *Methodist Quarterly Review*, 76(1927), 193-201.

"In the foregoing sketch I have set forth the strong points in the Cabala, passing by the conceits of its adherents." Discusses mythic history of Kabbalah, creation and cosmology, and suggests that the kabbalistic approach could be an aid in interpreting the New Testament.

C41 Waite, Arthur Edward. *The Holy Kabbalah: A Study of the Secret Tradition in Israel as Unfolded by Sons of the Doctrine for the Benefit and Consolation of the Elect Dispersed through the Lands and Ages of the Greater Exile*. London: Williams and Norgate Ltd., New York: Macmillan Co.,

1929. Rpt., with an introduction by Kenneth Rexroth, Secaucus, New Jersey: University Books, Inc., 1960.

Incorporates his earlier works (C30, I23) to include a study of virtually all aspects of Kabbalah: Post-Christian Literature of the Jews; Source and Authority of the Kabbalah and the Age of the Chief Texts; The Written Word of Kabbalism; The Doctrinal Content of the Kabbalah in Respect of God and the Universe; Hierarchies of Spiritual Being; Ways of God with Man; The Higher Secret Doctrine; Some Christian Students of the Kabbalah; The Kabbalah and Other Channels of Secret Tradition; Final Considerations; and Indices on Sephirotic Developments, The Four Worlds in Later Kabbalism, The Instruments of Creation, Divine Names, and Phases of the Soul.

C42 Waton, Harry. *The Kabbalah and Spinoza's Philosophy as a Basis for an Idea of Universal History.* Vol. 1: *The Philosophy of the Kabbalah.* Vol. 2: *The Philosophy of Spinoza.* New York: Spinoza Institute of America, Inc., 1931-32.

The first volume of Waton's study, *The Philosophy of the Kabbalah*, "does not purport to be an exhaustive presentation of the Kabbalah," but rather, "a prolegomena to a philosophy of history.... our vital concern lies in the universal doctrines, i.e., the philosophy of the Kabbalah, particularly in those doctrines that are applicable and requisite to a philosophy of history." To that end, Waton considers: What is the Kabbalah? What is Cause? What is Substance? The Six Worlds; The Primordial Serpent; The Genesis of Existence; The Sephiroth; and Adam: Nephesh, Ruach, Neshamah. "While in [the second] volume we are concerned with the transition from metaphysics to philosophy, nevertheless, a succinct statement of the underlying thread of the Philosophy of the Kabbalah is indispensable, for all that philosophy can hope to do is but to formulate the implications of metaphysics in a more explicit and rigorous manner." Book II has two parts: 1. De Intellectus Emendatione, Translated and Expounded; and 2. Cogitata Metaphysica, Translated and Expounded.

C43 Fuller, J.F.C. *The Secret Wisdom of the Qabalah: A Study in Jewish Mystical Thought.* London: Rider & Co., 1937.

"This small book is in no sense a treatise on the Qabalah. Instead, it is a speculative study on one of several secret doctrines which it contains, and, I believe, the key-doctrine of all the others. Should this be correct, then it follows that, unless this doctrine is understood, the whole symbolism of Jewish mysticism must remain obscure, and it is this mysticism, so it seems to me, which constitutes the foundations of Jewish culture and Jewish aspirations." After an introduction focusing on the mystical foundation of the world order, Fuller discusses: I. The Wisdom of the Qabalah; II.

The Cosmogony of the Qabalah; III. The Problem of Good and
Evil; IV. The Fall of the Tetragrammaton; V. The Redemption
of Tetragrammaton; VI. The Source of Mystic Power; and VII.
The Anatomy of Illuminism.

C44 Hertz, J.H. "Rise and Development of Cabala." In his A21.
III.296-318.

Traces the "Rise and Development of Cabala" by examining
"the claims of Neo-Platonism, for which alone of all the
above systems [Babylonian, Zoroastrian, Gnostic, Sufi] any
can be made out as the primary source of speculative Jewish
mysticism.

C45 Scholem, Gershom G. *Major Trends in Jewish Mysticism.* New
York: Schocken Books, 1941; 2nd ed. 1946; 3rd ed. 1954.

Compilation of lectures intended "not to give a complete
historical account of Jewish mysticism but an outline of its
principal features in the form of an analysis of some of its
most important phases." The lectures discuss: General Characteristics of Jewish Mysticism; Merkabah Mysticism and Jewish Gnosticism; Hasidism in Mediaeval Germany; Abraham Abulafia and the Doctrine of Prophetic Kabbalism; The Zohar; Isaac
Luria and His School; Sabbatianism and Mystical Heresy; and
Hasidism: The Latest Phase.

C46 Jones, Rufus M. "Jewish Mysticism." *Harvard Theological
Review*, 36(1943), 155-63.

Summary of C45.

C47 Minkin, Jacob S. "Jewish Mysticism." *Journal of Religion*,
24(1944), 188-200.

Historical survey of Jewish mystics who "touched and influenced Jewish life and thought at every turn and left their
records everywhere--in the Bible, in Apocrypha, in the Talmud, in the innumerable saintly volumes of Hebrew thought, in
the liturgy of both ancient and medieval times; in the creative things of the spirit which delight and instruct us; and
in Hasidism, wherein mysticism expressed itself as one of the
most heroic and surprising movements in modern Jewish history."

C48 Müller, Ernst. *History of Jewish Mysticism.* Trans. Maurice
Simon. Oxford: Phaidon Press, 1946. Rpt. New York: Yesod,
1978.

"The object of this work is to give a comprehensive survey
of the history of Jewish mysticism--one which shall cover the
whole field and not only that commonly known as Cabbalah."
After a brief introduction which divides the historical deve-

lopment of Kabbalah into four epochs--the biblical period, old Jewish esoteric teaching, the period of the Kabbalah proper, and the period of Hasidism--Müller discusses: Mystical Aspects of the Bible; Agada, Allegory and Apocalypse; First Traces of a Mystical Doctrine; The Origin of the Cabbalah; Cabbalah in Europe; The Zohar, The Luria and Later Cabbalah; Chassidism; and Cabbalistic Tendencies outside Judaism. In the Appendix, Muller provides translations of selections from *The Wisdom of Solomon*, the works of Philo, the Hebrew Book of Enoch, the Pirke Hechaloth, the Talmud Babli and Midrash, the *Zohar*, and some Hassidic tales.

C49 Scholem, Gershom G. "Jewish Mysticism and Kabbala." In A26. I.308-47.

As a basic introduction, Scholem divides his topic into six sections: I. General Characteristics; II. Rise of Jewish Mysticism; III. The Merkabah Mysticism; IV. The German Hasidism; V. The Sephardic Kabbala; and VI. The Kabbala after the Expulsion from Spain.

C50 Heschel, Abraham J. "The Mystical Element in Judaism." In A31. I.602-23.

Essay divided into eight parts: 1. The Meaning of Jewish Mysticism, discusses the attitude of Kabbalists towards God, whom "they want to feel and to enjoy ... not only to obey but to approach Him"; 2. The Exaltation of Man, explores the "paradoxical idea that not only is God necessary to man but that man is also necessary to man"; 3. The En Soph and His Manifestations, "That this world is charged with His presence and every object is a cue to His qualities"; 4. The Doctrine of the Shekinah, that "when Adam was driven out of Eden, an aspect of the Divine, the *Shekinah*, followed him into captivity"; 5. Mystic Experience, that "The ultimate goal of the cabbalist is not his own union with the Absolute but the union of all reality with God"; 7. The Torah--A Mystic Reality, that "The Torah is the main source from which man can draw the secret wisdom and power into the essence of things"; 7. The Mystic Way of Life, that "A longing for the unearthly, a yearning for purity, the will to holiness, connected the conscience of the cabbalists with the strange current of mystic living"; and 8. The Concern for God, that "the pattern of Jewish mysticism [is] to have an open heart for the inner life of God."

C51 Baeck, L. "Jewish Mysticism." *Journal of Jewish Studies*, 2(1950-51), 3-16.

Concludes that mysticism "has given to Judaism a sense of the mysterious, the non-rational; it has always aroused the sense of the infinite and the eternal, and thereby ever stimulated piety and prayer; it has preserved religion from spending itself in the world below."

C52 Krakovsky, Levi Isaac. *Kabbalah: The Light of Redemption.* Brooklyn: Kabbalah Foundation, 1950. Rpt. Jerusalem and New York: Research Centre for Kabbalah, 1970.

"My purpose in issuing this book is to establish in the hearts of the present generation of Jews the faith in the divinity and supreme power of Torah which characterized our prophets and sages; to make known to them that the prophets as well as the sages of all generations because of this faith were able to unfold the heavenly light which is hidden in the Torah.... Thus, we must concentrate with all our might and effort to establish the study of Kabbalah to its rightful place, so that Israel may rise above her enemies and be redeemed from exile." Discusses the origin and essence of Kabbalah as a received doctrine.

C53 Ginzberg, Louis. "The Cabala," In his A37. Pp. 187-238.

Reprint of Ginzberg's article from the *Jewish Encyclopedia*, B27.

C54 Wallman, Joseph. *The Kabalah: From Its Inception to Its Evanescence.* Brooklyn: Theological Research Publishing Company, 1958.

"In the following pages we shall meet with this segment of Jewry, examine their reasons for refusing to accept the traditional notion of the nature of God and His relation to the universe as well as getting acquainted with their own definition. The members of this faction had made the solution of this problem their especial study. These are the Kabalists and their field of enquiry--the Kabalah." Discusses: I. The Kabalah, The Various Connotations of the Word; II. The Kabalists, Their View on the Torah and the Form of their Religiosity; III. Antiquity of the Kabalah; IV. Development of the Kabalah; V. The Influence of the Babylonians and the Persians; VI. Kabalistic Literature; VII. The Doctrines of the Zohar; VIII. The Kabalah of Isaac Luria and its Consequences; IX. Evaluation of the Kabalah and Its Influence on the Jews; and X. Christian Kabalists.

C55 Jacobs, Louis. "What is Kaballah?" *Jewish Heritage*, 2,1(Spring 1959), 17-22.

Basic introduction to Kabbalah, including discussions of: Origins and Development; The Zohar; Isaac Luria and the Safed Brotherhood; Kabbalah and Hasidism; The Teachings of Kabbalah; Doctrine of the Sephirot; Doctrine of Tzimtzum; and Kabbalah in Modern Time.

C56 Rexroth, Kenneth. "The Holy Kabbalah." In his A49.

Reprint of his Introduction to C41.

Introductory Surveys 61

C57 Scholem, Gershom. *Jewish Mysticism in the Middle Ages.* The 1964 Allan Bronfman Lecture Delivered at Congregation Shaar Hashomayim, Westmount Quebec, Canada, October 5th 1964. New York: Judaica Press, 1966.

Unavailable for annotating.

C58 Rabinowicz, H. "Kabbolah." *Jewish Life,* 37(1969), 32-37.

Very brief introduction to Kabbalah, including discussions of origin, contemplative and theoretical Kabbalah, the *Sefirot, Sefer Yetzirah,* the Zohar and Isaac Luria.

C59 Scholem, Gershom G. "General Characteristics of Jewish Mysticism." In A75. Pp. 217-57.

Excerpts from the introductory lecture of C45.

C60 Schaya, Leo. *The Universal Meaning of the Kabbalah.* Trans. Nancy Pearson. London: George Allen & Unwin Ltd., 1971; Secaucus, New Jersey: University Books, Inc., 1972; Baltimore, Md.: Penguin Books, 1973.

Schaya "in no wise claims to have exhausted the doctrinal wealth of the Kabbalah ... but has concentrated on one of its most essential teachings, dealing with the *Sefiroth*; this concerns the ten principal aspects of God, which, in the form of 'spiritual keys', will help us to look towards his all-reality." Schaya includes chapters on Torah and Kabbalah; Contemplation of the Divine Aspects--The Unity of the *Sefiroth,* and the *Sefirothic* Hierarchy; Creation, the Image of God; The Kingdom of Heaven; The Corporeal World and the Cosmic Abyss; The Mystery of Man; The Return to the One; and The Great Name of God.

C61 Albertson, Edward. *Understanding the Kabbalah.* For the Millions Series. Los Angeles: Sherbourne Press, Inc., 1973.

Basic introduction to Kabbalah as "a term covering every school of Jewish mysticism and occultism,... therefore, similar to all other religions in which the goal is an immediate and personal knowledge of Reality." Contents: I. The Hidden Knowledge; II. Origins; III. Otz Hiim; IV. The Columns; V. The Triangles; VI. The Tree and the World; VII. The Tree and the Four Worlds; VIII. The Individual Sephiroth; IX. The Qliphoth; X. The Paths; and XI. Work upon the Tree.

C62 Heschel, Abraham J. "The Mystical Element in Judaism." In A89. Pp. 279-300.

Reprint of C50.

C63 Ponce, Charles. *Kabbalah: An Introduction and Illumination for the World Today.* San Francisco: Straight Arrow Books, distributed by Quick Fox, Inc., 1973; London: Garnstone Press, 1974.

"I have attempted to do nothing more than simply present the background and basic principles of Kabbalism. Beyond that, we are all students." The study is divided into three parts: I. The Background of the Kabbalah; II. The Doctrines of Kabbalism; and III. The Kabbalah Today.

C64 Scholem, Gershom G. "General Characteristics of Jewish Mysticism.." In A89. Pp. 245-75.

Reprint of the first chapter of C45.

C65 Scholem, Gershom G. *Kabbalah*. Library of Jewish Knowledge. Jerusalem: Keter Publishing House Jerusalem Ltd., and New York: Quadrangle, The New York Times Book Co., 1974.

Compilation of Scholem's articles for the *Encyclopaedia Judaica*, (B40), plus the article on Moses Cordovero by J.B. Ben Shlomo. Covers: The Historical Development of Kabbalah, The Basic Ideas of Kabbalah, The Wider Influences of and Research on Kabbalah, Topics and Personalities.

C66 Bloom, Harold. "Kabbalah." *Commentary*, 59(March 1975), 57-65.

Basic survey of Kabbalah written from the perspective that Kabbalah is "more a mode of intellectual speculation than a way of union with God. Like the Gnostics, the kabbalists sought *knowledge*, but unlike the Gnostics they sought knowledge in the Book. By centering upon the Bible, Kabbalah made of itself, at its best, a critical tradition, though distinguished by more invention than critical traditions generally display. In its degeneracy, Kabbalah has sought vainly for a magical power over nature, but in its glory it sought, and found, a power of the mind over the universe of death."

C67 Safran, Alexandre. *The Kabbalah: Laws and Mysticism in the Jewish Tradition*. Trans. Margaret A. Pater. New York and Jerusalem: Feldheim Publishers, 1975.

"My main concern was to shed light on the Jewish tradition by examining the living interaction between, and yet organic unity of, mysticism and the Law. I hope to succeed in rediscovering in the word *'Kabbalah'*, which means *'tradition'* in the Hebrew language, its original content and lasting values. This is not intended to be a historical study of Jewish mysticism, nor of the Jewish doctrine of the Law. Neither is suited to objective investigation or impersonal, factual presentation. I have chosen to pursue a constant, the unity of mysticism and the Law in the Kabbalah, which belongs to

Introductory Surveys 63

the essence of true Judaism." Safran divides his study into two parts: I. The Unity of the Kabbalah; and II. The Doctrine of the Kabbalah. The Appendix contains a discussion of The Science of the Kabbalah and the Science of Today.

C68 Halevi, Z'ev ben Shimon [Warren Kenton] *A Kabbalistic Universe*. New York: Samuel Weiser, Inc., 1977.

"... a general account of the origin and cosmic scheme of Creation and its inhabitants.... The aim of this work is to set out the macrocosmic order with its different levels of reality, the hierarchy of beings and their function, especially that of mankind which can exist throughout the Worlds."

C69 Epstein, Perle. *Kabbalah: The Way of the Jewish Mystic*. New York: Doubleday, 1978.

Three-part study of the practice of Jewish mysticism: I. The Mystic Life; II. Kabbalistic Practices; and III. Devekuth. The Epilogue contains Epstein's Personal Musings on a Future Kabbalah.

C70 Steinsaltz, Adin. "Worlds, Angels and Men." *Shefa Quarterly*, 1,4(September 1978), 4-14.

Selections from C74.

C71 Halevi, Z'ev ben Shimon [Warren Kenton] *Kabbalah: Tradition of Hidden Knowledge*. New York: Thames and Hudson, 1979.

Its "long and broadly spread history has given Kabbalah a remarkably rich and wide variety of images of reality which appear to the unversed eye as strange, obscure and even at times contradictory or corrupt." Introduction covers: Manifestation, Four Worlds, Adam, Anatomy, Seeking, Training, Work of Unification, Work of Creation, and Completion; text is comprised of examples of images on the themes of: Changing forms of Kabbalah, Views of eternity, Four levels of existence, Alternative systems, Angels and demons, Miracles and magic, Christian and occult Kabbalah, Kabbalistic methods (of action, devotion and contemplation), Death--rebirth--fate, Masters and Messiahs, Inner ascent, Work of Unification, and The End of Days.

C72 Kaufman, William E. *Journeys: An Introductory Guide to Jewish Mysticism*. New York: Bloch Publishing Company, 1980.

"A basic introductory guide to Jewish mysticism," with four parts: Heaven, God, Man and Earth. Ends with an Epilogue on Gateways to God.

C73 *Keeping Posted*, 25(March 1980).

Special Issue on mysticism. Unavailable for annotating.

C74 Steinsaltz, Adin. *The Thirteen Petalled Rose.* Trans. Yehuda Hanegbi. New York: Basic Books, 1980. Sel. rpt. C70.

Introduction to basic aspects of Jewish mysticism: I. Worlds; II. Divine Manifestation; III. The Soul of Man; IV. Holiness; V. Torah; VI. The Way of Choice: An Answer to Ethics; VII. The Human Image; VIII. Repentance; IX. The Search for Oneself; X. *Mitzvot*; XI. An Additional Note on the *Kiddush* Ritual.

C75 Berg, Philip S. *Kabbalah for the Layman: A Guide to Cosmic Consciousness.* Jerusalem: Research Centre of Kabbalah, 1981.

"The purpose of this book ... is not just to provide the reader with a taste of the vast world of Jewish mystical thought, and an experience of how Kabbalah can be brought to bear on the problems facing the world today, but to argue the appropriateness and necessity of returning to the understanding of the universe and its law that is provided for us by the Kabbalah." Divided into three parts: Origins and History of Kabbalah; The Body of Knowledge; and Making the Connection--Practical Applications. Berg also includes appendices on: Stages of Emanation and Creation; The Sefirot and its [sic] relationship to man; The Sefirot and the Twelve Tribes, Months and Astrological Signs; and The Magen David.

C76 Dan, Joseph. "Mysticism in Jewish History, Religion and Literature." In A117. Pp. 1-14.

"It is my purpose in the following remarks to point out briefly a few examples of major phenomena in Jewish religion, history and literature where the necessity of such an integration [of Jewish mysticism within the general framework of Jewish scholarship] is acutely felt."

C77 Berg, Philip S. *The Kabbalah Connection.* New York: Research Centre for Kabbalah, 1983.

Unavailable for annotating.

C78 Maller, Allen S. *God, Sex and Kabbalah (Messianic Speculations).* Los Angeles: Ridgefield Publishing Company, 1983.

"This book is designed to reflect the character and personality of the various elements in the Kabbalah. It contains stories, interpretations of Bible and Jewish history, prophecies of future developments, translations of famous Kabbalistic texts, meditation exercises; and an advocacy of performing the mitzvot, without which no book of Kabbalah can be considered authentic. The purpose of this book is to be a beginning: to provide the reader with an introduction to the various aspects of Kabbalah in order that the reader may determine which path to pursue in raising his or her spiritual consciousness." Contents: 1. The Golem of Rabbi Judah Loew; 2. The Mystic Sources of the Kabbalah; 3. The Hidden Code of the Kabbalah; 4. Sex and Divine Intercourse in the Zohar; 5. The Secrets of Creation; 6. The Shekinah; She as God; 7. Lilith: Queen of the Demons; 8. Hell No. We won't go; 9. Reincarnation; 10. The Mystery of Israel's Survival; 11. The Coming of the Messianic Age; 12. Intelligent Life in Outer Space; 13. The Tree of Life; 14. The First Step; 15. For Further Reading.

D. TOPICS IN JEWISH MYSTICISM

This chapter contains material which spans the history of Jewish mysticism, rather than being confined to a specific historical period or figure. The topics include: Critical Approaches; Magic; Messianism; God and Creation; Emanations and the Concept of the *Sefirot*; The Problem of Evil; Man and His Soul; Torah; The Mystic Way; Myth and symbol; Prophecy and Apocalyptic; and Psychology.

Critical Approaches

D1 Blumenthal, David R. "Some Methodological Reflections on the Study of Jewish Mysticism." *Religion*, 8(1978), 101-14.

"The order of business, then, is twofold: to define the scope of the field and, then, to comment upon its current shortcomings. As to scope, the field of Jewish mysticism, at its fullest, should encompass the following types of approach: historical studies, phenomenological studies, an appreciation of Jewish mysticism, and pedagogic studies."

D2 Katz, Steven T. "Language, Epistemology and Mysticism." In his A105. Pp. 22-74.

"Our primary aim has been to mark out a new way of approaching the data, concentrating especially on disabusing scholars of the preconceived notion that all mystical experience is the same or similar. If all mystical experience is always the same or similar in essence, as is so often claimed, then this has to be demonstrated by recourse to, and accurate handling of, the evidence, convincing logical argument, and coherent epistemological procedures. It cannot be shown to be the case merely by supported and/or unsupportable assertions to this effect, no matter how passionately these are advanced, nor again can it be demonstrated by *a priori* assumptions on the matter which 'prove' them in what is essentially circular fashion." Discusses Jewish mysticism on pp. 33-36.

D3 Katz, Steven T. "Models, Modeling and Mystical Training." *Religion*, 12(1982), 247-75.

Unavailable for annotating.

D4 Katz, Steven T. "The 'Conservative' Character of Mystical Experience." In his A120. Pp. 3-60.

"... the aim of this paper is to reveal the two-sided nature of mysticism, that it is a dialectic that oscillates between the innovative and traditional poles of the religious life. To recognize only one of these poles--it does not matter which--is to misrepresent the phenomenon." Considers Jewish mysticism throughout the paper, especially on pp. 7-11.

D5 Katz, Steven T. "Ethics and Mysticism." in A122. Pp. 184-202.

Explores the relationship between ethics and mysticism from the perspective that "mystics share both the ontological problem and its solutions with their particular traditions. They are fully situated in the metaphysical, theological, and social contexts of their traditions." Considers ethics and the kabbalistic tradition on pp. 196-199.

Magic

Primary Sources

D6 Gaster, Moses, ed. "The Sword of Moses, an Ancient Book of Magic." *Journal of the Royal Asiatic Society of Great Britain*, n.s. 28(1896), 149-98. Rpt. London: D. Nutt, 1896. Rpt. New York: S. Weiser, 1970. Rpt. D10.

Translation of a thirteenth- fourteenth-century mystical treatise comprised of two parts: "the Introductory of historical, as it gives the explanation of the heavenly origin of this text, and deals with all the preliminary incidents connected with the mode of using the text in a proper and efficacious manner," and "the theurgical or magical part," the former in a mixture of Hebrew and Aramaic, the latter with Arabic. In the first appendix, Gaster includes a smaller treatise, also called "The Sword of Moses," which consists of a list of mystical Names; and in the second, two Aramaic conjurations found within the manuscript of the *Sword*.

D7 Goldmerstein, L. "Magical Sacrifice in the Jewish Kabbala." *Folk-Lore*, 7(1896), 202-4.

Translation of an extract from *Sefer Raziel Hamalaleh*, or *The Book of the Angel Raziel*, made from the Warsaw edition of 1881, which is a reprint of the Wilna edition of 1877. The extract describes a sacrificial ceremony which "is not any part of the Jewish sacrificial rites, and in some points openly contradicts it."

D8 Conybeare, F.C., trans. "The Testament of Solomon." *Jewish Quarterly Review*, 11(1899), 1-45.

Translation of a pseudepigraphic magical text, written between the first and third centuries, which is a syncretistic blend of Jewish, Christian, Oriental and Hellenistic motifs.

D9 Block, Chayim. *The Golem: Legends of the Ghetto of Prague*. Trans. Harry Schneiderman. Vienna: The Golem, 1925. Rpt. New York: Rudolf Steiner Publications, 1972.

Collection of stories about the Golem, "a servant who would serve his people in their sufferings and struggles, bringing help to the community in its hour of greatest need." Although Bloch attributes the tales to a three-hundred-year-old manuscript, according to Scholem, "the book was written by one Y. Rosenberg around the year 1908 and contains not ancient legends but modern fiction" (C45).

D10 Gaster, Moses, ed. "The Sword of Moses, an Ancient Book of Magic." In his A12. I.228-337; III.69-103.

Reprint of D6.

D11 Thieberger, Frederic, trans. *The Great Rabbi Loew of Prague: His Life and Work and the Legend of the Golem*. London: East and West Library, 1955.

Provides information about both the man, the great Rabbi Loew of Prague, and the legends surrounding him. After an historical introduction to sixteenth-century Prague, Thieberger discusses The Reality and the Secret of his Life; Liwa's Idea of Man and Universe; and The Legend, with Extracts from the Works of the Great Rabbi Loew, and a Collection of Legends.

D12 Isbell, Charles D. *Corpus of the Aramaic Incantation Bowls*. Dissertation Series, Number 17. Missoula, Mont.: Society of Biblical Literature and Scholars Press, 1975.

"This dissertation is a collection of all the published Aramaic magic bowls."

D13 Winkler, Gershon. *The Golem of Prague: A New Adaptation of the Documented Stories of the Golem of Prague, with an Introductory Overview*. New York: Judaica Press, 1980.

"In this new rendition of the Golem of Prague, we have included all of the adventures of the Golem which were reportedly chronicled by R. Yitzchak ben Shimshon HaKohen Katz, a disciple and son-in-law of R. Yehuda Loevy ben Bezalel

(Maharal of Prague, 1513-1609). The original manuscript was transcribed and published by R. Yehuda Yudel Rosenberg in Warsaw, 1909, under the title, *Niflaos Maharal: HaGolem M'Prague* ("The Wonders Of The Maharal: The Golem Of Prague"). Our book is not the first English translation of the above, but is rather an original attempt to heighten the impact of the Golem episodes for the contemporary Western reader. We took the liberty of developing the factual accounts of the Katz document by filling in personal and historic data to cushion abrupt transitions in the original. We also inserted a reasonable amount of dramatization and dialogue, which we felt would best represent and convey the enduring charisma of the Golem of Prague to readers of all backgrounds, Jew or Non-Jew."

D14 Wiesel, Elie. *The Golem: The Story of a Legend.* Trans. Anne Borchardt. New York: Summit Books, 1983.

Secondary Sources

D15 Waite, Arthur E. *The Occult Sciences: A Compendium of Transcendental Doctrine and Experiment, Embracing An Account of Magical Practices; of Secret Sciences in Connection with Magic; of the Professors of Magical Arts; and of Modern Spiritualism, Mesmerism and Theosophy.* London: K. Paul, Trench, Trubner & Co. Ltd., 1891, 1923.

Presents "in a compressed and digested form, the whole scope of occult knowledge, expressed in the language of a learner." Part II, Secret Sciences in Connection with Magic, contains a seven-page discussion of Kabbalism (pp. 181-87), which discounts the pseudepigraphic while trying to establish the actual history of Kabbalah.

D16 Pilcher, E.J. "Two Kabbalistic Planetary Charms." *Proceedings of the Society of Biblical Archaeology*, 28(1906), 110-18.

Describes two talismans which are based on kabbalistic principles of astrology, though both charms "contain blunders arising from the carelessness or ignorance of the engraver; but these probably had no effect on their magical virtues, or the estimation in which they were held by their possessors."

D17 Daiches, Samuel. *Babylonian Oil Magic in the Talmud and in the Later Jewish Literature.* Publications of the Jews' College, no. 5. London: Jews' College, 1913.

Short monograph on the mystical uses of oil, discussing: oil as a mystic element in antiquity; Talmudic passages referring to oil magic; and later Jewish texts (which Daiches translates and annotates).

D18 Casanowicz, I.M. "Jewish Amulets in the United States National Museum." *Journal of the American Oriental Society*, 36(1916), 154-67.

Description of thirty-five Jewish amulets in the National Museum, Washington, D.C., the basis of which is "the use of the names of God and angels and in the application of Biblical verses unchanged or in permutation of the words and letters," according to the practices of what Casanowicz labels kabbalists. He also includes a transcription and translation of one of the amulets.

D19 Casanowicz, I.M. "Two Jewish Amulets in the United States National Museum." *Journal of the American Oriental Society*, 37(1917), 43-56.

Descriptions of two amulets, one "for the protection of Daniel, Son of Berakah, against evil spirits, sickness, the evil eye and magic." Provides transcriptions and translations for both.

D20 Kohler, Kaufmann. "The Tetragrammaton (Shem ham-M'forash) and Its Uses." *Journal of Jewish Lore and Philosophy*, 1(1919), 19-32.

Discusses the pronunciation of the Name, the meaning of J.H.V.H., the invocation of the Name, avoidance of the Name, and the magical use of the Name.

D21 Diserens, Charles M. "Mediaeval Magic in Its Relation to the Cabala." *Hebrew Union College Monthly*, 6(1920), 102-11.

"Indeed, the belief in, or practice of magic or its later analogue, occultism, certain types of mysticism of [sic] spiritualism seems generally to have been associated with a knowledge of the Cabala, and we may conclude that this was equally true during the middle ages in so far as cabalistic documents were accessible."

D22 Redgrove, H. Stanley. "The Kabbalah and Word-Magic." *Occult Review*, 50(1929), 176-79.

"Gematria, Notariqon and Temuria: these may, indeed, be recommended as alternatives to cross-word puzzles, and of no more significance and importance except as remarkable instances of the aberration of the human intellect. The real mystery of the Kabbalah lies deeper than these."

D23 Trachtenberg, Joshua. *Jewish Magic and Superstition: A Study in Folk Religion*. New York: Behrman's Jewish Book House, Inc., 1939. Rpt. New York: Atheneum, 1970.

"This book offers a contribution to an understanding of folk Judaism, the beliefs and practices that expressed most eloquently the folk psyche--of all the vagaries which, coupled with the historic program of the Jewish faith, made up the everyday religion of the Jewish people." Tangentially deals with various aspects of practical Kabbalah.

D24 Trachtenberg, Joshua. *The Devil and the Jews: The Medieval Conception of the Jew and Its Relation to Modern Antisemitism.* New Haven: Yale University Press, and London: Oxford University Press, 1943. Rpt. Cleveland and New York: Meridian Books, and Philadelphia: Jewish Publication Society of America, 1961.

Book devoted to "the accusation of sorcery against the Jews." Chapter 5, Europe Discovers the Kabbalah (pp. 76-87), explores the "ironic paradox" of the Renaissance conception of the Jew as sorcerer. Much anti-Semitism derived from the misconception that the Jewish Kabbalah was the source of magic while, in fact, Jews had little to do with the "Practical Kabbalah" which Christian Kabbalists appropriated for their own alchemical, astrological and magical pursuits.

D25 Castiglioni, Arturo. *Adventures of the Mind.* New York: Alfred A. Knopf, Inc., 1946. Rpt. Freeport, New York: Books for Libraries Press, 1972.

In this study of the history of medicine, Chapter 15, Hebrew Magic and the Dawn of Monotheism (pp. 167-77), discusses magical medicine in terms of: 1. The Magic Idea in its Various Aspects; 2. The Blood-Rite, The Evocation of the Name; and 3. The Cabala.

D26 Goodenough, Erwin R. "A Jewish-Gnostic Amulet of the Roman Period." *Greek and Byzantine Studies,* 1(1958), 71-80.

Completes the discussion of the amulet begun in F46. After fully describing the amulet, Goodenough concludes that "It seems highly likely that the cosmic scenes of the main face reflect the Deity of a Jewish-gnostic sect, and brought the wearer that Deity's protection."

D27 Bokser, Ben Zion. "The Thread of Blue." *Proceedings of the American Academy for Jewish Research,* 31(1963), 1-32.

Historical analysis of "The Thread of Blue" in the fringe on each corner of a garment as being influenced by "the efficacy of the fringe in the mystical powers possessed by the thread of blue."

D28 Scholem, Gershom G. "The Idea of the Golem." Trans. Ralph Manheim. In his A59. Pp. 158-204.

The popular literary form of the Golem, "which has achieved considerable fame, owes very little to the Jewish tradition, even its corrupt, legendary form. An analysis of the main Jewish traditions concerning the golem will show how little."

D29 Scholem, Gershom. "Prague and Rehovot: Tale of Two Golems." *Jerusalem Post*, June 18, 1965. Rpt. D30, D33.

In this dedication of a new computer at the Weitzman Institute at Rehovoth, named Golem I, Scholem applies the mystical theories of the Golem and numerology to contemporary scientific pursuits.

D30 Scholem, Gershom. "The Golem of Prague and the Golem of Rehovoth." *Commentary*, 41(1966,) 62-65.

Reprint of D29.

D31 Schrire, T. *Hebrew Magic Amulets: Their Decipherment and Interpretation*. London: Routledge & K. Paul, 1966. Rpt. New York: Behrman House Inc., Publishers, 1982.

"It has been our object to enable the inscription on a Hebrew amulet to be deciphered and interpreted and to permit the student, by a simple process of deduction, to determine the purpose for which the particular amulet had been made and when, how and where it was used." In Chapter 6, Mysticism, Ecstasy and the Belief in Amulets (pp. 26-32), Schrire discusses the ways in which mystical activities are involved in writing, making and wearing amulets; and Chapter 7, Kabbalism, Hasidism and the Spread of Kabbalistic Lore (pp. 33-41), explores the connection between inscriptions originating in the Middle East "and those found in mediaeval Western Jewish mystical literature."

D32 Hirschman, Jack. "On the Hebrew Letters." *Tree*, 2(Summer 1971), 34-45.

Unavailable for annotating.

D33 Scholem, Gershom. "The Golem of Prague and the Golem of Rehovoth." In his A81. Pp. 335-40.

Reprint of D29.

D34 Schiffman, Lawrence H. "A Forty-Two Letter Divine Name in the Aramaic Magic Bowls." *Bulletin of the Institute of Jewish Studies*, 1(1973), 97-102.

Interpretation of the Divine Name found on the bowls.

D35 Polen, N. "Hebrew Letters and Their Mystical Qualities." *Response*, 9,4(1975-76), 105-10.

Unavailable for annotating.

D36 Scholem, Gershom. "Colours and Their Symbolism in Jewish Tradition and Mysticism." Trans. Audrey Wilson and Johanna Pick Margulies. *Diogenes*, #108(Winter 1979), 84-111; #109(Spring 1980), 64-76.

The "status and meaning [of colors] in the Jewish world from the Bible to the Kabbalah."

D37 Winkler, Gershon. *Dybbuk*. New York: Judaica Press, 1981.

"A selection of six documented and dramatized accounts of possession and exorcism in the Jewish experience--the Dybbuks of Safed, Smyrna, Bagdad, Brisk and Radun. Included, as well, is a comprehensive exploration of traditional Judaic perspectives concerning the soul, reincarnation, death, suffering, infant mortality, ghosts, apparitions, magic and superstition."

Messianism

Primary Source

D38 Patai, Raphael. *The Messiah Texts*. Detroit: Wayne State University Press, and New York: Avon, 1979.

"The purpose of the present book is to put before the reader the texts of Jewish legends dealing with the coming of the Messiah and the events preceding, accompanying, and following his advent. These texts are excerpts from an exceedingly voluminous literature spanning three millennia, beginning with early Biblical indications and concluding with Messiah legends written, and Messiah dreams dreamt, by modern authors. The material scattered especially in the Talmudic, Midrashic, and Kabbalistic books and presented here is astounding in its riches, even though I cannot be sure that I succeeded in locating all the significant variants on each and every theme.... Each chapter opens with a few brief introductory remarks intended to serve as general orientation for the specific topic dealt with, and to provide continuity between it and the subject matter of the preceding chapter. Then follow the texts of the legends in a roughly chronological order."

Secondary Sources

D39 Ellinger, Moritz. "Quabbala." *Menorah*, 33(1902), 108-14, 227-32.

Summary of D40.

Messianism

D40 Fluegel, Maurice. *Philosophy, and Vedanta: Comparative Metaphysics and Ethics, Rationalism and Mysticism, of the Jews, the Hindus and Most of the Historic Nations, as Links and Developments of One Chain of Universal Philosophy.* Baltimore: Sun Printing Office, 1902.

"This volume continues the series of the 'Biblical Legislations' and the 'Messiah Ideals,' on the great social, intellectual and ethical issues of history; since Manu, Zoroaster, Kapila, Buddha, and Sankara, to Plato, Philo, Plotin, Apochryphae, Talmud, Gebirol, Maimonides, Qabbala, Zohar, Spinoza, Schelling, Hegel, etc. It treats of the Qabbala in juxtaposition with Hindu philosophy, the Vedanta, and most of the leading philosophical systems of the world."

D41 Greenstone, Julius H. *The Messiah Idea in Jewish History.* Philadelphia: Jewish Publication Society of America, 1906; rpt. 1948. Rpt. Westport, Conn.: Greenwood Press, 1972.

"It is the object of the present volume to trace the development of [the messianic] ideal from its early origins to the present day, to elucidate the influences it exerted upon the lives and habits of the Jews, and to explain the causes by which it, in turn, was influenced, giving in outline the historical conditions of every period." Divides the subject into seven chapters: I. In Biblical Times; II. The Second Commonwealth; III. The Talmudic Period; IV. The Rise of Rationalism; V. The Development in the Kabbalah; VI. The Effects of Kabbalistic Speculations; and VII. Religious Reform and Zionism. He also includes an appendix on The Messianic Hope in the Jewish Liturgy.

D42 Silver, Abba Hillel. *A History of Messianic Speculation in Israel from the First through the Seventeenth Centuries.* New York: Macmillan, 1927. Rpt. Boston: Beacon Press, 1959.

"To trace the story of these Messianic calculations in Israel from the destruction to the Shabbetai Zebi movement, to analyze their method and technique, to point to their historic consequences, and also to disclose the consistent opposition to them throughout the centuries are the objects of this study." Throughout the study, Silver includes information about the mystical influence on messianic movements, from references to pseudepigraphic texts through various false messiahs.

D43 Scholem, Gershom G. "Messianic Movements after the Expulsion from Spain." In A26. I.335-47.

Distinguishes between earlier messianic movements and those since 1500 by "the mystical imagery common to [their] chief representatives, whence all Messianic ideas acquired a peculiar intensity. All these movements reflected the tribulations and persecutions of their period, as well as the popular conceptions of the Messiah and the redemption which were current among the masses in the ghettos. They also incorporated, to an ever-increasing degree, elements of the Kabbala."

D44   Steinberg, A. "Messianic Movements up to the End of the Middle Ages." In A26. I.328-34.

Traces the phenomenon of "the succession of great popular movements ... whose sole aim is the hastening of the time when the Supra-historic Messianic ideal would, in accordance with the words of the ancient prophets, be realized. After the Introduction, Steinberg discusses: Messianic Movements under Roman and Byzantine Rule; Messianic Movements under Islamic Rule; and Messianic Movements during the Christian Middle Ages.

D45   Arendt, Hannah. "Jewish History, Revised." *Jewish Frontier*, March 1948, pp. 34-38. Rpt. D58.

Using Scholem (C45) as a guide, Arendt revises the established view of the origin of the Reform movement from "the consequences of the emancipation granted to sections of the Jewish people and as the necessary reactions of a new adjustment to the requirements of the Gentile world," to "the outgrowth of the debacle of the last great Jewish political activity, the Sabbatian movement, of the loss of Messianic hope and of the despair about the ultimate destiny of the people."

D46   Buber, Martin. *Israel and Palestine--The History of an Idea.* Trans. Stanley Godman. London: East and West Library, 1952. Rpt. D56.

"The book demonstrates the centrality of Zion to biblical life and thought--how it was dominant in talmudic thought, how it inspired medieval thinkers and Kabbalists, and finally how it moved modern Jews, from the lonely Moses Hess through the rationalist Ahad Ha'am to the saintly mystic Rav Kook ... and A.D. Gordon, the Halutz. It has been said that Jews survived the terrors and tribulations of history because the ideal of a Messianic Zion was forever alive and refused to perish." (Nahum Glatzer's Forward) After an Introduction on Zion and the Other National Concepts, Buber discusses: I. The Testimony of the Bible; II. Interpretation and Transfiguration; III. The Voice of the Exile (including discussions of the 'Kusari,' The Zohar, Rabbi Liva and Rabbi Nahman of Brazlav); and IV. The Zionist Idea (including a section on Rav Kook).

D47 Scholem, Gershom G. "Jewish Messianism and the Idea of Progress: Exile and Redemption in the Cabbala." Trans. Moses Hadas. *Commentary*, 25(1958), 298-305. Rpt. D53.

"Traditionally,... the coming of the Messiah was supposed to shake the foundations of the world. In the view of the prophets and Aggadists, redemption would only follow upon a universal revolutionary disturbance, unparalleled disasters in which history would be dislodged and destroyed. The nineteenth-century view is blind to this catastrophic aspect. It looks only to progress toward infinite perfection. In probing into as man's infinite progress and perfectability, we find, surprisingly, that they stem from the Kabbalah."

D48 Werblowsky, R.J. Zwi. "Crises of Messianism." *Judaism*, 7(1958), 106-20.

Explores two crises of messianism, the destruction of the Second Temple and the Shabbatean movement, in order to evaluate the messianic aspects of Zionism.

D49 Berger, Abraham. "The Messianic Self-Consciousness of Abraham Abulafia." In A43. Pp. 55-61.

Studies Abulafia, not "in a typology of Jewish Messianic personalities," but in comparison with "Hellenistic mystagogues, Islamic Sufis, and Greek Orthodox Spirituals," to conclude that "Abulafia opened up curious religious possibilities, resembling in many respects the development of early Christianity in its separation from the parent faith, and the radical Sufis, who preached that the pilgrimage to Mecca may be undertaken in contemplation without leaving the physical confines of one's own room."

D50 Zeitlin, Solomon. "The Origin of the Idea of the Messiah." In A57. Pp. 447-59.

"Belief in a supernatural *mashiah*, a scion of the family of David, was first brought forth by the Apocalyptic Pharisaic group. It did not greatly influence the Judaeans during the Second Commonwealth, but after the Destruction of the Second Temple, and particularly after the revolt of Bar Kokba, it gained stimulus and shaped the life of the Jewish people throughout the centuries. The idea of a supernatural *mashiah* became the cornerstone of Jewish survival, as is admirably portrayed by Doctor Abba Hillel Silver in his book *A History of Messianic Speculation in Israel*" (D42).

D51 Cohen, Gerson D. *Messianic Postures of Ashkenazim and Sephardim (Prior to Sabbathai Zevi)*. Leo Baeck Memorial Lecture 9. New York: Leo Baeck Institute, 1967.

"In examining some of the roots of pre-modern messianism, we must inevitably touch on a second subject, which is also not without interest to us: that is, the Jewish response to pressure and persecution, to alternatives of life through compromise or of death through steadfastness and martyrdom. For messianism provided the energy and ideological substance for Jewish resistance in a world in which the Jews were always outnumbered and in which they frequently had to content with unbridled animosity."

D52 Werblowsky, R.J. Zwi. "Messianism in Jewish History." *Cahiers d'histoire mondiale*, 11(1968), 30-45. Rpt. D55.

"For the student of Jewish history the problem of messianic movements in historical rather than purely phenomenological, i.e. the question is not so much one of deciding whether or not a certain movement deserves the epithet 'messianic', but rather one of describing the continuity of messianic belief and expectation as it manifested itself in the events and crises of Jewish history."

D53 Scholem, Gershom. "The Messianic Idea in Kabbalism." In his A81. Pp. 37-48.

Reprint of D47.

D54 Scholem, Gershom G. "Towards an Understanding of the Messianic Idea in Judaism." Trans. Michael A. Meyer. In his A81. Pp. 1-36.

"The objects of these remarks is not the initial development of the Messianic idea but the varying perspectives by which it became an effective force after its crystallization in historical Judaism. In this connection it must be emphasized that in the history of Judaism its influence has been exercised almost exclusively under the conditions of the exile as a primary reality of Jewish life and Jewish history. This reality lends its special colouring to each of the various conceptions with which we shall be dealing here."

D55 Werblowsky, R.J. Zwi. "Messianism in Jewish History" In A77. Pp. 30-45.

Reprint of D52.

D56 Buber, Martin. *On Zion: The History of an Idea.* New York: Schocken Books, 1973.

Reprint of D46.

D57 Smith, Morton. "Messiahs: Robbers, Jurists, Prophets and Magicians." *Proceedings of the American Academy for Jewish Research*, 44(1977), 185-95.

"I submit that these four ultimately messianic careers--the robber's, the teacher's, the prophet's, the magician's--are all of them credible within the society of first-century Palestine. If so, this fact would resolve the apparent contradiction set forth at the beginning of this paper: The variety of the meanings of the terms 'messiah' remains clear, and the basis for the distinction of Christianity as a peculiar sect remains, not messianic belief as such, but the libertine consequences drawn by many members of the sect from the teachings and practices of this particular messiah."

D58 Arendt, Hannah. "Jewish History, Revised." In A102. Pp. 96-105.

Reprint of D45.

D59 Shamir, Yehuda. "Mystic Jerusalem." *Studia Mystica*, 3,2(Summer 1980,) 50-60.

"Perhaps no other element in Jewish life is more symbolic of redemption than Jerusalem, the Holy City. Throughout the centuries, the vision of Jerusalem redeemed served to comfort and console an exiled people. With the destruction of the Temple, the conviction grew that parallel to the 'earthly Jerusalem' there existed a 'celestial Jerusalem' established even before the creation of the world itself. This vision ignited the imagination of sages, enthralled mystics of the Kabbalah, and still inspires the souls of modern day poets and writers."

D60 Taubes, Jacob. "The Price of Messianism." *Journal of Jewish Studies*, 33(1982), 595-600.

"I would like to argue that the historic material presented by Gershom Scholem allows for a different reading, one that presupposes a more inflected theoretical frame of reference than that which guides his inquiry towards an understanding of the Messianic idea in Judaism. His criterion of the interiorization of the Messianic experience is a case in point."

D61 Agus, Jacob B. "The Messianic Ideal and the Apocalyptic Vision." *Judaism*, 32(1983), 205-14.

"Since messianism reflects the most powerful motivations of Jewish life, it is essential that we take account of the psychic roots of this belief. Gershom Scholem pointed out that messianism combined two opposing motivations--a restorative hope, affirming the return of Israel to its status in the days of Kings David and Solomon, and a utopian vision of a trans-historical future. In this essay, we shall employ a modified version of Scholem's distinction, one that is more suited to an analysis of the choices confronting our people in our time. We draw the line between the Messianic Ideal and the Apocalyptic Vision of the future. The former is a projection of the moral-rational faith of the prophets; the latter is a dream-like affirmation of myth and mystery that afford gratification to the distressed and the persecuted. The two versions of messianism derive respectively from two fundamentally different patterns of faith."

God and Creation

D62 Abelson J. "The Talmud and Theosophy." *Theosophical Review*, 37(1905-6), 9-27.

In this paper read at the Bristol Lodge, Abelson discusses the similarities between the Talmud and Theosophy, especialy in relation to the doctrines of the Unity of God. Atonement, the Immortality of the Spirit, and the "ordinary duties of manhood and citizenhood."

D63 Abelson, Joshua. *The Immanence of God in Rabbinical Literature*. London, 1912. Rpt. New York: Hermon Press, 1969.

A study of "Talmudic Kabbalah ... all those mystic pronouncements which lie scattered and dispersed throughout the extensive realms of the Talmudic literature." Treats "mainly of the aspects of Divine Immanence which the Talmudic sages envisaged under the name 'Shechinah' and 'Ruah-ha-Kodesh' (Holy Spirit)." After exploring biblical and non-rabbinic treatments of the subject of immanence, Abelson provides a detailed analysis of both the Shekhinah and Holy Spirit, including: General View, personification, relation to sin, Torah, the Word, prophecy, etc., compatibility of mysticism and rabbinic theology, and interchange of the terminology of the two concepts.

D64 Abdul-Ali, Sijil. "Metaphysical Outlook in Jewish Mysticism: An Introductory Study." *Occult Review*, 24(1916), 350-56.

"The Kabalah inculcates that the Absolute is, in its very essence and withdrawal, unknowable; and in order to explain the intelligibility of the manifest world, it posits a group of Emanations, which, proceeding from the Absolute, make known its existence, and constitute together the Primordial or Heavenly Man. It is these Emanations alone that are the ultimate objects of knowledge, and even they in their entirety are withdrawn and well-nigh inscrutable. Thus the Universe is known or knowable, is, by hypothesis, in the likeness of man, but in respect of ultimate Being it is *Ain Soph*, the Limitless, which is beyond all possibility of Knowledge, and therefore, in the strictest sense, outside even the predicate of existence. Evidently this doctrine involves a confession of inability to solve the root-problem of creation and of knowledge, but it is at least a sign that the Kabbalists recognized, in their own manner, the peculiar difficulty of the task to which they had addressed themselves."

D65 Scholem, Gershom G. "Philosophy and Jewish Mysticism." *Review of Religion*, 2(1938), 385-402.

"Jewish mysticism in its various forms represents an attempt to interpret the religious values of Judaism in terms of the idea of the living God, who manifests Himself in the acts of creation, revelation, and redemption." Scholem concludes that the value of Jewish mysticism is its "attempt to discover the hidden life under the eternal shapes of reality, and to make visible that abyss in which the symbolical nature of all that exists reveals itself."

D66 Altmann, Alexander. "God and the Self in Jewish Mysticism." *Judaism*, 3(1954), 142-46.

Given "the perennial theme of all mysticism," that "God and man's self are essentially one," Altmann asks: "How does Jewish mysticism experience and conceive the bond between God and the Self? The answer to this question is not without its complications nor can it be a clear-cut and uniform one. Yet a certain bold line of development emerges once we focus attention on the problem."

D67 Altmann, Alexander. "A Note on the Rabbinic Doctrine of Creation." *Journal of Jewish Studies*, 7(1956), 195-206. Rpt. D68.

Analyzes the rabbinic doctrine of creation by emanation, which "expresses itself in favour of the Platonic doctrine of pre-existent matter, and ... differentiates between the pre-existence in the Divine Mind of the essences of things and their actual 'innovation' (in time) as a result of a process of emanation. Moreover, the background of this doctrine is no longer hellenistic philosophy and mythology but a certain type of Neoplatonism such as we find in Isaac Israeli,... there is a direct line from Israeli's concept of Supernal Wisdom to the one we find in the incipient Qabbala of R. Isaac the Blind and the Gerona mystics."

D68 Altmann, Alexander. "A Note on the Rabbinic Doctrine of Creation." In his A71. Pp. 128-39.

Reprint of D67.

D69 Scholem, Gershom G. "The Name of God and the Linguistic Theory of the Kabbala." *Diogenes*, 79(1972), 59-80; 80(1972), 164-94.

Explores the questions of "What precisely we are to understand by the voice and what is uttered through it ... The indissoluble link between the idea of the revealed truth and the notion of language--is as much, that is, as the word of God makes itself heard through the medium of human language, if, otherwise, human experience can reach the knowledge of such a word at all--is presumably one of the most important, if the the most important, legacies bequeathed by Judaism to the history of religions."

D70 Albertson, Edward. *Kabbala: God--Demon of Beiden?* Ary Verhaar, 1973.

Unavailable for annotating.

D71 Katz, Steven T. *Jewish Ideas and Concepts.* New York: Schocken Books, 1977.

"In the preparation of this volume two goals were kept in mind. The first was to present an accurate, informative, rich picture of Jewish thought which could serve as the basis for a proper understanding of Judaism.... Our second related but distinct goal was to bring to the surface the uniquely *Jewish* understanding of concepts which Judaism shares with its theological offspring." The first part contains a section, God in the Kabbalah (pp. 26-28), and there are references to Kabbalah throughout the text.

D72 Jacobs, Louis. "Kabbalistic World View." *Ultimate Reality and Meaning: Interdisciplinary Studies in the Philosophy of Understanding*, 2(1979), 321-29.

The "Kabbalistic World View" is a synthesis of "two contradictory tendencies in Jewish thought; that of the Rabbis, who appear to be saying that God really does have merciful and compassionate dispositions, and that of the philosophers like Maimonides who advocate a theology of negation, limiting the idea of *Imitatio Dei* solely to God's acts."

Emanations and the Concept of the *Sefirot*

D73 Hunt, John. *Pantheism and Christianity.* London: Isbister, Limited, 1884. Rpt. Port Washington, New York: Kennikat Press, 1970.

"The object of this book is to show not only that [Christianity and Pantheism] can be reconciled, but that Christianity will be a great gainer by the reconciliation." In discussing Kabbalah from a pantheistic perspective (pp. 84-88), Hunt focuses primarily on creation by emanation to conclude that "all is a manifestation of God.... all, so far as they do exist, have their existence in that which is divine."

D74 Criswell, K.A.C. "A Comparison of the Hebrew Sephiroth with the 'Paut Neteru' of Egypt." *Occult Review*, 16(1912), 349-57.

"I propose to compare the 'Paut Neteru,' or members of 'Great Company' of the gods of the city of Heliopolis, with the Hebrew scheme of the Sephiroth."

D75 Power, J.H. "The Kabalistic Tree of Life." *Occult Review*, 21(1915), 331-38.

"This, then, is a sketch of the Tree of Life, and of the Kabalist's idea of the origin of the numbers with which he works."

D76 Abdul-Ali, Sijil. "The Doctrine of Transcendence and Emanation in Jewish Mysticism." *Occult Review*, October 1917, pp. 214-22.

Unavailable for annotating.

D77 Halevi, Z'ev ben Shimon [Warren Kenton] *The Tree of Life: An Introduction to the Cabala*. London: Rider & Company, and New York: S. Weiser, 1972, 1975, 1980.

"In our account the origin of the Tree of Life is traced, then the power of its illumination and formulation. Following the development of its conception we see that cosmic principles apply to any whole entity. Observing its workings we are shown how the tree gathers into an intelligible order all aspects of phenomena and demonstrates them in a reflective picture, a Universe wherein the Creator is present even in the densest of matter."

D78 Jacobs, Louis. *A Jewish Theology*. London: Darton, Longman & Todd, 1973; and New York: Behrmann House, 1974.

"This book attempts a systematic presentation of the main themes of Jewish theology." In conjunction with his purpose, Jacobs includes information on Kabbalah where pertinent, especially discussions of the *Sefirot*, (pp. 28-34), Eternity (pp. 86-92), Creation (pp. 104-107), The Goodness of God (pp. 129-31), The Names of God (pp. 148-51), and Worship and Prayer (pp. 184-92).

The Problem of Evil

D79 Carmell, L. "The Problem of Evil: The Jewish Synthesis--Some New Insights from a Kabbalistic Source." *Proceedings of the Associations of Orthodox Jewish Scientists*, 1(1966), 92-100.

Investigates Saadya Gaon's belief "that if sin were impossible everyone would be entitled to the same reward, and as a consequence the reward would not be appreciated."

D80 Scholem, Gershom. "On Sin and Punishment: Some Remarks Concerning Biblical and Rabbinical Ethics." In A72. Pp. 163-77.

"The remarks I want to make on sin and punishment as they became apparent in Judaism will concern three different levels which correspond to the three dimensions of the Judaic religious world: (1) the Hebraic Bible, (2) the sources of Rabbinical Judaism in the Talmud and Midrash, and (3) the Judaic esoteric teachings or secret doctrine, regardless of whether we want to call it Jewish Gnosis or Mysticism, as it is expressed in the literature of the Kabbalists. In this study I shall stress a few points which are significant for the phenomenology of Judaism as a historical manifestation."

D81 Dan, Joseph. "The Desert in Jewish Mysticism: The Kingdom of Samael." *Ariel*, #40(1976), 38-43.

Explores "the duality in the concept of the desert in Jewish mysticism,... According to the Zohar, the desert is Satan's kingdom, home of the Serpent, the most vivid symbol of Evil. At the same time, the desert is the place from which redemption must come, for, unless Samael is defeated, redemption is impossible, and it had to take place in the desert, both in the past, in Moses' time, and in the present."

D82 Goldman, Norman Saul. "Mythology of Evil in Judaism." *Journal of Religion and Health*, 15(1976), 230-40.

Analysis of rabbinic "mythology of evil that ... is not only comparable [to Freud] in providing a functional myth for understanding evil or sin, but also serves as a theoretical basis for the rabbinic resolution of the problem of sin." Includes a discussion "of the vivid systematic theology of evil constructed by the Sabbatian and Frankist movements" (pp. 237-40).

D83 Dan, Joseph. "Samael, Lilith, and the Concept of Evil in Early Kabbalah." *AJS Review*, 5(1980), 17-40.

"In this paper an attempt is made to clarify both the sources and the original contribution to the mythological concept of evil as developed by Rabbi Isaac ben Jacob ha-Kohen in Spain in the second half of the thirteenth century.... The following analysis is divided into two parts: the first is an attempt to discover two types of sources which were used by Rabbi Isaac--mythological sources and theological sources; the second part is an attempt to point out the reasons for Rabbi Isaac's mythological attitude and his relationship to other kabbalists, both earlier and later. In this fashion, a conclusion might be reached concerning the role of mythological elements in the development of early kabbalah."

Man and His Soul

D84 Leiningen, C. de. "The Soul According to the Qabalah." A Paper Read before the Psychological Society of Munich, March 5, 1887. Trans. Thos. Williams. *Theosophical Siftings*, 2(1889-90), #18.

"Everywhere, and in all ages, various and contradictory systems and dogmas have rapidly succeeded one another on [the subject of the immortality and spirituality of the Soul], and the word Soul has been used to explain the most opposite states of existence and the most different shades of opinion. Of these antagonistic systems of thought there can be no doubt that the transcendental philosophy of the Jews, the Qabalah, is the most ancient, and perhaps for this reason, it may be held in part the product of that tranquil intelligence, of that acute perception of truth, which, according to tradition, man originally possessed."

D85 Scholem, Gershom. "Religious Authority & Mysticism." Trans. Ralph Manheim. *Commentary*, 38(November 1964), 31-39.

Explores "not the mystic's inner fulfillment but his impact on the historical world, his conflict with the religious life of his day and with his community." Included in somewhat different form in his A59.

D86 Jacobs, Louis. "The Doctrine of the 'Divine Spark' in Man in Jewish Sources." In A60. Pp. 87-114.

"We have tried to trace the doctrine of the divine spark in the soul from its beginnings in Philo, through the cabbalists, and down to its significant place in the *Ḥabad* system. Admittedly, the doctrine is a highly unconventional one for Jewish religious thinkers, but the evidence we have adduced in this essay demonstrates convincingly that there were subterranean currents in Jewish thought on the soul which occasionally burst to the surface. For all the emphasis in normative Jewish teaching on the impassible gulf between God and His Creatures, these currents carried across the centuries the daring idea that in the soul of man the abyss had been bridged."

D87 Olan, Levi A. *Judaism and Immortality*. New York: Union of American Hebrew Congregations, 1971.

"How the Jewish idea of life after death has evolved from the early more physical concept of the resurrection of a united body and soul to a belief in the immortality of the soul alone is traced by Rabbi Olan in the Bible, in the Apocrypha, in medieval philosophy, in the Kabalah and Chasidism, in the eighteenth century's Period of Englightenment and in Judaism today." (Editor's note) The fifth chapter is devoted to Jewish mysticism (pp. 71-79).

D88 Linder, Gary. "Is Mysticism an Alien Element in Judaism: The Scholem Thesis." *Gesher: Bridging the Spectrum of Orthodox Jewish Scholarship*, 6(1977-78), 123-40.

"To summarize, the Kabbalah accomplished two tasks: it provided Jews who had mystical inclinations with a uniquely Jewish outlet for their religious sensibilities, and it also helped restore the potency of traditional Judaism for many of the latter's devotees.... The genius of the Jewish mystics lies in their transformation of traditional Judaism while retaining its essential ideas and forms."

D89 Klapholtz, Israel Jacob. *The 36 Hidden Saints*. Ed. Yisrael Yaakov. Trans. Sheindel Weinbach. Bnei Brak: Peer Hasefer, 1981.

Unavailable for annotating.

D90 Sharot, Stephen. *Messianism, Mysticism, and Magic: A Sociological Analysis of Jewish Religious Movements*. Chapel Hill: University of North Carolina Press, 1982.

"This book is a sociological study of popular religious traditions and movements in Jewish communities. It deals primarily with the religion of the Jewish folk or masses; thus it is concerned with the religious doctrines and speculations of the intelligentsia only insofar as they were influential in, or in some way relevant to, popular expressions of religion." Sharot discusses: 1. Sociology and Jewish Historiography; 2. Concepts and Perspectives; 3. Religion and Magic in the Traditional Jewish Community; 4. Normative Jewish Millenarianism and the First Jewish Millenarian Movements in the Diaspora; 5. Sephardim, Ashkenazim, and Italian Jews; 6. The New Christians; 7. The Sabbatian Movement; 8. Developments in Sabbatianism; 9. Millenarianism and Mysticism in Eighteenth-Century Poland; 10. Hasidism and the Routinzation of Charisma; 11. Hasidism in Modern Society; 12. The Secularization of Millenarianism; and 13. Religious Zionism in Israel--A Return to Messianism.

Torah

D91 Abdul-Ali, Sijil. "The Unwritten Law in Jewish Mysticism." *Occult Review*, March 1918, pp. 150-58.

Unavailable for annotating.

D92 Altmann, Alexander. "Saadya's Theory of Revelation: Its Origin and Background." In A23. Pp. 4-25. Rpt. D97.

Although it is generally believed that Saadya's theory of revelation was borrowed from the Mu'tazilite concept of the *Created Kalam* of *Allah*, Altmann first demonstrates that this attribution of origin is erroneous, and then posits the theory that Saadya's theory of Revelation "has a mystical background, namely that of the targumic *Memra.*"

D93 Ginzberg, Louis. "Allegorical Interpretation of Scripture." In his A37. Pp. 125-50.

Reprint of article in the *Jewish Encyclopedia*, B27. Focuses on the two modes of "Allegorical Interpretation ... found dealing with the Bible: the one, symbolic or typologic interpretation, derived mainly from Palestinian Jews; the other, the philosophical or mystical mode, originated with the Alexandrian Jews of Egypt." In both, "allegorism is ... in some sense an incipient phase of rationalism."

D94 Scholem, Gershom G. "The Meaning of the Torah in Jewish Mysticism." Trans. Ralph Manheim. In his A59. Pp. 32-86.

"The Kabbalistic conceptions of the true nature of the Torah are based on three fundamental principles. They are not necessarily connected, although in our texts they often appear together, but it is not difficult to see how a relation can be established between them. These principles may be identified as 1. The principle of God's name; 2. The principle of the Torah as an organism; and 3. The principle of the infinite meaning of the divine word. Historically and presumably also psychologically, they do not all have the same origin.

D95 Scholem, Gershom G. "Tradition and Commentary as Religious Categories in Judaism." Trans. Henry Schwarzschild. *Judaism*, 15(1966), 23-39. Rpt. D98, D99.

"In Judaism, tradition becomes the reflective impulse that intervenes between the absoluteness of the Divine word-- revelation--and its receiver. Tradition thus raises a question about the possibility of immediacy in relationship to the Divine, even though it has been incorporated in revelation.... Every religious experience after revelation is a mediated one. It is the experience of the voice of God rather than the experience of God. But all reference to the 'voice of God' is highly anthropomorphic--a fact from which theologians have always carefully tried to escape. And here we face questions which, in Judaism, have been thought through only in the mystic doctrines of the Kabbalists." Expanded version under title "Revelation and Tradition as Religious Categories in Judaism," D100.

D96 Vajda, Georges. "The Dialectics of the Talmud and the Kabbalah." Trans. Alissandro Ferace and Nelda Cantarella. *Diogenes*, 59(1967), 63-79.

Examination of talmudic and kabbalistic dialectics, "not only the intellectual but in certain cases, also the allegedly suprarational steps which within Judaism (which is polymorphous) confront the given facts, the fundamental ideas whether complementary or contradictory which impose themselves with equal authority upon the conscience of the believer. Dialectics, in this sense, tend to synthesize these fundamental data reducing to a minimum the destruction of the components."

D97 Altmann, Alexander. "Saadya's Theory of Revelation: Its Origin and Background." In his A71. Pp. 140-60.

Reprint of D92.

D98 Scholem, Gershom G. "Tradition and Commentary as Religious Categories in Judaism." Trans. Henry Schwarzschild. *Studies in Comparative Religion*, 3(1969), 147-63.

Reprint of D95; expanded version under title "Revelation and Tradition as Religious Categories in Judaism," D100.

D99 Scholem, Gershom G. "Tradition and Commentary as Religious Categories in Judaism." In A74. Pp. 300-22.

Reprint of D95; expanded version under title "Revelation and Tradition as Religious Categories in Judaism," D100.

D100 Scholem, Gershom G. "Revelation and Tradition as Religious Categories in Judaism." Trans. Michael A. Meyer. In his A81. Pp. 282-303.

Expanded version of D95.

D101 Van Der Heide, A. "PARDES: Methodological Reflections on the Theory of the Four Senses." *Journal of Jewish Studies*, 34, 2(Autumn 1983), 147-59.

"My aim is to review a very popular characterization of Jewish exegesis--the 'Pardes' scheme--and to demonstrate its limitations. On the other hand, this very critique will offer an opportunity to suggest a broader perspective for the study of Jewish exegesis and for its relation to the study of Jewish religion in general."

The Mystic Way

Primary Source

D102 Gaster, Moses. *The Ma'aseh Book: Book of Jewish Tales and Legends from the Judeo-German*. The Schiff Library of Jewish Classics. 2 vols. Philadelphia: Jewish Publication Society of America, 1934.

Medieval *exempla*; comprised of three cycles: 1. those taken from the Talmud; 2. cycle of legends concerning medieval rabbis, including Rabbi Samuel the Hasid, Rabbi Judah the Hasid, Rashi, and R. Jehiel of Paris; and 3. primarily anonymous stories, though including a few by Jacob Luzzatto.

Secondary Sources

D103 Enelow, H.G. "Kawwana: The Struggle for Inwardness in Judaism." In A7. Pp. 82-107. Rpt. D119.

Explores the Jewish search for inwardness through the doctrine of Kavvanah, which "may mean intention, concentration, devotion; it may mean purpose and the right spirit; it may mean pondering, meditation, and mystery. The word kawwana connotes all these things, for the reason that it kept on gathering significance from the religious experience of the Jewish people. The doctrine of the Kawwana is thoroughly Jewish, and in its history we catch a glimpse of the struggle for the maintenance of inwardness in Judaism."

D104 Schechter, Abraham I. "Cabbalistic Interpolations in the Prayer Book." In his A18. Pp. 39-60.

Approaching the Jewish prayer book as, in addition to "a mere collection of prayers and supplications.... also a collection of historical, theological and philosophical compositions"; examines "The presence of compositions in our prayer book that were introduced by the mystics of the Cabbalistic school."

D105 Lauterbach, Jacob Z. "The Origin and Development of Two Sabbath Ceremonies." *Hebrew Union College Annual*, 15(1940), 367-424.

"In the following I shall describe the course taken by two Jewish ceremonies [the use of fragrant herbs and spices] observed respectively on Friday evening and Saturday night. Both of these ceremonies grew out of a mere custom or habit and originally were similar in character and form. The one, after being recognized as a religious ceremony, experienced in the course of time, (due probably to some objections raised against it) some reinterpretations. With some modifications, it has been preserved to this day. The other seemingly met with greater obstacles. And even though, or just because, it was given some new mystic significance and assumed a new character, it was not generally favored. It encountered strong objections and was discarded by the great majority of the people, so that it finally fell into utter disuse and became almost completely forgotten."

D106 Efros, Israel. "Holiness and Glory in the Bible: An Approach to the History of Jewish Thought." *Jewish Quarterly Review*, 41(1950-51), 363-77.

"My purpose in this essay is to present two fundamental concepts which, though they tend in opposite directions, always operated in the history of Jewish philosophy. Indeed, their very oppositeness stimulated Jewish thinking and steered its course. These concepts we may call holiness (*qedushah*) and glory (*kavod*), the first lifting the God-idea even higher, and the second--pulling it back and bringing it down nearer to man."

D107 Zaoui, Andre. "The Mystical Element." Trans. Eric Conrad. In A38. Pp. 99-107.

"In order to describe the relation of man to his God we shall examine two fundamental characteristics of Jewish prayer: the 'Kavana' and man 'standing before God.'"

D108 Wind, Solomon. *The Mystic Approach to Prayer: The Doctrine of the Ten Sephiroth in the Kabbalistic Prayer "Petach Eliyahu."* New York: Department for Torah Education and Culture, The Jewish Agency, 1957.

"The present article is an endeavor towards a personal adjustment to what appears as complexity or perplexity via the medium of prayer. In the accepted sense prayer is a solution for life's beneficence or a process of self judgment in order to establish a proper ratio between one's estimated worth and expected beneficence. In the mystic sense, however, prayer is an attunement to the Creator--the source of all life and benevolence."

D109 Bowers, Margaretta K., and Samuel Glasner. "Auto-Hypnotic Aspects of the Jewish Cabbalistic Concept of *Kavanah*." *Journal of Clinical and Experimental Hypnosis*, 6(1958).

D110 Scholem, Gershom. "The Doctrine of the Righteous in Jewish Mysticism." *Synagogue Review*, 34(1960), 189-95.

Unavailable for annotating.

D111 Zaoui, Andre. "Dialectics of Purification." In A58. Pp. 325-31.

"We shall examine particularly the relation that the texts of mystic theology in our tradition established between creation and repentance, and we shall thus define what could be called the dialectic of purification."

D112 Scholem, Gershom G. "Religious Authority and Mysticism." Trans. Ralph Manheim. In his A59. Pp. 5-31.

"In general, then, the mystic's experience tends to confirm the religious authority under which he lives; its theology and symbols are projected into his mystical experience, but do not spring from it. But mysticism has another, contrasting, aspect: precisely because a mystic is what he is, precisely because he stands in a direct, productive relationship to the object of his experience, he transforms the content of the tradition in which he lives. He contributes not only to the conservation of the tradition, but also to its development. Seen with new eyes, the old values acquire a new meaning, even where the mystic had no such intention or was not even aware of doing anything new. Indeed, a mystic's understanding and interpretation of his own experience may even lead him to question the religious authority he had hitherto supported."

D113 Jacobs, Louis. *The Via Negativa in Jewish Religious Thought*. Third Allan Bronfman Lecture. New York: Judaica Press, 1967.

Unavailable for annotating.

D114 Scholem, Gershom G. "Three Types of Jewish Piety." *Eranos-Jahrbuch*, 38(1969), 331-48. Rpt. D116, D117.

"I wish to talk here about the basic attitudes, about the ideal human types which the history of rabbinic Judaism has evolved and I should like to discuss the tensions that are possible between them. The basic tension in the religious society of Judaism is that between rational and emotional factors, rational and irrational forces. The ideal types formed by this society will necessarily reflect such tension." The types are: "*Talmid Hakham*, the rabbinic scholar, the *Zaddik*, the just Man, and the *Hasid*."

D115 Scholem, Gershom G. "The Tradition of the Thirty-Six Just Men." Trans. Michael A. Meyer. In his A81. Pp. 251-56.

Study of the historical origins and development of the legend.

D116 Scholem, Gershom. "Three Types of Jewish Piety." *Ariel*, #32(1973), 5-24.

Reprint of D114.

D117 Scholem, Gershom. "Three Types of Jewish Piety." *SIDIC: Journal of the Service International de Documentation Judéo-Chrétienne*, 8,1(1975), 4-13.

Reprint of D114.

D118 Steinsaltz, Adin. "Repentance." *Shefa Quarterly*, 1,1(Summer 1977), 3-9.

"The penitant thus does more than return to his proper place. He performs an act of amendment of cosmic significance; he restores the sparks of holiness which had been captured by the powers of evil. The sparks that he had dragged down and attached to himself are now raised up with him, and a host of forces of evil return and are transformed to forces of good. This is the significance of the statement in the Talmud that in the place where a completely penitant person stands, even the most saintly cannot enter; because the penitant has at his disposal not only the forces of good in his soul and in the world, but also those of evil, which he transforms into essences of holiness."

D119 Enelow, Hyman G. "Kawwana: The Struggle for Inwardness in Judaism (Meditation as a Preparation for Prayer)." In A104. Pp. 98-104.

Reprint of D103.

D120 Kramer, William M. "On Meditation in the Jewish Mystical Tradition." In A104. Pp. 68-71.

"The Jewish mystic did not feel deprived because he was not in possession of or possessed by 'visible and audible representations of God.' Judaism has long walked the *via negativa*. The mystic was, as the phrase has it, God-intoxicated."

D121 Shiloah, Amnon. "The Symbolism of Music in the Kabbalistic Tradition." *World of Music*, 20,3(1978), 56-65.

Because of the "close interrelationships of music and certain basic kabbalistic concepts,... we have to penetrate the hidden worlds sought by the mystic and to seize the scattered musical references in them, in order to understand the mystical symbolism assigned to this art." Shiloah discusses: Music and meditation; Man as protagonist of the drama of the universe; and The whole cosmos sings.

D122 Glazerson, Mattithias. *The Mystical Glory of Shabbath and Pesach*. Trans. Seth Sprecher. Jerusalem and New York: Feldheim, 1980.

"The goal of this book is to show the reader how the content and significance of Shabbath and the Festivals are revealed through the letters of the written words; the relevance of these letters in different combinations, and of their numerical values."

D123 Dan, Joseph. "The Emergence of Mystical Prayer." In A117. Pp. 85-120.

"The mystical concept of prayer emerged in the same period during which Hebrew mystical literature began to flourish among the Jews of Europe, the second half of the twelfth century and the beginning of the thirteenth.... It is evident that the development of a new attitude toward the liturgy is closely connected with the emergence of the various Jewish mystical schools, so that the analysis of this particular problem may shed some further light upon a crucial phase in the history of Jewish mysticism and religious thought in general."

D124 Ginsburg, Elliott. "The Sabbath in the Kabbalah." *Judaism*, 31(1982), 26-36.

"Over a period of several centuries, the Kabbalists developed a rich body of lore and ritual that articulated a new vision of the Sabbath. Several outstanding examples of it are the reformulation of the Sabbath as a mystical marriage ceremony, extensive discussion of the 'feminine' aspect within God, and an emphasis on the motif of human transformation marked by the devotees assimilation of the Sabbath-soul. Owing largely to the efforts of the 16th century Safed Kabbalists and their subsequent popularizers, the mystical understanding and celebration of the Sabbath was transmitted to, and assimilated by, virtually every Jewish community. In this essay I will discuss several of the central motifs of the Kabbalistic Sabbath, focusing on the mythic paradigms that lend emotional resonance to the day and the ritual that dramatizes it."

D125 Kaplan, Aryeh. *Meditation and Kabbalah: Containing Relevant Texts from* The Greater Hekhalot, *Textbook of the Merkavah School,* The Works of Abraham Abulafia, *Joseph Gikatalia's* Gates of Light, The Gates of Holiness, Gate of the Holy Spirit, *Textbook of the Lurianic School, Hasidic Classics.* York Beach, Maine: Samuel Weiser, 1982.

"It is with great trepidation that one begins to write a work such as this, involving some of the most hidden mysteries of the Kabbalah.... But so much misinformation has already been published that it is virtually imperative that an authentic, authoritative account be published." Discusses: Meditation, Talmudic Mystics, Rabbi Abraham Abulafia, Other Early Schools, Safed, The Ari, and The Hasidim.

D126 Kaplan, Lawrence. "Response to Joseph Dan." In A117. Pp. 120-28.

Response to D123: "While I do not wish to deny that the status of prayer is more problematic in philosophy than in Kabbalah, I would like to modify the rather stark contrast drawn by both Professors Scholem and Dan. I believe that medieval Jewish philosophy did not fail quite so miserably with regard to the problem of prayer as Professor Dan's thesis would suggest, nor, on the other hand, was mysticism that successful in resolving the problem, as Professor Dan would apparently have us believe."

Myth and Symbol

D127 Abelson, J. "Mysticism in Rabbinical Literature." *Hibbert's Journal*, 10,2(January 1912), 426-43.

"Having now made clear, as I hope, what is in a general way the pith and marrow of mysticism, let us now come to close grips with our main subject and see of what nature is the mysticism embedded in the vast and variegated domain of the Rabbinical literature. Investigation has led me to divide the subject off into two independent departments. These are *(a)* the mysticism of the Shechinah, *(b)* the mysticism of the 'Ruach Ha-Kodesh,' or Holy Spirit."

D128 Montgomery, James A. "The Lilith Legend." *The Museum Journal*, 4(1913), 62-65.

Unavailable for annotating.

D129 Abelson, J. "Seeing the Shekinah at Death." *Quest*, 6(1915), 92-108.

"But whereas the great majority of the Rabbinical pronouncements about seeing the Shekinah apply to the living man, there is a small minority of Talmudic and Kabbalistic *dicta* about catching a sight or sound or even a smell of the

Shekinah when a man is at the point of death. The latter theme is an aspect of the Shekinah problem which has affinities with many an interesting point in other systems of theology. Hence I have thought it might not be a vain thing to offer a few remarks about it in as simple a way as the technicalities of the literature will permit."

D130 Box, C.H. "The Significance of Metatron and Sandalfon." *Quest*, 21(1930), 197-99.

"In this brief article it is proposed: (1) to give a short statement regarding the general significance of Metatron; (2) to discuss the origin and meaning of the name; and (3) to consider some objections that have been raised."

D131 Scholem, G. "The Curious History of the Six-Pointed Star: How the 'Magen David' Became the Jewish Symbol." *Commentary*, 8(1949), 243-51.

"... traces the obscure story of the Magen David through its long and curious career, and reveals that the true story of the symbol is quite different from that asserted by most accepted 'authorities.'" (Editor's note)

D132 Buber, Martin. "Myth in Judaism." Trans. Ralph Manheim. *Commentary*, 9(1950), 562-66.

"When the editor of *Commentary* suggested that a translation of this essay be published, I re-read it for the first time in many years. (It was the fourth of my seven *Speeches on Judaism* and dates from 1913; my last reading of it was in preparation for the issuing of a collected edition of the *Speeches* in 1923). Upon re-reading, I have the impression that it may be of some importance even today for those wanting to know about the spiritual history of Israel, and so I willingly agreed. But I should like to inform the reader that had I written the essay some years later, I would have made it clearer that real myth is the expression, not of an imaginative state of mind or of mere feeling, but of a real meeting of two Realities."

D133 Bamberger, Bernard Jacob. *Fallen Angels*. Philadelphia: Jewish Publication Society of America, 1952.

Traces the myth of the rebel angels "within the Jewish religion and in the religions that sprang from Judaism." Part VII, "Jewish Mysticism" (pp. 163-99), traces the theme through German and Spanish Kabbalah, the Zohar, the later mystics and the Hasidic movement.

D134 Patai, Raphael. "Matronit: The Goddess of the Kabbala." *History of Religions*, 4(1964), 53-68.

Comparison of the Shekhinah to the major goddess of ancient Near Eastern mythology from the perspective that "The same three traits, chastity, promiscuity, and bloodthirstiness, characterize the daughter-goddess who figures prominently in Kabbalistic literature and is referred to by a great variety of names of which two, the *Matronit* and the *Shekhina*, are standard designations."

D135   Patai, Raphael.   "The Shekhina."   *Journal of Religion*, 44(1964), 275-88.

"We have followed in this paper the development of the Shekhina concept from its early targumic beginnings in the first or second century B.C. to the first stage it reached a thousand years later, just prior to its being taken up by Kabbalism and made into one of the fundamentals of its mystical theosophy." Included in D138.

D136   Scholem, Gershom G.   "Kabbalah and Myth."   Trans. Ralph Manheim.   In his A59.   Pp. 87-117.

"The reappearance of myth in the Kabbalah can be envisaged most clearly from two different standpoints, which are precisely the two poles of Jewish religious thinking: the idea of God and the idea of the Law. For it is evident that the mystical transformation of a religion sets in at the points that are most essential to the content of that religion, and so preserves its character as a specific historical phenomenon within a concrete religion."

D137   Scholem, Gershom G.   "Tradition and New Creation in the Ritual of the Kabbalists."   Trans. Ralph Manheim.   In his A59.   Pp. 118-57.

Purpose "is to examine the practical implications of [the re-emergence of myth in a monotheistic religion]. For the truth is that the Kabbalistic conceptions which exerted an influence on ritual were exclusively those in which contact was renewed with a mythical stratum, whether disguised in allegory or directly communicated in symbols. The speculative interpretations, however sublime, that are frequently enough intertwined with mythical images in the Kabbalah produced no new rites, and it is interesting to note that many of those Kabbalists who made a conscious effort to bar mythical images from their thinking showed extreme reserve toward such new rites as those which the Kabbalah brought forth with lavish abundance in Safed. But such scruples did not prevent the Kabbalah from achieving its widest popularity precisely by providing new rites, and in the following we shall note several striking examples of this intimate connection between the ritual and myths of the Kabbalists."

D138   Patai, Raphael.   *The Hebrew Goddess*.   New York: Ktav Publishing House, Inc., 1967.   Sel. rpt. D135.

"Historical scrutiny ... shows that for many centuries following the traditional date of the Sinaitic revelation, [Judaism], idealized in retrospect, remained a demand rather than a fact. Further study, undertaken in the present volume, indicates that there were among the Biblical Hebrews other religious trends, powerful in their attraction for the common people and their leaders alike, in which the worship of goddesses played as important a role as it did anywhere else on comparable stages of religious development. It will also be attempted to show that the female deities of the early, monarchic period, did subsequently not disappear but underwent transformations and succeeded in their changed forms to retain much of their old sway over religious sentiments." After the Introduction, Patai discusses: I. The Goddess Asherah; II. Astarti-Anath; III. The Cherubim; IV. The Shekhina; V. The Kabbalistic Tetrad; VI. Matronit--The Goddess of the Kabbala; VII. Lilith; and VIII. The Sabbath-Virgin, Bride, Queen and Goddess.

D139 Scholem, Gershom G. "The Star of David: History of a Symbol." Trans. Michael A. Meyer. In his A81. Pp. 257-81.

"What, then, is the true history of the Star of David in Jewish tradition? Is it rooted in that tradition? Did it for larger or smaller circles possess dignity as the symbol of Judaism, or at least as a Jewish symbol? And if not--when did it receive this function and status, and as a result of what circumstances? If we seek to clarify these questions, we must distinguish between the appearance of the sign itself, i.e., the figure of the two interlocked equilateral triangles, and the history of the designation which it bears today as the Shield of David. The symbol and its designation were not always connected. The history of the symbol, its career and its reception by Judaism, are however of great interest, especially if we remove the inventions and fantasies which certain recent Jewish scholars have woven around it."

D140 Lantero, Erminie Huntress. *Feminine Aspects of the Divinity*. Pendle Hill Pamphlet no. 191. Wallingford, Penn.: Pendle Hill Publications, 1973.

In the biblical and post-biblical tradition, "Male symbols are dominant and male theologians have frozen them into patterns of abstraction; but the feminine images are also there, awaiting that fuller appreciation for which we were not ready till now. What is needed is to redress the balance by restoring the feminine to its proper importance in the over-all pattern." The section on The Shekinah as Presence in Exile (pp. 24-29) explores "The full flowering of the Shekinah doctrine" which "came about through the complex late-medieval phenomenon known as Kabbalism."

D141 Martin, Bernard. "The Lure of Kabbalah: A Need for Myth." *CCAR Journal*, 22(1975), 3-12.

"It is difficult to believe that *Kabbalah* could have obtained such a widespread following among Jewish masses and retained its hold on them for so many generations unless it enshrined some perennial values and answered some deeply felt religious needs."

D142 Patai, Raphael. *The Jewish Mind.* New York: Charles Scribner's Sons, 1977.

"This book is an attempt to consider the Jewish mind as a product of Jewish culture, and Jewish culture as a product of the Jewish mind. Jewish religion--unquestionably the most important element in Jewish culture--is likewise considered as a product of the Jewish mind. We shall see how this collective mind reacted to the incessant flow of outside cultural influences to which the Jews were exposed throughout their history. And the reverse influences, those exerted by Jews on the Gentile world, will be treated, albeit briefly, as manifestations of the extraordinary force of the Jewish mind which has made itself felt around the globe for two thousand years." The ninth section of Chapter 6, Kabbala and Hinduism (pp. 134-51), considers Hinduism "the one ancient Oriental religion which [Kabbalah] resembles more than any other," and Chapter 8, Jewish Dionysians: The Hasidim (pp. 180-221), asserts that "What Hasidism effected was to introduce a strongly Dionysian element into traditional Jewish culture, which had earlier been characterized by an overwhelming Apollonian configuration."

D143 Steinsaltz, Adin. "The Imagery Concept in Jewish Thought." *Shefa Quarterly*, 1,3(April 1978), 56-62.

"In other words, Jewish thought uses pictorial or imagery concepts instead of abstract concepts.... Furthermore, a wealth of such phrases and imagery concepts are used in the Kabbalah and the Aggadah to express abstractions that would be described in other systems by means of abstract concepts."

Prophecy and Apocalyptic

D144 Agus, Jacob B. "The Prophet in Modern Hebrew Literature." *Hebrew Union College Annual*, 28(1957), 289-324.

In this analysis of the prophet as "The central hero-image in Jewish religious culture," Agus includes a discussion of prophets as "mystics as well as humanists, yielding alternately to the Divine command and to the ethical challenge in the unshakable conviction that the two imperatives were somehow one in the ultimate mystery of the Divine Will."

D145 Kalir, Joseph. "Of Jewish Prophecy and Mysticism." *Religious Education*, 69(1974), 451-62.

"Prophecy and mysticism, myth and faith, are interpreted in a way that will be helpful to all Scripture teachers."

D146 Collins, John J. "The Jewish Apocalypses." *Semeia*, 14(1979), 21-59.

"In this essay we are not concerned with the historical origin of apocalypticism but the identification of a literary genre "apocalypse" as represented in Jewish literature. Accordingly, we will confine our attention to the analysis of Jewish texts. We will begin with those texts in the prophetic corpus which are most frequently adduced in discussions of 'apocalyptic'--Zechariah and the later parts of Isaiah. The two main views of apocalypticism, the 'historical' view which emphasizes temporal eschatology and the 'vertical' view which stresses the spacial symbolism of the heavenly world, both find analogies and precedents in these books. We will then proceed to the apocalyptic writings of the Hellenistic and Roman periods."

Psychology

D147 Roback, A.A. "Freud, Chassid or Humanist." *B'nai B'rith Magazine*, January 1926, pp. 118-30.

Unavailable for annotating.

D148 Farwell, Arthur. "Sonata Form and the Cabbala." *Musical Quarterly*, 27(1941), 26-37.

"The *form* of the working of the primeval creative principle, in its abstract sense, in the cosmos as in the microcosmic 'inner man', is perhaps more happily exemplified in the abstract sonata than in any other of man's creations. This applies to the classic sonata (and to all its cognate classic forms) in its four movement completeness, as well as in its so organically important first movement. The student of these matters can scarcely wonder that Pythagoras adopted music and number as the symbolic vehicles for the teaching of the cosmic and human scheme. If the Cabbala's exposition of the sacred name, IHVH, reveals the ultimate formative principle of the sonata, the 'psyche' which it reflects, and the universe which the psyche reflects, in a more complete and vivid presentation than can readily be found elsewhere, it may well be thought to be worth our attention. Its application to science and art will probably be found to be universal."

D149 Gordon, Hirsch Loeb. "Psychiatry in Bible, Talmud and Zohar." In A36. Pp. 53-63.

Unavailable for annotating.

D150 Hurwitz, Siegmund. "The God Image in the Cabbala." Trans. Gustav Dreifuss, and Hildegard Nagel. *Spring: Journal of the Analytical Psychology Club of New York* (1954), 39-51.

"Mysticism in general, and particularly Jewish mysticism, may seem a remote and alien subject to many people. However, the knowledge and understanding of Jewish symbols are not without significance for the psychotherapist as well as for the religious historian, or for anyone interested in the psychology of religion. I should like to demonstrate this to you by a specially striking example"--analysis of a dream recounted by a Protestant.

D151 Ben-Horin, Meir. "The Ineffable: Critical Notes on Neo-Mysticism." *Jewish Quarterly Review*, n.s. 49(1956), 321-54.

"The following critical notes on recent Jewish expositions of mysticism may therefore be regarded as a link, however weak and inadequate, in the unbroken chain of our tradition of rationality which neither denies nor deprecates the irrational facets of human nature but which, in Freudian terms, seeks to sublimate the chaotic behavior of 'id' into responsible conduct of 'I, you, and we.'"

D152 Werblowsky, R.J. Zwi. "Some Psychological Aspects of the Kabbalah." *Harvest: Journal of the Analytical Psychology Club of London*, 3(1956), 77-96.

Analysis of the *Sefirot* "to suggest some tentative psychological hints. In fact, a few psychological viewpoints were already smuggled in fairly obviously when attention was drawn to the projection of the whole *unio*-problem as the divine personality, to the greater differentiation of the male as compared with the female, and to the male 'demonization' of the feminine symbol. The implicit suggestion was that the kabbalistic image of the divine is a numinous and complex projection of the unconscious psyche in its totality."

D153 Bakan, David. "Moses in the Thought of Freud: An Ambivalent Interpretation." *Commentary*, 26(1958), 322-31.

Condensation of a chapter from D154.

D154 Bakan, David. *Sigmund Freud and the Jewish Mystical Tradition*. New York: Schocken Books, 1958. Rpt. Boston: Beacon Press, 1975. Sel. rpt. D153, D156.

"The hypothesis of this essay is that a full appreciation of the development of psychoanalysis is essentially incomplete unless it be viewed against the history of Judaism, and particularly against the history of Jewish Mystical thought.... One point is ... that Freud's repeated affirmation of his Jewish identity had a greater significance for the development of psychoanalysis than is usually recognized." Bakan's study is comprised of five sections: I. The Background of Freud's Development of Psychoanalysis; II. The Milieu of Jewish Mysticism; III. The Moses Theme in the Thought of Freud; IV. The Devil as Suspended Superego; and V. Psychoanalysis and Kabbala.

D155 McClelland, David C. "Religious Overtones in Psychoanalysis." *Princeton Seminary Bulletin*, 52(1959), 15-32. Rpt. in *Theology Today*, 16(1959), 40-64.

Exploration of "the resemblance of psychoanalysis to a religious movement": "The goal of psychoanalysis is practically identical with that of Jewish mysticism--to release and fulfill the individual by contact with emotional, irrational forces."

D156 Bakan, David. "Freud and the Zohar: An Incident." *Commentary*, 29(1960), 65-66.

Selection from D154.

D157 Steindletz, E. "Hasidism and Psychoanalysis." *Judaism*, 9(1960), 222-28.

Comparison of Hasidism and psychoanalysis, not intended to provide an analytic study of Hasidism, but to "have it draw its points of reference, explanations and systematic clarifications from specific problems in psychoanalysis."

D158 Gelberman, Joseph H., and Dorothy Kobak. "Psychology and Modern Hasidism." *Journal of Pastoral Care*, 17(1963), 27-30.

Analysis of the Hasidic Rabbi as "an intuitive psychiatrist": "This, then, is the psychology of the true neo-Hassidism: namely, that the greatest value on earth is the holiness (or wholeness) of each individual. Every person is significant and can be helped to find the God (or good) in himself, while maintaining a trust in life."

D159 Couzin, Robert. "Leibnitz, Freud and Kabbalah." *Journal of the History of the Behavioral Sciences*, 6(1970), 335-48.

Psychologist Gordon Allport identifies two poles of psychology, the Lockean and the Leibnitzian, and David Bakan's "demonstration of Freud's place within another tradition, Jewish mysticism or Kabbala [D154], could serve to further this identification if any evidence could be found that associated Leibnitz with this latter movement. The presentation of such evidence is the first purpose of this paper. This link being established, we will be in a position to suggest a characterization of the 'Leibnizian [sic] tradition' itself, of which Leibnitz, Freud and the Kabbalists are all expressions."

D160 Singer, June. *Androgyny: Toward a New Theory of Sexuality*. Garden City, New York: Doubleday, 1976.

Postulates "a theory of human sexuality based on androgyny, for the old theories, founded on the dominance of one sex and the compliance of the other, have brought about an imbalance in society that needs to be remedied. In Chapter 13, Adam Kadmon in Kabbalah: The Tree of Life as Androgyne (pp. 151-70), Singer has a dual purpose: "The first is to make more comprehensible the way in which [the terms 'God' and 'Love'] are used throughout Kabbalistic material. The second has to do with an application of our own day, and perhaps to relieve some of the pressure on those who object to the designation of certain characteristics of the personality as 'masculine' and 'feminine.'"

D161 Bulka, Reuven P. "Hasidism and Logotherapy: Encounter through Anthology." *Journal of Psychology and Judaism*, 3(1978), 60-74. Rpt. D171.

"Various hasidic anecdotes or statements concerning free will, the nature of human striving, value orientation, the element of meaning, attitudes to despair, suffering, and death, the nature of love, perspectives on work and material gain, are presented along with the statements made by Viktor Frankl in developing his system of logotherapy. The similarities between the hasidic and logotherapeutic approaches are readily apparent. It is suggested that because both Hasidism and logotherapy focus on the metaclinical situation and attempt to reorient distorted thinking, their ideas are similar, even though working from different dimensions." (Abstract)

D162 *Journal of Psychology and Judaism*, 3,1(Fall 1978).

Special Issue--*Mystics and Medics: A Comparison of Mystical and Psychotherapeutic Encounters*. The issue "is concerned with philosophical and meta-clinical types of encounters within mystical tradition and their similarities with modern clinical practice." See: D161, D164, D165, D167, D169.

D163 Kuperstok, Nathan. "Extended Consciousness of Hasidic Thought." *Journal of Psychology and Judaism*, 2,2(Spring 1978), 41-51. Rpt. D172.

"Because consciousness is a personal-cultural construct, different states of consciousness lead to different models of reality. The Torah, as a coherent metaphysical system, structures a model of reality and a state of consciousness. Particularly, its esoteric aspect, as taught in Jewish mysticism, parallels the objectives of other eastern disciplines, in destructuring the distortion and reduction of reality produced by ego-centered consciousness and facilitating the development of an extended consciousness." (Abstract)

D164 Safier, Judah. "Hasidism, Faith, and the Therapeutic Paradox." *Journal of Psychology and Judaism*, 3(1978), 38-47. Rpt. D173.

"The concept of paradox in the therapeutic situation is explored. The therapeutic paradox is a special case of an intense and powerful interpersonal situation. Hasidism has channeled the energy of paradox in directions which sustain the hasid's search for meaning. The role of paradox in the perpetuation of Jewish values is illustrated through hasidic tales and discussed in terms of the significance of faith for the transcendence of paradox." (Abstract)

D165 Schachter, Zalman M. "The Dynamics of the Yehudit Transaction." *Journal of Psychology and Judaism*, 3(1978), 7-21. Rpt. D174.

"The Yehidut, or private encounter between hasid and rebbe, is analyzed. Attention is focused on the nature of the transaction and elements involved in the relationship, such as acceptance, love of fellow Jew, the rebbe as an archetypal model, and the rebbe as an accessible model. Also delineated are the many levels on which the rebbe, or master, interacts. They include the rebbe's interaction with himself, his interaction with the various selves of the hasid, or disciple, the interaction with the hasid's life process, and the aspect of arrangement making the yehidut transaction." (Abstract)

D166 Schachter, Zalman M. "The Management of Feeling in the Yehidut Transaction." *Journal of Psychology and Judaism*, 3(1978), 109-25.

"The management of feeling in the Yehidut (private encounter between hasid and rebbe) is explored through study of the investment of the rebbe and the hasid in the relationship. Empathy and anxiety are key ingredients in the encounter. The rebbe faces the possibility of missing the mark in perceiving the reality of the hasid. Attention is also given to the elements of countertransference and divestment." (Abstract)

D167 Spero, Moshe Ha Levi. "Discussion: On the Nature of the Therapeutic Encounter Between Hasid and Master." *Journal of Psychology and Judaism*, 3(1978), 48-59. Rpt. D175.

"Based on the assumptions of two earlier essays by Woocher (1978) [D169] and Safier (1978) [D164], an attempt is made to clarify ways to approach the issue of the therapeutic nature of the hasid-rebbe relationship. Basic distinctions between the hasid-rebbe relationship, general psychotherapeutic relationships, the 'I-Thou' encounter, and the psychoanalytic relationship are drawn. Final discussion examines the ways in which Hasidism may be construed as a scientific exploration of the human problematic." (Abstract)

D168 Wallace, Edwin R. "Freud's Mysticism and Its Psychodynamic Determinants." *Bulletin of the Menninger Clinic*, 42(1978), 203-22.

"In this paper I will examine Freud's mysticism and attempt to discern its primary psychodynamic determinants by examining the superstitious elements and unusual experiences in his personal life, his sober scientific evaluations of the occult, and his more speculative or mystical writings. Furthermore, I will briefly examine other determinants which I feel are less important but also present (ambivalence toward the mother, Freud's Jewishness, and the tension between rationalistic-positivistic and romantic elements in his education). In this way I hope to demonstrate how Freud's father conflict runs like a red thread through his mystical experiences and writings."

D169 Woocher, Jonathan S. "The Kabbalah, Hasidism, and the Life of Unification." *Journal of Psychology and Judaism*, 3(1978), 22-37. Rpt. D176.

"After a brief explanation of the kabbalistic notions of exile, separation, and the work of unification, as well as the hasidic notions of intent, ecstasy, and humility, and the role of the zadik in the healing process, attention is focused on how these concepts relate to modern psychological thinking. It is shown that many kabbalistic and hasidic notions are part of the contemporary therapeutic framework, although the ultimate objective of Jewish mystical tradition transcends the clinical realm." (Abstract)

D170 Bilu, Yoram. "Sigmund Freud and Rabbi Yehudah: On a Jewish Mystical Tradition of 'Psychoanalytic' Dream Interpretation." *Journal of Psychological Anthropology*, 2,4(1979), 443-63.

Unavailable for annotating.

D171 Bulka, Reuven P. "Hasidism and Logotherapy: Encounter through Anthology." In A106. Pp. 104-18.

Reprint of D161.

D172 Kuperstok, Nathan. "Extended Consciousness of Hasidic Thought." In A106. Pp. 87-97.

Reprint of D163.

D173 Safier, Judah. Hasidism, Faith, and the Therapeutic Paradox." In A106. Pp. 53-62.

Reprint of D164.

D174 Schachter, Zalman M. "The Dynamics of the Yehudit Transaction." In A106. Pp. 7-36.

Reprint of D165.

D175 Spero, Moshe Ha Levi. "Discussion: On the Nature of the Therapeutic Encounter Between Hasid and Master." In A106. Pp. 63-74.

Reprint of D167.

D176 Woocher, Jonathan S. "The Kabbalah, Hasidism, and the Life of Unification." In A106. Pp. 37-52.

Reprint of D169.

D177 Hoffman, Edward. "The Kabbalah: Its Implications for Humanistic Psychology." *Journal of Humanistic Psychology*, 20(1980), 33-47.

"The purpose of this article is to highlight six major principles of the Kabbalah, and whenever possible, to identify similarities to other psycho-spiritual traditions. These principles include: (a) That the cosmos is a unity, with all aspects in interrelation; (b) That the forces of creation represent an eternal interplay between an active force and a passive one; (c) That the human individual is a microcosm of the universe; (d) That in daily life, we are attuned to only one state of consciousness among many; (e) That each individual may attain higher states of consciousness, but careful preparation is necessary; and (f) That to achieve such transcendent states of consciousness various specific practices and techniques are utilized."

D178 Knapp, Bettina L. *Theatre and Alchemy*. Detroit: Wayne State University Press, 1980.

Alchemical interpretations of plays. Chapter 7, *The Dybbuk: The Spagyric Marriage* (pp. 154-86), views Shloyme Ansky's hasidic play as "a religious mystery, a drama of possession and of eternal love. For the alchemist it is the paradigm of a 'spagyric marriage': an inner union which takes place beyond the physical realm, in a retort, as a projection. Psychologically, such a wedding acts as an escape from life into an atemporal world."

D179 Hoffman, Edward. *The Way of Splendor: Jewish Mysticism and Modern Psychology*. Boulder and London: Shambhala, 1981. Sel. rpt. D180.

"My aim here has been to introduce the Kabbalah's psychological insights to the general public, unfamiliar with the intricacies of either jewish philosophy or mysticism. This book is intended to serve as a bridge to the actual body of Kabbalistic lore; it has not been planned as a substitute or replacement for the primary sources, but rather, as a guide across their often complex and difficult terrain." After a brief introduction, Hoffman discusses: 1. Jewish mystics: Seekers of Unity; 2. We are the Cosmos; 3. The Sacred Realm of the Body; 4. Techniques for Inner Development; 5. Awakening Ecstasy; 6. Returning to the Source: Dreams and Music; 7. The Dimension Beyond; 8. Life and Death: The Immortal Soul; and 9. The New Land of the Mind.

D180 Hoffman, Edward. "Jewish Mystics." *Jewish Spectator*, 47(Spring 1982), 56-60.

Selections from D179.

D181 Cleghorn, Spencer. *Kabbalistic Discoveries into Hebrew and Aegyptian Mysteries*. Albuquerque: American Institute for Psychological Research, 1983.

Unavailable for annotating.

D182 Rotenberg, Mordechai. *Dialogue with Deviance: The Hasidic Ethic and the Theory of Social Contraction*. Philadelphia: Institute for the Study of Human Issues, 1983.

"In the present book, the social-contraction theory will be introduced by drawing on the Hasidic-cabalistic ethic. Thus man's concrete ability to affect his actualizing future and his interpersonal relations is explained as patterned according to the Hasidic-cabalistic doctrine, which posits that by contracting himself to evacuate space for the human world, God in fact bestowed upon man the responsibility and power to determine his own future and to affect God's disposition by his 'corrective' behavior." The book is divided into three parts: "In Part I, the sociological-structural concept of mono versus multiple ideal-labeling is introduced.... On the social-psychological level (Part II) the concepts of interpersonal deassertiveness via material ('inconspicuous consumption') and spiritual (verbal modesty) contraction is introduced.... In Part III, on the psychological level, the functional approach to deviance and deviants is developed by introducing the 'ascent through descent' model."

D183 Schachter, Zalman M., and Edward Hoffman. *Sparks of Light: Counseling in the Hasidic Tradition.* Boulder: Shambhala, 1983.

    Unavailable for annotating.

THE HISTORY OF KABBALAH

The following chapter contains studies dealing with particular periods of Jewish mysticism, from its inception to the present. The first section, Antecedents, includes studies of biblical and post-biblical literature, and the Dead Sea Scrolls, which suggest that mysticism has always, to some degree, been present in Jewish literature. The section on Antecedents is followed by Merkabah Mysticism and Jewish Gnosticism, Medieval Hasidism, The Crystallization of the Kabbalah, The Zohar, Isaac Luria and His School, Shabbateanism and Mystical Heresy, and Hasidism. The last section, the Latest Phase, includes entries on twentieth-century attitudes towards mysticism, including Neo-Hasidism, defined as the accommodation of Hasidism to the modern world.

E. Antecedents

Primary Sources

E1 Laurence, Richard, trans. *The Book of Enoch the Prophet*. Oxford, 1821, 1828. 3rd ed., rev. and enlarged, Oxford: J.H. Parker, 1833. New ed. Glasgow: J. Thomson, 1878. Rpt. with new index, London: K. Paul, Trench, 1883, 1890, 1892. Rpt. Benton Harbor, Mich.: House of David, 1912. Rpt. Secret Doctrine Reference Series. Minneapolis: Wizards Bookshelf, 1973. Rpt. Thousand Oaks, Calif.: Artisan Sales, 1980.

E2 Murray, Edward, ed. *Enoch Restitutus; or, An Attempt to Separate from the Books of Enoch the Book Quoted by St. Judes; Also, A Comparison of the Chronology of Enoch with the Hebrew Computation, and with the Periods Mentioned in the Book of Daniel and in the Apocalypse*. London: J.G. & F. Rivington, 1836.

E3 Kenealy, Edward V.H. *Enoch, the Second Messenger of God*. London, 1878.

E4 Schodde, George H., trans. *The Book of Enoch: Translated from the Ethiopic, with Introductions and Notes*. Andover: W.F. Draper, 1882. Rpt. Saint Clair Shores, Mi.: Scholarly Press, Inc., 1976.

E5 Charles, R.H., trans. *The Book of Enoch*. Translated from Professor Dillman's Ethiopic Text. Oxford: Clarendon Press, 1893. Rev. ed. Oxford: Clarendon Press, 1906, 1912. Rpt. with intro. by W.O.E. Oesterley. Series I. Palestinian Jewish Texts (pre-rabbinic). London: Society for Promoting Christian Knowledge, 1917, and New York: Macmillan, 1925, 1929, 1942. Rpt. Jerusalem: Makor, 1973.

E6 Gaster, M. "Hebrew Versions of Hell and Paradise." *Journal of the Royal Asiatic Society*, July 1893, 571-611. Rpt. E24.

"I intend publishing now, for the first time in English garb, the oldest extant Revelations which must have served as a source to that of Peter, then to that of Paul, Ezra, Abraham, Isaiah, Virgin Mary, St. Macarius, and the host of others down to Dante and St. Patrick": I. The Revelation of Moses (A); II. The Revelation of Moses (B); III. The Revelation of R. Joshua ben Levi (A); IV. The Revelation of R. Joshua ben Levi (B); V-VII. Hell; VIII. Paradise.

E7 Conybeare, Fred C. "On the Apocalypse of Moses." *Jewish Quarterly Review*, 7(1894), 216-35.

Translation "from the ancient Armenian Version, which in turn seems to have been made not from a Greek, but from a Syriac or Ethiopic, or even Arabic text.... It is almost certain that in this Apocalypse we have one of those Jewish apocryphs which, like the Book of Enoch, exercised a formative influence upon the earliest Christianity. For two ideas are prominent in it which have been perpetuated in the younger religion, namely, that of baptism by trine immersion after repentance and forgiveness of sins, and that of the resurrection in the flesh and restoration to the Garden of Eden of the descendants of Adam."

E8 Gaster, M. "The Hebrew Text of One of the Testaments of the Twelve Patriarchs." *Proceedings of the Society of Biblical Archaeology*, 16(1894), 33-49, 109-17. Rpt. E23.

Textual introduction and translation of the apocryphal book; Hebrew version on pp. 109-17.

E9 Charles, R.H., trans. *The Apocalypse of Baruch*. London: A. and C. Black, 1896.

E10 Gaster, M. "Two Unknown Hebrew Versions of the Tobit Legend." *Proceedings of the Society of Biblical Archaeology*, 18(1896), 208-22. Rpt. E25.

E11 Morfill, W.R., trans. *The Book of the Secrets of Enoch*. Ed. R.H. Charles. Oxford: Clarendon Press, 1896.

E12 Charles, R.H., trans. *The Assumption of Moses*. London: A. & C. Black, 1897.

E13 Charles, R.H., trans. *The Book of Jubilees; or, The Little Genesis*. London: A. and C. Black, 1902. Translations of Early Documents. Series I. Palestinian Jewish Texts (pre-rabbinic), 4. London: Society for Promoting Christian Knowledge, and New York: Macmillan Company, 1917.

E14 Duff, Archibald, ed. *The First and Second Books of Esdras*. The Temple Bible. London: J.M. Dent & Co., 1903.

E15 Charles, R.H., trans. *The Testaments of the Twelve Patriarchs*. Oxford: Clarendon Press, 1908.

E16 Box, G.H., trans. *The Ezra-Apocalypse; Being Chapters 3-14 of the Book Commonly Known as 4 Ezra (or II Esdras)*. London: Sir I. Pitman & Sons, Ltd., 1912. Rpt. Translations of Early Documents, Series I. Palestinian Jewish Texts (pre-rabbinic), 8. London: Society for Promoting Christian Knowledge, 1917.

E17 Charles, R.H., ed. *The Apocrypha and Pseudepigrapha of the Old Testament in English, with Introductions and Critical and Explanatory Notes to the Several Books*. 2 vols. Oxford: Clarendon Press, 1913.

E18 Box, G.H., trans. *The Apocalypse of Ezra (II Esdras III-XIV)*. Translations of Early Documents, Series I. Palestinian Jewish Texts (pre-rabbinic), 8. London: Society for Promoting Christian Knowledge, 1917.

E19 Box, G.H., and J.I. Landsman, eds. and trans. *The Apocalypse of Abraham*. Translations of Early Documents, Series I. Palestinian Jewish Texts (pre-rabbinic), 10. London: Society for Promoting Christian Knowledge, and New York: Macmillan Company, 1918.

E20 Charles, R.H., trans. *The Apocalypse of Baruch*. Translations of Early Documents, Series I. Palestinian Jewish Texts (pre-rabbinic), 9. London: Society for Promoting Christian Knowledge, and New York: Macmillan Company, 1918.

E21 Charles, R.H., trans. *The Ascension of Isaiah*. Translations of Early Documents, Series I. Palestinian Jewish Texts (pre-rabbinic), 7. London: Society for Promoting Christian Knowledge, and New York: Macmillan Company, 1918.

E22 James, Montague Rhodes, ed. *The Lost Apocrypha of the Old Testament: Their Titles and Fragments*. London: Society for Promoting Christian Knowledge, and New York: Macmillan Company, 1920.

"The object of this book is to collect in a form convenient to English readers the remains of some of the apocryphal writings connected with the Old Testament which have not survived in their entirety."

E23 Gaster, M. "The Hebrew Text of One of the Testaments of the Twelve Patriarchs." In his A12.I.69-85, III.22-30.

Reprint of E8.

E24 Gaster, M. "Hebrew Versions of Hell and Paradise." In his A12. I.124-64.

Reprint of E6.

E25 Gaster, M. "Two Unknown Hebrew Versions of the Tobit Legend." In his A12. I.1-38.

Reprint of E10.

E26 Box, G.H., trans. *The Testament of Abraham, with an Appendix Containing a Translation from the Coptic Versions of the Testaments of Isaac and Jacob.* [Trans. S. Gaselee] Translations of Early Documents, Series II. Hellenistic-Jewish Texts. London: Society for Promoting Christian Knowledge, and New York and Toronto: Macmillan Company, 1927.

E27 Odeberg, Hugo, trans. *3 Enoch; or, The Hebrew Book of Enoch.* Cambridge: University Press, 1928. Rpt. The Library of Biblical Studies. New York: Ktav Pub. House, 1973.

E28 Oesterley, W.O.E., ed. *II Esdras (The Ezra Apocalypse).* Westminster Commentaries. London: Methuen & Co., Ltd., 1933.

E29 Gaster, Theodor H., trans. *The Dead Sea Scriptures.* Garden City, New York: Doubleday & Co., 1956.

"The purpose of this book is to provide a complete and reliable translation of the celebrated Dead Sea Scrolls, insofar as the original Hebrew texts have yet been published. Everything that is sufficiently well preserved to make connected sense has been included," except for fragments and versions of biblical texts. Includes: The Service of God: Rules of the Brotherhood; The Praise of God: Hymns and Psalms; The Word of God: The Study of the Scriptures; and The Triumph of God: Descriptions of the Final Age.

E30 Strugnell, J. *The Angelic Liturgy at Qumrân 4Q Serek Širôt 'Ôlat Haššabbāt.* In *Vetus Testamentum, Supplements,* 7 (1959), 318-45.

"The purpose of this paper is not a general description of the angelology of the published Qumrân texts, nor a discussion of the place that it holds in the theology of the Qumrân sect and in the evolution of angelology in the intertestamental period. Its aim is more modest. Among the manuscripts from the fourth cave at Qumrân there are numerous fragments of a work which is more consistently concerned with the angels and the heavens than any other surviving work from Qumrân. Since this will be published only in the last of the volumes dealing with Cave IV, in other words not for three more years, it may be expedient to make available in advanced samples of its text such as will give a reliable impression of the contents and literary genre of this work."

E31 Dupont-Sommer, A. *The Essene Writings from Qumran*. Trans. G. Vermes. Oxford: B. Blackwell, and Cleveland: World Publishing Company, 1961.

"It is essentially intended as a collection of the non-biblical Jewish sectarian documents recovered since 1947 from the caves in the region of Wadi Qumran.... All the non-biblical scrolls and scroll fragments are assembled here in their entirety, in translations and with comments." Chapter 9, Apocrypha and Pseudepigrapha (pp. 295-305); and Chapter 11, Fragments of Apocalyptical, Liturgical and other Writings (pp. 320-38).

E32 Vermes, Geza, trans. *The Dead Sea Scrolls*. Harmondsworth: Penguin Books, 1962; New York: Heritage Press, 1967.

"The present work gives the actual text of the non-biblical religious writings."

E33 Yadin, Yigael, ed. *The Scroll of the War of the Sons of Light against the Sons of Darkness*. Trans. Batya and Chaim Rabin. Oxford: Oxford University Press, 1962.

"The main purpose of the scroll seems to consist in supplying the members of the sect with a detailed set of regulations and plans in accordance with which they were to act on the day of destiny appointed 'from of old for a battle of annihilation of the Sons of Darkness'."

E34 Stone, Michael E., trans. *The Testament of Abraham: The Greek Recensions*. Texts and Translations 2. Pseudepigrapha Series, 2. Missoula, Mont.: Society of Biblical Literature, 1972.

Bi-lingual edition.

E35 Myers, Jacob M., trans. *I and II Esdras*. The Anchor Bible, 42. Garden City, New York: Doubleday, 1974.

E36 Milik, J.T., trans. *The Books of Enoch: Aramaic Fragments of Qumrân Cave 4*. Oxford: Clarendon Press, 1976.

"The main purpose of this edition is to present, in transcription (with restorations), and with translations and notes, all the fragments identified among the manuscripts of Qumrân Cave 4 as forming part of different Books of Enoch. In the Introduction the importance of this discovery is first briefly indicated; then an attempt is made to resolve the familiar problems of literary criticism concerning the Enochic literature in the light of fresh data furnished by the specimens of the original text; the character of the Greek version and of other ancient translations dependent on it is evaluated; and finally a description is given, in rapid outline, of works attributed to Enoch from Roman times down to the late Middle Ages, with emphasis on the profound gap which separates later writings from the Judeo-Aramaic documents; a delicate problem is that of the origin and dating of the Book of Parables, which forms the second section of the Ethiopic Enoch." Enoch in Cabbalistic Literature, pp. 125-35.

E37 Knibb, Michael A., ed. *The Ethiopic Book of Enoch: A New Edition in the Light of the Aramaic Dead Sea Fragments.* 2 vols. Oxford: Clarendon Press, 1978.

"This work offers a new edition (volume 1) and translation (volume 2) of the Ethiopic text of Enoch. The edition is based on Rylands Ethiopic MS. 23, and full account has been taken of the Aramaic fragments of Enoch that were discovered at Qumrân. The intention is not to produce a new conflated text of Enoch, but rather to present the sum total of the evidence for the text of Enoch in as clear a way as possible."

E38 Charlesworth, James H., ed. *The Old Testament Pseudepigrapha.* Vol. 1: Apocalyptic Literature and Testaments. Garden City, New York: Doubleday & Company, Inc., 1983.

Volume 1 contains two sections: Apocalyptic Literature and Related Works; and Testaments (often with Apocalyptic Sections).

Secondary Sources

E39 Schurer, Emil. *A History of the Jewish People in the Time of Jesus Christ.* Trans. John MacPherson, Sophia Taylor and Peter Christie. 5 vols. Clark's Foreign Theological Library, new series, vols. 23, 24, 25, 41, 43. Edinburgh: Clark, and New York: Charles Scribner's Sons, 1885-90. Rpt. Jerusalem, Raritas: Israel Project for University Libraries, n.d.

An examination and description of "that realm of thought and history in which the universal religion of Christ grew up." Covers some of the Jewish mystical literature produced during the time of Christ, especially Pseudepigraphic Prophecies (Div. II, vol. 3, section 32, chapter 5, pp. 44-133), where Schurer discusses *The Book of Daniel*, *The Book of Enoch*, *The Assumptio Mosis*, *The Apocalypse of Baruch*, *The Fourth Book of Ezra*, *The Testament of the Twelve Patriarchs*, and "The Lost Pseudepigraphic Prophecies."

E40 Montefiore, C.G. "Mystic Passages in the Psalms." *Jewish Quarterly Review*, o.s. 1(1889), 143-61.

Concludes that mystical passages in the Psalter indicate that the Psalmists "recognized that the religious life is expressed in the affections"; that "the communion with God is closely restricted to the righteous"; that "mystic passages of the Psalter are ... free from the Pantheistic tendencies of later mysticism"; and that "it does not make the communion with God dependent upon knowledge."

E41 Conybeare, Fred C. "On the Jewish Authorship of the Testaments of the Twelve Patriarchs." *Jewish Quarterly Review*, o.s. 5(1893), 375-98.

"... the Testaments, as they have come down to us in the Greek MSS., have been copiously interpolated, for the most part in a Christian sense. If the original document had been from the first a Christian one, then there was no necessity to so interpolate it. The conjecture of Grabius [Johannes Ernestus Grabius, *Spicilegium SS. Patrum*, 1714] that they were, to begin with, a purely Hebrew Apocryph, and were subsequently interpolated by Christians, is thus raised to a certainty."

E42 Kohler, K. "The Pre-Talmudic Haggadah I." *Jewish Quarterly Review*, o.s. 5(1893), 399-419.

"It is the purpose of this article to call the attention of scholars to a number of Midrashim that date back to the Maccabean era, and throw new light on the character of the ancient *Haggada*." Discusses: A. The Testaments of the Twelve Patriarchs; and B. The Second Baruch or Rather the Jeremiah Apocalypse.

E43 Kohler, K. "The Pre-Talmudic Haggada II C: The Apocalypse of Abraham and Its Kindred." *Jewish Quarterly Review*, o.s. 7(1895), 581-606.

Argues Jewish origins for the Testament of Abraham: "The grand topic of the *Divine Comedia*--I sum up our inquiry--occupied the minds of Jewish Essenes long before the Church took hold of it.... Before David, the son of Jesse, was placed by the Pauline Apocalyptic in the centre of Paradise as singer of the Hallelujah Psalms, the Essenes had placed their cup of wine into his hands to sing the praise of

God at the great banquet of the just ... But the New Year's Day, in its character of annual Day of Divine Judgment, turned the mind of the Jew more and more away from prying into the secrets of the hereafter, leaving the subject to the few mystics who maintained the ancient lore, whereas with the Church the question of salvation and doom grew ever of higher moment."

E44 Burkitt, F. Crawford. *Jewish and Christian Apocalypses*. The Schweich Lectures, 1913. London: Published for the British Academy by Humphrey Milford, Oxford University Press, 1914.

Burkitt confines himself to "the fundamental idea which underlies the great series of Jewish Apocalypses, *viz.* the idea of the immanent Judgment to Come, and further, to exhibit this Idea in connexion with ... its true historical setting and the ultimate cause of its manifestation." The lectures are divided into four chapters: I. The Apocalyptic Idea; II. The Book of Enoch; III. The Minor Jewish Apocalypses; and IV. Early Christian Apocalyptic Writing. The Appendices are: I. On the Greek Text of Enoch (subdivided into: 1. The Descent of the Angels, 2. The Prologue to Enoch, 3. Enoch and the Valleys of the Dead, 4. Miscellaneous Conjectures, and 5. On the Astronomical Teaching of Enoch); II. On the Martyrdom of Isaiah; and III. On some Other Kinds of Apocalypses.

E45 Ruach, Joseph. "Apocalypse in the Bible." *Journal of Jewish Lore and Philosophy*, 1(1919), 163-95.

"The latest studies on the subject have shown that the beginnings of apocalypse are already found in pre-exilic times, i.e., in so far as apocalypse is based on the conviction that in the future Israel as God's chosen people will be directing the destinies of the world, it may be traced to the age which gave shape to the stories of the patriarchs. This article attempts to show how this thought grew in biblical literature until it was fully developed in the Book of Daniel."

E46 Ginzberg, Louis. "Some Observations on the Attitude of the Synagogue Towards the Apocalyptic-Eschatological Writings." *Journal of Biblical Literature*, 41(1922), 115-36. Rpt. A9. Pp. 115-36.

"In the following few remarks I intend to give some facts about the attitude of the synagogue towards the apocalyptic writings which I hope may throw some light on the very intricate problems connected with the eschatological doctrines and beliefs of the Jews at the time of the Apostles and Apostolic fathers."

E47 Hertz, J.H. "Mystic Currents in Ancient Israel." In his A10. Pp. 126-56. Rpt. E54.

Survey of the Bible which "indicate[s] the mystic currents in the Law, the Prophets, and the Sacred Writings."

E48 McCown, C.C. "Hebrew and Egyptian Apocalyptic Literature." *Harvard Theological Review*, 18(1925), 357-411.

Study of the problem of Hebrew borrowings from Egyptian apocalyptic literature. Considers: I. The Relationships between Egypt and Israel; II. Hebrew and Egyptian Literature; III. Egyptian Apocalyptic Literature of the Middle Kingdom; IV. Egyptian Apocalyptic Literature of Greek and Roman Times; and V. The Influence of Egyptian Apocalyptic. Concludes that "Egyptian apocalypticism is another item which assists in demonstrating that, with all their peculiarities and their moral and religious superiority, the Jews and Christians did not bring to the world an absolutely new Gospel, but one for which the people at large had been prepared in many and various ways. The naturalness and inevitableness of the process by which the new religion spread and developed became clearer also through the study of Egyptian apocalytpic literature."

E49 Schmidt, Nathaniel. "The Apocalypse of Noah and the Parables of Enoch." In A14. Pp. 111-23.

"It is obviously a very delicate task to determine from these scanty remains the original language, character, and age of the Apocalypse of Noah. But some light may be thrown on these questions by the nature of the work in which the interpolations were made as well as by a closer examination of the fragments themselves."

E50 Kaplan, Chaim. "The Hidden Name." *Journal of the Society of Oriental Research*, 13(1929), 181-84.

"One of the enigmas of the Book of Enoch that have puzzled the commentators, is the Hidden name referred to in ch. LXIX. Michael is said to be entrusted with it. The satans made a futile attempt to persuade him to disclose it to them. In the following I shall endeavor to throw some light on the Hidden name problem by the help of Rabbinic references that deal with the explicit name and the powers contained therein."

E51 Abelson, J. "Psalms and Kabbalah." *Jewish Forum*, 16(1933), 133-37.

"The truth is that the central spiritual convictions of the Psalms ... played a specifically Jewish part. They became interwoven in the texture of all subsequent Jewish intellectual thought. They came to form, as I humbly maintain, a solid substratum of the Jewish Kabbalistic teachings."

E52 Hooke, S. H. "The Myth and Ritual Pattern in Jewish and Christian Apocalyptic." In his A19. Pp. 213-33.

"... this Essay will be confined to three main points. First, the relation between the attitude implied by the existence of those religious beliefs and practices described ... as the myth and ritual pattern, and the general outlook of the apocalyptic literature. Second, a discussion of the characteristic symbolism of this literature and its relation to the ritual forms and symbols which appear in the ritual pattern of the ancient East. Lastly, it will be suggested that the general plan to which the apocalyptic visions conform is based on the early myth and ritual pattern referred to, and is evidence for its persistence long after the social structure and outlook of the early civilizations which had given birth to it had decayed and passed away."

E53 Oesterley, W.O.E. *A Fresh Approach to the Psalms.* London and New York: C. Scribner's Sons, 1937.

Compilation of information regarding the Psalms, specifically: I. The Psalms as part of World Literature; II. The Dates of the Psalms; III. The Collections Embodied in the Book of Psalms; IV. The Titles of the Psalms; V. The Music of the Ancient East; VI. Music Among the Israelites; VII. The Poetical Structure of the Psalms; VIII. The Liturgical Use of the Psalms; IX. The Psalms in the Worship of the Ancient Synagogue; X. The Psalms in the Christian Church; XI. The Psalms and Messianic Interpretation; XII-XIV. The Theology of the Psalms--Belief in God, Sin and Retribution, and Belief in the Hereafter; and XV. Angelology and Demonology.

E54 Hertz, J.H. "Mystic Currents in Ancient Israel." In his A21. Pp. 169-95.

Reprint of E47.

E55 Rowley, H.H. *The Relevance of Apocalyptic: A Study of Jewish and Christian Apocalypses from Daniel to the Revelation.* London and Redhill: Lutterworth Press, 1944. 2nd ed. 1952; New York: Harper, 1955. 3rd ed. New York: Association Press, 1963.

Contains four lectures: I. The Rise of Apocalyptic; II. The Apocalyptic Literature--During the Last Two Centuries B.C.; III. The Apocalyptic Literature--During the First Century A.D.; and IV. The Enduring Message of Apocalyptic. Also includes Notes on: A. The Date of the Earliest Sections of the Ethiopic Book of Enoch; B. The Date of the Book of Jubilees; C. The Figure of Taxo in the Assumption of Moses; D. The Unity of 4 Ezra and 2 Baruch; E. The Duration of Antichrist's Reign in the Ascension of Isaiah; and F. The Source and Unity of the Little Apocalypse of the Gospels.

Antecedents 119

E56 Bloch, Joshua. *On the Apocalyptic in Judaism.* The Jewish Quarterly Review. Monograph Series, Number II. Philadelphia: Dropsie College for Hebrew and Cognate Learning, 1952.

Attempts to answer questions about Jewish apocryphal literature: "What position does it occupy in Jewish literature? What role did it play in the teachings of Judaism? What is the character of the books comprising that literature, especially those which are apocalyptic in character and why were they neglected by the Jews?" Includes chapters on Angelology and Demonology (pp. 65-70); Apocalyptic Thought in the Kabbalah (pp. 82-85), and Apocalyptic Lore in the Zohar (pp. 115-18).

E57 Dupont-Somer, A. *The Dead Sea Scrolls: A Preliminary Survey.* Trans. E. Margaret Rowley. Oxford: Basil Blackwell, 1952.

"In the present work Professor Dupont-Sommer not only presents his own view of the source and significance of the texts, but offers a fuller account of their finding and their contents than can be found in any other one place in English." (Translator's Preface) Contents: I. The Cave of the Manuscripts; II. The Two *Isaiah* Scrolls; III. The *Habakkuk Commentary* and the "New Covenant"; IV. The *Rule* of the "New Covenant"; V. The "New Covenant in the Land of Damascus"; VI. The *Psalms of Thanksgiving* of the "New Covenant"; VII. The *Rule of Battle for the Sons of Light*; VIII. The "New Covenant" and the Essenes; and IX. The Jewish "New Covenant" and the Christian "New Covenant."

E58 Frost, Stanley Brice. *Old Testament Apocalyptic.* London: Epworth Press, 1952.

Unavailable for annotating.

E59 Rabinowitz, Isaac. "The Authorship, Audience and Date of the De Vaux Fragment of an Unknown Work." *Journal of Biblical Literature,* 71(1952), 19-32.

"... an improved translation, a number of instructive parallels to the language, and a suggested solution to the problem of authorship," of a Dead Sea Scroll fragment which Rabinowitz attributes to the Hasidim under early Hasmonean leadership.

E60 Dupont-Sommer, A. *The Jewish Sect of Qumran and the Essenes: New Studies on the Dead Sea Scrolls.* Trans. R.D. Barnett. London: Valentine, Mitchell & Co., Ltd., 1954; and New York: Macmillan Company, 1956.

Sequel to E57, incorporating discoveries of "absolutely reliable information concerning the organization of the

Jewish sect of the Covenant, its rites, its doctrines, and its mystical and moral principles." Chapter 8, Mystical and Moral Ideals (pp. 131-46).

E61 Franken, Hendricus Jacobus. *The Mystical Communions with JHWH in the Book of Psalms*. Leiden: E.J. Brill, 1954.

"Our main interest is not the psychological side of the attitude of the pious expressing himself in the religious poetry of the psalms, although this side of the problem has to be considered also. The scope of this study is to describe a religious aspect, namely the mystical aspects of the relationship with God, as they are found in the psalms." After the Introduction, Franken discusses The Study of Magic and Mysticism in the Old Testament; The Terminology of Jewish Mysticism; Personality, Its Restriction and Extension; and A Treatment of Some Psalms--Mystic Ideas in their Context.

E62 Russell, D.S. *Between the Testaments*. London: SCM Press Ltd., and Philadelphia: Muhlenberg Press, 1960.

"In this small volume an attempt is made to review these years [between the Testaments] in the light of recent study and discoveries and in particular to assess the religious contribution made by that rather strange company of men known as 'the apocalyptists' ... indicating the part which the apocalyptics had to play within the religious development of Judaism and in the preparation of men's minds for the coming of Christianity." Part I: The Cultural and Literary Background; Part II: The Apocalyptists.

E63 Glasson, T.F. *Greek Influence on Jewish Eschatology*. London: Society for Promoting Christian Knowledge, 1961.

Unavailable for annotating.

E64 O'Dell, Jerry. "The Religious Background of the Psalms of Solomon (Re-evaluated in the Light of the Qumran Texts)." *Revue de Qumran*, 3(1961), 241-57.

"If the *Psalms of Solomon* were written by a Pharisee, they are not typical for the Pharisaic attitude. The writer must have been on the extreme outer fringes of the Pharisaic circle if we are to judge from the *Psalms of Solomon* themselves. It is much more likely that the milieu out of which these psalms originated was that of the Chasidim. By Chasidim I do not mean a closed, narrow party, but rather a general trend of pious, eschatological Jews whose piousness was one of an individual nature rather than something imposed upon them by the group. It is not necessary, indeed it is misleading, to dissect all the Jewry of the inter-testamental period into distinct religious and political groups. They were without a doubt a number of deeply spiritual and eschatologically orientated men who belonged neither to the Pharisees, Sadducees nor to the priestly minded Qumran Essenes, but were nonetheless religius Jews. Such a man, or group of men, was the author of the *Psalms of Solomon*."

E65 Ploeg, Jean van der. "The Belief in Immortality in the Writings of Qumran." *Bibliotheca Orientalis*, 18(1961), 118-24.

Analysis of "the belief in immortality in the writings of Qumran ... against the background of contemporary Judaism, with which it shared most of its beliefs and its Holy Writ."

E66 Heschel, Abraham J. *The Prophets*. Philadelphia: Jewish Publication Society of America, and New York: Harper & Row, Publishers, 1962.

"My aim therefore is to attain an understanding of the prophet through an analysis and description of his *consciousness*, to relate what came to pass in his life--facing man, being faced by God--as reflected and affirmed in his mind. By consciousness, in other words, I mean here not only the perception of particular moments of inspiration, but also the totality of impressions, thoughts, and feelings which make up the prophet's being." Chapter 19, Prophecy and Ecstasy (pp. 324-34); Chapter 20, The Theory of Ecstasy (pp. 335-50); and Chapter 21, An Examination of the Theory of Ecstasy (pp. 351-66).

E67 La Sor, William. "The Messianic Idea in Qumrân." In A50. Pp. 343-64.

"In this study 'conclusions' are premature. There are, however, certain observations that can be made. 1. The Qumrân Community did have an eschatological viewpoint and a Messianic viewpoint.... 2. There was a strong emphasis upon the priestly office, perhaps influenced by Ezekiel 40-48, where we also find the prominence of the Zadokite line ... 3. The 'Son of Man' or apocalyptic element is absent from Qumrân literature.... 4. The Zoroastrian influence on the ideas of Qumrân ... must therefore be restudied."

E68 Russell, D.S. *The Method & Message of Jewish Apocalyptic: 200 BC--AD 100*. Philadelphia: Westminster Press, 1964.

Three-part study of Jewish Apocalyptic literature. Part One--The Nature and Identity of Jewish Apocalyptic: I. The Milieu of Apocalyptic; II. The Apocalyptic Literature. Part Two--The Method of Jewish Apocalyptic: III. The Decline of Prophecy and the Rise of Apocalyptic; IV. Characteristics of the Apocalyptic Writings; V. The Apocalyptic Consciousness; VI. Apocalyptic Inspiration; VII. Apocalyptic and the

Interpretation of Prophecy. Part Three--The Message of Jewish Apocalyptic: VIII. Human History and Divine Control; IX. Angels and Demons; X. The Time of the End; XI. The Messianic Kingdom; XII. The Traditional Messiah; XIII. The Son of Man; and XIV. Life After Death.

E69 Stone, Michael E. "Paradise in 4 Ezra iv:8 and vii:36, vii:52." *Journal of Jewish Studies*, 17(1966), 85-88.

"It appears, therefore, that the passage under discussion must be the rejection of a specific tradition or type of special knowledge, and the technical language employed strongly suggests that the mystic tradition is intended. If this is so then it may supply one criterion for isolating the circle within Judaism after 70 C.E. from which *4 Ezra* issued."

E70 Widegren, Geo. "Iran and Israel in Parthian Times with Special Regard to the Ethiopic Book of Enoch." *Temenos: Studies in Comparative Religion*, 2(1966), 139-77.

"In what follows four circles of motifs will be analyzed though with the accent on possible Iranian influence. These motifs are: 1. God and His relation to the dualistic conception of the world. 2. The apocalyptic pattern. 3. The end and the final judgement. 4. The apocalyptic visionary and his visions."

E71 Russell, D.S. *The Jews from Alexander to Herod.* The New Clarendon Bible, Old Testament, Vol. V. Oxford: University Press, 1967.

Update of G.H. Box's *Judaism in the Greek Period, from the Rise of Alexander the Great to the Intervention of Rome (333-63 B.C.)* (The Clarendon Bible, Old Testament, Vol. V [Oxford: Clarendon Press, 1932]); "enlarged to include the years between Pompey's capture of Jerusalem in 63 B.C. and the death of Herod the Great in 4 B.C. Greater space has been given to the development of religious ideas and religious parties within Judaism, whilst a somewhat different selection of writings has been made to illustrate the literary activity of the times." Three Parts: I. The History; II. The Religion (including a discussion of Religious Ideas--1. The Idea of Mediation: Angels, Demons, and other Intermediaries, 2. Eschatological Expectation, 3. The Messianic Hope, 4. Resurrection and the Life to Come); and III. The Literature, with sections on the Qumran Literature, The Book of Daniel, and the Book of Enoch.

E72 Russell, D.S. *Apocalyptic: Ancient and Modern.* Philadelphia: Fortress Press, 1968, 1978.

"... attempt to see more clearly the message which the early Jewish apocalyptic writers had for the days in which they lived and, again hopefully, something for its meaning for us today. The subject is 'Apocalyptic, ancient and modern'. The treatment in the event may be more ancient and less modern, but I hope I have conveyed my conviction that these writers, for all their strange and bizarre ideas, still have something worth while to say to our modern generation." Contents: I. An Age of Crisis; II. From Creation to Consummation; and III. Kingdom and *Kerygma*.

E73 Stone, Michael. "The Concept of the Messiah in IV Ezra." In A69. Pp. 295-312.

"In IV Ezra the Messiah is mentioned or referred to only in certain sections of the book. While this raises problems about the literary unity of the work, it also facilitates an examination of its views bearing on the Messianic idea. These we here explore along three lines of question. These concern first, the nature and functions attributed to the Messiah; second, the consistency with which these are found in the passages dealing with him; and third, his function in the total eschatological scheme of the book."

E74 Pines, S. "Eschatology and the Concept of Time in the Slavonic Book of Enoch." In A76. Pp. 72-87.

"It is to my mind very probable indeed that the passage of the Slavonic Book of Enoch concerning the time of creation has been decisively influenced by Zoroastrian doctrines. We are unable to date the Slavonic Book of Enoch. The importance it attributes to sacrifices may however indicate that it is a relatively early work. It is certainly much earlier than the Pahlevi works which treat Finite Time as the Time of the Long Dominion opposed to Infinite Time. Its direct testimony to the existence of these notions may be the earliest one preserved."

E75 Hanson, Paul D. "Jewish Apocalyptic against Its Near Eastern Environment." *Revue Biblique*, 78(1971), 31-58.

"Periodically it becomes necessary in virtually every field of research to recognize that old theories no longer can be reconciled to new data, thus giving rise to the search for more satisfactory solutions. A case in point is the traditional theory which explains Jewish apocalyptic as the product of Persian dualism. Here we feel that new data leads to the conclusion that far from being a transplant from another religious sphere, apocalyptic represents the final phase of a very long development very much at home on Israelite soil. Foreign elements are not lacking, but more important than certain peripheral elements taken directly from third and second century Zoroastrianism are those central ideas which reach back to third and second millenium Near Eastern mythology, ideas which had become naturalized within Israel's

League, royal cult, and prophetic movement centuries before reaching the apocalyptic seers."

E76 Hanson, Paul D. "Old Testament Apocalyptic Re-Examined." *Interpretation*, 25(1971), 454-79.

Unavailable for annotating.

E77 Erling, B. "Ezekiel 38-39 and the Origins of Jewish Apocalyptic." In A82. I.104-14.

Analyzes "the great influence the oracle of God has exerted on later apocalyptic which suggests that some kinship must exist."

E78 Nickelsburg, George W.E., Jr. *Resurrection, Immortality, and Eternal Life in Intertestamental Judaism*. Cambridge: Harvard University Press, and London: Oxford University Press, 1972.

"This will be a study in the history of theology. In writing such a history, we must take seriously the fact that theological conceptions and the literature that contains them do not evolve in a vacuum. They are the products of real people, living in conrete historical situations. In no small measure, they are posed as answers to the problems which these people have seen arising from the situations they confront. Hence the historian of theology will ask: What (kinds of) situations or problems do the author and his community see themselves facing? How do they respond to this situation or solve this problem? To pose these questions in terms of the present study: 1) What (kind of) situations and problems have called forth such answers as resurrection, immortality, and eternal life? 2) What are the specific functions of these answers?" Contents: I. Religious Persecution--Apocalyptic Texts; II. Religious Persecution--The Story of the Persecution and Exaltation of the Righteous Man; III. Religious Persecution--The Story of the Persecution and Vindication of the Righteous; IV. The Oppression of the Righteous Poor--Enoch 94-104; V. Resurrection--Unrelated to Persecution, Oppression, and Injustice; and VI. The Qumran Scrolls and Two-Way Theology.

E79 North, Robert. "Prophecy to Apocalyptic via Zechariah." *Vetus Testamentum Supplements*, 22(1972), 47-71.

"Apocalyptic, as a 'more excellent way' of either prophecy or history or both, is being intensely reappraised in current biblical research. This ferment points up a prior and unsolved question: What does history itself mean in an Old Testament context and as an alternative to prophecy? A truism of the discussion has been this: 'Apocalyptic (meaning chiefly Daniel) is the child of prophecy (chiefly Ezekiel)'.

Far less clear is the extent to which this filiation implies continuity rather than opposition. In any case the line of succession involves Zechariah more pivotally than has been adequately investigated." Considers: I. What is Zechariah? II. What is apocalyptic? III. What is prophecy? IV. What is history? V. Conclusion.

E80 Black, M. "The Fragments of the Aramaic Enoch from Qumran." In A91. Pp. 15-28.

General analysis of the Aramaic Enoch, covering: I. The Enoch Apocalyptic Texts; II. The Original Language[s]; III. The Character of the Greek and Ethiopic Versions; and IV. The Language of I Enoch. Concludes that "these Enoch fragments are among the nearest extant compositions in the original to compositions behind the Words of Jesus."

E81 Hengel, Martin. *Judaism and Hellenism: Studies in Their Encounter in Palestine During the Early Hellenistic Period.* 2 vols. London: SCM Press, Philadelphia: Fortress Press, 1974.

"... sets out to make a better contribution to the better understanding of the development of Judaism in the period between the Testaments, which to a considerable degree coincides with the age of Hellenism, and at the same time to illuminate the social, religious and historical background from which primitive Christianity emerged." Chapter III, section 6, The Hasidim and the First Climax of Jewish Apocalyptic, an analysis of Hellenistic influences on early Apocalyptic literature, considers: 1. The Hasidim as a Jewish party at the time of the Hellenistic reform; and 2. The first climax of Jewish apocalyptic (The universal picture of history in early apocalyptic, resurrection, immortality and judgment, Wisdom through revelation); and Higher wisdom through revelation as a characteristic of religion in late antiquity (pp. 175-218).

E82 Collins, John J. "Jewish Apocalyptic against Its Hellenistic Near Eastern Environment." *Bulletin of the American Schools of Oriental Research,* #220(December 1975), 27-36.

"In this essay we wish to consider some of the more conspicuous features which Jewish apocalyptic shared with its Hellenistic Near Eastern environment. While occasional examples of literary borrowings can be found, we will be chiefly concerned with the parallel developments in different national traditions, each of which retained its distinctive character. The similarities which we find throughout the Hellenistic Near East are due primarily to the fact that traditions which had much in common to begin with (e.g. the idea of the kingship of the national deity) were subjected to the same new circumstances. In particular the alteration of political

conditions by the advent of the Greeks must be considered a
root cause of the new developments in the Hellenistic age."

E83 Collins, John J. "The Mythology of Holy War in Daniel and
the Qumran War Scroll: A Point of Transition in Jewish
Apocalyptic." *Vetus Testamentum*, 25(1975), 596-612.

"The high point of Jewish apocalyptic came ... when
the order of Israel's history was plunged into the chaos of
war and persecution, in the time of Antiochus Epiphanes. It
is not surprising then that the old mythology of the conflict
between God and chaos should again be evoked. In particular,
the books of Daniel and the Qumran War Scroll are replete
with the imagery of holy war. In this paper I wish to discuss the particular ways in which the imagery is modified or
transformed in those books. Specifically, I wish to
study the difference between the two books in their basic
conception of holy war, a difference which, I believe, marks
a highly important point of transition in the development of
Jewish apocalyptic."

E84 Hanson, Paul D. *The Dawn of Apocalyptic: The Historical and
Sociological Roots of Jewish Apocalyptic Eschatology.*
Philadelphia: Fortress Press, 1975; rev. ed. 1979.

"It is the author's hope that this endeavor may help
to refocus the discussion of apocalypticism upon the ancient
texts themselves and upon the sociological matrices within
which those texts took form." Contents: I. The Phenomenon of
Apocalyptic in Israel: Its Background and Setting; II. Isaiah
56-66 and the Visionary Disciples of Second Isaiah; III. The
Origins of the Post-Exilic Hierocracy; IV. Zechariah 9-14 and
the Development of the Apocalyptic Eschatology of the Vision-
aries; and V. An Allegory and Its Explication.

E85 Smithals, Walter. *The Apocalyptic Movement: Introduction &
Interpretation.* Trans. John E. Steely. Nashville: Abing-
don Press, 1975.

An examination of apocalyptic, including chapters on Apocalyptic and the Old Testament (pp. 68-88), and The Origin of
the Apocalyptic Movement in Judaism (pp. 127-50).

E86 Hanson, Paul D. "Prolegomena to the Study of Jewish Apocalyptic." In A96. Pp. 389-413.

"Among students of both Testaments, Jewish apocalyptic
remains an unsolved riddle. While it would be rash to claim
that the riddle is about to be broken, there are new bits of
data which raise hopes that the groundwork is being laid for
penetration into the dark riddle of apocalyptic from a new
perspective. That groundwork is located not on virgin territory, however, but on scarred battleground of old

controversies; that is to say, it is being worked out in lively dialogue with the works of previous generations of scholars. In our attempt to describe that groundwork, it seems prudent to begin with the dialogue with earlier scholarship, and only with the insights gained from that dialogue to proceed to outline a program for the study of apocalyptic from the new perspective opening before us." Considers: I. The Study of Jewish Apocalyptic in Past Scholarship; II. Suggestions for the Restudy of Jewish Apocalyptic: 1. Textual and Literary Criticism, 2. Form-Critical Investigation--The Analysis of Genres and of the History of Transmission, 3. History of Religions, and 4. Typology.

E87   Kolenkow, Anitra Bingham. "The Angelology of the Testament of Abraham." In A97. Pp. 153-62.

"The angelology of the Testament of Abraham (hereafter TA) is similar to that of other works of Hellenistic Jewish literature in its elaboration of biblical angelic characteristics. TA especially uses angelic characteristics to show both heaven's present concern for men and a correlate concerned judgment after death. This paper will emphasize both the 'history of religions' background of TA's angelology and TA's use of such angelology for its own theological purposes."

E88   Loewenstamm, Samuel E.   "The Death of Moses." In A97. Pp. 185-217.

Deals with the questions of "why Moses was doomed to die in the wilderness of Moab," and "How could it even be imagined that the man of God was mortal": "From these two basic questions developed the traditions with which we will attempt to deal below. In our treatment we shall distinguish between the answers given to each of these questions, although in the tradition itself one recognizes here and there a certain dovetailing of the two spheres. In addition, we will include in our survey a treatment of an extraordinary apocryphal text *[The Assumption of Moses]* that transforms the theme of Moses' death into a dispute over the theological doctrine of dualism."

E89   Loewenstamm, Samuel E. "The Testament of Abraham and the Texts Concerning Moses' Death." In A97.   Pp. 219-25.

"A comparison of the Testament of Abraham with the legends concerning the death of Moses hardly calls for justification. The forceful emphasis in the Torah upon the bond which connected these prominent men with God leaves no doubt about their unique affinity to the Divine Sphere. It is this affinity which made it difficult to acquiesce in the thought that Abraham and Moses should have suffered death like simple mortals. In a sense, therefore, the legends about their deaths may be considered as answers to analogous questions."

E90 Millar, William R. *Isaiah 24-27 and the Origin of Apocalyptic*. Harvard Semitic Monograph Series, Number 11. Missoula, Mont.: Scholars Press, 1976.

"It is not the purpose of this study to present a comprehensive discussion of apocalyptic origins. The goal is simply to glean from Isaiah 24-27 material that is important to that discussion. In the process, it is hoped that light is shed on our understanding of these important chapters in Isaiah." Contents: I. Unsettled Problems in Isaiah 24-27; II. The Text and Prosody of Isaiah 24-27; III. The Structure of Isaiah 24-27; and IV. Isaiah 24-27 and the Origin of Apocalyptic.

E91 Nickelsburg, George W.E., Jr. "Eschatology in the Testament of Abraham: A Study of the Judgment Scenes in the Two Recensions." In A97. Pp. 23-64.

"This paper will address itself to significant aspects of the judgment scene in the T Abr. The problem presented by the Long and Short Recensions (A & B) is especially magnified in this section, where, aside from some broad similarities, there are a multitude of important differences between A and B. Indeed, these differences are so numerous and significant that it is unfeasible to discuss the two recensions in parallel. My discussion will be confined mainly to Rec. A, with a concluding section on the relationship between A and B."

E92 Nickelsburg, George W.E., Jr. "Structure and Message in the Testament of Abraham." In A97. Pp. 85-93.

"My purpose here is to sketch out the structure of *the whole* of Rec. A, with a view toward discerning in it the author's message. In the second section, I shall deal with related matters in Rec. B. Against this background, I shall raise the question of priority."

E93 Stone, Michael E. "Lists of Revealed Things in the Apocalyptic Literature." In A96. Pp. 414-52.

"In a number of places in the apocalyptic literature there occur lists between which a striking similarity may be observed. This relationship cannot be explained away on the basis of coincidence alone. A comparative examination of the lists in the light not only of details of content and language, but also of their function and place within the vision structure puts this relationship beyond doubt."

E94 Nickelsburg, George W.E. "The Apocalyptic Message of 1 Enoch 92-105." *Catholic Biblical Quarterly*, 39(1977), 309-28.

"The current discussion of apocalyptic has focussed, in large part, on three issues: (1) the nature or essence of apocalyptic; (2) its origins; (3) the genre question (i.e., the distinction between apocalyptic eschatology and the literary genre 'apocalypse'). In the present paper I shall address myself to the first of these issues, as it relates to a single writing in the apocalyptic corpus: *1 Enoch* 92-105. Secondarily, I shall raise the question of origins. A discussion of genre involves comparison with similar works. Although this is beyond the scope of this study, I shall be comparing individual forms in these chapters with their counterparts elsewhere."

E95 Gruenwald, Ithamar. "Jewish Apocalyptic Literature." *Aufstieg und Niedergang der Römischen Welt*, Section II, volume 19, #1(1979), 89-118.

Eight-part study of Jewish Apocalyptic: I. Apocalypse and Prophecy; II. Gods and Angels; III. Pseudepigraphy; IV. "Outside Books"; V. The Status of Apocalyptic; VI. Apocalyptic and the Apocrypha; VII. Apocalyptic and History; and VIII. Apocalyptic and Eschatology.

E96 Rowland, Christopher. "The Vision of God in Apocalyptic Literature." *Journal for the Study of Judaism in the Persian, Hellenistic and Roman Period*, 10(1979), 137-54.

Study of "The Visions of God in Apocalyptic Literature" to conclude, in part: "Apocalyptic must be recognised as an important, indeed valuable, source for the reconstruction of the origins of Jewish mysticism, even if at present we are not in a position to ascertain whether it is the parent of the kind of meditation which was practiced among the rabbis and, for that matter, the predecessors of the rabbis who flourished before the fall of Jerusalem. Whatever its precise background this material from the apocalyptic literature offers us a much needed means of ascertaining the character of the earliest meditation on Ezekiel and the important role it played in the Jewish religion of the period.

E97 Skehan, Patrick W. "The Divine Name at Qumran, in the Masada Scroll, and in the Septuagint." *Bulletin of the International Organization for Septuagint and Cognate Studies*, 13(1980), 14-44.

Unavailable for annotating.

E98 Nickelsburg, George W.E. *Jewish Literature Between the Bible and the Mishnah: A Historical and Literary Introduction.* Philadelphia: Fortress Press, 1981.

"This volume has been designed primarily as a first introduction to the Jewish literature of the so-called intertestamental period." Includes chapters on The Exposition of Israel's Scriptures (pp. 231-78), and Revolt--Destruction--Reconstruction (pp. 277-309).

E99 Petuchowski, Jakob J. "Judaism as 'Mystery'--The Hidden Agenda?" *Hebrew Union College Annual*, 52(1981), 141-52.

"It has long been considered an established fact that Hellenistic Judaism not only conducted missionary propaganda, but also, in the process, adopted some of the concepts and terminology of the competing mystery cults. This article raises the question whether similar phenomena can also be detected in Palestinian Judaism. A number of rabbinic passages are examined here, in which the Community of Israel is presented as 'the Lord's vineyard,' inaccessible to outsiders, and in which the Greek word, *mysterion*, is variously applied to the God of Israel, circumcision, the Paschal sacrifice, and the Oral Torah. Specifically, an attempt is made to understand Seder Eliyahu Rabbah, ch. 8, ... Leviticus Rabbah 32:4 (end), ... and Canticles Rabbah II, vii, 1. While Palestinian Judaism in Late Antiquity was definitely *not* a mystery cult, it did, when competing on the market place of ideas, adopt some of the trappings of its competitors--particularly within contexts which would affect the would-be proselyte." (Abstract)

E100 Schiffman, Lawrence. "Jewish Sectarianism in Second Temple Times." In A116. Pp. 1-46.

"Our study of the sectarianism of the Second Jewish Commonwealth will seek to fulfill two primary purposes. First, it will describe the main sects and their relationships to one another. Second, it will investigate the underlying cause of the deep divisions which we will see in the period under discussion. Others have seen the causes of the rift in the political, social or religious circumstances of the Hellenistic period. We will argue, however, that almost every sectarian trend was already present in biblical times, and that Hellenism, while certainly a factor in encouraging sectarianism, was not its overriding cause. Hellenism simply heightened conflicts which had begun centuries before. In demonstrating this thesis, we will avoid the usual cataloguing of sects, choosing instead to concentrate on basic issues among the sects and how each group reacted to them."

E101 Schiffman, Lawrence H. *"Merkavah* Speculation at Qumran: The 4Q *Serekh Shirot 'Olat ha-Shabbat."* In A119. Pp. 15-47.

"In the light of our study, it is possible to conclude that *Merkavah* mysticism had its origin at Qumran or in related sectarian circles. From there it somehow penetrated and was absorbed by Pharisaic and then tannaitic tradition.

It would be through these channels that this speculation entered into the mainstream of Judaism."

E102 Van der Horst, Pieter. "Moses' Throne Vision in Ezekiel the Dramatist." *Journal of Jewish Studies*, 34,1(Spring 1983), 21-29.

Analysis of the throne vision in the poet Ezekiel's *Exagōgē* (first century BCE) to conclude: "Compared to later merkavah-literature, Moses' vision is very rudimentary. It contains no elaborate descriptions of the hosts of angels and their leaders, or of the heavenly palaces, or of the throne itself. Furthermore, the human shape of God receives no elaborate treatment, and no attention is paid to the fabulous dimensions of his limbs, so often discussed in detail in the Shi'ur Qomah speculations of later hekhalot-treatises. Even when compared with the earliest post-biblical merkavah-vision, *1 Enoch* 14, Ezekiel's description is much more sober. He was not interested in merkavah-mysticism in itself. But he did see that the literary form of a merkavah-vision was quite suitable as a medium for expressing a notion of more importance to him: namely that Moses is God's viceregent, that the man who liberated the people of Israel from the Egyptians is not merely a personage from the distant past but still present and ruling over the universe, and that through his heavenly enthronement the nation of the Jews is validated as divinely established."

F. Merkabah Mysticism and Jewish Gnosticism

Primary Sources

F1 Yonge, C.D. *The Works of Philo Judaeus, The Contemporary of Josephus.* 4 vols. London: H.G. Bohm, 1854-55.

F2 Kalisch, Isador, trans. *Sepher Yezirah. A Book on Creation; or the Jewish Metaphysics of Remote Antiquity.* In his *A Sketch of the Talmud.* New York: L.H. Frank & Co., 1877. Rpt. Hollywood: Symbols and Signs, 1974. Intro. rpt. in his F36.

F3 Deane, William J., ed. *The Book of Wisdom: The Greek Text, The Latin Vulgate and The Authorized English Version.* Oxford: Clarendon Press, 1881.

Prolegomena: I. 1. The Book of Wisdom: Its Claims of Attention; 2. Sketch of the Progress of Greek Philosophy; 3. The Jewish-Alexandrian Philosohy; 4. Its Influence on the Theology of the New Testament; II. Title. Plan. Contents; III. Language and Character; IV. Place and Date of Composition. Author; V. History. Authority. Relation to the Canon of Scriptures; VI. Text; VII. Versions, Editions, and Commentaries.

F4 Edersheim, Alfred, trans. *Sefer Yetzirah*. In his *The Life and Times of Jesus the Messiah*. 2 vols. London: Longmans, Green and Co., 1883. 2nd ed. London and New York: Anson D.F. Randolph and Company, 1884. II.691-98.

F5 Westcott, Wm. Wynn, trans. *Sepher Yetzirah: the Book of Formation, and the Thirty-Two Paths of Wisdom*. Bath: Robert Fryar, 1887. Rev. ed. Collectanea Hermetica. London: Theosophical Publishing Society, 1893. London: John Watkins, 1911. Rpt. New York: Occult Research Press, 1956; Cambridge, Eng.: I.A.M., 1978.

F6 Conybeare, Fred C., ed. *About the Contemplative Life; or, the Fourth Book of the Treatise Concerning Virtues*. Oxford: Clarendon Press, 1895.

Selections from Philo.

F7 Gaster, M. "The Wisdom of the Chaldeans: An Old Hebrew Astrological Text." *Proceedings of the Society of Biblical Archaeology*, 22(1900), 329-51. Rpt. F13.

Critical introduction and translation of text.

F8 Ginzberg, Louis. *The Legends of the Jews*. Trans. Henrietta Szold. Vol. 3 trans. Paul Radin. 7 vols. Philadelphia: Jewish Publication Society of America, 1909-38.

"In the present work,... I have made the first attempt to gather from the original sources all Jewish legends, in so far as they refer to Biblical personages and events, and reproduce them with the greatest attainable completeness and accuracy." In addition to exoteric sources, Ginzberg includes "The works of the older Kabbalah [which] are likewise treasuries of quotations from lost Midrashim, and it was among the kabbalists, and later among the Hasidim, that new legends arose. The literature produced in these two circles are therefore of great importance for the present purpose." Vol. 7, Index, compiled by Boaz Cohen. Shorter, one-volume version, F19.

F9 Mordell, Phineas. "The Origin of Letters and Numerals according to the Sefer Yesirah." *Jewish Quarterly Review*, n.s. 2(1911-12), 557-83, 3(1912-13), 517-44. Rpt. Philadelphia: Phineas Mordell, 1914. Rpt. New York: Weiser, 1975.

Claims that "the Sefer Yetzirah, as the earliest Hebrew grammar, contains not only the fundamental rules of Hebrew orthography, but also an account of the origin of letters and numerals. This account it is my present purpose to set forth." After explaining the origin of letters and numerals,

Mordell discusses the text and authorship, and provides a translation of the first part of the *Sefer Yetzirah*.

F10 Friedlander, Gerald, trans. *Pirķê de Rabbi Eliezer (The Chapters of Rabbi Eliezer the Great)*. According to the Text of the Manuscript belonging to Abraham Epstein of Vienna. London: K. Paul, Trench, Trubner, and New York: Bloch Pub. Co., 1916. 2nd Am. ed. New York: Hermon Press, 1965. Rpt. New York: B. Blom, 1971. 4th ed. New York: Hermon Press, 1981.

Text, attributed to Rabbi Eliezer b. Hyrkanos, first to second century A.D., comprised of three parts: 1. "Ten descents" from heaven to earth; 2. "a detailed account of Rabbinic mysticism, more particularly the ancient mysteries of the Creation..., the Divine Chariot..., as well as the secret of the Calendar ... and the secret of the Redemption"; and 3. "the fragment of a Midrash on the *Shemoneh 'Esreh*." Introduction covers: 1. Short account of the Book and its History; 2. Plan and contents of the book; 3. *Pirķê de Rabbi Eliezer* in Jewish and Christian Literature; 4. *Pirķê de Rabbi Eliezer* and the Talmud, Targum, Midrash, Zohar and Liturgy; 5. *Pirķê de Rabbi Eliezer* and the pseudepigraphic and apocryphal literature; 6. *Pirķê de Rabbi Eliezer* and Patristic Literature; 7. Date and origin of *Pirķê de Rabbi Eliezer*; 8. Polemical Tendency of *Pirķê de Rabbi Eliezer*; 9. Theology of *Pirķê de Rabbi Eliezer*.

F11 Tilden, Frank William. *Philo Judaeus, on the Contemplative Life*. Indiana University Studies, vol. ix, no. 52. Bloomington: Indiana University Press, 1922.

F12 Stenring, Knut, trans. *The Book of Formation, by Rabbi Akiba ben Joseph; including The 32 Paths of Wisdom, Their Correspondence with the Hebrew Alphabet and the Tarot Symbols*. Philadelphia: D. McKay, 1923. Rpt. New York: Ktav Publishing House, 1970.

F13 Gaster, M. "The Wisdom of the Chaldeans: An Old Hebrew Astrological Text." In his A12. I.338-55.

Reprint of F7.

F14 Colson, F.H., and G.H. Whitaker, trans. *Philo*. 10 vols. Loeb Classical Library. Greek Authors. London: Heinemann, New York: Putnam, and Cambridge: Harvard University Press, 1929-62.

Bi-lingual edition.

F15 *Sepher Yetzirah, the Book of Creation; a Verse by Verse Analysis by Dr. M. Doreal*. Denver: Brotherhood of the White Temple, Inc., 1941.

F16 Lewy, Hans, ed. *Philosophical Writings: Philo*. Oxford: East and West Library, 1946. Rpt. F20.

I. God and World; II. God and Man; III. Man and World; IV. The Knowledge of God; V. The Mystic Way; VI. The Soul and Her God; VII. On Man's Humility, Hope, Faith and Joy; VIII. On Vices and Virtues; and IX. Israel and the Nations.

F17 Raskin, Saul. *Kabbalah in Word and Image; with the Book of Creation and from the Zohar*. New York: Printed by Academy Photo Offset, 1952.

F18 Glatzer, Nahum N., trans. "The Messiah as Teacher: Two Selections from the Traditional Literature." *Commentary*, 18(1954), 466-67.

Selections from the *Alphabet of Rabbi Akiba* and a medieval Yemenite manuscript.

F19 Ginzberg, Louis. *Legends of the Bible*. New York: Simon and Schuster, 1956.

Abridged version of F8.

F20 Heinemann, Isaak. *Three Jewish Philosophers*. Philadelphia: Jewish Publication Society of America, and New York: Meridian Books, 1960.

Section on Philo is reprint of F16.

F21 *Book of Formation (Sepher Yetzirah). The Letters of Our Father Abraham*. Hollywood: Work of the Chariot, 1970. Enlarged ed. 1971.

F22 Glatzer, Nahum N., ed. *The Essential Philo*. New York: Schocken Books, 1971.

F23 *The Sepher Yetzirah*. Bray: Guild Press, 1975. 2nd ed. 1976.

F24 Suarès, Carlo, trans. *The Sepher Yetsirah, Including the Original Astrology according to the Qabala and Its Zodiac*. Trans. from the French by Micheline and Vincent Stuart. Boulder and London: Shambhala, 1976.

F25 Friedman, Irving, trans. *The Book of Creation*. New York: Samuel Weiser, Inc., 1977.

F26 Winston, David, trans. *Philo of Alexandria: The Contemplative Life, the Giants and Selections*. New York, Ramsey, and Toronto: Paulist Press, 1981.

Translation of "those passages that are the most significant and representative of his religious philosophy," taken from *The Contemplative Life*, *The Giants*, and other works, including sections on Scriptural Exegesis (pp. 79-82), Cosmogony (pp. 96-118), Souls, Angels and Daemons (pp. 118-123), and Mysticism (pp. 164-74). The third section of the Introduction is devoted to Philo's Mysticism (pp. 21-35), with sections on: 1. Divine Transcendence, 2. Rational Mysticism: Faith, Reason, and Intuition; 3. *Apatheia/Eupatheia*; and 4. The Mystical Experience.

F27 Cohen, Martin Samuel. *The Shi'ur Qomah: Liturgy and Theurgy in Pre-Kabbalistic Jewish Mysticism.* Lanham, Md.: University Press of America, 1983.

"A translation and commentary of the Sefer haqqomah recension of the text, Oxford manuscript 1791, ff. 58-70." Unavailable for annotating.

Secondary Sources

F28 Edersheim, Alfred. *History of the Jewish Nation After the Destruction of Jerusalem Under Titus.* Edinburgh: T. Constable, London: Hamilton Adams and Co., 1856, 1857. Rpt. Grand Rapids, Mich.: Baker Book House, 1954.

In the section, Mysticism and Philo (pp. 404-424), Edersheim discusses the development of mystical thought among both the Palestinian and Egyptian Jews in the post-commonwealth period of Jewish history. In Palestine, mysticism evolved slowly, culminating in the Kabbalism of the Middle Ages, but in Egypt, spurred by the Hellenistic influence, Jewish mysticism developed more quickly through the writings of Philo Judaeus.

F29 Benamozegh, E. *Jewish and Christian Ethics, with a Criticism on Mahomedism.* San Francisco: E. Blochman, 1873.

Opposed to Christianity's "alleged superiority to Judaism," Benamozegh traces the origins of Christianity to "the then setting sun of Judaism," to demonstrate that "Even the real *peculiarities* of the new system, such as *Justification by Faith, Freedom from the Law,* &c., are ... misapplications of old rabbinical doctrines or traditions." In the second chapter, The Doctrines upon which the Christian Code of Morals is Founded (pp. 12-29), he uses Kabbalah to "affirm that the tripple [sic] distinction of the Gnostics, and the spiritual of Paul become quite intellgible only by linking them with the equivalent Cabalistical doctrine."

F30 Schechter, S. "Fragments of the Sifre Zuta." *Jewish Quarterly Review*, o.s. 6(1894), 656-63.

Describes part of Codex Heb. C.18 at the Bodleian Library, which contains fragments of the Sifre Zuta, a fourth-century Midrash to the Book of Numbers.

F31 Buttenwieser, Moses. *Outline of the Neo-Hebraic Apocalyptic Literature.* Cincinnati: The author, 1901.

"The following outlines of the separate apocalypses will illustrate the points already mentioned as characteristic of the Neo-Hebraic Apocalyptic Literature," specifically: The Hebrew Book of Enoch; An Apocalyptic Fragment; The Ascension of Moses; The Ascension of Moses--A Fragment; The Revelation of R. Joshua B. Levi; The Alphabets of Rabbi Akiba; The Hebrew Elijah Apocalypse; The Apocalypse of Zerubbabel; The Wars of King Messiah; The Revelation of R. Simon b. Yohai; The Prayer of R. Simon B. Yohai; The Midrash of the Ten Kings; The Persian Apocalypse of Daniel; and Eschatological Descriptions.

F32 Porter, Frank Chamberlain. "The Pre-existence of the Soul in the Books of Wisdom and in the Rabbinical Writings." In A4. I.207-69.

"It has long been my conviction that the current language in regard to the Hellenism of the *Book of Wisdom* is misleading, and that it is more important to define the kind and degree of this Hellenism than to assert its reality. In particular in regard to the pre-existence of the soul, not only in *Wisdom* but in rabbinical and other Jewish books, it is not so useful to assert or deny as to define. What did the Jews mean by pre-existence, and above all what did they mean by soul?"

F33 Montefiore, C.G. "Jewish Apocalypses and Rabbinic Judaism." *Quest,* 7(1916), 137-67.

Analysis of the "antagonism of the Rabbis to the Apocalypses" as resulting from the Apocalypses' anticipation of "an early coming of the Redemption, the New Order and the Messianic Age;... The Rabbinic doctors, however,... mainly because they did not want to foster false hopes, or to encourage a hopeless contest with Rome, were against these foretellings and calculations.... It would seem that they also objected to the circulation and reading of speculations about the origins of the world and cognate matters, with which many of the Apocalyptic writings are concerned, and which ... made them then alluring and seductive."

F34 Büchler, Adolph. *Types of Jewish-Palestinian Piety from 70 B.C.E. to 70 C.E.: The Ancient Pious Men.* Jews' College, Publications, no. 8. London: Jews' College, 1922. Rpt. New York: Ktav, 1968, and Farnborough: Gregg, 1969.

"The present essay undertakes the modest task of collecting and re-examining the reports preserved in the rabbinic literature about the pious men, [Hasidim], who lived in Jerusalem in the period extending from 70 B.C.E. to 70 C.E.; of supplementing by a detailed examination of all the early records about the ways in which the pious men expressed their religious sentiments and ideas, the generalizing presentations by scholars of the rank of Jost, Gratz, Derenbourg, Geiger, Wellhausen, and Kohler, of the religious life of all the sections of Palestinian Jewry in the first century; of describing one representative class of typically pious individuals, and incidentally, throwing some new light on the inner life of the Jews of Jerusalem, which hitherto has not been considered worthy of special attention."

F35 Wright, Dudley. "The Mysteries of Merkabah." *Open Court*, 37(1923), 402-7.

Discussion of the "Society of the Merkabah, a Rabbinical school, the members of which gained divine knowledge by direct contemplation. There were grades of initiation and of sanctity, but among all of them the Mysteries were referred to in the terms of the deepest reverence and with bated breath."

F36 Kalisch, Isador. "Introduction to Sepher Yezirah." In his *Studies in Ancient and Modern Judaism*. New York: George Dobsevage, 1928. Pp. 344-50.

Reprint of the introduction to F2.

F37 Mordell, Phineas. "Notes on the Sepher Yetzirah." *Jewish Quarterly Review*, 19(1928), 79-80.

Criticism of Stenring's translation of the *Sefer Yetzirah*, (F12).

F38 Willoughby, Harold R. *Pagan Regeneration: A Study of Mystery Initiations in the Graeco-Roman World*. Chicago: University of Chicago Press, 1929; rpt. 1960.

Study of "the problem of the genesis of Pauline mysticism. How did it come about that, with Judaism and primitive Christianity essentially unmystical in character, Pauline Christianity developed in a way to accentuate the mystical phases of religious experience?" In Chapter 9, The Mysticism of Philo (pp. 225-62), Willoughby explores "a third Egyptian syncretism which was characterized by a mysticism peculiarly its own, yet resembling in important ways the other types of mystical experience current in Alexandria. This, strange to say, was a Jewish syncretism--the religion of Philo the philosopher, the great Jewish contemporary of Jesus and Paul."

F39 Goodenough, Erwin. *By Light, Light: The Mystic Gospel of Hellenistic Judaism*. London: Oxford University Press, and New Haven: Yale UniversIty Press, 1935. Rpt. Amsterdam: Philo Press, 1969.

Focusing on the question, "Was there ever such a mystic Judaism?", Goodenough "begins with Philo because he is our only extended source in Hellenistic Judaism," and explores the problem: "If then he has not invented mystic Judaism, once that term has become clear through analyzing his presentation, how far back does it go, and how did the movement develop?" After the Hellenistic Mysteries, Goodenough includes an Epilogue on Traces of the Mystery in the Kabbalah (pp. 359-69).

F40 Bamberger, Bernard J. "A Messianic Document of the Seventh Century." *Hebrew Union College Annual*, 15(1940), 425-31.

From analyzing chapters 34-37 of the *Pesikta Rabbati*, Bamberger concludes that "These chapters (which have perhaps been considerably reworked from their original form) bear the same relation to the classic midrash that the old apocalypses bear to classic prophecy. As the apocalypse is an imitation of the prophets and is ascribed to some ancient worthy, so our chapters are cast in the form of a midrashic exposition and every so often mention the name of a famous Tanna or Amora. The real intent, however, is apocalyptic and apologetic.... This work can be understood only as the expression of enthusiasts in a time of world crisis."

F41 Goodenough, Erwin R. *An Introduction to Philo Judaeus*. New Haven: Yale University Press, and London: Oxford University Press, 1940. 2nd ed. 1962.

Introduction to the thought of Philo. Chapter 7, The Mystic (pp. 178-213), asserts that "What interests Philo is not the demonstration that the immaterial is the only reality, but religious experience of that reality."

F42 Altmann, Alexander. "Gnostic Themes in Rabbinic Literature." In A25. Pp. 19-32.

"The present study attempts to show how Gnostic thought is reflected in some of the central themes of Rabbinic cosmology.... Gnosis presented a system of thought which was comprehensive and compelling in many respects. In the defence of Judaism, the Rabbis had to face this powerful movement, and it is no wonder that their own minds became engaged in speculations similar to those which they sought to combat."

F43 Altmann, Alexander. "The Gnostic Background of the Rabbinic Adam Legends." *Jewish Quarterly Review*, n.s. 35(1945), 371-91.

By deriving Gnostic origins for "The motif of the enmity of the angels towards Man," Altmann sheds light "upon the meaning of the other variations of the theme as well," specifically The Angels before Adam, and Adam's Sleep, both of which also reflect Gnostic influences.

F44 Goodenough, Erwin R. "Philo on Immortality." *Harvard Theological Review*, 39(1946), 85-108.

Close examination of all of "Philo's remarks upon immortality, with the double purpose of depicting an instance of mystic-thinking, and of finding perhaps some suggestion which can be used elsewhere as to what may have been in the minds of the Jews who adopted for their graves and synagogues the pagan symbol of life after death."

F45 Baeck, Leo. "The Origin of Jewish Mysticism." In his A28. Pp. 93-105.

Examination of the early period of Jewish mysticism, through the *Hekhalot* writings and the *Sefer Yetzirah*, to demonstrate that "an increasingly intense longing for the future entered this mysticism. It acquired a messianic tone. Its aim was not to release man from will and from the world, but to reconcile human will and the world with God, and to bring the beyond down to this earth, to transform the Sabbath, to whose poetry all its love is directed, into the breath of the world, into the life and fulfilment of mankind. This challenging, imperative, active, messianic element, this emphasis on personality and on the idea of the future, which is nevertheless combined with immersion in the bliss of peace, in the mystery of the Sabbath, became the distinctive feature, which is nevertheless combined with immersion in the bliss of peace, in the mystery of the Sabbath, became the distinctive feature of Jewish mysticism. And this evolution is the result of the distinctive nature of Judaism itself."

F46 Goodenough, Erwin R. *Jewish Symbols in the Greco-Roman Period*. Bollingen Series, xxxvii. 13 vols. New York: Pantheon Books, 1953-68.

"The immediate purpose of the study which follows is to try to discover the religious attitudes of the Jews in the Greco-Roman world." While not directly kabbalistic, the study contains numerous references to kabbalistic works, in order to indicate the manifestation of these symbols in Jewish mysticism.

F47 Jacobs, L. "The Concept of Ḥasid in the Biblical and Rabbinic Literature." *Journal of Jewish Studies*, 8(1957), 143-54.

Traces the concept of hasid as it occurred before eighteenth-century Hasidism, "showing that there is a gradual development of the concept of *ḥasid* from the Biblical down through the Rabbinic period.... With the addition of mystical and ascetic elements of various kinds the *ḥasid* in subsequent Jewish life and thought belongs to this later Rabbinic type."

F48 Scholem, Gershom G. *Jewish Gnosticism, Merkabah Mysticism, and Talmudic Tradition*. Based on the Israel Goldstein Lectures, Delivered at the Jewish Theological Seminary of America, New York. New York: Jewish Theological Seminary of America, 1960; 2nd ed. 1965.

Purpose is "to prove that there is much more to the subject than is immediately apparent. Indeed, I hope to establish proof that new findings, some of which I shall set forth in the following discussion, warrant a reconsideration of the entire problem." The first edition contains ten chapters: 1. General Remarks; 2. The Halakhic Character of Hekhaloth Mysticism; 3. The Four Who Entered Paradise and Paul's Ascension to Paradise; 4. The Merkabah Hymns and the Song of the Kine in a Talmudic Passage; 5. Some Old Elements in the Greater Hekhaloth; 6. The Age of *Shiur Komah* Speculation and a Passage of Origen; 7. Some Remarks on Metatron and Akatriel; 8. Some Aggadic Sayings Explained by Markabah Hymns. The Garment of God; 9. The Relationship Between Gnostic and Jewish Sources. Jewish Sources on the Ogdoas. Yaldabaoth and Ariel. Elijah and Lilith; and 10. The Theurgic Elements of the Lesser Hekhaloth and the Magical Papyri. Included in the second edition are four appendices: 1. A New Interpretation of an Aramaic Inscription; 2. On the Magical Formulae AKRAMACHAMAREI and SESENGEN BARPHARANGES; 3. *Ma'asseh Merkabah*--An Unpublished Merkabah Text; and 4. *Mishnath Shir ha-Shirim*--by Professor Saul Lieberman.

F49 Neusner, Jacob. "Essay on Ezekiel's Chariot." *Students' Annual, Teachers' Institute*. New York: Jewish Theological Seminary of America, 1961. Pp. 31-42.

Unavailable for annotating.

F50 Cohn, Jacob. "Two Studies in Classical Jewish Mysticism." *Judaism*, 11(1962), 242-48.

Two brief notes which "form part of the posthumous literary legacy of the late Rabbi Jacob Cohn ... The first, 'The Esoteric Tradition in Talmud and Midrash,' focuses on the earliest esoteric traditions of Jewish history; and the second, 'The Term *Shechina*,' discusses the concept of Immanence in rabbinic literature." (Editor's note)

F51 Finkel, Joshua. "The Alexandrian Tradition and the Midrash Ha-Ne'elam." In A51. Pp. 77-103.

Counters the objections of Werblowsky (in "Philo and the Zohar," 1959 [N57]), to the evidence presented by Samuel Belkin (*Sura*, 3(1958), 25-92, Hebrew), which "opposes Scholem's view that the [Midrash Ha-Ne'elam] is essentially medieval in content and tenor, and insists that it is rather stupid in the notions and theological tenets of antiquity."

F52 Neusner, Jacob. *A Life of Johanan ben Zakkai.* Studia Post-Biblica Volumen Sextum. Leiden: E.J. Brill, 1962; 2nd ed. 1970.

"This book does not offer a full-length portrait of Yohanan ben Zakkai. Such a portrait is not possible, for ... the sources do not provide us with adequate information.... It is useful mainly as a collection of sources about a specific sage."

F53 Neusner, Jacob. "Jewish Use of Pagan Symbols after 70 C.E." *Journal of Religion*, 43(1963), 285-94.

"I have suggested that the impact of the catastrophic event of 70 and 132-35 C.E. is reflected in new concern for personal, as well as cosmic, salvation; and that this concern was expressed by some of the rabbis of the Talmud, as well as by other Jews for outside their circles, through devotion to mystical lore, without attempting to delineate precisely what elements of this lore were exploited, and with what results. I have therefore interpreted the use by Jews of such relevant pagan symbols as part of a much more widespread Jewish devotion to mysticism. This was phenomenologically as normal a characteristic of Judaism in that age as was study of the law, though the users of pagan symbols may not have been very avid students of the law."

F54 Smith, Morton. "Observations on *Hekhalot Rabbati.*" In A53. Pp. 142-60.

An outline of the text, followed by an analysis of its contents, "a collection of pieces illustrating different aspects of a single tradition of speculation concerning the throne of God and the heavens beneath it."

F55 Loewe, Raphael. "The Divine Garment and Shi'ur Qomah." *Harvard Theological Review*, 58(1965), 153-60.

Explores the possibility that Scholem's conclusion "that the description of the garment was part of the *Shiur Komah* traditions" (F48), is "confirmed by the circumstance that in the great magical papyrus of Paris the visionary sees Helios revealed as 'a youthful god, well-favoured, fiery-haired, in a white *chiton* and a scarlet cloak.' Whatever the immediate or ultimate source of this, the *Shi'ur Qomah* at any rate derives from the Song of Songs; and it is to be emphasised that the relevant verses of the Song make no reference whatsoever to any garment at all."

F56 Scholem, Gershom. "Judaism and Gnosticism." *Report of the 1965-1966 Seminar on Religions in Antiquity*. Comparative Studies Centre, Dartmouth College, (7.10.1965), 139-45.

Report of a paper on "Merkabah Mysticism and Jewish Gnosticism."

F57 Cohn, Jacob. "Mystic Experience and Elijah-Revelations in Talmudic Times." In A62. English Section, pp. 34-44.

"The power of Elijah in performing miracles and answering all manner of difficult problems, was so firmly entrenched in the Talmudic mind that any feat that could not be otherwise explained was attributed to his interference. When by some mysterious telepathy the same lesson was taught in the Academy at Sura as at Pumbeditha, and at the same time, the fact was ascribed to Elijah. Many miraculous escapes from trouble were ascribed to his activity. Thus Elijah gradually emerged from his mystic character into a figure in Jewish folklore. However, the mystic technique was very persistent, and survived to a very late date. Even as late as the ninth century, in the days of Mar Joseph Gaon of Pumbeditha, intimacy with Elijah was known to have been vouchsafed to a chosen few."

F58 Dan, Joseph. "The Beginnings of Jewish Mysticism in Europe." In A63. II.282-90.

Brief introduction to medieval Jewish mysticism, which focuses on: The Doctrine of the Holy Names; *Hekalot* and *Merkava* mysticism; Mystery of the Divinity and of the Creation; and a kind of Gnosticism influenced by early Eastern sources.

F59 Rosh-Pinnah, Eliyahu [Ernst E. Ettish] "The Sefer Yetzirah and the Original Tetragrammaton." *Jewish Quarterly Review*, n.s. 57(1966-67), 212-26.

Using Mordell's shortcomings as a basis (F9), explores "the methods and work of the authors of the S[efer] Y[etzirah]."

F60 Sperber, Daniel. "On a Meaning for the Word [Milah]." *Revue des études juives*, 125(1966), 385-89.

"To sum up: in the above study we have tried to prove that the word [milah] means at all times more than merely a word; it bears the meaning of a spell, magical formula or incantation. This usage is to be found in both Talmuds and in the later literature of both Palestine and Babylon. Furthermore this meaning was correctly appreciated by the early mediaeval Jewish commentators (Rashi, R. Hananel, Arukh). That their understanding was accurate is borne out not only by the above Rabbinic texts, but also secular Aramaic ones, themselves hitherto insufficiently understood."

F61 Bronznick, Norman M. "Qabbalah as a Metonym for the Prophets and Hagiographa." *Hebrew Union College Annual*, 38(1967), 285-95.

In studying the etymology of the term "Qabbalah," Bronznick concludes that "In both tannaitic and amoraic texts, the rabbis,... frequently refer to the Prophets by the generic term Qabbalah.... Thus Qabbalah proves itself to be a truly felicitous term of reference for both the *Nevi'im* and *Kethuvim* whenever the rabbis, in their discourses, have need to invoke the authority of the extra-pentateuchal portions of the Bible--and such instances are numerous indeed."

F62 Baer, Richard A., Jr. *Philo's Use of the Categories Male and Female.* Leiden: E.J. Brill, 1970.

Asserts that "the categories male and female occupied more than an incidental place in Philo's thinking, and that much of his theology could be illuminated by an understanding of his use of these terms." After the Introduction on Philo's Method and Basic Concerns, Baer discusses: The Categories Male and Female in Relationship to Philo's Understanding of the Nature of Man; and The Categories Male and Female in Relationship to Soteriology and Prophetic Inspiration.

F63 Neusner, Jacob. *Development of a Legend: Studies on the Traditions Concerning Yohanan ben Zakkai.* Studia Post-Biblica Volumen Sextum Decimum. Leiden: E.J. Brill, 1970.

"My purpose is thus not to produce a connected history of the man and his time, but to offer systematic observations on the tradition about him and through it, on the development of a sample body of talmudic literature."

F64 Urbach, E.E. "Redemption and Repentance in Talmudic Judaism." In A76. Pp. 190-206.

"It is my intention in this paper to examine the relationship between two ideas--that of repentance and that of redemption--in the religious thought of the ancient rabbis of the tannaitic and the amoraic periods. On the one hand, we shall enquire to what extent the two concepts have become integrated into a single system, and on the other, we shall endeavour to determine if this integration, or the lack of it, contributed to the creation of various patterns in the conception of 'Redemption.'"

F65 Bowker, J.W. "'Merkabah' Visions and the Visions of Paul." *Journal of Semitic Studies*, 16(1971), 157-73.

"In *The Targums and Rabbinic Literature* [Cambridge, 1969, p. 38] I drew attention to the possible connection between *merkabah* visions (visions of the Heavenly Chariot based on, and arising from, contemplation on the 'chariot' chapters of Ezekiel, chs. i and x) and the visions of Paul. The purpose of this article is to make more conveniently available the basic evidence on which the suggestion is based."

F66 Gruenwald, Ithamar. "A Preliminary Critical Edition of *Sefer Yezira.*" *Israel Oriental Studies*, 1(1971), 132-77.

"As the title emphatically indicates, the following text and critical apparatus should by no means be considered a final and definitive edition of the *Sefer Yezira*, the Hebrew 'Book of Creation'.... The present edition has no intention of solving the riddles of the *Sefer Yezira*,... its only aim is to provide a provisional critical edition of the text." In the English introduction to the Hebrew edition, Gruenwald discusses the main textual problems of the text: 1. the relationship among the three recensions of the text; 2. the correct text of each of the three recensions; and 3. how "to do justice to all the 3 recensions without, however, unnecessarily complicating the critical edition of the text."

F67 Lachs, Samuel Tobias. "Midrash Hallel and Merkabah Mysticism." In A80. Pp. 193-203.

"Midrash Hallel is essentially an obscure work which has remained in virtual oblivion for centuries.... It is our contention that the fate of this midrash was not the result of accident. We feel that it was actually suppressed because of the nature of its content. Midrash Hallel contains esoteric material traceable to the Merkabah school of mysticism."

F68 Neusner, Jacob. "The Development of the *Merkavah* Tradition." *Journal for the Study of Judaism*, 2(1971), 149-60.

In order to demonstrate "that versions of a single event or saying appearing in documents of successive age do proceed from the simpler to the more complex as they pass from an earlier to a later document," Neusner compares "the four versions of the Story of Yohanan ben Zakkai and the *Merkavah*-sermon of his disciple Eleazar ben 'Arakh.... present[ing] a translation of each version, followed by some comments from a historical point of view, and then ... a synoptic study of several versions."

F69 Vermes, Geza. "Hanina ben Dosa: A Controversial Galilean Saint from the First Century of the Christian Era." *Journal of Jewish Studies*, 23(1972), 28-50; 24(1973), 51-64.

"The purpose of this study, which includes a full survey of the data, is not merely analytical; it aims also at determining and assessing the various stages of literary development [of texts by masters of subsequent generations]. An attempt will be made, furthermore, to discover historically reliable references to Hanina's life and to discern which other historical phenomena helped or hindered the transformation of a tradition into a legend." Considers four categories of references to Hanina: 1. The Healer; 2. The Miracle-Worker; 3.

The Teaching of Ḥanina; and 4. Ḥanina's Praises. Then, in the last section, Vermes provides A Historian's Evaluation of the Ḥanina Tradition.

F70 Gruenwald, Ithamar. "Knowledge and Vision: Towards a Clarification of Two 'Gnostic' Concepts in the Light of their Alleged Origins." *Israel Oriental Studies*, 3(1973), 63-107.

"The aim of the present study is to look into two of the main concepts of gnosticism, knowledge and vision of God, as part of this historical process of reciprocity between Judaism and gnosticism against the background of the other major oriental religions that played a similar role in the history of gnosticism."

F71 Gruenwald, Ithamar. "Some Critical Notes on the First Part of *Sefer Yezira*." *Revue des études juives*, 132(1973), 475-512.

Critical analysis of *Sefer Yetzirah* based on the text in his "Preliminary Critical Edition" (F66). "The main conclusions reached in the paper are: The text is divided into two main sections: paragraphs 1-16, which deal with the ten *sefirot*; and paragraphs 17-end, which deal with the twenty-two letters of the alphabet. In both cases, that of the *sefirot* and that of the twenty-two letters, the centre of the discussion is the creation of the world and its inner organization in the hierarchical paradigms. The work of a late editor, or editors, is clearly discernible in the first part of the book, where elements drawn from the second part are introduced apparently for the purpose of literary harmonization. The analytical approach adopted by the present writer seems to account in a reasonable way for these attempts towards the editorial harmonization of the two parts of the book."

F72 Leiter, Samuel. "Worthiness, Acclamation, and Appointment: Some Rabbinic Terms." *Proceedings of the American Academy for Jewish Research*, 41-42(1973-74), 137-68.

"... it would be convenient to consider, in addition to terms of worthiness and acclamation, several physical attributes and to trace schematically the evolution of each." On pp. 143-5, Leiter discusses *lifut* "as a special term of Merkabah mysticism."

F73 Neusner, Jacob. "The Traditions Concerning Johanan ben Zakkai: Reconsiderations." *Journal of Jewish Studies*, 24(1973), 65-73.

"In *Development of a Legend: Studies on the Traditions Concerning Yohanan ben Zakkai* [F63], I studied the history of a sample of rabbinic traditions. As subsequent research has expanded and perfected the methodological and conceptual framework for such an inquiry, it is now not without interest to reconsider the problems approached in my former work, to single out some of its weaknesses, and bring up to date the results of *Development*."

F74 Gruenwald, Ithamar. "The Jewish Esoteric Literature in the Time of the Mishnah and Talmud." *Immanuel*, 4(1974), 37-46.

Attempts to answer the question: "What do we really mean by qualifying Jewish apocalyptic and Merkavah mysticism by the term 'esoteric literature'?"; by examining: A. The esoteric qualities of apocalyptic literature; and B. The esoteric qualities of Jewish Merkavah mysticism; to conclude that "Merkavah mysticism is principally an exclusive revelation and not an esoteric revelation."

F75 Scholem, Gershom. "Jaldabaoth Reconsidered." In A88. Pp. 405-21.

"In summing up, I would suggest that by creating the seemingly enigmatic name Jaldabaoth out of *Jald-[s]abaoth*, a Jew who had joined the Gnostic camp of the *minim* consciously produced a secret name which, in accordance with the usage in Jewish esoteric circles, could rightly be claimed to represent the *[ermeneia]* of Saklas,... This seems to me a possible solution of the riddle."

F76 Wilson, R. McL. "'Jewish Gnosis' and Gnostic Origins: A Survey." *Hebrew Union College Annual*, 45(1974), 177-89.

Surveys the origins of Gnosticism and the part played by Jewish Gnosis to answer the questions: "Where did it come from? Who started it? How did it all begin? What is its relation to the other movements, earlier or contemporary or later, to Judaism, Christianity, Manicheism, Mandaeism and so on? Is it something limited to a particular period, a particular stage in the history of civilization, or is it something more endemic, liable to erupt at other times and in other ages?"

F77 Schiffman, Lawrence H. "The Recall of Rabbi Neḥunia ben Ha-Qanah from Ecstasy in the *Hekhalot Rabbati*." *AJS Review*, 1(1976), 269-81.

"The text that has been studied here demonstrates again that the *hekhalot* and magical literature must be studied together if we are to attain a full understanding of either. Further, evidence from the Hellenistic magical tradition must be given sufficient attention. This is true not only for 'esoteric' Jewish texts, but for many passages in Talmudic and Midrashic literature as well. Most important, this study shows that while Scholem is correct in his assertion that there is a halakhic element in the *hekhalot* texts [F48], that element is often modified and even transmogrified by the context in which it appears. Only careful philological analysis can bring it to the surface."

F78 Alexander, P.S. "The Historical Setting of the Hebrew Book of Enoch." *Journal of Jewish Studies*, 28(1977), 156-80.

"The present essay deals primarily with one of the Hekhaloth-Merkabah texts, the so-called Hebrew Book of Enoch or 3 Enoch, and its aim is to put this work into its historical setting. 'Historical setting' may be taken as defined by the following questions: (1) Firstly, when and where was 3 Enoch written? (2) Secondly, what sort of literature is it? In the language of form-criticism, What is its *Sitz-im*-Leben? (3) Thirdly, where do its teachings stand on the spectrum of Rabbinic thought? Are they 'orthodox', 'fringe' or 'heretical'?"

F79 Gruenwald, Ithamar. "Jewish Sources for the Gnostic Texts from Nag Hammadi?" In A101. III.45-56.

"In my opinion, however close some of the gnostic texts may have come to certain parallel Jewish material, the two cases discussed in this paper [*The Hypostasis of the Archons*, cod. p. 94, 3-15 (labib plate 142, 3-15), and cod. p. 95 = pl. 143, 13 sq.] render no conclusive proof for the direct dependence of the gnostic writers on Jewish sources. Jewish material which is projected onto the gnostic screen may well belong to those waves of syncretistic ideas that permeated the East in the first centuries of the Christian era. This Jewish material could have reached the gnostic writers in a hundred other ways besides a real and consciously conceived Jewish source. On the other hand, the assertion that there was direct knowledge of Jewish sources within gnostic literary circles cannot be dismissed. There are many passages in the gnostic writings from Nag Hammadi which can still be interpreted as directly depending on Jewish sources. It is only that the two peculiar test-cases examined here have not rendered proof to the direct dependence of gnostic ideas on Jewish sources."

F80 Fallon, Francis T. *The Enthronement of Sabaoth: Jewish Elements in Gnostic Creation Myths*. Nag Hammadi Studies, Vol. X. Leiden: E.J. Brill, 1978.

"We shall examine two related pericopes from Nag Hammadi documents to show first of all that they derive from a Jewish background, as a contribution to this wider scholarly discussion on the origins of Gnosticism and on the relationship of Judaism to Gnosticism. Secondly, we shall determine which segment or segments of Judaism have contributed to these pericopes. Thirdly, of course, we shall study these pericopes in terms of their relation to one another, the traditions upon which they draw, and their function within the given documents."

F81 Dan, Joseph. "The Concept of Knowledge in the *Shi'ur Qomah.*" In A109. Pp. 67-73.

"It is therefore the purpose of this article to try to analyze some aspects of the basic text of this literature, the *Shi'ur Qomah*, and the reader will judge for himself whether or not this analysis, if substantiated, brings this text closer to the usual connotation of the term 'gnostic.'"

F82 Saldarini, Anthony J. "Apocalypses and 'Apocalyptic' in Rabbinic Literature and Mysticism." *Semeia*, 14(1979), 187-205.

"No sure theory has been developed to account for the demise of apocalypse as a major genre in rabbinic literature, though Akiba's ban on books with biblical pretensions and the reaction against anything smacking of revolt after the end of the War of Bar Kosiba in 135 CE seems most likely ... Gershom Scholem has proposed the thesis that the Jewish mystical literature is the heir to apocalyptic literature and it is to his thesis and the mystical writings we shall turn first."

F83 Gruenwald, Ithamar. *Apocalyptic and Merkavah Mysticism.* Arbeiten zur Geschichte des Antiken Judentums und des Urchristentums, Band XIV. Leiden and Köln: E.J. Brill, 1980.

"This book is a description of Jewish Merkavah ('Divine Chariot') mysticism, its history, structure and main thematic features." In the first part of the book, Gruenwald discusses: I. Two Essential Qualities of Jewish Apocalyptic; II. The Mystical Elements in Apocalyptic; III. The Attitude Towards the Merkavah Speculations in the Literature of the Tannaim and Amoraim; and IV. The Hekhalot Literature. Part Two "contains detailed introductions to the various *Hekhalot* writings we possess": *Re'uyot Yehezkel*; *Hekhalot Zutreti*; *Hekhalot Rabbati*; *Merkavah Rabbah*; *Ma'aseh Merkavah*; *"Hekhalot"* Fragments; *Sefer Hekhalot* (3 Enoch); *Masekhet Hekhalot*; *Shi'ur Qomah*; Physiognomy, Chiromancy and Metaposcopy; and *Sefer Ha-Razim*. There are two Appendices by Saul Lieberman: 1. Metatron, the Meaning of His Name and His Functions; and 2. The Knowledge of *Halakha* by the Author (or Authors) of the *Heikhaloth*.

F84 Halperin, David G. *The Merkabah in Rabbinic Literature.* American Oriental Series, V. 62. New Haven: American Oriental Society, 1980.

"First, I hope to shed light on a particularly obscure, yet important, aspect of Jewish religious perception in Tannaitic and Amoraic times. Many of the implications of the present study can be explored only in subsequent investigations. But any clarification of *ma'aseh merkabah* that we can achieve will certainly sharpen our understanding of the character and role of mysticism, and of supernatural belief in general, within antique Judaism. It will add to our knowledge of the varieties and uses of early Jewish Scriptural interpretation. Second, by applying certain methodological principles to this one issue, I hope to demonstrate the general utility of an approach such as this in dealing with other, similar issues." Considers: I. Overview of the Sources; II. Mishnaic Restrictions on the Merkabah; III. The "Mystical Collection"; IV. Johanan b. Zakkai and the Merkabah; V. The Opening of PT Hag. 77a on the Merkabah; and VI. BT Materials on the Merkabah.

F85 Chernus, Ira. "Individual and Community in the Redaction of the Hekhalot Literature." *Hebrew Union College Annual*, 52(1981), 253-74.

"The 'hekhalot' texts appear to be the product of a series of redactional stages. Surveying the major texts, we find that in come cases the redactors molded their material to reflect a prominent concern for the social/communal roles and responsibilities of the 'merkavah' mystics. Hekhalot Rabbati is the best example of such concern; here the redaction betrays a rather explicit conception of the mystics as intermediaries who harmonize the upper and lower worlds, particularly in the liturgical and eschatological realms. In a text such as Ma'aseh Merkavah, on the other hand, the redactors seem to have been interested almost solely in the private experiences of the individual mystic. The other 'hekhalot' texts take intermediate positions on this issue, reflecting varying degrees of both individual and communal concerns. Yet all of these texts draw on the same basic stock of early traditions, indicating that in its earliest stages 'merkavah' mysticism was relatively neutral on this question, allowing both individualistic and communal orientations to develop within in." (Abstract)

F86 Cohn-Sherbok, Dan. "The Alphabet in Mandaean and Jewish Gnosticism." *Religion*, 11,3(1981), 227-34.

Unavailable for annotating.

F87 Blumenthal, David R. "A Philosophical-Mystical Interpretation of a Shi'ur Qomah Text." In A117. Pp. 153-71.

"The conclusion to be drawn here is, then: that while the Shi'ur Qomah no longer represented an articulation of a visual experience of God or of a theophany of His majesty and power achieved after a long ascent through the heavenly palaces, it did still function as an expression of another kind of experience of God--an experience of contact with the intellectual and vital forces that emanated from Him. The Shi'ur Qomah lost completely its direct visual meaning but it took on a symbolic meaning, not only in the objects it referenced but also in the experience it bespoke. As the nature of Jewish mystical consciousness varied, so did the interpretation and meaning of Shi'ur Qomah. As the nature of Jewish mystical conscious modulated, the ancient tradition of Shi'ur Qomah changed--in its reference and in its meaning-- from 'deliberate and excessive indulgence in anthropomorphism' to intellectual illumination and to contemplative spirituality. Therein lay the true impulse of the living Tradition."

F88 Gruenwald, Ithamar. "Jewish Merkavah Mysticism and Gnosticism." In A117. Pp. 41-55.

"In sum, we have seen that there are a number of connecting points between Jewish Merkavah mysticism and Gnosticism. However, it seems that the gnostic writers were more acquainted with the Merkavah tradition than the opposite. With all the points of connection between Gnosticism and Merkavah mysticism, no justification could be found for the allegation that there was a Jewish type of Gnosticism, which either served as the origin of heretical Gnosticism or coexisted with it. As it appears, there is equally no justification to see in Merkavah mysticism a Jewish concomitant of Gnosticism."

F89 Rodal, Alti B. "Response to David R. Blumenthal." In A117. Pp. 173-83.

Response to F87: "I would suggest in conclusion that, given the interpenetration, affinities and overlapping obtaining between the philosophical and mystical trends in Judaism, from Philo of Alexandria and the Merkavah mystics onwards, the philosophical-mystical approach of Ḥoṭer had numerous ancient precedents and contemporary parallels, not only among philosophers with mystic leanings, but also among philosophically inclined Kabbalists."

F90 Winston, David. "Was Philo a Mystic?" In A117. Pp. 15-39.

"... analysis of Philo's mystical passages, [to determine] if in addition to the distinction between complete or undifferentiated identity with the transcendent as opposed to mere union with it, we further distinguish between a union with the ultimate itself and one that is limited to only an aspect of it, for we shall soon see that man's highest union with God, according to Philo, is limited to the Deity's manifestation as Logos."

G. Medieval Hasidism

Primary Sources

G1 Collins, Edwin, trans. *Duties of the Heart (Ḥovot ha-Levavot)*. Wisdom of the East, no. 3. London: Orient Press, 1904; London: J. Murray, 1905. 2nd impression London: J. Murray, 1909. The Wisdom of the Heart Series. New York: E.P. Dutton, 1910. The Jewish Library, first series. New York: Macmillan Company, 1928.

According to Scholem, "Extremism in ethical and religious behavior,... found their classical literary expression, first and foremost, in 11th-century Spain in the *Ḥovot ha-Levavot* ("Duties of the Heart") by Baḥya ibn Paquda, originally written in Arabic. The material dealing with the life devoted to communion of the true 'servant'--who is none other than the Hasid yearning for the mystical life--is taken from Sufi sources and the author's intention was to produce an instructional manual of Jewish pietism which culminated in a mystical intent" (C65).

G2 Hyamson, Moses, trans. *Duties of the Heart*. New York: Bloch Pub. Co., 1925, 1941, 1943, 1945, 1947. Rpt. Jerusalem: Boys Town Jerusalem Publishers, 1962.

Bi-lingual edition.

G3 Rosenblatt, Samuel, ed. *The High Ways to Perfection*. 2 vols. New York: Columbia University Press, 1927-38.

Edition of Abraham Maimonides' ethical treatise intended to enable men to achieve union with God. In Vol. 1, Rosenblatt includes a detailed introduction covering the manuscript, historical and intellectual background of the author, Maimonides' philosophical system, and the text and translation of the first part of the treatise. The second volume completes the text and translation of the work.

G4 Cronbach, Abraham. "Social Thinking in the Sefer Ḥasidim." *Hebrew Union College Annual*, 22(1949), 1-147.

Approaches this medieval hasidic work as "it reflects the actualities of the world about it.... The notion that all mediaeval Jews were saints hardly finds validation in the *Sefer Ḥasidim*." In addition to discussions of Social Justice, Charity, Types of Charity, Intermediaries, and Restrictions of Charity, Cronbach includes translations of important passages (pp. 46-145).

G5 Goitein, S.D., trans. "A Treatise in Defense of the Pietists." *Journal of Jewish Studies*, 16(1965), 105-14.

Text and translation of Abraham Maimonides' defense of the pietists (Bodleian Library, MS Heb. c28, fol. 45 and 46), "obviously ... intended to be sent out as a circular of the *Nagid* to the communities under his control and to be read there in the synagogues."

G6 Kramer, Simon G., ed. *God and Man in the Sefer Hasidim (Book of the Pious)*. New York: Bloch Publishing Company, 1966.

"In my effort to bring [The Sefer Hasidim] before the English reading public, I have essayed this study in the hope that the publication of this volume will stimulate concern and discussion of the entire field of Jewish Ethics." After an Introduction which covers Historic Background, The Author--Rabbi Judah Hehasid (The Pious), Spanish and German Jewish Literature, Sefer Hasidim--General Characteristics of the Book, Its Contents and Piety and the Pious, Man's Relation to God, Methodology and Goals, and The Literature on the Sefer Hasidim; Kramer discusses: The Fear and Love of God, Sin and Repentance, Prayer, and Study and Education.

G7 Singer, Sholom Alchanan, trans. *Book of the Pious*. Northbrook, Ill.: Whitehall Company, 1971. Sel. rpt. G9.

Introduction discusses: The Times; The Man [Judah ben Samuel, the Pious of Regensberg]; and *Sefer Hasidim* in terms of authorship, as well as teachings; The Pious, as a movement; Pietism and Asceticism, The Texts; and The Translation.

G8 Mansoor, Menahem, trans., with Sara Arenson, and Shoshana Dannhauser. *The Book of Direction to the Duties of the Heart*. The Littman Library of Jewish Civilization. London: Routledge & Kegan Paul, 1974.

G9 Singer, Sholom Alchanan, trans. *Book of the Pious*. In A89. Pp. 303-13.

Selections from G7.

G10 Eleazar ben Judah, of Worms. *Three Tracts*. Trans. Jack Hirschman and Alexander Altmann. Tree Text: 2. Berkeley: Tree, 1975.

Selections from: *The Book of Prophecy*, *The Book of Words*, and *Hokmath Ha-'Egoz*.

Secondary Sources

G11 Kaufmann, David. "A Hitherto Unknown Messianic Movement Among the Jews, Particularly those of Germany and the Byzantine Empire." *Jewish Quarterly Review*, o.s. 10(1898), 139-51.

Based on evidence from a letter found in the Cairo Geniza, Kaufmann concludes that in the eleventh century, there were "hopes of a rising of the ten tribes, especially among the Jews of the German Empire ... The belief in the ten tribes prevailed so strongly among the Jews of Germany, that not even the horrible awakening by the terrors and death blows of the crusades was strong enough to dispel the dream."

G12 Joseph, Morris. "The Introduction to the 'Rokeach.'" In A3. Pp. 171-90.

Analysis of the Introduction to Eleazar ben Jehudah ben Kalonymos of Worms' *Rokeach*, to conclude: "Medieval in form, its spirit transcends the limits of time, and mirrors the thoughts and yearnings of the great souls of every age. The work of a Jewish Rabbi, it witnesses to a saintliness of life and a longing for communion with the Highest that recall in another religious literature a Thomas a Kempis and an Augustine."

G13 Friedlaender, Israel. "Jewish-Arabic Studies: Shiitic Elements in Jewish Sectarianism." *Jewish Quarterly Review*, n.s. 1(1910-11), 183-215; 2(1911-12), 481-516; 3(1912-13), 235-300.

Detailed study of the interaction between Jewish and Shiitic sectarians.

G14 Schechter, Solomon. "Jewish Saints in Mediaeval Germany." In his A11. Pp. 1-24.

"In the book entitled *Tur Orah Hayyim* (The Path of Life) by R. Jacob b. Asher, which became the prototype of R. Joseph Caro's *Shulhan 'Aruk* there occurs a reference to the 'German Saints' [Hassidei Ashkenaz], who interpreted the very dots and traces of writing. The term has now become typical, and a certain historical meaning is now attached to it. It is those 'German Saints' whom I propose to introduce you to in this paper."

G15 Goitein, S.D. "A Jewish Addict to Sufism: In the Time of the Nagid David II Maimonides." *Jewish Quarterly Review*, n.s. 44(1953), 37-49.

"Thus far, the participation of Jews in the mystic sessions of Sufi masters had been attested to only by Muslim sources. It is now corroborated by the document published here, a letter found in the Cairo Geniza and preserved in the Taylor-Schechter Collection of the Cambridge Library, which will be shown to date from the period, when Sufic influence on the Jews was at its highest."

G16 Goitein, S.D. *Jews and Arabs: Their Contacts through the Ages*. New York: Schocken Books, 1955.

In this "book on the relationships between Jews and Arabs through the ages," Goitein devotes the fourth section of Chapter Nine to Islamic and Jewish mysticism (pp. 148-54), in order to demonstrate that: "In its earlier stages,... as has become evident recently, *Sufism* is a direct outcome of the ascetic trend of religiosity, prevailing in original Islam itself which, later, was supplanted and enriched by foreign sources, in particular Christianity and Buddhism. To these oft-discussed borrowings, we have to add those taken from Judaism."

G17 Harris, Monford. "The Concept of Love in *Sefer Hassidim*." *Jewish Quarterly Review*, 50(1959), 13-44.

"It is the aim of this study to present a critique of the love between man and woman as reflected and evaluated in *Sefer Hassidim* and to advance an historical explanation for the sudden appearance of this whole problem.... *Sefer Hassidim*, then, is mid-point between these two traditions--the patriarchal, Jewish, semi-puritan tradition, and the knightly, romantic, semi-hedonistic tradition which was typical of the upper strata of Christian society of the later Middle Ages."

G18 Altmann, Alexander. "Eleazar of Worms' *Ḥokhmath Ha-Egoz*." *Journal of Jewish Studies*, 11(1960), 101-12. Rpt. G27.

Explores the theme of the nut as an image of the *Merkabah* by first presenting relevant passages, and then discussing the theme "within the larger conspectus of Eleazar's mystical doctrine."

G19 Katz, Jacob. *Exclusiveness and Tolerance: Studies in Jewish-Gentile Relations in Medieval and Modern Times*. Oxford: Oxford University Press, New York: Schocken Books, 1962.

"This book sets out to throw light on the changes of attitude on the part of the Jews towards their non-Jewish environment during the Middle Ages and down to the Era of the Enlightenment." Chapter VIII, The *Hasid*, (pp. 93-105), asserts that "the religious revival of the Franciscans had its counterpart in Jewish history in the Hasidim of the age of Rabbi Judah *He-Hasid*."

G20 Harris, Monford. "Dreams in *Sefer Ḥasidim*." *Proceedings of the American Academy for Jewish Research*, 31(1963), 51-80.

"These thirteenth century pietists were interested in shaping a community's diurnal life. This pragmatic flair is equally evident in the dream material. While here and there are insights of high originality and great theoretical implications, the dream material in *Sefer Ḥasidim* is centered on the practical concern of deriving a practical lesson so that one might live a more pious and holy life."

G21 Singer, Sholom A. "An Introduction to *Sefer Ḥasidim.*" *Hebrew Union College Annual*, 35(1964), 145-55.

First defines the Pietist movement and then introduces: The Man, Judah ben Samuel, the Pious of Regensburg; *Sefer Ḥasidim*; The Pious; Pietism and Asceticism; and The Texts."

G22 Rubin, A. "The Concept of Repentance among the Ḥasidey 'Ashkenaz." *Journal of Jewish Studies*, 16(1965), 161-76.

Analysis of beliefs about repentance of the Ḥasidey 'Ashkenaz: "they not only believed in the efficacy of suffering and pain in achieving atonement--they were convinced of its absolute necessity. Repentance was an impossibility without ascetic acts."

G23 Dan, J. "Ḥokhmath Ha-'Egoz, Its Origin and Development." *Journal of Jewish Studies*, 17(1966), 73-82.

"We intend to add some information drawn from manuscripts of Ashkenazic-hasidic literature, which tend to show that some of 'Alexander Altmann's views about Ḥokhmath Ha-'Egoz [G18] have to be modified."

G24 Goitein, S.D. "Abraham Maimonides and His Pietist Circle." In A65. Pp. 145-64.

Explores the thesis "that the pietist movement among the Jews of the Muslim East was not confined to the circle of Abraham Maimonides and of his elder companion and perhaps guide, Abraham ibn Abu'l-Rabi'--that is, Solomon, *he-ḥasīd*. In any case, the movement embodied in Abraham Maimonides was very remarkable and deserves a special place in the history of religion at large. For Abraham united in one person three spiritual trends which were mostly opposed to each other: strict legalistic orthodoxy, ecstatic pietism, and Greek science--sober, secular humanism. He represented all the best found in medieval Judaism, as it developed within Islamic civilization."

G25 Soloveitchik, Haym. "Topics in the Ḥokhmath Ha-Nefesh." *Journal of Jewish Studies*, 18(1967), 65-78.

Exploration of three topics in Eleazar of Worms' Ḥokhmath Ha-Nefesh: I. The Structure of the Soul and Da'ath; II. The Origin of the Soul, its Sojourn in the Body, After-life; and III. Demuth [mirror images of man fashioned at the beginning of Creation].

G26 Marcus, Ivan G. "The Organization of the *Haqdamah* and *Hilekhoth Ḥasiduth* in Eleazar of Worms' *Sefer ha-Roqeaḥ.*" *Proceedings of the American Academy for Jewish Research*, 36(1968), 85-94.

"The author of several mystical works, Eleazar ben Judah of Worms (*ca*. 1160-*ca*. 1230) is best known for his halakhic compilation *Sefer ha-Roqeaḥ*. Eleazar prefaced this compendium with a *Haqdamah* and an introductory pietistic tract, the *Hilekhoth Ḥasiduth* (Laws of Saintliness). At first glance the *Haqdamah* appears to be '... a collection of maxims thrown together without much regard to order or subject.' However, a close analysis of the text will reveal a carefully arranged composition in which name-acrostics and word patterns reflect transitions in meaning and style."

G27   Altmann, Alexander. "Eleazar of Worms' Symbol of the Merkabah." In A71. Pp. 161-71.

Reprint of G18, without the critical edition of Text 4.

G28   Agus, Irving A. "The Use of the Term *Ḥakham* by the Author of the *Sefer Ḥassidim* and Its Historical Implications." *Jewish Quarterly Review*, n.s. 61(1970), 54-62.

"The term 'sage' in the *Sefer Ḥassidim*, therefore, is applied to an 'erudite scholar' when he is in the process of fulfilling his obligations toward his neighbors or his fellow Jews--religious obligations imposed upon him by Jewish public law, even though he was not elected for, nor was he appointed to, a public, salaried office. His talmudic scholarship alone imposes upon him these obligations."

G29   Dan, Joseph. "Rabbi Judah the Pious and Caesarius of Heisterbach: Common Motifs in Their Stories." In A79. Pp. 18-27.

"One of the main subjects which interested scholars, who studied the history and literature of the Ashkenaz, Hasidic movement in the twelfth and thirteenth centuries, was the nature and the degree of outside, Christian influences upon this movement. It is the purpose of this discussion to add some material to the enquiry into this problem by comparing supernatural stories contained in the writings of Rabbi Judah the Pious of Regensburg and of his Christian contemporary, the preacher Caesarius of Heisterbach."

G30   Soloveitchik, Haym. "Three Themes in the *Sefer Ḥasidim*." *AJS Review*, 1(1976), 311-57.

"... this essay questions whether the celebrated remarks of the *Sefer Ḥasidim* about *talmud torah* and *talmide hakamim* constitute a theoretical evaluation of these institutions and thus expressed a basic axiological critique, or whether these words arose from a distinct historic context and possessed a specific address. It is the Tosafist movement--surely not one of the more bashful events of Jewish history--which forms the backdrop to *Ḥaside 'Ashkenaz*. Much of the *Sefer*

Medieval Hasidism

Hasidim, both good and bad, is a product of and a response to the disruptive effects of the new dialectic. The Hasidic movement was a reaction to, and at the same time part of, the intellectual revolution that was sweeping Ashkenaz in the twelfth century."

G31 Mansoor, Menahem. "Arabic Sources on Ibn Pakuda's Duties of the Heart." In A101. III.81-90.

"In Bahya's times theology encountered philosophy. A real or alleged gap separated the world from God and there occurred a twofold reaction. Rationalists attempted to provide a firm intellectual and scientific grounding for religion. Mystics responded by overlooking the duality itself, denying that there was any world apart from God. In the Arabic sources available by Bahya, both responses appear.... The very fact that the *Al-Hidaya* ("Duties of the Heart") was written in Arabic leads one to speculate about Arab influence on the work. Though the work is replete with references to traditional Jewish teaching, Bahya's dependence on Islamic philosophers and moral ascetics is indisputable, though he fails to credit them explicitly in his work."

G32 Dan, Joseph. "Teraphim: From Popuar Belief to a Folktale." *Scripta Hierosolymitana*. Volume 27: *Studies in Hebrew Narrative Art Throughout the Ages*. Eds. Joseph Heinemann and Shmuel Werses. Jerusalem: Magnes Press at the Hebrew University, 1978. Pp. 99-106.

Study of the narrative aspects of interpretations of the *teraphim* (Genesis 31.16), among the Ashkenazic Hasidim.

G33 Marcus, Ivan G. "The Recensions and Structure of *Sefer Hasidim*." *Proceedings of the American Academy for Jewish Research*, 45(1978), 131-53.

"Yet, despite a considerable amount of subsequent scholarly debate, several problems concerning the textual development of the book remain unsolved. Among these, two separate but interrelated questions are especially perplexing: What is the relationship between the two published versions of the book? Can a substantive structure of the book as a whole be discovered? This essay intends to advance some new observations towards the solution of both problems."

G34 Dan, Joseph. "The Ashkenazi Hasidic 'Gates of Wisdom.'" In A111. Pp. 183-89.

Conclusions: "the method of interpretation of scripture according to a list of 'gates' was not invented by Rabbi Eleazar of Worms when he set out to write down his esoteric tradition after Rabbi Judah's death, that it was known to a wide circle of disciples of Rabbi Samuel the Pious and his son, Rabbi Judah, and thus comprised an integral part of Ashkenazi Hasidic tradition concerning the meaning and form of the Bible.... From a historical point of view, this seems to enforce the conclusion that Ashkenazi Hasidism should not be regarded as one school,..."

G35   Marcus, Ivan G. "The Politics and Ethics of Pietism in Judaism: The *Hasidim* of Medieval Germany." *Journal of Religious Ethics*, 8(1980), 227-58.

"Judah the Pietist's program of socio-religious innovation in *Sefer Hasidim* led to tensions in the medieval Rhineland Jewish communities between the norms of Jewish *piety* and the demands of a new version of Jewish *pietism*. Because Judah sought to impose his vision of God's complete will on other Jews (the politics of pietism), Pietists came into conflict with non-Pietist Jews in child rearing, choice of marriage partner, style of public worship and philanthropy. This tension (the ethics of pietism) was resolved when Judah's disciple, Rabbi Eleazar of Worms, adapted his teacher's program into an accepted form."

G36   Marcus, Ivan G. *Piety and Society: The Jewish Pietists of Medieval Germany*. Études sur le Judaïsme, v. x. Leiden: E.J. Brill, 1981.

"The German-Jewish Pietists constitute a case study of religious revival and adjustment, the first in medieval European Jewish history. Our concern here is to reexamine the Qalonimides and their followers as a religious sub-culture in pre-modern Jewish history and to understand the Pietist authors' goals and how they sought to reinterpret Judaism to achieve them. In the course of reconsidering the historical meaning of their pietistic works, such as *Sefer Ḥasidim*, it becomes clear that Samuel, Judah and Eleazar not only agreed with one another that the ideal Jew or *ḥasid* must pursue a personal goal of otherworldly salvation in a peculiar way, but they also differed about the social implications of their shared vision." The study is divided into three parts: The Shared Vision; Judah the Pietist's Sectarian Program; and Eleazar of Worms' Personal Transformation. In addition, there are three appendixes: I. The Complementary Structures of Pietism, Sin, and Atonement; II. The Authorship of the Major Pietistic Sources; and III. Penitential Terminologies in *Sefer Ḥasidim*.

G37   Marcus, Ivan G. "*Ḥasidei 'Ashkenaz* Private Penitentials: An Introduction and Descriptive Catalogue of their Manuscripts and Early Editions." In A117. Pp. 57-83.

"The Jewish Pietists of medieval Germany *(ḥasidei 'ashkenaz)* expressed and sought to implement their views on atonement in a variety of tracts and manuals which have not yet been surveyed and clearly differentiated from one another. Whereas a number of different texts bear the same title, identical ones sometimes have different names. After distinguishing between two functionally distinctive types, I present an annotated catalogue of the manuscripts and early editions of these texts." The two types are the "sage-penitential" and "private penitentials."

G38 Shatzmiller, Joseph. "Doctors and Medical Practice in Germany around the Year 1200: The Evidence of Sefer Hasidim." *Journal of Jewish Studies*, 33(1982), 583-93.

"I suggest that ... a study of *Sefer Hasidim* (The Book of the Pious), the well known compilation of some 2,000 Hebraic short moral stories *(exampla)*, composed around 1200 A.D., could provide us with a most welcome opportunity to learn concerning the status of the medical profession in *Ashkenazic* Jewish society and to ascertain the level of professionalism attained at that time."

H. The Crystallization of the Kabbalah

Primary Sources

H1 Lask, I.M., trans. "Every Man his Own Messiah." In A24. Pp. 21-29.

Abridged selection from *Ozar Eden Ganuz*, in which Abulafia "represented himself as the Messiah to both Christians and Jews. As a result of his own spiritual experiences and researches, he gave a new interpretation to the function of the Messiah, which he declared himself prepared to fulfil; but, as the following confessions indicate, it seems to have comprised the propagation of a method of individual and spiritual regeneration rather than of political salvation. Abulafia's account has been combined with that of an anonymous disciple who reflects the immense influence of the master."

H2 Newman, Jacob, trans. *The Commentary of Nahmanides on Genesis, chapters 1-6.* Pretoria Oriental Series, Vol. IV. Leiden: E.J. Brill, 1960.

Nahmanides' commentary to the first six chapters of Genesis is important for "To him philology is not always the last word in Biblical exegesis; he has an open mind, for mystical interpretation and allusions to Qabbalistic interpretation are found scattered throughout his work. The history of Jewish mysticism in medieval times ... has not been treated in a way which satisfies our just demand that it should be based on sound historical knowledge.... It is evident that a future historian ... could not pass by Nahmanides' work." After the Introduction and sections on The Secret Wisdom (Kabbalah), and Mysticism versus Philosophy, Newman provides the text, in both English and Hebrew, and notes.

H3   Silverstein, Shraga, trans. *The Gates of Repentance (Shaarei Teshuvah)*. The Torah Classics Library. Boys Town Jerusalem, and New York: Yaakov Feldheim, 1967.

Bi-lingual edition of an ethical treatise by Yohan ben Avraham of Gerona, based less upon mystical speculation than *halakhah* and *aggadah*, with emphasis upon social justice and ethics.

H4   Blumenthal, David R., trans. *The Commentary of R. Hoter Ben Shelomo to the Thirteen Principles of Maimonides*. Études sur le Judaïsme Médiéval, dirigées par G. Vajda, Tome VI. Leiden: E.J. Brill, 1974.

Analytic Introduction on The Author, The Philosophical Analysis and Some Grammatical Notes precedes The Translation and The Notes.

H5   *Iggeret Hakodesh*. In A87. Pp. 102-8.

Selections from *Iggeret Hakodesh*, attributed to Moses ben Nahman, on the subject of sex. The two themes treated are: "the subsequent effect of the thoughts of the couple on any child conceived during coitus"; and "the essential beauty or at least naturalness of sex--both act and organs."

H6   Cohen, Seymour J., trans. *The Holy Letter: A Study in Medieval Jewish Sexual Morality Ascribed to Nahmanides*. New York: Ktav Publishing House, 1976.

Bi-lingual edition, containing a critical introduction which discusses both the question of authorship and the meaning of the text.

H7   Meltzer, David, ed. *The Path of the Names, Writings by Abraham ben Samuel Abulafia*. Trans. Bruria Finkel, Jack Hirschman, David Meltzer and Gershom Scholem. Tree Texts: 4. London, Berkeley: Trigram, 1976.

Selections from *Sha'erei Zedek* (Gates of Justice), *The Question of Prophecy*, *Haye Olam Ha-Ba* (The Book of Eternal Life, or The Book of the Life of the Afterlife), and *Sefer Ha-Ot* (The Book of the Letter).

H8   Chavel, Charles B., trans. *Ramban (Nachmanides): Writings and Discourses*. 2 vols. New York: Shilo Publishing House, 1978.

Vol. 1: Discourses on A Wedding; The Law of the Eternal is Perfect; The Words of Koheleth; Rosh Hashanah. Vol. 2: Letter to the French Rabbis; The Gate of Reward; The Book of Redemption; The Disputation at Barcelona; Prayer at the Ruins of Jerusalem.

H9 Kaplan, Aryeh, trans. *The Bahir: An Ancient Kabbalistic Text Attributed to Rabbi Nehuniah ben HaKana, First Century C.E.* New York: Samuel Weiser, Inc., 1979.

Translation of one of the oldest and most important kabbalistic texts which marks the reappearance of myth within Judaism. Kaplan provides, in addition to the translation, a detailed introduction on the history and contexts of the treatise, notes to the Bahir, the Hebrew text, and an index. Kaplan divides the text into five parts: 1. The first verses of Creation (1-16); 2. The alphabet (27-44); 3. The Seven Voices and Sefirot (45-123); 4. The Ten Sefirot (123-93); and 5. Mysteries of the soul (194-200).

Secondary Sources

H10 Myer, Isaac. *Qabbalah. The Philosophical Writings of Solomon ben Yehudah ibn Gebirol or Avicebron, and Their Connection with the Hebrew Qabbalah and Sepher ha-Zohar, with Remarks upon the Antiquity and Content of the Latter, and Translations of Selected Passages from the Same. Also, An Ancient Lodge of Initiates, Translated from the Zohar, and an Abstract of an Essay upon the Chinese Qabbalah, Contained in the Book Called Yih King; a Translation of Part of the Mystic Theology of Dionysios, the Areopagite; and an Account of the Construction of the Ancient Akkadian and Chaldean Universe, etc.* Philadelphia: The Author, 1888. Rpt. New York: S. Weiser, 1970.

"The following pages are devoted to a short account of the life and writings of the philosopher, Solomon ben Yehudah Ibn Gebirol or Avicebron; proofs of the antiquity of the Zoharic writings and the Qabbalah, a condensed statement of some parts of the Qabbalistic philosophy, quotations from the Zoharic books, and various articles pertaining to the same, in Appendixes." Excerpts from the Zohar, Chapters 18 and 19 (pp. 335-414). Appendix A, An Ancient Lodge of Initiates, pp. 439-43.

H11 Neubauer, A. "The Bahir and the Zohar." *Jewish Quarterly Review*, o.s. 4(1892), 357-68.

Argues that orthodox rabbis should consider neither the Bahir nor the Zohar a work of authority since both texts have been proved to be spurious.

H12 Schechter, S. "Notes on Hebrew MSS. in the University Library at Cambridge." *Jewish Quarterly Review*, o.s. 4(1892), 245-55.

Describes MS. Add. 434, a unique, small, 230-page quarto in Spanish Rabbinic characters, in different hands, which is "the programme of the author, who thinks that the prayers, though introduced by the Men of the Great Synagogue, are nevertheless based not only on the Scriptures, but influenced also by the Aggadoth and the Midrashim." While the author cites a number of rabbinic sources, "Of more importance are his quotations from the [Sefer Hekhaloth] and the [Sefer Yetzirah], which greatly contribute to giving his work" a mystical character.

H13 Margoliouth, George. "The Doctrine of the Ether in the Kabbalah." *Jewish Quarterly Review*, o.s. 20(1908), 825-61.

Examination of the position which the doctrine of the ether occupies in thirteenth-century Jewish mysticism.

H14 Marx, Alexander. "An Aramaic Fragment of the Wisdom of Solomon." *Journal of Biblical Literature*, 40(1921), 57-69.

Discussion of passages from the Aramaic fragment of the Wisdom of Solomon which "are found in a commentary on the Zohar which was written in Spain, perhaps in Sargossa, in 1325 and has the title [Pavement of Sapphire]," by Joseph Angelino.

H15 Marmonstein, A. "Gnosis and Qabbala." *Search Quarterly*, 3(1933), 377-94.

Concludes that "one thing is quite clear, that there was a liberal and frequent give and take between the two many-times hostile camps. This interdependence became even more intensive at the time when the earliest attempts of the Qabbalists unearthed some long-forgotten and well-hidden treasures of the Gnosis and translated them into the language and re-wrote them in the style of the Qabbala."

H16 Sarachak, Joseph. *Faith and Reason: The Conflict over the Rationalism of Maimonides*. Williamsport, Pa.: Bayard Press, 1935. Rpt. New York: Hermon Press, 1970.

"The present study is the first attempt which has been made to give in connected form a history of the anti-Maimonidean controversy." In Part III, chapter 12, Rationalism and the Cabala (pp. 128-35), Sarachek explores the "age-old deposit, of layer upon layer of irrational thought derived from the many cultures with which Judaism had come into contact," in order to determine whether or not Kabbalah was "causally related to the anti-Maimonist sentiment of the time."

H17 Rosenthal, Franz. "A Judaeo-Arabic Work under Sufic Influence." *Hebrew Union College Annual*, 15(1940), 433-84.

Rosenthal studies "the treatise in the Ms. or. Hunt. 382, fol. 1b-57b (=Catalogue Uri No. 358 = Catalogue Neubauer No. 1422), which precedes the unique text of the Arabic original of Ibn Gabirol's Tikkun middot han-nefes," as "a rare example of the deep penetration of Sufic thought ... into the minds of certain of the intellectual Jewish elite. The same treatise seems likewise to be unique in its adaptation of Sufic terminology to Jewish modes of thought."

H18 Efros, Israel. "Some Aspects of Yehuda Halevi's Mysticism." *Proceedings of the American Academy for Jewish Research*, 11(1941), 27-41. Rpt. H38.

"It is the philosopher in whom, according to the summary of that viewpoint given at the beginning of the *Kuzari*, hereditary and environmental factors developed intellectual, moral, and practical capacities which, then perfected through instruction and training, cause a divine light to dwell with him so that he and the Active Intellect become one. Indeed reason was not only a condition but also, in itself, a reliable source of physical and metaphysical knowledge, even though slow, gradual, syllogistic, as compared with prophecy which gives truth in a timeless flash. It is this rationalism, both as metaphysics and epistemology, to which Halevi is opposed."

H19 Netanyahu, B. *Don Isaac Abravanel: Statesman and Philosopher*. Philadelphia: Jewish Publication Society of America, 1953.

Study of Don Isaac Abravanel, "Statesman, diplomat, courtier and financier of international reknown,... an encyclopedic scholar, a philosopher thinker, a noted exegete and a brilliant writer.... also a mystic and apocalyptist of the highest stature and influence." Part II, chapter 4, Messianism (pp. 195-257), asserts that "the messianic concept of Abravanel comprises all the aspects of his world outlook in its fullest and broadest sense. Consequently, it embodies drastic changes not only in the history of the Jewish people, but also in that of mankind as a whole, and it entails, in addition, cataclysmic changes in nature, especially manifested by the miracle of resurrection and by the absolute domination of the spirit over the flesh. In brief, this is the Messianism of the Jewish mystics and apocalyptists, and not of the realists and the rationalists.... This is not a worldly Messianism, although it is not otherly-worldly; it is not a heavenly paradise, although it is not an earthly one either. It is the dream of man in wonderland. It is something humanity has never experienced and never will, in the ordinary course of events. Hence it is not historical but post-historical. It belongs to the End of Days."

H20   Vajda, Georges. "The Mystical Doctrine of Rabbi 'Obadyah, Grandson of Moses Maimonides." *Journal of Jewish Studies*, 6(1955), 213-25.

Analyzes the Judeo-Arabic manuscript Oriental 661 of the Bodleian Library, the first document of which contains "an introduction to the spiritual life or, if you prefer, a guide to perfection.... The goal of spiritual progression is a kind of union with God."

H21   Altmann, Alexander. "Isaac Israeli's 'Chapter on the Elements' (Ms Mantua)." *Journal of Jewish Studies*, 7(1956), 31-57.

"A Ms. (28c) preserved in the *Biblioteca Comunale di Mantova* (Mantua) contains a Hebrew text entitled *Sha'ar ha-yesodot le-Aristo* ('Chapter on the Elements by Aristotle') which can be shown to represent a translation from the Arabic of a treatise written by none other than Israeli. A suggestion to this effect was put forward first by Prof. G. Scholem in a letter dated 18th July, 1955 to the present writer. The text is published here for the first time, and the attempt has been made to prove Israeli's authorship."

H22   Lehmann, O.H. "The Theology of the Mystical Book Bahir and Its Sources." In A39. I.477-83.

"The derivation of the Bahir originally from Mesopotamia explains its strange symbolism and gnostic imagery, its ready acceptance by the pious halachists in the west--Jewish philosophy and law were also derived from Babylonia--, on the other hand its close relation to Catharist, Manichaean, and Valentinian speculations. When the Catharist heresy was suppressed in the crusade against the Albigensians, the theology introduced by the Bahir continued to flourish. Far from being a late fabrication the Bahir contains remnants of old Jewish gnostic speculations. In fact, for the pre-Zoharic mystics the Bahir became almost a canonic book."

H23   Weiss, J.G. "A Contemporary Poem on the Appearance of the Zohar." *Journal of Jewish Studies*, 8(1957), 219-21.

"The present note seeks to shed light on a controversy then current within Spanish-Jewish society about the origin and value of the new mystical teaching by discussing" Todros ben Jehuda Abulafia's Poem No. 797.

H24   Altmann, Alexander. "The Motif of the 'Shells' (Qelipoth) in 'Azriel of Gerona." *Journal of Jewish Studies*, 9(1958), 73-80. Rpt. H36.

"In this paper research into the antecedents of the Zoharic concept of the *qelipoth* is carried a stage further by the attempt to trace yet another, hitherto unsuspected, literary source. 'Azriel of Gerona, a younger contemporary of Eleazar's [of Worms], is known to have influenced Moses de Leon in certain respects. We suggest that 'Azriel's notion of *qelipah* had a share in the evolution also of Moses de Leon's doctrine of the 'shells.'"

H25 Harris, Monford. "Marriage as Metaphysics: A Study of the *'Iggereth Hakodesh." Hebrew Union College Annual*, 33(1962), 197-220.

"It is in the thirteenth century Spanish Jewish community, a community in which *Woman* and marriage have become problematic that we find for the first time in the history of Jewish thought a treatise devoted completely to the mystical understanding of marriage, the *'Iggereth Hakodesh* usually attributed to Moses Nahmanides. It purports to be a personal letter written for the education and edification of a young man. Nothing is known of this young man. The letter is written on two levels, an exoteric and an esoteric. The exoteric furnishes the skeletal frame for the esoteric."

H26 Twersky, Isadore. *Rabad of Posquières: A Twelfth-Century Talmudist.* Cambridge: Harvard University Press, 1962.

"The following book on an outstanding medieval Talmudist, Rabad of Posquières, who lavishly enriched the major genres of halakic literature and perceptibly accelerated the development of a critico-conceptual method of halakic study, is offered as a modest contribution to this field of historical research." In the section "Rabad and Kabbalah" (pp. 286-300), Twersky concludes that "the teachings attributed to Rabad, as fragmentary and disjoined as they may be, are representative, adumbrating the nuclear motifs of its two major aspects: the devotional-practical aspect, that is, mysticism of prayer; and the speculative-theoretical aspect, that is, God and the sefirot."

H27 Altmann, A. "The Delphic Maxim in Medieval Islam and Judaism." In his A53. Pp. 196-232. Rpt. H33.

Explores the various meanings "associated in the medieval Islamic and Jewish mind with this exhortation to know oneself in order to know God." Considers specifically: 1. The Motif of the Soul's "Likeness" to God; 2. The Microcosm Motif; and 3. Soul and Intellect.

H28 Wijnhoven, Jochanan. "The Mysticism of Solomon Ibn Gabirol." *Journal of Religion*, 45(1965), 137-52.

"In this article we will consider first the major aspects in Gabirol's personality and thinking, which give us an insight into his mysticism. Then we will deal with the real and alleged traces that Gabirol has left in the history of Jewish mysticism, and with the scholarship that has treated his influence on the Kabbala."

H29   Wilensky, Sara Heller. "Isaac Ibn Latif's *The Gate of Heaven:* A Mystical Guide of the Perplexed." In A64. II.17-25.

"The peculiar contribution of Isaac ibn Latif to the development of Spanish Kabbalah is in the ontological, rather than the anthropological aspect of mysticism. As a result of his double disappointment--in both philosophy and Kabbalah--to which he explicitly testifies in his *Zurath ha 'Olam*, Latif embarks on his declared mission of guiding the perplexed of his time. To achieve this end he joins to Kabbalah Neoplatonic philosophy in general, and that of Gabirol in particular. In his interesting and unique attempt to strike a synthesis between Neoplatonic philosophy and Kabbalah, we observe the influence of the former upon the latter. We see rather clearly the process of transition from philosopher to Kabbalistic perceptions and we note how mystic symbols are born out of philosophic terms."

H30   Altmann, A. "'The Ladder of Ascension.'" In A67. Pp. 1-32. Rpt. H34.

Study of the allegorical interpretation of Muhammad's nocturnal journey from the "holy mosque" to the "'further mosque' ... which originally denoted the celestial sanctuary or the seventh heaven near the throne of Allah," as a type of "allegoricism [which] is neoplatonic in character, and for this reason it made an impact on medieval Jewish philosophers and mystics. The term *sullam ha-'aliyyā* which is found in medieval Hebrew literature derives from this impact."

H31   Altmann, Alexander. "Moses Narboni's 'Epistle on *Shi'ur Qōma.*'" In A65. Pp. 225-54. Rpt. H35.

After briefly summarizing the reactions of Jewish philosophers and kabbalists to the *Shi'ur Qōma*, "the most obnoxious document of Jewish mysticism," Altmann presents Moses Narboni's epistle on the subject, and then explores the reasons why Narboni dealt with the *Shi'ur Qōma*.

H32   Wilensky, Sara O. Heller. "Isaac Ibn Latif--Philosopher or Kabbalist?" In A65. Pp. 185-223.

Explores this borderline figure whose contribution "to the development of speculative Kabbala is in the ontological, rather than the anthropological, aspect of mysticism. In his interesting and unique attempt to strike a synthesis between neoplatonic philosophy and Kabbala, we observe the influence of the former upon the latter."

H33 Altmann, Alexander. "The Delphic Maxim in Medieval Islam and Judaism." In his A71. Pp. 1-40.

Reprint of H27.

H34 Altmann, Alexander. "The Ladder of Ascension." In his A71. Pp. 41-72.

Reprint of H30.

H35 Altmann, Alexander. "Moses Narboni's 'Epistle on *Shi'ur Qoma.'*" In A71. Pp. 180-209.

Reprint of H31, excluding the critical edition of the Hebrew text of the "Epistle" and annotated English translation.

H36 Altmann, Alexander. "The Motif of the 'Shells' in Azriel of Gerona." In A71. Pp. 172-79.

Reprint of H24.

H37 Hruby, K. "Jewish Mysticism from Provence to Safed." *Encounter Today*, 8(1973), 95-97, 99, 140-44.

Unavailable for annotating.

H38 Efros, Israel Isaac. "Some Aspects of Yehudah Halevi's Mysticism." In his A86. Pp. 141-54.

Reprint of H18.

H39 Sharf, A. *The Universe of Shabbetai Donnolo*. Warminster, Engl.: Aris & Phillips Ltd., and New York: Ktav, 1976.

Studies the cosmology which emerges from Shabbetai Donnolo's *Sefer Ḥakhmoni*, a commentary on the *Sefer Yetzirah* because: "Firstly, some of its elements are original and valuable in their own right.... Secondly, his cosmology blinds in a striking way the mystical and obscure with the plain and practical.... Thirdly, his cosmology can be related to his surroundings." The book has seven chapters: 1. Shabbetai Donnolo and the Sefer Ḥakhmoni; 2. The Rule of the Stars; 3. The Celestial Dragon; 4. Man the Microcosm; 5. Man in God's Image; 6. Donnolo and Byzantine Medicine; 7. Byzantine Jewry and Donnolo's Universe; and four appendices: Texts; Donnolo and the Baraita de Mazzalot; Comparative Melothesia and Stellar Analogues; and Byzantine and Muslim Rulers of the Tenth Century.

H40 Blumenthal, David R. "Maimonides' Intellectual Mysticism and the Superiority of the Prophecy of Moses." *Studies in Medieval Culture*, 10(1977), 51-67.

"It will be the thesis of this paper that, for Maimonides: (1) The phenomena of prophecy fall within that which the modern world can rightly call 'intellectualist mysticism'; (2) that the phenomena of providence, cognition, and piety also fall within the definition of 'intellectualist mysticism'; (3) that the prophetic experience, unlike the mystical experience, had special socio-political functions; and (4) that in both the mystical and the socio-political conceptualizations, the prophecy of Moses was superior and unique."

H41 Blumenthal, David R. "An Illustration of the Concept of 'Philosophic Mysticism' from Fifteenth Century Yemen." In A111. Pp. 291-308.

Illustration of Georges Vajda's theory "that the philosophic and mystical traditions meet at the point where knowledge, experience, and piety intersect," through the doctrine of prophecy in the thought of Hoter ben Shelomo, a fifteenth-century Yemenite savant.

H42 Matt, Daniel Chanan. "David ben Yehudah Hehasid and His *Book of Mirrors*." *Hebrew Union College Annual*, 51(1980), 129-72.

"An important feature of the *Book of Mirrors [Sefer Mar'ot Hazove'ot*, 13-14 century] is the large number of passages from the Zohar which R. David translates into Hebrew from the original pseudo-Aramaic. His renderings represent the first lengthy translations of the Zohar.... In fact, he appropriates the literary format of the Zohar ... in order to introduce his own teachings. The Zohar thus becomes a model and a springboard for creative mystical exegesis.... The second half of this article discusses his original formulations in the context of 13th century Kabbalah. These include: the relation of the mystic to the Infinite; the doctrine of *'Eser Ẓaḥẓahot*, ten translucent lights which precede the emanation of the Sephirot; and the independent quality of Shekhinah, who is described as *Sod Ha'efshar*, the Secret of the Possible."

H43 Shahar, Shulamith. "The Relationship between Kabbalism and Catharism in the South of France." In A114. Pp. 55-62.

"The existence of similarities is not an indisputable proof of mutual influence between the Cathars and the Kabbalists. The similarity could also be the result of autonomous developments in each of these sects, and expression of motifs and ways of thought which developed in different religious groups close to one another in atmosphere and in the fundamental problems which concerned them, rather than the result of mutual influence between them. Nevertheless, while not indisputable, this evidence of similarity does constitute a prima facie case for assuming the existence of mutual influence between the sects."

H44 Faierstein, Morris M. "'God's Need for the Commandments' in Medieval Kabbalah." *Conservative Judaism*, 36,1(Fall 1982), 45-59.

"This article will deal with the Kabbalistic response to the problem of *ta'amei hamiẓvot*, the reasons for the commandments. It will attempt to trace the theoretical understanding of *ta'amei hamiẓvot* rather than deal with reasons for specific miẓvot. Though this problem is important for understanding kabbalistic theology, it was not dealt with by kabbalists until Menachem Recanati's *Sefer Ta'amei Hamiẓvot*, where the first significant theoretical explanation is found. The issue has not as yet been dealt with by the modern students of Kabbalah. Therefore, this article will attempt to trace the dominant motifs of *ta'amei hamiẓvot* in the development of Kabbalistic thought as a preliminary to more intensive investigations."

H45 Funkenstein, Amos. "Nahmanides' Symbolical Reading of History." In A117. Pp. 129-50.

Determines five reasons why, in contrast to the Christian exegetical tradition, "Nahmanides' typological attempts are limited despite the promising methodological declarations he made.... (1) Caution. Nahmanides was aware of the force of the figurative imagination in Christianity and of its consequences.... (2) Even Nahmanides did not altogether shift the focus from the apocalyptic to the structural implications of figural interpretations, especially of the days of creation.... (3) The speculative energies of Nahmanides and his generation were concentrated in theosophical rather than historiographical issues.... (4) Even where the early kabbalah indulges in historical speculations, these are, as in the *Sefer ha-temunah*, much more detached from the content and attached to the form of Scriptures, to letter-and-name symbolism.... (5) Typologies, and for that matter all forms of historical speculations in Christianity, express a distinct sense of steady progress *within* history: progress from the old to the new dispensation, progress within the further history of the *ecclesia militans et triumphans*, extensive progress (mission) as well as intensive progress (articulation of faith and dogma). Jews lacked such a sense of progress and hence the desire to show how matters repeat themselves periodically on a higher level."

H46 Lieber, David. "Response to Amos Funkenstein." In A117. Pp. 151-52.

Criticism of Funkenstein's last point in H45, "which he considers to be the most fundamental. Christianity, which has a sense of progress in history, he suggests, avails itself more readily of typological, or what [Erich] Auerbach characterizes as 'figural interpretation.' Traditional Judaism, on the other hand, is 'outside the turmoil of history' and has no special need for this kind of hermeneutics."

I. The Zohar

Primary Sources

I1 Mathers, S. Liddell MacGregor. *Kabbala Denudata, The Kabbalah Unveiled, Containing the Following Books of the Zohar: The Book of Concealed Mystery, The Greater Holy Assembly, The Lesser Holy Assembly. Translated into English from the Latin Version of Knorr von Rosenroth, and Collated with the Original Chaldee and Hebraic Text.* London: Redway, 1887. New ed. London: Routledge & K. Paul, 1926, 1954. Rpt. New York: S. Weiser, 1968; New York: Weiser, and London: Routledge & Kegan Paul, 1970; and New York: Krishna Press, 1974.

I2 Myer, Isaac. *Qabbalah: Quotations from the Zohar and Other Writings, Treating of the Qabbalistic or Divine Philosophy.* New York: The Author, 1893.

Printed from the *Oriental Review:* "We will now give some quotations from the Zoharic and other Qabbalistic writings, to show the estimation in which the Qabbalists held the primordial Thought, and the Word of the Unknown Deity as Its first manifestation."

I3 *Hebrew Literature; Comprising Talmudic Treatises, Hebrew Melodies and the Kabbalah Unveiled.* Intro. Epiphanius Wilson. New York: Colonial Press, 1901.

In an anthology intended to "give a good idea of ... interest, beauty, and subtlety of thought" of Hebrew literature, Mathers' translation (I1) of "The Lesser Holy Assembly" (pp. 301-61) is included as an example of the "profound spirituality of [the Hebrew] philosophical mysticism."

I4 Manhar, Nurho de, trans. "The Sepher Ha-Zohar; or, the Book of Light." *Word,* 5(1907), 8-18, 86-100, 155-68, 237-48, 303-14, 344-49; 6(1907-8), 48-56, 116-24, 184-92, 248-56, 376-81; 7(1908), 54-64, 121-24, 185-90, 246-53, 313-18, 379-83; 8(1908-9), 57-64, 126-28, 188-89, 314-18; 9(1909), 53-56, 252-53, 306-10, 372-76; 10(1909-10), 58-62, 116-21, 187-90, 250-54, 313-17, 376-80; 11(1910), 123-27, 187-90, 247-54, 307-15, 368-77; 12(1910-11), 56-59, 186-89, 381-82; 13(1911), 59-62, 121-26, 374-84; 14(1911-12), 60-64, 120-28, 188-92, 251-56, 381-84; 15(1912), 125-27, 185-88, 251-

54, 307-16, 377-82; 16(1912-13), 189-91, 311-16, 376-80; 17(1913), 316-18, 379-83. Rpt. I8.

"Containing the doctrines of Kabbalah, together with the discourses and teachings of its author, the great Kabbalist, Rabbi Simeon ben Jochai, and now for the first time translated wholly into English, with notes, references, and expository remarks." Contains the Prologue, Bereshith and Lech Lecha.

I5 Scholem, Gershom G. "Cheiromancy in the Zohar." *Quest*, 17(1926), 255-56.

Translation of *Zohar* (II.74 a,b), a "highly symbolical passage ... partly bearing on cheiromancy as perhaps of special interest to those who would study the history of this curious form of 'divination' which has won a new popularity in our own day."

I6 Sperling, Harry, and Maurice Simon, with Paul P. Levertoff, trans. *The Zohar*. Intro. J. Abelson. 5 vols. London and New York: Soncino Press, 1931-34. Rpt. London and New York: Soncino Press, 1973; New York: Rebecca Bennett Publications, 1977.

I7 Scholem, Gershom G., ed. *Zohar: The Book of Splendor*. New York: Schocken Books, 1949, 1963. Sel. rpt. I9.

Attempts "to present ... a sequence of passages which might be expected to arouse an immediate interest in the reader: by the colorfulness with which the life of the soul is pictured, by the curious poignancy of scriptural exegesis, by the outright paradoxicality of the thoughts asserted." After an introduction on The Historical Setting of the Zohar, Literary Character, and Origin and Authorship, Scholem "selected such passages as would throw light on the mystical ideas concerning God, together with the various stages of his manifestation, and on the idea of the soul, its grades and its destiny, as taught by the Zohar."

I8 Caplan, Samuel, and Harold U. Ribalow, eds. *The Great Jewish Books and Their Influences on History*. New York: Horizon Press, 1952. New York: Washington Square Press, 1963.

"The aim of this volume is to present, in popular form, the essence of those masterworks of Jewish literature which have most decisively molded the life of the Jewish people from their earliest beginnings down to the present era." In the section devoted to Moses de Leon (pp. 191-213), Jacob B. Agus provides an introduction to the composition, message and influence of the Zohar, and two brief selections: "Serve the Lord with Gladness," and "An Allegorical Explanation of Jonah."

I9   Scholem, Gershom, ed. "The Tree that Reaches into Both Worlds: Selections from the Zohar." *Commentary*, 14(1952), 485-88.

   Selections from I7.

I10 Shahn, Ben. *The Alphabet of Creation: An Ancient Legend from the Zohar*. With drawings by Ben Shahn. New York: Schocken Books, 1954.

   "*The Alphabet of Creation* is one of the legends from the *Sefer Ha-Zohar*, or *Book of Splendor*, an ancient Gnostic work written in Aramaic by ... Moses de Leon who presented the work ... as mystic knowledge revealed many centuries earlier to Rabbi Simeon ben Yohai." In a free interpretation from the English translation of Maurice Samuel and other sources, Shahn "turned the words and letters into a kind of visual magic in which the true spirit of the wonderful is magnificently suggested. There are forty-six pictures all together, and twenty-two letters of the Hebrew alphabet and twenty-four drawings."

I11 Glatzer, Nahum N., ed. "Mystic Drama of Jerusalem: From the Zohar." *Commentary*, 21(1956), 365-66.

   Selections to "illustrate the typical blend of the rational and the supernatural, the heavenly and the earthly, which is Jerusalem."

I12 Runes, Dagobert D., ed. *The Wisdom of the Kabbalah, as Represented by Chapters taken from the Book Zohar*. New York: Philosophical Library, 1957.

   Contains "The Greater Holy Assembly," "Taken with only essential revisions, from the English translation by S.L. MacGregor Mathers" (I1).

I13 *Sifra Detzniyutha*. Work of the Chariot, 2. Hollywood: Work of the Chariot, 1971.

   Text, translation and commentary; no translator or editor cited.

I14 Horowitz, Michael, ed. *A Freak's Anthology: Being a Golden Hits from Buddha to Kubrick*. Edited with Countercultural Commentary. Los Angeles: Sherbourne Press, Inc., 1972.

   Selections from and commentary on the *Zohar*, pp. 81-93.

I15 Rosenberg, Roy A., trans. *The Anatomy of God: The Book of Concealment, The Greater Holy Assembly and The Lesser Holy Assembly of the Zohar, with The Assembly of the Tabernacle*. New York: Ktav Publishing House, 1973.

"Taken together, these three texts offer a coherent and poetic account of the emanation of God as the Holy Ancient One, the Small Countenance and the Shekhinah, a process that resulted also in the emergence of the physical universe. The Assembly of the Tabernacle is a smaller composition that focuses part of The Zohar to the Book of Exodus." In addition to the translation, Rosenberg provides a general introduction to the Zohar, separate introductions for each text, and an Index of Scriptural Citations.

I16 Zahavy, Zev, ed. *Idra Zuta Kadisha: The Lesser Holy Assembly*. New York: Sage Books, Inc., 1977.

"The purpose of the ensuing modest enterprise is to offer the serious student of Kabbalistic literature an opportunity to delve into the recondite Aramaic text, by placing a convenient translation at its side. Through such an exercise, it is felt, the researcher in Kabbalah mysticism may become more proficient in discerning the clandestine connotation of the symbolic terminology." The English is Mathers' (I1), and the Aramaic text is taken from the Vilna edition of *Sefer ha Zohar*, 1894.

I17 Sassoon, George, trans., and Rodney Dale, ed. *The Kabbalah Decoded: A New Translation of the "Ancient of Days" Texts of the* Zohar. London: Duckworth, 1978.

Contains four Zoharic texts: "The Greater Holy Assembly," "The Lesser Holy Assembly," "The Book of Mystery" and "The Assembly of the Tabernacle." Neither Sassoon nor Dale is a linguist or an Hebraist, but they feel that this makes them more qualified to deal with what they consider "essentially technical descriptions,... written in a simple form of a simple language."

I18 Manhar, Nurho de, trans. *Zohar: Bereshith, Genesis: an Expository translation from Hebrew. Complete with Three Hundred Paragraphs of Footnotes Extracted from the Secret Doctrine, Exordium, and Copious Notes Assembled and Compiled by John Drais.* Secret Doctrine Reference Series. San Diego: Wizards Bookshelf, 1980.

Reprint of I4.

Secondary Sources

I19 Rubinsohn, Theoph. "The System of the Jewish Cabbalah, as Developed in the Zohar." *Bibliotheca Sacra and American Biblical Repository*, 9(1852), 563-81.

Intention is to prove "that the Zohar cannot be Rabbi Simeon's production in the entire form in which we now have

it; and ... that if the author of the Zohar lived in the
thirteenth century, the chief principles of the system are,
however, not his own, but of high antiquity; and as to the
sources from which he has taken them, it is indifferent
whether they were Christian or Jewish, written or traditional."

120 Fluegel, Maurice. "Philosophy and Qabbala: The Zohar, Copernicus and Modern Astronomy." *Menorah*, 29(1900), 77-84.

Translates and analyzes *Zohar* III, pages 9 and 10, in order
to determine why this passage, which predates Copernicus,
discusses a cosmos in which a circular earth revolves around
the sun: "But it was no forgery; it was gems mixed up with
the dust, and thus it may be that our modern astronomy had
been anticipated by the ancients."

121 Gaster, Moses. "The Origin and Antiquity of the Zohar."
Israel's Messenger, (Shanghai), 3,10(Ellul 3rd 5606/24
August 1906). Ed. N.B. Ezra.

Unavailable for annotating.

122 Pick, Barnhard. "The Zohar and Its Influence on the Cabala."
Open Court, 24(1910), 233-43.

After introducing the *Zohar* through discussions of the Name
and Contents of the Zohar and the Question of Authorship,
Pick explores the History of the Development of the Cabala in
the Post-Zohar Period through Sabbathai Zevi and Jacob Frank,
to conclude that "The Cabalists of the eighteenth century,
with the exception of Moses Chayim Luzzatto (born 1707, died
1747), are of little importance. Modern influences gradually
put a stop to the authority of the Cabala, and modern Judaism
sees in the Cabala in general only a historical curiosity or
an object of literary historical disquisitions."

123 Waite, Arthur Edward. *The Secret Doctrine in Israel: A Study
of the Zohar and Its Connections*. New York: Occult Research Press, n.d. London: William Rider & Son, Ltd.,
1913. Boston: Occult & Modern Thought Book Centre, 1914.
Rpt. Mokelumne Hill, Calif.: Health Research, 1976.

"... a work of critical analysis and collation for the
exposition of Zoharic doctrine on the several subjects indicated by the teachings of its sections, and this has been
attempted for the specific purpose of proving that behind
each and all there lies a single radical and essential thesis
which is spoken of in general terms as the Mystery of Faith.
It is this thesis which constitutes the vital part of the
Secret Doctrine in Israel." Waite surveys the major topics
covered in the Zohar, Occult Sciences, Developments of Later

Kabalism, The Alleged Christian Elements, and Jewish Theosophy.

I24 Gaster, M. "A Gnostic Fragment from the Zohar: The Resurrection of the Dead." *Quest*, 14(1923), 452-69. Rpt. I25.

Analysis of the "Midrash Hane'elam" ("The Hidden or Veiled Midrash") to demonstrate that "It had been taken over from a special Gnostic school and adapted to the Biblical text in a very deft manner"; and a translation in which "I am simply joining together the portions which seem to belong to one continuous text referring to death and resurrection, leaving out all the Biblical references which have been adjusted in such manner to the text as to form the apparent basis for this interpretation which has been placed upon the original."

I25 Gaster, M. "A Gnostic Fragment from the Zohar: The Resurrection of the Dead." In his A12. I.369-86.

Reprint of I24.

I26 Bension, Ariel. *The Zohar in Moslem and Christian Spain*. London: G. Routledge and Sons, Ltd., 1932. Rpt. New York: Sepher-Hermon Press, Inc., 1974.

"The principal idea of this research is not only to judge the immediate influences which each brought to bear on the other, through a close cultural contact, but more especially to draw attention to that particular mystical atmosphere to which the mysteries of Spain were subjected, and to that spirit of fantastic adventurousness with which all currents of Spanish life were impregnated. Furthermore, I trust this book will succeed in dissipating the prejudices created by the anti-Kabbalists, and in proving that, despite the doubts surrounding its authorship, the time of its composition, and the place of its origin, the ethical and aesthetical value of the Zohar is indisputable." Study is divided into three parts: Before the Exile; The Zohar; and After the Exile.

I27 Garstin, E.J. Langford. "The Doctrine of 'The Son' in the Zohar." *Search Quarterly*, 3(1933), 286-302.

"As a conclusion it will therefore suffice to point out that it is by virtue of 'Son element' alone in man that he can achieve his destiny; that it is, as it were, the rescuing force operating in him whereby the equilibrated and exalted Ruach, raised to that degree where it can be considered as Daath or Tetragrammaton, is united to Elohim, so that the 'full Name,' as it is called, appears, which is Tetragrammaton Elohim. Not altogether inappropriately, therefore, have the Christian Qabalists, wishing thereby to denote the Christ state, added the letter Shin, the symbol of Ruach Elohim, to the Tetragrammaton, forming therefrom the name Jeheshua, whereby they denote Jesus."

128 Levertoff, Paul P. "Some Aspects of Jewish Mysticism." *Journal of the Transactions of the Victoria Institute, or, Philosophical Society of Great Britain*, 65(1933), 71-87.

Quotes a few brief passages from the *Zohar* and other works of Jewish mysticism, and then explains them.

129 Stern, S.M. "Rationalism and Kabbalists in Medieval Allegory." *Journal of Jewish Studies*, 6(1955), 73-86.

Analysis of Isaac ibn Abi Sahula's *Meshal Ha-Kadmoni* which contains passages from the Zohar, "to give an account of the social and religious tendencies of the *Meshal Ha-Kadmoni* as far as they may be discerned."

130 Ashlag, Yehuda. *An Entrance to the Zohar: Key to the Portals of Jewish Mysticism*. Ed. Philip S. Berg. Jerusalem and New York: Research Centre for Kabbalah, 1974.

Compilation and translation of commentary by Rabbi Yehuda Ashlag, to "prepare the student with proper guidelines, fundamental rules correlating to the general principles contained in the text, defined limits to which the Zohar does or does not allude to, and finally the unraveling of its mystical terminology. When a mastery of this introduction will have been achieved, the individual will then find the portals to the Zohar unlocked." The commentary is divided into two main categories: A Preface to the Zohar, and An Introduction to the Zohar.

131 Wijnhoven, Jochanan H.A. "The Zohar and the Proselyte." In A92. Pp. 120-40.

"The following is an analysis and commentary upon ten passages in the Zohar dealing with the proselyte. Together they form, as one could say, Moses de Leon's 'theology of the proselyte.'" The passages are: Under the Wings of the Shekhinah; Abraham, the Proselyte in the Sefirot; The Guests at the Banquet; Jethro the Proselyte, Bringer of Wisdom; The Soul of the Convert and the Discourse of the Donkey Driver; The Golden Calf and the Proselyte; The Proselyte and Those who Stood at Sinai; The Heavenly Schoolmaster and the Soul of the Proselyte; The Proselytes in the Days of the Messiah; and Ruth, the Proselyte.

J. Isaac Luria and His School

Primary Sources

J1 Bloch, Chaim. "Legends of The Ari." Trans. Clifton P. Fadiman. *Menorah Journal*, 14(1928), 371-84, 466-77.

"Selections from Chaim Bloch's collection of Chassidic legends centering in the famous Cabalist, Isaac Luria ha-Levi, called ha-Ari (The Lion).... The tales themselves ... are significant, it is worth noting, not only as a narrative transformation of Cabalistic lore, but also as an authentic and indigenous outgrowth of the Jewish mythopoeic faculty. As such they may well furnish a basis for further investigation into the sources and qualities of late medieval Jewish folklore."

J2 Kaplan, Mordecai M., trans. *Mesillat Yesharim: The Path of the Upright by Moses Hayyim Luzzatto*. Philadelphia: Jewish Publication Society of America, 1936, 1964.

Bi-lingual edition.

J3 Glatzer, Nahum N., ed. "Rules for the House of Study: An 18th-Century Religious Document." *Commentary*, 11(1951), 480-83.

Moses Hayyim Luzzatto's regulations governing the study group founded by Luzzatto in Padua.

J4 Jacobs, Louis, trans. *The Palm Tree of Deborah*. London: Valentine, Mitchell, 1960. New York: Sepher-Hermon Press, 1974, 1981.

"Moses Cordovero (1522-1570), a leading figure in the inner circle of mystics in sixteenth-century Safed, was one of the most profound and systematic exponents of the teachings of the Zohar. In *The Palm Tree of Deborah* he presents a detailed program of observances and attitudes of mind by means of which the ideal of the 'Imitation of God' may be realized. In its ten chapters, each of which is devoted to one of the ten *Sephiroth*, he shows how the *Sephiroth* can be 'perfected' by man's deeds and thoughts in the light of the qualities each *Sephirah* reveals."

J5 Cohen, Seymour J., trans. *Orchot Tzaddikim. The Ways of the Righteous*. Jerusalem: Feldheim Publishers, 1969.

Bi-lingual edition of a compilation of Luria's teaching and personal traits as found in the writings of Hayyim Vital (Salonika, 1770).

J6 Luria, Isaac, and Hayyim Vital. *Tree of Life.* Work of the Chariot, 6. 2nd ed. Los Angeles: Work of the Chariot, 1970.

   Text, translation and commentary; no editor or translator cited.

J7 Luzzatto, Moses Hayyim. *General Principles of the Kabbalah.* Trans. Research Centre of Kabbalah. New York: Press of the Research Centre of Kabbalah, distributed by S. Weiser, 1970.

   A textbook for beginners, compiled from the writings of Luzzatto. Divided into two parts: A Detailed Outline of the Wisdom of the Kabbalah, and Luzzatto's explication of the major aspects of Lurianic Kabbalah.

J8 Marmorstein, Jenny, trans. "The Way of the Tree of Life." *Tradition*, 11,3(Fall 1970), 46-67.

   "Thanks to a renaissance talent harnessed to the Kabbalah, [Moses Hayyim Luzzatto] was in a position to play an influential role in the distribution of Lurianic concepts and insights from small groups of adepts to the widest circles of literati Jews. The following work, in English for the first time, represents this aspect of his endeavour. Based on the *magnum opus* of Luria's outstanding disciple, Chaim Vital (1543-1620) it contains an outspoken defense of mystical study and an ardent call to engage in it."

J9 Kaplan, Aryeh, trans. *Derech haShem: The Way of God; and An Essay on Fundamentals: Ma'amar haIkkarim.* Jerusalem and New York: Feldheim Publishers, 1977.

   "Besides being a brilliant thinker, however, Rabbi Moshe Chaim Luzzatto was also a foremost Kabbalist. All his writings therefore take into account the teachings of Kabbalah with all their depth. To a large measure, the system presented in this work is that which is assumed by the Kabbalah, and therefore, it finds itself right in the center of the mainstream of Jewish thought. Besides this, even though this is not a Kabbalistic work, it can serve as an excellent introduction to the subject."

Secondary Sources

J10 Isaacs, A.S. *A Modern Hebrew Poet: The Life and Writings of Moses Chaim Luzzatto.* New York: Office of "The Jewish Messenger," 1878.

   "In the following essay, the author has suggested the forces which tended to mould Luzzatto's manner of life and thought." Believing mysticism to be a guiding force in the life of Luzzatto, Isaacs first sketches the development of Jewish mysticism, and then briefly traces the life of Luzzatto in order to demonstrate "that every fresh trial, every new wondering, only developed in a greater degree the mystical tendencies of Moses Chaim Luzzatto."

J11 Schechter, S. "Safed in the Sixteenth Century: A City of Legists and Mystics." In his A5. Pp. 202-306. Rpt. J20, J24.

Analyzes the fame of the city as provided by the eminence of two of its sixteenth-century residents, R. Joseph Caro and R. Isaac Luria. Appended to the essay in the original edition are four lists of moral precepts and usages observed by the saints of Safed (in Hebrew), and a list of the names of the sages and saints of sixteenth-century Safed.

J12 Hersch, Emil G. "R. Moses 'Hayim Luzzato's 'Path of the Righteous.'" In A7. Pp. 147-64.

Studies Luzzatto's *Path of the Righteous* as a treatise on rules of conduct which "attempts to throw light on the foundations rather than the facts of consecrated conduct. It is oriented towards philosophy much more intently than towards practice. Sound comprehension of the ends at which moral conduct aims is its important solicitude. Practice is seen to be the outflow of principle, conduct the offspring of conviction."

J13 Spiegel, Shalom. "A Messiah." In his A17. Pp. 27-45.

General discussion of Moses Chaim Luzzatto.

J14 Ginzburg, Simon. *The Life and Works of Moses Hayyim Luzatto: Founder of Modern Hebrew Literature.* Philadelphia: Dropsie College, 1931. Rpt. Westport, Conn.: Greenwood Press, 1975.

Presents an "English sketch of Luzzatto's life and works,... some new facts relating to his life, a short appreciation of his cabbalistic and rabbinic writings, and a more extended appreciation of his dramatic and lyric poems. This [is] followed by a discussion of his place and rank in Hebrew literature,... and of his style.... Finally a selection of some most important letters is given, so that the letters serve as an appendix to the sketch or the sketch serves as an introduction to the documents." Chapter 4 (pp. 77-89) covers Luzzatto's kabbalistic works.

J15 Krakovsky, Levi Isaac. *The Kabbalah: A Study of Rabbi Isaac Luria's "Tree of Life."* Brooklyn: National Institute for Research in Kabbalah, 1942.

"The aim of the author is to present to the reader a popular version of the Kabbalah, which will open for him a door to the heretofore unrevealed and inexhaustible fountain of sublime Kabbalah wisdom." After the Introduction, Krakovsky discusses: Spiritual Substance and Its Symbolic Representation; God the Source of All; The Divisions of the Soul; The Language of the Kabbalah; The Ten Luminous Emanations; Kabbalistic Terminology; and Questions and Answers on Kabbalistic Matters.

J16 Menes, Abraham. "The Ethical Teachings of Moses Hayim Luzzatto." *Proceedings of the American Academy for Jewish Research*, 17(1947-48), 61-68.

"A close analysis however, will show us that even the Mesillat Yesharim [of Luzzatto] is thoroughly permeated with an exalted messianic mysticism."

J17 Gordon, Hirsch Loeb. *The Maggid of Caro: The Mystic Life of the Eminent Codifier Joseph Caro, as Revealed in His Secret Diary*. Based on Unpublished Manuscripts. New York: Pardes Publishing House, Inc., 1949.

Introduced by "a biography, in order to penetrate the trait of Caro's personality.... The authenticity of Caro's authorship is established in the next chapter while two more chapters discuss the various means of communication between God and man accepted by men of faith. A revaluation of the traditions that other men, besides Caro, were granted the grace of a Maggid, has also been made. In the last chapter an attempt is made to 'diagnose' the 'Case of Joseph Caro' on the basis of the numerous events of his long, rich, and creative life, his unusual environment and unique cultural background."

J18 Bokser, Ben Zion. *From the World of the Cabbalah: The Philosophy of Rabbi Judah Loew of Prague*. New York: Philosophical Library, 1954. London: Vision Press, 1957.

Study of an "important figure who helped pave the way for the" transformation of Kabbalah from a movement whose "language abounds in all kinds of strange imagery" into its hasidic form, as a movement which "re-establishes its contact with reality, and takes as its goal the hallowing of life, not its transcendence." Discusses: I. The World of the Cabbalah; II. A Portrait of the Master; III. Human Destiny; IV. Faith and Reason; V. Judaism and Christianity; and VI. The Legacy of Rabbi Judah.

J19 Tishby, I. "Gnostic Doctrines in Sixteenth-Century Jewish Mysticism." *Journal of Jewish Studies*, 6(1955), 146-52.

Studies the Lurianic doctrines of the "Breaking of the Vessels" and the "Fall of the Sparks," because "Yet in

Lurianic Kabbalism we see before us a broad pattern of mythical Gnosis which, in its structure and tendencies, comes very close to Manicheism. The mere fact of the existence of a late gnostic-manicheistic system in Judaism might well invalidate the assumption prevalent in many studies on the subject that the growth of Gnosticism can only be understood as the result of a collision and coalescence of pagan mythological with monotheistic religions."

J20 Schechter, S. "Safed in the Sixteenth Century: A City of Legists and Mystics." In his A42. Pp. 231-97.

Reprint of J11.

J21 Werblowsky, R.J. Zwi. "Mystical and Magical Contemplation: The Kabbalists in Sixteenth-Century Safed." *History of Religions*, 1(1961), 9-36.

Purpose is "to describe the varieties in the techniques and practice of meditation and contemplation as exemplified by one apparently homogeneous and narrowly circumscribed group.... the remarkable community of saints that lived in Safed in Upper Galilee in the sixteenth century and which brought about the great kabbalistic renaissance that influenced Judaism for many generations to come." The two types of contemplation are the mystical and the magical, "in the sense that they [kabbalists] assume 'scientific,' albeit esoteric, causal laws regulating our connections with 'higher' spheres."

J22 Werblowsky, R.J. Zwi. *Joseph Caro: Lawyer and Mystic*. Scripta Judaica-IV. London: Oxford University Press, 1962.

A study of Joseph Karo's "halakhic activity, his kabbalistic speculations and his intimate mystical life." Contains chapters on: 4. Spiritual Life in Sixteenth-century Safed: Mystical and Magical Contemplation (pp. 38-83); 9. The Doctrine of the Sefiroth (pp. 189-205); 10. The Living Garment of the Deity: *Shekinah* (pp. 206-33); and 11. Man and his Soul (pp. 234-56). Appendix F discusses The Mystical Life of the Gaon Elijah of Vilna (pp. 307-12).

J23 Ashlag, Yehuda L. *The Kabbalah: A Study of Ten Luminous Emanations from Rabbi Isaac Luria, with Two Commentaries Sufficient for the Beginner Called: Inner Reflecting and Inner Light*. Trans. Levi I. Krakovsky. 2 vols. Old City Jerusalem: Research Centre for Kabbalah, 1969-73.

Volume I covers: Spiritual Substance and Its Symbolic Representation; The Language of the Kabbalah; Ten Luminous Emanations or Spiritual Substances; The Tree of Life-- Contraction and Line of Light; The Inner Reflection; Kabbalistic Terminology; Questions and Answers. Volume 2 has two parts: I. Explaining the Ten Circular Sefirot that were revealed after the Restriction, surrounded by the Light of the Endless, and how these Circular Sefirot receive Light from the Line; and II. Explaining the Ten Sefirot of Straightness, their emergence, their devolvement, and what they comprise. The volume concludes with a discussion of Inner Reflection.

J24 Schechter, S. "Safed in the Sixteenth Century: A City of Legists and Mystics." In A75. Pp. 258-321.

Reprint of J11.

J25 Shamir, Yehudah. *The Spider and the Raven: Six Kabbalists of Sixteenth Century Safed.* Austin, Texas: by the author, 1971.

"This is the first draft for a book to include an essay researching the Kabbalah of Safed in the sixteenth century." After the Introduction, Shamir discusses: Solomon Alkabez; Moses Cordovero; Moses Alshekh; Abraham Galante; Hayim Vital; and Israel ben Moses Najara.

J26 Newman, Eugene. *Life & Teachings of Isaiah Horowitz.* London: by the author, 1972.

"This study, based on original sources, is the first systematic presentation of 'The Life and Teachings of Isaiah Horowitz' (ca. 1570-1626).... His work, originally published in Amsterdam in 1649, comprises Halakhah, Kabbalah (mysticism), Exegesis, Homiletics, Liturgy, Ethics and Methodology of Talmud, to each of which Isaiah Horowitz made a distinct contribution as will be shown in the following pages." Chapter 16, Isaiah Horowitz as Kabbalist (pp. 141-69), presents Horowitz as "an eclectic, who explains and expounds the ideas and theories of the former Kabbalists, especially those who follow the Zohar."

J27 Barzilay, Isaac. *Joseph Shlomo Delmedigo (Yashar of Candia): His Life, Works and Times.* Studia Post-Biblica. Leiden: E.J. Brill, 1974.

Comprehensive study of Yashar (1591-1655), including a section on Yashar and the Cabbalah which discusses: The Historical Development of the Cabbalah in Italy and Poland (pp. 223-39); Yashar's Attitude to the Cabbalah (pp. 240-59); In the Domain of Spiritualism and Occultism (pp. 260-79); *Masref La-Hokhmah:* A Concealed Anti-Cabbalistic Work (pp. 280-91); and Philosophication of the Cabbalah and Its Failure (pp. 292-96).

J28 Borowitz, Eugene B. "TZIMTZUM: A Mystic Model for Contemporary Ledership." *Religious Education,* 69(1974), 687-700.

"I believe we can find a fresh model for contemporary leadership in the mystic speculations about God of Isaac Luria (1534-1572) of Safed in the Holy Land.... I herely [sic] follow Ludwig Feuerbach's insight that statements about God are, in fact, projections of our sense of what it is to be a person. Hence to Feuerbach, concepts of God are essentially concepts of man and theses about the way God relates to his creatures are implicitly theses about the way people ought to relate to each other."

J29 Bland, Kalman P. "Neoplatonic and Gnostic Themes in R. Moses Cordovero's Doctrine of Evil." *Bulletin of the Institute of Jewish Studies*, 3(1975), 103-29.

"Beyond the intrinsic value of an exposition in English of Cordovero's conception of evil, such a work might to serve to fulfill an important task for the historian of Jewish mysticism. Looking back to the *Zohar* and chronologically preceding Luria, Cordovero occupies a position in the watershed out of which the new Kabbalah emerged. The Lurianic revolution can only be gauged in the light of what Cordovero taught. Given the centrality of the problem of evil in Luria, it is crucial to possess a clear view of what Cordovero said on this issue."

J30 Ashlag, Yehuda. *An Entrance to the Tree of Life: A Key to the Portals of Jewish Mysticism.* Ed. Philip S. Berg. Old City Jerusalem and New York: Research Centre of Kabbalah, 1977.

"This work is an introduction to a major Kabbalistic treatise by Rabbi Isaac Luria known as 'The Tree of Life.' It was written by Rabbi Judah Ashlag, a contemporary writer of great stature in the interpretation of the Lurianic system. In a broader sense, the 'Introduction' surveys the concepts of Jewish mystical thought by the technique of posing pertinent questions and, then, in the second part of the work begins a more technical explanation of the specific development of spiritual forces as understood by Rabbi Luria--the Ari. As such, this book forms a link in the chain of esoteric works that gives one an insight into the concepts of the Kabbalah." (Editor's note)

J31 Patai, Raphael. "Exorcism and Xenoglossia among the Safed Kabbalists." *Journal of American Folklore*, 91(1978), 823-33.

"In the following, I first summarize the Kabbalistic beliefs about sin and the *post mortem* punishment which followed it, secondly discuss the rituals and incantations performed for the purpose of exorcising spirits from the persons of whom they took possession in order to escape their punishment, and thirdly present a sample account of a case of spirit possession and exorcism written by an eyewitness and containing a rare instance of xenoglossia."

J32 Bokser, Ben Zion. "Rabbi Judah Loew of Prague." *Proceedings of the Rabbinical Assembly*, 40(1979), 128-38.

Unavailable for annotating.

J33 Werblowsky, R.J. Zwi. *"O Felix Culpa:* A Cabbalistic Version." In A109. Pp. 355-62.

Examination of Rabbi Isaiah Horowitz's (known as SHeLaH) doctrine of *felix culpa* in which "Adam's sin is the major and decisive mechanism of purification by precipitating and then ejecting the latent elements of evil. In other words, SHeLaH applies--albeit in a mitigated form--the Lurianic scheme of *qelipah*, evil and a cathartic process, to man's 'original sin,' rather than to a primordial event in the recesses of the creating godhead."

J34 Schimmel, Solomon. "Education of the Emotions in Jewish Devotional Literature: Anger and Its Control." *Journal of Religious Ethics*, 8(1980), 259-76.

"This paper analyzes the discussions of the emotion of anger in medieval Jewish devotional literature, particularly as summarized and interpreted in the 16th century ethical-mystical treatise *Reshit Hochma* by Elija de Vidas. Among the issues considered are the causes of human anger, its moral and theological status, its relationship to broad dispositions of character and religious attitudes, and affective cognitive and behavioral methods for controlling it. The paper also notes the tension and even conflict, explicit or implicit, between the attitudes of Jewish law and those of Jewish devotional literature towards material possessions and the acceptance of economic misfortune." (Abstract)

J35 Robinson, Ira. "Messianic Prayer Vigils in Jerusalem in the Early Sixteenth Century." *Jewish Quarterly Review*, 72(1981), 32-42.

Analysis of the messianic speculation of Abraham ben Eliezer ha-Levi (1460?-1530?), a Spanish Kabbalist who "argued that the Messiah will come in the year A.M. 5290 (1530 C.E.), and that the decade prior to his advent will be marked by events demonstrating the immanence of Israel's redemption. In the face of this advent and in anticipation of the accompanying 'birthpangs,' Abraham called for universal repentance by Jews as individuals and as a community. He also called the Jews to prayer."

J36 Schorsch, Ismar. "The Holocaust and Jewish Survival." *Midstream*, 27,1(1981), 38-42.

"The catastrophic expulsion of Spanish Jewry in 1492 has often been pointed to as an instructive model for post-Holocaust Jewry. The relative size of the communities, the traumatic psychic effects, and the length of time required to formulate a viable theological response all seem comparable. Conspicuously, however, students of the Holocaust have failed to explore the utility of Lurianic Kabbalah for neutralizing the theological waste left in the debris of Hitler's Europe, despite the universal celebration of its primary expositor, Gershom Scholem."

J37 Sherwin, Byron L. *Mystical Theology and Social Dissent: The Life and Works of Judah Loew of Prague*. Littman Library of Jewish Civilization. Rutherford, New Jersey: Fairleigh Dickinson University Press, 1981.

J38 Altmann, Alexander. "Lurianic Kabbala in a Platonic Key: Abraham Cohen Herrera's *Puerta del Cielo*." *Hebrew Union College Annual*, 53(1982), 317-55.

"In what follows an attempt is made to depict the manner in which Abraham Cohen Herrera tried to reconcile, at varying levels, Lurianic Kabbala with Italian Renaissance Platonism, of which he was a belated representative. It will be shown that he recognized both the possibilities and severe limitations of harmonizing Kabbala in its highly developed form with the *philosophia perennis*. He succeeds best in the relatively simple coordination of the basic structure of the Lurianic system (à la Vital) and the neoplatonic ontology. He is less sure and hence inclined toward a variety of options when it comes to specifics such as the triadic pattern of the supernal world above the *Sefirot*, and especially so when confronting the often bewildering features of the Lurianic cosmogony. Yet he manages to find surprising analogies even for such outspoken mythological elements as the death of the primordial kings, restitution and rebirth. What is completely missing is the messianic orientation and a sense of salvation being imminent, something he might have caught from Lurianism. The final part of the paper deals with Herrera's multifaceted yet unambiguous effort to impart a neoplatonic significance to Luria's innovative and daring theory of *zimzum*. As the introductory section points out, Herrera considered Kabbala a divinely revealed and esoterically transmitted body of truths that was independent of rational verification, yet could be comprehended, in large measure, by human understanding." (Abstract)

J39 Fine, Lawrence. "Maggidic Revelation in the Teachings of Isaac Luria." In A119. Pp. 141-57.

"The phenomenon of maggidism which developed within Kabbalistic communities in the sixteenth century constitutes an extremely interesting example of mystical experience. This study seeks to elucidate the theory of maggidic revelation in the teachings of Isaac Luria. The sources for our knowledge of Luria's doctrine of maggidism are *Sha'ar Ruah ha-Qodesh* and *Sha'ar ha-Yihudim*, versions of his teachings formulated by Hayyim Vital."

J40 Fine, Lawrence. "Recitation of *Mishnah* as a Vehicle for Mystical Inspiration: A Contemplative Technique Taught by Hayyim Vital." *Revue des études juives*, 141(1982), 183-99.

"The aspect of his spiritual life with which we are concerned here in the present study is Hayyim Vital's continuous efforts to achieve altered states of consciousness and merit esoteric communications and revelations. Specifically, we will consider a unique meditative technique which Vital himself developed and practiced for such purposes."

J41 Krabbenhoft, Kenneth. "Structure and Meaning of Herrera's *Puerta del cielo.*" *Studia Rosenthaliana*, 16(1982), 1-20.

In *Puerto del cielo*, Abraham Cohen de Herrera "casts the basic issues of cabala in a mold that takes in far more than the doctrines of the medieval masters and the Safed school of the sixteenth century, including the remarkable Ari: he embraces the entire history of Platonic theology from the pagan authorities Pythagoras and Plato, Plotinus and Proclus, to the Christian Pseudo-Dionysus, scholasticism and the Spanish theologians Francisco Suárez and Domingo Báñez. Furthermore, he wrote in Spanish, and while this, along with Portuguese, was the language of everyday communication and the secular arts in the Sephardic community, the languages of Cabala were then biblical Hebrew and Aramaic, as they always had been."

K. Shabbateanism and Mystical Heresy

Primary Sources

K1 Scholem, Gershom. "A Sabbathaian Will from New York." *Miscellanies of the Jewish Historical Society of England*, 5(1948), 193-211. Rpt. K5.

Presents the will of Gottlieb Weble, "a member of the Sabbathaian sect in Prague, who later (1849) settled in America as a member of a group of Sabbathaian families ... It is ... the latest document written by a Jewish Sabbathaian who obviously never abandoned the basic tenets of the doctrine which he was taught in his father's house."

K2 Eybeschutz, Jonathan. "Babel, the Flood, and Space Travel: A Cabbalist's View." Trans. Shabtai Rosenne. *Commentary*, 29(1960), 63-64.

Selections from Eybeschutz's commentary on the Tower of Babel which appears in his *Tiferet Yonatan*.

K3 Scholem, Gershom. "The Sprouting of the Horn of the Son of David: A New Source from the Beginnings of the Doenme Sect in Salonica." In A57. Pp. 368-86.

Translation of a manuscript containing texts ascribed to Nathan of Gaza, and a preface to the text of the Eighteen Commandments which "served as the basis for the organization of the first nucleus of apostates ... The name of our treatise is 'The Sprouting of the Horn of the Son of David.' Its purpose is to explain why the Redemption had not yet come even though the Messiah had already revealed himself in the world. The answer is: the Princes of the Nations obstructed it.... The historical importance of the tale under discussion is that we can see from it how the historical life of Sabbatai Zevi becomes progressively obscured, starting immediately after his death: mystic legend replaces the events."

K4 Salomon, H.P. "Midrash, Messianism and Heresy in Two Spanish-Hebrew Hymns." *Studia Rosenthaliana*, 4(1970), 169-80.

Translation and study of two Spanish hymns in Hebrew letters, interspersed with Hebrew words, found in the two-part pamphlet, *Shir Emunim* and *Shir Neeman*, found in Amsterdam, 1793; the hymns reflect medieval kabbalistic traditions and possibly Sabbathaian influences.

K5 Scholem, Gershom. "A Sabbathaian Will from New York." In his A81. Pp. 167-75.

Reprint of K1.

K6 Frank, Yakov. *Sayings*. Trans. Harris Lenowitz. Berkeley, Oakland: Tree/Tzaddikim Book, 1978.

Collection of sayings based on the Hebrew of N. Sokolow, derived from A. Kraushar's quotations from Polish recensions of Frank's sayings.

Secondary Sources

K7 Anon. *A True and Exact Account of a Famous New Prophet Now Residing at Alkair, a City in Egypt, 1687, Faithfully Translated from the Aegyptian Language by Rabbi Ben Haddi*. London, 1687. Rpt. K23.

A letter purported to be of Egyptian origin, used by Christian conversionists against the Jews.

K8 Anon. *The Devil of Delphos, or the Prophets of Baal: Containing An Account of a Notorious Impostor, Call'd Sabatai Sevi, Pretended Messiah of the Jews, in 1666. Who Afterwards Turn'd Turk: And of Many Other Impostors in Church and State; as, False Christs, and False Prophets from the Rise of Christianity to the Present Times.* London, 1708.

In a book intended "to shew thee the Danger that many have fallen into thro' the Delusions of pretended Prophets, who have not been wanting to appear in almost all Ages of the World," *The Devil of Delphos* contains a section on Sabatai Sevi, The Pretended Messiah of the Jews in the Year 1666 (pp. 56-73), "because it borders very much on the same Ground with the Pretensions of our Prophets. For the Messiah which the Jews expect, has been a great Snare to them, and produced as many Warnings of his Coming, as the Christian Notion of the Return of Christ to live and reign a Thousand Years on Earth, and call home the Jews, and build a new Jerusalem."

K9 Asher, D. "The History of the Sabbatheans." *Voice of Jacob*, 5, #113(10 October 1845), 4.

One-page summary (perhaps from his *Outline of the Jewish Religion; in a Series of Questions and Answers for the Use of Schools and Families* [Manchester: the author, 1845]?).

K10 Schauffler, William G. "Shabbathai Zevi and His Followers." *Journal of the American Oriental Society*, 2(1851), 1-26.

After a brief biography of Shabbetai Zevi, and a kabbalistic explanation of his claim to be the Messiah, Schauffler provides an English translation of "a communication, addressed to me by one of their chief men [contemporary Sabbatian], in which the writer makes a simple and candid statement of some of the articles of their faith."

K11 Schechter, S. "The 'Baalshem'--Dr. Falk." *Jewish Chronicle*, 9 March 1888, pp. 15-16.

Discussion of the contents of Falk's diary.

K12 Gaster, Moses. "Messiahs and False Messiahs." *Jewish World*, 10 December 1897; 7 January, 11, 18 February; 11, 18 March 1898.

Lecture delivered by Gaster on the subject of False Messiahs. The fourth part (11 March 1898) is devoted to "the period of Cabbalah, where mysticism and esoteric speculations take the place either of legal decisions or of clear interpretation of the law."

K13 Ezra, N.E.B. "Shabbethai Sebi: The Pseudo-Messiah." Lecture delivered before a meeting of the Literary Circle of the Shanghai Zionist Association on Sunday, 18th November, 1906. *Israel's Messenger*, 30 November 1906.

Summary of the history of Shabbetai Zevi to warn of "the 'false prophets' who vainly seek to glorify themselves by aspiring undeserved positions in the history of Israel."

K14 Adler, H. "The Baal Shem of London." *Transactions of the Jewish Historical Society of England*, 5(1908), 148-73.

"I fear that I shall have to ... cast something of a shadow upon a character that has hitherto loomed before the mind of Anglo-Jewry encircled with a halo," Samuel Jacob Hayyim Falk, and his kabbalistic practices.

K15 Hills, Gordon P.G. "Notes on Some Contemporary References to Dr. Falk, the Baal Shem of London, in the Rainsford MSS. at the British Museum." *Transactions of the Jewish Historical Society of England*, 8(1915-17), 122-28.

References by Charles Rainsford, an eighteenth-century occultist, found in the Rainsford MSS 23644 to 23680 in the Catalogue of Additional MSS.

K16 Bernheimer, Carlo. "Some New Contributions to Abraham Cardoso's Biography." *Jewish Quarterly Review*, n.s. 18(1927-28), 97-129.

Summary and Hebrew edition, primarily containing biographical information, of a new-found writing of Abraham Cardoso.

K17 Kastein, Joseph [Julius Katzenstein] *The Messiah of Ismir: Sabbatai Zevi*. Trans. Huntley Paterson. London: John Lane, and New York: Viking Press, 1931.

Fictionalized version of the life of Shabbetai Zevi.

K18 Fearnsides, W.E. "Sabbatai, The Turkish Messiah." *Papers of the Manchester Literary Club*, 61(1935), 81-92.

Biographical sketch of Shabbetai Zevi which concludes that "*He* was surely the true leader and statesman who led [the Jews] wisely out of a state of subservience into the enjoyment of full citizenship and co-operation; and *he* was the true prophet who interpreted to them the will of Jehovah, not along the lines of Moses but as applying to their difficulties and the circumstances of their times."

K19 Zeitlin, Solomon. "Remarks on the Sabbatai Zevi Movement." In A20. Pp. 34-36.

Analysis of one of the causes of the popularity of the Shabbetean movement: "the great catastrophe of the Ukraine Jews in the years 1648-49, in which were seen signs of the Messiah, since according to the doctrines of the Kabbalists, suffering and disaster must precede his coming."

K20 Buber, Martin. "Spinoza, Sabbatai Zevi, and Baalshem." In his A29. Pp. 95-116.

Reprint of part of L111.

K21 Cohen, Mortimer J. "Was Eibeschuetz a Sabbatian?" *Jewish Quarterly Review*, 39(1948-49), 51-62.

Examines the contention of Scholem (C45), and Moshe Arie Perlmuter (in *R. Yehonatan Eibeschuetz Ve'yahaso el Ha'shabtaut*, in Hebrew) that Eibeschuetz was a Sabbatian to conclude that while it unlikely, we cannot be certain.

K22 Leveen, Jacob. "An Autograph Letter of the Pseudo-Messiah Mordecai ben Hayyim of Eisenstadt." In A30. I.393-99.

An introduction to the pseudo-messiah Mordecai of Eisenstadt, and a transcription of a letter he wrote to Abraham ben Michael Raphael Rovigo, "a wealthy Jewish scholar of Modena, a Cabbalist and follower of Shabbethai Sebhi." The letter provides new information about Mordecai's life, as well as a revelation of himself as "the Messiah, the son of David, for the Soul of David shines within me."

K23 Schnur, Harry C. "Sabbatai Zevi--The Cabalistic Messiah." In his A32. Pp. 159-234.

Explains the phenomenon of the false messiah "who shied from martyrdom, [yet] managed to become a myth in his lifetime and to exert an influence that inspired a mass movement on a tremendous scale," as the result of "The religious intensity of Jewish homesickness ... the nation's longing for rehabilitation, for redemption in freedom." Appendix I (pp. 229-232), contains a reprint of K7.

K24 Duker, Abraham G. "The Tarniks (Believers in the Coming of the Messiah in 1840)." In A34. Pp. 191-201.

"Evidently, the Tarniks were sufficiently widespread to create a problem in some Jewish communities in Eastern Europe, so much so, that the fear arose among the rabbinical leadership lest the disappointment engendered by the Messiah's failure to come that year would result in apostasy, along the lines of the debacle that followed Sabbatai Zevi's conversion to Islam in 1666. Evidence of this fear is to be found in folk tales."

K25 Greenberg, Hayim. "Sabbatai Zevi--The Messiah as Apostate." In his A33. II.84-98.

Deals with the questions: "Why did Sabbatai Zevi become an apostate? How did it come about that the man who considered himself the redeemer of his people, the Messiah, the messenger of God announcing the salvation of the world, bowed his head before the Sultan's court Mufti, donned a Turkish turban and adopted the Moslem name Mohammed?"

K26 Ben-Zvi, Itzhak. *The Exiled and the Redeemed*. Trans. Isaac A. Abbady. Philadelphia: Jewish Publication Society of America, 1957, 1961.

"... study of three different categories of Jews: 1. Jews belonging to communities that were originally dispersed in Moslem countries.... 2. Certain religious sects that consider themselves to this day as belonging to the House of Israel, and whose members continue openly ... to observe Jewish religious practices in their own way.... 3. Certain groups of Jewish extraction who were coerced by their Moslem conquerors into adopting the Moslem faith." Book II, chapter 2, The Sabbateans of Salonica (pp. 110-28), discusses: 1. Sources of Information; 2. Communal Structure and Organization; 3. Their Liturgy; and 4. Sabbateans in Modern Turkey.

K27 Buber, Martin. "Spinoza, Sabbatai Zvi, and the Baal-Shem." In his A47. Pp. 89-112.

Different translation of part of L111.

K28 Scholem, Gershom. "In Search of Sabbatai Zevi." *Hadassah Magazine*, 41,10(1961), 4-5.

Unavailable for annotating.

K29 Simonsohn, S. "A Christian Report from Constantinople Regarding Shabbethai Sevi (1666)." *Journal of Jewish Studies*, 12(1961), 33-58.

Description and transcription of "a letter from Constantinople of the 15th December, 1666. It contains a full report on Shabbethai Sevi and his movement until after his apostasy. It is unsigned,... It contains 16 pages, written in a clear Italian hand of the 17th century. From the absence of a signature it would appear to be either a copy or a translation of the original letter."

K30 Duker, Abraham G. "The Mystery of the Jews in Mickiewicz's Towianist Lectures on Slavic Literature." *Polish Review*, 7,3(Summer 1962), 40-66.

"Thus the idea of the mystical synthesis or symbiosis of the Jews and Poles, to which the poet [Adam Mickiewicz] alluded so often in his *Lectures on Slav Literature*, continued foremost in his thoughts until his death. This idea as we see runs parallel if not closely to Frankist notions about the place of the Jews in Poland. To conclude, Mickiewicz's mysticism cannot be understood without taking into account Frankist influences."

K31 Lewis, Geoffrey L., and Cecil Roth. "New Light on the Apostasy of Sabbatai Zevi." *Jewish Quarterly Review*, n.s. 53(1962-63), 219-25.

A "hypothetical" reading of the apostasy of Shabbetai Zevi, based on an allusion made by Edward Browne in his *Brief Account of Some Travels in Hungaria, Servia &c.* (London, 1673, p. 58), to a Turkish song.

K32 Roth, Cecil. "The King and the Cabalist." In his A52. Pp. 139-64.

Relationship between Samuel Jacob Hayyim Falk and Theodore King of Corsica.

K33 Duker, Abraham G. "Polish Frankism's Duration: From Cabbalistic Judaism to Roman Catholicism and from Jewishness to Polishness--A Preliminary Investigation." *Jewish Social Studies*, 25(1963), 287-333.

"This is an attempt to reconstruct in part the journey of the Polish followers of the false messiah Jacob Frank (d. 1791) away from the extremist Cabbalistic Judaism of the 'Higher Torah' into the Roman Catholic Church and Polish belongingness, some generations after their insincere baptism at the end of the 1750's. Particular attention will be given to a famous branch of the Frankist large Wolowski clan, namely, the family of Maria Wolowska Szymanowska, the first Frankist musical artiste of note whose daughter, Celina, was married to Poland's outstanding poet, Adam Mickiewicz."

K34 Zenner, Walter P. "The Case of the Apostate Messiah: A Reconsideration of the Failure of Prophecy." *Archives de sociologie des religions*, 21(1966), 111-18.

Uses the example of the Shabbatian movement to explore the paradox that when a prophecy fails to be fulfilled, the movement around the prophet should disintegrate; however, "this does not occur. The aim of this paper is to examine this aspect of a messianic movement, using some hypotheses about reactions to the 'failure of prophecy.'"

K35 Alter, Robert. "Sabbatai Zevi and the Jewish Imagination." *Commentary*, 43(June 1967), 66-71.

Studies modern attitudes towards Sabbatai Zevi to conclude that "perhaps ... there is a greater truth in [Isaac Bashevis] Singer's fictional version of Sabbatianism than in [Gershom] Scholem's massive reconstruction of it [K41], for Singer knows in the very quick of his imagination what Scholem understands finely but often seems unwilling to concede--that the would-be redeemer opened the gates to a world of chaos, not of redemption."

K36 Scholem, Gershom. "The Crisis of Tradition in Jewish Messianism." In his A81. Pp. 49-77.

Analysis of the Sabbatian movement which "first encompassed the collective Jewish community and later broke into radical and sectarian forms, and into forces smoldering beneath the surface--in all of this affecting wide circles of the Jewish people in Europe and the Near East."

K37 Scholem, Gershom. "The Crypto-Jewish Sect of the Dönmeh (Sabbatians) in Turkey." Trans. Michael A. Meyer. In his A81. Pp. 142-66.

"The phenomenon with which I shall deal in the following pages represents one of the strangest and most paradoxical episodes in the history of the Jewish religion. In concerns the existence of an important religious group which nearly three hundred years ago voluntarily left Judaism, or rather the religious framework of the social and religious organization of the Jewish people. Its members became formally Muslims but remained Jews at heart--though Jews of a most peculiar kind. They continued as a separate entity, preserving their Jewishness in this twofold existence. Deeply motivated, even fanatical adherents of a Jewish mystical heresy, they succeeded in maintaining their identity almost untouched for more than two hundred and fifty years. Moreover, with amazing success they shrouded everything pertaining to their beliefs and religious practices with an impenetrable veil of secrecy. There are few sects in the recent history of religions like the crypto-Jewish sect of the Dönmeh. It has existed for centuries, been known both in its environment and, later, through the literature, yet scholars have had very little trustworthy information on which to proceed. It is therefore not surprising that reports concerning the sect in the scholarly literature on religions are most sparse. This has been true less because of lack of interest than because of the extreme paucity of information that was available to the outside world."

K38 Scholem, Gershom. "The Holiness of Sin." Trans. Hillel Halkin. *Commentary*, 51(January 1971), 41-70. Rpt. under title "Redemption Through Sin," K39.

"Since its original appearance in Hebrew in the mid-30's under the title 'Mitzvah ha-Ba'ah ba-Averah,' Scholem's study of those Jews of the 18th and 19th centuries who clung to their belief in the Messiahship of Sabbatai Zevi even after his conversion to Islam, has been widely regarded as one of the classics of modern Jewish scholarship and one of the great works of the historical imagination in our time." (Editor's note)

K39 Scholem, Gershom. "Redemption through Sin." In his A81. Pp. 78-141.

Reprint of K38.

K40 Yerushalmi, Yosef Hayim. *From Spanish Court to Italian Ghetto: Isaac Cardoso--A Study in Seventeenth-Century Marranism and Jewish Apologetics.* New York: Columbia University Press, 1971.

Exploratory attempt to combine inquisitorial documents with rabbinic sources, Iberian with Hebrew literature, Peninsular social history with Jewish communal history, "and to see what can be learned by applying them to one man: the seventeenth-century Marrano physician, philosopher, and apologist, Isaac Cardosa." In Chapter 7, Abraham, Isaac, and the Messiah (pp. 302-49), Yerushalmi studies the effects of the Sabbatian movement on the Marranos, as it is revealed in the conflict between Isaac Cardoso and his brother Abraham, "the prime architect of postconversion Sabbatian ideology."

K41 Scholem, Gershom. *Sabbatai Ṣevi: The Mystical Messiah, 1626-1676.* Trans. R.J. Zwi Werblowsky. Bollingen Series XCIII. Princeton: Princeton University Press, 1973.

"The present work is a synthesis that offers a comprehensive history of the movement up to the deaths of Sabbatai Ṣevi and of his prophet, Nathan of Gaza,... In this book I hope to prove that those sources which historians have tended to regard with particular contempt are the very sources which can make an essential contribution to an understanding of the period. What I have in mind are the documents of kabbalistic literature and the theological writings of the followers of Sabbatai Ṣevi." The study is divided into seven parts: 1. The Background of the Sabbatian Movement; 2. The Beginnings of Sabbatai Ṣevi (1626-1664); 3. The Beginnings of the Movement in Palestine (1665); 4. The Movement up to Sabbatai's Imprisonment in Gallipoli (1665-1666); 5. The Movement in Europe (1666); 6. The Movement in the East and the Center in Gallipoli until Sabbatai's Apostasy (1666); 7. After the Apostasy (1667-1668); and 8. The Last Years of Sabbatai Ṣevi (1668-1676).

K42 Duker, Abraham G. "Frankism as a Movement of Polish-Jewish Synthesis." In A93. Pp. 133-64.

"A new factor entered in the middle of the nineteenth century, namely, the transformation of antisemitism in Poland from mainly religiously motivated views into racial, racial-religious, and finally, racial-religious-folkish ideological solutions of the Jewish problem. These changes brought theoretical and speculative antisemitic interpretations of Frankism, possibly more far-reaching than that of the Nazis, as will be mentioned later. It is my intention to bring out, within the limited space allotted, the main lines as well as examples of the developments." Sections: The Founder and His Sect; Ambivalent Acceptance; World Rule; Continued Separatism, Complications in Accepting Christian Beliefs; The Frankists as a Social Group; Expansion of Class of Wealthy Jews; The Jewish War of 1859; Defense Tactics; Racism and Anti-Frankist Fears; Rejection of Other Converts' Intermarriage; and "Intellectuals" Go Racist.

K43 Gratus, Jack. *The False Messiahs*. London: Victor Gollancz, Ltd., 1975; New York: Taplinger Pub. Co., 1976.

"Beginning with the messianic ideology of the Old Testament, I have endeavoured to trace the history of messianism through its many claimants to the present day." Chapter 11, Sabbatai Zevi, pp. 143-60.

K44 McKeon, Michael. "Sabbatai Sevi in England." *AJS Review*, 2(1977), 131-69.

"In the following discussion, I hope to establish the major significance of Sabbatai Sevi for England by examining several questions ... concerning the English awareness of him 300 years ago. How and in what form did the unparalleled developments in the Levant from 1665 to 1667 first become known to English-speaking people? What contribution was made by the Sabbatian movement to Christian eschatology and to the expectations aroused among its devotees by the approach of the 'wonderful year' 1666? What was the range of response to the movement among English observers; what was its ideological or sectarian meaning to contemporaries?"

K45 Mandel, Arthur. *The Militant Messiah, or The Flight from the Ghetto: The Story of Jacob Frank and the Frankist Movement*. Atlantic Highlands, New Jersey: Humanities Press, 1979.

Biography of Frank.

K46 Waugh, Daniel Clarke. "News of the False Messiah: Reports on Shabbetai Zevi in Ukraine and Muscovy." *Jewish Social Studies*, 41(1979), 301-22.

"The purpose of this article is to present some previously ignored information about the extent to which the Shabbetaian movement became known in eastern Europe. In the first part, some material published long ago concerning Ioanikii Haliatovs'kyi's *Mesia pravdivy* [The True Messiah], an anti-Jewish polemic that appeared in its first edition in Kiev in 1669 will be reviewed and supplemented. The second part concerns some translations made for Tsar Aleksei Mikhailovich in 1666 from newspapers and pamphlets containing information about Shabbetai Zevi. The texts of these hitherto unstudied and unpublished Muscovite translations are appended, since they should be of interest to students of the Shabbetaian movement as well as to those whose primary concern is Muscovite cultural history."

K47 Ostow, Mortimer. "The Hypomanic Personality." In A110. Pp. 387-93. Rpt. K49.

"I attempt to establish in this essay that Nathan [of Gaza] may have exhibited the qualities of a normal variant of manic-depressive illness, namely, hypomanic personality, which is not only not disabling, but which actually confers supernormal capacities that often make for success and leadership. Nathan used [Shabbatai] Zvi as a fascinating figurehead, and through him, gave expression to his own antinomian tendencies."

K48 Falk, Avner. "The Messiah and the Qelippoth: On the Mental Illness of Sabbatai Sevi." *Journal of Psychology and Judaism*, 7,1(Fall-Winter 1982), 5-29.

"This article surveys the psychoanalytic theories of manic-depressive illness and connects them with the facts of Sabbatai Sevi's life, both his childhood and his later bizarre behavior. It also discusses Sabbatai Sevi's married and sexual life in light of these theories. It investigates the unconscious symbolism of the Kabbalah, the centerpiece of Jewish mysticism, in terms of Sabbatai Sevi's own pathology, since he used the language of the Kabbalah to express his thoughts and feelings. It finally attempts to show that the antipsychoanalytic bias of Gershom Scholem was the pitfall which made it impossible for him to truly understand the person he was studying so carefully." (Abstract)

K49 Ostow, Mortimer. "The Hypomanic Personality." In A118. Pp. 221-30.

Reprint of K47.

K50 Wacholder, Ben Zion. "Jacob Frank and the Frankists Hebrew Zoharic Letters." *Hebrew Union College Annual*, 53(1982), 265-93.

"This publication reproduces and interprets the Hebrew-Zoharic letter written by three disciples of Jacob frank in 1800 and addressed to the Jews of Hungary. The document may be divided into two parts. Part one contains copies of two letters ascribed to Jacob Frank written in 1767 and 1768. The second part, written in 1800, affirms that Frank's predictions concerning European Jewry are soon to be realized. The document as a whole represents a frantic attempt to sustain the Frankist movement nearly a decade after the Master's death. According to our document, Frank foresaw the doom of Europe's Jewry unless the Jews adopted 'the holy faith of Edom,' i.e. Christianity. The conversion to Christianity, however, was to serve as an instrument leading to Christianity's ultimate defeat. The patriarch Jacob, reincarnated in Frank, was destined to rise as Israel's leader in its war against Edom. The significance of this document lies in its representation of Frank's own formulation of both his messianic role and the movement's doctrine. Of the Frankist literature, our text is the only one which purports to reproduce the Master's own words in Hebrew." (Abstract)

K51 Duker, Abraham G. "Some Cabbalistic and Frankist Elements in Adam Mickiewicz's 'Dziady.'" In A 123. Pp. 213-35.

"The many puzzling passages in this most discussed mystical work of Mickiewicz, *Dziady* (Forefather's Eve), *Part III*, have been subjected to manifold attempts at solutions. His contacts with cabbalists and Frankists are a matter of record. I brought out elsewhere the Jewish factor in Towiański's cure of Celina, the poet's wife, as well as possibilities of Frankist influence in the poet's Paris lectures on Slav literature [K30]. I shall now attempt to trace similar ideas and influences in his pre-Towianist *Dziady, Part III*."

L. Hasidism

Primary Sources

L1 Buber, Martin. "Hasidica: Stories and Sayings of the Ba'al Shem and Others." *Quest*, 13(1921-22), 370-85.

Collection of stories and sayings: "The Power of Community," "Blessing and Impediment," "The Initiation of Tears," "Unadvised," "The Reception," "Samael," "The Heavy Penance," "That Which Goeth into the Mouth," "True Wisdom," and "Sayings of Rabbi Nahman ben Simha of Bratzlav."

L2 Buber, Martin. "Sayings of the Baal-Shem-Tov." Trans. Clifton Fadiman. *Menorah Journal*, 17(1929), 52-58.

"These writings consist of a collection of fragments handed down to us in the books of disciples and disciples of disciples, as quotations from the Baal-Shem-Tov. They are what is left of the living speech of one who himself wrote no books." Selections include: "Of Knowledge and Belief," "Of Zeal and Work," "Of the Holy Sparks and their Redemption," "Of Man's Service to God," "Of the Near and the Far," "Solitude," "A Parable of Prayer," "Of the Power of Words," "Of Devotion," "Of Evil and Good," and "Of Arrogance and Humility."

L3 Unger, Manasseh. "How the Rabbi of Kalev Freed a Song." Trans. Edward Robbin. *Menorah Journal*, 16(1929), 276-7.

Hasidic tale about the Rabbi from Kalev.

L4 Buber, Martin. *Jewish Mysticism, and the Legend of Baalshem*. Trans. Lucy Cohen. London and Toronto: J.M. Dent and Sons Ltd., 1931. Sel. rpt. L19, L25.

Tells the stories of the Chassidim and "describes the founder's religion and that of some of the more remarkable of his successors." Contents: The Life of the Chassids, pp. 1-38; Twenty-one Chassidic Stories, pp. 39-211; and A Fragment from Baalshem's Life, and Some of His Sayings, pp. 212-24.

L5 Levin, Meyer. *The Golden Mountain: Marvellous Tales of Rabbi Israel, Baal Shem, and of His Great-Grandson, Rabbi Nachman, Retold from Hebrew, Yiddish and German Sources*. New York: J. Cape & R. Ballou, 1932. Rpt. L37.

"I have tried to put the scattered legends of the Baal Shem Tov together so as to form a legendary life-story of Rabbi Israel, who was born in 1700 in Okup and died in 1760 in Medzibuz. His great-grandson, who was born in Medzibuz in 1772, and died in Uman in 1810, left thirteen tales, which were written down by his pupil, Nathan. Of these, I have here translated eleven; the other two are fragmentary and confused."

L6 Levin, Meyer. "How Satan Defeated Rabbi Israel in His Struggle against the False Messiah: A Tale of the Baal Shem." *Menorah Journal*, 20(1932), 21-25.

"This is one of the group of stories forming a legendary biography of Rabbi Isreal ben Eleazer, known as the Baal Shem Tov.... The tale here given, though also found in the Yiddish sources, follows a version by Martin Buber. Jacob Frank, mentioned here, was one of a number of false messiahs who appeared in that time and was successful in attracting followers."

L7 Birnbaum, Salomo, comp. *The Life and Sayings of the Baal Shem*. Trans. Irene Birnbaum. New York: Hebrew Publishing Company, 1933.

Anthology of Hasidic stories, divided into three parts: The Life of the Baal Shem, Three Letters of the Baal Shem, and Sayings of the Baal Shem.

L8 Newman, Louis I. *The Hasidic Anthology: Tales and Teachings of the Hasidim*. Translated from Hebrew, Yiddish and German. In collaboration with Samuel Spitz. New York: Charles Scribner's Sons, 1934. Rpt. New York: Schocken Books, Inc., 1963.

"This Anthology of Hasidic lore and wisdom derives its material from the utterances attributed to the leaders and sages of the religious movement of Hasidism which originated during the middle of the 18th century in Podolia, with the appearance of Israel ben Eliezer (1700-1760),... The parables, tales, aphorisms, epigrams, fables, anecdotes, exegetical comments and interpretations ascribed to the Besht formed the foundation for the sayings and writings of his contemporary Disciples and their descendants,... An oral tradition incorporated first in manuscripts and later printed in book form, arose among the millions of the followers of Hasidism, remaining fluid until today,... The stories and sayings of this Anthology portray the message of Hasidism more eloquently than any commentary regarding them."

L9 Buber, Martin. "The Prayer-Book." Trans. Simon Chasen. *Menorah Journal*, 24(1936), 272-75.

A tale of the Baal Shem Tov.

L10 Meckler, David L. *Miracle Men: Tales of the Baal Shem and His Chassidim*. New York: Covici, Friede, 1936. Rpt. New York: Bloch Pub. Co., 1964.

"The present volume does not comprise a large measure of the Chassidic legends, but it is the writer's belief that they represent the Chassidic tale at its best. That they be kept true to tradition, with their original spirit unimpaired, they have been woven around the lives of the Baal Shem, his forerunners and followers, thus providing a requisite unity and a fair idea of Chassidism itself. As a matter of fact, no dissertation and no description of any kind will do so much justice to Chassidism as does its legends."

L11 Margolis, Meir. "A Trip with Israel Baalshem." Trans. Leo W. Schwartz, from A. Kahann's *Sefer ha-Hasiduth*. In A24. Pp. 190-91.

"The following brief reminiscence, not entirely untouched by legendry, is a unique portrait by a contemporary. Meir is said to have been a pupil of the Baalshem. He was a rabbi of the community of Lemberg, the center of Poland then ruled by Austria-Hungary, and the author of a number of works dealing with ethics and mysticism."

L12 Buber, Martin. *For the Sake of Heaven.* Trans. Ludwig Lewisohn. Philadelphia: Jewish Publication Society of America, 1945; 2nd ed. 1953. Rpt. New York: Meridian Books, 1958; Westport, Conn.: Greenwood Press, 1970.

Contains a cycle of stories about several Zaddikim who "actually attempted by means of theurgic or magic activities (the so-called Practical Cabala) to make of Napoleon that 'Gog of the Land of Magog,' mentioned by Ezekiel, whose wars, as is proclaimed by several eschatological texts, were to precede the coming of the Messiah."

L13 Buber, Martin. "The Ladder from Man to God: Sayings of the Hasidim." *Commentary*, 4(1947), 478-82.

Selections from L16.

L14 Buber, Martin. *Tales of the Hasidim.* Trans. Olga Marx. Vol. 1. *The Early Masters.* Vol. 2. *The Later Masters.* New York: Schocken Books, 1947-48. Sel. rpt. L15, L17.

Purpose "is to picture the zaddikim and their lives from extant written (and some oral) material." Vol. 1 includes: Israel ben Elizer, The Baal Shem Tov; Barukh of Mezbizh; Dov Baer of Mezritch, the Great Maggid; Abraham, the Angel; Pinhas of Koretz and His School; Yehiel Mikhal of Zlotchov; Zev Wolf of Zbarazh; Mordecai of Neskhizh; From the Circle of the Baal Shem Tov; Menahem Mendel of Vitebsk; Shmelke of Nikolsburg; Aaron of Karlin; Levi Yitzhak of Berditchev; Zusya of Hanipol; Elimelekh of Lizhensk; Shneur Zalman of Ladi ("The Rav"); Shelomo of Karlin; Israel of Koznitz; and Jacob Yitzhak of Lublin ("The Seer"). Vol. 2 includes: Descendants of the Great Maggid; From the School of Rabbi Shmelke of Nikolsburg; From the School of Rabbi Elimelekh of Lizhensk; From the School of Rabbi Shelomo of Karlin; From the House of the Maggid of Koznitz; From the School of the Rabbi of Lublin; and Pzhysha and Its Daughter Schools.

L15 Buber, Martin. "Tales of the Hasidim" and "More Tales of the Hasidim." *Commentary*, 3(1947), 73-78, 175-80.

Selections from L14.

L16 Buber, Martin. *Ten Rungs: Hasidic Sayings.* Trans. Olga Marx. New York: Schocken Books, 1947, 1962. Sel. rpt. L13.

"This book contains a small selection of hasidic sayings: ... They all revolve around a single question: How can we fulfill the meaning of our existence on earth? And so, dear reader, these pages are not concerned with the mysteries of heaven, but with your life and mine, in this hour and the next. These sayings were scattered throughout hundreds of books, in versions largely distorted in the speeches and writings of the disciples who transmitted them. I have selected, reduced to the quintessence of meaning, and arranged them according to major themes, not because they are beautiful and interesting, but because of my belief that, in this selection, arrangement and form, they may serve to show even the reader who is very remote from their origins the way to the true life."

L17 Buber, Martin. "Hasidic Tales: Second Period--A Selection." *Commentary*, 6(1948), 363-68.

Selections from L14, vol. 2.

L18 Hayim ben Isaac. "Man, the Master of All Created Worlds." Trans. Michael Wyschogrod. *Commentary*, 14(1952), 595-97.

Selections from Rabbi Hayim ben Isaac of Volozhin's *Nefesh Hachayim* (1749-1821), a book whose doctrine "was a mystical humanism that gave the everyday precepts of rabbinic law cosmic proportions." Rabbi Hayim ben Isaac was an opponent of Hasidism.

L19 Buber, Martin. *The Legend of the Baal-Shem*. Trans. Maurice Friedman. New York: Harper & Row, 1955. Rpt. New York: Schocken Books, 1969, 1977.

"This book consists of a descriptive account and twenty stories. The descriptive account speaks of the life of the Hasidim, a Jewish sect of eastern Europe which arose around the middle of the eighteenth century and still continues to exist in our day in deteriorated form. The stories tell the life of the founder of this sect, Rabbi Israel ben Eliezer, who was called the Baal-Shem, that is, the master of God's Name, and who lived from about 1700 to 1760, mostly in Podolia and Wolhynia." "The Life of the Hasidim," pp. 17-50; Twenty Hasidic Stories, pp. 51-208. (Different translation of L4).

L20 Dresner, Samuel H., trans. "The Zaddik and the People: Teachings of Jacob Joseph of Polonoye." *Commentary*, 19(1955), 71-73.

Selections from the writings of Rabbi Jacob Joseph of Polonoye, "the foremost literary disciple of the Baal Shem," and "the first to collect Hasidic teachings and set them into treatise form."

L21 Buber, Martin. *The Tales of Rabbi Nachman*. Trans. Maurice Friedman. New York: Horizon Press, 1956. Rpt. London: Souvenir Press, 1974.

"My re-creation of the tales of Rabbi Nachman first appeared in print fifty years ago. I have not translated these tales, but retold them with full freedom, yet out of his spirit as it is present to me." In "Rabbi Nachman and Jewish Mysticism," Buber introduces Jewish mysticism, Rabbi Nachman of Bratzlav, Sayings of Rabbi Nachman, and the Stories. Specific stories "re-created" are: "The Rabbi and His Son," "The Steer and the Ram," "The Clever Man and the Simple Man," "The King's Son and the Son of the Maid," "The Master of Prayer," and "The Seven Beggars." The final chapter is "Rabbi Nachman's Journey to Palestine."

L22 Schneersohn, Joseph I. *Lubavitcher Rabbi's Memoirs.* Trans. Nisan Mindel. 2 vols. Brooklyn: Otzar Hachassidim, 1956-60.

"The 'Memoirs' reveal an important phase in Jewish history in recent centuries, and, particularly, in the history of Chassidism. They portray a gallery of Jews who paved the way for the founders of the Movement, and who, as *Nistarim* (scholars and mystics in disguise), prepared the ground for the movement to take root and flourish. The material in which the 'Memoirs' are based represents an accumulation of memoranda preserved in the family archives or in the oral tradition of the Lubavitcher Rabbis since the time of Rabbi Shneur Zalman of Liady, founder of Chabad Chassidism." (Translator's note)

L23 Weiner, Herbert, trans. "The Tanya and the Gaon." *Commentary,* 21(1956), 67-68.

Excerpt of a letter written in 1789 by Schneur Zalman of Ladi to his congregation, "which describes the unsuccessful efforts made by [Schneur Zalman] to engage the Gaon [of Vilna] or his followers in a public dispute, gives some indication of the bitterness that rent Jewry for many years."

L24 Weiner, Herbert, ed. "From the Teachings of Habad Hasidism: Anecdote and Discourse." *Commentary,* 24(1957), 64-65.

Selections of teachings from various Lubavitcher Rebbes.

L25 Buber, Martin. "The Baal-Shem-Tov's Instruction in Intercourse with God." In his A41. Pp. 179-222.

Different translation of L2.

L26 Buber, Martin. *Tales of Angels, Spirits and Demons.* Trans. David Antin and Jerome Rothenberg. New York: Hawk's Well Press, 1958.

"The source of the first story is a tale of the Riziner Rabbi. The second story, whatever its original source, derives from a little book containing several new tales of Rabbi Nachman of Bratslav and titled accordingly. *The House of Demons* is a very free adaptation of a tale found in one of the most significant Jewish folk collections, the *Kav Hayashar* of 1705. The remaining stories are all versions of Hasidic legends."

L27 Rabinowicz, Harry M. *The Slave Who Saved the City, and Other Hassidic Tales*. A Wonderful World Book. New York: A.S. Barnes and Company, Inc., and London: Thomas Yoseloff Ltd., 1960.

Anthology of legends which "have been lovingly collected and suitably adapted for the younger reader. They are presented in the hope that they may recall the brilliance of the *Hassidic* martyrs of this tormented age and rekindle the fires that burned so brightly in the Golden Era of *Hassidism*." In addition to the tales, Rabinowicz includes a biographical sketch of the Besht.

L28 Shamblatt, Sanford D., ed. "The Testament of Israel Baal Shem Tov." *Judaism*, 9(1960), 282-84.

Quotations on Equality, Prayer, The Sinner and Repentance, and The Righteous from *Tsaraat HaRivash*.

L29 Steinman, Eliezer. *The Garden of Hasidism*. Trans. Haim Schachter. Jerusalem: World Zionist Organization, 1961.

Unavailable for annotating.

L30 Newman, Louis I., trans. *Maggidim & Hasidim: Their Wisdom, A New Anthology of the Parables, Folk-Tales, Fables, Aphorisms, Epigrams, Sayings, Anecdotes, Proverbs, and Exegetical Interpretations of the Leading Maggidim (Folk-Preachers), and the Hasidic Masters and Their Disciples*. In collaboration with Samuel Spitz. A Companion Volume to L8. New York: Bloch Publishing Company, 1962.

"This Anthology is presented to readers in the hope that it may augment the treasuries of new homiletical material." The material is divided into four categories: 1. "items chosen from the works of folk-preachers, known as Maggidim"; 2. "items from the works of the Hasidic Maggidim"; 3. "aphorisms, epigrams, reflections and comments of the Zaddikim, namely, the Saintly, Righteous spiritual leaders of Hasidism"; and 4. material "culled from the writings of distinguished Rabbis and scholars, who, in addition to being authorities in the domain of Halakah or Jewish jurisprudence, were also outstanding preachers."

L31 Schneur Zalman of Liadi. *Liqqutei Amarim (Tanya)*. 5 vols. New York: Kehot Publication Society, 1962-68.

Translation of Rabbi Schneur Zalman's explanation of "Chassidus in general, and Chabad Chassidus in particular":

1. *Tanya*. Trans. Nissan Mindel. 1962
2. *Shaar Hayichud Vehaemunah*. Trans. Nisen Mangel. 1965
3. *Igeres Hateshuva*. Trans. Zalman I. Posner. 1965
4. *Igeres Hakodesh*. Trans. Jacob I. Schochet. 1968
5. *Kuntres Achron*. Trans. Zalman I. Posner. 1968

L32 Alter, Yehudah Leib. "Reflections on Passover." Trans. David S. Shapiro. *Judaism*, 12(1963), 206-209.

"The following selections are from the *Sefath Emeth* on the Torah by the second 'Gerer Rebbe,' Rabbi Yehudah Leib Alter, who is known throughout Jewry by the name of his *magna opera*.... The selections on Passover here presented may help the reader to gain some understanding of the method and approach of this great master of the Hassidic Midrash." (Editor's note)

L33 Dov Baer of Lubavitch. *Tract on Ecstasy*. Trans. Louis Jacobs. London: Valentine, Mitchell, 1963. Rpt. Chappaqua, New York: Russel Books, 1982.

Treatise "in the form of a letter, sent by Dobh Baer to his followers, advising them on the role of ecstasy in the religious life"; advocates reflection "on the divine mysteries, on God and his relationship to the created world" in order to "infuse the soul with the divine light so that the evil in man would be vanquished of itself." In addition to the tract, Jacobs includes a translation of Dov Baer's First Letter, and a discussion of his Technique of Contemplation.

L34 Dresner, Samuel H. "Humility and Rabbi Levi Yitzhak." *Jewish Heritage*, 6,1(Summer 1963), 18-22.

Parable to illustrate the humility of Levi Yitzhak.

L35 Schachter, Zalman M. "Thrice He Won." *Jewish Heritage*, 6,1(Summer 1963), 23-26.

Story of Rabbi Levi Yitzhak.

L36 Dresner, Samuel, trans. "Spirit in Matter and Faith in Works." *Judaism*, 14(1965), 220-23.

Selections from Rabbi Levi Yitzhak of Berdichev's book *Kedushat Levi* which as "A good introduction to Jewish mysticism, it remains one of the finest works of Hasidic literature." (Editor's note)

L37 Levin, Meyer. *Classid Hassidic Tales: Marvellous Tales of Rabbi Israel Baal Shem and of His Great-Grandson, Rabbi Nachman, Retold from Hebrew, Yiddish, and German Sources*. New York: Citadel Press, 1966. Rpt. New York and Baltimore: Penguin Books, 1975; Tel Aviv: Greenfield, 1978.

Reprint of L5.

L38 Dawidowicz, Lucy S. *The Golden Tradition: Jewish Life and Thought in Eastern Europe.* New York: Holt, Rinehart and Winston, 1967.

"This is a book about Eastern European Jews in crisis, challenge, and creativity from the end of the eighteenth century until their cataclysmic destruction in the Second World War.... I have here assembled autobiographies, memoirs, reminiscences, and letters of some sixty persons whose lives document these Eastern European Jewish responses to modernity." The chapter on Early Hasidism (pp. 93-110), contains: "The Proselytizer: Zosya of Annopol"; "A Hasid Prays for Napoleon: Menahem Mendel of Rymanow"; "Hasid of Inwardness: Simha Bunim"; "Rebbe of Mystery: Menahem Mendel of Kotsk"; and "The Rebbe of Lubavich Beats Count Uvarov," by Chaim Meir Hellman.

L39 Dresner, Samuel H., trans. "Sexual Purity and Redemption." Trans. Samuel H. Dresner. *Judaism*, 17(1968), 65-67.

Kalonomos Kalman Epstein's "book *Maor Vashmesh*, from which I have translated the following selection, became one of the most popular of all Hasidic works and is studied widely until this day."

L40 Buber, Martin. *From the Treasure House of Hassidism.* A Selection of "Or Haganuz." Leket. Jerusalem: Cultural Division, Department for Education and Culture in the Diaspora, World Zionist Organization, 1969.

"For the most part, these aphorisms were gleaned from the oral teachings of the 'Zaddikim', as the great teachers of Hassidism--that great and audacious religious movement, which had set itself the purpose of reviving and renewing the religious experience of the ordinary Jew--were called.... From these sayings there emanates the voice of implicit faith that takes precedence over religious worship."

L41 Schneersohn, Shalom Dov Ber. *Kuntres Uma'ayon Mibais Hashem.* Trans. Zalman I. Posner. Brooklyn: Kehot Publication Society, 1969. 2nd ed. 1973.

"The *Kuntres* here translated was written by Rabbi Shalom Dov Ber at the turn of the century as an indirect result of the establishment of the *Machazikei Hadas*. He weaves Chassidic doctrine, Kabala thoughts, Biblical and Talmudic texts and candid insights into human frailties into a document structured and systematic, yet informal and personal, a text for study and meditation. It has become one of the foremost ethico-philosophical works of Chabad."

L42 Ben-Amos, Dan, and Jerome R. Mintz, trans. and eds. *In Praise of the Ba'al Shem Tov*. Bloomington and London: Indiana University Press, 1970.

"Although small portions of *In Praise of the Baal Shem Tov* (particularly the opening tales) have been rendered in English and have appeared as parts of collections of Hasidic tales, the present edition is the first complete translation into English. The present work follows the original Kopys edition. The present translators have tried to keep faith with Rabbi Dov Ber and the printer of Kopys,..."

L43 Klapholtz, Yisroel Yaakov. *Tales of the Baal Shem Tov: A Collection of Stories and Biographical Sketches Taken from Reliable Sources*. 3 vols. Bnei Brak: Pe'er Hasefer: Institute for Translation and Publication of Torah Literature for All Ages, 1971-1979.

L44 Fleer, Gedaliah. *Rabbi Nachman's Fire: An Introduction to Breslover Chassidus*. New York: Hermon Press, 1972, 1975.

"This booklet is meant as an introduction to Breslover Chassidus. The first and largest section is a detailed, yet concise, chronological biography of Rabbi Nachman's life, superimposed upon the time in which he lived.... The second part contains the translated words of Rabbi Nachman in the area of both man's relationship to man and his relationship to G-d.... Later in the same section is a sample of some of the Breslover Rebbe's more lengthy Chassidic discourses translated from his sefer 'L'kutey Maharan,' ... The final section consists of reprints of letters taken from among my correspondence with people in various circumstances, asking me for further elaboration of the Breslover way of looking at G-d, the world, or their own personal lives and problems."

L45 Applefeld, Aharon, ed. *From the World of Rabbi Nahman of Bratzlav*. Leket II. Jerusalem: Cultural Division, Department for Education and Culture in the Diaspora. World Zionist Organization, 1973.

"Rabbi Nahman's teachings are not systematic; the reader will even find some of them a bit obscure. But we have chosen to present them as he gave them. We felt that in the sections dealing with his outlook, and even more so in the dream chapters, there is a certain value in preserving the original style, which in this case testifies to the great effort and the amount of courage and spiritual flexibility which were needed to grapple with questions which deviated widely from the accepted bounds of thought in those days." The five parts of the book are: Tales; Discourses and Teachings; Prayers; About Himself; and Dreams.

L46 Kaplan, Aryeh, trans. *Rabbi Nachman's Wisdom: Shevachay HaRan, Sichos HaRan.* By Rabbi Nathan of Nemirov, a Disciple of Rabbi Nachman. Brooklyn, 1973.

"This work is a translation of *Shevachay HaRan* and *Sichos HaRan*, a combined work that was first published several years after [Rabbi Nachman's] passing. It contains his most often quoted teachings, its subjects ranging from simple everyday advice to the most esoteric Kabbalistic mysteries. It is where the Rebbe presents a way of life that has both depth and meaning." In addition to the text and notes, there are also three appendices: A. The Life of Rabbi Nachman; B. A History of this Work; and C. On Breslov.

L47 Metzger, Alter B.Z. "Kaitz--The Time of Messianic Redemption: A Letter attributed to Fraide, the Baal Hatanya's Daughter." *Tradition*, 13,4 and 14, 1(Spring-Summer 1973), 180-85.

"Highly relevant to a normal person and somewhat similar but not quite identical to the three aforementioned levels of *Iscaphia* [conquest and control of evil inherent in man]--the control of evil, 'Binah Ilaah' or 'Shekhinah'--man as a bearer of Godliness and finally 'Yichudah Ilaah'--is the following description of man's spiritual labor during the course of an individual's daily prayers described by the contemporary Lubavitcher Rebbe, Rabbi Menachem M. Schneerson as particularly as reflecting the spiritual concepts relayed [sic] to the months of Nisan, Iyar, and Sivan."

L48 Lamm, Norman, trans. "The Letter of the Besht to R. Gershon of Kutov." *Tradition*, 14,4(Fall 1974), 110-25.

"The letter is a personal recommendation of the bearer, R. Yaakov Yosef, to R. Abraham Gershon Ashkenazi of Kutov, brother-in-law of the Besht, who was then in Palestine. It was written in 1750 or 1751, perhaps 1752 ... It consists of three parts, all interwoven. One deals with personal and familial matters.... The second aspect of the letter is a reflection of the era--the anti-Semitic excesses ... Most significant for Hasidic scholarship is the main part of the letter--the Besht's revelation to his brother-in-law of his most intimate religious experience. Two such events are related by the Besht in this remarkable autobiographical disclosure, both characterized as *aliyot neshamah*, 'ascents of the soul,' and both taking place on Rosh Hashanah."

L49 Wengrov, Charles, trans. *The Baal Shem Tov on Pirkey Avoth: Thoughts, Interpretations, Explanations on the* Ethics of the Fathers. Jerusalem: Feldheim Publishers, 1974.

"... the selections in this work have been gathered from a great variety of sources not available to the general reader.

The passages are generally given in their original form, with no emendations whatever."

L50 Sufrin, A.D., and E.Z. Gorman. *Sefer Haminhagim: Chabad-Lubavitch Customs.* London: Lubavitch Foundation, 1975.

Translation of the *Sefer Haminhagim* of Chabad Lubavitch, "not a Shulchan Aruch. It quotes our custom when there are several opinions on Shulchan Aruch, but it does not substitute for the Shulchan Aruch."

L51 Avidor, Shmuel Hacohen, comp. *Touching Heaven, Touching Earth: Hassidic Humor & Wit.* Tel-Aviv: Sadan Publishing, 1976.

L52 Fleer, Gedaliah, trans. *Rabbi Nachman's Foundation.* New York: Ohr MiBreslov, distributed by Sepher-Hermon Press, Inc., 1976.

"I have chosen to call this book *Rabbi Nachman's Foundation* since it deals with the concept of *Tikun HaBris*, the basic premise upon which all selfless devotion to G-d is structured." Selections include: Rabbi Nathan's Preface to *Tikun HaKelali*; The Ten Psalms; A Deeper Look; In the Spirit of the Law; and A Letter to David.

L53 Unterman, Alan, trans. *The Wisdom of the Jewish Mystics.* New York: New Directions Book, 1976.

"The selections from the writings of the Jewish mystics, down the ages, which are included here ... all belong to what we have called the human face of the Kabbalah.... we have drawn on tales about the mystics, on some of their sayings scattered throughout kabbalistic and non-kabbalistic texts, and primarily on the writings of some of the great Hasidic mystics who produced a new genre of mystical literature aimed at the layman."

L54 Green, Arthur, and Barry W. Holtz, trans. *Your Word is Fire: The Hasidic Masters on Contemplative Prayer.* New York, Ramsey and Toronto: Paulist Press, 1977.

"Because Hasidic literature contains no systematic manual of contemplative prayer, the texts included in the present volume have been culled from many sources.... While the notes may be of some interest to students of Hasidism, the primary purpose of the present translation is devotional rather than academic. We offer these texts for the enrichment of the personal religious lives of our readers, for use as readings in the context of worship, and as a source of inspiration to those who seek to uncover the oneness of religious truth behind the garb of various mystical traditions." After an Introduction on the contemplative prayer of Hasidism, Green and Holtz present writings on: The Power of Your Prayer; Preparing the Way; Meet Him in the Word; Beyond the Walls of Self; Prayer for the Sake of Heaven; In His Presence; Thoughts That Lead Astray; The Way of the Simple; After the Hour of Prayer; and A Final Parable.

L55 Steinsaltz, Adin. "The King's Son and the Son of the Maid." Trans. Yehuda Hanegbi. *Shefa Quarterly*, 1,2(Autumn 1977), 55-66. Rpt. L61.

Story of Nachman of Bratzlav, with commentary by Adin Steinsaltz, pp. 66-75.

L56 Steinsaltz, Adin. "The Merchant and the Pauper." Trans. Yehuda Hanegbi. *Shefa Quarterly*, 1,1(Summer 1977), 47-62. Rpt. L61.

Story of Nachman of Bratzlav, with commentary by Adin Steinsaltz, pp. 62-67.

L57 Band, Arnold J., trans. *Nahman of Bratslav--The Tales*. The Classics of Western Spirituality. New York, Ramsey and Toronto: Paulist Press, 1978.

Thirteen tales in which Band has "tried to capture ... the oral familiarity and charm of the Yiddish and the metaphysical rigor and grandeur of the Hebrew." Each tale is prefaced by a brief Prologue, and at the end of the volume is a fuller commentary. The Introduction contains a brief biography of R. Nachman.

L58 Handler, Andrew, trans. *Rabbi Eizik: Hasidic Stories about the Zaddik of Kallo*. Rutherford: Fairleigh Dickinson University Press, and London: Associated University Presses, 1978.

Stories about Rabbi Eizik Taub, whose "reputation established Nagykallo as the first center of the hasidic movement in Hungary."

L59 Koenig, Ester, trans. *The Thirteen Stories of Rebbe Nachman of Breslev*. Ed. Mordechai Kramer. Jerusalem: Hillel Press, 1978.

"This work is the first authentic and complete English translation of the stories of Rebbi Nachman of Breslav. Previous translations of Martin Buber and Meyer Levin have missed the point and have tried to present fairy-tales.... We have maintained all efforts to keep in mind Rebbe Nachman's statement and admonition, that every word of these stories has great meaning, and anyone that changes one word of these stories from what he himself said, detracts from them greatly. Just as medicine contains various ingredients which make up the final compound, so we have endeavored to accurately preserve the Rebbe's words." (Editor's note)

L60 Brown, Moshe, trans. *Light of Chanukah*. Brooklyn: Z. Berman Books, 1979.

Translation of "the *Sefas Emes* by the great Rabbi Yehudah Aryeh Leib Alter (1847-1905), the second leader of the famed Chassidic dynasty of Gur. His analysis is a combination of depth and clarity that has made the author's works famous among all Judaic scholars."

L61 Steinsaltz, Adin. *Beggars and Prayers: Adin Steinsaltz Retells the Tales of Rabbi Nachman of Bratslav*. Trans. Yehuda Hanegbi. New York: Basic Books, Inc., Publishers, 1979.

Six tales with commentary: "The Losing of the King's Daughter," "The Merchant and the Pauper" (rpt. of L56), "The King's Son and the Son of the Maid" (rpt. of L55), "The Master of Prayer," "The Clever Man and the Simple Man," and "The Seven Beggars."

L62 Greenbaum, Avraham, trans. *Restore My Soul! Meshivat Nefesh*. Jerusalem: Yeshivat Chasidey Breslov, and Brooklyn: American Friends of Zvi La Tzadik, 1980.

"Rabbi Alter of Teplik was one of the leading Breslover Chassidim in Europe at the turn of the century. He foresaw the spiritual holocaust that was descending upon the Jewish people. Inspired by Rabbi Nachman's cry, *'Gevalt!* Never give up *hope!'* R. Alter collected from Rabbi Nachman's book *Lekutey Moharan*, and from that of his disciple R. Nathan, *Lekutey Halachot*, all the sections dealing with inner fortitude and optimism. A clear message emerges. Man should know that he can always return to God, regardless of the condition he may be in. R. Alter called the book *Meshirat Nefesh.*" Including all of the original edition's passages from R. Nachman, but only a selection from R. Nathan, "The text ... is accompanied by notes which are intended to serve as a guide to the sources of the many quotations from the Bible, the Talmud, the Midrash and the Kabbalistic writings. There are also notes aimed at clarifying certain ideas found in the text."

L63 Kaplan, Aryeh, trans. *Gems of Rabbi Nachman*. Published by Rabbi Aryeh Kaplan and Yeshivah Chasidei Breslov, 1980.

"This work contains many sayings from *Rabbi Nachman's Wisdom* [L46], some of which are grouped under specific headings. In addition, it presents for the first time, a translation of some of his parables and tales, as well as a number of his most famous teachings from his major work, *Likutey Moharan.*" (Publisher's Preface)

L64 Nachman of Bratslav. *Outpouring of the Soul.* Trans. Aryeh Kaplan. Jerusalem: Yeshivat Chasidei Breslov, 1980.

Unavailable for annotating.

L65 Schneersohn, Joseph Isaac. *Bosi l'Gani: The Last Series of Discourses Written by the Previous Rebbe.* Trans. Eliyahu Touger. Sichos in English. Brooklyn: Empire Press, 1980.

Translations of four discourses: 1. Ma'amar Bosi L'Gani; 2. Ma'amar Hayosheves B'Gannim; 3. The Ma'amar Released for Purim, 5710; and 4. The Ma'amar Released for Bais Nissan, 5710.

L66 Shick, Eleazer Shlomo. *A Voice Calls out to God; Based on the Works of Rabbi Nachman of Breslov and His Holy Disciples.* Trans. Kalman David Serkez. Brooklyn: Mesirta Heichal HaKodesh, 1980.

Unavailable for annotating.

L67 Zevin, Shlomo Yosef. *A Treasury of Chassidic Tales on the Torah: A Collection of Inspirational Chassidic Stories Relevant to the Weekly Torah Readings.* Trans. Uri Kaploun. New York: Mesorah Publications, Ltd., and Jerusalem: Hillel Press, 1980.

Volume I: Stories on Genesis and Exodus.

L68 Kaplan, Aryeh. *The Light Beyond: Adventures in Hassidic Thought.* New York and Jerusalem: Maznaim Publishing Corporation, 1981.

Almost half of this "collection of Hassidic thought" comes "from the words of the Baal Shem Tov himself. As the founder of Hassidism, he also laid its philosophical foundations, and to a large degree, it is his thoughts that influenced later Hasidic literature." In addition, Kaplan includes "representation of the works of" Rabbi Shneur Zalman of Lyady and Rabbi Nachman of Breslov. The thirteen topics covered are: God; Creation; Man; Israel and the Torah; Faith, Love and Reverence; Meditation and Prayer; The Commandments; Torah Study; The Sabbath and Holy Days; Life and Society; Sin and Repentance; Divine Providence; and The Ultimate Future.

L69 Zevin, Shlomo Yosef. *A Treasury of Chassidic Tales on the Festivals: A Collection of Chassidic Stories Relevant to the Festivals.* Trans. Uri Kaploun. 2 vols. New York: Mesorah Publications, Ltd., and Jerusalem: Hillel Press, 1981-82.

Volume I: Rosh Hashanah, Ten Days of Penitance, Yom Kippur, Sukkos, Koheles, Hoshanah Rabbah, Shemini Atzeres, Simchas

Torah, Rosh Chodesh, Yud-tes Kislev, Chanukah, Purim and Esther. Volume II: Pesach, The Seder, The Haggadah, Shir Hashirim, Lag Baomer, Shavuos, The Giving of the Torah, The Ten Commandments, Ruth, The Three Weeks and Lamentations.

L70 Green, Arthur, trans. *Upright Practices; The Light of the Eyes*. The Classics of Western Spirituality. New York, Ramsey and Toronto: Paulist Press, 1982.

"In this volume, two of Rabbi Nahum's [of Chernobyl] works are made available to the general reader for the first time in English. *Upright Practices* is a devotional manual of personal practices recommended by the Hasidic master for his disciples. *The Light of the Eyes* is a collection of homilies based on the Book of Genesis. Until now chiefly the sacred property of the Hasidim, these homilies are prime examples of the genre that, more than any other, reveals the earnestness and depth of Hasidic spirituality."

L71 Schwartz, Howard, trans. "The Lost Princess." *Judaism*, 31(1982), 225-28.

A tale by Rabbi Nahman of Bratslav.

L72 Schwartz, Tsila, and Howard Schwartz, trans. "The Tale of the Menorah." *Judaism*, 31(1982), 225.

A tale by Rabbi Nahman of Bratslav.

L73 Auerbach, Uri. *Reb Maerl Premishlaner: His Life, Works and Divrei Torah*. New York and Jerusalem: Moznaim Publishing Corporation, 1983.

Anthology of stories intended "to describe some of the unusual strengths of Reb Maer'l including his *Ruach Hakodesh*, his piety, his devotion to the Mitzvah of Tzedakah and some of his *Divrei Torah*."

L74 Dan, Joseph, ed. *The Teachings of Hasidism*. Library of Jewish Studies. New York: Behrman House, Inc., 1983.

"The present anthology offers the English reader a selection of texts from the classical period. The texts have been chosen for the importance of the ideas they express and also because they are representative of the thought of the individual author. The choice of selections has in part been governed by the desire to avoid passages heavily burdened with homiletical formulations or detailed kabbalistic discussions. Kabbalistic terminology has been kept to the minimum required for accuracy. The main goal has been to present the most significant works of early Hasidism on the central themes that preoccupied the first Hasidic rabbis." Part One: God, Man and Israel; Part Two: The Zaddik; Part Three: The

Hasidism

Religious Life. Also includes an Introduction on the history of Hasidism.

L75 *The Divine Conversation; Order of the Day; Golden Advice*. New York: Chassidei Breslov, n.d.

Selections based on the teachings of Rabbi Nachman of Breslov and his disciples.

Secondary Sources

L76 McCaul, Alexander. *Sketches of Judaism and the Jews*. London: B. Wertheim, 1838.

The second Sketch, "The Chasidim, a Fanatical Sect" (pp. 17-42), examines the history of Hasidism to prove the Jews "a credulous and superstitious people in the highest degree," Hasidism being "a numerous and powerful sect, whose fanaticism almost exceeds the bounds of belief."

L77 Lazarus, J.G. "The Sect of the Khasidim in the North of Europe." *The Israelite* (Cincinnati), 27 May 1859, p. 375; and 3 June 1859, p. 382.

Unavailable for annotating.

L78 Schechter, S. "The Chassidim." A Paper Read before the Jews' College Literary Society, November 13th, 1887. London: "Jewish Chronicle" Office, 1887. Rpt. L80, L138.

"As an active force for good, Chassidism was shortlived. For, as I propose to show, among its central tenets there lurked the germs of the degeneracy which so speedily came upon it. But its early purposes were high, its doctrines fairly pure, its aspirations ideal and sublime."

L79 Maimon, Solomon. *Autobiography*. Trans., with an essay on Maimon's philosophy, J. Clark Murray. Paisley: A. Gardner, and Boston: Cupples and Hurd, 1888. Rpt. New York: Schocken Books, 1947, 1967; London: East and West Library, 1954.

The autobiography of Solomon Maimon (1754-1800) reflects not only the philosophical, intellectual, historical and scientific background of an original thinker who rebelled against the structures of the Jewish community, but also, the state of the contemporary Jewish community outside Germany. In Chapter 12, I Study the Kabbalah, and Even Become a Physician (pp. 36-43), Maimon describes his introduction to kabbalistic studies; and Chapter 16, A Secret Society: the Hasidic Sect (pp. 49-55), is a critique of Hasidism.

L80   Schechter, S. "The Chassidim." In his A1. Pp. 1-45.

      Reprint of L78.

L81   Schechter, Solomon. "Rabbi Elijah Wilna, Gaon." In his A1.
      Pp. 73-98. Rpt. L139.

      "The subject of the present essay will be R. Elijah Wilna,
      who, among the Jews, as Lessing among the Germans, represent-
      ed truth, both by his life and by his literary activity."

L82   Eichler, M.M. "Chassidism and Modern Judaism." *Jewish
      Exponent*, 33,18(23 August 1901), 1.

      Believing "that Chassidism, with certain modifications,
      could be propagated in modern Israel or Western Europe and
      America," Eichler answers two questions: "1. What is Chassi-
      dism, and what historical conditions brought about the move-
      ment and caused it to flourish? 2. What conditions in modern
      Israel justify a revival of Chassidism, and how could it be
      made a constructive factor in the new phases of Judaism that
      have resulted from the reform movement on the one hand and
      the progress in the natural sciences and higher criticism on
      the other?"

L83   Gordon, Nathan. "Joseph Perl's Megalleh Temirin." In A2.
      Pp. 235-42.

      "Joseph Perl's work has been praised as a most brilliant
      satire. He is not unjust, nor does he omit the minutest
      detail in order to complete the picture of Chasidic life.
      Indeed it must have been a terrible strain for him to wade
      through the undelectable literature, but what he derived from
      it he used with marvellous ability. He was one of the modest
      champions of the Haskalah. He had seen how Mendelssohn's
      school had succeeded after hard struggles in instilling into
      the minds of some Jews a desire for culture, for scientific
      research, and the impediment caused by Chasidism drove him to
      despair. His attacks were poignantly felt by them, and thus
      be [sic] contributed in the repulse of their further
      progress."

L84   Davidson, Israel. *Parody in Jewish Literature*. Columbia
      University Oriental Studies, Vol. II. New York: Columbia
      University Press, 1907.

      "The purpose of this book is to trace the development of
      that branch of Jewish satire which on account of its form
      goes by the name of parody, and to throw as much light upon
      the social life of the Jew as is possible to obtain from this
      peculiar class of literature." The first section of Part I,
      chapter 5, Parody from the Beginning of the 19th. Century to
      the Present Day (pp. 60-77), is devoted to Parodies against
      the Hasidim.

L85 Schechter, Solomon. "Saints and Saintliness." In his A5. Pp. 148-81. Rpt. L140.

"Here we shall confine ourselves to the subject of Saints and Saintliness in Judaism, an aspect of Judaism almost entirely neglected by our 'theologians.' ... Some mystics defined the saint, or the Chasid, as one who acts Chasid-like with his Maker, which may be interpreted to mean that not only does he not insist upon the letter of the Law, but all his worship is an act of grace without any hope of reward or fear of punishment."

L86 Sperling, H. "Jewish Sectaries. III: The Chassidim." *Jewish Review*, 3(1912), 130-46.

Attempts to answer the questions: "What, then, is the essence of Chassidism? Whence its strength? What are its antecedents? Who was its originator, and what are its relations to the rest of Jewry?"

L87 Wassilevsky, I. "Chassidism: A Resume of Modern Hebrew Mysticism." Intro. C.H. Herford. Read before the Annual Conference in London of the International Society of Philology, Science and Fine Arts, June 2, 1916. Blackburn: Geo. Toulmin & Sons, 1916.

Unavailable for annotating.

L88 Gaster, M. "The Chasidim and Their Modern Literature." *Jewish Forum*, 3(1920), 606-11.

"Whatever [literature about Chasidism] will appear henceforth must of necessity bear the imprint of the tragedy through which they [the Chasidim] have passed. And this modern Chasidic Literature carefully preserved and properly studied will in time contribute a very important page to the history of the Chasidic movement. It shows us the form it had assumed at the beginning of the 20th century. It is the most faithful reflex of the inner life of the Chasidim at that period, and in a way a monument to their piety and credulity. It well deserves a little love and much charity."

L89 Gasler, M. [Gaster?] "Mysticism among Jews." *Forum*, 66(July 1921), 55-63.

"This Chasidic movement, regarded from an historic point of view, started at just the parting of the ways. A new era was coming of political emancipation when the Jews would be called to participate to the full in the modern life of the nations of the world. It was the real parting of the ways, and to some extent it prepared the mind for the new changes which were coming.... On the one hand, it prepared them for changed conditions of life, and it put a check on the growing legal sophistry; and on the other hand, it was a warning against exaggerated spiritual exaltation and mystical aberration, which might lead them away from that moral sanity so characteristic of the Jewish faith."

L90 Gordon, Leib. "What is Chassidism?" Trans. L.M. Herbert. *Jewish Forum*, 5(1922), 142-44, 177-81.

"Rabbi Gordon wrote the present essay at a time when the Russian Government proposed to prohibit Chassidism and began to close their houses of prayer,... To the inquiry made by the Government, the Rabbi, though not a Chassid himself, replied, defending Chassidism. However, for the sake of truth, we may as well admit that the worthy Rabbi has not told the whole story." (Editor's note)

L91 Levertoff, Paul P. *Love and the Messianic Age in Hitherto Untranslated Hasidic Writings; with Special Reference to the Fourth Gospel.* Studies in Jewish and Christian Piety. London: Episcopal Hebrew Christian Church Publications, 1923.

"This little book forms the basis of lectures on 'Hasidic Teaching in the Light of the New Testament' delivered by me in 1920 before the Origen Society, Lincoln College, Oxford, and at the Community of the Resurrection, Mirfield.... I hope by means of this short study to prove that traditional orthodox Judaism has no lack of spiritual fervour. Even 'the Sea of the Talmud' has its Gulf Stream of Mysticism." Contents: I. Knowledge of Love; II. The Law and Love; III. Fear and Love; IV. Joy and Love; V. Prayer and Love; VI. Repentance and Love; Epilogue: Love in the Fourth Gospel.

L92 Levertoff, Paul. "The Use of Parables in Ḥasidic Literature." *Quest*, 16(1925), 209-16.

Studies the use of parables in Hasidic literature, most of which, "like those in the Gospels, deal with sin and forgiveness, law and love, prayer and worship, fatherhood and sonship."

L93 Levertoff, Paul P. "The Wisdom of the Ḥasids." *Quest*, 18(1926), 29-38.

"The author has not only written the most sytematic account of the doctrine of the Hasids, based on first-hand acquaintance with their by no means easily accessible literature, which we possess, but he was also brought up among them, and so he knows intimately the spirit of this mystical Jewish Messianic movement from within." (Editor's note)

L94 Zhitlowsky, Chaim. "A Note on Chassidism." In *The Dybbuk, A Play in Four Acts*, by S. Ansky. Trans. Henry G. Alsberg and Winifred Katzin. New York: Boni & Liveright, 1926. Pp. 11-20.

"It was Ansky's purpose to draw us a picture of life in a Chassidic community, a life hovering on the boundary between two worlds, the world of reality and the faith-created world of supernatural forces. This life, with all its richness of spirit, will be found depicted in the pages of 'The Dybbuk.'"

L95 Bension, Ariel. "The Sephardic Chassidim of Beth-el." *Menorah Journal*, 13(1927), 269-81.

Description of "the Sephardic Chassidim of Jerusalem, whose sanctuary Beth-El was," and "Shalom Sharaabi, the Master Builder, [who] appeared among the Chassidim of Beth-El in the eighteenth century. It was he who molded their Chassidism into an order that inspired Jewish life in Jerusalem for many generations, unifying and harmonizing its varied elements by the power of mystic love with which he infused it."

L96 Gaster, Moses. "Hasidism." *Jewish Forum*, 11(1928), 288-90.

Brief attempt to analyze the causes of Hasidism through a survey of the historical, psychological and mystical influences which contributed to the movement.

L97 Ginzberg, Louis. "The Gaon, Rabbi Elijah Wilna." In his A16. Pp. 125-44.

Biographical sketch of the eighteenth-century scholar.

L98 Horodetzky, S.A. "The Essence of Chassidism." *Reflex*, 3(October 1928), 11-18.

Answers the questions: "What has Chassidism given the Jewish people? What has it innovated in addition to all that was created before in the field of Jewish religious mysticism? What has Chassidism discovered that it should attract hundreds of thousands of people in all parts of the world and to make Chassidism such a tremendous force in Jewish life in the last two hundred years?"

L99 Horodezky, Samuel A. *Leaders of Hassidism*. Trans. Maria Horodezky-Magasanik. London: Hasefer, 1928.

"In this book an attempt has been made to describe the lives and deeds of the leaders of Hassidism." The leaders include: Rabbi Israel Baal Shem Tov; Rabbi Baer of Meseritz; Rabbi Jacob Joseph of Polona; Rabbi Nachum of Tchernobyl; Rabbi Levi Yitzhak of Berditchev; Rabbi Abraham "The Angel"; Rabbi Leib Sorahs; Rabbi Shneur Zalman of Ladi; The "Grand-Sire" of Shpola [Rabbi Loeb]; Rabbi Nahman of Bratzlav; and The Maid of Ludomir [Hanna Rachel Werbemacher]. Horodezky also includes chapters on The Communal Life of the Hassidim, and Palestine and Hassidism.

L100 Doppelt, Frederic A. "The Besht in Chassidism." *Reflex*, 4(May 1929), 57-64.

Analysis of the Baal Shem Tov, "this hero of our people, the outlines of whose spirit are stamped upon our hearts for the last two hundred years, has an actual image and a legendary image created in the minds of the people; and both are dissimilar."

L101 Idelsohn, A.Z. *Jewish Music in Its Historical Development*. New York: Henry Holt and Company, Inc., 1929. Rpt. New York: Tudor Pub. Co., 1948; New York: Schocken Books, 1956, 1967; Westport, Conn.: Greenwood Press, 1981.

"The aim of this book is to give a description and an analysis of the elements and characteristics of Jewish music, in their historical development, from the earliest times of its appearance as a Semitic-Oriental song, throughout the ages and countries." Chapter 19, Chassidic Song (pp. 411-34), explores the ramifications of the fact that "The chassidic leaders believed that vocal music is the best medium of rising to salvation."

L102 Spiegel, Shalom. "A Wonder-Worker." In his A17. Pp. 119-59.

Popular approach to Hasidic literature.

L103 Yisroel ben Baruch haChassid. "A Jewish Mystical Movement." *Occult Review*, 55(1932), 83-88, 167-73.

"There exists, however, yet another and most significant system of Jewish mysticism--*Chassidism*--concerning which surprisingly little appears to be known. In the works of W. Wynn Westcott and Arthur Edward Waite there are casual statements as to the existence of the Chassidim--and no more. This revivalist movement is, in reality, so important, and of so recent a date, that I am moved to present a few of its major tenets. Those which have most strongly impressed me are given here, hand in hand with some verbatim statements of those of its exponents who rightfully acquired the laudatory title of *Tsaddik* or saint, together with a few comparative and explanatory remarks on the Qabalah."

L104 Minkin, Jacob S. *The Romance of Hassidism*. New York: Macmillan Company, 1935. Rev. ed. North Hollywood: T. Yoseloff, 1955, 1971.

"It is the author's opinion that the story of Hassidism, its struggles and triumphs, its faith and ideals, can best be told through the outstanding personalities who created this movement of romantic mysticism and spread it among the masses. From the comparatively large number of Hassidic saints and teachers, the author has selected men whose faith reflected not only their own soul's conflicts and harmonies, but who also had the widest influence on the movement they created."

L105 Lapson, Dvora. "The Chassidic Dance." *Dance Observer*, November 1937. Rpt. L157.

"For Chassidism, unlike any other reform movement known to us, has made dancing a part of life, of the everyday life of millions of Jewish people. The Chassidic dance was not composed deliberately, nor did it originate as a folk dance. It arose as a conscious attempt to create human joyousness out of misery."

L106 Mahler, Raphael. "Censorship of Hasidic, Kabbalistic and Yiddish Literature in Galicia during the Period of Reaction (1815-1848)." *Journal of Jewish Bibliography*, 1(1938-39), 35-39, 71-82.

"We shall examine in this article the influence of Hasidism during this period as reflected in the contemporary Hasidic literature, in official government documents, and in some utterances of the bitter opponents of Hasidism, the *maskilim*."

L107 Bloch, Joshua. "A Legendary Edition of the *Toledot Yaakob Yosef* by Jacob Joseph ha-Kohen." *Jewish Quarterly Review*, n.s. 31(1941), 245-57.

History of "the *Toledot Yaakob Yosef (=Toledot)*, written by Rabbi Jacob Joseph ha-Kohen of Polonnoye to gain followers for the Zadikim, not only stimulated enthusiasm and admiration for their teachings and practices among their followers, but also became a useful instrument against the vigorous opposition in the ranks of the Mithnagedim."

L108 Pinson, Koppel S. "The Poetry of Hassidism." *Menorah Journal*, 29(1941), 287-311.

"I shall rather deal with the imaginative, emotional and aesthetic aspects of Hassidism, and their influence on artistic and imaginative Jewish life as a whole. For it is here that the modernity of Hassidism becomes most apparent. Unlike the rabbinic works of the period and even of the Hasklah writers, the creations of Hassidic fantasy still appeal to us today despite their crudity and superstitious dressing. We appreciate the sense of poetry inherent in them; we view them as true types of aesthetic creation; and we experience a sense of emotional kinship with them."

L109 Finkel, Joshua. "A Psychoanalytic Prefiguration in Hasidic Literature." In A22. Pp.. 55-66.

Finds prefigures of psychoanalysis in hasidic writings to conclude that "One sphere of Jewish thought may be closer than another to certain ideas from without, but no single segment of Jewish thought may claim sole kinship with an intellectual system outside its fold. A psychoanalytic prefiguration might as well be found in the Talmud, Responsa, Qabbala or even in the humblest *Ma'ase Buch*. The Jewish mind is far from explored."

L110 Buber, Martin. "The Beginnings of Chassidism." In his A27. Pp. 149-80. Rpt. L113. Another translation L146.

"The decisive factor for the nature and greatness of Chassidism is not found in a teaching, but in a mode of life; and, indeed, in a mode of life which shapes a community, and regulates a community in accordance with its own nature.... It is the new mode of life which presses towards a conceptual expression, a theological interpretation; and the practical point of reference, which determines the selection, has its origin in this need for theological interpretation."

L111 Buber, Martin. "The Interpretation of Chassidism." In A27. Pp. 65-148. Rpt. L118, L119. Another translation L151, L153, L154.

Contains "Spirit and Body in the Chassidic Movement"; "Spinoza, Sabbatai Zwi, and Baalshem"; and "Symbolism and Sacramental Existence in Judaism": "Like my other studies of Chassidism they are not concerned with a historical presentation or an analytical investigation, but with the interpretation of the religious content, and still more of the religious attitude, of Chassidism. Though the three works bear the imprint of their common task, they differ in their approach to the problem. The first considers the Chassidic movement principally from the point of view of mankind's way of faith; the second sets Chassidism in juxtaposition to two earlier manifestations of Jewish, spiritual life, manifestations of an attack on faith, and of a distortion of faith; the third work is an attempt to compare, on a point of essential importance, the attitude of the faith of the prophets and of the chassids. It is hoped that the joint publication of these three works may help to draw attention to the vital importance of chassidic teaching and chassidic life for present-day Jewry, and for mankind."

L112 Mindel, Nissan. *Rabbi Joseph I. Schneersohn, The Lubavitcher Rabbi (A Short Biography)*. Rev. ed. Brooklyn: Kehot Publication Society, 1947.

"His selfless devotion to his people, his martyrdom for Torah and Judaism, his inspiring leadership in the most critical era of Jewish history, makes [sic] the Lubavitcher Rabbi stand out as one of the most reverend and saintly figures of the entire world of Jewry."

L113 Buber, Martin. "The Beginnings of Hasidism." Trans. Greta Hort. In A29. Pp. 1-33.

Reprint of L110.

L114 Buber, Martin. "Foundation Stone." Trans. Carlyle Witton-Davies and Mary Witton-Davies. In A29. Pp. 34-59. Different translation L147.

"The first revolt of the Am-haaretz [unlearned people of the land], the revolt of early Christianity, rushed out of the gates of Judaism. The second revolt, the Hasidic one, remained within the confines of Judaism. For unlike the first, which demanded that men should live as if the kingdom of God had dawned, Hasidism affirmed the natural reality of the still unmessianic time as the material to be hallowed, and thereby it affirmed the people as such, the great unholy body, which is destined to be hallowed."

L115 Buber, Martin. "God and the Soul." Trans. Carlyle Witton-Davies and Mary Witton-Davies. In his A29. Pp. 145-58. Different translation L148.

"In Hasidism--and in it alone, so far as I can see, in the history of mankind--has mysticism become Ethos. Here the original mystical unity, to which the soul desires to ascend, is no other form of God than the demander of the demand, and the mystical soul cannot become real, if it is not one with the moral soul."

L116 Buber, Martin. "Love of God and Love of One's Neighbor." Trans. Immanuel Olsvanger. In his A29. Pp. 159-83. Different translation L136.

"You cannot truly love God if you do not love your fellow man, and you cannot truly love your fellow man if you do not love God. This is the stage which Hasidism has reached, though the new mode of life instituted by it remains fragmentary and transitory. One must have essential intercourse only with God, says Kierkegaard. It is impossible, says Hasidism, to have truly essential intercourse with God when there is no essential intercourse with men."

L117 Buber, Martin. "The Place of Hasidism in the History of Religion." Trans. Carlyle Witton-Davies and Mary Witton-Davies. In A29. Pp. 184-201. Different translation L149.

Comparison of Hasidism and Zen: "The realism of Zen is dialectic, it means annulment; the Hasidic realism is messianic, it means fulfilment. Just as, linked with revelation, it heeds the past, so, linked with redemption, it heeds the future--both in contrast to Zen, for which absolute reality is only accorded to the *moment*, as this is the possibility of inner illumination, and before the moment the dimension of time disappears. Hasidism is, so far as I can see, the only mysticism in which *time* is hallowed."

L118   Buber, Martin. "Spirit and Body of the Hasidic Movement." Trans. Greta Hort. In his A29. Pp. 60-94.

Reprint of part of L111.

L119   Buber, Martin. "Symbolical and Sacramental Existence in Judaism." In A29. Pp. 117-44.

Reprint of part of L111.

L120   Kranzler, Gershon. *Rabbi Shneur Zalman of Ladi: A Brief Presentation of the Life, the Work, and the Basic Teachings of the Founder of Chabad Chassidism*. Based on talks with Rabbi Mendel Schneerson. Brooklyn: Kehot Publication Society, 1948.

Brief pamphelt providing Genealogy of Shneur Zalman, Biography, Facsimile of a Letter in the Rabbi's Handwriting, Important dates in the Life of the Rav, Published Works of the Rav, and a Bibliography.

L121   Buber, Martin. *The Way of Man According to the Teachings of the Hasidim*. London: Routledge & K. Paul, 1950. Rpt. Wallingford, Pa.: Pendle Hill, 1960; New York: Citadel Press, 1966. Rpt. L137, L167, L174.

"The task of man, of every man, according to hasidic teaching, is to affirm for God's sake the world and himself and by this very means to transform both." Buber discusses this task in terms of: I. Heart-Searching; II. The Particular Way; III. Revolution; IV. Beginning with Oneself; V. Not to be Preoccupied with Oneself; and VI. Here Where One Stands.

L122   Rabinovich, Wolf. "Karlin Hasidism." *Yivo Annual of Jewish Social Science*, 5(1950), 123-51.

Study of the history of Karlin Hasidism--"the historical development of the movement in Karlin, the role of its representatives who were the pioneers of hasidism in rabbinic Lithuania and their fate during the persecutions by the Lithuanian communities and rabbis, their battle with the *misnagdim*, their intellectual niveau and their later relationship with the other hasidic currents."

L123 Scholem, Gershom G. "Devekuth, or Communion with God." *Review of Religion*, 14(1950), 115-39. Rpt. L203.

Explores the doctrine of Devekuth as the central point of Hasidism by considering both "its 'prehistory' and its position in Hasidism."

L124 Buber, Martin. "Israel's Land: Habitation of God: The Zionism of Rabbi Nahman." Trans. Francis C. Golffing. *Commentary*, 12(1951), 345-54.

"In this essay on Rabbi Nahman of Bratzlav (1772-1810), Martin Buber gives us an understanding of one of the most significant modern manifestations of the spiritual tie between the idea and soil of Eretz Israel and the believing Jew. At the same time, Dr. Buber continues one of his lifelong tasks: to explore the myths and legends of Judaism--and especially of Hasidism--in order to arrive, indirectly as it were, at philosophic and religious truths." (Editor's note) Buber covers: The Hasidim and the Holy Land; The Sabbatianic Danger; The Baal-shem-tov and Palestine; Rabbi Nahman's Decision; The Voyage; The Holiness of the Soil; The Earthly Way; The Soil of Faith; and The Doorway to Redemption.

L125 Zborowski, Mark, and Elizabeth Herzog. *Life is with People: The Jewish Little-Town of Eastern Europe*. New York: International Universities Press, Inc., 1952. Rpt. New York: Schocken Books, 1962.

"This book is an attempt to bring our anthropological discipline to the task of preserving something of the form and the content, the texture and the beauty, of the small-town life of Eastern European Jews, as it was lived before World War I, in some places up to World War II,..." Chapter 6, The Rebbeh Makes Miracles (pp. 166-88), discusses the Hasidim in Eastern Europe.

L126 Chavel, Charles B. "Shneyur Zalman of Liady." In A35. Pp. 53-76. Rpt. L220.

Biographical sketch.

L127 Perlmutter, Philip. "The Hasidim of Williamsburg." *Chicago Jewish Forum*, 12,1(Fall 1953), 26-30.

Description of the Hasidim of Williamsburg.

L128 Weiss, J.G. "Contemplative Mysticism and 'Faith' in Hasidic Piety." *Journal of Jewish Studies*, 4(1953), 19-29.

Explores the hypothesis that while "A certain degree of uniformity can be seen in the realm of folklore and in some forms of religious life.... Both from the theological point of view and as far as religious values are concerned, this standardisation of the Hasidic schools and their doctrines must be rejected. The postulated artificial unity and uniformity disappear when we look for their verification in the theoretical literature of Hasidic authors."

L129 Poppers, Harry L. "Hasidism and Rabbinic Judaism." *Judaism*, 4(1955), 70-77.

"A brief sketch of the bitter historic conflict engendered by the rise of Hasidism will serve to highlight the actual points of divergence that emerged between it and traditional rabbinic Judaism."

L130 Weiss, J.G. "R. Abraham Kalisker's Concept of Communion with God and Men." *Journal of Jewish Studies*, 6(1955), 87-99.

"It is intended in this article to analyse one of R. Abraham's letters--which is unfortunately undated--dealing mainly with *devekuth*, the ideal way of life in Hasidic theory and practice."

L131 Wilensky, Mordecai L. "The Polemic of Rabbi David of Makow against Hasidism." *Proceedings of the American Academy for Jewish Research*, 25(1956), 137-56.

"In this article, we will deal with the following: A) A description of an anti-Hasidic document, as yet unpublished, whose author is Rabbi David of Makow, the outspoken opponent of Hasidism toward the end of the 18th century and the beginning of the 19th century. B) A disclosure of previously unknown material concerning Rabbi David."

L132 Finkel, Joshua. "A Link between Hasidism and Hellenistic and Patristic Literature." *Proceedings of the American Academy for Jewish Research*, 26(1957), 1-24; 27(1958), 19-41.

In Part I, Finkel traces a parable about Rabbi Israel of Rizin (the Riziner) back to a parable in Philo to demonstrate that "It is more likely than not that Philo's present parable was a time-worn fixture of Greek moral edification." And in Part II, he explores "the problem of transmission of the Greek motif from antiquity to modern times."

L133 Kazis, Israel J. "Hasidism Re-examined." *Reconstructionist*, 23(31 May 1957), 7-13.

Using Louis Ginzberg's assertion that with the exception of Habad, "other forms of Hasidism ... represent the acme of systematic cant and irrational talk," [C53, p.215], Kazis examines "the elements of irrationality and fantasy in Hasidic doctrine [that it] may have a sobering effect upon those who have been overly influenced by the current romanticist conception of Hasidism."

L134 Weiss, J.G. "A Circle of Pre-Hassidic Pneumatics." *Journal of Jewish Studies*, 8(1957), 199-213.

"The following note aims at analysing certain aspects of the life of 'the circle of Nahman of Kossov' with a view to establishing its historical position between the late Sabbatian and early Hasidic movements."

L135 Buber, Martin. "The Life of the Hasidim." In his A41. Pp. 74-122.

Study of four hasidic concepts--Hitlahavut: Ecstasy; Avoda: Service; Kavana: Intention; and Shiflut: Humility.

L136 Buber, Martin. "Love of God and Love of Neighbor." In his A41. Pp. 225-55.

Different translation of L116.

L137 Buber, Martin. "The Way of Man According to the Teachings of the Hasidim." In his A41. Pp. 126-76.

Reprint of L121.

L138 Schechter, S. "The Chassidim." In his A42. Pp. 150-89.

Reprint of L78.

L139 Schechter, S. "Rabbi Elijah Wilna, Gaon." In his A42. Pp. 298-320.

Reprint of L81.

L140 Schechter, S. "Saints and Saintliness." In his A42. Pp. 123-49.

Reprint of L85.

L141 Weiss, J.G. "Is the Hasidic Book 'Kethoneth Passim' a Literary Forgery?" *Journal of Jewish Studies*, 9(1958), 81-83.

Refutation of Dubnow's assertion (in *Toledoth ha-hasiduth*, Tel Aviv, 1930-32), that the Hasidic book *Kethoneth Passim* is a literary forgery.

L142 Weiss, J.G. "The Kavvanoth of Prayer in Early Hasidism." *Journal of Jewish Studies*, 9(1958), 163-92.

From examining secondary sources, the biography of Israel Baal Shem (published 1815), and passages in the writings of his disciples, Weiss concludes that "no consistent concept of *Kavvanoth* of prayer seems to appear and the picture which emerges of Israel Baalshem's views and practice is somewhat vague. The evidence predominantly suggests that he had abandoned *Kavvanoth* as a method of meditation in the strict Kabbalistic sense, or rather never practised them at all."

L143   Katzoff, Louis. "Aspects of Mental Hygiene in Hasidism." *Jewish Heritage*, 2,2(Fall 1959), 20-24.

Asserts that "*Hasidism* was able to win so many Jews to its view because it was not a system of thought, a teaching,... not based on a rational system of philosophy or theology, but on a 'way of living.' *Hasidism* intuitively knew the needs of the human soul and in meeting them found the key to the fulfillment of the human personality. Without benefit of the science of psychology, it nevertheless demonstrated an amazing understanding of individual behavior and group interaction."

L144   Newman, Louis I. "The Baal Shem Tov." In A44. Pp. 281-307.

Introduces the "life and the new religious orientation ... [which] helped to fill the spiritual needs of Polish Jewry during the declining years of the Polish Kingdom and to insure the survival of Polish Jewry for another two centuries." Newman discusses the Baal Shem Tov as Teacher and Healer, His Psychological Insight, Character of His Message, Role of Joy in Hasidism, Religious Ideas, Importance of Love, Ethical Virtues, Role of Zaddik, and The Legacy of Hasidism.

L145   Rabinowicz, H. "Music and Dance in Hassidism." *Judaism*, 8(1959), 252-57.

Examination of the importance of music and dance to Hasidism since "Song was an integral part of Hassidic life and 'service through joy,' was the ideal of the Besht."

L146   Buber, Martin. "The Beginnings." In his A47. Pp. 24-57.

Different translation of L110.

L147   Buber, Martin. "The Foundation Stone." In his A47. Pp. 59-88.

Different translation of L114.

L148   Buber, Martin. "God and the Soul." In his A47. Pp. 183-99.

Different translation of L115.

L149 Buber, Martin. "The Place of Hasidism in the History of Religion." In his A47. Pp. 219-39. Rpt. L243.

Different translation of L117.

L150 Buber, Martin. "Redemption." In his A47. Pp. 201-18.

"I want to show now how in Hasidism the national element was combined with the cosmic element, with the individual element, with the religious element, and how they became a real unity, according to the order of these four kinds of exile and redemption. I shall illustrate with passages from Hasidic literature."

L151 Buber, Martin. "Spirit and Body of the Hasidic Movement." In his A47. Pp. 113-49.

Different translation of L111.

L152 Buber, Martin. "Supplement: Christ, Hasidism, Gnosis." In his A47. Pp. 241-54.

"In Rudolf Pannwitz's essay on Hasidism [*Merkur*, 8, 79(September 1954), 810-30], one finds, along with a penetrating understanding, some no less basic misunderstanding that ought in some measure to be clarified." Pannwitz's response to Buber: "Mythos, Gnosis, Religion." *Merkur*, 8, 81(November 1954), 1068-71.

L153 Buber, Martin. "Symbolic and Sacramental Existence." In his A47. Pp. 151-81.

Different translation of L111.

L154 Buber, Martin. "Symbolic and Sacramental Existence in Judaism." Trans. Ralph Manheim. *Spiritual Disciplines*. Papers from the Eranos Yearbook, vol. 4. New York: Pantheon Books, 1960. Pp. 168-85.

Different translation of L111.

L155 Dresner, Samuel H. *The Zaddik: The Doctrine of the Zaddik According to the Writings of Rabbi Yaakov Yosef of Polnoy*. New York: Schocken Books, 1960.

"Told through the medium of the writings of Yaakov Yosef of Polnoy, here is a study of the Zaddik, the saint--mystic and holy leader, as he was created by the crisis of eighteenth-century Judaism that produced the Hasidic movement." Dresner divides his discussion of the Zaddik into two parts: The Problem (The Conditions of the Time, The Life of Rabbi

Yaakov Yosef, The Writings of Rabbi Yaakov Yosef, and A Critique of Leadership); and The Solution (The Zaddik, Humility, The Descent of the Zaddik, Transgression and Danger, and The Circle of Musar).

L156 *Judaism*, 9,3(Summer 1960).

Special issue on Hasidism. See: B4, L28, L158, L159, L162, L163, L166, M41, M42.

L157 Lapson, Dvora. "The Chassidic Dance." In A46. Pp. 20-26.

Reprint of L105.

L158 Margolius, Hans. "On the Ethics of Hasidism." *Judaism*, 9(1960), 207-15.

"The primary purpose of Hasidism was to effect ... the justification of the ignorant as opposed to the learned man, the justification of the simple acts of the pure of heart as opposed to the demands of tradition, custom, learning and law."

L159 Orent, Joel. "The Transcendent Person." *Judaism*, 9(1960), 235-52.

Study of the *Tsaddik*, "a new type of Jewish personality" who "in his fulness [sic] of mind, did not need to imitate any other human being, and was able to appropriate for himself his own right to self-fulfilment."

L160 Patterson, D. "The Portrait of Hasidism in the Nineteenth-Century Hebrew Novel." *Journal of Semitic Studies*, 5(1960), 359-77.

"The purpose of this paper is to present a picture of Hasidism as it is portrayed in the Hebrew novel over a period of twenty years, namely 1868-88. In no sense does it purport to be a scientific study of Hasidism, but represents rather an attempt to describe the attitude adopted by Hebrew novelists toward that movement in the second half of the nineteenth century."

L161 Rabinowicz, H. *A Guide to Hassidism*. New York and London: Thomas Yoseloff, 1960.

Intended "as an introduction to Hassidism," containing twelve essays: 1. The Background; 2. Rabbi Israel Baal Shem Tov; 3. Three Great Teachers [Rabbi Dov Baer of Meseritz, Rabbi Jacob Joseph of Polona, Rabbi Levi Isaac of Berdychev]; 4. The Wrath of Elijah [Vilner Gaon]; 5. The Legacy of Habad; 6. Rabbi Nachman of Bratslav; 7. Pioneers of Polish Hassidism; 8. The Three Great Dynasties [Rizhyn-

Sadagura, Belz, Ger]; 9. The Role of Hassida; 10. The Hassidic Way of Life; 11. Hassidism and Israel; and 12. Hassidism in the Twentieth Century.

L162 Shauli, A. "Hasidic Legend and Aphorism as Literary Art Form." *Judaism*, 9(1960), 229-34.

"The religious movement which Rabbi Israel Baal Shem Tov began was also the beginning of a great Jewish esthetic revival. The Hasidic tale, the Hasidic aphorism and idea were nourished by an imagination which suddenly blossomed anew and gave birth to new visions and new melodies."

L163 Unger, Menashe. "The Study of Hasidism." *Judaism*, 9(1960), 253-59.

"A brief survey of the major modern works of the Hasidic movement would appear to be in order, now that we are observing the 200th anniversary of the death of its founder, Rabbi Israel Baal Shem Tov. We will confine ourselves to books which have been published in the twentieth century, and deal only with those which we regard as absolutely indispensable to the research student, as well as to the general reader who wants to understand the history of Hasidism."

L164 Weiss, J.G. "The Great Maggid's Theory of Contemplative Magic." *Hebrew Union College Annual*, 31(1960), 137-47.

"In the bulk of writings which was handed down and printed in the name of R. Dobh Baer of Mezritch, the first theoretician of the Hasidic movement, a fully developed theory of speculative magic is discernible. It appears often, but by no means exclusively, connected with his theory of the religious leader (Zaddik) who is particularly supposed to make use of the methods prescribed by this speculative doctrine of magic which forms an integral part of the Great Maggid's system of magical idealism animated by the concept of contemplation as the highest religious activity."

L165 Weiss, J.G. "Via Passiva in Early Hasidism." *Journal of Jewish Studies*, 11(1960), 137-55.

"The claim is that passivity is conducive to ecstasy, and indeed instrumental in attaining it; and it is this that I shall attempt to trace in the literature of early Hasidism. If the mystical spirit be present in that literature, as I believe it to be in abundance, Hasidism will show affinities to all other mystical trends and the aspect of passivity will not be lacking."

L166 Werner, Alfred. "Max Weber: Hasidic Painter." *Judaism*, 9(1960), 260-68.

Analysis of the hasidic influences on the American-Jewish artist Max Weber.

L167 Buber, Martin. "The Way of Man According to the Teachings of the Hasidim." In A48. Pp. 425-41.

Reprint of L121.

L168 Reimer, Jack. "Franz Kafka and Rabbi Nachman." *Jewish Frontier*, 28,4(April 1961), 16-20.

"We have examined three literary themes: transformation, the closed door, and the letter as they appear in the writings of Franz Kafka and Rabbi Nachman. In each case we have seen that these two artists make use of the very same motifs but that they use them to provide opposing answers to the same questions. It is in this sense that we believe Rabbi Nachman's comment to be true: 'Two men who live in different places, or even in different generations, may still converse.'"

L169 Schochet, Jacob Immanuel. *Rabbi Israel Baal Shem Tov: A Monograph on the Life and Teachings of the Founder of Chassidism.* Toronto: Lieberman's Publishing House, 1961.

Originally a series of articles in the Toronto *Daily Hebrew Journal* (from 1 May to 20 September 1960). Schochet "discarded all legendary, or otherwise questionable sources and material, not in the least to repudiate them as such or to deny their own merits, but rather to trace a somewhat definite and accurate based on genuine documents and historically sound facts," of Rabbi Israel Baal Shem Tov. In addition to biography, Schochet includes background material on kabbalistic influences on the founder of Hasidism.

L170 Mailer, Norman. "Responses & Reactions." *Commentary*, 34(1962), 504-6; 35(1963), 146-48, 335-37, 517-18; 36(1963), 164-65.

"Every other month in this magazine, a short story, or two, or possibly three, all very short, from Martin Buber's *Tales of the Hasidim* [L14] will be printed, followed by a terse commentary by me."

L171 Schneersohn, Joseph I. *The "Tzemach Tzedek" and the Haskala Movement.* Trans. Zalman I. Posner. Brooklyn: Kehot Publication Society, 1962, 1969.

"The pamphlet here translated, presents a view of that critical period of ingress of Haskala into Russia in the 1840's, written from the position of the traditional Jew. The author, Rabbi Joseph I. Schneersohn, the late Lubavitcher Rabbi, was a great-grandson of Rabbi Menachem

Mendel, the central figure of these pages. He drew his material from unpublished sources, memoirs of participants, and family traditions, as well as documents. Like many of his discursive writings, it has the informality of reminiscence and attention to detail. The footnotes, unless otherwise noted, are his, except for occasional citations, etc." (Translator's note)

L172 Wilensky, Mordecai L. "Some Notes on Rabbi Israel Loebel's Polemic against Hasidism." *Proceedings of the American Academy for Jewish Research*, 30(1962), 141-51.

Discussion of Rabbi Israel Loebel, an example of the paradox "that from the circles of the Maggidim, from whose ranks came many of the founders of Hasidism and its first expounders, came also its most ardent opponents, who expressed and spread their opinions both orally and in written form."

L173 Block, Irving. "Chabad Psychology and the *Benoni* of *Tanya*." *Tradition*, 6,1(Fall 1963), 30-39.

"The purpose of the present article is to present one of the basic notions of the *Tanya* in a language closer to the understanding of the contemporary Jew. Unfortunately, limitations of space necessitate that the ideas and concepts introduced here be simplified. This article intends no more than to point out the *general direction* of Chabad thought on the topics discussed and does not attempt anything like a full exposition of them."

L174 Buber, Martin. "The Way of Man According to the Teachings of the Hasidim." In A55. Pp. 243-87.

Reprint of L121.

L175 Patterson, D. "The Portrait of the 'Saddik' in the Nineteenth-Century Hebrew Novel." *Journal of Semitic Studies*, 8(1963), 170-88.

Sequel to L160: " ... many of the episodes relating to the Saddikim in these novels preserve the flavour of first-hand observation by actual, if sceptical, spectators. Although their presentation of the scene is obviously very different from that of fervent adherents, their descriptions frequently sound the note of truth. Their most biting satire is directed against the charlatanism which such unrestrained credulity is bound to occasion; and as exponents of the doctrine of enlightenment, they lose no opportunity of pillorying the undesirable obscurantism of many of the Hasidic leaders towards any form of secular knowledge."

L176 Shazar, Zalman. "The Idea of Redemption in Hassidic Thought." In A57. Pp. 401-20.

Explains the absence of Messianism in the Hassidic movement as "the great price that Hassidism paid in order to mount the breach and to rescue the messianic hope and with it the belief of the Jewish people in its future. There was a strict embargo both external and internal, on every practical expression. Every Hassid had to divert the essence of this belief and desire internally into his own soul, strictly eschewing all public and overt acts to a point of pitilessness, lest the nation fall once again."

L177   Glitzenstein, Abraham C. *The Arrest and Liberation of Rabbi Shneur Zalman of Liadi.* As compiled and edited from the writings and traditions of the leaders and followers of Chabad-Chassidism. Trans. Jacob Immanuel Schochet. Brooklyn: Kehot Publication Society, 1964.

Translation and adaptation of Rabbi Abraham C. Glitzenstein's compilation of all available material relating to the arrest and liberation of the Hasidic rabbi. In addition to the history of the event, Schochet includes a Pastoral Letter of Rabbi Menachem Mendel Schneerson of Lubavitch, Genealogy of the Founder of General Chassidism and the Leader of Chabad, Facsimile of a Letter in R. Shneur Zalman's Handwriting, History of the Letter, Glossary, Important Dates from the Life of R. Shneur Zalman, and Published Works of R. Shneur Zalman.

L178   Jacobs, Louis. *Seekers of Unity: The Life and Works of Aaron of Starosselje.* New York: Basic Books, and London: Valentine, Mitchell, 1966.

"The subject of this study, Rabbi Aaron ben Moses Ha-Levi Horowitz of Starosselje (1766-1828), is a little-known contemplative and Hasidic master, whose thought is of much interest to students of mysticism and religion in general.... It would have been futile to attempt to understand the thought of an unconventional but orthodox Kabbalist without reference to his Kabbalistic antecedents. To these, Chapters 2, 3 and 4 of the present work are devoted. Chapter 1 is a largely biographical introduction, and Chapter 5 discusses Rabbi Aaron's general approach. Rabbi Aaron's works are three in number: *Sha'are Ha-Yihud We-Ha-'Emunah* (his philosophy of religion), *Sha'are 'Abhodah* (his understanding of the meaning of worship) and *'Abhodath Ha-Levi* (his commentaries on the Pentateuch). Chapter 6 deals mainly with the first of these works, Chapter 7 with the second and Chapter 8 with the third. Chapter 9 is an attempted brief summary of Rabbi Aaron's philosophy and a consideration of its significance."

L179   Hilsenrad, Zalman Aryeh, trans. *The Baal Shem Tov: His Birth and Early Manhood.* Brooklyn: Kehot Publication Society, 1967.

"Who and what was the founder of Chasidus? What was there about him and about his teachings which attracted--and continues to attract--both the greatest Torah scholars and also the least learned of our people? To learn something of the times of the Baal Shem Tov, of his parents, his birth, upbringing, and early manhood ... that is the purpose of this little book. It is offered in the fond hope that it will inspire us to aspire to follow ... and to shteig with the saintly men we know as Chasidim. And if but one reader adopts but one Chasidic trait ... that will be my reward."

L180 Lipschitz, Max A. *The Faith of a Hasid*. New York: Jonathan David, Publishers, 1967.

"Thus, to sum up, the following are the objectives, purposes, and aims of this book: 1. A Study of the lives, works, and influences of the first two *Zaddikim* of the city of Gur; Rabbi Yitzhak Meir Alter, known as the Rym by the initials of his names; and Rabbi Yehuda Aryeh Leib Alter, commonly called the Sefath Emeth from the title of his commentary. 2. A critical and impartial examination of Hassidism, with major emphasis on the Gerer *Zaddikim*'s Hassidic thinking." The study is divided into four parts: I. Basic Hassidism; II. The School of Gur and Their Rabbis; III. The Philosophy of Gur; and IV. The Literature of Gur.

L181 Schatz, R. "Contemplative Prayer in Hasidism." In A67. Pp. 209-26. Rpt. L251.

The spiritual significance of Hasidic prayer is certainly not to be found in a (non existent) abolition of its concrete elements. The same applies to the attitude of Hasidism to other concrete elements in the cosmos. Its real contribution lies in the breaking of the concrete framework of prayer in an effort to illuminate thereby the 'dark letters'. The same applies to the Hasidic doctrine of the annihilation of all concrete things in order to raise the divine sparks imprisoned in them. The real revolution took place in the change of meaning of the concept of *kawwanah* (originally 'concentrated attention and devotion', later 'mystical intention'): the intention is now intended 'upwards' in the sense of divesting the spiritual of the material and attaining the 'pure', divine thought. It is this change which characterizes the role of the spirit in Hasidic doctrine."

L182 Shapiro, David S. "The Basis of Habad Philosophy: A Study in the *Tanya*." *Judaism*, 16(1967), 324-39.

Attempt "to enlighten the student as to the doctrines, both theological and psychological, and the way of life of the Lubavitcher."

L183 Eliach, Yaffa. "The Russian Dissenting Sects and Their Influence on Israel Baal Shem Tov, Founder of Hassidism." *Proceedings of the American Academy for Jewish Research*, 36(1968), 57-83.

Posits the thesis that "contrary to current theories, the founder of the Hassidic movement of Judaism--the Baal Shem Tov ... was inspired by non-Jewish sources,... Today a close examination of Hassidic sources, its customs, dances, songs, and dress shows that Hassidism indeed drew heavily on sources foreign to Judaism: the Russian Schismatics and Dissenters of the seventeenth and eighteenth centuries."

L184 Ettinger, S. "The Hassidic Movement--Reality and Ideals." *Journal of World History*, 11(1968), 251-66. Rpt. L201.

"The success of Hassidism sprang from the fact that it brought mysticism to the 'intelligentsia' of the time in a form they could accept. It particularly appealed to young students and religious functionaries. On the other hand it found an echo among the masses, for instead of the ideal personality of the pre-Hasidic generation, the remote, self-mortifying mystic, Hassidism idealised the mystic who leads the people and lives among them."

L185 Fackenheim, Emil L. "Two Types of Reform: Reflections Occasioned by Hasidism." In A68. Pp. 169-87.

Analyzes the relationship between Hasidism and the two kinds of reform in Judaism: "The rationalistic kind of reform, it is now very plain, is largely negative in character; and an additional positive reform is needed if Judaism is not to be dissipated into generalities and irrelevancies. But those who seek such a reform have learned to look on Hasidism, not as a quaint and superseded phenomenon, but rather as a source of inspiration and hope."

L186 Hurwitz, Siegmund. "Psychological Aspects in Early Hasidic Literature." Trans. Hildegard Nagel. In A70. Pp. 149-239.

Using both the psychology of C.G. Jung and the modern research in Kabbalism of G. Scholem, Hurwitz examines the older Hasidic writings of Rabbi Dov Baer of Meseritz as forerunners of the psychological theory "of a preconscious or unconscience which precedes human consciousness," and "for an interpretation of the symbol content of mystical texts." The study is divided into six parts: 1. The Great Maggid and Hasidism; 2. Consciousness and the Unconscious *(Sekhel and qadmut-ha-sekhel)*; 3. Sefiroth Symbolism; 4. The Symbolism of Numbers and Names; 5. *Coniunctio* Mysticism; and 6. The Unconscius-Dream-Prophecy.

L187 Lamm, Norman. "Pukhovitzer's Concept of Torah Lishmah." *Jewish Social Studies*, 30(1968), 149-56.

"R. Yehudah Leib Pukhovitzer is, hence, a typical rabbinic scholar and preacher of his period [late seventeenth century], drawing heavily on Kabbalistic sources, in the fashion then prevailing, in order to persuade his audience of his noble but unexceptional ethical and religious preachments. His view of the study of *Torah lishmah* runs the whole gamut of acceptable, normative definitions of the concept, and he deserves credit for anticipating the approach of R. Hayyim of Volozhin by about a century and a half. But there is nothing in what Pukhovitzer writes to warrant the conclusion that he advocates schools for mystics, or that he identifies the study of Kabbalah as yet another definition of the term 'the study of Torah *lishmah.*'"

L188 Alfassi, Yitzhak. "Love of Israel in Hasidism." *Jewish Heritage*, 11(Spring 1969), 37-38.

"Love of Israel occupies a central place in the teachings of Hasidism. The Besht, Israel Baal Shem Tov, the founder of Hasidism, was the first to lay down: 'Everyone who judges Israel judges as if it were the Almighty because Israel is in complete unison with the Holy One.'"

L189 Aron, Milton. *Ideas and Ideals of the Hassidim*. New York: Citadel Press, 1969.

Survey of Hassidic thought, including sections on: Jewish Universalism and the Teachings of Hasidut; R. Israel Baal Shem Tov: In the Shade of the Lord; R. Dov Ber, Heir to the Besht and First of a Dynasty; R. Yaakov Yoseph: In the Shadow of the Besht; Teachers, Disciples, and Descendants; Three Sets of Brothers and Three Different Disciples; R. Shneur Zalman of Ladi: Wisdom, Understanding, Knowledge; The Karleener: Hassidism Comes to Lithuania; R. Nakhman of Bratzlav: Genius of Hassidism; The Worlds of Six Hassidic Masters; Leaders, Teachers, and Giants of Hasidut; A Tale of Four Cities in Poland; On the Highways and Byways of Hasidut; and Gleanings from the Field of Hasidut.

L190 Kopp, Sheldon B. "The Zaddik as Therapist." *Jewish Heritage*, 12,1(1969), 58-61.

"At its peak, however, Hasidism left a great legacy: reverence for life and an openness toward the world. It taught not only a spiritual gusto and feeling for the moment at hand, but also a joy in the sensual life, a joy which hallows and sanctifies that life. Salvation was not a reward for self-sacrifice and ascetic denial of the body, but the ecstasy of giving oneself to life.... It was the calling of the Zaddik to help men free themselves. Their teachings are still therapeutic."

L191 Mindel, Nissan. *Rabbi Schneur Zalman.* 2 vols. New York: Kehot Publication Society, 1969-74.

Vol. I is a *Biography* of Schneur Zalman. Vol. 2, *The Philosophy of Chabad*, "is an attempt at presenting an outline of Rabbi Schneur Zalman's thought, namely, the Chabad philosophical system which he created. It complements the biographical volume on the founder of the Chabad movement,... " Vol. II is divided into four parts: I. The Human Personality; II. The Cosmic Entity; III. Ends and Means, and IV. The Fulfillment. The Supplement consists of Selected Readings from *Likutei Amarim (Tanya).*

L192 Pinsker, Sanford. "Mendele Mocher Seforim: Hasidic Tradition and the Individual Artist." *Modern Language Quarterly*, 30(1969), 234-47.

"For Mendele, folk literature was always 'of' and 'for' the people but it was never *by* them. His was a progress out of a world which looked at Yiddish literature with disdain to a world which gradually moved from satire toward folk humor. Behind it all is the huge backdrop of a Hasidic tradition which provided an audience for Yiddish 'story' and then was forced out by more skilled practitioners of the art."

L193 Scholem, Gershom. "The Neutralisation of the Messianic Element in Early Hasidism." *Journal of Jewish Studies*, 20(1969), 25-55. Rpt. L204.

Takes up the question of "the messianic element in early Hasidism, e.c., from Israel Ba'al-Shem to the pupils of the Maggid of Mezeritch at the end of the eighteenth century. Was Messianism at the centre of the movement? Was it one of the prime elements that pervaded its teaching, as it had pervaded the teachings of the lurianic school which formed the basis of hasidic doctrine? Or did it disappear as an essential part in the formation of the movement and its doctrine so that we can speak of a 'liquidation' of Messianism as a living force? Or ought we rather take a more dialectical view, and speak of the transformation which it underwent, and which brought about a profound change to be defined not so much as the liquidation, but as the neutralisation of this element?"

L194 Katz, John. "Chasidism in Jazz." *Journal of Synagogue Music*, 2,4(1970), 28-33.

"This article cannot, nor should it, discuss all the compex historical points of contact or isolated non-parallel developments of Jazz-Chasidism; rather my main concern is to analyze what is musically 'true' to both forms."

L195 Rabinowicz, Harry M. *The World of Hasidism*. London: Vallentine, Mitchell, and Hartford, Conn.: Hartmore House, 1970.

Attempt to provide, in English, "a concise account of the movement as a whole, particularly during the last century. In this respect, 'The World of Hasidism' breaks new ground. This book is based on my 'Guide to Hasidism', published in 1960 [L161]. It has been rewritten and expanded and new chapters have been added."

L196 Rabinowitsch, Wolf Zeev. *Lithuanian Hasidism from its Beginnings to the Present Day*. Trans. M.B. Dagut. London: Vallentine, Mitchell, 1970; and New York: Schocken Books, 1971.

"In the present study of the history, offshoots, and teachings of Lithuanian hasidism, I have made use of both written and oral sources.... From a study of all this material, it emerges that Lithuanian hasidism had three main branches. The first and most important of these, to which the great majority of Lithuanian hasidim belonged, comprised the 'Karlin dynasty' and the dynasties of the Karlin *heder* [school] formed by generations of disciples. Secondly, there was Amdur hasidism. And thirdly there were the dynasties which originated in Volhynia and subsequently established themselves in Lithuania." Contents: I. The Beginnings of Hasidism in Lithuania; II. Karlin Hasidism; III. Amdur Hasidism; IV. The Karlin "Heder"; V. Other Hasidic Dynasties in Polesia; and VI. The Final Tragedy.

L197 Rose, Neal. "Eretz Israel in the Theology and Experience of Rabbi Nahman of Bratzlav." *Journal of Hebraic Studies*, 1(1970), 63ff.

Unavailable for annotating.

L198 Schatz-Uffenheimer, Rivka. "Self-Redemption in Hasidic Thought." In A76. Pp. 207-12.

"In the following presentation I shall attempt to illuminate certain basic points in Hasidic thought which account, I believe, for the peculiar Hasidic conception of individual self-redemption."

L199 Ury, Zalman F. *The Musar Movement: A Quest for Excellence in Character Education*. Studies in Torah Judaism, 12. New York: Yeshiva University Press, Department of Special Publications, 1970.

Analysis of Rabbi Israel Salanter's Musar "as an eclectic ethical theory, placing special emphasis on the importance of the *interplay* of thought and deed. In Musar, the idea and the act are inextricably intermingled." Contents: I. Historical Background; II. Theoretical Foundations; III. Musar as a Process; IV. The Kelm School of Musar; V. The Navaradock School of Musar; and VI. Musar's Relevance to Contemporary Problems. While the Musar movement was not, in itself, mystical, it was responsible for the "popularization of the Kabbalistic vocabulary" (C45).

L200 Berger, Abraham. "Approaches to Rabbi Nachman and His Tales." In A78. Pp. 11-19.

"In the tales of Rabbi Nachman we can detect echoes of the Bible (of which he was a master), Midrash *Agada*, medieval philosophic works, Kabbalistic texts such as *Bahir*, Zohar and *Sefer ha-Kanah*, and Lurianic literature. But these are mere tracings in the web of his memory, the Mother of Muses, and are utterly assimilated by the best of his imagination."

L201 Ettinger, S. "The Hassidic Movement--Reality and Ideals." In A77. Pp. 251-66.

Reprint of L184.

L202 Pasternak, Velvel, ed. *Songs of the Chassidim*. 2 vols. Plainview, New York: Harold Branch Publishing, Inc., 1971. Sel. rpt. L209.

"... practical handbook of chassidic music."

L203 Scholem, Gershom. "Devekuth, or Communion with God." In his A81. Pp. 203-227.

Reprint of L123.

L204 Scholem, Gershom. "The Neutralization of the Messianic Element in Early Hasidism." In his A81. Pp. 176-202.

Reprint of L193.

L205 Silberschlag, E. "Interpretations and Reinterpretations of Hasidism in Hebrew Literature." *Yearbook of Comparative Criticism*, 4(1971), 218-58.

Unavailable for annotating.

L206 Wiesel, Elie. "Souls on Fire." *Jewish Heritage*, 13(Winter 1971-72), 7-13.

Excerpts from L212.

L207 Heschel, Abraham J. "Hasidism as a New Approach to Torah." *Jewish Heritage*, 14(Fall-Winter 1972), 14-21.

"The Baal Shem took the tradition of Jewish learning, the Talmud and Kabbalah, mysticism, and gave it a new luster and a new meaning. He was very much influenced by and adopted quite a number of ideas from Jewish mysticism, Kabbalah, but he gave them a new slant, a new accent. To use a Hasidic term, he tried to consolidate the abstractions and philosophic reflections of Jewish mysticism into what he called a way of worship, an existential way, an application to human terms rather than letting them stay in their naked abstraction."

L208 Jacobs, Louis. *Hasidic Prayer*. The Littman Library of Jewish Civilization. London: Routledge & Kegan Paul, 1972; and New York: Schocken Books, 1973.

"This book is a study of one very important aspect of Hasidic thought; the attitudes of the Hasidic masters to prayer. While the stress is on the theoretical side, the practical manifestations of Hasidic prayer have also been noted. The book seeks to portray the major tendencies among the Hasidim in the matter of prayer from the earliest period down to the present." Jacobs discusses: I. Hasidism; II. The Nature of Hasidic Prayer; III. The Hasidic Prayer Book and Prayer House; IV. Preparations for Prayer; V. Gestures and Melody in Prayer; VI-VII. Contemplative Prayer; VIII. Ecstatic Prayer; IX. The Elevation of "Strange Thoughts"; X. Prayer as Inspiration; XI. The Prayers of the Zaddik; XII. The Polemic on the Recital of *Le-Shem Yihud*; and XIII. Hasidic Prayer in the Responsa.

L209 Pasternak, Velvel. "Chasidic Music." *Congress: A Journal of Opinion and Jewish Affairs--bi-Weekly*, 39,1(14 January 1972), 14-18.

Condensation of the Introduction to L202, vol. 2.

L210 Schatz, Rivka. "Some Problems of Hassidic Thought." *Orot: Journal of Hebrew Literature*, 13(1972), 51-61; 14(1973), 87-97.

"Our discussion will therefore center ... around purely theoretical questions in the theological, psychological and social spheres; for these are the aspects that have been least studied and worked on. If the questions posed by Hassidism can be presented so as to avoid either the cloying sweetness of the popular approach or the disparagement that arises out of lack of understanding of religio-social phenomena, there seems to be no reason why we should not try and look at Hassidic thought in such a manner."

L211 Wiesel, Elie. "Hasidism and Man's Love of Man." *Jewish Heritage*, 14(Fall-Winter 1972), 6-12.

"A Hasid, therefore, is he who yields to despair but who somehow, when his friend is involved, can turn that despair into joy and fervor. Therefore what is Hasidism? Hasidism is compassion, Hasidism is love. Hasidism is fervor. I believe it is also hope against hope. But above all, it is a call to friendship, an act of friendship, the most beautiful act in human life, and the most moving one in recent history."

L212 Wiesel, Elie. *Souls on Fire: Portraits and Legends of Hasidic Masters.* Trans. Marion Wiesel. New York: Random House, 1972. Sel. rpt. L206.

Portraits and legends of Israel Baal Shem Tov and his disciples, The Maggid of Mezeritch and his disciples, Levi-Yitzhak of Berditchev, Elimelekh of Lizensk and his disciples, Israel of Rizhin and his disciples, Nahman of Bratzlav, The School of Pshiskhe and Menahem-Mendl of Kotzk.

L213 Albert, Ada Rapoport. "Confession in the Circle of R. Nahman of Braslav." *Bulletin of the Institute of Jewish Studies,* 1(1973), 65-96.

"Why was R. Nahman among those few ṣaddiqim who did,... institute the practice of confession? He belonged to that school of thought in the hasidic leadership which saw the ṣaddiq as a being qualitatively different from his followers--a man different in essence from ordinary people. In his teachings this concept of the ṣaddiq finds one of its strongest formulations in the hasidic movement. In a circle where the ṣaddiq was seen in such a light, his position as an intermediary between God and man in confession was, perhaps, the more easily acceptable."

L214 Heschel, Abraham Joshua. *A Passion for Truth.* New York: Farrar, Straus and Giroux, 1973.

Compares and contrasts the teachings of the Baal Shem Tov, the founder of Hasidism, and Menahem Mendl of Kotzk, in whom Hasidism "reached both its climax and its antithesis." In the first chapter, Heschel compares The Two Teachers; and then in Chapter 2, The Kotzkes and Kierkegaard; Chapter 3, The Power of the Will; Chapter 4. Radicalism; Chapter 5, The Battle for Faith; Chapter 6, Personality; Chapter 7, Resignation; Chapter 8, Differences; Chapter 9, The Kotzker and Job; and Chapter 10, The Kotzker Today.

L215 Hilburg, Erwin. *Collected Studies in Hassidism and Frankism.* Westphalia: Lindlar, 1973.

Unavailable for annotating.

L216 Lowenkopf, Anne N. *The Hasidim: Mystical Adventurers and Ecstatics.* Los Angeles: Sherburne Press, Inc., 1973.

"This book provides a history of the brotherhoods, thumbnail sketches of Hasidic saints, and an insightful introduction to their modern plans and applications." The twelve chapters are: 1. The Rebel; 2. Holy Man and Renigade; 3. Burning Words and Burning Books; 4. The Maggid of Meseritz; 5. Excommunication; 6. The Charade, Chains and Two Czars; 7. The Occult as a Practical Art; 8. Growing Up in a Hasidic Family; 9. Corruption; 10. The Whirlwind with a Glib Tongue; 11. The Rav; and 12. Chabad: The Average Man's Path to God.

L217 Schultz, Joseph P. "The Religious Psychology of Jonathan Edwards and the Hassidic Masters of Habad." *Journal of Ecumenical Studies*, 10(1973), 716-27.

"The eighteenth century religious polarization between intellect and emotion, between thought and feeling, was successfully bridged by Jonathan Edwards and by the *Habad* branch of Hasidism. Both Edwards and the *Habad* masters in their psychology of religious experience aimed at clarifying the difference between authentic religious fervor and sham enthusiasm, and at showing that feelings have a legitimate place in the intellectual process."

L218 Werblowsky, R.J. Zvi. "Mysticism and Messianism: The Case of Hasidism." In A85. Pp. 305-14.

"Indeed, messianism was neither liquidated nor discarded by the early Hasidic masters. It was very much there, but not as an acute, pivotal and consuming concern; it had moved to a different *locus standi* in their spiritual universe. The most accurate definition of this development is Professor Scholem's term 'neutralisation of messianism'."

L219 Bosk, Charles. "Cybernetic Hasidism: An Essay on Social and Religious Change." *Sociological Inquiry*, 44(1974), 131-44.

"This paper employs a cybernetic model of a religious symbol system to explain the competition among Rabbinists, Hasidim, and Messianists in the Jewish communities of eighteenth-century Poland. Hasidism's ability to attract adherents is explained by the great flexibility of its constitutive belief, 'communion with God' when compared with Rabbinic Torah or the Messianic belief in the 'lifting of sparks.' This flexibility is traced through all levels of the cybernetic hierarchy."

L220 Chavel, Charles B. "Shneyur Zalman of Liday." In A89. Pp. 317-32.

Reprint of L126.

L221   Dresner, Samuel H. *Levi Yitzhak of Berditchev: Portrait of a Hasidic Master.* New York and Bridgeport: Hartmore House, 1974.

"In this book I have sketched the life and the spirit of Rabbi Levi Yitzhak of Berditchev. My principal sources have been the stories and legends which have been handed down for more than a century and a half since his death, as well as his book *Kedushat Levi.*"

L222   Mazor, Yaacov, and Andre Hadju, in collaboration with Bathja Bayer. "The Hasidic Dance--*Niggun:* A Study Collection and Its Classificatory Analysis." *Yuval,* 3(1974), 136-265.

"It is well known that a musically sensitive Hasid is able to distinguish between the styles proper to each dynasty, and can even single out the niggunim characteristic of a certain 'dynastic style'. Perhaps it will also become possible, following the classification described here, to define which are the elements, and combinations of elements, that characterize the style of a certain dynasty--and to use these criteria to distinguish between one style and another.... Our classification considers only two main parameters: a) form structure, b) scalar structure and ambitus."

L223   Schochet, Jacob Immanuel. *The Great Maggid: The Life and Teachings of Rabbi Dov Ber, of Mezhirech.* Brooklyn: Kehot Publication Society, 1974. 2nd ed. 1978.

Volume I. Rabbi Dov Ber of Mezhirech and His Leadership of Chassidism: A Biography.

L224   Schwartz, Dannel I. "The Rebbe of Kotzk." *Jewish Spectator,* 39,2(Summer 1974), 32-38.

Menachem Mendel of Kotzk "was an altogether new type of Rebbe, obsessed as he was with the search for absolute truth grounded in introspection and learning and in relentlessness, untiring pursuit of the perfection that is Truth."

L225   Steinsaltz, Adin. "The Losing of the Princess: An Interpretation." Trans. Yehuda Hanegbi. *Ariel,* #35(1974), 65-70.

"The theme of this story is fairly widespread and appears in several different traditions and cultures. This very repetition seems to prove Rabbi Nahman's point, since, like other Hassidim, in all the creative efforts of a man he saw a secret striving to approach the Divinity, and consequently, as he said of all the stories of the nations, 'the glory of God cries out from them.' Rabbi Nahman felt that, with only a little adjustment and addition, the inner, Divine meaning of these folk tales could be made manifest."

L226 Arden, Harvey. "The Pious Ones." Photographs by Nathan Benn. *National Geographic*, 148(1975), 276-98.

Photo essay of the Hasidim of Williamsburg.

L227 Berk, Fred. *The Chasidic Dance*. American Zionist Youth Foundation and Union of American Hebrew Congregations, 1975.

"The collection of articles in this book offers the reader a glimpse into the world of Chasidic dance, a truly authentic dance style of the Jewish people.... The religious beliefs and feelings of the Chasidim are expressed in the rhythms of the dance." Selections include: Haim Leof, "Chasidism"; Lois Bar-Yaacov, "A Chasidic Wedding"; Marsha Seid, "Wedding Dances"; Jill Gellerman, "With Body and Soul: The Dance of the Chasidim"; Zvi Friedhaber, "Chasidic Dances at the Festivities of Rabbi Shimon bar Yochai in Meron"; and Lillian Shapero, "Chasidic Dance in the Jewish Theater." The volume concludes "with step-by-step instructions for ten Chasidic dances in Israeli style."

L228 Folberg, Neil. *We Are Thy People: Glimpses of Lubavitcher Life*. Berkeley: Bet-Alpha Press, 1975.

"By living with Habad families in major Habad communities, I have attempted to make intimate photographs that show the physical and spiritual aspects of a traditional Jewish way of life, emphasizing the unique character of the Habad Hasidic approach."

L229 Gotlieb, Phyllis. "Hassidic Influences in the Work of A.M. Klein." In A94. Pp. 47-64.

Examination of "the influence of Hassidism on the work of A.M. Klein," which concludes that "throughout Klein's work he found no solution for his angst.... There is no epiphany in this work, no mystic vision.... there is a certain vacuum behind Klein's work, a lack of presence, of the blood and bone he tried so hard to celebrate."

L230 Green, Arthur. "Rabbi Nachman Bratzlaver's Conflict Regarding Leadership." In A92. Pp. 141-57.

"The superhuman demands which Nahman constantly placed upon himself, his alternating senses of personal greatness and personal failure, and the ceaseless striving for the redemption of the individual from the seemingly unbearable burden of guilt--all these proceed directly from the psychic makeup of Nahman the tortured man of faith, and all have left their mark upon the uniquely tortuous face of Bratzlav Hasidism."

L231 Jacobs, Louis. "Hasidism and Prayer." *SIDIC: Journal of the Service International de Documentation Judéo-Chrétienne*, 8,1(1975), 21-25.

Analysis of Hasidic prayer: Prayer of Petition; Preparation for Prayer; and Hitlahavut.

L232 Kaplan, Abraham. "Hasidism and Zen-Buddhism." In A104. Pp. 175-85. Reprinted from *Japanese Religions*, 1975.

Comparison of Hasidism and Zen in terms of *Kavvanah*.

L233 Lamm, Norman. "The Phase of Dialogue and Reconciliation." In A93. Pp. 115-29.

"The end of the phase of hostility between the Hasidim and the Mitnaggedim, and the beginning of geniune dialogue between them, was occasioned by a multiplicity of causes, ranging from the political and economic to the historical and psychological. However, in order to isolate, insofar as it is possible to do so, the basic mechanism of reconciliation that made possible the existence of vigorous dissent within a pattern of 'tolerance,' I shall restrict myself to the realm of ideas and the interplay of religious values and theological concepts. By thus limiting the scope of this inquiry, we can perhaps sharpen the focus on what I think marks the beginning of the reconciliation which ultimately assured that Hasidism would remain within the fold of traditional Judaism, and whereby the Mitnaggedim, although they continued to reject the foundations of Hasidism, accepted the Hasidim as authentically traditional Jews, thereby implying indirectly, their acceptance of Hasidism as a legitimate variant of Judaism."

L234 Pye, Faye. "A Brief Study of an Hasidic Fairy Tale." *Harvest: Journal for Jungian Studies of the Analytical Psychology Club*, 21(London, 1975), 94-104.

"Psychologically the tale of 'The Lost Princess' is interesting in several ways: first as a fairy tale in its own right: secondly as fantasy material manifesting the author's individuation process: thirdly as part of a spate of symbolic material brought forth by the rabbi while he was still a relatively young man, but approaching death: and lastly because of the symbolic and social context in which the tale arose."

L235 Rubinstein, Aryeh, ed. *Hasidism*. Popular History of Jewish Civilization. New York and Paris: Leon Amiel Publishers, and Jerusalem: Keter, 1975.

"This book does not purport to be a full history of Hasidism nor an exhaustive account of its doctrines. It does hope to give the reader a taste of Hasidism--the flavor, however faint, of the movement which swept Eastern Europe and which may have something to say even today." Twelve chapters: 1. In the Wake of Shabbetai Zevi; 2. Bringing Heaven Down to Earth (on Baal Shem); 3. Hasidism Becomes a Movement; 4. Cleaving to God; 5. The Zaddik; 6. Fervor Plus Reason (Shneur Zalman of Lyady); 7. Bans and Book-Burnings (The Gaon of Vilna); 8. The Zaddik Who Talked Back to God; 9. The Rebel of Kotsk; 10. The Hasidic Life; 11. Satmar, Lubavich--and In Between; and 12. Continuity or Revolt? (Hasidism's place in history).

L236 Wilensky, Mordecai L. "The Hostile Phase." In A93. Pp. 89-113.

Analysis of polemics written by Mitnaggedim against Hasidim: "I will deal with the accusations: changes in prayer; changes in ritual slaughter; bizarre actions; suspicion of Sabbatianism. I shall end with the accusation that hurt the Lithuanian and White Russian Mitnaggedim, that the new sect was causing neglect of Torah Study and disrespect for Torah Scholars."

L237 Applebaum, S., and A.B.Z. Metzger. "Chasidism and Psychotherapy: An Overview." *Intercom*, 6,2(1976), 15-24.

Unavailable for annotating.

L238 Raphael, Chaim. "The Litvak Connection & Hasidic Chic." *Commentary*, 61(May 1976), 48-53.

In response to the "simplistic" accounts found in most histories, Raphael provides a fuller picture of the attitude of Rabbi Elijah ben Solomon, the Gaon of Vilna, to Hasidism.

L239 Ehrmann, Naftali Hertz. *The Rav: A Historical Narrative of the Life and Times of Rabbi Shneur Zalman of Liady*. Trans. Karen Paretzky. Jerusalem and New York: Feldheim Publishers, 1977.

L240 Green, Arthur. "The Zaddiq as Axis Mundi in Later Judaism." *Journal of the American Academy of Religion*, 45(1977), 327-47.

"The present paper,... seeks to expand the use of [Mircea Eliade's symbol of *axis mundi* 'for the organization of sacred space'] by pointing to a link between the imagery of *axis mundi* and the tradition of the *zaddiq* or holy man in the mystical sources of Judaism."

L241 *Keeping Posted*, 23(November 1977).

Special Issue on Hasidism; unavailable for annotating.

L242 Kirsch, James. "Rabbi Nachman: The Question of His Self-Understanding." *Journal of Psychology and Judaism*, 2(1977-78), 29-40. Rpt. L261.

"After presenting a brief historical perspective on Rabbi Nachman of Bratzlav, a lengthy dream of Rabbi Nachman is presented. The view that this dream is concerned with Rabbi Nachman's sexual desire is rejected. Instead, the entire dream is analyzed from a Jungian perspective and is shown to revolve around Rabbi Nachman's relationship to the self. The analysis offers some meaningful psychological insights into the character of Rabbi Nachman." (Abstract)

L243 Buber, Martin. "Zen and Hasidism." In A104. Pp. 165-74.

Reprint of L149.

L244 Gelber, S. Michael. "Psychoanalytic Insights that Spark the Tales of the Hassidim." In A103. Pp. 79-116.

"It is clear that Hassidism's concepts of nature, dreams, fellowship with God, and prayer have, then, much in common with many of the mainstays of psychoanalytic theory and practice. The tales of the Hassidim, it has been shown, that deal with these four major categories of Hassidic interest, all smack of Freudian insight. In one or another of them, in some or all of them, the presence of perceptions about transference, resistance, working alliance, free association of thought, dreams, and interpretation, is brightly apparent."

L245 Heschel, Abraham Joshua. "Rabbi Pinhas of Koretz and the History of Poland." Trans. Samuel H. Dresner. In A103. Pp. 171-80.

Rabbi Pinhas' response to the *Haidamak* Pogroms and the partition of Poland.

L246 Jacobs, Louis. *The Doctrine of the Zaddik in the Thought of Elimelech of Lizensk.* The Rabbi Louis Feinberg Memorial Lecture in Judaic Studies. Cincinnati: University of Cincinnati, 1978.

"Although Gershom Scholem and others have demonstrated that it is a serious blunder to see the doctrine of the Zaddik--the Hasidic saint and miracle-worker--as a later aberration unknown to the founder and earliest teachers of the sect, it is generally acknowledged, with justice, that the doctrine receives its fullest treatment in the *Noam Elimelekh*, setting the pattern for future developments, particularly in Poland. In view of Elimelech's importance it is surprising that, so far as I am aware, there has hitherto been little detailed study of his teachings. This lecture seeks to fill the gap."

L247 Klapholtz, Yisrael, comp. *Dawn of Greatness: Great Rabbis When They Were Young.* Trans. Devorah Friedman. Bnei Brak: Pe'er Hasefer Publications, 1978.

For children; "A Collection of Stories and Biographical Sketches of the Grand Rabbis of Sanz, Zidichov and Kamarna."

L248 Lai, Whalen W-L. "Inner Worldly Mysticism: East and West." In A104. Pp. 186-207.

"In the end, the Hasidic tradition remained faithful to history and to its theistic basis. The extravagance of the spirit, latent messianic hope, the reverence for the Zaddik are some consequences. In the end, too, the Zen tradition remained faithful to the Buddhist outlook. Zen is concerned with the enlightenment, gnosis. To find this transcendental wisdom, it dares even to break reason itself and doubts all premises so that it verges on an enlightened atheism. More contrast and comparison can be drawn. The scholar, I suppose, will dwell on the ideological differences. The more mystic-inclined will search out spiritual kinships. The two have never been mutually exclusive within the traditions or within the complex nature of man himself."

L249 Peli, Pinchas Hakohen. "Sabbath: A Hasidic Dimension." In A103. Pp. 335-53.

"It will, probably, remain debatable whether Hasidism deliberately undertook to 'change' Kabalah or to 'neutralize' it. The changes were inevitable, though, because of the nature of Hasidism as a social movement. The Hasidic concept of Sabbath also changed: while Hasidism draws its teachings and inspiration about Sabbath from all the sources that preceded it, particularly the Kabalah, the Hasidic Sabbath is yet a new one, the revered queen transformed once again into a young, glowing bride. From a background crowded with customs and Kawanoth, it sprouts forward in new melodious song, in newly heralded harmony spun between the Zaddik and his followers, between one Hasid and another."

L250 Rotenberg, Mordechai. *Damnation and Deviance: The Protestant Ethic and the Spirit of Failure.* London: Collier Macmillan Publishers, and New York: The Free Press, 1978.

"Since the main endeavor of this work is to reveal the impact of 'Protestant bias' on Western theories of deviance, it is essentially 'nondisciplinarian' in its theoretical-empirical orientation, although it is categorically 'social-scientific.' ... To conclude the book, I present what I regard as a more optimistic paradigm of man, the Hassidic salvation ethic, to counter the Protestant deterministic concept of the inherently damned or elect man." Hassidism, pp. 189-202.

L251 Schatz, R. "The State of Nothingness and Contemplative Prayer in Hasidism." In A104. Pp. 83-93.

Reprint of L181.

L252 Schneerson, Menachem M. *On the Essence of Chassidus: A Free Translation of an Essay.* Trans. Y.H. Greenberg and S.S. Handelman. Brooklyn: Kehot Publication Society, 1978.

"The following discourse ... is a definitive explanation of the nature and idea of Chassidic philosophy. Indeed, Chabad (or Lubavitcher) Chassidus has as one of its prime aims the elaboration and definition of general Chassidus in intellectual and systematic terms,... " (Translator's Preface) Appendix: Excerpts from a Discourse Given on the Last Day of Passover 5730 (1970).

L253 Teshima, Jacob Yuroh. "The Problem of 'Strange Thoughts' and Its Treatment." In A103. Pp. 421-42.

"A total difference between the Hasidic and Zen attitudes of distracting thought is seen in the appreciation of thoughts. While Zen Buddhism denies their significance from the outset, Hasidism came to discover a cosmic significance in 'strange thoughts': their descent and ascent is a necessary process to mend the damage caused by the Breaking of the Vessels in the higher worlds and to restore the original order of the universe. Hasidism opened a completely new way of life through this unique and positive view: celebration and sanctification of life through this unique and positive view: celebration and sanctification of life under any circumstances. Man shall no longer be under an obsession of guilt feeling on account of bad thoughts. Those thoughts remind him that he, too, can be a partner of God by lifting them up to heaven."

L254 Teshima, Jacob Yuroh. "Self-Extinction in Zen and Hasidism." In A104. Pp. 108-17.

"The idea of self-extinction is probably a most desirable subject in ethics and morality as well as in religion. From the ethical point of view, it is felt as a sort of endless pain to man to maintain its implementation. There is pain of conflict at any subject which is imposed on man by force, even by the force of his own highest ethos. But Zen and Hasidism have found it as a goal available to man to attain, because they consider self-extinction as the gate through which one can return and reunify oneself with the source of the ultimate reality. Return is an authentic wish and aspiration of man's soul. It is a spontaneous act of man, therefore pains are no more pains. As we have seen above, Hasidism and Zen, despite their similarity, differ from each other in details. The self-extinction results in independence of man from life and death in Zen, but in submission of man to God in Hasidism. The more careful clarification of other aspects in both religions is awaited."

L255 Wiesel, Elie. *Four Hasidic Masters and Their Struggle against Melancholy.* Ward-Phillips Lectures on English Language and Literature, no. 9. Notre Dame and London: University of Notre Dame Press, 1978.

Not a "systematic theology, [but] constructed from stories woven together into a cable so tautly made that it responds like a musical instrument to the complex nuances of the potential union" of traditions. "In these lectures it makes little difference that the Jew waits for the Messiah while the Christian waits for the Messiah's Second Coming. Both wait. It is the human condition." Wiesel's lectures are about: Rebbe Pinhas of Koretz; Rebbe Barukh of Medzebozh; The Holy Seer of Lublin; and Rebbe Naphtali of Ropshitz.

L256 Wineman, Aryeh. "The Metamorphosis of a Hasidic Legend in Agnon's ''Al 'Even 'Aḥat.'" *AJS Review,* 3(1978), 197-201.

"In ''Al 'even 'aḥat,' Agnon did not retell this tradition concerning Rabbi Adam [from *Shivḥei ha-Besht--The Praises of the Besht*] ... rather, he composed a story which relates to that tradition in a way which very subtly invites comparison with the hasidic source itself."

L257 Berman, Dennis. "Hasidism in Rabbinic Traditions." *Society of Biblical Literature, Seminar Papers,* 2,17(1979), 15-33.

"This is a summary of the hasid traditions in rabbinic literature," with emphasis on "Profiles of the Righteous Person."

L258 Green, Arthur. *Tormented Master: A Life of Rabbi Nachman of Bratslav.* Judaic Studies Series. University: University of Alabama Press, 1979.

Critical biography of Nahman of Bratslav, based on three kinds of sources: "his own writings, the works of his leading disciple and *de facto* successor as leader of the community, Nathan of Nemirov (1780-1845), and the writings of later Bratslav *ḥasidim*. References to Nahman outside Bratslav literature are scant and often highly polemical; while they are considered where appropriate in our study, they hardly constitute a major source of understanding." The six major divisions of the biography are: 1. Childhood and Early years: 1722-1798; 2. Nahman's Journey to the Land of Israel; 3. Conflict and Growth; 4. Bratslav: Disciples and Master; 5. Messianic Strivings; and 6. Nahman's Final Years.

L259 Jacobs, Louis. "Eating as an Act of Worship in Hasidic Thought." In A109. Pp. 157-66.

"With few exceptions Hasidism is not ascetic. Indeed, the movement arose partly in opposition to Lurianic asceticism. Nor, as Buber would evidently have it, is the attitude of Hasidism that of thankful acceptance. As we shall endeavor to demonstrate, Hasidism is puritanical in essence but with certain subtle ideas of its own. We are concerned, however, not with the more general question of how Hasidism views physical pleasure but with the Hasidic idea of eating as an act of worship. That the Hasidic masters themselves thought this worthy of treatment as a separate and most important theme is justification enough for us to do so."

L260 Jung, Leo. "The Gracious Power of the Pietists." In A108. Pp. 209-18.

"What is the message of Hassidism to the Jews of our time? 'As for our enemies, our "revenge" is unchanging: They afflict us, but we survive them, Brethren! Don't ever be frantic with terror! Stand up and prepare defense, attack, and never neglect steadfast work in the Lord's vineyard!'"

L261 Kirsch, James. "Rabbi Nachman: The Question of His Self-Understanding." In A106. Pp. 75-86.

Reprint of L242.

L262 Kirsch, James. "The Zaddik in Nachman's Dream." *Journal of Psychology and Judaism*, 3(1979), 227-34.

"The Jungian approach to dreams is employed in order to understand fully the significance of the Zaddik in Rabbi Nachman of Bratzlav's dreams. One particular dream of Rabbi Nachman is analyzed. It is shown that the Zaddik referred to is Nachman himself. The Zaddik contains the spiritual and animal qualities of the human being. The tensions in the dream reflect on the tensions in Nahman's life. In Nachman, the archetype of the anthropos was constellated very early and was the cause of persecution for him and may have been the cause of his early death. Special attention is given to the concept of Zaddik Hador (Saint of the Generation) and its significance in Nachman's dream." (Abstract)

L263 Rapoport-Albert, Ada. "God and the Zaddik as the Two Focal Points of Hasidic Worship." *History of Religions*, 18(1979), 296-325.

"It seems, then, that right from the start, and more unequivocally so with the institutionalization of the leadership of Hasidism, it was the duty of a minority of spiritually endowed men to 'cleave' to God, while it was the duty of the majority of ordinary people to 'cleave' to their leaders. It is not by accident that the same weighty term, to cleave, is used to describe the nature of the affiliation in both cases. The ordinary person stands in relation to the Zaddik as the Zaddik stands in relation to God. Just as God is the focus of the Zaddik's religious life, so the Zaddik is the focus of the ordinary person's religiosity."

L264 Syrkin, A. "About One Hassidic Parable." *Darshana International*, 19,1(1979), 43-47.

Analysis of a parable told by Rabbi Simhah Bunem about Rabbi Eisik from Cracow, son of Rabbi Jekel.

L265 Band, Arnold J. "Folklore and Literature." In A113. Pp. 33-43.

Subtitled "A Study of the Braslav Theory of the Folktale and Its Implication for Our Understanding of Narrative Art and Genres of Literary Composition"; analysis of the Breslav cycle according to "a threefold classification of tales": "(a) standard tales with no specific sefirotic association; (b) tales classified as 'in the midst of days,' thus connected with the lower seven spheres; (c) tales classified as 'of the years of antiquity,' thus associated with the three upper spheres."

L266 Berger, Alan. "Hasidism and Moonism." *Sociological Analysis*, 41(1980), 375-90.

Unavailable for annotating.

L267 Dresner, Samuel H. "Hasidic Truth." *Shefa Quarterly*, 2,2(1980), 58-76; 2,4(1981), 9-37. Another version L272.

Attempts to answer the questions: "What could Hasidic truth, the parochial teachings of some benighted, superstitious Jews of the Medieval East, possibly mean to those newly acculturated Jews of the West, then panting after the promises of the 'civilized' society whose golden doors had at last opened to them? What could it mean to the gentile? And what meaning can it possibly have for us of the twentieth century?"

L268 Maccoby, Hyam. "Judaism in Extremis: The Messiah of Bratslav." *Commentary*, 71,3(September 1980), 49-56.

Questioning the current assumption that celebrates Hasidism "as a joyous alternative to the aridity of the Jewish intellectual tradition," Maccoby studies Nahman of Bratslav to conclude that "A movement that had aimed at freedom thus became paralyzed by guilt, for which an apt symbol is the asceticism of a figure like Nahman. As Freud might have explained it, the breaking of the hold of the rational self delivered the hasidic psyche into the grip of the superego, the irrational conscience whose prohibitions are much crueler than those of the rational conscience. The whole process, necessary as it may have been, demonstrated that it is after all the ego and reason that are the chief guardians of freedom and creativity."

L269 Sharot, Stephen. "Hasidism and the Routinization of Charisma." *Journal for the Scientific Study of Religion*, 19(1980), 325-36.

"The spread of Hasidism in the Jewish communities of eastern Europe in the last decades of the eighteenth and first decades of the nineteenth century is related to the routinization of charisma in the form of the dynasties of the *zaddikim*, the leaders of the movement. The coexistence of two principles of charismatic succession, together with multiple succession, resulted in features which contributed to the success of the movement: the continual formation of many new branches, a decentralized and segmental structure, and diversity of religious values and practices."

L270 Shick, Eleazar Shlomo. *Golden Advice, Based on the Works of Rabbi Nachman of Breslow and the Holy Disciples*. Trans. Kalman David Sirkez. Brooklyn: Mesivta Heichal HaKodesh, 1980.

Unavailable for annotating.

L271 Steinsaltz, Adin. "The Psychology of the Soul." *Shefa Quarterly*, 2,2(1980), 3-9.

Study of a central doctrine of Habad Hasidism--"the relationship between the external manifestation of the human soul (its 'aspects,' forces) and the essence of the soul itself." Asserts that "The hasidic theory of moral growth was based on what may be called a species of sublimation. In the Habad doctrine, this was developed into a system that prescribed the way in which the individual could become a more complete human being--by directing the Intellect towards more noble objects."

L272 Dresner, Samuel H. "Hasidism and Its Opponents." In A116. Pp. 119-75. Version of L267.

"This essay is a contribution toward an understanding of the conflict between Hasidism and its opponents, from the Hasidic point of view. Its substance is the examination of two doctrines that early Hasidism promulgated which were central to the dissension. Its method is: (1) to justify the selection of these two doctrines for examination through the testimony of a unique document; (2) to describe both the conditions which gave rise to the emergence of Hasidism and the salutary effects of its victory, as exemplified by the substitution of joy for despair; (3) to argue that this victory and transformation of values was in large measure due to two Hasidic doctrines, which are then taken up for analysis."

L273 Green, A.O. "Hasidism's Discovery and Retreat." In A115. Pp. 104-30.

"The fact that we shall here study, within the very heart of a group that saw itself as completely faithful to that heritage [belief in transcendance], formulations of experience that seem entirely contradictory to whatever we think of as biblical-western understandings of God, should teach us as much about the history of religions altogether as it does about the particular case of Judaism."

L274 Knapp, Bettina. "Tradition and Revelation in Rabbi Nachman's 'The Master of Prayer.'" *Research Studies*, 49,1(1981), 1-22.

Unavailable for annotating.

L275 Korn, Y. "Yiddish and Hasidism." *Jewish Frontier*, 48(1981), 13-15+.

Unavailable for annotating.

L276 Rakeffet-Rothkoff. "Reb Chayim of Volozhin." *Jewish Life*, 5(Summer/Fall 1981), 53-59.

Unavailable for annotating

L277 Schiller, Mordechai. "Some Thoughts on Hasidism." *Tradition*, 19,2(Summer 1981), 99-111.

Study of a Galician hasid, Menahem Ekstein, whose *T'naei Nefesh LeHasagat HaHasidut* "presents a program of mental exercises for stimulating and developing spiritual consciousness," in order to answer the question: "Does Judaism--and, in particular, Hasidism--recognize an intuitive, non-linear mode of mental activity, as a means of developing areas of the mind and soul considered inaccessible to the probing intellect?"

L278 Band, Arnold J. "The Function of the Enigmatic in Two Hasidic Tales." In A117. Pp. 185-209.

"While the historical background is indispensable for an understanding of these tales, a more detailed analysis will often yield unexpected results of interest to the historian of religions too. The literary sophistication so patent in the two tales we shall investigate implies a heightened sense of form and an acute awareness of the semiological interplay between author/narrator and his audience. It shall become abundantly clear that the traditional concept of the Hasidic tale and its milieu which posits a naive storyteller and a naive audience is not supported by the evidence of these tales or many others like them. Finally, the dichotomy so often drawn between the didactic and aesthetic in the treatment of Hasidic tales--or hagiographic literature, in general--will be found to be an obfuscating simplification."

L279 Green, Arthur. "Rabbi Nahman Bratslaver's Journey to the Land of Israel." In A119. Pp. 181-212.

"Our explanation of Nahman's journey as a death-defying *rite de passage* does not necessarily contradict any of the interpretations that Nahman himself offered and that have been mentioned above. On the contrary, it provides them with that clarity of focus they had previously lacked. The granting of higher wisdom, *hokhmah 'ila'ah* or 'garbed' wisdom, as a result of such initiation, corresponds directly to that claimed for rites of initiation in the most varied religious cultures."

L280 Schwartz, Howard. "Rabbi Nachman of Bratslav: Forerunner of Modern Jewish Literature." *Judaism*, 31(1982), 211-24.

Analysis of the impact of Rabbi Nachman's tales: "... he had a significant influence on the modern Yiddish literary tradition. For with the model of Nachman's broad acceptance in Yiddish to support them, the formative figures of modern Yiddish literature, especially Sholem Aleichem and I.L. Peretz, had the confidence to write in their native tongues.... The wide currency of Nachman's tales also proved influential in other direct and indirect ways. Nachman's style was the direct model for Yiddish writers such as Der Nister and Dovid Ignatow. But, more importantly,... [he] created an atmosphere in which it was possible to approach the sacred literatures from a consciously literary perspective.... above all,... [he] inspired to inspire subsequent Jewish authors."

L281 Wiesel, Elie. *Somewhere a Master: Further Hasidic Portraits and Legends*. Trans. Marion Wiesel. New York: Summit Books, 1982.

Portraits and legends of: Pinhas of Koretz, Aharon of Karlin, Wolfe of Zbarazh, Barukh of Medzibozh, Moshe-Leib of Sassov, The Holy Seer of Lublin, Meir of Premishlan, Naphtali of Ropshitz, and The School of Worke.

L282 Wolpin, Nisson, ed. *The Torah World: A Treasury of Biographical Sketches.* Brooklyn: Masorah Publications, Ltd., in conjunction with Gudath Israel of America, 1982.

"This book takes the reader into the far-flung corners of the Torah world, from Baranovich to Shanghai, from New York City to Jerusalem, from Telshe, Lithuania to Telshe, Ohio ... to sit at the feet of the teachers of Chassidic teachings ... to walk in the footsteps of Torah pioneers and to find shelter in the shadow of custodians of a sacred heritage--the leaders of the Torah world." Chassidic Mentors: Rabbi Meir Shapiro, Rabbi Menachem Zienba, Rabbi Daniel Goldberg and Lipa Geldwerth (pp. 64-112).

L283 Faierstein, Morris M. "The Friday Night Incident in Kotsk: History of a Legend." *Journal of Jewish Studies*, 34,2 (Autumn 1983), 179-89.

"The antinomian legend of the 'Friday night incident' in Kotsk ... reports that on a Friday night in the winter of 1839 Rabbi Menachem Mendel of Kotsk, at a gathering of his followers, either touched the candlesticks or extinguished the candles, thereby desecrating the Sabbath. While doing this he is alleged to have muttered, 'There is no Law and there is no Judge.' In other words, there is no God. Shortly thereafter, Menachem Mendel either locked himself, or was locked, into his study, where he remained until his death, approximately twenty years later. This essay presents an overview of the legend's literary history and an analysis of the truth or falsity of its story."

M. The Latest Phase

Primary Sources

M1 Weiner, Herbert, trans. "From the Teachings of Rav Kuk." *Commentary*, 17(1954), 490-92.

Extracts from the writings of Rabbi Kook on the topics: The Value of God-Denial; Appearance and Essence; Prayer; Those Designated for the Mysteries; Effect of Sin; and The Sage and the Prophet.

M2 Langer, Jiri. *Nine Gates to the Chassidic Mysteries.* Trans. Stephen Jolly. New York: McKay Company, Inc., 1961. Sel. rpt. M10.

"Above all I have aimed to introduce my readers to some of the more recent representatives of the Chassidic movement.

Furthermore I have been lured on by the realization that I have an opportunity in this book of publishing various stories which have possibly never been written down before--not even in Hebrew--and which I have learnt only from verbal tradition."

M3   Kuk, Abraham Isaac.   "The Experience of Mysticism."   In A55. Pp. 99-101.

Selection in which Kook "describes some of the elements of the mystical experience--the sense of unity, the experience of freedom and the resolution of conflicts."

M4   Metzger, Alter B.Z., trans.   *Rabbi Kook's Philosophy of Repentance: A Translation of "Orot ha-Teshuvah."*   Studies in Torah Judaism, #11.   New York: Yeshiva University Press, and Jerusalem: Hillel Press, 1968; 2nd ed. 1978.

Translation of the book begun before World War I and completed in 1924, subsequently edited and structured by Rabbi Zvi Yehuda Kook. "The introductory chapter by Dr. Metzger focuses on the psychological dimensions of Rabbi Kook's thoughts and the Appendix is an attempt by the author to convey in simply [sic] language the mystical, poetic and often elusive concepts of Rabbi Kook's mystical but radiant insights." (Editor's note)

M5   Wiesel, Elie.   *Legends of Our Time.*   New York: Avon Books, 1968.

The grandson of a Hasid, Dodye Feig, Elie Wiesel continues the tradition of the Hassidim with this collection of stories, creating "a new mythology" for our time.

M6   Kook, Abraham Isaac.   "The Road to Renewal."   Intro. Ben Zion Bokser.   *Tradition*, 13,3(Winter 1973), 137-53.

English translation of "Derek Hatechiah" (1909), an essay in which Rabbi Kook "offers one of the most comprehensive statements of Rabbi Kook's philosophy of Judaism. The force which directs the world toward the absolute good that pulsates throughout existence, declares Rabbi Kook, is a spiritual illumination from the Divine source of all existence. It is what we commonly call a mystical experience, though Rabbi Kook does not use this term. This illumination is initially experienced by certain qualified individuals who channel it to society. There an imperative is released 'for the perfection of the moral, social, intellectual and practical world.' Rabbi Kook warns, however, that this inflow of psychic and spiritual energy may, in fact, be distorted and become a source of idolatrous aberations. The decisive factor is a moral and rational refinement which must precede in the medium where the illumination is to act. Only where such refinement has preceded will the illumination be grasped in its full authenticity and evoke as its response the passion to perfect life."

M7 Kushner, Lawrence. *The Book of Letters: A Mystical Alef-Bait*. New York and San Francisco: Harper & Row Publishers, 1975.

Mystical interpretation of the Hebrew alphabet; written for children.

M8 Kushner, Lawrence. *Honey from the Rock: Visions of Jewish Mystical Renewal*. San Francisco: Harper & Row Publishers, 1977.

"The following pages are about 'having been close.' They are not so much about 'knowing' as 'being.' Once it must have made sense to say that you believed in something, or had faith in something. But not any more.... And this must surely mean it is time once again to set out for the wilderness."

M9 Bokser, Ben Zion, trans. *Abraham Isaac Kook: The Lights of Penitence, The Moral Principles, Lights of Holiness, Essays, Letters, and Poems*. New York, Ramsey and Toronto: Paulist Press, 1978.

This volume presents "the major writings of Rabbi Kook in a form that makes them accessible to the English reader. Rabbi Kook belongs among the truly great masters of spirituality in the history of Judaism.... The present study begins with an introductory essay, which presents the basic outline of Rabbi Kook's biography as well as an assessment of his religious philosophy. Then follow in translation his basic writings, each prefaced with a brief prefatory statement indicating the literary and ideological context in which it appeared. These include *The Lights of Penitence* (Orot Hateshuvah); selected essays from his three volume work *The Lights of Holiness* (Orot Hakodesh); *The Moral Principles* (Midot Harayah); ten of his philosophical essays which appeared in different publications; selected letters from his three volumes of correspondence (Igrot Harayah); and his poems."

M10 Langer, Jiri. "Life in a Hasidic Yeshiva." In A104. Pp. 29-37.

Selection from M2.

M11 Schneerson, Menachem M. *Sichos in English: Excerpts of Sichos Delivered by Rabbi Menachem M. Schneerson, The Lubavitcher Rebbe, Delivered at His Periodic Public Addresses, Translated into English*. 6 vols. Brooklyn: Committee for Sichos in English, 1978.

"Free translation" of Sichos, "structured to appeal to an English speaking reader who is somewhat familiar with the teachings of Chassidus. The Sichos are not adapted or altered in context, but are presented, with slight changes, in the same form and thought style in which they were originally presented. Great effort has been made to ensure the accuracy of the translations; however, they carry no official authority."

M12   Carlebach, Shlomo. *Holy Beggar Teachings: Jewish Hasidic Stories, 1975-1977*. Steven L. Maimes and Elana Rappoport, eds. Oakland, Calif.: S.L. Maimes, 1979.

Unavailable for annotating.

M13   Halevi, Z'ev ben Shimon [Warren Kenton] *Kabbalah and Exodus*. Boulder: Shambhala, and London: Rider & Co., 1980.

A kabbalistic text, "in the same tradition of midrash or investigation, in that it examines a Biblical text in terms of Kabbalistic theory, ancient legend and contemporary knowledge so as to find what the scribes buried deep within the Book of Exodus." After an Introduction, and a discussion of the general Kabbalistic Scheme, Halevi divides his discourse into ten major sections: Incarnation; Sleep and Awakening; Action; Rebellion and Rules; Initiation; Knowledge of Existence; Knowledge of Man; Revolt; Experience; and Work.

M14   Eliach, Yaffa. *Hasidic Tales of the Holocaust*. New York: Oxford University Press, 1982.

"This collection of Hasidic tales is not a mystification of the Holocaust, nor is it a negation of the value of armed resistance and the physical struggle for one's life or death with honor. It is simply an attempt to bring to light yet another, unexplored aspect of the Holocaust. The tales become a link, a historical continuum between the spiritual world of the period before the Holocaust and the rebirth afterward." Subjects of tales: 1. Ancestors and Faith; 2. Friendship; 3. The Spirit Alone; and 4. At the Gates of Freedom.

M15   Eliach, Yaffa. "The Holocaust and New Hasidic Tales." *Tradition*, 20(Fall 1982), 228-34.

Selections from M14.

Secondary Sources

M16   Grossman, Mordecai. "A Mystical Approach to Judaism." *Menorah Journal*, 16(1929), 97-111.

"Neo-Chassidism, in its spirit and content, is in such harmony with the declaration of independence of the human spirit from the bonds of mechanism. A movement like Neo-Chassidism would be, therefore, not merely Jewishly creative; it would be at the same time a movement auxiliary to the large human movement making for a freer, more creative human life. By its own life it would help in the creation of human conditions necessary for its continued living."

M17 Scholem, Gershom. "Kabbala at the Hebrew University." *Reconstructionist*, 3,10(1937), 8-12.

"One of the main functions of the Institute of Jewish Studies at the Hebrew University is the formulation of a new approach to Jewish history, based on an attempt to view that history objectively and as a whole.... Among the branches of religious history, one of those most requiring such a fresh approach is Jewish mysticism, or Kabbala; and this fresh approach goes hand in hand with the new attitude towards medieval poetry, folk literature, folklore and customs."

M18 Krakovsky, Levi I. *The Omnipotent Light Revealed: Wisdom of the Kabbalah*. Hollywood: Kabbalah Culture Society of America, 1939. Rpt. New York: Yesod.

Believing that "the Kabbalah was destined by Providence to be unveiled in our perverse era," Krakovsky reveals the "omnipotent light" by applying kabbalistic teachings to the exigencies of the twentieth century, including discussions of: Retrospect of Philosophers and Religions; To Attune Our Will to the Will of God Means Complete Enhancement of the Human Race; and Kabbalistic Analysis of Truth."

M19 Schneersohn, Joseph I. *Some Aspects of Chabad Chassidism*. Brooklyn: Machne Israel, 1944, 1957, 1961, 1971.

"... translation of a letter written some time ago by the Rabbi ... to one of his noted correspondents, in reply to query whether the study of Chabad would bring practical results to that type of intellectual Jew who, though previously estranged from Judaism, has become conscious of a desire to return to his people and to learn something of his spiritual heritage, in an academic way." Also contains a Biographical Sketch of Rabbi Schneersohn, by Nissan Mindel.

M20 Heller, Bernhard. "A Faith's Mystic Quest." *Christendom*, 10(1945), 188-99.

"In this article an aspect of Jewish thought will be delineated. While the facts in and of themselves should be of interest to a non-Jew, they are of further significance in that they disclose the parallel response of Christian and Jew to the mystery of Divine Being and the irrepressible quest of the human mind to comprehend and commune with the Source and Center of all that is."

M21 Agus, Jacob. *The Banner of Jerusalem: The Life, Times and Thought of Abraham Isaac Kuk, The Late Chief Rabbi of Palestine.* New York: Bloch Pub. Co., 1946. 2nd ed. M84.

"The theme of this book is the life and thought of a great genius of faith. Chief Rabbi Kuk, one of the leading authorities of Orthodox Judaism in the modern period, was a genuine and gentle philosophical mystic, of rare scope and profundity.... Kuk is a unique and fascinating subject of study, since he is virtually the first literary mystic of Orthodox Judaism in post biblical days."

M22 Rosenberg, Harold. "Inner World of the Hasid: A Jewish Mystical Experience Projected for Moderns." *Commentary*, 1,5(March 1946), 35-38.

"Buber's novel *[For the Sake of Heaven]* is interesting, even fascinating, and extremely suggestive, precisely because the Hasidic rabbis who are its heroes are so different from us, and because Buber has preserved that difference. *For the Sake of Heaven* tells of the Hasidic congregation, the communion, of Lublin in the years of the Napoleonic wars, and of the strange process whereby a second communion was formed inside the body of the first under the shaping pressures of world history. Such a communion is a thing that we today in America know nothing about; we can hardly imagine it; its inner phenomena, its assumptions, its real relations are as strange to us as the life of the Hindus in E.M. Forster's *Passage to India.*"

M23 Gourary, S. "The Story of the United Lubavitcher Yeshivot." *Jewish Education*, 20,1(1948), 43-46.

In the light of the spiritual regeneration provided by the Lubavitcher Yeshivot, Gourary reviews "briefly how these institutions have developed, their role in Jewish life and the ideology motivating their educational objectives."

M24 Feldman, Louis H. "Another Parallel to the Maenadism of the Bacchae: Hasidism in Modern Jewry." *Harvard Theological Review*, 42(1949), 65-67.

Describes "the dancing and ecstasy characteristic of that unique movement in modern Jewry known as Hasidism," as a parallel "to the Dionysiac practices mentioned in Euripides' Bacchae."

M25 Heschel, Abraham Joshua. *The Earth is the Lord's: The Inner Life of the Jew in East Europe.* New York: Henry Schuman, 1950. Rpt. London and New York: Abelard-Schuman, 1964; New York: Farrar, Straus, Giroux, 1975. Sel. rpt. M149.

Book is "about the life of the Jews in Eastern Europe ... about their daily life, about their habits and customs, about their attitudes toward the basic things in life, about the scale of values which directed their aspirations"; deals with a number of topics related to mysticism, including: Kabbalah, Hasidim, and Thirty-Six Zaddikim.

M26 Weiner, Herbert. "A Mystic Philosopher on East Broadway: The Life and Studies of S.H. Setzer." *Commentary*, 14(1952), 421-32.

Portrait of S.H. Setzer, a "devoted scholar, mystic, and original thinker [who] has been giving years of unremitting study to the understanding of the Zohar."

M27 Chabad-Lubavitch. *Outlines of the Social and Communal Work of Chabad-Lubavitch: A Brief Outline of Some Instances of the Social and Rehabilitation Work Carried on in Various Parts of the World, by the Heads of the Chabad Movement since Its Beginning to the Present Day.* New York: Kehot Publication Society, 1953.

"In the following outline we are relating some instances of the social work of the Chabad leaders, beginning with the founder of Chabad to the present day."

M28 Weiner, Herbert. "Rav Kuk's Path to Peace with Israel." *Commentary*, 17(1954), 251-63.

As "a study in Judaism through personality," Wiener attempts "through personal contact with Rav Kuk's son, Zvi Yehudah Kuk, to find his way to the teachings of Rav Kuk and the tradition which his son carries on." (Editor's note)

M29 Goodman, Walter. "The Hasidim Come to Williamsburg: New Settlers and Old, Just across the Bridge." *Commentary*, 19(1955), 269-74.

"Walter Goodman describes the impact of the Hasidim on crowded Williamsburg, and speculates about what may in the long run be the impact of Williamsburg--and of America--on them." (Editor's note)

M30 Heschel, Abraham Joshua. *God in Search of Man: A Philosophy of Judaism.* New York: Farrar, Straus & Cudahy, 1955. Rpt. New York: Meridian Books, 1961; New York: Octagon Books, 1972.

Heschel's philosophy of Judaism, covering God, Revelation and Response. Though a book on philosophy, *God in Search of Man* deals with a number of mystical topics, including: Ways to His Presence, The Sublime, Wonder, The Sense of Mystery, Awe, Glory, Revelation and Kavanah.

M31 Weiner, Herbert. "The Lubavitcher Movement." *Commentary*, 23(1957), 231-41, 316-27.

> Two-part article in which Weiner first describes "the headquarters in Brooklyn of the Lubavitcher Hasidic movement, reporting on his conversations with several prominent members of the sect and describing an all-night festive gathering of the Hasidim at which the rebbe 'gave Torah.'" In the second part, he "pursues rather more intensively his investigation of the movement's 'inner meaning.'" (Editor's note)

M32 Bergmann, Samuel Hugo. "Death and Immortality in the Teachings of Rabbi Kook." *Judaism*, 7(1958), 242-47.

> Explores the teachings of Rabbi Kook, "The only Jewish thinker of the last generation, who faced the problem of death in all its concreteness, and tried to provide a bold explanation,... His answer was: *Death is a defect in Creation. The people of Israel are called upon to remove this disgrace from the world.*"

M33 Buber, Martin. "Hasidism and Modern Man." In A40. Pp. 9-21.

> Reprint of M34.

M34 Buber, Martin. "Hasidism and Modern Man." In his A41. Pp. 21-43. Rpt. M33, M35.

> Written to clarify points which have been misunderstood in earlier writings: "The most important element in Hasidism ... [is] the strong tendency, both in personal life and in that of the community, more and more to overcome the fundamental division between the sacred and the profane.... Man cannot approach the Divine by going beyond the human. But he can approach it by becoming the man that he, this individual man, was created to become. This seems to me the eternal essence of Hasidic life and Hasidic teaching."

M35 Buber, Martin. "Hasidism and Modern Man." *Review of Religion*, 22(1958), 109-20.

> Reprint of M34.

M36 Bokser, Ben Zion. "Jewish Universalism: An Aspect of Thought of Harav Kook." *Judaism*, 8(1959), 214-19.

> "The late Chief Rabbi Abraham Isaac Kook has been described as the last authentic creative Jewish mystic. Characteristic in his mystical thought is his insistence that antagonism and conflict are rooted in limited provincialism. Only the realization of the all-embracing harmony that is God, in whom the familiar polarities are resolved, can lead to human

accommodation and harmony. His pantheistic thought enabled him to look beyond one's particular and immediate loyalty and find the Divine reflected in other commitments. In a day of growing denominationalism, political as well as religious, his thought,... brings a refreshing note."

M37 Gersh, Harry, and Sam Miller. "Satmar in Brooklyn: A Zealot Community." *Commentary*, 28(1959), 389-99.

Description of the Satmar Hasidim, whose Rebbe "has won for himself a rather special place by his unrelenting, pure, and active hostility to what he regards as the 'sacrilege of' the State of Israel and the 'apostasy' of all non-Hasidic Jewry. The other sects of Hasidim have made their peace with Israel."

M38 Schneersohn, Joseph I. *On Learning Chassidus (Kuntres Limud haChassidus)*. Trans. Zalman I. Posner. Brooklyn: Kehot Publication Society, 1959, 1965, 1971, 1974.

Unavailable for annotating.

M39 Schneersohn, Joseph I. *On the Teachings of Chassidus (Kuntres Toras haChassidus)*. Trans. Zalman I. Posner. Brooklyn: Kehot Publication Society, 1959, 1971, 1974.

Unavailable for annotating.

M40 Ben-Horin, Meir. "The Ultimate and the Mystery: A Critique of Some Neo-Mystical Tenets." *Jewish Quarterly Review*, n.s. 51(1960-61), 55-71, 141-56.

Criticism of "The 'ultamatisms,' 'absolutisms,' 'ineffabilisms,' expounded by [twentieth-century mystical] writers, [which] reflect the intellectual as well as the social, political, and economic crises of our century. They are created by and contribute to the aggressive onslaught of irrationalist totalitarianism upon the morality of man's intelligence, the logic of his compassion, the power of his drive to achieve a worthwhile life, not by faith in 'humanly impossible divine possibilities,' but through experimental reorganization of the expanding realm of tangible conditions."

M41 Friedman, Maurice. "Hasidism and the Contemporary Jew." *Judaism*, 9(1960), 197-206.

Discusses the "challenge of Hasidism to the contemporary Jew": "But we do need genuine fervor if the quantitatively greatest body of Judaism in the world is not also to be the thinnest and most meaningless. Community and the overcoming of dualism, too, are elements of Hasidism without which no renewal of Judaism is possible."

M42 Schachter, Zalman S. "Hasidism and Neo-Hasidism." *Judaism*, 9(1960), 216-21.

Evaluates "the Hasidic movement and its survival to our day, despite the many premature obituaries which have been published during the past fifty years, announcing its decadence and demise."

M43 Schachter, Zalman. "How to Become a Modern Hasid." *Jewish Heritage*, 2,4(Spring 1960), 33-40.

Traces his own history as "An adolescent refugee from Austria who loved Goethe," to his initial encounter with Hasidism through his association with Lubavitch Hasidism.

M44 Kegan, Judith. "Hasidism and Neo-Hasidism." *Mosaic*, 2,1(Spring 1961).

Unavailable for annotating.

M45 Kranzler, George. *Williamsburg, A Jewish Community in Transition: A Study of the Factors and Patterns of Change in the Organization and Structure of a Community in Transition.* New York: Philipp Feldheim, Inc., 1961.

"This study will attempt to analyze the process of change in the Jewish community of Williamsburg since its origin at the beginning of the century. Particular stress is laid on the last fifteen years, when the intense valuational attitude of the new population reversed the process of deterioration."

M46 Schachter, Z.M. "A Contemporary Attempt at the Perennial Questions." *Judaism*, 10(1961), 112-18.

"Here, employing a dialogic framework but going beyond it to include the categories of *It* and *He*, the author essays a fresh solution of the problems, perennial and contemporary, implicit in the Jewish Triad [God, Torah and Israel]. The use of certain Kabbalistic concepts in the scheme of thought here advanced bespeaks a new and unconventional use of Kabbalistic and Hasidic teaching."

M47 Scholem, Gershom. "Kabbala and Historical Criticism: Acceptance Speech at the Rotschild Prize's Ceremony." *Jerusalem Post*, 10,421, 23 Nissan 5722 (27.4.1961), II.

Unavailable for annotating.

M48 Weiner, Herbert. "The Dead Hasidim." *Commentary*, 31(1961), 234-42, 420-27.

Description of the Bratzlaver Hasidim, "followers of Rabbi Nachman--who are unique among the various Hasidic sects for never having replaced their founder with another Rebbe."

M49 Weiner, Herbert. *The Wild Goats of Ein Gedi: A Journal of Religious Encounter in the Holy Land.* Garden City, New York: Doubleday, 1961. Rpt. Cleveland and New York: Meridian Books, and Philadelphia: Jewish Publication Society of America, 1963.

"My hope was to engage the reader in a kind of journey to the Holy Land which was not only a trip abroad but, like the pilgrimage of old, a search for personal source springs of spirit--and that involved, I thought, encounters with real people." Some of these real people include Hasidim from Meah Shearim, and Rabbi Abraham Isaac Kook and his son.

M50 Poll, Solomon. *The Hasidic Community of Williamsburg.* New York: Free Press of Glenco, Inc., 1962; 2nd ed. New York: Schocken Books, 1969.

"The major area of inquiry of this volume ... deals with the economic activities of the Hasidic community. To put these activities into proper perspective and to evaluate them, it was considered necessary to give some background of the group in the preliminary chapters." In Part One, The Problem and its Setting, Poll discusses: 1. An Ultrareligious Group; 2. The Structure of the Jewish Community in Hungary; 3. The Structure of the Jewish Community in the United States; 4. The Transplantation of Hasidic Culture; 5. The Threat of Assimilation; 6. The Hasidic Family; 7. The Social Stratification of the Hasidic Community; and 8. Organizations and Social Control. In Part Two, Economic Activities of the Hasidic Community, he covers: 9. The General Patterns of Hasidic Economic Behavior; 10. The Hasidic Occupational Hierarchy: Religious and Professional Services; 11. The Hasidic Occupational Hierarchy: Nonprofessional Occupations; and 12. A Sociological Analysis of the Hasidic Community. The Appendix explores Some Problems in Studying the Hasidic Community.

M51 Vernoff, Charles. "Neo-Hasidism--A Defense." *Mosaic*, 3,1(Winter 1962), 18-26.

Taking issue with Judith Kegan's "Hasidism and Neo-Hasidism" (M44), Vernoff attempts "to treat some of the issues she presents from a more commitedly Chassidic perspective." Discusses: Chassidism Past, Chassidism Present, and Chassidism Future.

M52 Agus, Jacob B. "Abraham Isaac Kuk." In A56. Pp. 73-96.

Asserts that all of Kook's "attitudes and ideas can be understood in reference to his deep and genuine mysticism." Agus discusses: Kuk's Early Years and Study, Spokesman for Orthodoxy, Concept of Zionism, The Holy Land, European Interlude, Chief Rabbi of Palestine, Last Years, His Religious Ideas, Kuk Essentially a Mystic, Influence of Kabbalah,

Personal Mystical Experiences, Kuk's Religious Nationalism, Nationalistic Value of Ritual, and The Legacy.

M53 Rubin, Israel. "Chassidic Community Behavior." *Anthropological Quarterly*, 37(1964), 138-48. Rpt. in M124.

"The present analysis is based on a field study of the contemporary Satmarer Chassidim of Brooklyn, New York, as well as historical research. After summarizing the circumstances that gave rise to Chassidism, we shall attempt to isolate two behavior clusters that seem to have characterized practically all Chassidic communities of the last two centuries, though with minor variations in actual form and relative emphasis. These behavior patterns ... shall then be viewed as the clue to the understanding of the lasting viability, as well as the wide appeal of the Chassidic culture."

M54 Weiner, Herbert. "Braslav in Brooklyn." *Judaism*, 13(1964), 351-60. Rpt. M71.

Portrait of "a group of Bratslaver Hasidim in Brooklyn, composed of young American-born men and women, many of them from completely non-religious homes."

M55 Bokser, Ben Zion. "Rabbi Kook: Builder and Dreamer of Zion." *Conservative Judaism*, 19(Winter 1965), 68-78.

Study of Rabbi Kook's writings as "an example of the Jewish mystical tradition in its pure form. He was inspired by Rabbi Judah Loew of Prague, a Cabbalist who freed the Cabbalah from superstitious admixtures, seeing in it largely a way to the immediacy of God. The immediacy of God shines through all of Rabbi Kook's writings. All things, for Rabbi Kook, were a crust with an inner essence, a divine dimension; seen aright all things have the capacity to reveal the light of holiness. His vision of the Jewish people and the Return to the Holy Land was within this basic concept which gives unity to all his thought."

M56 Poll, Solomon. "The Role of Yiddish in American Ultra-Orthodox and Hassidic Communities." *YIVO Annual of Jewish Social Science*, 13(1965), 125-52.

"This is a paper on the role and position of Yiddish among American ultra-Orthodox and Hassidic Jews. The members of these groups consider their goal in life to be the perpetuation of Jewish laws, practices and observances, and their conduct is entirely defined by religious dogma and principles. Many migrated to the United States after World War II and most of them settled in Williamsburg, a section of Brooklyn, in New York City."

M57 Weiner, Herbert. "A Wedding in B'nai Brak." *Commentary*, 40(July 1965), 39-46.

Description of Weiner's "first experience of Hasidism—flesh-and-blood Hasidism, that is, as opposed to its literary counterpart. The occasion was an observance by the Belzer Hasidim of the 'Third Meal'—the weekly ritual marking the end of the Sabbath which, in Hasidic practice, serves as an occasion of communion between the Rebbe and his disciples."

M58 Zenner, Walter P. "Saints and Piecemeal Supernaturalism among the Jerusalem Sephardi." *Anthropological Quarterly*, 38(1965), 201-17.

"In this article I shall describe various aspects of the saints-complex of Sephardic, or Middle Eastern and Mediterranean, Jews in Jerusalem. An attempt will be made to analyze the motives which people attribute to themselves and others when engaged in the behavior appropriate to the reverence for saints. The material was collected while I was conducting research on one Sephardic origin-group, the Jews from Aleppo (otherwise referred to as Halebim). While the greater part of the study was carried out on that group, the total sephardic scene was taken into account since Halebim were a small part of it."

M59 Frenkel, Isser. *Men of Distinction: Biographies of Great Rabbis*. 2 vols. Tel-Aviv: "Sinai" Publishing, 1967.

"In these short stories of but a few pages each, I have endeavoured to portray the man and his life in condensed yet readable form." Includes biographies of Rabbi Abraham Isaac HaCohen Kook (II.41-50), and Rabbi Joseph Isaac Schneersohn (II.109-18).

M60 Rudavsky, David. *Emancipation and Adjustment: Contemporary Jewish Religious Movements, Their History and Thought*. New York: Diplomatic Press, Inc., 1967. Rev. ed. M147.

"This book focuses on the origin, evolution, and growth of the ideologies of the contemporary religious alignments in principally the Orthodox, Reform, and Conservative tendencies in religious Judaism, and their variants. Since these movements were not born or evolved in a vacuum but have arisen and developed in conditions and events in the Jewish experience of Europe, they are treated in their general and Jewish historical contexts." Chapter 6, Hassidism and Neo-Hassidism (pp. 116-55), discusses Hassidism "as a variant of Orthodoxy," and Neo-Hassidism "as a synthesis of Hassidism and Western religious ideas. Though Neo-Hassidism, unlike Hassidism, does not represent a religious party in Judaism, it is of considerable interest because of its influence on current Western progressive religious thought." Section on Neo-Hassidism is an expansion of N23.

M61 Scholem, Gershom. "Mysticism and Society." *Diogenes*, 58(Summer 1967), 1-24.

Takes the "dialectical view" in answering the question: "Can the mystical impulse still retain its vigor and meaning once it is directed towards the activity of the mystic within his group? In other words: if it is true that mysticism is [sic] its original appearance should be seen as a phenomenon of a strictly personal and individualistic nature, may it not be equally true that this phenomenon at the same time involves a dialectic of its own which the critical observer will quickly discover and which may or may not be separated from the phenomena of mysticism themselves?"

M62 Singer, Isaac Bashevis. "The Extreme Jews." Photographs by Nancy Rudolph. *Harper's Magazine*, 234(April 1967), 55-62.

"One thing is clear--their [Hasidim] way of life is based on a profound religious logic and a historic reason. The long beards and sidelocks, the old-fashioned garments, and the clinging to all the rigors and customs are directed toward one purpose only--complete segregation from the gentile, and even more from the Jew who is heading toward ultimate disappearance. This segregation is as old as Jewish exile itself and has maintained the Jews through the two thousand years of his existence in the diaspora."

M63 Jochnowitz, George. "Bilingualism and Dialect Mixture among Lubavitcher Hasidic Children." *American Speech*, 43(1968), 182-200.

"... Lubavitcher children are as fluent in English as they are in Yiddish. Their English pronunciation improves as they grow older, and girls above the age of eight speak English with little or no foreign accent. Boys, whose education is much more religiously oriented, have more trouble with English.... The teen-age girls who will be the mothers of the next generation speak English very well. There is no doubt that in another generation the English of Lubavitcher children will be absolutely native. Religion, however, is the central fact in Lubavitcher life, and religious education and discussion is exclusively in Yiddish. It is therefore reasonable to conclude that the Lubavitcher community will remain bilingual indefinitely."

M64 Mintz, Jerome R. *Legends of the Hasidim: An Introduction to Hasidic Culture and Oral Tradition in the New World*. Chicago and London: University of Chicago Press, 1968.

"This work is both a study of the contemporary hasidic community in New York and a collection of hasidic oral tradition. Part I, the study, is an attempt to describe and analyze a culture through its oral tradition. Its aim is to produce an integrated description of both the culture and the themes in the oral tradition. The study relies on the analysis of the tales collected and on data obtained through customary anthropological methods--participant observations, interviews, photography, and the collection of life histories. Part II consists of the collection of tales recorded in New York City, for the most part in 1959-61 and the summer of 1963. The bulk of tales collected are legends--stories believed by the narrators to be true. Most tales are based therefore on actual experiences or observations which have been cast into narrative form in accord with traditional models and established points of view. The tales, presented completely and accurately, enable the reader to evaluate the analysis for himself."

M65 Blomster, W.V. "A Theosophy of the Creative Word: the *Zohar*-Cycle of Nelly Sachs." *Germanic Review*, 44(1969), 211-27.

"The poems of Nelly Sachs' *Zohar* cycle, particularly appealing in their synoptical brevity, present an ideal subject for a study of her concept of the word in the light of Jewish tradition. Both the thought and the imagery of the cycle reveal the contribution of this heritage. However, it also becomes apparent that the poetry of Nelly Sachs is universal in its essence. From this Jewish background she develops a metaphysical *ars poetica*, making of the word the instrument by which every creative act is accomplished. Her esteem for the creative work makes it possible to discover in her works a verbally-oriented theosophy, the contemporary validity of which is totally comprehensible on a non-dogmatic plane."

M66 Mark, Faygah. "The Work of Isaac Bashevis Singer: Its Mystical Roots." *Jewish Heritage*, 11(Spring 1969), 48-56.

"Singer poses the eternal question: how account for the existence of evil in the world? The sages' answer was: 'both good and evil come from God, and we finite beings with our finite minds cannot understand His infinite way.' The Kabbalah explains: in creating the world, God has also released destructive forces into existence, which constitute the realm of evil that stands ever ready to assail life. It is ruled by the prince of darkness, Samael, and his mistress Lilith. These destructive forces constantly encounter the good forces which propel life onto the path of righteousness."

M67 Schreiber, Mordecai. "Rav Kuk and Martin Buber on Teshuvah." *CCAR Journal*, 16,3(June 1969), 31-35.

"Kuk's concept of teshuvah finds strikingly and surprisingly close parallels in the thought of a younger contemporary, Martin Buber, whose position in the ideological spectrum of Judaism was quite removed. In contradistinction to Kuk's stance as a strict halachist, Buber's non-halachic position is well-known,... While Kuk spoke with the voice of normative Judaism, Buber's voice was distinctly his own. It should follow that the two would part ways in dealing with a concept so tightly intertwined with the halacha, as is the case with teshuvah. But the opposite is true."

M68 Shmueli, Efraim. "The Appeal of Hasidism for American Jewry Today." *Jewish Journal of Sociology*, 11(June 1969), 5-30.

"This article is not primarily about Hasidism itself (the pietistic movement among eastern European Jews) in any of its intrinsic aspects, but about the astonishing acceptance of some Hasidic ideas, if not practices, by American (particularly Jewish) intellectuals today, and even by the wider public. The emotional impetus and the intellectual and psychological insights of reinterpreted Hasidism seem paradoxically to have an intimate connexion with types of emotion and patterns of thought generated in a modern technological society." Shmueli considers: Hasidism interpreted; Older attitudes towards Hasidism; The legitimacy of the traditional trends; Psychological dimensions; Hasidism and existentialism; The development of Jewish individualism; and The Establishment and salvation.

M69 Sherwin, Byron L. "Elie Wiesel and Jewish Theology." *Judaism*, 18(1969), 39-52.

"To the neo-Maimonidean mind, Wiesel might not be Elisha the prophet but Elisha the heretic. But it can easily be shown that he is firmly within a tradition which finds its sources in Biblical theology and which develops within Jewish literature, notably Kabbalistic writings."

M70 Weiner, Herbert. "The Fragrance of Eden." *Midstream*, 15(October 1969), 56-71.

Selection from M71.

M71 Weiner, Herbert. *9 1/2 Mystics: The Kabbala Today*. New York: Holt, Rinehart and Winston, 1969. Rpt. New York: Collier Books, 1971. Sel. rpt. M54, M70, M79.

"... records a search for the life secret of a mystical tradition sometimes known as the Kabbala. It describes a series of encounters wherein individuals and groups who claim intimate acquaintance with this tradition are challenged to relate their hidden wisdom to problems of our own day. It also contains a good deal of historical and technical information about Jewish mysticism, but frankly, anyone interested in a purely objective, scholarly account of this latter subject will be better served by other books; this journal is on a more personal and popular level."

M72 Garvin, Philip, photographs. *A People Apart: Hasidism in America*. Text by Arthur A. Cohen. New York: E.P. Dutton & Co., Inc., 1970. Sel. rpt. M80.

Photographic study of "a full year's worth of Hasidic life including all the holy days, the life of the winter and the summer, the schools and camps, the businesses and vacation places."

M73 Harris, Monford. "Pre-Marital Sexual Experience: A Covenantal Critique." *Judaism*, 19(1970), 134-44.

Exploration of the sexual experience as an aspect of the Jewish concept of covenant. Includes a section on kabbalistic attitudes toward Sex as Coventantal Affirmation (pp. 142-43).

M74 Kahana, Boaz. "Stages of the Dream Concept among Hasidic Children." *Journal of Genetic Psychology*, 116(1970), 3-9.

"This study investigated the extent to which cognitive stages in the dream concept are invariant among Hasidic children. It gathered evidence regarding the universal validity of the concept of fixed stages in the development of thinking.... The findings of this study did not support the invariance of the process of emerging cognitive structures in the development of the dream concept. The study underscored the importance of cultural influences in affecting the sequence of cognitive development and suggested that the demand characteristics of the environment may cause reversals in cognitive development."

M75 Lubavitch Foundation of Great Britain. *Challenge: An Encounter with Lubavitch-Chabad*. London: Lubavitch Foundation, 1970, 1973.

"*Challenge* offers both to the friends of Lubavitch-*Chabad* and to those who have not yet encountered it, an introduction to its history, philosophy and activities." Contains sections on: The Beginning of Chassidism; Chabad Chassidism; Lubavitch Spans the Globe; What Chabad Says; Encounters; and An Extra Dimension.

M76 Pinsker, Sanford. "The 'Hassid' in Modern American Literature." *Reconstructionist*, 36(6 March 1970), 7-15.

Study of "the *hassid*-as-metaphor [which] occupies a very central position in the American Jewish writer's fictional fabric." Considers fiction by Abraham Cahan, Michael Gold, Philip Roth, Edward Lewis Wallant and Bernard Malamud.

M77 Raddock, Charles. "The Bachelor Chossid from Prague." *Jewish Life*, 37,5(1970), 42-47.

Brief biography of Jiri Langer, focusing on his becoming a Hasid.

M78 Scholem, Gershom. "Reflections on the Possibility of Jewish Mysticism in Our Time." *Ariel*, #26(1970), 43-52. Rpt. M83.

Considering the possibility of future mysticism, Scholem suggests that "mysticism, in its new guise, will not conform to the conservative precepts of the traditional mystics, but will be of secular significance.... For future generations, however, this mystical experience was destined to take on forms of higher naturalistic consciousness rather than religious devotion, a different secular awareness, only outwardly devoid of traditional religiosity but with the substance of mystical experience still there, preserved and reverberating."

M79 Weiner, Herbert. "And So? The Yearning to Know." *Jewish Heritage*, 12,3(1970), 5-9.

Excerpt from M71.

M80 Cohen, Arthur A. "Hasidic Encounter," *Jewish Heritage*, 13,2(1971), 46-53.

Excerpt from M72.

M81 Lamm, Norman. "The Ideology of the Neturei Karta According to the Satmarer Version." *Tradition*, 13,1(Fall 1971), 38-53.

Examines "four major premises in the Neturei Karta ideology as formulated by the Satmarer": A. Divine Redemption and Human Passivity; B. Sequence of Redemption; C. Agents of Redemption can only be the Pious; and D. The Messianic State--a Complete Theocracy.

M82 Schealtiel, Nochum J. "Jewish Mysticism in the Modern Age." *Judaism*, 20(1971), 194-203. Rpt. M93.

"This sterile type of life and 'scholarship' [eighteenth-century pilpul] is quite symptomatic of our present age and its method of rational inquiry, of logical positivism with its atomizing games of linguistic analysis. Jewish mysticism forcefully counters it and bears a very relevant message for modern man by means of which he is able to extricate himself from contemporary mind- and soul-polluting forces that threaten to stifle him, and to find himself. Paraphrasing Psalms 42:8, mysticism is the *zinor*, the conduit, the voice which causes 'deep to call unto deep,' the profound depth of man's soul calling unto the profound depth of the universal soul to find and absorb itself therein."

M83 Scholem, Gershom. "Reflections on the Possibility of Jewish Mysticism in Our Time." *Israel Year Book*, 1971. Pp. 133-39.

Reprint of M78.

M84 Agus, Jacob. *High Priest of Rebirth: The Life, Times, and Thought of Abraham Isaac Kuk.* New York: Bloch Pub. Co., 1972.

Second edition of M21.

M85 Friedman, Maurice. *Touchstones of Reality: Existential Trust and the Community of Peace.* New York: E.P. Dutton & Co., Inc., 1972.

More than a "text for a wide-gauge introductory religion course,... an address to the seeking and concerned reader of whatever age, vocation, life situation and of whatever persuasion or lack of one ... its chief focus is the substitution of 'touchstones of reality' for that special sphere of religious feelings, experiences, creeds, and institutions that Martin Buber once called 'the great enemy of mankind' because such 'religion' confirms us in that dualism in which what really matters in our lives remains untouched and unconcerned." In Chapter 8, Friedman focuses on Hasidism and Contemporary Man (pp. 143-81), as "touchstones of reality."

M86 Gutwirth, Jacques. "The Structure of a Hassidic Community in Montreal." *Jewish Journal of Sociology,* 14(1972), 43-62.

Demonstrates that "in the case of the Montreal Hassidic community, still close to its centuries-old roots, we are able to see how Judaism, Hassidic and orthodox, as the main source of Jewishness and ethnic identity, is connected with a typical economic structure and middle-class ideology."

M87 Kranzler, George. *The Face of Faith: An American Hassidic Community.* Photographs by Irving I. Herzberg. Baltimore: Baltimore Hebrew College Press, 1972.

Photographic essay of Williamsburg, to portray the distinctiveness of this American Hassidic community, in order "to demonstrate a technique of creative and imaginative Verstehen of the intricate fabric of objective and subjective factors in the study of the total Gestalt of social dynamics."

M88 Rubin, Israel. *Satmar: An Island in the City.* Chicago: Quadrangle Books, 1972.

"My purpose in this book is ... to investigate one core group which is the recognized dominant force in Hasidic Williamsburg. The organizational framework for this core community is the Congregation Yetev Lev D'Satmar.... In undertaking this study, I had two basic objectives in mind: first, to provide an accurate description of Satmar life, and, second, to attempt to answer, on the basis of the facts, a number of questions about the internal structure of the community as well as its place in the American cultural scene." The six parts of Rubin's study are: 1. The Historical Background; 2. Religion, the Core of Satmar Life; 3. Family and Education; 4. Economics, Politics, and Welfare; 5. Vital Processes; and 6. Implications and Conclusions.

M89 Schochet, J. Immanuel. "The Philosophy of Lubavitch Activism." *Tradition*, 13,1(Summer 1972), 18-35.

"The following is an attempt to formulate, more or less systematically, the philosophy of Lubavitch activism which inspires the Hassid to pursue his ideals unaffected by his environment. It is taken from the writings and talks of the present Lubavitcher Rebbe, R. Menachem M. Schneerson, *Shelita*,... In these sources it will seek the answer, and its philosophical rationale, to the general questions: 1. What is a Hassid? 2. What is the Hassid's mission? 3. How is he to go about realizing it in the context of Lubavitch activism? 4. What is the role of the Rebbe?"

M90 Sherwin, Byron L. "Jewish Mysticism and Jewish Youth." *Congress bi-Weekly: A Journal of Opinion and Jewish Affairs*, 39,2(28 January 1972), 7-9.

"A purpose of this essay will be to determine whether the current fascination with Jewish mysticism is simply a passing fad or whether it reflects concern with an authentic aspect of Jewish life and thought too long forgotten and too successfully suppressed."

M91 Bokser, Ben Zion. "Mysticism and Judaism." *Congress bi-Weekly*, 40(9 November 1973), 16-18.

Deals with the questions: "What is mysticism, and what is the secret of its fascination for many in our time? What are the implications of this development for the Jewish community which is as vitally concerned with maintaining--and deepening--the loyalties of Jewish youth to their Jewish heritage?"

M92 Fehl, Philipp. "Hasidism and Elie Wiesel." *Theology Today*, 30(1973), 148-53.

Wiesel's "purpose is not to negate the old tales [of Hasidic rabbis] and their pious interpretations, but to show, without endorsing them, their loveliness and inner coherence, and to prove to us that Hasidism in a confrontation with the philosophy of despair can hold its own--not necessarily in truth (he delicately avoids this point) but in majestic picturesqueness."

M93 Schealtiel, Nochum J. "Jewish Mysticism in the Modern Age." In A84. Pp. 242-51.

Reprint of M82.

M94 Schindler, Pesach. "The Holocaust and Kiddush Hashem in Hassidic Thought." *Tradition*, 13,4 and 14,1(Spring-Summer 1973), 88-104.

"Hassidic responses of *Kiddush Hashem* are interpreted on the background of both the *Kiddush Hahayim* manifestations, especially as these were reflected in spiritual-passive resistance and physical resistance, and presently, *Kiddush Hashem*, the manner in which death was faced."

M95 Singer, Isaac Bashevis, and Ira Moskowitz. *The Hasidim*. New York: Crown Publishers, Inc., 1973.

Primarily a pictorial essay on Hasidism, preceded by several introductory essays: Singer, "The Spirit of Jewishness" (pp. 6-13), and "The Spirit of Hasidism" (pp. 14-24); and Moskowitz, "Hasidism and the Artist" (pp. 25-31).

M96 Bokser, Ben Zion. "A Commentary on Rabbi Kook: A Review Essay." *Conservative Judaism*, 29(1974), 72-80.

Review of Zvi Yaron's *Mishnato shel HaRav Kook* (Hebrew), in which Bokser explains how "all currents of Jewish and secular thought impinged on Rabbi Kook, and out of them all he molded a new mystical-philosophic system--a rich treasure of wisdom, still to be examined by the modern Jew."

M97 Gonzalez-Wippler, Migene. *A Kabbalah for the Modern World: How God Created the Universe*. New York: Julian Press, Inc., 1974.

"Dear Reader: This is a book about God." Explores the thesis that "in the Kabbalistic view, the Act of Creation was essentially an Act of Love. And, since according to the established laws of physics, the Universe renews itself continuously throughout eternity, we can say with reasonable certainty that God ARE well, alive and forever loving." Eight chapters: 1. The Creation; 2. The Cosmic Egg; 3. The Creation; 4. The Body of God; 5. God and Sex; 6. Kabbalah; 7. The Tree of Life; and 8. The Nature of the Soul.

M98 Gordon, Haim. "Existentialist Education as Expressed in the Hasidic Stories of Martin Buber." *Religious Education*, 69(1974), 579-92.

"The following analysis of the stories 'The Seven Beggars' and 'The Werewolf' is based on Buber's interpretation of Hasidism as an existentialist religious sect whose unique approach to life is best recorded in its legends. By focusing on educational goals and means I shall show what these stories can contribute to contemporary educational thought."

M99 Halevi, Z'ev ben Shimon [Warren Kenton] *Adam and the Kabbalistic Tree*. London: Rider and Company, and New York: S. Weiser, 1974.

Reflects "one individual's understanding of what he has been taught"; presents the "archetypal scheme" of the Tree of Life as a "divine model for the Universe and Man. Using its analogue we examine Adam, our study taking us up from the Earthly Kingdom of the body, through the Worlds of Soul and Spirit, to the Crown of Heaven. Using ancient concepts, modern observation, and the Tree, the interaction of the Micro and Macrocosm is seen, reflecting in detail and total their source in the ultimate One."

M100 Isaacs, Stephen. "Hasidim of Brooklyn." *Washington Post*, 17 February 1974. Rpt. M122.

Description of the reclusiveness of the Hasidim of Brooklyn.

M101 Scholem, Gershom. "Jewish Theology Today." *Center Magazine*, 7,2(March-April 1974), 58-71.

Addresses four central questions: "The question about the authoritative sources from which such a theology can draw; in other words, the question as to the legitimacy of Revelation and Tradition as categories which can form the foundations of a Jewish theology.... The question about the central values, or about the ideas underlying such values, that can be established from such sources and from the conviction that God does exist.... The question about the position of Judaism and its tradition in a secularized and technologized world.... The question about the meaning, in this context, for the lives and thoughts of the Jews, of the decisive events of recent Jewish history, that is, of the catastrophe of the Holocaust and everything connected with it, as well as the establishment of a Jewish commonwealth in Israel, the *Judenstaat*."

M102 Shaffir, William. *Life in a Religious Community: The Lubavitcher Chassidim in Montreal*. Cultures & Communities: A Series of Monographs. Community Studies. Toronto and Montreal: Holt, Rinehart & Winston of Canada, Limited, 1974.

"This study, which is both an extended and compact version of my doctoral dissertation on the Lubavitch chassidic community in Montreal, examines how such a community of orthodox Jews persists in an urban setting." Shaffir considers: 1. The Chassidic Movement; 2. My Introduction to Lubavitch; 3. Establishing a Distinctive Identity; 4. Maintaining a Tenable Way of Life; 5. The Schools; 6. Lubavitcher and Their Neighbours: Gentiles and Jews; 7. The Community's

Proselytization Work: A Latent Consequence; and 8. Newcomers to the Lubavitch Community.

M103 Steinberg, Harry. "New Square: Bridge over the River Time." *The Times of Israel*, March 1974. Rpt. M126.

Description of Squarer Hassidim.

M104 Bloom, Harold. *Kabbalah and Criticism*. A Continuum Book. New York: Seabury Press, 1975.

Bloom establishes Kabbalah as a basis for his own approach to literature. In the first essay, Kabbalah, he traces the history and basic doctrines of Kabbalah to conclude that "Kabbalah made of itself, at its best, a critical tradition, though distinguished by more invention than critical traditions generally display." In the second essay, Kabbalah and Criticism, Bloom discusses Kabbalah as an interpretative paradigm, for "The Kabbalists read and interpreted with excessive audacity and extravagance; they knew that the true poem is the critic's mind." Finally, Bloom concludes with The Necessity of Misreading, which explains "that a reading, to be strong, must be a misreading, for no strong reading can fail to insist on itself."

M105 Bloom, Harold. *A Map of Misreading*. Oxford and New York: Oxford University Press, 1975.

Establishes Bloom's theories of "misreading" or "misprision" by displacing terminology "from the context of later or Lurianic Kabbalism, which I take as the ultimate model for Western revisionism from the Renaissance to the present." In the first five chapters, Bloom explains his theory of and technique for "misprision," and in the last six, interprets poems by Milton, Emerson and poets whom they influenced.

M106 Kaufman, William E. "Mysticism and the Modern Jew." *Reconstructionist*, 41(March 1975), 7-11.

Attempt "to examine the phenomenon of mysticism objectively, especially as it affects the modern Jew, by raising these questions: Is mysticism a live option for the modern Jew? What are the arguments for and against it? Is mysticism the answer to the deep seated emotional needs of today's questing Jew?"

M107 Mitchell, Douglas, and Leonard Plotnicov. "The Lubavitcher Movement: A Study in Contexts." *Urban Anthropology*, 4(1975), 303-15.

"Anthropological studies of primitive and peasant societies have invariably furnished good descriptions of the contexts that provide the ethnographic setting. That is a convention intrinsic to holism and functional analysis. When anthropologists turned to the study of contemporary urban sociocultural phenomena the use of context has in some cases been neglected. A holistic approach to anthropological urban studies still offers the advantages that have been developed in ethnology, but the complexity of modern society requires a more self-conscious awareness in the employment of relevant contexts. This is illustrated with a report of the Lubavitch Chassidic proselytizing activities in Pittsburgh, Pennsylvania, which are described and analyzed in terms of several of the most significant contexts"--ethnic, historical, international political, religious, behavioral and cultural.

M108   Pinsker, Sanford. "Piety as Community: The Hasidic View." *Social Research*, 42(1975), 230-46.

Exploration of "the pivotal sense of community" characteristic of Hasidic culture, specifically considering: The World of the Hasidim; The Lubavitcher Hasidim; and The Satmar Hasidim.

M109   Potok, Chaim. *The Place of Hasidism and Hasidic Thought in the Life of Modern Man*. Leo Dehon Lecture Series, Monograph No. 1. Franklin, Wisc.: Sacred Heart School of Theology, 1975.

Unavailable for annotating.

M110   Schachter, Zalman M. *Fragments of a Future Scroll: Hassidism for the Aquarian Age*. Germantown, Pa.: Leaves of Grass Press, 1975.

Reflections on mysticism: "Treat this book as a study guide. It is not a textbook. Read a page, think about it, sift the ideas through your consciousness. Let what floats from your mind float free, and follow gently. More than what stimulated it, your own production is what counts in spiritual life."

M111   Halevi, Z'ev ben Shimon [Warren Kenton] *The Way of Kabbalah*. London: Rider, and New York: Weiser, 1976.

"*The Way of Kabbalah* is a study of the ancient inner teaching of Judaism as it has been applied and adapted to universal needs." Specifically, Halevi discusses: The Tradition; Language; The Great Tree of Azilut; The Work of Creation; Natural Adam: The Body; Natural Adam: The Psyche; Slaves in Egypt; The Promised Land; Jacob and Esau; The Zadek; Kabbalah; Objective Knowledge; Groups; Group Structure; Group Dynamics; Meeting; Out of Egypt; Preparation; Literal; Allegorical; Metaphysical; Will; Minor and Major

States; Neshamah: Soul; Kavvanah: Intention; Preparation; The Approach of Action; The Approach of Devotion; The Approach of Contemplation; and Ascension.

M112 Kegan, Robert. *The Sweeter Welcome: Voices for a Vision of Affirmation: Bellow, Malamud and Martin Buber.* Needham Heights, Mass.: Humanities Press, 1976.

Eploration of "The philosophy of Martin Buber in relation to the literary voices of Saul Bellow and Bernard Malamud," particularly in relation to Buber's Neo-Hasidism.

M113 Rajneesh, Bhagwan Shree. *The True Sage.* Hasids Series. Rajneeshparam, Oregon: Rajneesh Foundation, International, 1976.

Unavailable for annotating.

M114 Scholem, Gershom. "With Gershom Scholem: An Interview." In his A98. Pp. 1-48.

Interview conducted by Muki Tsur and Abraham Shapira. Includes sections on: Into the World of the *Kabbalah*; Secular Messianism; An Encounter with Kabbalists in Eretz Yisrael; and There's Mystery in the World.

M115 Singer, Isaac B., and Ira Moskowitz. *A Little Boy in Search of God: Mysticism in a Personal Light.* Garden City, New York: Doubleday, 1976.

"This essay will try to relate the experiences of one who considers himself a bit of a mystic both in his life and in his literary creations. Whether this individual case merits a detailed description is something for the reader to judge. I believe myself to be the best authority to describe this particular study with all its uniqueness and--if you will-- peculiarities. I came from a Hasidic household and began early in life to probe into Hasidic and cabalistic lore as well as take an interest in what's called psychic research, and I will touch on these subjects as they relate to me and to my feelings about mysticism."

M116 Spiegel, Irving. "The Rebbe: In his Torah There is Room for All Jews." *National Jewish Monthly,* March 1976. Rpt. M125.

Description of Menachem Mendel Schneerson, spiritual leader of the Lubavitcher movement.

M117 Berger, Alan. *Witness to the Sacred.* Chico, Calif.: New Horizons Press, 1977.

Unavailable for annotating.

M118 Berger, Rhonda Edna. *An Exploration into the Lubavitcher Hasidic Leadership Kinship Alliance Network.* Working Papers in Yiddish and East European Jewish Studies, no. 27. New York: Max Weinreich Center for Advanced Jewish Studies of the YIVO Institute for Jewish Research, 1977.

"The purpose of this paper is to describe and analyze the political kinship alliance network of the Lubavitcher Hasidic leadership family, the Schneersohns. The political alliance network of the Hasidic group not only represents an interesting example of a group's adaptation to historical situations, but also presents an unusual case in genealogical kinship studies." The paper has three sections: "The first section provides a general overview of the Lubavitcher Hasidic leadership's alliance network. The second section analyzes the actual genealogical data and examines how the political alliance based on kinship that evolved interacted with their environment. The final portion of this paper analyzes the trends of the actual political kinship alliance network."

M119 Bokser, Ben Zion. "Hidden Meanings in the Writings of Rabbi Kook." *Proceedings of the American Academy for Jewish Research,* 44(1977), 19-27.

"One of the themes which occurs frequently in the thought of Rabbi Abraham Isaac Kook (1865-1935) is the call to reckon with the inner meaning which inhabits the world of external forms. In the Torah as in the phenomena of the outer world, we are impinged upon by objects and events that reveal their essence but dimly, when seen in their formal appearance. Behind their outer form there is always an inner content which needs to be recovered from its outer shell. This is the light of the inner world which radiates ultimately from the opaqueness of all existence. This concept has its roots in the classics of the Cabbala, but it was given fresh application by Rabbi Kook."

M120 Gellerman, Jill. *The* Mayim *Pattern as an Indicator of Cultural Attitudes in Three American Hasidic Communities: A Comparative Approach based on Labananalysis.* Working Papers in Yiddish and East European Jewish Studies, Number 26. New York: Max Weinreich Center for Advanced Jewish Studies, 1977.

"By using the system of Labananalysis as a research tool for describing, comparing, and interpreting *what* is performed and *how* it is executed in three Hasidic performances, this study will explore the central question of how this dance behavior shapes and is shaped by the attitudes, values, and beliefs of the Hasidism, members of a mystic branch of Orthodox Judaism born in late eighteenth-century Eastern Europe." After the Introduction, Gellerman discusses

Hasidism: Background and Beliefs; The Role of Dance in Hasidic Culture; The *Mayim* Dance Pattern; and Stylistic Analysis.

M121 Gordon, Haim. "Religious Education as Expressed in the Hasidic Stories of Martin Buber." *Religious Education*, 72(1977), 61-73.

Continuation of M98: "In this paper ... on the basis of three of Buber's Hasidic stories, I shall discuss three significant questions which face the religius educator: How does one convey the spirit of a religious heritage (in this case Judaism)? How does one help one's pupils become aware of the nearness of God? How does one prepare one's pupils for future battles with evil? My analysis of the stories 'The Rabbi and his Son,' 'The Psalm-Singer,' and 'The Shepherd' will provide only a partial answer to these questions; but the discussion and the summary will indicate a direction--a mode of existence--which can be adopted by the religious educator who wishes to grapple with these questions in daily encounters with his pupils."

M122 Isaacs, Stephen. "Hasidim of Brooklyn." In A100. Pp. 189-94.

Reprint of M100.

M123 Mintz, Jerome R. "Brooklyn's Hasidism." *Natural History*, 86,1(January 1977), 46-59.

"It is this devotion to their mystical and social heritage, together with their loyalty to the law and to their leaders, that enables the hasidim to flourish in twentieth-century New York."

M124 Rubin, Israel. "Chassidic Community Behavior." In A100. Pp. 180-88.

Reprint of M53.

M125 Spiegel, Irving. "The Rebbe: In His Torah There is Room for All Jews." In A100. Pp. 202-7.

Reprint of M116.

M126 Steinberg, Harry. "New Square: Bridge over the River Time." In A100. Pp. 195-201.

Reprint of M103.

M127 Weinberg, Bernard. "Satmar and Lubavitch: The Dynamics of Disagreement." *Jewish Life*, 2,2-3(Fall-Winter 1977-78), 55-65.

"Lubavitch and Satmar are really poles apart. Externally, they seem to be identical in their lifestyle and in their yearnings, but, they really operate with diametrically opposed assumptions about themselves and the world about them. Ironically, their philosophical differences as well as their external similarities are distinct sources of friction. Their philosophical differences place them on opposite sides of some of the basic issues of our time. Their external similarities render them competitors for the same political and social influences."

M128 Bullivant, B.M. *The Way of Tradition: Life in an Orthodox Jewish School.* Australian Council for Educational Research Series No. 103. Victoria: Australian Council for Educational Research, 1978.

Sociological study of a Lubavitcher school in Victoria, Australia: "This is an account of how a number of boys tried to come to terms with the pressure of the 'Yoke' in their formal religious schooling, while at the same time coping with the many demands of the secular education system." Part I: The Roots of Tradition (1. The Great Tradition of Chassidic Judaism; 2. The academic tradition); Part II: The Social Organization of Tradition (3. The structuring of tradition in Lubavitcher School; 4. The organization of time and activity; 5. The ceremonial organization of tradition; 6. The formal organization of knowledge); Part III: The Millstones of Tradition (7. Patterns of social interaction; 8. The countervailing curriculum; 9. The rhythm of the year; 10. The millstones of tradition); Appendix: Towards a neo-ethnographic research method.

M129 Green, Arthur E. "The Role of Jewish Mysticism in a Contemporary Theology of Judaism." *Shefa Quarterly*, 1,4(September 1978), 25-40.

"I have tried to seek out, in this presentation, four areas in which the model of Jewish mysticism should prove instructive to us in our attempts at formulating a contemporary theology of Judaism. 1. The reassertion of faith after the Holocaust,... as the ultimate act of courage in the face of the absurd. 2. The revival of spirituality or inwardness as the central core of our lives as religious Jews,... 3. An assertion that the truth-claims of our tradition are to be renewed on the level of mythic and symbolic truth,... 4. A call for the reopening of the channels of religious imagination and creative sacred fantasy in various areas affecting the life of the Jewish religious community."

M130 Gutwirth, Jacques. "Fieldwork Method and the Sociology of Jews: Case Studies of Hassidic Communities." *Jewish Journal of Sociology*, 20(1978), 49-58.

Study of the relationship between Boston's Hasidic community and the larger Jewish community to illustrate the theory that "starting with an intensive fieldwork study of a given Jewish group, one comes--of necessity--to know and to analyse for the sake of the research itself a whole sector, or even in some cases the entire spectrum, of the larger Jewish community."

M131 Jacobson, David C. "The Recovery of Myth: M.Y. Berdyczewski and Hasidism." *Hebrew Annual Review*, 2(1978), 119-30.

Berdyczewski's "hope is that just as in the Eighteenth Century Hasidism was able to convince large numbers of traditional Jews to adopt its revolutionary set of cultural values, so might traditional Jews and Maskilim find in the values and world-view of Hasidism a basis for a cultural renaissance at the beginning of the Twentieth Century. When they do, B's myth of modern Jewish history will have reached its conclusion. The Jewish people will then have transcended the dichotomies of its perverted identities and returned to the ancient Hebrew people's harmonious relationship with nature and with life."

M132 Kantor, Mattis. *Chassidic Insights: A Guide for the Entangled.* New York: Ktav Publishing House, Inc., 1978.

"This is not a book about Kabbala or Chassidic thought. It is a book of Kabbala and Chassidic thought--in English. What I say here is not new. It is mostly explicit and partly implicit in Torah. To indicate sources, however, would make reading the book too tedious." I. Tradition (The Communication, The Withdrawal, The Truth); II. Transition (The Purpose, The Reason, The Development); and III. Transcendence (The Reality, The Choice, The People).

M133 Posner, Zalman I. *Think Jewish: A Contemporary View of Judaism, A Jewish View of Today's World.* Nashville, Tenn.: Kesher Press, 1978.

"This book endeavors to bridge that gap between the Jewish knowledge and the academic, to demonstrate that Judaism's teachings must be examined with the care and rigor one examines, say, political or economic or social or scientific offerings." Posner "draws on Chassidic sources and orientation in an endeavor to contribute the Chassidic perspective to the subjects at hand, though citations are seldom directly made." Includes discussions of: What is Chasidus? What is Chabad? (pp. 11-21); Rebbe and Chassid (pp. 22-29); and Chassidic Attitudes to Other Jews (pp. 93-108).

M134 Rajneesh, Bhagwan Shree. *The Art of Dying: Talks on Hasidism.* Poona, India: Rajneesh Foundation, 1978.

"These are ten of the daily discourses of Bhagwan Shree Rajneesh, given at his ashram in Poona. Five are based on Hasidic stories, five are his answers to questions put by his followers." The discourses are: The Art of Dying; Confusion is my Method; Walking the Tightrope; Let It Be So; Peasant Wisdom; Why No Women?; The Treasure; A Child on the Seashore of Time; "I see what I need to see"; and Just a Hotch-potch.

M135 Semi, Emanuela Trevisan. "A Note on the Lubavitch Hassidim in Milan." Trans. Judith Djamur. *Jewish Journal of Sociology*, 20(1978), 39-47.

Study of the wider Jewish community, and the small Lubavitch community of Milan to conclude "that the Jews of Milan have until now made use of the Lubavitch group in so far as it could help in the maintenance of the community's *Jewish* identity, but that they have dissociated themselves from that group when there was a risk of casting doubt upon their specific identity as a *Milanese* community."

M136 Singer, Merrill. "Chassidic Recruitment and the Local Context." *Urban Anthropology*, 7(1978), 373-83.

"There has been a growing recognition of the importance of contextual reference in urban anthropological research. A recent paper by Mitchell and Plotnicov (1975) [M107] explored the relationship between Lubavitcher Chassidic proselytizing in Pittsburgh and a broad range of cultural, geographic, and temporal contexts. The present paper focuses on a different branch of the same movement (Los Angeles) to point out how important just one of those contexts can be with regard to Chassidic behavior and community response."

M137 Bosk, Charles L. "The Routinization of Charisma: *The Case of the Zadik.*" *Sociological Inquiry*, 49,2-3(1979), 150-67. This issue of the journal is published separately under the title *Religious Change and Continuity: Sociologial Perspectives*. Ed. Harry M. Johnson. San Francisco, Washington and London: Jossey-Bass Publishers, 1979.

"Hasidism survives today as a vocal and vibrant segment of the Jewish religion; however, the Hasidism of today is much transformed from the original. A group that began as a fervent revival movement emphasizing personal discovery in individual experience survives today as the most traditional and ritual bound of organized groups within the Jewish religion. A role that was once a religious office earned through a demonstration of inner illumination, that of Zadik, has become a hereditary office. Both these occurrences index the routinization of charisma within Hasidism. This routinization represents the continual accommodation of ethical and exemplary action and not the triumph of one over the other; it represents, in Weber's terms, a case of 'incomplete rationalization.'"

M138 Elmen, Paul. "Isaac Singer at Jabbok's Ford." *Christian Century*, 96(16 May 1979), 546-49.

"To a marked degree, Singer possesses the Hasidic sense of the excitement hidden in the commonplace, the theology which recognizes a cosmic act in the proffer of a glass of water."

M139 Epstein, Perle. "In Search of Hasidism." *Shefa Quarterly*, 2,1(1979), 55-71.

Selection from M140.

M140 Epstein, Perle. *Pilgrimage: Adventure of a Wandering Jew*. Boston: Houghton Mifflin Company, 1979. Sel. rpt. M139.

Description of personal search for knowledge of Jewish mysticism.

M141 Gealy, Marcia B. "Malamud's Short Stories: A Reshaping of Hasidic Tradition." *Judaism*, 28(1979), 51-61.

"These 'particles of culture' which characterize Malamud's best writing, particularly some of his finest short stories, I would identify with Hasidism,... If Malamud recalls for us the humor of Shalom Aleichem and, more significantly, the irony of I.L. Peretz, if his tales infuse us with the same sense of mystery that we find in the recreated Hasidic tales of Martin Buber, it is because he shares a common past with all of these writers."

M142 Glatzer, N.N. "Was Franz Rosenzweig a Mystic?" In A109. Pp. 121-32.

"Mystical imagery, symbolism, terminology (some of it vaguely, some incorrectly quoted and some borrowed from contemporaries) do not make Rosenzweig a mystic. His negative view of mysticism never changed and must be taken as an authentic repudiation of the *unio mystica*, the mystic's rejection of this world and of the discursive intellect, his ethical passivity, his defiance of expression, his disallowance of the law. What the use of mystical notions by Rosenzweig does show is that he was aware of the preeminent position of mysticism in the shaping of Jewish religious thought and of the viability of the mystical verb for the expression of his own (nonmystical) thinking."

M143 Manashe, Abraham. "Learning the Holy Tongue." *Parabola*, 4,4(1979), 17-24.

Photographic essay of the children of Gehulah, a Hasidic section of Jerusalem, as they study.

M144   Marx, Tzvi. "An Alternative to Mysticism: Halakhic Empiricism." *Shefa Quarterly*, 2,1(1979), 46-54.

Response to Green, M129: "However, while his proposal deserves serious consideration, it seems to me that Green has not taken seriously enough the dangers inherent to such an approach [using Jewish mysticism to revitalize Jewish education]. I believe that these dangers outweigh its positive aspects, and that the Jewish tradition does offer an alternative, sounder path to the modern Jew: the way of halakhic empiricism. In presenting this latter approach and comparing it to Green's, I do not claim it to be descriptive of Jewish reality today or of rabbinic thought as it has been perceived and interpreted during the last two hundred years. Rather, like Green's proposal, it represents a way in which we might begin to retrieve some of the latent spiritual and educational energies that lie buried within the rich tradition of Judaism."

M145   Mintz, Jerome R. "Ethnic Activism: The Hasidic Example." *Judaism*, 28(1979), 449-64.

Examines American hasidic communities of the 1960s to conclude: "Certain features of hasidic life--their sense of common religious purpose, their division into small groups under the leadership of inspired rebbes, their discipline and their submission of self interest--have enabled the hasidim to maintain their Orthodoxy and at the same time to cope with social change."

M146   Roditi, Edouard. "Neo-Kabbalism in the American Jewish Counter-Culture." *Midstream*, 25,8(October 1979), 8-13.

"Even in contemporary Judaism, one can thus observe a marked deviation from traditionally rationalistic and legalistic Talmudic thought in the general direction of Hassidism, Kabbalah, and other intuitional, quietistic, or mystical modes of thought or of life that for centuries have been generally discouraged or considered 'dangerous' except for the rare initiate who, in most cases, moreover, was advised to seek guidance from an older and more experienced 'master.' The increasing popularity of the writings of Martin Buber, of the magnificently scholarly research of Gershom Scholem, of the fiction of Isaac Bashevis Singer, and, at a more popular level, of Chaim Potok, too, then also of the 'pop' singing of San Francisco's 'hippy' Rabbi Schlomo Carlebach, are all symptoms of this kind of increasingly revivalist interest expressed in recent decades."

M147   Rudavsky, David. *Modern Jewish Religious Movements*. New York: Behrman House, 1979.

Revised edition of M60.

M148 Stahl, Abraham. "Ritualistic Reading among Oriental Jews." *Anthropological Quarterly*, 52(1979), 115-20.

"It was the custom among Jews in the Middle East and North Africa, for groups of men to meet in order to read the Zohar, the principle text of Jewish mysticism. This very difficult text was read with great devotion although the readers were unable to understand its language and its meaning. People formed 'Zohar Societies' which regularly held reading sessions. This practice is continued by Oriental immigrants in Israel. The paper describes such sessions among Moroccan Jews: the way in which the meeting is conducted, the manner of recitation, and the general atmosphere."

M149 Heschel, Abraham Joshua. "The Earth is the Lord's." *Keeping Posted*, 25(March 1980), 18-19.

Excerpts of M25.

M150 Prager, Moshe. *Those Who Never Yielded: The History of the Chasidic Rebel Movement in the Ghettoes of German-Occupied Poland*. Vol. I. Mattisyahu's Men. Trans. Y'hoshua Leiman. Brooklyn: Lightbooks, 1980.

"... detailed report, based entirely on authentic documents and reliable testimony," of "the Chassidic lads of the spiritual-moral rebel movement," who "completely ignored the tyrants' regime, paid no attention to their decrees, and never yielded in the face of their fury. They absolutely refused to recognize the shocking circumstances as reality, and they did nothing at all--neither outwardly nor inwardly--to adapt to Satan's rule. In the ghetto blackness, those young Chassidim created their own nobly spiritual super-reality that became even more refined, even more holy in the crucible of suffering and tribulation. By virtue of this super-reality they were able to overcome Satan and his henchmen."

M151 Rosenberg, Ruth. "Contemporising Kabbalah: Saul Bellow Confirms the Cosmic Connection." *Journal of Reform Judaism*, 27(Spring 1980), 40-54.

Analysis of Bellow's *Humboldt's Gift* to conclude that "Three kabbalistic concepts symbolize Humboldt's failure of *kavvanah*. First, the shrinking of his 'significant space' signifies his loss of that cosmic stage on which each gesture, word and look assumes deeper meaning,... Secondly, Humboldt's running out of drapery material when he reached his shaggy belly, as he attempted to clothe himself in radiance, is based on a kabbalistic notion.... Third, Humboldt's insomnia testifies to the disrupted communication. According to the Zohar, when the soul departs in the night and fails to illumine one with dreams on its return, this is a warning that one is about to die."

M152 Singer, Merrill. "The Use of Folklore in Religious Conversion: The Chassidic Case." *Review of Religious Research*, 22(1980), 170-85.

"An analysis is presented of religious conversion and of the conscious use of folklore as a proselyting tool among the Lubavitcher Chassidim. It is demonstrated that folklore, as a medium of communication and persuasion, contributes in identifiable ways to the attraction, attachment, and resocialization of the neophyte. Consequently, it is proposed that the examination of folklore usage in the missionary setting will advance our understanding of religious conversion."

M153 Urzidil, Johannes. "Two Recollections." Trans. Chris Waller. In A112. Pp. 56-68.

One of Urzidil's recollections, The Golem (pp. 61-68), provides a history of the Golem legend of Prague from the sixteenth through the eighteenth centuries, as an "outside" influence on Kafka.

M154 Biale, David. "The Kabbala in Nachman Krochmal's Philosophy of History." *Journal of Jewish Studies*, 32(1981), 85-97.

D.H. Joel's (1815-1882) "treatment of the Kabbala points to the work of the most important exception to the general hostility towards Jewish mysticism in the nineteenth century: Nachman Krochmal (1785-1840). Like Joel, Krochmal's positive attitude toward the Kabbala could only find expression by transforming mysticism into philosophy. Yet, a study of the precise status of the Kabbala in Krochmal's thought is of much greater interest than in the case of Joel, for Krochmal's attitudes toward irrationalism were inextricably linked to his coherent and subtle philosophical system."

M155 Dekro, J. "Love of Neighbor in Later Jewish Mysticism." *Response*, 13(1981), 74-83.

Unavailable for annotating.

M156 Dicker, Herman. *Piety and Perseverance: Jews from the Carpathian Mountains*. New York: Sepher-Hermon Press, 1981.

"Thus, I made it my goal to trace the historical development of the region, describing the political, social and economic conditions of these 100,000 Jewish men, women and children." Not only "a memorial to past generations," the book is intended to "acquaint us with the survivors of the

Holocaust, and provide a bridge to better understanding of some Hasidic communities in the United States." The study's two parts are: The History and The People.

M157 Kushner, Lawrence. *The River of Light: Spirituality, Judaism, and the Evolution of Consciousness.* San Francisco: Harper & Row, Publishers, 1981.

"*The River of Light* boldly recasts traditional Jewish spiritual resources in a modern idiom, relating them to psychoanalysis, physics, and biology and to other traditions of mysticism.... Taken simply, *The River of Light* is a narrative of the emergence into consciousness of Abraham, the father of our Western path. On another level, it is an evocative manual for all who would attempt that journey in our times, a guide to the religious meaning of both self-discovery and scientific inquiry." After Abraham's Journey: A Legend, Kushner discusses: Like Ones in a Dream; The River of Light; The Self-Reflection at Sinai; Protoplasm of Consciousness; The Light of Creation; Return to Nothing; and Living in the River.

M158 Bloom, Harold. *The Breaking of the Vessels.* The Wellek Library Lectures at the University of California, Irvine. Chicago and London: University of Chicago Press, 1982.

Application of Bloom's kabbalistic literary theory--see M104, M105.

M159 Gerson, Jessica. "Norman Mailer: Sex, Creativity and God." *Mosaic*, 15,2(June 1982), 1-16.

"An over-all evaluation of Mailer's sexual views reveals a dichotomy which is typical of his dualistic views in general, and reflects the Manichean values of Jewish mysticism. The question to be weighed is whether or not Mailer achieves, in his insights into sexuality, the unity and wholeness which is the goal of all mystical speculation and action."

M160 Nadler, Allan L. "Piety and Politics: The Case of the Satmar Rebbe." *Judaism*, 31(1982), 135-52.

"Unlike most New York City street violence, then, the case of Satmar vs. Belz (or Satmar vs. Lubavitcher, or Satmar vs. Agudah, or Satmar vs. Mizrachi, etc.) is not the result of that city's social ills. It is, rather, an outcome of the Talmudic teachings of a most remarkable Rabbi and scholar [R. Joel Teitelbaum]. Doctrine, not poverty, and certainly not a tendency to hatred and violence inherent in Hungarian Hasidim, inspires Satmar youths as they vandalize 'Zionist' synagogues and burn Belzer school buses. In examining the anti-Zionist doctrine of the Satmar Rebbe one discovers that there is method, and even a little wisdom, to the Satmarer's madness."

M161   Rabinowicz, Harry. *Hasidism and the State of Israel*. The Littman Library of Jewish Civilization. Rutherford, Madison and Teaneck: Fairleigh Dickinson University Press, and London and Toronto: Associated University Presses, 1982.

"This study is divided into two parts. The first section describes the deep yearning Hasidim felt for the Holy Land from the time of the founder of Hasidism, Rabbi Israel Baal Shem Tov, to the outbreak of World War II. The second part describes the Hasidic Rabbis now in Israel, their lifestyles and their followers. This book attempts to deal with this vast subject within the restricted confines of a single volume."

M162   Rivlin, Leanne G. "Group Membership and Place Meanings in an Urban Neighborhood." *Journal of Social Issues*, 38,3(1982), 75-93.

"The changing nature of cities has raised serious questions concerning the quality of neighborhood and community life. It is essential to reflect on the meaning of neighborhoods and their function for urban dwellers. The role of group membership in place meanings is considered, using an environmental perspective that acknowledges the importance of places to an individual's sense of identity. A small case study of a Hasidic sect with a distinctive life style provides an opportunity to assess the contribution of group affiliation to connections to a neighborhood. Sources of commitment to an area are discussed as are the qualities of group affiliations that affect this commitment. A conception of generic and specific place meanings, based on individual and group experiences, is proposed." (Abstract)

M163   Sheridan, Judith Rinde. "Isaac Bashevis Singer: Sex as Cosmic Metaphor." *Midwest Quarterly*, 23(1982), 365-79.

"... without question Singer's concern with sexuality and perversion is prominent. Yet the basis of his interest must be understood in terms of the ancient Jewish traditions and attitudes found in the Kabbalah. For Singer, as well as for Kabbalistic sages, sexuality provides the consummate metaphor for man's proximity to salvation in damnation. Although Kabbalistic study has been subject to an uneasiness among Jewish intellectuals similar to that felt by Singer's Yiddish readers, Singer's use of sexuality influenced by the Kabbalah is central to Jewish theological and ethical matters."

M164   Schachter-Shalomi, Zalman, with Donald Gropman. *The First Step: A Guide for the New Jewish Spirit*. Toronto, New York, London, Sydney: Bantam Books, 1983.

"We need new models, alternative ways of practicing Judaism, but until recently few have been generally available. This book does not pretend to be the last word on the matter. On the contrary, it is our hope that it will encourage others to share their thoughts, experiences, and know-how about getting more out of being a Jew." Contents: A Note to the Reader; Rx for a Working Jew; Relationships: Marriage, Divorce, and Remarriage; The Teachings of the Body; Jewish Orientation; Prayer--Fact or Feeling; Praying in God's Corner; Singing to God; How to Deal with a Jewish Issue: Circumcision; The Dance of Sabbath; A Time for Lovers; God-birthing; and I Believe We Can Rise Up.

N. MAJOR SCHOLARS

As a relatively new field of study, Kabbalah has been strongly influenced by several major scholars. This chapter contains material dealing with the critical approaches of Leo Baeck, Martin Buber, Abraham Joshua Heschel, and Gershom G. Scholem.

Leo Baeck

N1   Wilhelm, Kurt. "Leo Baeck and Jewish Mysticism." Trans. William Wolf. *Judaism*, 11(1962), 123-30.

In his approach to Jewish mysticism, Baeck "wants to know what place mysticism occupies in the history of Jewish religion, what function it has in the Essence of Judaism, in that continuity of Jewish teaching from the ancient times of the Bible to the present. Baeck looks for theology in Jewish mysticism. Furthermore, he interests himself in special problems of exegesis,... The present essay, too, will reflect that double interest: Wherein does Baeck's significance lie as the theologian of Jewish mysticism; and what results did his research have in the field of Jewish history? Finally we shall try to answer the question as to how Baeck,... became interested in the field of the Kabbalah."

N2   Altmann, Alexander. *Leo Baeck and the Jewish Mystical Tradition*. Leo Baeck Memorial Lecture 17.   New York: Leo Baeck Institute, 1973.

"His research in the field of Jewish mysticism commands respect, but his chief merit lies in his effort as a theologian to integrate an awareness of our mystical tradition--at least some of its strata--into the fabric of modern Jewish thought. It is here that Baeck the thinker comes into his own, and that his interpretation of Kabbala is significant in the context of Jewish intellectual history in our time. No other Jewish theologian among his contemporaries--liberal or orthodox--has a comparable achievement to his credit."

Martin Buber

N3 Tepfer, John J. "Martin Buber and Neo-Mysticism." *Central Conference of American Rabbis, Yearbook,* 44(1934), 203-19.

Exploration of Buber's Hasidism to demonstrate "that Buber's thinking, whether it relates to his theory of knowledge or reality, religion, nationalism or society is totally within the realm of mysticism--his knowledge is not that of ratiocination, his ethics are something irrational and an ecstasy, his nationalism is rooted in a mystical notion of tendencies in the blood."

N4 Kohn, Hans. "The Religious Philosophy of Martin Buber." *Menorah Journal,* 26(1938), 173-85.

"The ultimate reality, the being in itself, cannot be conceived by pure reason, it can only be lived by what Kant called the practical reason. Without this reality there would be no ethical life. Buber teaches that this reality cannot be expressed, but only addressed; it cannot be defined, but it can be realized in our life. Here Buber gives a modern expression to what the prophets and the hasidim taught and lived."

N5 Buber, Martin. "My Road to Hasidism." Trans. Libby Benedict, from Buber's *Die Chassidischen Bucher.* In A24. Pp. 514-22.

"This autobiographical excursion indicates dramatically how Buber brought into harmony two divergent veins of culture--the mystical heritage of Israel and the tradition of the West. He has combined them in practical life too, for he taught Religion and Ethics at the University of Frankfurt until 1933, and for the past several years has been a member of the faculty of the Hebrew University of Palestine." (Editor's note)

N6 Pfuetze, Paul E. "Martin Buber and Jewish Mysticism." *Religion in Life,* 16(1946-47), 553-67.

Examination of Buber's mysticism to conclude that "every aspect of Buber's thought stems from his Chassidic mysticism: his knowledge is intuitive, his ethics are an ecstasy, his Zionism is a spiritual nationalism grounded in a curious notion of tendencies in the blood."

N7 Blau, Joseph L. "Martin Buber's Religious Philosophy: A Review Article." *Review of Religion,* 13(1948), 48-64.

"Here, in these pages, is an attempt to sketch the major themes of [Buber's] religious thought, and to show forth as its central feature that without losing sight at any moment of man's need for God, it emerges in a social philosophy of redemption because of God's need for man. Here is mysticism, indeed, but it is not remote from the concerns of man. The meeting of the *I* and the eternal *Thou* takes place neither in the Heaven of Heavens, nor in the Holy of Holies, nor in the Heart of Hearts; man and God meet in the community."

N8 Cohen, Arthur A. *Martin Buber.* London: Bowes and Bowes, and New York: Hillary House, 1957. New York: Humanities Press, 1958.

"What I should like in this brief study of the life and contribution of Martin Buber is to concentrate upon his pursuit of the holy. It is a pursuit, both reasonable and intuitive, eschewing mysticism, structured out of a complete awareness of Western history and thought." Contents: Introduction; I. The Bare Bones; II. First Principles: I and Thou; III. The Bible and Hasidism; and IV. Man's Way in the World.

N9 Buber, Martin. "My Way to Hasidism." In his A41. Pp. 47-69.

Different translation of N5.

N10 Rexroth, Kenneth. "The Hasidism of Martin Buber." In his A45. Pp. 106-42.

Written "to organize my own relationship to a thinker who has had a major influence on me"; approaches the writer as a "Romantic Traditionalist," the "creed and essence" of whose thought is Hasidism.

N11 Stace, W.T. *Mysticism and Philosophy.* Philadelphia and New York: J.B. Lippincott Company, 1960.

"The aim of this book is to investigate the question, What bearing, if any, does what is called 'mystical experience' have upon the more important problems of philosophy." Chapter 3, section 4, The Problem of Objective Reference (pp. 154-61), focuses on Buber as an example of "mystical Monadism."

N12 Scholem, Gershom. "Martin Buber's Hasidism: A Critique." Trans. Michael A. Meyer. *Commentary*, 32(1961), 305-16. Rpt. N17, N30, N31.

Critical analysis of Buber's work of Hasidism because of "his selective presentation of Hasidism": "To sum up, the merits of Buber's presentation of Hasidic sayings and legends are very great indeed and will to a large extent stand the test of time. But the spiritual message he has read into them in his more mature works is too deeply bound up with assumptions that have no root in the texts--assumptions drawn from his own very modern philosophy of religious anarchism."

N13 Buber, Martin. "Interpreting Hasidism." Trans. Maurice Friedman. *Commentary*, 36(1963), 218-25.

Response to Scholem (N12) and Rivka Schatz-Uffenheimer (*The Philosophy of Martin Buber*, W. Kolhammer Verlag; in German); Buber explains that in his work on Hasidism he attempts "to recapture a sense of the power that once gave it the capacity to take hold of and vitalize the life of diverse classes of people.... The man who remains true to the special task of renewing the vitality of [Hasidism] is obliged to proceed selectively: he must know precisely what he is to include in his work and what he must hand over uncontested to the scholar who follows the principles of historical completeness."

N14 Buber, Martin. "Reflections on Theology, Mysticism, and Metaphysics." Trans. Maurice Friedman. In A54. Pp. 52-55.

Adaptation of N19.

N15 Friedman, Maurice. "Martin Buber." In A56. Pp. 183-209.

Introduction to the "religious philosopher, translator of the Bible, and translator and re-creator of *Hasidic* legends and thought, but especially ... a religious personality who has provided leadership of a rare quality during the time of his people's greatest trial and suffering since the beginning of the Diasporah." The article contains sections on: Early Influences, Introduction to Zionism, Discovery of Hasidism, Academic and Scholarly Activities, Under the Nazis, and The Holy Land. Concerning Buber's philosophy, Friedman discusses The New Philosophy of Dialogue: I-Thou, Interpretation of the Bible, View of Jesus, Approach to Zionism, Jewish Law and Ritual, Buber the Teacher, and Influence of Buber.

N16 Potok, Chaim. "Martin Buber and the Jews." *Commentary*, 41(March 1966), 43-49.

In exploring the reasons why in spite of the fact that Martin Buber "regarded his thought as firmly rooted in Judaism,... Jews, however, have continued to look upon his efforts with suspicion and to regard them as outside the mainstream of Jewish thought," Potok discusses some of the influences which mysticism had on Buber.

N17 Scholem, Gershom. "Martin Buber's Hasidism: a Critique." In A61. Pp. 451-66.

Reprint of N12.

N18 Averbach, Charles. "Reflections on Martin Buber." *CCAR Journal*, 14,2(April 1967), 28-64.

Includes a section on "Hasidism--Hallowing the Every Day" (pp. 48-54), which asserts that "Buber finds in the Hasidic way a Jewish existentialism which has outgrown despair"; and that "Buber's evaluation of Hasidism was congruent with his theory of the dialogical life.... Through Hasidism he offered the world an insight, a life of radiance and joy in the service of God. If Buber gave no more to the world than this alone, his contribution would be of significance."

N19 Buber, Martin. "On Hasidism." In A66. Pp. 731-41.

Response to N24.

N20 Bergman, Hugo. "Martin Buber and Mysticism." In A66. Pp. 297-308.

Analyzes "the distinctive nature of Buber's mysticism and his positive attitude to this phenomenon.... this is his way to the ... 'Great Reality' or to the 'Great Experience' as Zen Buddhism would term it. It is reached through the highest intensification of our experience of things."

N21 Friedman, Maurice. *To Deny Our Nothingness: Contemporary Images of Man*. New York: Delacorte Press, 1967.

"Finally, through constructing a typology of contemporary images of man, we can throw fresh light on many of the figures and works with which we deal, while recognizing the interrelation and overlapping of types. Many of these thinkers, as we shall see, belong to more than one type; each has a uniqueness that cannot be captured by any type." In Part IV, Friedman considers Buber a "Modern Mystic" (pp. 108-14), and in Part IX, an "Existentialist" (pp. 287-304).

N22 Kaufmann, Walter. "Buber's Religious Significnce." In A66. Pp. 665-85.

Overall evaluation of Buber's work, containing a section on Buber and Hasidism (pp. 677-81), which describes Kaufmann's belief that Buber's *Tales of the Hasidim* (L14) is "one of the great religious books of all time."

N23 Rudavsky, David. "The Neo-Hasidism of Martin Buber." *Religious Education*, 62(1967), 235-44.

Analysis of Buber's Neo-Hasidism in terms of: The True Zion, Life as a Dialogue, The Eternal Thou, Love of God, Redemption from Evil, God and Torah, God of Paul and Judaism, Jesus and Judaism, The Ideal Community, with a conclusion on Buber's Influence.

N24 Schatz-Uffenheimer, Rivkah. "Man's Relation to God and World in Buber's Rendering of the Hasidic Teaching." In A66. Pp. 403-34.

"In this essay,... I have only one intention, in line with the purpose of this whole volume: to raise a few problems that come to mind when one reads Buber's works on Hasidism in the light of the Hasidic sources. And I refer to Buber's mature thought which crystalized in the 1940's."

N25 Oliver, Roy [Roy Walker] *The Wanderer and the Way: The Hebrew Tradition in the Writings of Martin Buber*. London: East and West Library, and Ithaca: Cornell University Press, 1968.

"It is not a full account of Buber's 'thought' but an attempt to show that it is his lifelong response to the Hebrew Bible that enables us to see his Hasidic writings and his I-Thou 'philosophy'--in all its varied applications--in their true dimensions." Uses "the Biblical archetypes--Adam, Noah, Abraham, Moses, Psalmist, Isaiah and Servant--[to] throw light on Buber as a man and not merely as an oracular source of doctrines or ideas. Each chapter moves from Buber's response to the Biblical human figure which is its subject, through the Hasidic material in which Buber traces the same theme, and finally to its expression in the contemporary formulation usually referred to as his I and Thou 'philosophy.'"

N26 Shaffer, Carolyn R. "A Jewish View of Redemption." *Commonweal*, 90(1969), 512-15.

"This is the secular or man-oriented conclusion that emerges from Buber's initial religious presupposition, his belief that God is in all the things of the earth. Thus, despite the simple, religious language of his hasidic writings, Buber offers men, not pious platitudes but a call to action in the world. He translates hasidic talk about making the world 'holy' by serving man. And, strange as it may seem, this secular challenge issued by a Jewish theologian may best express the meaning of Easter for Christians who, after all, believe not only that God is in man but that God is man."

N27 Curtis, C.J. *Contemporary Protestant Thought*. New York: Bruce Publishing Company, 1970.

In a book devoted "to the thought of the most significant representatives of Protestant theology in the twentieth century," Curtis includes Chapter 8, Christianity and Judaism: Buber (pp. 117-33), because Buber "has contributed both to the personalist and existentialist strains within Protestant theology.... For the purposes of this concise exposition of Buber's thought the following triadic division has been adopted: (1) Buber's philosophy of *I* and *Thou*, (2) Hasidism, and (3) Zionism."

N28 Friedman, Maurice. "Martin Buber's Encounter with Mysticism." *Human Inquiries: Review of Existential Psychology and Psychiatry*, 10(1970), 43-81.

Unavailable for annotating.

N29 Mosse, George L. "The Influence of the Volkish Idea on German Jewry." In his *German and Jews*. New York: Howard Fertig, 1970. Pp. 85-94.

Explores the influence of German Volkish ideas on Jewish youth of the late nineteenth century, focusing on "the similarity between Buber's rediscovery of the Hasidim and the contemporary German revival of mystics like Meister Eckhart and Jacob Bohme ... Buber's Hasidism performed a similar function by embodying a Judaism which was not rationalized, not fossilized, and surely not quiescent. Moreover, the dynamic nature of the Hasidim arose from a mysticism linked to a revived love for the Volk. The Hasidim represented a heritage with which modern Jews could forge a meaningful link."

N30 Scholem, Gershom. "Martin Buber's Interpretation of Hasidism." In A75. Pp. 397-418.

Reprint of N12.

N31 Scholem, Gershom. "Martin Buber's Interpretation of Hasidism." In his A81. Pp. 228-50.

Reprint of N12.

N32 Vermes, Pamela. "Martin Buber: A New Appraisal." *Journal of Jewish Studies*, 22(1971), 78-96.

Examines Buber's work from the perspective that "Hasidism remains the root out of which Buber's ideal flowered. And the soil out of which both drew their life was the Bible. Once this is realised, one is out of the alien territory of an *it-world* and a *you-world* and back on familiar ground."

N33 Oliver, Roy. "The Baal Shem's New Year's Sermon: The Hasidic Source of a Key Phrase in the Writings of Martin Buber." *Jewish Quarterly*, 20,2(1972), 9-13.

"The importance of Hasidism in Buber's development was not that he found in it something new in the sense of novelty. What he sensed in Hasidism was a living renewal of original Hebrew insights which made the Hebrew Bible--particularly the prophetic tradition--live again for him as an inspiring guide to his own way of living. If the 'narrow ridge' expresses *'holy* insecurity' we may look for it in his Hasidic writings."

N34 Schaeder, Grete. *The Hebrew Humanism of Martin Buber.* Trans. Noah J. Jacobs. Detroit: Wayne State University Press, 1973.

Traces "the path of Hebrew humanism that [Buber] followed [which] unites the West with the East, the Western freedom of the spirit with the wisdom of the Orient for the sake of 'the one thing that is needful.'" Chapter 2, Mysticism and Myth (pp. 54-106), focuses on: Buber's Studies in German Mysticism, The Renewal of Hasidism, *Ekstatische Konfessionen* and Myth; and Chapter 6, The Message of Hasidism (pp. 287-338), discusses: Hasidism as Being-Tradition, The Zaddik, the Being-Tradition of Sanctification, and *For the Sake of Heaven* and *Tales of the Hasidim.*

N35 Moran, James A. "Martin Buber: Mystic of the Everyday." *Studies in Religion,* 5(1975-76), 162-70.

"Since there has been some confusion over the 'mystical' nature of the I-Thou relation, I have discussed the development of Buber's attitude towards mysticism and have compared and contrasted his acount of the I-Thou relation with the mystic's account of his experience. If we take more seriously the suggestion that many mystics were not simply concerned with 'other worldly' experiences, but interested in deepening and expanding human experience, then we shall understand the similarity between the language of the mystic and the language of *I and Thou*. *I and Thou* embodies a mysticism of everyday."

N36 Scholem, Gershom. "Martin Buber's Conception of Judaism." In A98. Pp. 126-71.

"Upon closer inspection, Hasidism's 'love affair' with the world turns out to be Buber's love affair with the world. The Hasidic attitude was much more dialectical than it appears in Buber. In Buber's later writings his heated polemic against all gnosis contributed to this unequivocal glorification of the 'concrete.' He considered Jewish *kabbalah* to be gnosis; with good reason, to be sure. While previously, in an excellent formulation, he had defined Hasidism as "*kabbalah* become ethos" he now sees Hasidim--precisely when it is most characteristic--as the opposite of *kabbalah*. What he had previously seen, in a no less felicitous expression, as the 'deschematization of mystery' is now polemically overstated in antithesis."

N37 Ben Horin, Meir. "Between Buber and Kaplan: The Issue of Hasidism." *Reconstructionist,* 44,3(1978), 7-15.

Comparison of Buber's and Kaplan's views of Hasidism, considering: Their Shared Views; Their Substantial Differences: Two Aphorisms on Hasidism; Kaplan Takes Hasidism Seriously;

Hasidism's Failure to Come to Terms with Modernism; Offered Spiritual Dignity to Illiterates; Kaplan Opposes Adherence to Supernaturalism; Buber is Not "Commanded" by Supernaturalist "Commands" Either: "Unity" as World Task, Not World's Trait; Buber Introduces "Mystery"; Buber's "Renewal" Versus Kaplan's "Reconstruction"; Buber's "Unity" and Kaplan's "Conscience."

N38 Breslauer, S. Daniel. "The Hasidic Anecdote in Martin Buber and Shmuel Yosef Agnon." *Hebrew Studies*, 19(1978), 8-15.

Uses Agnon as a "'control' text, another version of the same tales against which to measure [Buber's] variations," to establish "Buber's 'message' as a new disciple of Hasidic masters. He was to transform that message by revealing it as 'teaching.' To do this he molded his material so that dynamic religiousness was revealed. He selected and edited his tales so that the ritualistic and static elements could be disregarded. Buber's task was nothing less than changing a Jew's perception of his religion. In Buber's rendering, through Hasidism, the Jewish religion became a teaching rather than a set of laws and dogmas. Of course Buber wrestled with his texts and recreated their form and style. The contrast with Agnon, however, shows how well he succeeded in his aim of effecting the transformation of Hasidism into a living, dynamic religiosity."

N39 Goodman, Ruth. "Dialogue and Hasidism: Elements in Buber's Philosophy of Education." *Religious Education*, 73(1978), 69-79.

"Buber's insights into Dialogue and Hasidism are brought to bear on his reflections on education. He took issue with the view that the main goal of the educative process is the release of the creative powers of the child. He emphasized that it is precisely at this point that education must begin rather than end. It is the educative force that meets the criticism, which constitutes teaching."

N40 Hellwig, Monika K. "Gifts and Insights from the Hasidim." *Listening*, 13(Fall 1978), 268-78.

Buber's "studies not only of the legends but of the whole way of life of the Hasidim, have stimulated many further studies and translations, opening up a wealth of resources even for those who do not read either Hebrew or Yiddish. As this has happened, the pervasive influence of this traditional piety of poor and excluded and often persecuted Jews, has become interior and transforming not only for sophisticated Jews long alienated from their own traditions of piety, but also for increasing numbers of Christians alienated for various reasons from Christian traditions of piety, folklore, symbolism and ritual. An ever increasing number of readers is rediscovering or first discovering with a certain sense of homesickness, the healing power of this tradition and its whole way of life."

N41 Jospe, Eva. "Encounter: The Thought of Martin Buber." *Judaism*, 27(1978), 135-47.

"The following pages constitute an attempt to trace the influences that led to [Buber's] philosophy, and to present its premises and goals, and to give at least an indication of its validity by pointing out the principal areas to which it applies." Jospe discusses mysticism, in particular Hasidism, as one of the influences on Buber's thought.

N42 Katz, Steven. "Reflections on Martin Buber's Centennial." *Expository Times*, 90(1978), 71-76.

Analysis of the significance of Buber's work: "Buber's profound religious sensitivities ... go not only to the heart of his understanding of Hasidism, but even more importantly to his own independent vision of reality which here he shares with his readers."

N43 Kaufman, William E. "The Mysticism of Martin Buber: An Essay on Methodology." *Judaism*, 27(1978), 175-83.

"In this essay I shall show how [Buber's] conception of, and attitudes toward, mysticism furnish a way of understanding some aspects of his philosophical development as a religious thinker. Further, I shall demonstrate how an investigation of the mysticism of Buber offers an insight into the methodology required for a study of mystical experience."

N44 Walters, James W. "Martin Buber's Philosophy of Rationality and Mysticism." *Encounter*, 39(1978), 189-201.

"Martin Buber is variously known as a dialogical philosopher, as an existential theologian, as a philosophical anthropologist, and as a Jewish mystic. Each term is an accurate description of this original thinker, but I believe any single appelation slights the provocative richness of this religious thinker. Most fundamentally Buber is an existential mystic with Jewish roots.... my basic intent in this paper is to expound Buber's basic philosophy of religion. And this philosophy of religion, I suggest, is rooted in and inseparable from a profound mysticism of communion. A concomitant interest in this paper is the defense of the integrity of Buber's credentials as a mystic."

N45 Friedman, Maurice. *Martin Buber's Life and Work: The Early Years, 1878-1923*. New York: E.P. Dutton, 1981.

This book, "to coin a term, is a 'dialography,' an attempt to show Buber's thought and work as his active personal response to the events and meetings of his life." Part III, Mysticism (1898-1917) discusses: Encounter with Mysticism (pp. 76-93); The Discovery of Hasidism (pp. 94-123), and The Prague Bar Kochbans and the "Speeches on Judaism" (pp. 124-47).

N46 Glatzer, Nahum N. "Aspects of Buber's Thought." *Modern Judaism*, 1(1981), 1-16.

"True, the genius in Buber drove him to the study of many aspects of human endeavor. However, the student would fail in understanding Buber if he did not see that all (or nearly all) of Buber's contributions to these endeavors are organically interrelated. Indeed, after an initial period in which he freed himself from a form of mysticism and literary romanticism, Buber's works are dominated by *one* major theme, which he elaborates in a hundred variations. The theme is stated in the title of his central work, *I and Thou*."

N47 Oppenheim, Michael. "The Meaning of Hasidut: Martin Buber and Gershom Scholem." *Journal of the American Academy of Religion*, 49(1981), 409-23.

"In the following pages it will be demonstrated that one way of interpreting the disagreement about Hasidut is to focus on Buber's and Scholem's conflicting views about the concept of God that activated that movement. Buber holds that the power of Hasidic life emerged from the relationship between man and the God who is both Creator of the universe and partner in dialogue. Hasidut revealed the redemptive quality given to human life once it is touched by the I and Thou of God and man, and Buber sees this as the treasured heritage that Hasidut offers to the modern Jew as well as to mankind in general. In contrast, Scholem affirms that it is precisely Hasidut's pantheistic or acosmic view of God that permits it to speak to the Jewish--and the broader human--situation in the modern world."

N48 Katz, Steven T. "Martin Buber's Misuse of Hasidic Sources." In his A121. Pp. 52-93.

"The reason for this severe critique of Buber's work on Hasidism and Hasidic sources is to establish Buber's unreliability as a guide to this movement and to clear the stage for a new investigation, some outlines of which I shall suggest, of these materials and hence of the origin and meaning of Hasidism."

Abraham Joshua Heschel

N49 Lookstein, Joseph H. "The Neo-Hasidism of Abraham J. Heschel." *Judaism*, 5(1956), 248-55.

Heschel's "literary creativeness ... portrays a consistent, if not always systematic, line of thinking."

N50 Petuchowski, Jakob J. "Faith as the Leap of Action: The Theology of Abraham Joshua Heschel." *Commentary*, 25(1958), 390-97.

Explores the theology of Heschel from the perspective that "his constant harping on the 'ineffable,' his almost compulsive return to the theme of awe and wonder, his frequent disquisitions on the sublime," indicate that Heschel is a mystic.

N51 Cherbonnier, E. La B. "A.J. Heschel and the Philosophy of the Bible: Mystic or Rationalist?" *Commentary*, 27(1959), 23-29.

Refutation of N50.

N52 Kaplan, Edward K. "Mysticism and Despair in Abraham J. Heschel's Religious Thought." *Journal of Religion*, 57(1977), 33-47.

"A closer look reveals that Heschel's vision of human existence, like that of Pascal, was always both realistic and faithful. He is fully aware of humanity's loneliness without God, and he responds to our radical doubt and despair with an equally radical challenge: that of mystical experience, direct confirmation of the divine. How does this conform to Heschel's function as philosopher? How does his appeal to readers' intellectual assent encourage traditional religious belief? My view is that Heschel's apologetics has broader pertinence. Its fundamental intent follows Herbert Fingaretti's explanation of the mystical teacher: 'The mystic's words are like [a psychoanalyst's] therapeutic interventions: they are designed to be effective in producing specific change, not to embody universal truths. The "pattern" underlying the mystic's words is, in short, pragmatic, not logical.' Heschel philosophizes in order to cleanse our illusions. He first casts us adrift and so prepares a meeting with God which begins in meaninglessness and dread."

N53 Katz, Steven. "Abraham Joshua Heschel and Hasidism." *Journal of Jewish Studies*, 31(1980), 82-104.

From evaluating Heschel's "contribution to our understanding of Hasidism," Katz concludes that "Heschel succeeded in his three goals of (a) providing a historical picture of the Baal Shem Tov and, more especially, of the Kotzker; (b) constructing a phenomenology of religious types, and (c) fulfilling his existential-theological ambition of aiding his readers to find meaning in their own lives in the face of all the obstacles to this end."

N54 Klein, Zanvel E. "Heschel as a Hasidic Scholar." *Journal of Jewish Studies*, 32(1981), 200-202.

Criticism of N53.

N55 Dresner, Samuel H. "The Contribution of Abraham Joshua Heschel." *Judaism*, 32(1983), 57-69.

Selection from Dresner's introduction to Heschel's *The Circle of the Baal Shem Tov: Essays in Hasidism* (University of Chicago Press, forthcoming).

Gershom G. Scholem

N56 Werblowsky, R.J. Zwi. "Philo and the Zohar: A Note on the Methods of the *Scienza Nuova* in Jewish Studies." *Journal of Jewish Studies*, 10(1959), 25-44, 113-35.

Defense of Scholem from the criticism of Samuel Belkin (*Sura*, 3[1958], 25-92; in Hebrew), because "Prof. Belkin's article is merely the most recent and most pretentious salvo from a barrage that has been directed for a long time against the modern, critical study of kabbalism. Even the mild innuendo of contempt, conveyed by Prof. Belkin's reference to the representation of the modern *Wissenschaft des Judenthums* does not compensate for the woeful lack of scholarly standards with which Scholem's researches and conclusions are still being criticized."

N57 Wijnhoven, Jochanan H.A. "Gerhsom G. Scholem: The Study of Jewish Mysticism." *Judaism*, 19(1970), 468-81.

"Scholem defines a truly learned man as one who is bound to tradition through his inquiries. Tradition itself should be understood as 'a process that creates productivity through receptivity.' By penetrating deeply into the Jewish mystical tradition, and by shedding light upon forgotten episodes in the history of the Jewish people, he has brought the past and the present together, leaving us the challenge of the confrontation. That he fulfilled his task not as a 'prophet,' but as a scholar and professor, makes his work no less relevant and perhaps more enduring."

N58 Alter, Robert. "The Achievement of Gershom Scholem." *Commentary*, 55(April 1973), 69-77.

Evaluation of Scholem's scholarship to conclude that "what emerges from the multifarious mystical matters discussed by Scholem is a powerful sense of the protean nature of Jewish experience. Where we might have been inclined to view the various modern ideologies of Jewish survival as a splintering of classical Jewish unity, a fateful breaking away from the grand continuity of the Jewish past, Scholem shows us a historical Judaism itself fissured with sharp divisions and marked by the most extreme variety."

N59 Ben-Shlomo, Joseph. "The Influence of Gershom Scholem." *Ariel*, #32(1973), 25-28.

"Scholem's specific field of interest, Jewish mysticism, has been the medium rather than the source of his vision. Kabbalah is only the most striking instance of the incorporation of a profoundly revolutionary set of doctrines within the traditional framework of Judaism. Despite their radical character, these doctrines, which were put forth as a continuation of the tradition, became one of its legitimate representatives. Scholem turned the scientific study of Kabbalah, previously neglected if not despised, into a subject of serious scholarship."

N60 Davies, W.D. "From Schweitzer to Scholem: Reflections on Sabbatai Svi." *Journal of Biblical Literature*, 95(1976), 529-58.

"I shall offer reflections on the value of Scholem's study [*Sabbatai Ṣevi*, K41] for what could lead to a reassessment of Schweitzer's work.... and shall consider the purpose of this lecture fulfilled if only it helps to integrate Scholem's insight into the nature of Judaism more closely into the study of Christian origins."

N61 Alter, Robert. "Gershom Scholem: History and the Abyss." In his A99. Pp. 67-89.

In an anthology "concerned with Jewish writers as a symptomatic, if extreme, instance of the predicaments of twentieth-century literature," this essay analyzes Scholem's scholarship as showing "us a historical Judaism itself fissured with sharp divisions and marked by the most extreme variety.... What his researches actually do is to open the doors of the mind to a genuine Jewish pluralism, grounded in the spectacular plurality of Jewish historical experience."

N62 Kostelanetz, Richard. "Gershom Scholem: The Mystics' Medium." *Present Tense*, 4(Spring 1977), 29-33.

Explores the paradoxes of Scholem: "that this sane, largely rational man has spent more than sixty years tenaciously studying the most extraordinary bunch of eccentrics who ever called themselves religious Jews.... that most mystical thought implicitly disapproves of scholarly bookishness such as Scholem's."

N63 Rotenstreich, Nathan. "Symbolism and Transcendence: On Some Philosophical Aspects of Gershom Scholem's Opus." *Review of Metaphysics*, 31(1978), 604-14.

"The significance, from the philosophical point of view, of Scholem's analysis of kabbalah as an avenue of mysticism lies precisely at this point. Kabbalah defies the possibility of interpreting mysticism as amounting to *unio mystica* with its pantheistic corollary and thus defies the possibility of a philosophical system which pretends to be an interpretation and sublation of mysticism onto the level of reason. Moreover, it might be impossible to take a philosophical system as an adequate and exhaustive interpretation of historical events or trends, including religious or mystical currents.... Scholem has shown us that even Jewish mysticism remains aware of [the distance between man and God]. Thus, when one speaks about mysticism as a prelude to a philosophical system, one has to be more specific or more particular and speak about a certain mystical tradition, both in historical and phenomenological terms."

N64 Biale, David. *Gershom Scholem: Kabbalah and Counter-History*. Cambridge and London: Harvard University Press, 1979.

"Here in a nutshell is Scholem's whole program: Where the Wissenschaft des Judentums saw only an historical corpse, Scholem finds 'hidden life.' He accepts the nineteenth-century estimation that if one considers only the rational aspect of the Jewish tradition, Judaism appears dead indeed. But by also considering 'degeneracy' and 'impotent hallucinations' as equally legitimate within Judaism, one discovers hidden life--a 'great living myth,' which Scholem finds in Jewish Gnosticism and the Kabbalah.... For Scholem, the Kabbalah, a suppressed and esoteric tradition, holds the key to the continuing vitality of Judaism." Contents: 1. The Nineteenth-Century Legacy; 2. Revision and Revolution; 3. From Berlin to Jerusalem; 4. Theology, Language, and History; 5. Mysticism; 6. Myth; 7. Messianism; 8. The Politics of Historiography; 9. Counter-History; and Epilogue: Between Mysticism and Modernity.

N65 Scholem, Gershom G. *From Berlin to Jerusalem: Memoirs of My Youth*. Trans. Harry Zohn. New York: Schocken Books, 1980.

Memoirs of Scholem's youth, including his decision to devote his life to kabbalistic studies.

N66 Scholem, Gershom G. "How I Came to the Kabbalah." *Commentary*, 69(May 1980), 39-53.

Adapted from N65.

N67 Biale, David. "Gershom Scholem and Anarchism as a Jewish Philosophy." *Judaism*, 32(1983), 70-76.

"As the virtual creator of the study of Jewish mysticism as an academic discipline, Gershom Scholem enlarged the definition of Jewish history to include irrational elements along with rational and legal ones. Yet, Scholem's importance extends well beyond the walls of the academy, for the results of his historiography suggest a new philosophy of Judaism and, as such, his work constitutes a significant contribution to modern Jewish thought. It is only fitting, in the wake of his death in February 1982, that we reflect on the larger meaning of his legacy and what message it may convey for the urgent issues of Jewish life today."

N68 Breslauer, S. Daniel. "The Ethics of *Gilgul*." *Judaism*, 32(1983), 230-35.

"... *gilgul* has developed from a tradition stressing community and halakhah to an existentialist affirmation of the individual. Gershom Scholem was particularly adroit at finding the revolutionary aspects of Jewish mysticism and pointed to the possibility of just such a revolutionary existentialism in the idea of *gilgul*. The working out, however, of that potential, did not take place in Lurianic Kabbalah. It required first the identification of ethical and halakhic transgressions as found in Hasidism. It then required moving from the need for a mediator to the belief that the isolated self could accomplish the task of redemption. This last stage occurred only with the early modern Hebrew writers. Scholem's insight is relevant and helpful as a tool by which to understand the evolution of religious ideas, which develop slowly but still in unexpected and revolutionary directions. Seen as an indication of such dynamic development, Scholem's views about *gilgul* are perceptive insights into the process of ethical reflection in Jewish religious thought."

N69 Maccoby, Hyam. "The Greatness of Gershom Scholem." *Commentary*, 76,3(September 1983), 37-46.

Scholem "radically revised, and gave fresh life to, the entire field of Jewish studies. At the same time, the new insights which he brought to his reading of Jewish experience and ideology required, and have resulted in, a reorientation of all thoughtful Jews to their own tradition and to the implications of their religious history. A brilliantly panoptic mind, a true 'master thinker,' Scholem represented a force in the intellectual life of our century, and not only in Jewish intellectual life, whose influence will be felt for a long time to come."

O. NON-JEWISH KABBALAH

This awkward phrase refers to manifestations of Kabbalah outside of the realm of what could be considered "orthodox" Jewish mysticism. Primarily comprised of Christian occultist materials, the chapter also includes works by Jews who deviate from the generally accepted tradition. In evaluating these materials, I have selected only those which employ tenets of Jewish mysticism in a clearly identifiable manner. Therefore, works whose kabbalistic origins have been altered beyond recognition have been excluded, despite the appearance of the words "Cabala" or "Qabbalah" in their titles.

Primary Sources

O1 Agrippa von Nettesheim, Heinrich Cornelius. *Three Books of Occult Philosophy*. Trans. J.F. [John French] London, 1651.

The first text of Christian Kabbalah available in English. While all three books contain references to Kabbalism, four chapters in Book III are devoted specifically to the subject: Chapter 10, Of Divine emanations, which the Hebrews call Numerations, others attributes; The gentiles gods and Dieties [sic]; and of the ten Sephiroths and ten most sacred names of God which rule them, and the interpretations of them (pp. 366-70); Chapter 11, Of the Divine names, and their power and vertue (pp. 370-79); Chapter 27, Of the calculating Art of such names [of spirits] by the tradition of Cabbalists (pp. 430-34); and Chapter 30, Another manner of making Characters [letters of the Hebrew alphabet], delivered by Cabalists (pp. 439-44).

O2 More, Henry. *Conjectura Cabbalistica. Or, A Conjectural Essay of Interpreting the Minde of Moses, according to a Threefold Cabbala: Viz. Literal, Philosophical, Mystical, or Divinely Moral*. London, 1653; 1662; 1713.

"And therefore I thought fit to call this threefold interpretation that I have hit upon, Cabbala's, as if I had indeed light upon the true Cabbala of Moses in all the three senses of the Text, such as might have become his own mouth to have uttered for the instruction of a willing and well prepared Disciple.... That though I call this Interpretation of mine

Cabbala, yet I must confess I received it neither from Man nor Angel.... And I know nothing to the contrary, but that I have been so successful as to have light upon the old true Cabbala indeed."

03 Fludd, Robert. *Mosaicall Philosophy: Grounded upon the Essentiall Truth or Eternal Sapience.* London, 1659.

"My desire is ... to prove and maintaine the true and essentiall Philosophy, with the virtuous properties of that eternall Wisdom, which is the Foundation and Corner-stone, whereon it is grounded." Relying heavily on Agrippa, Fludd incorporates tenets of Christian Kabbalah throughout the work, especially in Part II, Chapter 2 of the second treatise: How and by what Attributes or properties the Hebrew Rabbies, and profoundest Cabalists do proove, that contrariety of natures doth proceed from one eternall Essence, as from the root of al things (pp. 171-77).

04 Helmont, Franciscus Mercurius van. *A Cabbalistical Dialogue in Answer to the Opinion of a Learned Doctor in Philosophy and Theology that the World was Made of Nothing. As it is Contained in the Second Part of the Cabbala Denudata & Apparatus in Lib. Sohar, p. 308 &c. To which is subjoyned A Rabbinical and Paraphrastical Exposition of Genesis 1.* London, 1682.

A dialogue explaining to the "Compiler" the fundamentals of Creation according to Christian Kabbalah. The second part consists of a kabbalistic explication of the first chapter of Genesis.

05 Helmont, Franciscus Mercurius van. *Two Hundred Queries Moderately Propounded Concerning the Doctrine of the Revolution of Humane Souls, and Its Conformity to the Truths of Christianity.* London, 1684.

A series of questions designed to justify van Helmont's interpretation of Isaac Luria's theory of *gilgul*, transmigration of the soul.

06 Helmont, Franciscus Mercurius van. *The Paradoxal Discourses ... Concerning the Macrocosm and Microcosm, or the Greater and Lesser World, and their Union.* London, 1685.

Primarily a medical treatise, but Chapter 4, Concerning the Revolution of Humane Souls (pp. 105-61), is devoted to van Helmont's interpretation of *gilgul*.

07 Conway, Anne. *The Principles of the Most Ancient and Modern Philosophy Concerning God, Christ and the Creatures.* London, 1692.

Considered one of the greatest female thinkers of the seventeenth century, Anne Conway was taught Kabbalah by van Helmont during the period when he served as her physician. Her treatise incorporates a number of kabbalistic teachings from van Helmont, as well as the *Kabbala Denudata*, and Chapter 5 (pp. 34-47) is devoted specifically to a kabbalistic justification of belief in Christ.

O8 Helmont, Franciscus Mercurius van. *Seder Olam: or, the Order, Series, or Succession of all the Ages, Periods, and Times of the Whole World is Theologically, Philosophically, and Chronologically Explicated and Stated. Also the Hypothesis of the Pre-existency and Revolution, of Humane Souls. Together with the Thousand Years Reign of Christ on the Earth, Probably Evinced, and Deliver'd in an Historical Enarration thereof, according to the Holy Scriptures. To which is also Annexed, Some Explanatory Questions of the Book of the Revelations of the Like Import. And an Appendix; containing Some Emendations and Explanations of Divers Passages, in the Two Foregoing Treatises, out of the Author's Original Manuscripts and Papers.* Trans. J. Clark. London, 1694.

Fully delineated treatise of Christian Kabbalah, based on van Helmont's kabbalistic theories.

O9 *Aesch Mezareph, or Purifying Fire, a Chymico-Kabalistic Treatise Collected from the Kabala Denudata of Knorr von Rosenroth.* Trans. Lover of Philalethes. London, 1714. Rpt. Collectanea Hermetica, Vol. IV. Ed. W. Wynn Westcott. London: Theosophical Publishing Society, 1894. Rpt. New York: Occult Research Press, 1956; Calif.: Health Research, 1974.

English adaptation of a kabbalistic alchemical text. The Hebrew source, probably based on an Italian original, is lost.

O10 More, Henry. "Expositio Mercavae." In R. Casway. *A Miscellaneous Metaphysical Essay: or, an Hypothesis Concerning the Formation and Generation of Spiritual and Material Beings. With Their several Characteristics and Properties, and How Far the Several Surrounding Beings Partake of Either Property. To which is Added, Some Thoughts upon Creation in General, upon Pre-existence, the Cabalistic Account of the Mosaic Creation, the Formation of Adam, and Fall of Mankind; and upon the Nature of Noah's Deluge. As also upon the Dormant State of the Soul, from the Creation to our Birth, and from our Death to the Resurrection. The Whole Considered upon the Principles of Reason, and from the Tenor of the Revelations in the Holy Scriptures.* London, 1748. Pp. 364-94.

In this eclectic compilation of esoteric notions, Casway tries to show that a "consistent Scheme of Providence may be chalk'd out, consistent with Reason and Revelation, agreeable to the Phaenomena we observe around us, carried on by Providence." While containing many references to Jewish mysticism, the text is not kabbalistic per se; however, the Appendix contains an abridged translation of Henry More's kabbalistic speculation about Ezekiel's chariot, taken from the *Kabbala Denudata*.

O11 Mathers, S.L. MacGregor, trans. *The Key of Solomon the King (Clavicula Salomonis): Now First Translated and Edited from Ancient MSS. in the British Museum*. London: G. Redway, 1889; rpt. London: Kegan Paul, Trench, Trubner, 1909. Rpt. L.W. de Laurence, ed. Chicago: De Laurence, Scott & Co., 1916; rpt. London: Routledge and K. Paul, 1972.

Magical treatise, *Mafteaḥ Shelomo*, attributed by Mathers to King Solomon but, according to Scholem, "not originally Jewish at all, and it was only in the 17th century that a Hebrew edition was brought out, a mélange of Jewish, Christian and Arab elements in which the kabbalistic component was practically nil" (C65).

O12 Abraham ben Simeon, of Worms. *The Book of Sacred Magic of Abra-Melin the Mage, as Delivered by Abraham the Jew unto his Son Lamech, A.D. 1458*. Trans. and ed. S.L. MacGregor Mathers. London: J.M. Watkins, 1898; 2nd ed. 1900. Rpt. Chicago: The de Laurence Company, 1932; London: J.M. Watkins, 1956; New York: Causeway Books, 1974; New York: Dover Publications, 1975.

Though extolled by Mathers as an English translation of a French translation of a Hebrew work written in the fifteenth century, *The Book of Sacred Magic* was originally written in the sixteenth century in German, and not by a Jew. According to Scholem, "the Hebrew mss of it found in Oxford (Neubauer 2051) [B1] is simply a bad translation" (C65). Nevertheless, occultists view the text as being genuine.

O13 Gollancz, Hermann, ed. *Sepher Maphteaḥ Shelomo (Book of the Key of Solomon. An Exact Facsimile of an Original Book of Magic in Hebrew*. London and New York: Oxford University Press, 1914.

Facsimile of the original of O11.

O14 White, Nelson and Anne White, eds. *Mafteach Shelomo. Lemegeton; Clavicula Salomonis: or, The Complete Lesser Key of Solomon the King*. Pasadena, Calif.: Technology Group, 1979. Index and Reference Volume, 1980.

Another edition of O11.

015 Reuchlin, Johann. *On the Art of the Kabbalah--De Arte Cabbalistica.* Trans. Martin Goodman and Sarah Goodman. Bilingual Editions of Classics in Philosophy and Science Series. New York: Abaris Books, Inc., 1983.

Bi-lingual edition.

Secondary Sources

016 Barrett, Francis. *The Magus, or Celestial Intelligencer; Being a Complete System of Occult Philosophy. In Three Books: Containing the Antient and Modern Practice of the Cabalistic Art, Natural and Celestial Magic, &c.; Shewing the Wonderful Effects that May Be Performed by a Knowledge of the Celestial Influences, the Occult Properties of Metals, Herbs, and Stone, and the Application of Active to Passive Principles.* London: Printed for Lackington, Allen, and Co., Temple of the Muses, 1801. Rpt. London: Knight and Compton, 1875; New Hyde Park, New York: University Books, Inc., 1967; Leicester: Vance Harvey Publishing, 1970; Secaucus, New Jersey: Citadel Press, 1975.

"In this Work,... we have ... collected whatsoever can be deemed curious and rare, in regard to the subject of our speculations in Natural Magic--the Cabala--Celestial and Ceremonial Magic--Alchymy--and Magnetism.... The Second Book forms a complete treatise on the mysteries of the Cabala and Ceremonial magic; by the Study of which, a man (who can separate himself from material objects, by the mortification of the sensual appetite--abstinence from drunkenness, gluttony, and other bestial passions, and who lives pure and temperate, free from those actions which denegrate a man to a brute) may become a recipient of Divine light and Knowledge" (pp. 33-72).

017 Anon. "Cabala." *Retrospective Review*, 9(1824), 62-72.

Study of Pico della Mirandola and "the Cabalists of the middle ages": *Cabalistarum Selectiora obscurioraque dogmata, a Pico ex eorum commentationibus pridem excerpta*, &c. (1569); *Abolita divinae Cabalae mysteria, contra Sophistarum logomachiam defensa*, by Jacques Gaffarel (1625); *Conjectura Cabbalistica; or a Conjectural Essay of interpreting the Minde of Moses according to a threefold Cabala*, by Henry More (1653) [O2]; and *Oeuvres* of Guillaume Postel.

018 Morley, Henry. *The Life of Henry Cornelius Agrippa von Nettesheim, Doctor and Knight, Commonly Known as a Magician.* 2 vols. London: Chapman and Hall, 1856.

"I wish to show how the man really lived, what the man really wrote, of whom these stories have so long been current." Included in Chapter V, Cornelius a Doctor of Divinity (I.69-81), is a long discussion of Kabbalah, based primarily on Brucker's *Historia Philosophiae* (English translation B47), and the *Kabbala Denudata*, which covers the basic texts, practical and theoretical Kabbalah, Christian kabbalists, cosmology, and the mystical uses of the name of God. Morley includes references to kabbalistic influences on Agrippa throughout the work, though primarily in relation to the *Third Book of Occult Philosophy* (O1). The exposition of the Kabbalah is reprinted in O41.

019 Story, William W. *The Proportions of the Human Figure, According to a New Canon, for Practical Use, with a Critical Notice of the Canon of Polycletus, and of the Principal Ancient and Modern Systems*. London: Chapman and Hall, 1866.

"In the present Essay on the Proportions of the Human Figure, a new system is proposed, by which the measures of all its parts may be exactly ascertained and determined without reference to the Figure itself. The first three Chapters are preliminary, and devoted to a consideration of the ancient Cabala of numbers and symbols, a critical examination of the famous Canon of Polycletus, as reported by Vitruvius, and a brief view of the principal systems of Proportion in use in ancient and modern time." The Cabala, pp. 1-13.

020 Jennings, Hargrave. *The Rosicrucians: Their Rites and Mysteries*. London: J.C. Hotten, 1870. London: Chatto and Windus, 1879. London: Nimmo, 1887. London: George Routledge & Sons, Ltd., and New York: E.P. Dutton & Co., 1887, 1907, 1921. Rpt. New York: Arno Press, 1976.

"This book ... concentrates in a small compass the results of very considerable labour, and the diligent study of very many books in languages living and dead. It purports to be a history (for the first time treated seriously in English) of the famous Order of the 'Rose-Cross', or of the 'Rosicrucians'." The last two chapters (pp. 442-464), deal with Kabbalism: Chapter 23, The Outline of the Cabala, or Kabbalah. Its Mystic Indications. The Purpose of the Great Architect of the Universe in the Sensible and Spiritual World (Natural and Supernatural), and the Character of their Reciprocity, and Double-Working; and Chapter 24, Cabalistic Profundities.

021 Pike, Albert. *Morals and Dogma of the Ancient and Accepted Scottish Rite of Freemasonry*. Published by the author, 1871; rev. ed. 1950.

"... contains the Lectures of the Ancient and Accepted Scottish Rite in [the Southern Jurisdiction of the United

States], and is specially intended to be read and studied by the Brethren of that obedience, in connection with the Rituals of the Degrees." Chapter 28, Knight of the Sun, or Prince Adept, contains a detailed explanation of the Freemasons' interpretation of Kabbalism since "All truly dogmatic religions have issued from the Kabalah and return to it: everything scientific and grand in the religious dreams of all the illuminati, is borrowed from the Kabalah" (pp. 744-71).

O22 Greene, William B. *The Blazing Star; With an Appendix Treating of the Jewish Kabbala*. Boston: A. Williams and Co., 1872. Appendix, pp. 27-108.

Appendix discusses: Books of the Kabbala; The Kabbalistic Balance; The Cherubim; Man, the Form of All Things; The Sephiroth--The First Triad; The Sephiroth--The Second Triad; The Sephiroth--The Third Triad; The Sephiroth--Matrona; The Ten Sephiroth. Conclusion: "Our exposition is wholly inadequate, and perhaps, in some points, incorrect; for the texts we have interpreted are very dark. We trust, however, that what we have said will suffice to break the ten seals of the lesser Zohar, and to make it an open book."

O23 Mackey, Albert G. *An Encyclopaedia of Freemasonry and Its Kindred Sources; Comprising the Whole Range of Arts, Sciences and Literature as Connected with the Institution*. Philadelphia: Moss & Co., 1873, 1878. New and rev. ed. Philadelphia: L.H. Everts & Co., 1894.

Collects "materials ... which, under one cover, would furnish every Mason who might consult its pages the means of acquiring a knowledge of all matters connected with the science, the philosophy, and the history of his Order." In addition to a brief entry on the *Sefer Yetzirah*, the *Encyclopaedia* contains a rather extensive article on Kabbalah, covering the mythical history, and sections on The Dogmatic Kabbala, with a discussion of the *Sefirot*, and The Literal Kabbala, which explains Gematria, Notaricon and Temurah.

O24 Skinner, J. Ralston. *Key to the Hebrew-Egyptian Mystery in the Source of Measures Originating the British Inch and the Ancient Cubit, by which Was Built the Great Pyramid of Egypt and the Temple of Solomon; and through the Possession and Use of Which, Man, Assuming to Realize the Creative Law of the Deity, Set it Forth in a Mystery, among the Hebrews Called Kabbala*. Cincinnati: Robert Clarke & Co., 1875; Philadelphia: D. McKay Co., 1876; Minneapolis: Wizards Bookshelf, 1972.

"The first step ... necessary to the deciphering of the hieroglyphic or symbolic meanings of the Hebrew Bible, is the restoration of the great pyramid after its architectural conception. This is the chief burden of this work; and it is thought that the intent of the architect has been so far recovered as to justify publication. Secondarily, it is to be shown that the Temple was but another architectural style of setting forth the same measures with the pyramid."

025 Blavatsky, H.P. "Mysteries of the Kabala." In her *Isis Unveiled: A Master-Key to the Mysteries of Ancient and Modern Science and Theology*. London: Bernard Quaritch, New York: J.W. Bouton, 1877. Vol. II, ch. 5, pp. 212-50. Rpt. in O88.

Blavatsky wants to "give attention to some of the most important Mysteries of the *Kabala*, and translate their relations to the philosophical myths of various nations." She considers: Ain-Soph and the Sephiroth; The primitive wisdom-religion; The book of *Genesis* a compilation of Old World legends; The Trinity of the Kabala; Gnostic and Nazarene systems contrasted with Hindu myths; Kabalism in the book of *Ezekiel*; Story of the resurrection of Jairus' daughter found in the history of Krishna; Untrustworthy teachings of the early Fathers; and Their persecuting Spirit.

026 Pancoast, S. *The Kabbala: or, The True Science of Light: An Introduction to the Philosophy and Theosophy of the Ancient Sages, Together with a Chapter on Light in the Vegetable Kingdom*. Philadelphia: J.M. Studdart & Co., 1877; New York: R. Washington, 1883.

"As we shall show, the old Kabbala, with its curious and comprehensive symbol language, is at once an elaborate System of Natural Philosophy and a profound system of Theology--an illuminated exposition of the mysterious truths of Nature and of that higher Science which the Book of Nature unfolds to the enlightened eye of the Soul, the Science of Religion." Pancoast uses Kabbalism to demonstrate the relationship between the science of light and life and health.

027 Blavatsky, Helena P. "Kabalistic Views on 'Spirits' as Propagated by the Theosophical Society." *Religio-Philosophical Journal* (Chicago), 23(January 26, 1878), 2. Rpt. in O88.

In this letter to the editor, Mme. Blavatsky defends her views on spirits which are "but the substance of what many kabalists have said before me," by citing the work of Heinrich Kunrath, "a most learned kabalist," and "Zeus ... a kabalist of more than twenty-five years' standing."

028 Pancoast, Seth. "Kabbalah." *Path*, 1(April 1886), 8-14.

Introduction to Kabbalah as "a system of philosophy and theosophy, that was obtained at a very remote period of time by the wise men of the east, through the unfoldment of the intuitive perceptions."

029 Pancoast, Seth. "The Mystery of Numbers." *Path*, 1(May 1886), 37-41.

"It is the Kabbalistic science of numbers of which we purpose to speak."

030 Skinner, J. Ralston. "Notes on the Cabbalah of the Old Testament." *Path*, 1(July, August 1886), 103-108, 134-39.

Explains "of what Cabbalah really consists ... that sublime science upon which Masonry is based, is in fact, the substance of Cabbalah,--which last is the rational basis of the Hebrew text of the Holy Writ."

031 Caithness, Marie, Duchess of Pomon. *Mystery of the Ages, Contained in the Secret Doctrine of All Religions.* London: Redway, 1887.

Contains a chapter written from the Theosophical standpoint, "The Kabbala, or Hebrew Theosophy"; unavailable for annotating.

032 Lazarus, Montague R. "The Kabbala and the Microcosm." *Theosophist*, 8(September 1887), 767-74; 9(October, November, December 1887), 45-52, 119-24, 167-71.

After giving "the general outlines of the *Anima*, and its component parts and the seats of their manifestation in terms that are more familiar to a large number of the readers of the *Theosophist* than the Kabbalistic ones," Lazarus goes "on to give an account of some of the theories propounded in the Tractate of Rabbi Moses of Cordova, on the reason of the soul's descent into matter, its garments, its sin and cutting off, its guardians and their influence upon it and other similar questions."

033 Pratt, Henry. "About the Kabbalah." *Theosophist*, 10(1889), 649-61.

Basic introduction to the theosophical attitude towards Kabbalah.

034 Westcott, W. Wynn. *Numbers: Their Occult Power and Mystic Virtue, Being a Résumé of the Views of the Kabbalists, Pythagoreans, Adepts of India, Chaldean Magi and Mediaeval Magicians.* Collectanea Hermetica, v. 9. London: Theosophical Publishing Society, 1890; 2nd ed. 1902; 3rd ed. 1911; 4th ed. 1974.

Exploration of the science of "associating the ancient doctrines of Numbers with the letters of the alphabet, the

Planets, Stars, Zodiacal signs and other Astronomical terms, a form of divination ... by which ... to foretell the future, life and death, good and evil Fortune, detection of theft, etc." Part III, Kabbalistic View of Numbers, pp. 9-16.

035 Westcott, W. Wynn. "The Kabalah." *Lucifer*, 8(1891), 465-69; 9(1891), 27-32.

"Whether there ever existed such a nexus between the Primary Kabbalah and the Wisdom Religion may never be known, but a study of Kabalistic books does show that a gradual degradation has been going on in the philosophy since medieval times. Some of the writings of the latest Rabbis sadly differ from the purer and more ancient treatises."

036 Blavatsky, Helene P. "The Kabalah and the Kabalists at the Close of the Nineteenth Century." *Lucifer*, 10(May 1892), 185-96. Rpt. Adyar Pamphlets, no. 105. Adyar, Madras: Theosophical Pub. House, 1919. Rpt. in 083, 088.

Defense of Kabbalah since "In the present age both Church and Science, the blindly-believing and the all-denying, are arrayed against the Secret Sciences, though both Church and Science believed in and practiced them--especially the Kabalah--at a not very distant period of history." Rpt. in 088 contains a brief bibliography of theosophical writers on Kabbalah.

037 Westcott, W. Wynn. "A Further Glance at the Kabalah." *Lucifer*, 12(1893), 147-53, 203-208.

Considers "only of certain particular Kabalistic dogmas, and of some historical side lights which can be thrown upon the subject," to conclude that "The old Kabalistic works are of a nature similar to the secrets of Freemasonry; there is much doctrine that is never written nor printed: these works often teem with imagery which seems folly, and with doctrines that seem absurd; yet they enshrine the highly Spiritual teachings which I have shortly outlined."

038 Hirsch, S.A. "Johann Reuchlin, The Father of the Study of Hebrew among Christians." *Jewish Quarterly Review*, o.s. 8(1896), 445-70.

Hirsch allows himself "the pleasure of considering [Reuchlin's] convictions, both religious and philosophical, and the circumstances that caused him to embrace them, in order to understand the stimulus that impelled him to take the road on which we find him." References to Reuchlin's interest in Kabbalah appear throughout the article.

039 Bjerregaard, C.H.A. "The Kabbala and 'Being.'" *Metaphysical Magazine*, 5(1897), 96-105.

"The Kabbala is a Theosophy that reveals Being in Nature rather than in man, though the great Being thus revealed is shown in the human form. In the Kabbala we see Being humanized in nature. We cannot begin to understand the Kabbala if we treat the books called by that name in the same manner as we ordinarily treat books. Its wisdom cannot be read by any intellectual process: it can only be attained by living it."

040 Stirling, William. *The Canon: An Exposition of the Pagan Mystery Perpetuated in the Cabala as the Rule of All the Arts.* London: Elkin Mathews, 1897. Rpt. London: Garnstone Press, 1974.

"The subject of *The Canon* is the ancient and esoteric Law that formerly regulated every aspect of human activity, providing a canonical standard for all the arts and sciences, as music, decoration, sculpture, astronomy and the art of government, and while, according to Plato, preserved over 10,000 years the stability of Egyptian culture." Chapter 3, The Cabala (pp. 39-67), is an "attempt to elucidate the principal doctrines of the Cabala. This singular work is known to have formed an important part of the Masonic traditions, and undoubtedly contains the nearest approach to a direct revelation of the ancient canonical secrets of the old world."

041 Morley, Henry. "Exposition of the Cabala." In Agrippa, Henry Cornelius. *Three Books of Occult Philosophy or Magic: Book One--Natural Magic.* Chicago: Hahn & Whitehead, 1898. Pp. 231-41. Rpt. London: Aquarian Press, New York: S. Weiser, 1971.

Reprint of 018.

042 L'Hoste Ranking, D.F. de. "The Kabbalah." *New Century Review*, 7(1900), 373-79.

In an attempt to explain "*Why* we have ten digits, and not more or fewer," l'Hoste Ranking explores the kabbalistic doctrine of the *Sefirot*.

043 Chamier, D. "The Kabalah and Its Doctrines." *Theosophist*, 24(1902), 90-97.

"This is but the merest outline of some of the teachings of the Kabalah."

044 Kohut, George Alexander, ed. *Ezra Stiles and the Jews: Selected Passages from His Literary Diary concerning Jews and Judaism.* New York: Philip Cowen, 1902. Rpt. from *The American Hebrew*, November 1901 to June 1902.

As a critical edition of Ezra Stiles' comments about the Jews, the book does not focus directly on Kabbalah, but does contain references to Kabbalism and the Zohar, indicating the attitude towards and information about Jewish mysticism of this eminent colonial Hebraist.

045 Gollancz, Hermann, ed. *Clavicula Salomonis*. London: D. Nutt, and Frankfort a. M.: J. Kaufmann, 1903.

Description and outline of "a Hebrew Manuscript of the 'Clavicula Salomonis', until this supposed to have been lost," dealing with mystical formulae attributed to King Solomon. See 011.

046 Moore, Edward. *Studies in Dante: Third Series--Miscellaneous Essays*. Oxford: Clarendon Press, 1903. Rpt. New York: Greenwood Press, 1968.

In the third section of the fourth essay, Symbolism and Prophecy in *Purg.* xxviii-xxxiii (pp. 253-83), Moore explains the DXV Prophecy through the use of Gematria, and then speculates about Dante's possible sources for the kabbalistic technique.

047 Bayley, Harold. *A New Light on the Renaissance Displayed in Contemporary Emblems*. London: J.M. Dent & Co., 1909. Rpt. New York: B. Blom, 1967.

Interprets various watermarks found in Renaissance paper in order to postulate the theory that they are symbolic protests against the Church by descendants of artisans who were persecuted for heresy. In Chapter 7, The Kabbalah (pp. 96-110), Bayley explores the influence of kabbalistic systems of numerology, primarily Notaricon, on emblems.

048 [Bennett, Allen] "A Note on Genesis." *Equinox: The Official Organ of the A.A. The Review of Scientific Illumination*, 1,2(1910?), 163-85.

Occult use of Kabbalah to interpret Genesis.

049 Bosman, Leonard A. *The Mysteries of the Qabalah*. London: Dharma Press, 1913. Rpt. 051.

Unavailable for annotating.

050 Lévi, Eliphas [Alphonse Louis Constant] *The History of Magic: Including a Clear and Precise Exposition of Its Procedure, Its Rites and Its Mysteries*. Trans. Arthur Edward Waite. London: W. Rider & Son, 1913; 2nd ed. 1922; 3rd ed. 1930; 4th ed. 1948; 5th ed. 1969.

According to A.E. Waite, "the most arresting, entertaining and brilliant of all studies on the subject with which I am acquainted.... The importance of Eliphas Lévi's account ...

arises from the fact (a) that he is the authoritative exponent-in-chief of all the alleged sciences; (b) that it is he who, in a sense, restored and placed them under a new and more attractive vesture ... (c) that he claimed ... the very fullest knowledge concerning them,... but (d) that ... it follows from his long examination that Magic,... has no ground in the truth of things, and is of the region of delusion only." Chapter 7, The Holy Kabalah (pp. 98-106), examines "the origin of true science by recurring to the Holy Kabalah, or tradition of the children of Seth, taken from Chaldea by Abraham, communicated by Joseph to the Egyptian priesthood, ingarnered by Moses, concealed by symbols in the Bible, revealed by the Saviour to St. John, and embodied in its fulness in hieratic images, analogous to those of all antiquity, in the Apocalypse of the Apostle."

051 Bosman, Leonard. *Esoteric Studies*. 5 vols. London, 1916-17.

1. *The Mysteries of the Qabalah* (rpt. of 049)

2. *The Cosmic Wisdom as Embodied in the Qabalah and in the Symbolical Hebrew Alphabet*, by El. Gewurz and Bosman

3. *The Music of the Spheres or Cosmic Harmony*

4. *The Music of the Spheres, Part II, also a Dissertation on the Derivation of the Hebrew Alphabet*

5. *The Sacred Names of God*

Unavailable for annotating.

052 Colville, W.J. *Kabbalah, the Harmony of Opposites: A Treatise Elucidating Bible Allegories and the Significance of Numbers*. New York: Macoy Publishing & Masonic Supply Co., 1916.

Approaching Kabbalism as "a form of theosophical teaching employing a Hebrew instead of a Greek or Sanscrit terminology," W.J. Colville's *Kabbalah* is a popularization of Kabbalah as a Hermetic pursuit. Considers: I. A General Outline of Kabbalah; II. Inner Significance of the 22 Letters Comprising the Hebrew Alphabet; III. Book of Concealed Mystery; IV. Book of Concealed Mystery. Humanity, Spiritual and Physical; V. The Kabbalistic Use and Significance of Numbers; VI. Kabbalistic Views of the Human Soul, Its Nature and Destiny; VII. Kabbalistic Doctrine Concerning Cause and Effect (Karma); VIII. The Secret Tradition in Israel. The Zohar--The Serpent and Fall of the Angels; IX. Biblical Traditions Kabbalistically Considered; X. Abraham, Melchisedec, Moses and the Law; XI. Doctrine of the 3 Temples of the Messiah; and XII. Kabbalistic Teachings Concerning the Soul, Its Nature and Destiny.

053 Gewurz, Elias. *The Hidden Treasuries of the Ancient Qabalah.* Vol. I: *The Transmutation of Passion into Power.* Chicago: Yogi Publication Society, 1918.

Interpretation of various aspects of Kabbalah: I. The Vessel in which Transmutation takes Place; II. The Feminine Elements in Man and their Redeeming Power; III. Spiritual Companionship between Man and Woman; IV. The Knowledge of God obtainable through Love Pure and Undefiled; V. The Mystery of Time and Space; VI. The Place that Passeth Understanding; VII. Justice and Mercy; VIII. On the Threshold of the Sanctuary; IX. The Eternal Light According to the Qabalah; and X. Regeneration according to the Qabalah. The book ends with a Qabalistic Prayer.

054 Moore, George Foot. "Ezra Stiles' Studies in the Cabala." *Proceedings of the Massachusetts Historical Society,* 51(1918), 290-306.

In the "quest of the Trinity and the suffering Messiah," Stiles turned from "the Talmud and the mediaeval Jewish commentators, the *Moreh Nebokim* (Guide of the Perplexed) of the rationalistic philosopher Maimonides," to "the theosophical literature to which collectively the name Cabala, i.e. *Secret Tradition,* is given." Stiles owned a copy of the Zohar, and learned from "three or four Cabalists [who] were for a longer or shorter time in Newport."

055 Covey-Crump, W.W. "How Has Kabalism Affected Freemasonry?" *The Craft and the Kabalah.* Rpt. from *The Transactions of the Author's Lodge.* Vol. III. Luton, 1919. Rpt. in 056. Pp. 14-16.

Parallels between the history of English masonry and Kabbalah.

056 Evans, Henry Ridgely. *The Cabala and Freemasonry.* Washington, D.C,: The Author, 1919. Rpt. from *New Age Magazine.* Includes rpt. of C34 and O55.

Discussion of *Sefer Yetzirah,* the *Zohar* and the Apocalypse to demonstrate parallels between Kabbalism and Freemasonry.

057 Jacobs, Joseph. *Jewish Contributions to Civilization: An Estimate.* Philadelphia: Jewish Publication Society of America, 1919.

The first part of what was intended to be a three-book work; considers "the Jewish contributions to civilization during the past two thousand years, showing that [the Jews] have made themselves thereby a constituent element of that civilization to which they are equally heirs with other nations, creeds, and people." Although Jacobs does not devote a section exclusively to Kabbalah, he does refer to the influence of Jewish mysticism, especially in Chapter 5, Influence of Jewish Thought in the Middle Ages (especially pp. 175-85).

058 Boyile, Veolia J. *The Fundamental Principles of the Yi-king, Tao, and the Cabbalas of Egypt and the Hebrews.* New York: Azoth Publishing Company, 1920. London: W. & G. Foyle, 1934.

Unavailable for annotating.

059 Fehr, Bernhard. "William Blake und die Kabbala." *Englische Studien*, 54(1920), 139-48.

Using the *Kabbala Denudata* as his source, Fehr traces the influence of Kabbalah on the eighteenth-century English poet. (In German)

060 Spence, Lewis. *An Encyclopaedia of Occultism: A Compendium of Information on the Occult Sciences, Occult Personalities, Psychic Science, Magic, Demonology, Spiritism, Mysticism and Metaphysics.* London: G. Routledge & Sons, Ltd., New York: Dodd, Mead & Co., 1920. Rpt. Secaucus, New Jersey: The Citadel Press, 1960; 1974.

Entry on the Kabala (pp. 240-42), contains a brief survey of the *Sefirot, Ein Soph,* the Four Worlds and Souls; traces the "almost wholly fabulous" origins of the Kabbalah and concludes that "this tradition ... wholly reposes on the single dogma of magic."

061 Miller, Laurel. *Kabbalistic Numerology, or the True Science of Numbers, Letters, Words and Their Astrological Allocations according to the Kabbala; Including the Art of the Name Horoscope and Divination by Numbers.* New York: Metaphysical Publishing Co., 1921.

Interpretation of the Hebrew alphabet according to Tarot.

062 Achad, Frater [Charles Robert Stansfeld Jones] *Q.B.L. or the Bride's Reception: being a Short Cabalistic Treatise on the Nature and Use of the Tree of Life.* Chicago: Private Printing for the Author, 1922. Rpt. New York: Samuel Weiser Inc., 1969.

"The intention of this essay is to supply a basis whereby all serious Students of the Occult and Mystic Lore may learn to attain to Equilibrium on all Planes, thus gradually taking up their Great Inheritance, and while climbing higher and higher towards the Summit of the Work, planting their feet yet more firmly upon a sure foundation, that of Direct Experience. To such as succeed in their endeavours, History will matter little, except in-so-far as it represents their own early struggles or it may be gives hints of the means to be employed, but in the End, they will find themselves at one with the Beginning, citizens of that Kingdom wherein all is HERE and NOW." Discusses: The Formation of the Tree of Life being a Qabalistic Conception of the Creative Process; Concerning the Natural Basis of Correspondences in the Hebrew Alphabet; Of the Twenty-two Paths with their Yetziratic and Colour Correspondences; Concerning the Tarot Trumps and Their Attributions to the Hebrew Alphabet; Some Account of the Ineffable Name and of the Four Worlds with their Correspondences to the Minor Arcana of the Tarot; Concerning the Macrocosm and the Microcosm and how by Means of the Tree of Life We May Learn to Unite Them; Concerning the Literal Qabalah and the Methods of Gematria, Notaricon and Temurah; Concerning Numbers, Symbols and Matters Cognate; Of that which Was and Is and Shall Be; Of the Kingdom of the Bride.

063 Gewurz, Elias. *The Mysteries of the Qabalah.* Vol. II. Chicago: Yogi Publication Society, 1922.

Compilation of the teachings of Elias Gewurz on: The Hebrew Alphabet and its Hieroglyphical Significance; Explanatory Note on the Letters; The Qabalistic Definition of the Snake Nachash; The Lessons of Nachash (The Snake); The Brotherhood of the White Lodge; Initiation According to the Qabalah, from a Scientific and Philosophical View; The Qabalah; The Soul of the Qabalah; Examples of Permutation and Numerical Valuation; and The Literature of the Qabalah Throughout the Ages.

064 Moore, George F. "A Cabalistic MS. from the Library of Judah Monis." *Publications of the American Jewish Historical Society,* 28(1922), 242-45.

After surveying Judah Monis' knowledge of Kabbalah, Moore then describes (in Hebrew) the contents of a kabbalistic manuscript which belonged to Monis and is, in part, in his hand.

065 Saurat, Denis. "Milton and the Zohar." *Quest,* 13(1922), 145-65; also in *Studies in Philology,* 19(1922), 136-51.

Saurat tries "to prove that Milton knew the Zohar and other Kabbalistic documents, that he used them freely as a source of inspiration; that practically all his philosophical ideas are Kabbalistic ideas, in such a way that the only tenable hypothesis is that he derived the most important part of his philosophy from the Kabbalah."

066 Abelson, J. "Swedenborg and the Zohar." *Jewish Chronicle Supplement,* no. xli, May 30, 1924, pp. vii-viii.

Because it is difficult to separate different strands of mysticism, "it is not to be wondered at that a writer like

Swedenborg should betray many an affinity of thought with a book like the Zohar. He may, of course, have been, as were many eminent Christian divines of his day, a student of the Zohar or other Kabbalistic writing. But there is a greater probability that he came to these conclusions as a result of his own independent thought."

067 Abrahams, Israel. "Pico Della Mirandola." In A13. Pp. 317-31.

As Abrahams sums up "in plain terms: Pico's permanent service to learning and thought arose from his obsession with the Cabala. The Cabala was not worth all his devotion to it, but out of that devotion, through Reuchlin whom he also impregnated with his Cabalistic obsession, Pico restored Hebrew to the academic world as the complement to Greek, thereby perfecting the Renaissance on its literary side. Further, again through the Cabala, Pico helped to give back Plato to modern theology and philosophy; and with the return of Plato, Idealism came to its own as a criticism and corrective--through [sic] not as a supplanter--of Rationalism. Finally, out of his mistaken idea that he could trace Cabala in Paganism, Hebraism, Hellenism, and Paulinism, he helped on the humanistic movement which believes in the continuity of the human spirit, the humanistic movement, which out of the belief in the values of all expressions of the human spirit, has created in our time comparative science as applied to religion and anthropology."

068 Blavatsky, H.P. "The Ten Sephiroth." *Theosophist*, 47(1925), 383-88. Rpt. in O88.

An explication of the *Sefirot*; found among the papers of H.P. Blavatsky after she left India in 1885.

069 Hall, Manly P. *The Sacred Magic of the Qabbalah: The Science of the Divine Names and Numbers*. 2nd ed. n.p.: G. Raymond Brown Printing Co., 1925; 3rd ed. rev. Los Angeles: Hall Publishing Company, 1929; 6th ed. Los Angeles: Philosophical Research Society, 1945.

"From the time of Moses, the Jews preserved by oral tradition certain spiritual laws or mystic principles, which, when applied to the exoteric documents of Scripture, reveal to those able to use them the unseen spiritual wonders of the Invisible. In the following papers will be found a series of concise statements intended to give the student of the invisible path a few principles or foundation stones upon where to build the superstructure of personal experience and first-hand knowledge."

070 Newman, Louis I. *Jewish Influence on Christian Reform Movements*. Columbia University Oriental Studies, Vol. 23. New York: Columbia University Press, 1925.

"This work is a study of a few typical 'Reform Movements' or heresies in the history of Catholicism during the Middle Ages and of Protestantism during the Reformation era." In addition to references to Kabbalah throughout the text, Newman specifically discusses The Kabbalah in Medieval Christendom (pp. 176-85), focusing on Agobard, Arnold of Vilanova, Abraham Abulafia and Raymond Lully; Zwingli and the Kabbalah (pp. 488-90); and Luther's Interest in Hebrew, the Kabbalah and the Rabbis (pp. 622-25).

071 Pullen-Burry, Henry Burry. *Qabalism*. Chicago: The Yogi Publication Society, 1925.

Attempt to prove that "To speak therefore of the Qabalah of the Jews in the sense that they were the recipients of the Secret Archaic Wisdom is entirely misleading. What they did receive was the Bible, which on its surface was a falsehood almost from beginning to end, but which hidden between its very words and letters did contain the Wisdom,... therefore we find that the Qabalah itself is the sacred lore of the ages, received by man in all later ages by sanction of the Lodge." In pursuit of his thesis, Pullen-Burry discusses Elohim, The Ten Sephiroth, The Four Worlds, Adam Qadmon, Philo Judaeus and The Absolute.

072 Saurat, Denis. *Milton: Man and Thinker*. New York: L. MacVeagh, The Dial Press, 1925. Rpt. London: J.M. Dent and Sons, Ltd., 1944; Hamden, Connecticut: Archon Books, 1964; New York: Haskell House Publishers, 1970; New York: AMS Press, 1975.

"The aim of this study is to determine the human and lasting element in Milton's thought." The first part of Part IV, Section II, Contemporary Sources and Influences, is devoted to the *Zohar* and the Kabbalah (pp. 281-300), because "roughly speaking, the whole of Milton's philosophy is found in the Kabbalah, except for his materialism."

073 Van der Naillen, Albert. *The Great Message*. San Francisco: California Press, 1925.

This book is written "to give the world the teachings, moral, ethical and spiritual philosophies of the ancient Aztec civilization and absolute brotherhood," known as "Cabala," as derived from medieval Jewish and Christian records, brought to Mexico by the Spaniards.

074 Waite, Arthur Edward. *The Secret Tradition in Alchemy: Its Development and Records*. London: Kegan Paul, Trench, Trubner & Co. Ltd., 1926. Rpt. London: Vincent Stuart & John M. Watkins Ltd., New York: Samuel Weiser Inc., 1969.

"I have set myself therefore to collect and estimate such evidence--if any--as it may be possible to ascertain of that which lies behind the surface sense of alchemical literature through the ages of Christendom." In the appendix on Kabalistic Alchemy (pp. 377-94), Waite analyzes *Aesh Mezareph*, the only extant Jewish alchemical text, to conclude that it "is a Kabalistic Light Alchemy ... only on the basis of analogy between things above and below, on the part of one whose chief concern was apparently for those which are above. After what manner this speculative and theoretical part can be said to exhibit the possibility of transmuting metals is for those to find who can."

075 Box, G.H. "Hebrew Studies in the Reformation Period and After: Their Place and Influence." In A15. Pp. 315-75.

While Box's article is not devoted strictly to Kabbalah, it does contain discussions of kabbalistic influences on Pico della Mirandola and Johann Reuchlin, The Cabala, and The Cabala and its place in Christian thought of the XVIth and XVIIth centuries (pp. 319-32).

076 Nicolson, Marjorie H. "Milton and the *Conjectura Cabbalistica*." *Philological Quarterly*, 6(1927), 1-18.

"In this paper, the attempt is threefold: to suggest a reason for the profound interest in cabbalism during the seventeenth century; to discuss in detail an English version of the Cabbala, popular during the years in which Milton was most concerned with the subjects treated in *Paradise Lost*; and to present a comparison between the *Conjectura Cabbalistica* and *Paradise Lost*, less with a desire to establish actual borrowing on the part of Milton than to indicate typically cabbalistic strains in *Paradise Lost*."

077 Hall, Manly P. *An Encyclopedic Outline of Masonic, Hermetic, Qabbalistic and Rosicrucian Symbolical Philosophy: Being an Interpretation of the Secret Teachings Concealed within the Rituals, Allegories and Mysteries of All Ages.* San Francisco: Printed for the Author, 1928. Rpt. Los Angeles: The Philosophical Research Society, Inc., 1962, 1975, 1977.

"It is my complete conviction that certain outstanding philosophers, seers, and prophets of antiquity perceived with inner clarity the very truths and facts so desperately necessary for our present situation. For that reason, I made the attempt to gather some of the fragments of the great wisdom of the past into an Encyclopedic Outline, that it might be readily available for modern use." Several sections are devoted to Kabbalah: The Qabbalah, The Secret Doctrine of Israel (pp. 113-16); Fundamentals of Qabbalistic Cosmogony (pp. 117-20); The Tree of the Sephiroth (pp. 121-24); and Qabbalistic Keys to the Creation of Man (pp. 125-28).

078 Saurat, Denis. *Blake & Modern Thought.* New York: L. Mac-
Veagh, The Dial Press, 1929. Rpt. London and New York:
Russell & Russell, 1964.

According to Saurat, "Blake is a curious witness of his own
time; and as his time was merely the dawn of ours, he is a
curious and important *witness of our own mentality."* The
section, The Cabala (pp. 98-106), is based on Saurat's belief
that "The Jewish Cabalists had worked out the identification
of God and Man to its furthest possible limits; and a long
string of Christian Cabalists from Pico della Mirandola to
Fludd and Swedenborg, had taught the European mind that in
the Cabala there was a living spring of fertilising ideas.
Blake is full of the Cabala and of its Christian exponents."

079 Budge, E.A. Wallis. *Amulets and Superstitions: The Original
Texts with Translations and Descriptions of a Long Series
of Egyptian, Sumerian, Assyrian, Hebrew, Christian, Gnostic
and Muslim Amulets and Talismans and Magical Figures, with
Chapters on the Evil Eye, the Origin of the Amulets, the
Pentagon, the Swastika, the Cross (Pagan and Christian),
the Properties of Stones, Rings, Divination, Numbers, the
Kabbalah, Ancient Astrology, Etc.* London and New York:
Oxford University Press, H. Milford, 1930. Rpt. under title
Amulets and Talismans. New Hyde Park, New York: University
Books, 1961.

"In this volume I have described the principal amulets
which were used by the Semitic peoples of Western Asia,
Egypt, Nubia and Ethiopia, beginning with those of the third
millenium B.C. from Sumer and Elam." Chapter 21, Kabbalah
(pp. 366-79), is "intended to give the general reader an idea
of the way in which the older Rabbis and their successors
employed letters and numbers as a means of interpretation."
And Chapter 23, The Kabbalistic Names and Signs, and Magical
Figures, and Squares of the Seven Astrological Stars or
Planets, describes "briefly the means which the Kabbalists
used to obtain for their purposes the most favourable of"
the influences of the planets.

080 Nicolson, Marjorie Hope. *Conway Letters: The Correspondence
of Anne, Viscountess Conway, Henry More, and Their Friends,
1642-1684. Collected from Manuscript Sources & Edited with
a Biographical Account.* New Haven: Yale University Press,
London: Oxford University Press, 1930.

A major intellect of seventeenth-century England, outstanding among men as well as women, Anne Conway was at the center
of a group including William Harvey, Robert Boyle, Isaac
Newton, René Descartes, Thomas Hobbes, Johann Gottfried van
Leibnitz, Ralph Cudworth, Henry More, William Penn, George
Fox, George Keith, and Franciscus Mercurius van Helmont. In
the *Conway Letters,* Nicolson provides an edition of the

correspondence of this unusual woman, devoting Chapter VI to van Helmont (pp. 309-77), who through Conway disseminated kabbalism throughout the Western European intellectual community.

081 Nicolson, Marjorie. "George Keith and the Cambridge Platonists." *Philosophical Review*, 39(1930), 36-55.

Primarily a "study of the relationship between the seventeenth-century Quakers and that other remarkable group, the Cambridge Platonists"; contains a brief section on the influence of van Helmont on George Keith (pp. 49-53).

082 Saurat, Denis. *Literature and Occult Tradition: Studies in Philosophical Poetry*. Trans. Dorothy Bolton. New York: L. MacVeagh, The Dial Press, 1930. Rpt. Port Washington, New York: Kennikat Press, New York: Haskell House, 1966.

"I propose, in this work, to study modern philosophical poetry.... [It] is the expression, varying according to the character, intelligence and surroundings of each poet, of a body of common ideas, related to neo-platonism and various occult doctrines, but original in its essence which represents the mind of modern man: the assertion of the liberty of man and of the sanctity of material nature of which he is a part." The second section of Chapter III, Occultism and Literature, devoted to The Cabala (pp. 74-149), discusses God the Unknown, The Sexual Law, The Left Side, and Reincarnation: The Quest of the Twin Soul. And the second section of Chapter V, The Philosophical Ideas of Edmund Spenser, focuses on Spenser and the Cabala (pp. 222-37), from the perspective that Spenser's *Sapience* corresponds to the *Shekhinah*, and "that in his 'Hymne of Heavenly Beautie' Spenser extolls the *Matrona* of the cabalists."

083 Blavatsky, Helena. "Kabalah and the Kabalists." *Theosophical Path*, December 1931, pp. 497-511.

Reprint of O36.

084 Givry, Grillot de. *Witchcraft, Magic & Alchemy*. Trans. J. Courtenay Locke. New York: Houghton Mifflin Company, 1931. Rpt. New York: Dover Publications, Inc., 1971.

"A collection of the iconography of occultism ... I have accordingly gathered together and explained in this book more than three hundred and fifty pictures, picked from the most curious, characteristic and rare of those illustrating works in sorcery, magic, astrology, cheiromancy, cartomancy, and alchemy." The section on Jewish and Christian Cabbalists, (pp. 205-19), focuses on the introduction "into the language of theology a complex vocabulary and fresh elements to which Christians attached a perhaps unmerited importance ... such sparkling formulas as the ten *sephiroth*, or numerations, the thirty-two Ways of Wisdom, and the fifty Doors of Knowledge; it furnished the names of many angels which make no appearance in the Bible, and, above all, it was provided with an armoury of seventy-two names of the Deity capable of seducing the imagination of seekers who had exhausted Christian theology without satisfying a curiosity ardent and avid for forbidden mysteries."

085 *The Book of Fate and Fortune: An Encyclopaedia of the Occult Sciences*. New York: R.M. McBride & Company, 1932.

"It is a popular compendium having for its main object the collection in one volume, easy to read and convenient to consult, of the facts and theories in the numerous special treatises which related to each of these sciences." Chapter 4, High Magic, (pp. 398-440), discusses Kabbalah as "a mystical doctrine of interpretation, an esoteric Tradition, the hidden science of ancient and modern Magi, especially the explanation of the Macrocosm (the Universe) and the Microcosm (Man), it is the Key of the Great Enigma; but in order to open the Lock with this Key, it is necessary to be an initiate." [Author wishes to remain anonymous]

086 Regardie, Israel. *A Garden of Pomegranates: An Outline of the Qabalah*. London: Rider & Co., 1932. 2nd ed. rev. St. Paul, Minn.: Llewellyn Publications, 1970.

Intended to be "a sort of Berlitz handbook, a concise but comprehensive introduction, studded with diagrams and tables of easily understood definitions and correspondences to simplify the student's grasp of so complicated and abstruse a subject." Contents: I. Historical Survey; II. The Pit; III. The Sephiros; IV. The Paths; V. Adam Kadmon; VI. The Literal Qabalah; VII. The Literal Qabalah (continued); and VIII. The Ladder.

087 Regardie, Israel. *The Tree of Life: A Study in Magic*. London: Rider, 1932. 2nd ed. New York: S. Weiser, 1969; 3rd ed. 1980.

"The writer desires to render intelligible and comprehensible to the ordinary intelligent layman, to the student of the Mysteries and those versed in the lore of other mystical systems and philosophies, the root principles from which the tremendous high-towering structure of Magic is built." The last section of Chapter 2 is devoted to The Tree of Life of the Qabalists; and throughout the text, Regardie includes numerous references to Qabalah.

088 Blavatsky, Helena P. *The Complete Works*. Ed. A. Trevor Barker. 4 vols. London: Rider, 1933-36. Rev. version, together with the remainder of the author's published works

was published under the title *Collected Writings*. Ed. Boris De Zirkoff. 12 vols. Madras: Theosophical Pub. House, Wheaton, Ill.: Theosophical Press, 1950-80. Supplement, 1975.

See 025, 027, 036, 068, 083.

089 Blau, Joseph L. "Browne's Interest in Cabalism." *PMLA*, 49(1934), 963-64.

Asserts that "The omniverous [Sir Thomas] Browne could scarcely have been expected to leave unread the many expressions of interest in Cabalistic speculation which Pico della Mirandola and John Reuchlin had aroused in the literati of the sixteenth and early seventeenth centuries."

090 Kelley, Maurice. "'Paradise Lost,' vii, 8-12, and the 'Zohar.'" *Modern Language Review*, 29(1934), 322-24.

Argument against Denis Saurat's Assertion that Milton was influenced by the Zohar (072): "The fact that Saurat's suggestion has not the support of the *De doctrina*, that the passage in *Tetrachordon* is not in consonance with the *Zohar*, and that other influences of the *Zohar* on the invocation of Book VII have not been proved, forces the rejection of Saurat's interpretation."

091 Fortune, Dion [Violet Mary Firth] *The Mystical Qabalah*. London: Williams and Norgate, Ltd., 1935, 1941, 1951, 1958. Rpt. London: E. Benn, 1972.

"... used as the basis of the tutorial system of the Fraternity" of the Inner Light; contains an occult interpretation of the ten *Sefirot*.

092 Franklyn, Julian, ed. *A Survey of the Occult*. London: Arthur Barker Limited, 1935.

"There are several encyclopaedias of the occult, but there has existed none that is abreast of modern science and modern psychology: this is the gap which the publishers have aimed to fill." The first fourteen paragraphs of Literature of Occultism (pp. 159-63), briefly survey the history of Kabbalah, primarily Christian.

093 Hambloch, Ernest. "The Power behind European Freemasonry." *English Review*, 63(1936), 568-79.

Study of the components of Freemasonry with a section on "The Cabbalah [which] is nothing but Jewish freemasonry."

094 Fuller, J.F.C. *The Secret Wisdom of the Qabalah: A Study in Jewish Mystical Thought*. London: Rider & Co., 1937.

"In this book is revealed the secret doctrine of the Qabalah--the Key to Hebrew mysticism and magic. In it the author discusses not only the origins of this occult science, but explains its symbolism as a world philosophy which may be made use of either for good or evil. Further, he traces its relationships with Illuminism and the most modern theories of Science, showing how ridiculous movements originate and why it is that they decay. This book is a veritable key to both past and present occultism, and, consequently, is of profound significance in understanding the nature of those hidden forces which to-day are still attempting to control the world." (Editor's note) After the Introduction, Fuller discusses: I. The Wisdom of the Qabalah; II. The Cosmogony of the Qabalah; III. The Problem of Good and Evil; IV. The Fall of Tetragrammaton; V. The Redemption of Tetragrammaton; VI. The Source of Mystic Power; and VII. The Anatomy of Illuminism.

095 Weston, Warren. *"Father of Lies."* London: M.C.P. Publications, 1938.

Attempt "to discover the principles of world theocracy for which powerful occult groups are labouring," by first examining "the general character of magic and magical symbolism. If these are found in the pagan religions which will be considered next, the same method will be followed in dealing with various esoteric sects and secret societies." Chapter 4, The Kabbalah, Key to Judaism (p. 49-72), explores the esoteric doctrine of this "pagan" faith from the perspective of the occult, in order to explain "some of the magical practices recorded in ancient Jewish history."

096 *The Encyclopedia of Occult Sciences.* Intro. M.C. Poinsot. New York: Robert M. McBride and Company, 1939. Rpt. Detroit: Gale Research Company, 1972.

"The author of this Encyclopaedia has begged me to tell the reader at the very start of the Introduction what he has been good enough to ask of me, that it does not constitute a complete treatise of the sciences called Occult (this would require ten volumes at the least), nor will it be found to be new to the 'initiated.' It is a popular compendium having for its main object the collection in one volume, easy to read and convenient to consult, of the facts and theories in the numerous special treatises which relate to each of these sciences." Discusses Kabbalah in relation to Alchemy (Chapter 3) and High Magic (Chapter 4).

097 Blau, Joseph L. "The Diffusion of the Christian Interpretation of the Cabala in English Literature." *Review of Religion*, 6(1941-42), 146-68.

Blau traces the appearance of Kabbalism throughout the history of English literature, from Dean Colet and John

Fisher, through Everard Digby, Henry Howard, Early of Northampton, Henry Smith, Edmund Spenser, Sir Philip Sidney, Arthur Golding, the Cambridge Platonists, Francis Bacon, Robert Burton, John Owen, John Brinsley, Archbishop John Tillotson, Thomas Godwyn, John Milton, William Blake, Philip Bailey, the Reverend Richard Harris Barham (pen-name Thomas Ingoldsby, Esq.), George Eliot, W.B. Yeats, Madame Blavatsky, Anna Kingsford, Edward Maitland, Wynn Westcott, and others, to conclude that "Fludd, Thomas Vaughan, and Henry More were the only Christian Cabalists who wrote in English," though because "Christian Cabalism pervaded the atmosphere of Europe, many English writers were touched by its ideas.... Cabalism was an intellectual fad, a day's fashion."

098 Blau, Joseph Leon. *The Christian Interpretation of the Cabala in the Renaissance.* New York: Columbia University Press, 1944. Rpt. Port Washington, New York: Kennikat Press, Inc., 1965.

Pursues the thesis that "the use of Cabala by Christian thinkers was a fad of no lasting significance; that, no matter what type of interpretation was momentarily aided by cabalistic speculation, this type of speculation rapidly proved a blind alley." After a brief introduction to kabbalistic thought, Blau traces Christian interest in Kabbalah from the Latin translations of texts at the request of Pope Sixtus IV and Edigio di Viterbo, through the work of Pico della Mirandola, John Reuchlin, Paul Ricci, Cornelius Agrippa, Jean Thenaud, of Angouleme, and various other Christian kabbalists of the sixteenth century. Blau concludes with four appendices: A. Cordovera; B. Was Raymond Lull a Cabalist?; C. Archangelus of Borgo Nuovo; and D. Selections from Thenaud, La Saincte et Trescrestienne Cabale (in French).

099 Adolf, Helen. "The *Esplumoir Merlin:* A Study in Its Cabalistic Sources." *Speculum,* 21(1946), 173-93.

Comparison of the characters of Merlin in "Esplumoir Merlin" of Grail literature, based on passages from the *Zohar* and *Seder Gan Eden:* "If we have interpreted and dated the Bird's Nest correctly, then the *Esplumoir Merlin,* in itself a detail of little importance, would stand out as a guiding fossil, commemorizing the imprint of one civilization upon the other."

0100 Steele-Smith, William. *Wonders of the Hebrew Alphabet, for the Plain English Reader.* Sydney: Central Press Pty. Ltd., 1947.

Uses kabbalistic explanations for the letters of the Hebrew alphabet and practices of Gematria in order to explain the development of the English alphabet and discover prophecies concerning Christ in patriarchal history.

0101 Williams, Jerry Turner. "Words into Images in Chaucer's *Hous of Fame.*" *Modern Language Notes*, 62(1947), 488-90.

Suggests the Zohar (Exodus 217a-217b) as a parallel for Chaucer's description of the Eagle in the second book of the *Hous of Fame:* "Although it is not impossible that Chaucer may have heard about the work, it is improbable, in the light of existing evidence, that he could have known it well. I present the passage in the *Zohar* not as a source, but merely as an interesting parallel."

0102 Seligmann, Kurt. *The History of Magic.* New York: Pantheon Books Inc., 1948. Rpt. under title *Magic, Supernaturalism, and Religion.* New York: The Universal Library, Grosset & Dunlap, 1968.

"The aim of this book is to present to the general reader a condensed account of magical ideas and operations in the civilized Western world." The section on Cabala (pp. 338-58) discusses Christian Cabalists and the Jews, Secrets of the Bible, Magic of Letters and The Book *Yetzirah*.

0103 Butler, E.M. *Ritual Magic.* Cambridge: University Press, 1949.

"The chief focus of interest lies in the Faustian rituals and the conclusions they have suggested, which I believe to be important, although they do not exhaust the many and various aspects of the underlying problem: the relationship between ritual and legend, the burning 'hen or egg' question of priority." The third chapter of Part I, Pre-Christian Rites and Ceremonies, covers Jewish Elements in Magic, specifically the *Testament of Solomon* (pp. 29-36), and the Kabbalah (pp. 36-44).

0104 Ziegler, Julian. "Two Notes on J.T. Williams' 'Words into Images in Chaucer's *Hous of Fame.'*" *Modern Language Notes*, 64(1949), 73-76.

Response to 0101: "Thus, while doubting any relationship between *The Zohar* lines and those in the *Hous of Fame*, and putting forward a conjectured source for the latter work in Boethius, through Chaucer's own translation, I feel that the passages cited by Mr. Williams may well have been used by Milton."

0105 Baeck, Leo. "Judaism on Old and New Paths." *International Review of Missions*, 39(1950), 190-200.

Brief survey of Jewish mysticism, with reference to Christian counterparts of Jewish movements, to suggest that "When

Jews and Christians, Christians and Jews seek to understand each other, then will be fulfilled something of the meaning of the words of the Psalm (LXXXV, vv. 10 and 11): 'Mercy and truth are met together;... ' Here there are not old and new paths, here there is only the way, the one way, for ever."

0106 Parkinson, Thomas. "The Sun and Moon in Yeats's Early Poetry." *Modern Philology*, 50(1952), 50-58.

"It is the intent of this paper to analyze in detail the meaning of [the sun and the moon as symbols] both by examining the texts of Yeats's poems and by investigating his prose writing and certain works with which he was familiar," including Mathers's *The Kabbalah Unveiled* (I1).

0107 Waton, Harry. *The Key to the Bible*. New York: Spinoza Institute of America, 1952.

Believing that "Mathematics is the key to all knowledge and understanding," that "Philosophy interprets what mathematics reveals," and that "the philosophy of the Bible is the Kabbalah," Waton first discusses "the three orders of mathematics"; then he considers "the Kaballah, so as to acquire an idea of the philosophy involved in the Bible itself. And then only shall we take up the study of the Bible itself." The sixth chapter, An Introduction to the Kabbalah (pp. 86-96), briefly discusses the *Ain Sof*, the four Worlds and the *Sefirot*.

0108 Bouwsma, William J. "Postel and the Significance of Renaissance Cabalism." *Journal of the History of Ideas*, 15(1954), 218-32.

Survey of "the uses to which Postel put Cabala, with the broad purpose of attempting to determine why one leading Christian intellectual of the Renaissance was attracted to such unlikely material." Two general explanations are "that Cabala, as of Jewish origin, provided a sanction for hellenistic conceptions previously regarded with distrust," and "that, as the reaction of religions against philosophizing Judaism, Cabala reinforced an important aspect of Renaissance thought. Through Postel we can make our explanations more specific."

0109 Werblowsky, R.J. Zwi. "Milton and the *Conjectura Cabbalistica*." *Journal of the Warburg and Courtauld Institutes*, 18(1955), 90-113.

Takes issue with Denis Saurat [065, 072] to explode "the fallacy of the Zoharic Milton.... Milton is influenced not by the Lurianic *tsimtsum*, still less by the *Zohar* but by Christian post-Renaissance Kabbalah in its pre-Lurianic phase, and, more particularly, by those aspects of it which interested seventeenth-century English Platonism."

0110 Fletcher, Harris Francis. *The Intellectual Development of John Milton.* 2 vols. Urbana: University of Illinois Press, 1956.

In the section, Milton's Beginnings and Early Training in Semitics (I.276-83), Fletcher confronts the question of Milton's knowledge of Kabbalah. After discounting the argument of Saurat (O72) on the basis that it lacks any scholarly foundation, Fletcher himself lays the groundwork for a study of kabbalistic influences on Milton, asserting that Alexander Gill, the Elder, Milton's teacher, knew Latin translations of kabbalistic texts, and that much of this Latinized and Christianized Kabbalah was readily available to seventeenth-century Englishmen.

0111 James, Laura De Witt. *William Blake: The Finger on the Furnace.* New York: Vantage Press, 1956.

"My main thesis in this study is an interpretation of one of Blake's most deftly hidden doctrines: the doctrine of the False Tongue beneath Beulah." In order to prepare the reader for her exposition on the False Tongue, James offers several preliminary essays dealing with Blake and Kabbalah, including: The Tree of Life, Hierarchy, The Dead in Ulro, and Chaos.

0112 Spitz, Lewis W. "Reuchlin's Philosophy: Pythagoras and Cabala for Christ." *Archiv für Reformationsgeschichte,* 47(1956), 1-20.

Analysis of Reuchlin's use of Kabbalah to conclude that "It is quite clear that, although Reuchlin's essential Christianity was rooted in northern piety, the positive philosophical influences in his constructive theology were essentially Italian in origin. What was novel came from the South, from Italy and indirectly from Spain. But the nature of that influence has been misunderstood. Now that we appreciate more fully the Christian concerns of the Italian humanists,... we are in a better position to assess the goals and methods of the northern humanists, such as Reuchlin. In the *Guerre de Savants* that has raged over this question, some right, as usual, must be conceded to both sides. Reuchlin is one more demonstration ... that the philosophy of the Quattrocento was essentially theology. Reuchlin's design was to use Pythagoras and Cabala for Christ."

0113 Bardon, Franz. *The Key to the True Quabbalah: The Quabbalist as a Sovereign in the Micro- and the Macrocosm.* Trans. Peter A. Dima. Freiburg: Verlag Hermann Bauer, 1957; Wuppertal: Dieter Rüggeberg, 1975.

Two-part study: "In its first part, the theory, I prepare the reader for the difficult field of the Quabbalah, whereas the second part contains the actual practice."

0114 Bouwsma, William J. *Concordia Mundi: The Career and Thought of Guillaume Postel (1510-1581).* Harvard Historical Monograph, 33. Cambridge: Harvard University Press, 1957.

"Postel is at once one of the most interesting and one of the most puzzling figures of the sixteenth century," among other things, "the most learned Christian cabalist of his day." In *Concordia Mundi*, William Bouwsma "tried to show that a generally consistent and well-considered world-view lay at the heart of Postel's particular interests and activities, giving them meaning and focus; and beyond this that once the inner coherence of his life and thought have been grasped, Postel proves richly suggestive for our understanding both of the sixteenth century and of its place in the broader development of western thought."

0115 Hall, Manly Palmer. *Old Testament Wisdom: Keys to Bible Interpretation.* Los Angeles: Philosophical Research Society, Inc., 1957.

First volume of a trilogy, *How to Understand Your Bible*. Chapter 2, Keys to Old Testament Mysteries (pp. 26-49), provides a History of Cabala as "a body of religious instruction, [which] was ensouled by a spiritual mystery, ancient and medieval scholars unfolded a secret magical, philosophical, and religious doctrine as a key to the inner interpretation of the traditional form of their religion." Also includes Kabbalistic interpretations of the various doctrines discussed throughout the book.

0116 Schwartz, F. Schneider. *The True Mysteries of Life: the Psychology of the Bible, the Kabbalah, and the Dead Sea Scrolls.* New York: Vantage Press, 1957.

In "a strictly non-sectarian view,... I have undertaken the task of writing several volumes on the most important subject in the world, *Know Thyself*, as explained in the Bible and the Kabbalah. Though I am not college trained or a professional writer, I am sure my kind of people, who need this knowledge most, will understand what I have to say. To explain all the mysteries of the Bible and the Kabbalah in detail would be impossible, even for an experienced writer, but fortunately the small details are not very important." The six chapters are: I. Man: Who or What are You?; II. The Soul: What is it?; III. The Universal, Scientific, Proved God; VI. What is Religion?; V. The Cause of all Trouble; and VI. Who Created Evil?

0117 Adamson, J.H. "The War in Heaven: Milton's Version of the Merkabah." *Journal of English and German Philology*, 57(1958), 690-703.

"The Cabbalistic interpretation of the Merkabah then postulates a cosmic cycle of creation, consequent separateness from the Divine, and finally a re-creation in which the Divine Will is again all in all. The re-creation is accomplished through the Heavenly Man or Logos. It is obvious that this is also Milton's basic pattern for the War in Heaven in *Paradise Lost*. The Angelical Polity, intuitively obedient to the Divine Will, has been shattered by rebellion in which sons of the Angels deny their Creator and seek to live according to the dictates of their own creaturely wills. The Son restores the Divine Polity by ascending the Divine Chariot and defeating the Powers of Darkness."

0118 Benbow, R. Mark. "Cabalism in Renaissance England." *Notes and Queries*, n.s. 5(1958), 54-55.

Adds *The Earle of Gowries Conspiracie against the Kings Maiestie of Scotland* (anon., Edinburgh, 1600), to the group of books cited by Blau (O98) which indicates the diffusion of kabbalistic knowledge in Renaissance England.

0119 Gundersheimer, Werner L. "Erasmus' Humanism, and the Christian Cabala." *Journal of the Warburg and Courtauld Institutes*, 26(1963), 38-52.

Although Erasmus's letters evince a "coolness" towards Kabbalah, Gundersheimer has investigated this prominent humanist's attitude towards Christian Kabbalah in order to present "at least a major (if not the dominant) Christian position towards it. Moreover, such an investigation may shed some light on the complexity and differentiation of Erasmus's responses to the serious problems which cabalistic studies had indirectly brought about in Germany in the second decade of the [sixteenth] century. Finally, this study should provide the basis for a more precise assessment of the importance of cabalistic study as an aspect of Renaissance humanism."

0120 Spitz, Lewis W. *The Religious Renaissance of the German Humanists*. Cambridge, Mass.: Harvard University Press, 1963.

"Two major themes dominated the concerns of the German humanists, romantic cultural nationalism and religious enlightenment, and both were of tremendous importance to the Reformation movement itself. This book is a study of the leading men and their ideas about ecclesiastical reform and religious renewal. It has to do with the time-honored theme *de spiritu* et littera." In addition to frequent references to Kabbalah throughout the text, in Chapter IV, Reuchlin, Pythagoras Reborn (pp. 61-80), Spitz discusses the influence on and importance of the Kabbalah to Reuchlin.

0121 Butler, W.E. *Magic and the Qabalah*. London: Aquarian Press, 1964. New York: Weiser, 1972.

"It would appear, therefore, that the body of knowledge and tradition which comes to us down the ages from some of the earliest experiences and speculations of the Hebrew race, has been augmented by many tributaries. In its Jewish aspect it still expresses some of the orthodox Jewish concepts of its eleventh century recension, but it also brings with it immemorial traditions which have come to us from the Night of Time; from times long past, and, we may also suggest, from a land now lost. This composite tradition is that with which we are concerned in this book."

0122 Hall, Manly P. *Cabalistic Keys to the Lord's Prayer.* Los Angeles: The Philosophical Research Society, Inc., 1964.

Interpretation of The Lord's Prayer through the use of an occult interpretation of the *Sefirot*.

0123 Hirst, Désirée. *Hidden Riches: Traditional Symbolism from the Renaissance to Blake.* Covent Garden: Eyre & Spottiswoode Ltd., New York: Barnes & Noble, 1964.

In an effort to understand the poetry of William Blake, Hirst traces the development of the mystical tradition through the eighteenth century, as it filtered through Western Christianity. While the study does not focus specifically on Kabbalah, Hirst is ever aware that these "concepts derived, it is true, from the ancient world, by a kind of Neo-Platonism blended with Hebrew symbolism." And she consistently demonstrates kabbalistic sources of and influences on this non-Jewish tradition.

0124 Josten, C.H., trans. "A Translation of John Dee's 'Monas Hieroglyphica' (Antwerp, 1564), with an Introduction and Annotations." *Ambix*, 12(1964), 84-221.

According to Dr. Meric Casaubon (1599-1671), "Monas Hieroglyphica" demonstrates that John Dee "was a Cabalistical man, up to the ears." This facsimile and translation of Dee's alchemical text, which "lends itself easily to digressive secondary interpretations of a numerological, cabbalistic, astrological, cosmological, or mathematical nature," is preceded by an Introduction (pp. 84-111), which discusses The Enigmatic Character of the Work; The Preparation of the 'Monas Hieroglyphica' and its First Reception in England; The Later History of the Text and of the Symbol of Dee's Monad; and Suggestions for an Interpretation.

0125 Secret, François. *Les Kabbalistes chrétiens de la Renaissance.* Paris: Dunot, 1964.

Chapter IX, La Kabbale chrétienne en Angleterre (pp. 228-38), is devoted to the Christian Kabbalah in sixteenth-century England. Covering essentially the same ground as

Blau (097), *Secret* discusses, among others, John Fisher, Thomas More, Everard Digby, John Dee, Henry Howard, Reginald Scott, Henry Smith, Henry Ainsworth, William Alabaster, Francis Bacon and Robert Fludd. (In French)

0126 Yates, Frances A. *Giordano Bruno and the Hermetic Tradition.* London: Routledge & Kegan Paul, Ltd., Chicago: University of Chicago Press, 1964.

Presents Bruno "as a variation on the Hermetic-Cabalist tradition." The fifth chapter, Pico Della Mirandola and Cabalist Magic (pp. 84-116), focuses on practical Kabbalah as introduced by Pico who believed that since "Cabala confirmed the truth of Christianity, Christian Cabala was a Hebrew-Christian source of ancient wisdom, and one which he found it most valuable and instructive to compare with Gentile ancient wisdoms, and above all with that of Hermes Trismegistus."

0127 Knight, Gareth. *A Practical Guide to Qabalistic Symbolism.* 2 vols. Toddington, Cheltenham (Glos.): Helios Book Service, 1965.

"This book [vol. 1] and its successor [vol. 2] deal with the Sephiroth and Paths of the Tree of Life as a basis for a study of many branches of esoteric symbolism.... Also, this book is written from a theosophic standpoint because it is meant to be used as a practical guide to opening up the higher aspects of the soul of man. It is not intended to be an academic or historical treatise."

0128 Nauert, Charles G., Jr. *Agrippa and the Crisis of Renaissance Thought.* Illinois Studies of the Social Sciences, 55. Urbana: University of Illinois Press, 1965.

Not devoted to Kabbalah; rather, a study of the life and thought of a man who "felt keenly the religious and intellectual problems, and even the political and social problems, of the sixteenth century." However, Nauert includes numerous references to Kabbalah, especially Chapter VI, Agrippa's Readings (see pp. 129-36).

0129 Cavendish, Richard. *The Black Arts.* London: Routledge & K. Paul, New York: Putnam, 1967.

Explores "the practice, theory and underlying rationale of black magic in all its branches." Chapter 3, The Cabala and the Names of Power (pp. 81-141), approaches "The Cabala [as] a body of occult doctrine, originally Jewish, which has been adopted with enthusiasm by non-Jewish occultists since the fifteenth century."

0130 Schulze, Wilhelm August. "Der Einfluss der Kabbala auf die Cambridger Platoniker Cudworth and More." *Judaica,* 23(1967), 75-126, 136-60, 193-240.

Extensive study of the influence of Kabbalah on Cudworth and More. Contents: Einleitung: Der christliche Kabbalismus; 1. Die Schopfung; 2. Der Gottesgedanke; 3. Der Raum; 4. Die Geisterwelt; 5. Die Natur; 6. Jacob Bohme; 7. Die Seele; 8. Die Ethic; 9. Die Erkenntnistheorie; 10. Die Materie; 11. Biblische Hermeneutik; Schluss: Fernwirkungen den Cambridger Platonismus. (In German)

0131 Wirszubski, Ch. "Giovanni Pico's Companion to Kabbalistic Symbolism." In A67. Pp. 353-62.

Examination of *Liber de Radicibus uel Terminis Cabale*, "a Latin translation of a book entitled in Hebrew *Sefer Hassorasim*" *(Cod. Vat. Ebr. 190, foll. 222-275)*, translated for Pico by Flavius Mithridates, which "is not a Kabbalistic treatise but a glossary of Kabbalistic symbols or, to put it more precisely, a glossary of miscellaneous words and expressions that are conceived of by the Kabbalists as names or representations of the ten *Sefirot*. It appears from the author's prefaces to the first and second parts that the book was meant to be an introduction to the study of the Kabbalah and at the same time a Kabbalistic companion to the interpretation of Scriptures and the sayings of the Rabbis."

0132 Gray, William. *The Ladder of Lights (or Qabalah Renovata): A Step by Step Guide to the Tree of Life and the Four Worlds of the Qabalists*. Toddington, Eng.: Helios Book Service, Ltd., York Beach, Maine: Samuel Weiser, Inc., 1968.

A "renovated" explanation of the *Sefirotic* tree which uses Jewish Kabbalah only as a starting place for Gray's theories. Companion volume, 0178.

0133 Ansari, Asloob Ahmad. "Blake and the Kabbalah." In A73. Pp. 199-220.

Blake "must have been attracted by the mythic content of the kabbalah which expressed itself as vengeful conquest of its upholders against the custodians of the rabbinic wisdom.... To uncover a few strata of significances common to this bold body of speculation and the cosmic drama enacted in Blake's major epics, therefore, promises to be a rewarding experience."

0134 Duncan, A.D. *The Christ, Psychotherapy and Magic: A Christian Appreciation of Occultism*. London: George Allen and Unwin Ltd., 1969.

"This book is in three parts. The first consists of three essays which will seek to establish the origins from which the Qabalistic tradition has sprung. These will discuss Gnosis and Gnosticism, the Qabalah in Judaism, and the relationship between magic and mysticism.... The second section contains an examination of the Qabalah as it is found in the modern occult tradition.... The third and last section deals with the practical applications of Qabalistic occultism; its meditational techniques and their affinities with modern psychotherapy. The relationship between occult meditation and Christian prayer is examined and a short study is made of ceremonial magic and clairvoyance."

0135 Epstein, Perle. *The Private Labyrinth of Malcolm Lowry: "Under the Volcano" and the Cabbala.* New York: Holt, Rinehart and Winston, 1969.

"Perle Epstein, drawing on her own researches and conversations with Mrs. Lowry and on unpublished material from Lowry's estate, analyzes the sources of Lowry's creative imagination in *Under the Volcano*, illuminating the influence that the Cabbala had on him--and why." (Editor's note) The study is comprised of three parts: I. Introduction (Malcolm Lowry; Lowry and the Cabbala; The Two Cabbalas); II. The Symbolism of *Under the Volcano*; and III. *Under the Volcano* and the Cabala.

0136 Heline, Corinne. *The Bible and the Tarot.* Oceanside, Calif.: New Age Press, Inc., 1969.

Discussion of astrologic uses of Kabbalah.

0137 Wirszubski, Chaim. "Giovanni Pico's Book of Job." *Journal of the Warburg and Courtauld Institutes*, 32(1969), 171-99.

Examination of Cod. Ottob. Lat. 607 of the Vatican Library, which "contains a remarkable composite translation of Job, annotated and in part rewritten by Giovanni Pico della Mirandola,... [whose] value lies in the opportunity they afford of seeing in detail how Pico's Biblical, philosophical, and Kabbalistic interests meet together in the interpretation of the Book of Job."

0138 Marcus, Jacob R. *The Colonial American Jew, 1492-1776.* 3 vols. Detroit: Wayne State University Press, 1970.

By no means a work devoted to Kabbalah, but still useful for indicating the limited influence of Kabbalah on Colonial America, particularly by Judah Monis (II.1096-1103), and Ezra Stiles (II.1104-1107).

0139 Miller, Arlene A. "The Theologies of Luther and Boehme in the Light of Their *Genesis* Commentaries." *Harvard Theological Review*, 63(1970), 261-303.

"Despite the many differences between Luther and Boehme which emerge in a detailed study of their *Genesis* commentaries, one can with certainty conclude that Boehme's writings would have been impossible without Luther. For though Boehme indeed brings Paracelsan alchemical terminology, Cabalistic philosophic thought and gnostic sophia symbolism into his work, his new metaphysical-theological gestalt would have been unthinkable without his Lutheran orientation."

0140 Suares, Carlo. *The Cipher of Genesis: The Original Code of the Qabala as Applied to Scriptures.* London: Stuart & Watkins, Berkeley: Shambhala Publications, 1970.

Believing that the Bible "is already hopelessly mistranslated in Hebrew," Suares tries to decode Genesis according to his belief that "The twenty-two graphs which are used as letters in the Hebrew alphabet are twenty-two proper names originally used to designate different states or structures of the one cosmic energy, which is *essence* and *semblance*, of all that is."

0141 Alazraki, Jaime. "Kabbalistic Traits in Borges' Narration." *Studies in Short Fiction*, 8(1971), 78-92.

"The Kabbalistic texture of [Borges' stories] adds to their manifold complexity and to their richness of meaning. Borges challenges the reader to activate all his resources, to become himself a Kabbalist. He seems to be saying: If man, powerless to solve the labyrinths of the gods, is left with the choice of weaving and deciphering his own, let us--at least--devise them as close as possible to the divine model, let us write a secular text in the manner that the Holy one was fashioned."

0142 Chiel, Arthur A. "Ezra Stiles--The Education of an 'Hebrician.'" *American Jewish Historical Quarterly*, 60(March 1971), 235-41.

Primarily a discussion of Stiles' Hebrew studies, but does refer to Stiles' interest in Hebrew mysticism, to the extent of purchasing a copy of the Zohar and studying with Rabbi Moses ben David of Apta, Poland.

0143 Sturzaker, James. *Kabbalistic Aphorisms*. London; Adyar, Madras; Wheaton, Ill.: Theosophical Publishing House, Ltd., 1971.

"The Mystical Kabbalah is a glyph or symbol system which consists of the Tree of Life and the twenty-two Major Arcana of the Tarot cards or, to give the cards their correct name, the Book of Thoth.... This book of Kabbalistic Aphorisms has been compiled to suit the needs of all. Churchman and atheist, materialist and occultist, highly intelligent and not so gifted will find satisfaction by a study of each section of the Aphorisms in relation to the aspect of the glyph with which they are concerned."

0144 Wirszubski, Ch. "Mors Osculi, Poetic Theology and Kabbala in Renaissance Thought." *Proceedings of the Israel Academy of Sciences and Humanities*, 1971.

Erroneous reference; unable to locate article.

0145 Alazraki, Jaime. "Borges and the Kabbalah." *TriQuarterly*, 25(1972), 240-67. Rpt. 0152.

"The impact of the Kabbalah on Borges' work far exceeds the random quotations or allusions the casual reader may find and which, after all, only confirm the interest Borges conceded.... Behind his transparent texts there lies a stylistic intricacy, a certain Kabbalistic texture, a spellbinding characteristic to which Borges finds himself attracted.... Most of his narratives do not exhaust themselves at the level of literal meaning--they present an immediate and manifest layer and a more oblique and allusive one. It is the latter which generates in his stories a Kabbalistic aura whose source goes far beyond a fortuitous familiarity with the Kabbalah." Considers: 1. A scrutiny of Borges' Kabbalah library; 2. The doctrine of the *Sefiroth*; 3. The legend of the Golem; 4. The doctrine of Ibbur; 5. Reality of the unreal; 6. Style; and 7. Unveiling and seventy faces of a text.

0146 Drury, Nevill, and Stephen Skinner. *The Search for Abraxas*. London: Neville Spearman, 1972.

Traces the historical quest for magic. The third chapter of Section I, Qabalah in Theory and Practice (pp. 19-44), reviews the history of practical Kabbalah, which "draws for its content from many Traditions, those of Chaldea, the Egyptian Mysteries, the Tyrian Mysteries, the wisdom of the Babylonian Magi, the teachings of the Essenes, the Greek and Christian Gnosis, the mathematical theology of Pythagoras, and in later days, the teachings of Rosicrucianism and Alchemy, all blended with the various mythological systems of Europe to make a composite and rich working whole."

0147 Suares, Carlo. *The Song of Songs: The Canonical Song of Solomon Deciphered according to the Original Code of the Qabala*. London and Berkeley: Shambhala Publications, 1972.

Considers the Song of Songs "truly the song of the two young lovers, it is true allegorically, it is true symbolically, and true inasmuch as it expressed most vividly the science of Qabala.... It is Knowledge as all Qabala is, but at its highest and deepest level. In this volume our purpose is to introduce that Knowledge. We deem it our duty to state, before any other development, that the views of the modern Jewish authorities on Qabala are erroneous.... Qabala, originally, was neither Jewish nor mysticism: it declared itself as a tradition issued from Abraham, who was an ancient Chaldean belonging to a much older period than Moses', and it asserted that Abraham's Revelation was direct knowledge, devoid of mysticism."

0148 Yates, Frances. *The Rosicrucian Enlightenment.* London and Boston: Routledge & K. Paul, 1972. St. Albans, Eng.: Paladin, 1975.

Focuses on the Rosicrucian movement of the early seventeenth century, the period in European culture "between the Renaissance and the so-called scientific revolution of the seventeenth century. It is a phase in which the Renaissance Hermetic-Cabalist tradition has received the influx of another Hermetic tradition, that of alchemy."

0149 Friedman, Jerome. "Michael Servetus: The Case for a Jewish Christianity." *Sixteenth Century Journal,* 4(1973), 87-110.

"The purpose of this paper is to analyze the use of Jewish literature in Servetus' writings in order to discover what pattern is formed. Rather than simply list citations of a Jewish nature this paper will attempt to demonstrate what function Judaica played in Servetus' thought." Includes a section exploring the possibility of kabbalistic influence on Servetus (pp. 99-102).

0150 Lévi, Eliphas [Alphonse Louis Constant] *The Book of Splendours.* Wellingborough: The Aquarian Press, New York: S. Weiser, Inc., 1973.

"This is the first part of Eliphas Lévi's last great discourse on the mysteries of occultism that was continued and concluded in *The Great Secret.* In it, Lévi examines with great precision and insight the inner meanings of Qabalism and their relationship to the occult sciences. Part One is a commentary on the *Siphra Dzeniuta* by Simeon Ben Jochai, which includes an examination of the affinities between Qabalism and Freemasonry. Part Two pursues the Correspondences between Qabalism, numerology and the Tarot." (Editor's note)

0151 Sosnowski, Saul. "The God's Script--A Kabbalistic Quest." *Modern Fiction Studies,* 19(1973), 381-94.

Borges' story "'The God's Script' may serve as an 'aleph' for other texts with Kabbalistic motifs. By comparing Tzinacan's journey with the mystic's path, we shall attempt to clarify the meaning of his search for an all-powerful formula and the effects of this search upon him. We shall also demonstrate that the steps that he must trace in order to arrive at the Divine Lights are structurally analogous to the prerequisites acknowledged by the Kabbalists. That there is a connection between these two elements is made clear in Borges' epilogue to *El aleph* when he says that he has caused Tzinacan to utter arguments of a Kabbalist or a theologian."

O152 Alazraki, Jaime. "Borges and the Kabbalah." In A90. Pp. 184-211.

Rpt. of O145.

O153 Cavendish, Richard, ed. *Encyclopedia of the Unexplained: Magic, Occultism and Parapsychology.* New York: McGraw-Hill, London: Routledge & K. Paul, 1974.

A compendium of material on "parapsychology and psychical research, including such 'psychic' abilities as clairvoyance, precognition and telepathy, mediumship, faith healing and Spiritualism; magic and the occult, an even broader and vaguer category, ranging from the astral plane to Atlantes to ritual magic to reincarnation, or in terms of people and groups from the Theosophical Society to the Rosicrucians to the Flat Earthers to the Golden Dawn to Jung, or from Gurdjieff to Steiner to Aleister Crowley to Reich to the witches; and the main systems of divination--astrology, the I Ching, the Tarot, and others." The section, Cabala (pp. 56-59), "considers the Cabala primarily from the point of view of modern occultists, who have interpreted it and mingled it with other traditions in ways which tend to raise the hackles of scholars of Jewish mysticism."

O154 Cook, Roger. *The Tree of Life: Images for the Cosmos.* London: Thames and Hudson, New York: Avon Books, 1974.

Explores "The image of the tree [which] symbolically reflects man's intense desire to grasp the essential reality of this world." An integral part of the study is the *Sephirotic* Tree, which Cook includes in his section on The Inverted Tree (pp. 18-20); illustrations and variations can be found throughout the text.

O155 Duncan, J. Ann. "The Early Novels of Paul Adam." *Modern Language Review,* 69(1974), 534-40.

Analysis of the early novels of Paul Adam, especially as influenced by the popular notion of Kabbalah in late nineteenth-century France.

O156 International Order of Kabbalists. *Conference--12th October, 1974.* London: Metatron Publications, 1974.

Contents: Sylvia M. Swinborne, "The Aims and Objectives of a Kabbalist"; Patrick Fullick, "The Kabbalist and Ecology"; Alan J. Goffin, "Physics and Metaphysics--A Synthesis"; Michael Defries, "Meaning, Purpose and Dangers of Ritual"; and Raymond C. Wilkie, "How and Why Mysticism and Occultism Should be Used by the Kabbalist."

0157 Lévi, Eliphas [Alphonse Louis Constant]. *The Mysteries of the Qabalah, or the Occult Agreement of the Two Testaments, as Contained in The Prophecy of Ezekiel and The Apocalypse of Saint John.* Studies in Hermetic Tradition, Vol. II. Wellingborough: Thorsons, 1974.

Explains "the resemblance in meaning" of Ezekiel and Revelation "to prove the identity of the ultimate goal of the Old and New Testament, and so establishes the reconciliation between the two main systems of salvation of the western world: Judaism and Christianity." Lévi interprets both prophecies, verse by verse.

0158 Richardson, Alan. *An Introduction to the Mystical Qabalah.* Wellingborough, Eng.: The Aquarian Press, 1974. New York: Weiser, 1981.

"This book is an attempt to give a basic understanding of the Qabalist philosophy and its application to magic, to people who are approaching this subject for the first time. It is an attempt to do away with the bogeys, and show the principles behind the various magical practices." The second chapter, The Magical Philosophy (pp. 13-23), contains an explanation of the *Sefirotic* tree; the fourth, The Middle Pillar (pp. 29-33), deals with the central column; and the remainder of the book applies these principles to magic.

0159 Banes, Daniel. *The Provocative Merchant of Venice.* Silver Spring, Md. and Chicago: Malcolm House, 1975. Addendum, 1976.

After noting some anomalous features of the play, and providing an edition and program notes, Banes hypothesizes "that the classical Kabbalistic scriptures, translated or paraphrased, may have been among the provocative texts that kindled Shakespeare's imagination when he wrote *The Merchant of Venice.*"

0160 Coudert, Allison. "A Cambridge Platonist's Kabbalist Nightmare." *Journal of the History of Ideas,* 36(1975), 633-52.

While early in his philosophic career, Henry More was drawn to Kabbalah and to the two leading contemporary exponents of Jewish mysticism, Lady Anne Conway and Franciscus Mercurius van Helmont, ultimately, More rejected Kabbalah because "the Kabbalists were neither modest nor charitable in their writings. They asserted the most monstrously complex theories and spoke about them as if they were fundamental truths.... In the end, More could not accept the Kabbala, nor could he convince Helmont and Lady Conway that his objections were valid."

0161 Davies, Ann. *Meditational Ascent on the Tree of Livingness: Authorized Religious Practices and Teachings of B.O.T.A., based upon the Holy Qabalah and Tarot.* Los Angeles: Builders of the Adytum, 1975.

Based on transcriptions of special class work conducted by Davies at the Temple of Tarot and Holy Qabalah; uses the *Sefirotic* tree as a "map for a journey into new dimensions of consciousness; upward and inward through the paths of livingness toward direct identity with the One Reality." Contains 104 lessons, ranging from an introduction to the *Sefirotic* tree through the thirty-two paths as interpreted with the use of Tarot.

0162 Denning, Melita, and Osborne Phillips. *The Sword and the Serpent.* The Magical Philosophy, Book III. St. Paul: Llewellyn Publications, 1975.

Study of Qabalah and Magical Art, including discussions of the *Sefirot* and the Paths.

0163 Hoeller, Stephan A. *The Royal Road: A Manual of Kabalistic Meditations on the Tarot.* A Quest Book. Wheaton, Ill.: Theosophical Publishing House, 1975.

"... chiefly intended to serve as a handbook of Kabalistic meditation on the Major Arcana of the Tarot.... Since this treatise does not presuppose any previous background of reading and study within the fields of either the Kabalah or the Tarot, it may be considered a primer of these subjects, in addition to being a guide to a specific practice of meditation." The introductory section contains two chapters: The Wisdom of the Tarot; and Tarot and Kabalah. The section, The Road and the Journey, is divided into seven: Preparing for the Journey; A Map for the Traveler; The Ten Way Stations; The Twenty-Two Highways; The Fool's Pilgrimage; Observing the Signposts; and The Road Goes Ever On. The appendix concerns Astral Travel: The Glamourous Road.

0164 International Order of Kabbalists. *Conference, 1975.* London: Metatron Publications, 1975.

"... there are no authoritative teachings concerning the Kabbalah or its allied subjects"; consequently, the papers delivered at the Conference represent individual interpretations of the participants. Contents: Frances A. Morris, "Animals in Relation to the Tree of Life"; James Sturzaker, "Colour and Kabbalah"; Silvia M. Swinborne, "The Gods in Relationship to the Tree of Life"; Alfred J. Lesser, "The Importance of the Mundane Chakvas in Kabbalah"; Doreen L. Sturzaker, "Gemstones and Kabbalah"; and A.J. Goffin, "Relationship of the Magical Weapons."

0165 Knight, Gareth. *Experience of the Inner Worlds: A Course in Christian Qabalistic Magic.* Toddington, Eng.: Helios Book Service, 1975.

Knight's "aim in this book has been to provide a system of occult teaching and practice that is founded on a framework of Christian tradition and belief." Believing that Christian magic is a product of Florentine magicians, the Rosicrucian Brotherhood, Robert Fludd, Eliphas Lévi, the Hermetic literature, pagan mystery tradition, visions of Dante, Jewish Qabalism, Alchemy, Courtly Love and the Holy Grail tradition, Knight traces the history of magic through all of these sources. And since most were, in one way or another, influenced by Kabbalah, various aspects of the Jewish system appear throughout the text.

0166 Newman, Beth S. "John Donne and the Cabala." *Jewish Quarterly,* 23,1-2(1975), 31-36.

"I would like to suggest that Donne's modern attitude toward the spirituality of sex was influenced by Cabalism, a Jewish Neoplatonism which elucidated the spiritual mysteries of God and the universe through explicitly sexual imagery."

0167 Poncé, Charles. *The Game of Wizards: Psyche, Science, and Symbol in the Occult.* Harmondsworth, Baltimore, Victoria: Penguin Books, 1975.

Attempts to answer the questions: "What psychological, metaphysical, or philosophical realities do [occult sciences] purport to reveal that so engage us? What is it about the nature of the psyche that is willing to support the existence of such systems? And even more importantly, What is it about the nature of the psyche that causes it to produce such systems?" Chapter 3, The Structure of God (pp. 117-47), "concentrate[s] on four major principles: the En-Sof and the configurations of the *Sefiroth*, the alphabet and its symbolism, and the four-world systems." Appendix C discusses The Influence of Kabbalism on Tarot (pp. 236-40).

0168 Smith, Richard Furnald. *Prelude to Science: An Exploration of Magic and Divination.* New York: Charles Scribner's Sons, 1975.

"... I have tried to define the boundaries of science as closely as possible and have acknowledged the presence of values on both sides of those boundaries. I then proceed to an overview of magic, a historical survey of divination, and a more detailed discussion of their most widespread and enduring forms: astrology, the Kabbalah, and Tarot." Chapter 9, The Kabbalah: Letters and Numbers of Power, pp. 85-91.

0169 Straughn, R.A. *The Realization of Neter Nu: A Kabalistical Guide to the Realization of Self.* Bronx: Maat Pub., 1975.

Unavailable for annotating.

0170 Sturzaker, Doreen, and James Sturzaker. *Colour and the Kabbalah.* Wellingborough: Thorsons Publishers Limited, New York: Samuel Weiser, Inc., 1975.

"This book is offered to those interested in the Kabbalah but who have not yet studied its colour aspect, for we feel that to gain a deeper, truer understanding of the subject the differing colours of the Sephiroth and the Paths must be taken into consideration.... In the following pages an attempt will be made to look more closely into these correspondences and to explain the Sephiroth and the Paths in the light of colour symbolism. In doing this we offer our own interpretation and would urge each serious student and fellow Kabbalist to consider the colour aspect, meditate and come to his own understanding, for in the end the validity of the system depends on its relevance for each individual."

0171 Wieczynski, Joseph L. "Hermetism and Cabalism in the Heresies of the Judaizers." *Renaissance Quarterly*, 28(1975), 17-28.

"The Jewish features which superficially invested [Renaissance] Hermeticism, Cabalism, and many scientific treatises from the West afforded Russian ecclesiastics a grand pretext for an attack upon all freethinking and humanism. In centuries to come Russian nationalists would find [Archbishop Gennadius of Novgorod's] scapegoat a convenience for similar purposes."

0172 Coudert, Allison. "A Quaker-Kabbalist Controversy: George Fox's Reaction to Francis Mercury van Helmont." *Journal of the Warburg and Courtauld Institutes*, 39(1976), 171-89.

Discusses van Helmont's relationship with the Quakers, and the way his belief in the kabbalistic doctrine of the revolution of souls caused him to leave the organization which he at one time thought was "a suitable foundation for his Kabbalist version of the Christian religion."

0173 Holroyd, Stuart. *Magic, Words, and Numbers.* A New Library of the Supernatural. Garden City, New York: Doubleday, London: Aldus Books, 1976.

Non-Jewish Kabbalah 351

Traces man's search for power and the answer to the question: "Are there laws, other than the familiar laws of Nature, that people can use to gain special and remarkable power?" Chapter 3, Mysteries of the Cabala (pp. 48-65), contains a basic explanation of the *Sefirot*, and a discussion of the use made of Kabbalah by various occultists and magicians.

0174 Leventhal, Herbert. *In the Shadow of the Enlightenment: Occultism and Renaissance Science in Eighteenth-Century America*. New York: New York University Press, 1976.

Examines "those aspects of eighteenth-century colonial thought which were not new, not the product of the Enlightenment, but rather, continuations of what E.M.W. Tillyard has called 'the Elizabethan world picture.'" Although Kabbalah did not play a major role in colonial intellectual history, it did influence Ezra Stiles (pp. 251-58).

0175 Straughn, R. *Meditation Techniques of the Kabalists, Vedantins and Taoists*. Bronx: Maat Pub. Co., 1976.

Unavailable for annotating.

0176 Zika, Charles. "Reuchlin's *De Verbo mirifico* and the Magic Debate of the Late Fifteenth Century." *Journal of the Warburg and Courtauld Institutes*, 39(1976), 104-38.

The significance of Reuchlin's *De Verbo mirifico* is as a "defense of Pico's work against the attacks of Garsias, and an important agent in the dissemination of this position north of the Alps. While the importance of Reuchlin for the dissemination of a Christian Kabbalah, largely instigated or at least circulated by Pico, is well attested, his place in the development of magical ideas from Pico to Cornelius Agrippa is either unrecognized or left very much understated."

0177 Copenhaver, Brian P. "Lefèvre d'Etaples, Symphorien Champier, and the Secret Names of God." *Journal of the Warburg and Courtauld Institutes*, 40(1977), 189-211.

Copenhaver's "intention simply to shed light on the significance and depth of the work by studying Lefèvre's development of one Cabalist theme--the secret names of God--in the final chapters of book two of *De magia naturali*."

0178 Gray, William G. *The Talking Tree*. York Beach, Maine: S. Weiser, Inc., 1977.

Applies the principles of the *Sefirotic* tree to an abstract system of thirty-two paths, no longer dependent on the Hebrew alphabet for articulation, but capable of talking "to us in our own ways about the Inner actualities Mankind has sought since his inception in the Mind of his Maker. More. The Tree will talk about anything we are interested in." Companion volume to O132.

0179 Papus [Gérard Encausse] *The Qabalah: Secret Tradition of the West*. Studies in Hermetic Tradition, Vol. IV. Wellingborough: Thorsons Publishers Limited, New York: Samuel Weiser, Inc., 1977.

"We have endeavoured to establish as clear a classification as possible of the books and traditions of which the Qabalah is a part, and we have done our best to draw up as extensive a bibliography as possible." The study is divided into four parts: I. The Divisions of the Qabalah (The Hebrew Tradition and the Classification of Related Works, The Massorah, The Mishna, and The Qabalah); II. The Teachings of the Qabalah (The Elements of the Qabalah in Ten Lessons by Eliphas Lévi, General Thoughts on the Qabalah by Sédir, and Systematic Résumé of the Qabalah); III. The Texts *(The Sepher Yetzirah)*; and IV. Summary Bibliography of the Qabalah.

0180 Sosnowski, Saul. "Borges and the Kabbalah--The Search for the Word." In A101. III.125-32.

"A close scrutiny of [Borges'] texts will show that he considers language to be *the* key that leads to ontological enrichment. The poet's task is analogous to the approach envisioned by the Kabbalists. The poet, however, does not have a text that circumscribes the space to be searched. His realm is rather the totality of language. This fact, however, does not set him apart from the Kabbalist. The Text that confronts the Kabbalist comprises Total Being." Illustrates the thesis through an analysis of Borges' story "The God's Script."

0181 Zika, Charles. "Reuchlin and Erasmus: Humanism and the Occult Philosophy." *Journal of Religious History* (Sydney), 9(1977), 223-46.

Not an article on Kabbalah; explores the fundamental distinctions between Reuchlin and Erasmus as humanists. However, that distinction lies in the respective attitudes of the two towards Kabbalah, and in exploring the distinction, Zika discusses both Erasmus' antipathy towards Jewish mysticism and Reuchlin's adaptation of Kabbalah for his own works.

0182 Banes, Daniel. *Shakespeare, Shylock and Kabbalah*. Silver Spring, Md.: Malcolm House, 1978.

"The purpose of this book is to identify some of the kabblistic themes in *The Merchant of Venice*, and to relate them to antecedents in the literature of the Kabbalah. The evidence that I have accumulated seems overwhelmingly abundant.... The thesis of the book is that the Playwright, inspired by the romantic symbolism and the exalted ideals of Jewish Kabbalah, artistically wove subtle kabbalistic embellishments into the multistranded tapestry of his complex drama." Part I: The Kabbalistic Tradition of Merrie England; Part II. Kabbalistic Theme in *The Merchant of Venice*; Part III: Shakespeare's Kabbalistic Sourcebooks.

0183 Halevi, Z'ev ben Shimon [Warren Kenton] *The Anatomy of Fate: Kabbalistic Astrology*. London: Rider & Company, New York: S. Weiser, 1978.

Using astrology in conjunction with kabbalistic principles, Halevi explores the principle of the Macrocosm/Microcosm, and "the processes of celestial influences," as well as "the nature of fate, free will and the purpose of destiny for each of us who are incarnate for so brief a time between birth and death."

0184 Howard, Michael. *The Runes and Other Magical Alphabets*. Wellingborough, Eng.: Thorsons, New York: S. Weiser, 1978.

"The subject of this book is *magical* alphabets which suggest something apart, distinctive from everyday use and probably surrounded by some supranormal awe." The section on The Alphabet of the Hebrews (pp. 69-73), deals with the *Sefer Yetzirah* and the tarot.

0185 La Dage, Alta J. *Occult Psychology: A Comparison of Jungian Psychology and the Modern Qabalah*. St. Paul: Llewellyn Publications, 1978.

"The purpose of this book is to describe, in as far as I understand it, some of the inner correspondences between the Qabalah and the psychology of C.G. Jung." Based on the Kabbalism of the Western Occult Tradition, "This book is not intended to be 'scientific' or even rational! It is rather to be taken intuitively ... as a source of dreaming and inspiration." La Dage considers: The Eternal Quest; The Roots of the Qabalah; The Teachings of the Qabalah; The Universal Force; The Collective Unconsious [sic]; The Archetypes as Psychological Factors; The Archetypes--the Gods on the Tree; The Four Functions; and The Process of Individuation.

0186 Sassoon, George, and Rodney Dale. *The Manna-Machine*. London: Sidgwick & Jackson, 1978.

Explores the thesis that "the *Zohar*--contains the answers to all our questions about manna--and contains proof that the Lord was a space visitor."

0187 Sturzaker, James. *First Steps to Kabbalah.* London: Metatron Publications, 1978.

   Unavailable for annotating.

0188 Godwin, David. *Cabalistic Encyclopedia: A Complete Guide to Cabalistic Magick.* St. Paul: Llewellyn, 1979.

   This "is not a comprehensive dictionary of the Hebrew language. Nor is it a complete dictionary of the cabala as understood by true cabalists, who are Jewish scholars and mystics of vast learning in the Talmud and Torah. Rather, it is a dictionary of cabalism as understood and interpreted by the Christian (or Christian-biased) mystery schools and hermetic societies of the West, in particular the Hermetic Order of the Golden Dawn as it existed in the waning years of the 19th century. This book is intended for those who wish a relatively complete dictionary, arranged alphabetically both in English and in Hebrew as well as numerically, of cabalism as thus understood."

0189 Godwin, Joscelyn. *Athanasius Kircher: A Renaissance Man and the Quest for Lost Knowledge.* London: Thames and Hudson, 1979.

   A Jesuit scholar, Athanasius Kircher (1602-80) was among the first to draw a parallel between the kabbalistic doctrine of *Adam Kadmon* and the concept of Jesus. An eclectic thinker, Kircher studied "Egyptian mystery wisdom, Greek, Cabbalistic and Christian philosophy,... as he reinterpreted the history of man's scientific and artistic collaboration with God and Nature." Book contains reproductions of illustrations from Kircher's work, many of which reflect kabbalistic influence.

0190 Godwin, Joscelyn. *Robert Fludd: Hermetic Philosopher and Surveyor of Two Worlds.* Boulder: Shambhala, 1979.

   Fludd not only summarized "esoteric teachings common to all ages and peoples," but "recognized the universality of truth, welcoming it whether it came from Catholic or Protestant sources, from the Hebrew Bible, from Pythagoras, Plato or Hermes Trismegistus." Chapter 2, Cabbala (pp. 34-41), contains kabbalistically inspired illustrations of "The Tetragrammaton in the Macrocosm and Microcosm," "The Emanation of the Sephiroth," and "The Sephirotic Tree."

0191 Hutin, Serge. "Note sur la création chez trois kabbalistes chrétiens Anglais: Robert Fludd, Henry More et Isaac Newton." In A107. Pp. 149-56.

   Studies the three English Kabbalists in terms of their attitudes towards the doctrine of creation *ex nihilo*. (In French)

0192 Merchant, Carolyn. "The Vitalism of Anne Conway: Its Impact on Leibnitz's Concept of the Mind." *Journal of the History of Philosophy*, 17(1979), 255-69.

Explores the basic elements of Leibnitz's concept of the monad, as influenced by, in addition to his generally recognized sources, "Chinese Philosophy, Maimonides, and the Cabala. The writings of Francis Mercury van Helmont and Anne Conway served to confirm and buttress his vitalistic view of nature and to stimulate the coalescence of his ideas into a 'monadology.'"

0193 Regardie, Israel. *Foundations of Practical Magic: An Introduction to Qabalistic, Magical and Meditative Techniques.* Wellingborough: Aquarian Press, 1979.

Unavailable for annotating.

0194 Yates, Frances A. *The Occult Philosophy in the Elizabethan Age.* London and Boston: Routledge & Kegan Paul, 1979.

Outgrowth of the chapter on Pico and Kabbalah in her *Giordano Bruno and the Hermetic Tradition* (0126); an exploration of the "Hermetic-Cabalist" tradition, the kabbalistic side being "fundamental because it was in touch throughout the period with the living tradition of Jewish Cabala, and, through its Christianization, it exercised a most powerful influence on the history of religion." Yates divides the book into three parts: The Occult Philosophy in the Renaissance and Reformation; The Occult Philosophy in the Elizabethan Age; and The Occult Philosophy and Rosicrucianism and Puritanism--The Return of the Jews to England. The discussion revolves around Christian-kabbalistic influences on figures such as Raymond Lull, Pico della Mirandola, Johannes Reuchlin, Francesco Giorgi, Cornelius Agrippa, Albrecht Dürer, John Dee, Edmund Spenser, Christopher Marlowe, Shakespeare, George Chapman and John Milton.

0195 Bronstein, Leo. *Kabbalah and Art.* Hanover, New Hampshire, and London: Published by Brandeis University Press, distributed by University Press of New England, 1980.

"Leon Bronstein's book has this thesis: (1) that in the thick overlay of categories of the Kabbalah there is contained an epistemology or theory of knowledge; (2) that that epistemology offers postulations about how to know the fundamentals of existence: God, the world, and mankind; (3) that man, in his ethical life of good and evil and in his passion for visionary understanding, and the world, in its germination of structure, both exhibit an equipoised dialectic of the masculine and the feminine, the name for which is "Presence" or *Shekhinah*; (4) that art, in its history and in its born-again incarnations as this painting, this vision, or that, is the Kabbalah itself (the 'same as itself'), knowing, knowledgeable, dazzling, and explosive of spirit." (Editor's note) Explores the kabbalistic spirit found in non-Jewish art.

0196 Copenhaver, Brian P. "Jewish Theologies of Space in the Scientific Revolution: Henry More, Joseph Raphson, Isaac Newton and their Predecessors." *Annals of Science*, 37(1980), 489-548.

"Theological speculations on God's relation to place and space were introduced into the Jewish tradition by the early rabbis, initially in response to the previous appearance of words like $m\bar{a}q\hat{o}m$ (place) in Biblical literature. In the Middle Ages, Jewish philosophers modified these rabbinical ideas in the context of Aristotelian, Neoplatonic, and anti-Aristotelian currents within Jewish thought. One development in medieval Jewish thought of special interest for the development of ideas of space was the rise of Cabala, which Christian thinkers of the Renaissance and early modern periods saw as a sacred and primeval deposit of wisdom akin to *prisca theologia*. Both Henry More and, under More's influence, Joseph Raphson made use of Cabalist ideas in developing their own theologies of space. Isaac Newton was aware of these Jewish ideas but for the most part repudiated them, while making some use of $m\bar{a}q\hat{o}m$ as an expression of God's omnipresence." (Summary)

0197 Schutz, Albert L. *Call Adonoi: Manual of Practical Cabalah and Gestalt Mysticism*. Goleta, Calif.: Quantal Publishing Co., 1980.

Unavailable for annotating.

0198 Hodson, Geoffrey. *The Hidden Wisdom in the Holy Bible: An Examination of the Idea That the Contents of the Bible Are Partly Allegorical*. 4 vols. Wheaton, Ill., Madras, India, and London: Theosophical Publishing House, 1981.

Theosophical interpretation of the Bible, including an examination of The Sephirothal Tree reprinted in the last three volumes: II.413-23; III.303-13; and IV.341-51.

0199 Swietlicki, Catherine. *"Terra nostra:* Carlos Fuentes' Kabbalistic World." *Symposium: A Quarterly Journal in Modern Foreign Literatures*, 35(Summer 1981), 155-67.

"Fuentes seems to have been intrigued by Kabbalism's 'concepto del mundo mutante y recreable.' It is this aspect of Kabbalah which facilitates comparisons with other thought systems and which permits Fuentes to use Kabbalism in structuring the novel and in unifying numerous ideas dispersed throughout the novel."

0200   Bischoff, Erich. *Kabbala: An Introduction to Jewish Mysticism and Secret Doctrine.* New York: S. Weiser, 1983.

Unavailable for annotating.

0201   Gray, William G. *Concepts of Qabalah.* The Sangreal Sodality Ser.: Vol. 3. New York: S. Weiser, 1983.

Unavailable for annotating.

0202   Sephariel [Walter Gorn Old] *A Manual of Occultism.* London: W. Rider & Son Ltd., n.d., 1914, 1918, 1920.

Intends "to place before the lay reader a number of methods by means of which he will be able to demonstrate to his own satisfaction, and that of others, that there is a deep substratum of truth in what is usually called 'Occultism,' and that the occult arts are sure and definite means of exploring them." Discusses practical Kabbalah in the section on Thaumaturgic Art, pp. 140-92.

0203   Westcott, W. Wynn. *An Introduction to the Study of Kabalah, with Eight Diagrams.* New York: Allied Publications, n.d. London: J.M. Watkins, 1910; 2nd ed. 1926. Rpt. Hastings, Sx.: Metaphysical Research Group, 1978.

"Being fully persuaded of the good to be thus derived, I desire to call attention to the dogmas of the old Hebrew Kabalah." Reprint of lecture delivered to a Society of Hermetic Students in 1888 on a theosophic interpretation of Kabbalah.

INDEX

The Index is divided into three parts. The first, Primary Materials, includes titles and authors of kabbalistic texts found in this bibliography. The second, Authors, includes the authors of secondary materials, editors of anthologies containing kabbalistic material, and individuals to whom *Festschriften* are dedicated. The Subject index includes subjects of both primary and secondary sources found in this bibliography.

Primary Materials

Abraham ben Mordecai Galante   C13
Abraham ben Simeon, of Worms   O12
Abraham ha-Yakhini   C13
Abraham Isaac Kook: The Lights of Penitence, The Moral Principles, Lights of Holiness, Essays, Letters, and Poems   M9
Abraham of Granada   C12
Abulafia, Abraham   C8, C10, C12, C13, C19, C20, H1, H7, D125
Aesch Mezareph   O9
Agrippa, Heinrich Cornelius   O1
Alkabiz, Solomon   C10
Alphabet of Rabbi Akiba   F18
Alshech, Moses   C10
Alter, Yehudah Leib   L32, L60
Apocalypse of Abraham   E19
Apocalypse of Baruch   E9, E20
Apocalypse of Moses   E7
Apocrypha and Pseudepigrapha of the Old Testament   E17
Applefeld, Aharon   L45
Aramaic incantation bowls   D12
Ascension of Isaiah   E21
Assumption of Moses   E12
Astrology, miscellaneous texts   F7, F13
Auerbach, Uri   L73
Avidor, Shmuel Hacohen   L51
Azikri, Eliezer   C9

Baal Shem Tov on Pirkey Avoth: Thoughts, Interpretations, Explanations on the Ethics of the Fathers   L49

"Baal-Shem-Tov's Instruction in Intercourse with God" L25
Band, Arnold J. L57
Beggars and Prayers: Adin Steinsaltz Retells the Tales of Rabbi Nachman of Bratslav L61
Ben-Amos, Dan L42
Birnbaum, Salomo L7
Book of Jubilees; or, The Little Genesis E13
Book of Letters: A Mystical Alef-Bait M7
Book of Prophecy G10
Book of Sacred Magic O12
Book of the Pious see *Sefer Hasidim*
Book of Wisdom C48, F3
Book of Words G10
Bosi l'Gani L65
Brown, Moshe L60
Buber, Martin L1, L2, L4, L9, L12-L17, L19, L21, L25, L26, L40
Buzaglo, Shalom C13

Cabbalistical Dialogue O4
Carlebach, Shlomo M12
Caro, Joseph C10, C12
Casway, R. O10
Classic Hassidic Tales: Marvellous Tales of Rabbi Israel Baal Shem and of His Great-Grandson, Rabbi Nachman L37
Clavicula Salomonis see *Mafteah Shelomo*
Cohen, Martin Samuel F27
Commentary of Nahmanides on Genesis H2
Commentary of R. Hoter Ben Shelomo on the Thirteen Principles of Maimonides H4
Conjectura Cabbalistica O2
Contemplative Life F6, F11, F26
Conway, Anne O7
Cordovero, Moses C8-C10, C13, C19, J4

Dan, Joseph L74
Dawidowicz, Lucy S. L38
De Arte Cabbalistica O15
Dead Sea Scrolls E29-E33, E36, E37
Derech haShem J9
"Derek Hatechiah" M6
Divine Conversation; Order of the Day; Golden Advice L75
Dov Baer of Mezhirech C12, C19, L33
Dresner, Samuel H. L20, L34, L36, L39
Duties of the Heart see *Hovot ha-Levavot*

Early Masters L14
Eliach, Yaffa M14, M15
Eliezar of Worms C12, C13, G10
Elijah, Gaon of Vilna C12
Enoch, Book of C48, E1-E5, E11, E27, E36, E37
Epstein, Kalonymus Kalman C12, L39
Eschatology, legends of E6, E24
Etz Hayyim J6, J8

Primary Materials										361

"Experience of Mysticism"   M3
"Expositio Mercavae"   O10
Eybeschutz, Jonathan   K2
Ezekiel   C12, C16
Ezra, Book(s) of   E14, E16, E18, E28, E35

Fleer, Gedaliah   L44, L52
Fludd, Robert   O3
For the Sake of Heaven   L12
Frank, Jacob   K6
"From the Teachings of Habad Hasidism: Anecdote and Discourse" L24
"From the Teachings of Rav Kuk"   M1
From the Treasure House of Hassidism   L40
From the World of Rabbi Nahman of Bratzlav   L45

Garden of Hasidism   L29
Gates of Repentance   see *Shaarei Teshuvah*
Gems of Rabbi Nachman   L63
Giants   F26
Gikatilla, Joseph   C19, C20, D125
Golden Mountain: Marvellous Tales of Rabbi Israel, Baal Shem, and of His Great-Grandson, Rabbi Nachman   L5
Golden Tradition: Jewish Life and Thought in Eastern Europe   L38
Golem, legends of   D9, D11, D13, D14
Gorman, E.Z.   L50
Green, Arthur   L54, L70
Greenbaum, Avraham   L62

Halevi, Z'ev ben Shimon   M13
Handler, Andrew   L58
Hasidic Anthology: Tales and Teachings of the Hasidim   L8
Hasidic Tales of the Holocaust   M14, M15
"Hasidic Tales: Second Period--A Selection"   L17
"Hasidica: Stories and Sayings of the Ba'al Shem and Others"   L1
Hasidism, Breslover   L44, L62
Hasidism, Classical Period   L74
Hasidism, Lubavitcher   L24, L47, L50
Hasidism--Miscellaneous legends   C4, C8, C11, C18-C20, C48, D125, L1, L3, L8, L10, L12-L17, L20, L26, L27, L29, L30, L34-L36, L38, L39, L51, L53, L54, L58, L67, L69
L69
Hasidism, modern   M2, M5, M10, M12, M14, M15
Haye Olam Ha-Ba   H7
Hayim ben Isaac of Volozhin   C6, C19, L18
Heikhalot literature   D125
"Hell"   E6, E24
Helmont, Franciscus Mercurius van   O4, O5, O6, O8
High Ways to Perfection   G3
Hokhmath Ha-Egoz   G10
Holtz, Barry W.   L54
Holy Beggar Teachings: Jewish Hasidic Stories, 1975-1977   M12
Holy Letter: A Study in Medieval Jewish Sexual Morality Ascribed to Nahmanides   H6

Honey from the Rock: Visions of Jewish Mystical Renewal M8
Horowitz, Isaiah C13
Horowitz, Israel C9
Hoter ben Shelomo C20, H4
Hovot ha-Levavot G1, G2, G8
"How Satan Defeated Rabbi Israel in His Struggle against the False Messiah: A Tale of the Baal Shem" L6
"How the Rabbi of Kalev Freed a Song" L3

Ibn Gabirol, Solomon C13
Ibn Paquda, Bahya C19, G1, G2, G8
Iggeret Hakodesh H5, H6, L31
Iggeret Hateshuva L31
In Praise of the Ba'al Shem Tov L42
Isaac ben Moses Najara C10
Isaac Eizik of Komarno C12
Israel b. Eliezer (Ba'al Shem Tov), stories of C8, C12, C19, L1, L2, L4-L7, L9-L11, L19, L25, L28, L37, L42, L43, L48, L49, L68
L48, L49, L68

Jacob Joseph of Polonoye L20
Jacobs, Louis L33
Jewish Mysticism, and the Legend of Baalshem L4
Judah Loew of Prague C19, D11, D13

Kabbala Denudata I1, O9, O10
Kabbalah and Exodus M13
"Kaitz--The Time of Messianic Redemption: A Letter Attributed to Fraide, the Baal Hatanya's Daughter" L47
Kalisker, Abraham C8
Kaplan, Aryeh L46, L63, L64, L68
Kedushat Levi L36
Key of Solomon the King see *Mafteah Shelomo*
"King's Son and the Son of the Maid" L55
Klapholtz, Yisroel Yaakov L43
Koenig, Ester L59
Kook, Abraham Isaac C9, C19, M1, M3, M4, M6, M9
Kuntres Achron L31
Kuntres Uma'ayon Mibais Hashem L41
Kushner, Lawrence M7, M8

"Ladder from Man to God: Sayings of the Hasidim" L13
Lamm, Norman L48
Langer, Jiri M2, M10
Later Masters L14
Legend of the Baal-Shem L19
Legends of Our Time M5
Legends of the Bible F19
Legends of the Jews F8, F19
Leon, Moses de C10, C13
"Letter of the Besht to R. Gershon of Kutov" L48
Levi Yitzhak of Berdichev L36
Levin, Meyer L5, L6, L37

Primary Materials 363

Life and Sayings of the Baal Shem L7
Light Beyond: Adventures in Hassidic Thought L68
Light of Chanukah L60
Light of the Eyes L70
"Lights of Holiness" M9
"Lights of Penitence" M9
Likutey Moharan L63
Liqqutei Amarim see *Tanya*
Little Genesis see *Book of Jubilees*
Lost Apocrypha of the Old Testament E22
"Lost Princess" L71
Lubavitcher Rabbi's Memoirs L22
Luria, Isaac C10, C13, C16, C19, D125, J1, J5, J6, J8,
Luzzatto, Moses Hayyim C12, C19, J2, J3, J7, J8, J9

"Ma'amar Bosi L'Gani" L65
Ma'amar haIkkarim J9
"Ma'amar Hayosheves B'Gannim" L65
"Ma'amar Released for Bais Nissan, 5710" L65
"Ma'amar Released for Purim, 5710" L65
Ma'aseh Book D102
Mafteah Shelomo O11, O13, O14
Maggidim & Hasidim: Their Wisdom L30
Maimonides, Abraham G3, G5
Maimonides, Moses C12, C19, C20
"Man, the Master of All Created Worlds" L18
Maor Vashmesh L39
Margolis, Meir L11
Meckler, David L. L10
Menachem Mendel of Chernobyl C19
Menachem Mendel of Vitebsk C19
Mendel of Kotzk C8
"Merchant and the Pauper" L56
Merkavah mysticism D125, O10
Mesillat Yesharim J2
Messianism, miscellaneous texts D38, F18
Metzger, Alter B.Z. L47
Midot Harayah M9
Mintz, Jerome R. L42
Miracle Men: Tales of the Baal Shem and His Chassidim L10
Miscellaneous Metaphysical Essay O10
Molko, Solomon C10
"Moral Principles" M9
Mordechai of Chernobyl C19
More, Henry O2, O10
"More Tales of the Hasidim" L15
Mosaicall Philosophy O3
Mysticism, miscellaneous stories C1, C2, C4, C11, C14, C15, C17-C19

Nachman of Bratslav C14, C19, L5, L21, L26, L37, L44-L46, L52, L55-L57, L59, L61, L63, L64, L66, L68, L71, L72, L75
Nahmanides H2, H5, H6, H8

Nahum of Chernobyl   L70
Nathan of Gaza   K3
Nefesh Hahayim   C6, L18
Newman, Louis I.   L8, L30
Nine Gates to the Chassidic Mysteries   M2, M10

Old Testament Pseudepigrapha: Apocalyptic Literature and Testaments   E38
Orchot Tzaddikim   J5
Orot ha-Kodesh   M9
Orot ha-Teshuvah   M4, M9
Outpouring of the Soul   L64
Ozar Eden Ganuz   H1

Palm Tree of Deborah   see *Tomer Deborah*
"Paradise"   E6, E24
Paradoxal Discourses   O6
Path of the Names   H7
Path of the Upright   see *Mesillat Yesharim*
Philo Judaeus   C48, F1, F6, F11, F14, F16, F20, F22, F26,
Pirke de Rabbi Eliezer   F10
Pirkei Heikhalot   C16, C48
"Prayer-Book"   L9
Premishlaner, Maerl   L73
Principles of the Most Ancient and Modern Philosophy   O7

Question of Prophecy   H7

Rabbi Eizik: Hasidic Stories about the Zaddik of Kallo   L58
Rabbi Kook's Philosophy of Repentance: A Translation of "Orot ha-Teshuvah"   M4
Rabbi Nachman's Fire: An Introduction to Breslover Chassidus   L44
Rabbi Nachman's Foundation   L52
Rabbi Nachman's Wisdom: Shevachay HaRan, Sichos Haran   L46
Rabinowicz, Harry M.   L27
Ramban (Nahmanides): Writingss and Discourses   H8
Reb Maerl Premishlaner: His Life, Works and Divrei Torah   L73
"Reflections on Passover"   L32
Restore My Soul! Meshivat Nefesh   L62
Reuchlin, Johann   O15
Reuveni, David   C10
"Revelation of Moses"   E6
"Revelation of R. Joshua ben Levi"   E6
"Road to Renewal"   M6
Rosenberg, Judah Yudel   D9, D13
Roth, Aaron   C12
"Rules for the House of Study"   J3

"Sayings of the Baal-Shem-Tov"   L2
Schachter, Zalman M.   L35
Schneersohn, Joseph Isaac   L22, L65
Schneersohn, Shalom Dov Ber   L41
Schneerson, Menachem M.   L47, M11

Schwartz, Howard L71, L72
Schwartz, Tsila L71, L72
Seder Olam (of van Helmont) O8
Sefath Emeth L32, L60
Sefer Baal Shem Tov C9
Sefer Ha-Bahir C10, C13, C19, H9
Sefer ha-Hasiduth L11
Sefer Haminhagim: Chabad-Lubavitch Customs L50
Sefer Ha-Ot H7
Sefer Hasidim C19, G4, G6, G7, G9
Sefer Raziel Hamalaleh D7
Sefer Yetzirah C7, C13, C16, C19, F2, F4, F5, F9, F12, F15, F17, F21, F23-F25
"Sexual Purity and Redemption" L39
Shaar Hayihut Vehaemunah C6, L31
Shaarei Teshuvah H3
Sha'arei Zedek H7
Shabbetai Zevi C13
Shabbetaian documents K1, K3-K5
Shamblatt, Sanford D. L28
Sharabi, Shalom C12
Shevachay HaRan L46
Shick, Eleazer Shlomo L66
Shir Emunim K4
Shir Neeman K4
Shi'ur Komah C13, F27
Shneur Zalman of Liadi C6, C19, L23, L31, L68
Shomer Emunim C9
Sichos HaRan L46
Slave Who Saved the City, and Other Hassidic Tales L27
Solomon, King O11, O13, O14
Solomon ibn Adret C8
Solomon Shloemel ben Hayyim Meinstrl C8
"Spirit in Matter and Faith in Works" L36
"Sprouting of the Horn of the Son of David" K3
Steinman, Eliezer L29
Steinsaltz, Adin L55, L56, L61
Sufrin, A.D. L50
Susskind, Alexander C9, C12
Sword of Moses D6, D10

"Tale of the Menorah" L72
Tales of Angels, Spirits and Demons L26
Tales of Rabbi Nachman L21
Tales of the Baal Shem Tov L43
Tales of the Hasidim L14, L15
Tanya L31
"Tanya and the Gaon" L23
Tausk, Jacob C13
Ten Rungs: Hasidic Sayings L16
Testament of Abraham E26, E34
Testament of Isaac E26
"Testament of Israel Baal Shem Tov" L28

Testament of Jacob E26
Testament of Solomon D8
Testaments of the Twelve Patriarchs E8, E15, E23
Thirteen Stories of Rebbe Nachman of Breslev L59
Three Books of Occult Philosophy O1
Tiferet Yonatan K2
Tobit, legends of E10, E25
Tomer Deborah C6, J4
Touching Heaven, Touching Earth: Hassidic Humor & Wit L51
Tract on Ecstasy C12, L33
Treasury of Chassidic Tales on the Festivals: A Collection of Chassidic Stories Relevant to the Festivals L69
Treasury of Chassidic Tales on the Torah: A Collection of Inspirational Chassidic Stories Relevant to the Weekly Torah Readings L67
Tree of Life see *Etz Hayyim*
"Trip with Israel Baalshem" L11
Tsaraat HaRivash L28
Two Hundred Queries O5

Unger, Manasseh L3
Unterman, Alan L53
Upright Practices; The Light of the Eyes L70

Vidas, Elijah de C9, C13
Vital, Hayyim C9, C10, C12, C19, J5, J6, J8
Voice Calls out to God; Based on the Works of Rabbi Nachman of Breslov and His Holy Disciples L66

Ways of the Righteous see *Orchot Tzaddikim*
Weble, Gottlieb K1
Weiner, Herbert L23, L24
Wengrov, Charles L49
Wiesel, Elie D14, M5
Wisdom of Solomon C48
"Wisdom of the Chaldeans" F7, F13
Wisdom of the Jewish Mystics L53

Yohan ben Avraham of Gerona H3
Your Word is Fire: The Hasidic Masters on Contemplative Prayer L54

"Zaddik and the People: Teachings of Jacob Joseph of Polonoye" L20
Zevin, Shlomo Yosef L67, L69
Zohar C6-C12, C16, C19, C48, F17, I1-I18

Authors

Abbady, Isaac A.   K26
Abdul-Ali, Sijil   D64, D76, D91
Abelson, Joshua   C35, C36, D62, D63, D127, D129, E51, I6, O66
Abrahams, Israel   B58, O67
Achad, Frater   O62
Adams, Hannah   B17, B49
Adamson, J.H.   O117
Adler, Cyrus   A14, B27
Adler, H.   K14
Adolf, Helen   O99
Agus, Irving A.   G28
Agus, Jacob B.   B69, B73, D61, D144, I8, M21, M52, M84
Aland, Kurt   A39
Alazraki, Jaime   O141, O145, O152
Albert, Ada Rapoport   L213, L263
Albertson, Edward   C61, D70
Alexander, P.S.   F78
Alfassi, Yitzhak   L188
Allen, John   B50
Alter, Robert   A99, K35, N58, N61,
Altmann, Alexander   A40, A53, A65, A71, A109, A119, B36, D66-D68, D92, D97, F42, F43, G10, G18, G27, H21, H24, H27, H30, H31, H33-H36, J38, N2
Ansari, Asloob Ahmad   O133
Antin, David   L26
Applebaum, S.   L237
Applefeld, Aharon   L45
Arden, Harvey   L226
Arendt, Hannah   A102, D45, D58
Arenson, Sara   G8
Aron, Milton   L189
Asher, D.   K9
Ashlag, Yehuda   I30, J23, J30
Auerbach, Uri   L73
Averbach, Charles   N18
Avidor, Shmuel Hacohen   L51

Baeck, Leo   A28, C51, F45, O105
Baer, Richard A., Jr.   F62
Baer, Yitzhak   B75
Bakan, David   D153, D154, D156
Baldwin, James Mark   B26
Bamberger, Bernard Jacob   D133, F40
Band, Arnold J.   L57, L265, L278
Banes, Daniel   O159, O182
Bardon, Franz   O113
Baron, Salo W.   A26, A43, B68, B71
Barrett, Francis   O16
Bar-Yaacov, Lois   L227

Barzilay, Isaac J27
Baskerville, Beatrice C. B59
Basnage, Jacques B43
Baumgardt, David A54
Bayer, Bathja L222
Bayley, Harold O47
Belmaker, Robert H. A110
Ben-Amos, Dan L42
Benamozegh, E. F29
Benbow, R. Mark O118
Benedict, Libby N5
Ben-Horin, Meir A50, D151, M40, N37
Benn, Nathan L226
Bennett, Allen O48
Ben-Sasson, H.H. A77, B97
Ben-Shlomo, Joseph B162, N59
Bension, Ariel I26, L95
Ben Zion, Raphael C6
Ben-Zvi, Itzhak K26
Berg, Philip S. C75, C77, I30
Berger, Abraham D49, L200
Berger, Alan L266, M117
Berger, Peter L. A115
Berger, Rhonda Edna M118
Bergman, Hugo N20
Bergmann, Samuel Hugo B76, M32
Berk, Fred A46, L227
Berlin, Charles A78
Berman, Dennis L257
Bernheimer, Carlo K16
Bevan, Edwyn R. A15
Biale, David M154, N64, N67
Bilu, Yoram D170
Bin Gorion, Emanuel C11
Bin Gorion, Micha C11
Binion, Samuel A. C28, C29
Birnbaum, Irene L7
Birnbaum, Salomo L7
Bischoff, Erich O200
Bjerregaard, C.H.A. O39
Black, M. E80
Bland, Kalman P. J29
Blau, Joseph L. A43, B38, B78, N7, O89, O97, O98
Blavatsky, Helena P. O25, O27, O36, O68, O83, O88
Bleeker, C. Jouco A76
Bloch, Chaim D9, J1
Bloch, Joshua E56, L107
Block, Irving L173
Blomster, W.V. M65
Bloom, Harold C66, M104, M105, M158
Blumenthal, David R. C16, C20, D1, F87, H4, H40, H41
Bokser, Ben Zion C19, D27, J18, J32, M6, M9, M36, M55, M91, M96, M119

Authors

Borchardt, Anne D14
Borchsenius, Poul B83
Borges, Jorge Luis A90
Borowitz, Eugene B. J28
Bosk, Charles L. L219, M137
Bosman, Leonard A. O49, O51
Bouwsma, William J. O108, O114
Bouyer, Louis B72
Bowers, Margaretta K. D109
Bowker, J.W. F65
Box, George H. B62, D130, E16, E18, E19, E26, O75
Boyile, Veolia J. O58
Brandon, S.G.F. A85
Breslauer, S. Daniel N38, N68
Bridger, David B35
Bridges, Hal B90
Bronstein, Leo O195
Bronznick, Norman M. F61
Brown, Francis A4
Brown, Moshe L60
Broyde, Isaac B27
Buber, Martin A27, A29, A41, A47, A66, D46, D56, D132, K20, K27, L1, L2, L4, L9, L12-L17, L19, L21, L25, L26, L40, L110, L111, L113-L119, L121, L124, L135-L137, L146-L154, L167, L174, L243, M33-M35, N5, N9, N13, N14, N19
Büchler, Adolph F34
Budge, E.A. Wallis O79
Bulka, Reuven P. A106, D161, D171
Bullivant, B.M. M128
Burkitt, F. Crawford E44
Burnet, Thomas B46
Butler, E.M. O103
Butler, W.E. O121
Buttenwieser, Moses F31

Cahn, Zvi B79
Caithness, Marie O31
Calmet, Augustin B16
Caplan, Samuel I8
Carlebach, Shlomo M12
Carmell, L. D79
Casanowicz, I.M. D18, D19
Castiglioni, Arturo D25
Casway, R. O10
Cavendish, Richard B38, O129, O153
Chambers, Ephraim B15
Chamier, D. O43
Charles, R.H. E5, E9, E12, E13, E15, E17, E20, E21
Charlesworth, James H. E38
Chasen, Simon L9
Chavel, Charles B. H8, L126, L220
Cherbonnier, E. La B. N51
Chernus, Ira F85

Chiel, Arthur A.   A103, O142
Cleghorn, Spencer   D181
Cohen, Arthur A.   A74, M72, M80, N8
Cohen, Gerson D.   D51
Cohen, Lucy   L4
Cohen, Martin Samuel   F27
Cohen, Mortimer J.   K21
Cohen, Seymour J.   H6, J5
Cohen, Simon   B31
Cohn, Jacob   F50, F57
Cohn-Sherbok, Dan   F86
Collins, Edwin   G1
Collins, John J.   D146, E82, E83
Colson, F.H.   F14
Colson, John   B16
Colville, W.J.   O52
Constant, Alphonse Louis   see Levi, Eliphas
Conybeare, F.C.   D8, E7, E41, F6
Cook, Roger   O154
Copenhaver, Brian P.   O177, O196
Costa, Isaac da   B53
Coudert, Allison   O160, O172
Couzin, Robert   D159
Covey-Crump, W.W.   O55
Criswell, K.A.C.   D74
Cronbach, Abraham   G4
Cross, F.L.   A39
Cross, Frank Moore   A96
Crouzet, Francois   A77
Curtis, C.J.   N27

Dagut, M.B.   L196
Daiches, Samuel   D17
Dale, Rodney   I17, O186
Damon, S. Foster   A73
Dan, Joseph   A117, C76, D81, D83, D123, F58, F81, G23, G29, G32, G34, L74
Dann, Charles A.   B22
Dannhauser, Shoshana   G8
Dannhauser, Werner J.   A98
Davidson, Israel   L84
Davies, Ann   O161
Davies, W.D.   N60
Dawidowicz, Lucy S.   L38
Deane, William J.   F3
Defries, Michael   O156
De Haas, Jacob   B30
Dekro, J.   M155
Denning, Melita   O162
Deutsch, Gotthard   B29
Dicker, Herman   M156
Dimont, Max I.   B80
Diserens, Charles M.   D21

Authors

Doppelt, Frederic A.   L100
Doreal, M.   F15
D'Oyly, Samuel   B16
Dreifuss, Gustav   D150
Dresner, Samuel H.   L20,   L34, L36, L39, L155, L221, L245, L267, L272, N55
Drury, Nevill   O146
Dubnow, Semen M.   B60, B64, B85
Duff, Archibald   E14
Duker, Abraham G.   K24, K30, K33, K42, K51
Duncan, A.D.   O134
Duncan, J. Ann   O155
Dupont-Sommer, A.   E31, E57, E60

Eban, Abba   B87
Edersheim, Alfred   F4, F28
Edwards, Paul   B38
Efros, Israel Isaac   A86, D106, H18, H38
Ehrmann, Naftali Hertz   L239
Eichler, M.M.   L82
Eisenmenger, Johann Andreas   B45
Eliach, Yaffa   L183, M14, M15
Eliade, Mircea   A72
Ellinger, Moritz   D39
Elmen, Paul   M138
Ember, Aaron   A14
Encausse, Gerard   see Papus
Enelow, H.G.   D103, D119
Enfield, William   B47
Epstein, Isidore   A25, B74
Epstein, Perle   C69, M139, M140, O135
Erling, B.   E77
Etheridge, John Wesley   B54
Ettinger, S.   A77, L184, L201
Ettish, Ernst E.   see Rosh-Pinnah, Eliyahu
Evans, Henry Ridgely   O56
Eybeschutz, Jonathan   K2
Ezra, N.E.B.   K13

Fackenheim, Emil L.   A68, L185
Fadiman, Clifton P.   J1, L2
Faierstein, Morris M.   B14, H44, L283
Falk, Avner   K48
Fallon, Francis T.   F80
Farwell, Arthur   D148
Fearnsides, W.E.   K18
Fehl, Philipp   M92
Fehr, Bernhard   O59
Feldman, Louis H.   M24
Feldman, Ron H.   A102
Ferguson, John   B42
Ferm, Vergilius   B32
Fine, Lawrence   J39, J40

Finkel, Bruria H7
Finkel, Joshua F51, L109, L132
Finkelstein, Louis A31
Finn, James B52
Firth, Violet Mary see Fortune, Dion
Fishbane, Michael A. A92
Fitzmyer, Joseph A. B10
Fleer, Gedaliah L44, L52
Fletcher, Harris Francis O110
Flohr, Paul R. A92
Fluegel, Maurice D40, I20
Folberg, Neil L228
Fortune, Dion O91
Franck, Adolphe C39
Frank, Joseph A54
Franken, Hendricus Jacobus E61
Franklyn, Julian O92
Freehof, Solomon B. A58
Frenkel, Isser M59
Friedhaber, Zvi L227
Friedlander, Gerald F10, G13
Friedman, Devorah L247
Friedman, H.G. B27
Friedman, Irving F25
Friedman, Jerome O149
Friedman, Maurice A66, L19, L21, M41, M85, N13-N15, N21, N28, N45
Frisch, Ephraim A2
Frost, Stanley Brice E58
Fuller, J.F.C. C43, O94
Fullick, Patrick O156
Funkenstein, Amos H45

Garstin, E.J. Langford I27
Garvin, Philip M72
Gasler, M [Gaster?] L89
Gaster, Moses A12, B28, C27, D6, D10, D102, E6, E8, E10, E23-E25, F7, F13, I21, I24, I25, K12, L88, L96
Gaster, Theodor H. E29
Gaynor, Frank B33
Gealy, Marcia B. M141
Gelber, S. Michael L244
Gelberman, Joseph H. D158
Gellerman, Jill L227, M120
Gersh, Harry B88, M37
Gerson, Jessica M159
Gewurz, Elias C3, O53, O63
Ginsburg, Christian D. B20, B24, B25, C25,
Ginsburg, Elliott D124
Ginzberg, Louis A16, A37, B27, C53, D93, E46, F8, F19, L97
Ginzburg, Simon J14
Givry, Grillot de O84
Glasner, Samuel D109
Glasson, T.F. E63

Glatzer, Nahum N.   A92, C8, F18, F22, I11, J3, M142, N46
Glazerson, Mattithias   D122
Glitzenstein, Abraham C.   L177
Godbey, J.E.   C40
Godman, Stanley   D46
Godwin, David   O188
Godwin, Joscelyn   O189, O190
Goffin, Alan J.   O156, O164
Goitein, S.D.   G5, G15, G16, G24
Goldin, Judah   A75
Goldman, Norman Saul   D82
Goldmerstein, L.   D7
Goldziher, Ignace   A30,
Golffing, Francis C.   L124
Gollancz, Hermann   O13, O45
Gonzalez-Wippler, Migene   M97
Goodenough, Erwin Ramsdell   A69, D26, F39, F41, F44, F46
Goodman, Martin   O15
Goodman, Ruth   N39
Goodman, Walter   M29
Gordis, Robert   A84
Gordon, Haim   M98, M121
Gordon, Hirsch Loeb   D149, J17, L90
Gordon, Nathan   L83
Gorman, E.Z.   L50
Gotlieb, Phyllis   L229
Gourary, S.   M23
Graetz, Heinrich Hirsch   B57, B61
Gratus, Jack   K43
Gray, William G.   O132, O178, O201
Green, Arthur   L54, L70, L230, L240, L258, L273, L279, M129
Greenbaum, Avraham   L62
Greenberg, Hayim   A33, K25
Greenberg, Louis   B70
Greene, William B.   O22
Greenstone, Julius H.   D41
Grossman, Mordecai   M16
Gruenwald, Ithamar   E95, F66, F70, F71, F74, F79, F83, F88
Gundersheimer, Werner L.   O119
Gutwirth, Jacques   M86, M130

Hadju, Andre   L222
Halevi, Z'ev ben Shimon   C68, C71, D77, M13, M99, M111, O183
Halkin, Hillel   K38, K39
Hall, Manly P.   O69, O77, O115, O122
Halperin, David G.   F84
Hambloch, Ernest   O93
Handler, Andrew   L58
Hanegbi, Yehuda   L55, L56, L61, L225
Hanson, Paul D.   E75, E76, E84, E86
Harper, Robert Francis   A4
Harper, William Rainey   A4
Harris, Michael H.   C2

Harris, Monford   G17, G20, H25, M73
Hastings, James   B28
Haupt, Paul   A14
Heckethorn, Charles William   C26
Heifetz, Harold   A104
Heinemann, Isaak   F20
Heinemann, Joseph   A79
Heline, Corinne   O136
Heller, Bernard   M20
Hellwig, Monika K.   N40
Hengel, Martin   E81
Herbert, L.M.   L90
Hersch, Emil G.   J12
Hershon, Paul Isaac   C1
Hertz, Joseph Herman   A10, A21, A25, C38, C44, E47, E54
Herzog, Elizabeth   L125
Heschel, Abraham J.   C50,   C62, E66, L207, L214, L245, M25, M30, M149
Hilburg, Erwin   L215
Hills, Gordon P.G.   K15
Hilsenrad, Zalman Aryeh   L179
Hinnells, John R.   A85
Hirsch, Samuel Abraham   A8, C31, O38
Hirschman, Jack   D32, G10, H7
Hirst, Desiree   O123
Hodson, Geoffrey   O198
Hoeller, Stephan A.   O163
Hoffman, Edward   D177, D179, D180, D183
Holroyd, Stuart   O173
Holtz, Barry W.   L54
Hook, Walter Farquhar   B19
Hooke, S.H.   A19, E52
Horodetzky, Samuel A.   L98, L99
Horodetzky-Magasanik, Maria   L99
Horovitz, Bela   A40
Horowitz, Michael   I14
Hort, Greta   L113, L118
Howard, Michael   O184
Hruby, K.   H37
Hunt, John   D73
Hurwitz, Siegmund   D150, L186
Hutin, Serge   O191
Hyamson, Moses   G2

Idelsohn, A.Z.   L101
International Order of Kabbalists   O156, O164
Isaacs, A.S.   J10
Isaacs, Stephen   M100, M122
Isbell, Charles D.   D12

Jacob, Walter   A58
Jacobs, Joseph   O57
Jacobs, Louis   B6-B8, B40, C9, C12, C55, D72, D78, D86, D113, F47, J4, L33, L178, L208, L231, L246, L259

Jacobs, Noah J.   N34
Jacobson, David C.   M131
James, Laura De Witt   O111
James, Montague Rhodes   E22
Jennings, Hargrave   O20
Jochnowitz, George   M63
Johnson, Harry M.   M137
Jolly, Stephen   M2
Jones, Charles Robert Stansfeld   see Achad, Frater
Jones, Rufus M.   C46
Joseph, Morris   G12
Jospe, Alfred   B76
Jospe, Eva   N41
Jospe, Raphael   A116
Josten, C.H.   O124
Jung, Leo   A35, A51, L260

Kadushin, Max   B82
Kahana, Boaz   M74
Kahann, A.   L11
Kalir, Joseph   D145
Kalisch, Isador   F2, F36
Kantor, Mattis   M132
Kaplan, Abraham   L232
Kaplan, Aryeh   D125, H9, J9, L46, L63, L64, L68
Kaplan, Chaim   E50
Kaplan, Edward K.   N52
Kaplan, Lawrence   D126
Kaplan, Mordecai M.   J2
Kaplan, Nathaniel   B89
Kaploun, Ari   L67, L69
Kasher, Menahem M.   A51
Kastein, Joseph   K17
Katsaros, Thomas   B89
Katsh, Abraham I.   A108
Katz, Jacob   B77, G19
Katz, John   L194
Katz, Shlomo   A33
Katz, Steven T.   A105, A120, A121, D2-D5, D71, N42, N53, N48
Katzenstein, Julius   see Kastein, Joseph
Katzoff, Louis   L143
Kaufman, William E.   C72, M106, N43
Kaufmann, David   G11
Kaufmann, Walter   A48, N22
Kavler, Vigdor W.   A58
Kazis, Israel J.   L133
Kedourie, Elie   B99
Kegan, Judith   M44
Kegan, Robert   M112
Kelley, Maurice   O90
Kenealy, Edward V.H.   E3
Kenton, Warren   see Halevi, Z'ev ben Shimon

Kertzer, Morris N.   B86
Kiev, I. Edward   A78
Kilman, Wolfe   A103
Kinzie, Mary   A90
Kiraly, Bela K.   A93
Kirsch, James   L242, L261, L262
Kitagawa, Joseph M.   A72
Kitto, John   B20
Klapholtz, Israel Jacob   D89, L43, L247
Klein, A.M.   A94
Klein, Zanvel E.   N54
Knapp, Bettina L.   D178, L274
Knibb, Michael A.   E37
Knight, Charles   B21
Knight, Gareth   O127, O165
Kobak, Dorothy   D158
Koenig, Ester   L59
Kohler, Kaufmann   A7, B27, D20, E42, E43
Kohn, Hans   N4
Kohut, George Alexander   O44
Kolenkow, Anitra Bingham   E87
Kopp, Sheldon B.   L190
Korn, Y.   L275
Kostelanetz, Richard   N62
Krabbenhoft, Kenneth   J41
Krakovsky, Levi Isaac   C52, J15, M18
Kramer, Simon G.   G6
Kramer, William M.   D120
Kranzler, Gershon   L120, M45, M87
Kraushar, A.   K6
Kravitz, Nathaniel   C10
Kuperstok, Nathan   D163, D172
Kushner, Lawrence   M7, M8, M157

Lachs, Samuel Tobias   A80, F67
La Dage, Alta J.   O185
Lai, Whalen W-L.   L248
Lamm, Norman   A51, A87, L48, L187, L233, M81
Landman, Isaac   B31
Landsman, J.I.   E19
Langer, Jiri   M2, M10
Lantero, Erminie Huntress   D140
Lapson, Dvora   L105, L157
Lask, I.M.   C11, H1
La Sor, William   E67
Laurence, Richard   E1
Lauterbach, Jacob Z.   D105
Lavender, Abraham D.   A100
Lazarus, J.G.   L77
Lazarus, Montague R.   O32
Lehmann, O.H.   H22
Leiningen, C. de   D84
Leiter, Samuel   F72

Authors

Lemke, Werner E.   A96
Lenowitz, Harris   K6
Leof, Haim   L227
Lesser, Alfred J.   O164
Leveen, Jacob   K22
Leventhal, Herbert   O174
Levertoff, Paul P.   I6, I28, L91-L93
Lévi, Eliphas   O50, O150, O157
Levin, Meyer   L5, L6, L37
Levine, Baruch A.   B91
Levine, Ephraim   A25
Lewis, Geoffrey L.   K31
Lewis, Thomas   B44
Lewisohn, Ludwig   L12
Lewy, Hans   F16
L'Hoste Ranking, D.F. de   O42
Lieber, David   H46
Lieberman, Saul   F48, F83
Linder, Gary   D88
Lipschitz, Max A.   L180
Loewe, H.   B28
Loewe, Raphael   A60, A109, F55
Loewenstamm, Samuel E.   E88, E89
Long, Charles H.   A72
Lookstein, Joseph H.   N49
Lowenkopf, Anne N.   L216
Lowinger, Samuel   A30
Lowy, Bella   B57

Maccoby, Hyam   L268, N69
Mackey, Albert G.   O23
Mahler, Raphael   B92, L106
Mailer, Norman   L170
Maimes, Steven L.   M12
Maimon, Solomon   L79
Maller, Allen S.   C78
Manashe, Abraham   M143
Mandel, Arthur   K45
Manhar, Nurho de   I4, I18
Manheim, Ralph   L154
Mansoor, Menahem   G8, G31
Marcus, Ivan G.   G26, G33, G35-G37
Marcus, Jacob R.   C5, O138
Margoliouth, George   H13
Margolis, Meir   L11
Margolius, Hans   L158
Mark, Faygah   M66
Marmonstein, A.   H15
Marmorstein, Jenny   J8
Martin, Bernard   B93, B96, D141
Marx, Alexander   H14
Marx, Olga   L14, L16
Marx, Tzvi   M144

Mathers, L. Liddell MacGregor   I1, I12, I16, O11, O12
Mathews, Shailer   B29
Matt, Daniel Chanan   H42
Mattuck, Israel I.   A38
Maurice, Thomas   B48
Mayne, Seymour   A94
Mazor, Yaacov   L222
McCaul, Alexander   L76
McClelland, David C.   D155
McClintock, John   B23
McCown, C.C.   E48
McKeon, Michael   K44
Meckler, David L.   L10
Meltzer, David   C13, H7
Menes, Abraham   J16
Merchant, Carolyn   O192
Metraux, Guy S.   A77
Metzger, Alter B.Z.   L47, L237, M4
Meyer, Michael   N12
Milik, J.T.   E36
Millar, William R.   E90
Miller, Arlene A.   O139
Miller, Laurel   O61
Miller, Patrick D.   A96
Miller, Sam   M37
Milman, Henry Hart   B51
Mindel, Nissan   L22, L31, L112, L191
Minkin, Jacob S.   B31, C47, L104
Minkowski, Helmut   A54
Mintz, Jerome R.   L42, M64, M123, M145
Mitchell, Douglas   M107
Montefiore, C.G.   E40, F33
Montgomery, James A.   D128
Moonan, Willard   B13
Moore, Edward   O46
Moore, George Foot   A4, O54, O64
Moran, James A.   N35
Mordell, Phineas   F9, F37
Morfill, W.R.   E11
Morley, Henry   O18, O41
Morris, Frances A.   O164
Morris, George S.   B56
Moskowitz, Ira   M95, M115
Mosse, George L.   N29
Müller, Ernst   B31, C48
Murray, Edward   E2
Myer, Isaac   H10, I2
Myer, Michael   K37
Myers, Jacob M.   E35

Nadler, Allan L.   M160
Nagel, Hildegard   D150, L186
Nahon, Gerard   A111

Authors

Nauert, Charles G, Jr., O128
Nemoy, Leon   A108
Netanyahu, B.   H19
Neubauer, Adolf   B1, B2, H11
Neugroschel, Joachim   C14
Neuman, Abraham A.   A50
Neusner, Jacob   A69, A83, A89, B91, F49, F52, F53, F63, F68, F73
Newman, Beth S.   O166
Newman, Charles   A90
Newman, Eugene   J26
Newman, Jacob   H2
Newman, Louis I.   L8, L30, L144, O70
Nickelsburg, George W.E., Jr.   A97, E78, E91, E92, E94, E98
Nicolson, Marjorie H.   O76, O80, O81
North, Robert   E79
Novek, Simon   A44, A55, A56
Noy, Dov   A79, A113

Odeberg, Hugo   E27
O'Dell, Jerry   E64
Oesterley, William O.E.   B62, E5, E28, E53
Olan, Levi A.   D87
Old, Walter Gorn   see Sephariel
Oliver, Roy   N25, N33
Olsvanger, Immanuel   L116
Oppenheim, Michael   N47
Orent, Joel   L159
Ostow, Mortimer   A118, K47, K49

Pancoast, Seth   O26, O28, O29
Papus   O179
Parkinson, Thomas   O106
Parrinder, Geoffrey   B98
Passow, Isidore David   A80
Pasternak, Velvel   L202, L209
Patai, Raphael   C18, D38, D134, D135, D138, D142, J31
Patterson, D.   L160, L175
Peli, Pinchas Hakohen   L249
Perlmutter, Philip   L127
Petuchowski, Jakob J.   E99, N50
Pfuetze, Paul E.   N6
Philipson, David   A13
Phillips, Osborne   O162
Pick, Bernhard   C32, C34, C37, I22
Pike, Albert   O21
Pilcher, E.J.   D16
Pines, S.   E74
Pinsker, Sanford   L192, M76, M108
Pinson, Koppel S.   L108
Ploeg, Jean van der   E65
Plotnicov, Leonard   M107
Podhoretz, Norman   A61
Poinsot, M.C.   O96

Polen, N. D35
Poll, Solomon M50, M56
Ponce, Charles C63, O167
Popenoe, Cris B11
Poppers, Harry L. L129
Porter, Frank Chamberlain F32
Posner, Zalman I. L31, L41, L171, M38, M39, M133
Potok, Chaim M109, N16
Poupko, Bernard Aaron A22
Power, J.H. D75
Praag, H.M. van A110
Prager, Moshe M150
Pratt, Henry O33
Puech, Henri-Charles A88
Pullen-Burry, Henry Burry O71
Pye, Faye L234

Rabinovich, Wolf Zeev L122, L196
Rabinowicz, Harry M. B84, C58, L27, L145, L161, L195, M161
Rabinowitz, Isaac E59
Raddock, Charles M77
Rajneesh, Bhagwan Shree M113, M134
Rakeffet-Rothkoff L276
Raphael, Chaim L238
Raphall, Morris J. C21
Rappoport, Elana M12
Raskin, Saul C7, F17
Redgrove, H. Stanley D22
Rees, Abraham B15
Regardie, Israel O86, O87, O193
Regensberg, Chaim David A20
Reimer, Jack L168
Reinharz, Jehuda A119
Revel, Bernard A22
Rexroth, Kenneth A45, A49, C41, C56, N10
Rhine, A.B. B61
Ribalow, Harold U. I8
Richardson, Alan O158
Ripley, George B22
Rivlin, Leanne G. M162
Roback, A.A. D147
Robbin, Edward L3
Robinson, Ira J35
Rodal, Alti B. F89
Roditi, Edouard M146
Rose, Neal L197
Rosenberg, D. C23
Rosenberg, Harold M22
Rosenberg, Roy A. I15
Rosenberg, Ruth M151
Rosenblatt, Samuel G3
Rosenfeld, Alvin H. A73
Rosenfeld, Leonard A51

Authors

Rosenne, Shabtai K2
Rosenthal, Erwin I.J. A23
Rosenthal, Franz H17
Rosenthal, Judah A62
Rosh-Pinnah, Eliyahu F59
Rotenberg, Mordechai D182, L250
Rotenstreich, Nathan N63
Roth, Cecil A25, A52, A63, B34, K31, K32
Roth, Leon A60
Rothenberg, Jerome C17, L26
Rothschild, Fritz B9
Rouner, Leroy S. A122
Rowland, Christopher E96
Rowley, H.H. E55
Ruach, Joseph E45
Rubenstein, Avraham B40
Rubin, A. G22
Rubin, Israel M53, M88, M124
Rubinsohn, Theoph. I19
Rubinstein, Aryeh L235
Rudavsky, David M60, M147, N23
Runes, Dagobert D. I12
Russell, D.S. E62, E68, E71, E72

Sachar, Abram Leon B65
Safier, Judah D164, D173
Safran, Alexandre C67
Saldarini, Anthony J. F82
Salomon, H.P. K4
Sarachak, Joseph H16
Sassoon, George I17, O186
Saurat, Denis B67, O65, O72, O78, O82
Schachter, Haim L29
Schachter, Zalman B5, D165, D166, D174, D183, L35, M42, M43, M46, M110, M164
Schaeder, Grete N34
Schatz-Uffenheimer, Rivka B40, L181, L198, L210, L251, N24
Schauffler, William G. K10
Schaya, Leo C60
Schealtiel, Nochum J. M82, M93
Schechter, Abraham I. A18, D104
Schechter, Solomon A1, A5, A11, A42, F30, G14, H12, J11, J20, J24, K11, L78, L80, L81, L85, L138-L140
Schiffman, Lawrence H. D34, E100, E101, F77
Schiller, Mordechai L277
Schilpp, Paul Arthur A66
Schimmel, Solomon J34
Schindler, Pesach M94
Schmidt, Nathaniel E49
Schneersohn, Joseph I. L22, L171, M19, M38, M39
Schneerson, Menachem M. L252
Schnur, Harry C. A32, K23
Schochet, Jacob Immanuel L31, L169, L177, L223, M89

Schodde, George H.   E4
Scholem, Gershom G.   A59, A67, A81, A98, B3, B40, C45, C49, C57,
    C59, C64, C65, D28-D30, D33, D36, D43, D47, D53, D54, D65, D69,
    D80, D85, D94, D95, D98-D100, D110, D112, D114-D117, D131, D136,
    D137, D139, F48, F56, F75, H7, I5, I7, I9, K1, K3, K5, K28, K36-
    K39, K41, L123, L193, L203, L204, M17, M47, M61, M78, M83, M101,
    M114, N12, N17, N30, N31, N36, N65, N66
Schorsch, Ismar   J36
Schreiber, Mordecai   M67
Schrire, T.   D31
Schultz, Joseph P.   L217
Schulze, Wilhelm August   O130
Schurer, Emil   E39
Schutz, Albert L.   O197
Schwartz, Dannel I.   L224
Schwartz, F. Schneider   O116
Schwartz, Frederick C.   A58
Schwartz, Howard   L71, L72, L280
Schwartz, Leo W.   A24, C4, L11
Schwartz, Tsila   L72
Schwarzschild, Steven S.   B4
Secret, Francois   O125
Seid, Marsha   L227
Seligmann, Kurt   O102
Seltzer, Robert M.   B100
Semi, Emanuela Trevisan   M135
Sephariel   O202
Serkez, Kalman David   L66
Shaffer, Carolyn R.   N26
Shaffir, William   M102
Shahar, Shulamith   H43
Shahn, Ben   I10
Shamblatt, Sanford D.   L28
Shamir, Yehuda   D59, J25
Shapero, Lillian   L227
Shapira, Abraham   M114
Shapiro, David S.   L32, L182
Sharf, A.   H39
Sharot, Stephen   D90, L269
Sharpe, Eric J.   A85
Shatzmiller, Joseph   G38
Shauli, A.   L162
Shazar, Zalman   L176
Sheridan, Judith Rinde   M163
Sherwin, Byron L.   J37, M69, M90
Shick, Eleazer Shlomo   L66, L270
Shiloah, Amnon   D121
Shinan, Avigdor   A101
Shmueli, Efraim   M68
Shulvass, Moses A.   A64
Siegel, Seymour   B9
Silber, Saul   A20
Silberschlag, Eisig   B94, L205

Silver, Abba Hillel   A57, D42
Silver, Daniel Jeremy   A57, B96
Silverstein, Shraga   H3
Simon, Leon   A6
Simon, Maurice   I6
Simonsohn, S.   K29
Singer, Charles   A15
Singer, Isaac Bashevis   M62, M95, M115
Singer, Isidore   B27
Singer, June   D160
Singer, Merrill   M136, M152
Singer, Sholom Alchanan   G7, G9, G21
Skehan, Patrick W.   E97
Skinner, J. Ralston   O24, O30
Skinner, Stephen   O146
Smith, Gerald Birney   B29
Smith, Morton   D57, F54
Smith, Richard Furnald   O168
Smith, William   B25
Smithals, Walter   E85
Sokolow, N.   K6
Soloveitchik, Haym   G25, G30
Soltes, Mordecai   A36
Somogyi, Joseph   A30
Sosnowski, Saul   O151, O180
Spence, Lewis   O60
Spencer, Sidney   B81
Sperber, Daniel   F60
Sperling, Harry   C33, I6, L86
Spero, Moshe Ha Levi   D167, D175
Spiegel, Irving   M116, M125
Spiegel, Moshe   B85
Spiegel, Shalom   A17, J13, L102
Spitz, Lewis W.   O112, O120
Spitz, Samuel   L8, L30
Stace, W.T.   N11
Stahl, Abraham   M148
Starr, Joshua   A34
Steele-Smith, William   O100
Stehelin, John Peter   B45
Stein, Siegfried   A109
Steinberg, A.   D44
Steinberg, Harry   M103, M126
Steindletz, E.   D157
Steinman, Eliezer   L29
Steinsaltz, Adin   C70, C74, D118, D143, L55, L56, L61, L225, L271
Steinschneider, Moritz   B55
Stenring, Knut   F12
Stern, J.P.   A112
Stern, S.M.   I29
Sternglass, Ernest J.   A54
Stirling, William   O40
Stone, Michael E.   E34, E69, E73, E93

Story, William W.   O19
Straughn, R.A.   O169, O175
Strong, James   B23
Strugnell, J.   E30
Sturzaker, Doreen   O164, O170
Sturzaker, James   O143, O164, O170, O187
Suares, Carlo   F24, O140, O147
Sufrin, A.D.   L50
Swetschinski, Daniel   A119
Swietlicki, Catherine   O199
Swinborne, Sylvia M.   O156, O164
Syrkin, A.   L264

Talmage, Frank   A113, A117
Taubes, Jacob   D60
Taylor, C.   B16
Tepfer, John J.   N3
Teshima, Jacob Yuroh   L253, L254
Thieberger, Frederic   D11
Tilden, Frank William   F11
Tishby, I.   J19
Touati, Charles   A111
Touger, Eliyahu   L65
Trachtenberg, Joshua   D23, D24
Tsur, Muki   M114
Twersky, Isadore   H26

Ueberweg, Frederich   B56
Uffenheimer, Rivka Schatz   see Schatz-Uffenheimer, Rivka
Unger, Manasseh   L3, L163
Unnik, W.C. van   A91
Unterman, Alan   L53
Urbach, Ephraim E.   A67, F64
Ury, Zalman F.   L199
Urzidil, Johannes   M153

Vajda, Georges   A111, B40, D96, H20
Van der Heide, A.   D101
Van der Horst, Pieter   E102
Van der Naillen, Albert   O73
Vermes, Geza   E32, F69
Vermes, Pamela   N32
Vernoff, Charles   M51

Wace, Henry   B25
Wacholder, Ben Zion   K50
Wagner, Stanley M.   A116
Waite, Arthur Edward   C30, C41, D15, I23, O74
Walker, Roy   see Oliver, Roy
Wallace, Edwin R.   D168
Wallman, Joseph   C54
Walters, James W.   N44
Wandycz, Damian S.   A123

Authors

Warner, Charles Dudley B129
Wassilevsky, I. L87
Waton, Harry C42, O107
Waugh, Daniel Clarke K46
Waxman, Meyer A62, B66
Waxman, Ruth B. A84
Webster, Nesta H. B63
Weinberg, Bernard M127
Weiner, Herbert L23, L24, M1, M26, M28, M31, M48, M49, M54, M57, M70, M71, M79
Weinryb, Bernard D. A50, B95
Weiss, J.G. H23, L128, L130, L134, L141, L142, L164, L165
Wengrov, Charles L49
Werblowsky, R.J. Zwi A67, A76, B37, B39, B99, D48, D52, D55, D152, J21, J22, J33, K41, L218, N56, O109
Werner, Alfred L166
Westcott, Wm. Wynn F5, O9, O34, O35, O37, O203
Weston, Warren O95
Whitaker, G.H. F14
White, Anne O14
White, Nelson O14
Widengren, Geo A82, E70
Wieczynski, Joseph L. O171
Wiesel, Elie D14, L206, L211, L212, L255, L281, M5,
Wiesel, Marion L212, L281
Wigoder, Geoffrey B37
Wijnhoven, Jochanan H.A. B12, H28, I31, N57
Wilensky, Mordecai L. L131, L172, L236
Wilensky, Sara O. Heller H29, H32
Wilhelm, Kurt N1
Williams, Jay G. B101
Williams, Jerry Turner O101
Willoughby, Harold R. F38
Wilson, R. McL. F76
Wind, Solomon D108
Wineman, Aryeh L256
Winkler, Gershon D13, D37
Winston, David F26, F90
Wirszubski, Ch. A67, O131, O137, O144
Witton-Davies, Carlyle L114, L115, L117
Witton-Davies, Mary L114, L115, L117
Wolf, William N1
Wolpin, Nisson L282
Woocher, Jonathan S. D169, D176
Woolf, Max C23
Wright, Dudley F35
Wright, G. Ernest A96
Wright, Wayne C15
Wyschogrod, Michael L18

Yadin, Yigael E33
Yardeni, Myriam A114
Yates, Frances A. O126, O148, O194

Yerushalmi, Yosef Hayim   K40
Yisroel ben Baruch haChassid   L103
Yonge, C.D.   F1

Zahavy, Zev   I16
Zaoui, Andre   D107, D111
Zborowski, Mark   L125
Zeitlin, Solomon   A50, D50, K19
Zenner, Walter P.   K34, M58
Zevin, Shlomo Yosef   L67, L69
Zhitlowsky, Chaim   L94
Ziegler, Julian   O104
Zika, Charles   O176, O181
Zinberg, Israel   B93

Subjects

Aaron b. Moses Ha-Levi Horowitz of Starosselje   L178
Aaron ben Samuel ha-Nasi   B62
Abrabanel, Isaac   H19
Abraham b. Eliezer ha-Levi   J35
Abulafia, Abraham   B78, B81, B89, C45, D49, D125, O70
Abulafia, Todros ben Jehuda   H23
Adam   F43
Adam, Paul   O155
Adam Kadmon   B42, D160, O71, O85, O189
Aesch Mezareph   O74
Afterlife   B79, D87
Agnon, Samuel Joseph   L256, N38
Agrippa, Henry Cornelius   O18, O41, O98, O128, O176, O194
Aharon of Karlin   L281
Akatriel   F48
Alchemy   D24, D178, O9, O74, O84, O146, O148
Alkabez, Solomon b. Moses   J25
Allegory   D93
Alphabet, Hebrew   D32, D35, F86, I10, M7, O1, O52, O61, O62, O63, O79, O100, O102, O140, O167, O168, O184
Alphabet of Rabbi Akiba   F31
Alshekh, Moses   J25
Alter, Yehuda Aryeh Leib   L180
Alter, Yitzhak Meir   L180
Altmann, Alexander   G23
America   O138, O174
American literature   M76
Amulets and talismans   D16, D18, D19, D31, D26, O79
Angelino, Joseph   H14
Angels and angelology   D133, E44, E53, E56, E71, E87, E95, F43, O84
Anski, S.   D178, L94

Subjects

Apocalypse and Apocalyptic   B46,   B85,   B97, B281, C48, D61, D146,
   E44-E46,   E48, E49, E52, E55, E56, E58, E62, E67, E68, E70, E72,
   E75-E79, E81-E86, E90, E93-E96, F31, F33, F40, F74, F82, F83
Apocalypse of Abraham   E43
Apocalypse of Baruch   E39
Apocalypse of Zerubbabel   F31
Apocrypha   E95
Archangelus of Borgo Nuovo   O98
Ariel   F48
Arnold of Vilanova   O70
Art   C71, O195
Ascension of Isaiah   E55
Ashlag, Yehuda   I30
Assumption of Moses   E39, E55, E88, F31
Astrology   C75, D16, D24, O79, O136, O183
Astronomy   E44, I20
Avodah   L135
Azriel b. Menahem of Gerona   B62, H24, H36
Aztecs   O73

Bacon, Francis   O97
Baeck, Leo   N1, N2,
Bakan, David   D159
Baruch (Jeremiah's scribe)   E42
Barukh of Medzebozh   L255, L281
Bellow, Saul   M112, M151
Berdyczewski, Micha Yosef   M131
Bible   see Torah
Blake, William   O59, O78, O97, O111, O123, O133
Blue, Fringe of   D27
Boehme, Jacob   N29, O139
Book(s) of Baruch   E55
Book of Mirrors   see *Sefer Mar'ot Hazove'ot*
Book of Wisdom   F32
Borges, Jorge Luis   O141, O145, O151, O152, O180
Brief Account of Some Travels in Hungaria, Servia &c.   K31
Browne, Edward   K31
Browne, Thomas   O89
Bruno, Giordano   O126
Buber, Martin   B13, B69, B76, L170, M22, M67, M98, M112, M121, N3-N48

Caesarius of Heisterbach   G29
Cahan, Abraham   M76
Cardozo, Abraham Miguel   K16
Cardozo, Isaac   K40
Caro, Joseph   G14, J11, J17, J20, J22, J24
Catharism   H43
Chapman, George   O194
"Chapter on the Elements"   see *Sha ar ha-Yesodot le-Aristo*
Chaucer, Geoffrey   O101, O104
Cheiromancy   I5

Christianity   B21, B24, B39, B43, B45, B93, C30, C33, C34, C37,
    C39, C41, C48, C54, D24, D49, F29, F87, G17, G19, I26, M20, N26,
    N27, O7, O8, O15, O50, O57, O70, O75, O78, O97, O98, O102, O105,
    O108, O109, O112, O114, O119, O120, O122, O123, O125, O126,
    O130, O134, O157, O165, O194, O196
Clavicula Salomonis   see *Mafteaḥ Shelomo*
Colors   D36, O170
Confession   L188
Conjectura Cabbalistica   O76, O109
Conway, Anne   O80, O160, O192
Cordovero, Moses   B66, B78, B85, J25, J29, O32, O98
Creation   B38, B39, B46, B65, B71, B78, C26, C34, C40, C41, C75,
    D67, D68, D73, D78, D111, D137, F58, J33, O4, O77, O191
Cudworth, Ralph   O130

Da'at   G25
Daniel   E39, E45, E71, E83, F31
Dante, Alighieri   O46
David b. Judah ha-Hasid   H42
David of Makow   L131
Dead Sea Scrolls   B10, E57, E59, E60, E64, E65, E67, E71,
    E78, E80, E83, E97, E101
Dee, John   O124, O194
Delmedigo, Yoseph Shlomo   J27
Demut   G25
Desert   D81
Devekut   C50, C69, L123, L130, L203, L235
Dialectics   D96
Dibbuk   D37
Divine Spark   D86
Dönmeh   see Shabbateans and Shabbateanism
Donne, John   O166
Donnolo, Shabbetai   H39
Dov Baer of Mezhirech   B97, L161, L164, L189, L212, L233
Dreams   D170, G20, M74
Dualism   E70
Dubnow, Semen M.   L141
Dürer, Albrecht   O194
Duties of the Heart   see *Ḥovot ha-Levavot*

Edwards, Jonathan   L217
Egyptian mysticism   D181, E48, F28
Ein-Sof   B22, B23, B39, C34, C50, C60, C72, O25, O60, O107, O167
Eisenstadt, Mordecai   K22
Ekstein, Menahem   L277
Eleazar b. Judah of Worms   G12, G18, G25-G27, G34, G36
Elijah   F31, F48, F57
Elijah, Gaon of Vilna   B65, B97, J22, L81, L97, L139, L161, L235,
    L238
Elimelech of Lizensk   L212, L246
Emblems and symbols   F46, O47
England   K44, O97, O118, O125, O130, O191, O194

Subjects 389

Enoch   E39, E44, E49, E50, E55, E70, E71, E74, E78, E80, E94, F31,
    F78, F83
Epstein, Perle   M139, M140
Erasmus, Desiderius   O119, O181
Eschatology   E46, E63, E71, E74, E84, E91, E95, F31
Eser Ẓaḥẓaḥot   H42
Esoteric literature   F74
Esplumoir Merlin   O99
Eternal life   E78
Eternity   D78
Ether, doctrine of   H13
Ethics   D5
Etz Ḥayyim   J15, J30
Evil   C34, D79, D82, D83, J29, J33
Exorcism   J31
Eybeschuetz, Jonathan   K21
Ezekiel, Book of   C26, E77, F49, O25, O157
Ezekiel, poet (first century B.C.E.)   E102
Ezra, Book(s) of   E39, E55, E69, E72, E73

Faith   D145
Falk, Hayyim Samuel Jacob   B63, K11, K14, K15, K32
Feuerbach, Ludwig   J28
Fludd, Robert   O78, O97, O190, O191
Folklore and legends   C11, C18, D102, G32, L128, L234, L278, M64
Fox, George   O172
Franck, Adolphe   C24
Frank, Jacob   B51, B59, B63, B73, B95, B97, C5, K45, K50
    Frankism   B59, B60, B64, B85, K33, K42, K45, K50, K51, L215
Frankl, Viktor   D161, D171
Freemasonry   O21, O23, O30, O37, O40, O55, O56, O63, O71, O77,
    O93, O150
Freud, Sigmund   D147, D153, D154, D156, D159, D168, D170
Fuentes, Carlos   O199

Gaffarel, Jacques   O17
Galante, Abraham   J25
Garment of the Deity   F48, F55, J22
Gate of Heaven   see *Zurath ha 'Olam*
Gates of Wisdom   G34
Geldwerth, Lipa   L282
Gematria   see Numerology
Genesis   O4, O25, O48, O140
Gennadius of Novgorod   O171
German Hasidism   B66, B71, B78, B81, B97, C45, C49, G11, G14, G22,
    G32, G34, G35, G37, N29
Gikatilla, Joseph   B78
Gilgul   see Soul(s), Revolution of
Gill, Alexander, the Elder   O110
Ginzberg, Louis   L133
Giorgi, Francesco   O194
Gnosticism   F48, F56, F70, F75, F76, F79, F80, F88, H15, J19, O25,
    O134

Gnosticism, Jewish B78, C45, D26, F42, F43, F48, F56, F58, F75,
    F76, F86, F88, H15, I24, I25
Goddess, Hebrew D138, D140
Gold, Michael M76
Goldberg, Daniel L282
Golem D9, D11, D13, D14, D28-D30, D33, M153
Good and evil C43, O94
Greek Orthodoxy D49

Haggada E42, E43
Halakah B82
Halevi, Judah B99, H18, H38
Hanina ben Dosa F69
Hasidism B7, B9, B32, B42, B53, B57, B60, B62, B64, B66, B68,
    B70, B73, B77, B81, B83, B85, B87, B94-B96, B98, B100, B101,
    C45, C48, C55, D90, D125, D147, E143, L76-L283, M25, M60, M108,
    M133, M147, M149, M156, N19, N47, N53
Hasidism, Amdur L196
Hasidism, American B4, B14, B86, L127, L166, M29, M45, M50,
    M53, M54, M56, M64, M68, M72, M80, M87, M100, M120, M122-M124,
    M130, M136, M145, M156, M162
Hasidism, anthropological analysis L125
Hasidism, Australian M128
Hasidism, Belzer L161, M57
Hasidism, Beth-el L95
Hasidism, Biblical F47
Hasidism, Breslover L44, L265, M48, M54
Hasidism, Canadian M86, M102
Hasidism, causes of L96
Hasidism, communal life L99, L110, L113, L146
Hasidism, definition and doctrine L90, L103, L111, L119, L121,
    L135-L137, L151, L153, L154, L158, L161, L167, L174, L176,
    L189, L198, L207, L210, L211, L249, L250, L267, L272, L273,
    M33-M35, M132
Hasidism, effects L89, L98, L106, L114, L129, L147, L172, L184,
    L185, L201
Hasidism, Gerer L161, L180
Hasidism, Habad see Hasidism, Lubavitcher
Hasidism, history B77, B85, B92, B93, B95, B97, L110, L113,
    L125, L131, L146, L161, L184, L201, L233, L235, L236, L269,
    L272, N48
Hasidism, Italian M135
Hasidism, Karliner L122, L189, L196
Hasidism, Kotzker L214
Hasidism, legends and folklore L206, L212, L264, L265, M64,
    M152
Hasidism, literature B14, L84, L88, L92, L102, L108, L160,
    L162, L163, L165, L170, L175, L186, L192, L200, L205, L225,
    L229, L234, L244, L256, L278, L280, M76, M92, M98, M121, M131,
    M141, N38
Hasidism, Lubavitcher L24, L120, L161, L173, L177, L182, L191,
    L217, L228, L235, L252, L271, M19, M23, M27, M31, M38,

Subjects 391

    M39, M43, M63, M75, M89, M102, M107, M108, M118, M127, M128, M133, M135, M152
Hasidism, messianism   L193, L204, L218
Hasidism, modern   B84, B88, B92, B94, C5, L82, L88, L161, M24, M33, M34, M35, M41, M49, M57, M62, M74, M85, M86, M90, M95, M109, M110, M113, M133, M134, M136, M137, M143, M150, M161, M164
Hasidism, music and dance   L101, L105, L145, L157, L202, L209, L222, L227, M24, M120
Hasidism, prayer   L181, L208, L231
Hasidism, psychology   D157, D158, D161, D163-D167, D169, D171-D177, D182, D183, L109, L133, L143, L186, L190, L210, L234, L237, L242, L244, L262, L271,
Hasidism, rabbinic   L257
Hasidism, Ruzhin-Sadagora   L161
Hasidism, Satmarer   L235, M37, M53, M81, M88, M108, M124, M127, M160
Hasidism, sociological analysis   D182, L210, L219, M128, M130
Hasidism, Squarer   M103, M126
Hasidism, Worker   L281
Hasidism, worship   L259, L263
Haskalah   L96, L171
Hebrew University   M17
Heikhalot literature   B62, F45, F48, F53, F54, F58, F77, F78, F83, F85, H12, L162
Hellenism   D49, E81, E82, E100, F28, F39, F46, L132
Helmont, Franciscus Mercurius van   O7, O80, O81, O160, O172, O192
Hermetism   O77, O171, O194
Herrera, Abraham Cohen   J38, J41
Heschel, Abraham Joshua   B90, N49-N55
Hinduism   D39, D40, E143, O25
Historiography, Jewish   K35, M47, M154, N1, N13, N57, N58, N61, N64, N67
Hokhmath Ha-Egoz   G18, G23, G27
Hokhmath Ha-Nefesh   G25
Holocaust   J36, M14, M15, M94, M156
Horowitz, Isaiah   J26, J33
Hoter b. Shelomo   F87, F89, H41
Hovot ha-Levavot   G31
Humanism   B93, O120

Ibn Gabirol, Solomon   B62, H10, H28
Ibn Latif, Isaac   H29, H32
Ibn Paquda, Bahya   B99, G31
Iggeret Hakodesh   H25
Imagery   C71, D143
Immanence   D63, F50
Immortality   D62, D87, E65, E68, E78, F44
Iran   E70
Isaac b. Jacob ha-Kohen   D83
Isaac the Blind   B55, B62
Isaiah   E44, E84, E90
Islam   D39, D40, D49, F29, G13, G15, G16, G31, H17, H27, H30, H33, H34, I26

Israel b. Eliezer (Ba'al Shem Tov)   B60,   B63-B65, B73, B97, K20,
   K27, L1,   L2, L4-L7, L9-L11, L19, L25, L42, L43, L49, L68, L99,
   L100, L111, L124, L142, L144, L161, L169, L179, L183, L189,
   L207, L212, L214, L235
Israel of Rizin   L132, L212
Israeli, Isaac   H21

Jacob b. Asher   G14
Jacob Isaac ha-Hozeh of Lublin   L255, L281
Jacob Joseph ha-Kohen   L99, L107, L161
Jaldabaoth   F75
"Jeremiah Apocalypse"   see Baruch (Jeremiah's scribe)
Jerusalem   D59
Jewish literature   L160, L175, L205, L280
Job, Book of   O137
Joel b. Uri Heilprin   B63
Johanan ben Zakkai   F52, F63, F73
Jubilees, Book of   E55
Judah b. Samuel he-Hasid   G21, G29, G36
Judah Hasid of Shidlov   G19
Judah Loew b. Bezalel (of Prague)   D11, D46, D125, J18, J32, J37
Jung, Carl G.   O185

Kabbala Denudata   O7, O9, O18, O59
Kabbalah (definition of word)   B20, B22, B23, B25, B31, B50, B52,
   C54, F61
Kabbalah, origin and history   B20, B23, B25, B28, B31, B41, B43-
   B45, B47, B49, B52, B54, B55, B66, B78, B79, B81, B96, B99,
   B100, C21, C24, C26-C33, C35, C37, C38-C40, C44-C49, C52, C54,
   C55, C58, C61, C63, C75, F45, F58
Kabbalah in Judaism, role of   D88
Kabbalah Unveiled   O106
Kafka, Franz   L168, M153
Kalisker, Abraham   L130
Kallo, Yizhak Isaac   L58
Kaplan, Mordecai Menahem   N37
Kavod   D106
Kavvanah   B82, C50, D103, D107, D109, D119, E66, L135, L142, L181,
   L232, M30, M151
Kedushah   D106
Keith, George   O81
Kelippah, kelippot   H24, H36, J33
Kethoneth Passim   L141
Khumrat, Heinrich   O27
Kierkegaard, Soren   L214
Kircher, Athanasius   O189
Klein, A.M.   L229
Kook, Abraham Isaac   B76, D46, D56, M21, M28, M32, M36, M49, M52,
   M55, M59, M67, M84, M96, M119
Kook, Zvi Yehudah   M28
Kotsk, Menahem Mendle of   L214, L224, L283
Krochmal, Nachman   M154
Kuzari   H18, H38, D46, D56

Langer, Jiri M77
Lefevre d'Etaples O177
Leibnitz, Gottfried Wilhelm D159, O192
Lévi, Eliphas O11, O179
Levi Yitzhak of Berditchev L99, L161, L212, L221
Lilith D83, D128, F48
Literary criticism M104, M105, M158
Loebel, Israel L172
Logotherapy D161, D171
"Lost Pseudepigraphic Prophecies" E39
Lowry, Malcolm O135
Lully, Raymond O70, O98, O194
Luria, Isaac B62, B64, B66, B81, B85, C5, J11, J15, J20, J24, J28, O109
Doctrines B39, B46, C45, C48, C54, C55, C58, J19, J23, J30, J33, J36, J38, J39, O5, O196
Luther, Martin O70, O139
Luzzatto, Moses Chaim J10, J12-J14, J16

Ma'asseh Merkabah F48, F83
Mafteaḥ Shelomo O45
Magen David see Star of David
Magic B39, B43, B71, B85, B91, D15-D37, D57, D90, E61, F48, F77, F83, J21, J22, L164, O11-O14, O16, O45, O50, O60, O69, O79, O84, O85, O87, O94, O95, O102, O103, O121, O126, O129, O134, O146, O153, O158, O162, O165, O168, O173, O176, O177, O188, O193, O197
Mailer, Norman M159
Maimon, Solomon L79
Maimonides, Abraham G24
Maimonides, Moses B57, B99, H16, H40, O54
Malamud, Bernard M76, M112, M141
Manasseh ben Israel B63
Marlowe, Christopher O194
Matronit see Shekhinah
Medicine G38
Meditation D113, D120, D125, J21, J22, J40, L128, O161, O175
Megalleh Temirin L83
Meir of Premishlan L281
Meister Eckhart E74
Menachem Mendel of Kotzk L212, L214, L224, L235
Mendele Mocher Seforim L192
Merkabah mysticism B42, B71, B78, C36, C45, C49, E101, E102, F35, F48, F56, F58, F65, F67, F68, F72, F74, F83-F85, F88, F89, G18, G27, O10, O117
Merkavah Rabbah F83
Meshal Ha-Kadmoni I29
Mesilat Yesharim J12, J16
Messiahs and Messianism B57, B64, B71, B79, B81, B85, B87, B97, C5, C34, C78, D38-D61, D90, E67, E71-E73, F31, F33, F40, F68, F74, G11, J16, J35, K34, L176, L193, L204, L218, O52
Messiahs, False B27, B51, B61, B64, B65, B87, D45, K8, K12, K13, K22, K24, K34, K43 (see also Jacob Frank, Frankism, Shabbetai Zevi and Shabbateanism)

Metatron C36, D130, F48, F83
Mickiewicz, Adam K30, K51
Midrash Hallel F67
Midrash ha-Ne'lam F51
Milah (Hebrew word) F60
Milton, John O65, O72, O76, O90, O97, O104, O109, O110, O117, O194
Mishnath Shir ha-Shirim F48
Molko, Solomon C5
Monas Hieroglyphica O124
Monis, Judah O64, O138
Moonism O194
More, Henry O17, O76, O80, O97, O130, O160, O191, O196
Moreh Nebhukhim O54
Moses B72, E88, E89, D153
Moses de Leon B62
Moshe-Leib of Sassov L281
Musar Movement B97, L199
Music and dance D121, D148, L101, L105, L145, L157, L194, L202, L209, L222, L227
Mystery literature F39
Mystical testimonies C12
Mysticism, modern B6, B41, B90, C55, C63, C69, C77, C78, D1, D150, D151, M17, M18, M20, M22, M40, M46, M49, M61, M70, M71, M78, M79, M82, M83, M90, M91, M93, M97, M99, M101, M106, M110, M111, M115, M129, M132, M144, M146, M148, M155, M157, M164, N3, N21, N44,
Myth D127-D143, E52, L152, M131
Mythology, Egyptian D74

Nachman of Bratslav D46, D56, L5, L21, L44, L61, L69, L75, L99, L124, L161, L168, L189, L197, L200, L212, L213, L225, L230, L242, L258, L261, L262, L268, L270, L274, L279, L280
Nahman of Kossov L134
Nahmanides H25, H45, H46
Nahum of Chernobyl L99
Najara, Moses J25
Name(s) of God B43, C41, D34, D69, D78, E50, E97, F58, O1, O84, O129, O140, O177
Naphtali of Ropshitz L255, L281
Narboni, Moses H31, H35
Nathan of Gaza K47, K49
Nehunia ben Ha-Qanah F77
Neo-Hasidism B14, D158, M16, M42-M44, M46, M51, M60, M62, M109, M110, M137, M146, M147, N23, N49
Neturei Karta M81
Newton, Isaac O191, O196
Noah, Apocalypse of E49
Noam Elimelekh L246
Numerology B15, B16, B18, B19, B22, B42, B44-B46, B48, C23, C34, D22, D32, D35, D122, O19, O23, O24, O29, O34, O42, O46, O47, O52, O61-O63, O69, O79, O84, O85, O100, O107, O143, O150, O161, O163, O168, O170

Obadiah b. Abraham Maimonides   H20
Occultism   D21, O16, O22, O26, O51-O53, O58, O60, O62, O73, O77, O82, O85, O86, O91, O92, O94-O96, O113, O115, O122, O134, O143, O147, O150, O153, O156, O157, O162, O164, O169, O170, O173, O179, O185, O188, O200-O202
Ogdoas   F48
Oral Law   D91

Pagan symbols   F53
Pannwitz, Rudolf   L152
Pantheism   D73
PARDES   D101
Pasqually, Martines   B63
Passivity   L165
Passover   D122
Path of Life   see *Tur Orah Ḥayyim*
Path of the Upright   see *Mesillat Yesharim*
Paul, Visions of   F65,
"Paut Neteru"   D74
Penitentials   G37
Perl, Joseph   L83
Perlmuter, Moshe Arie   K21
Pesikta Rabbati   F40
Philo Judaeus   B85, C36, C39, F28, F38, F39, F41, F44, F45, F62, F90, L132, N56, O71, O196
Philosophy and mysticism   B73, C20, D65, F87, F89, H32, H40, H41, M30, N11, N14, N19, N43, N44, N46, N63
Pico della Mirandola   O17, O67, O75, O78, O89, O98, O126, O131, O137, O176, O194
Pietism and Pietists   F34, F47, G20, G21, G24, G26, G30, G35-G37
Piety   D114, D116, D117, F34, L128, M108, M156
Pinhas of Koretz   L245, L255, L281
Plato   C39
Postel, Guillaume   O17, O108, O114
Prayer   D78, D102-D126, J35, L181, L231, L251,
Prophets and Prophecy   B99, C45, D57, D144, D145, E66, E79, E95, K34
    Pseudepigraphic   E39, E95
Proselytes   I31
Provence   B71, B78, H37
Psalms   E40, E51, E53, E61, E64
Psychiatry and psychology   B23, C3, D109, D147-D183, K48, L186, M157, O116, O134, O185, O197
Puerta del Cielo   J38, J41
Pukhovitser, Judah Leib   L187

Rabad of Posquieres   H26
Rabbinic Judaism   L129
Rabbinical literature   D17, D127, E99, F32, F33, F42, F43, F47, F48, F50, F53, F57, F60, F61, F64, F65, F67, F72, F78, F82-F84, H12
Raphson, Joseph   O196

Recanati, Menachem H44
Redemption B38, F64, L150, L176, L198, N26
Reformation O120, O194
Reincarnation B67
Religious authority D85, D112
Renaissance O125, O128, O144, O171, O194
Repentance C74, D111, D118, F64, G22, G37
Resurrection of the dead B79, E71, E78
Reubeni, David C5
Reuchlin, Johann O38, O75, O89, O98, O112, O120, O176, O181
Re'uyot Yehezkel F83
Revelation B38, D92, D95, D98, D99, D100, J39, M30
Revelation, Book of O157
"Revelation of R. Joshua B. Levi" F31
Ricci, Paul O98
Righteous, Doctrine of D110
Ritual D105, D137, E52
Rosenroth, Christian Knorr von see *Kabbala Denudata*
Rosenzweig, Franz M142
Rosicrucians O20, O77, O146, O148, O194
Roth, Philip M76
Ruaḥ ha-Kodesh D63, D127
Russian dissenting sects L183

Saadiah Gaon B85, D79, D92, D97, O196
Sabbath and festivals D105, D122, D124, L249
Sachs, Nelly M65
Safed mysticism B83, B85, B94, B101, C55, H37, J11, J20-J22, J24, J25, J31, J35
Sahula, Isaac b. Solomon Abi I29
Saints see *Ẓaddik*
Salanter, Israel L199
Samael D81, D83
Sandalfon D130
Satire L83, L84
Saurat, Denis O90, O109, O110
Schneersohn, Joseph I. L112, M59
Schneerson, Menachem Mendel L171, M116, M125
Scholem, Gershom G. D60, D88, K21, K35, K48, M114, N47, N56-N69
Schweitzer, Albert N60
Sectarianism, Jewish E100
Sefer ha-Bahir B65, H11, H22
Sefer Hakhmoni H39
Sefer Ha-Razim F83
Sefer ha-Rokeaḥ G12, G26
Sefer ha-Shorashim O131
Sefer Ḥasidim G4, G17, G20, G21, G28, G30, G33, G35, G36, G38
Sefer Mar'ot Ha-Ẓove'ot H42
Sefer Raziel B62
Sefer Ta'amei Hamiẓvot H44
Sefer Yetzirah B22, B26, B27, B42, B47-B49, B62, B65, B89, C26, C36, C39, C58, F35-F37, F45, F59, F66, F71, H12, H39, O23, O56, O62, O102, O179, O184

Subjects 397

Sefirot   B24, B39, B42, B43, B46, B66, B89, C21, C36, C41, C55,
  C58, C60, C75, D64, D74, D76, D78, D108, D152, F71, H42, J22,
  J23, O1, O22, O25, O42, O60, O68, O71, O77, O84, O87, O91, O107,
  O122, O127, O162, O167, O170, O173, O190
Sefirotic Tree C60, C61, D73-D78, D160, J23, M99, O62, O87, O127,
  O132, O143, O154, O158, O161, O178, O190, O198
Servetus, Michael O149
Setzer, S.H. M26
Sex and marriage in Kabbalah B39, B51, B67, C78, D160, F62, H25,
  M73, M163
Sha'ar ha-yesodot le-Aristo H21
Shabbateans and Shabbateanism B60, B64, B81, B85, B95, C45, K9,
  K12, K13, K16, K19, K21, K24, K26, K36, K41, K47, K49
  Doctrine D90, K10
  Effects D45, D48, D58, D90, K34, K40, L124, L235
  History K9, K37-K39
Shabbetai Zevi, B51, B53, B57, B61, B63-B65, B73, B85, B95, B97,
  B100, B101, C5, K7, K8, K10, K13, K17, K18, K20, K23, K25, K27,
  K28, K31, K35, K41, K43, K48, L111, N60
  Reports of K7, K8, K10, K28, K29, K31, K44, K46
Shakespeare, William O159, O182, O194
Shapiro, Meir L282
Shekhinah B82, C36, C50, D63, D127, D129, D134, D135, D138, F50,
  H42, J22, O22
Shi'ur Komah B62, F48, F55, F81, F83, F87, F89, H31, H35
Shneur Zalman of Lyady L68, L99, L120, L126, L177, L189, L191,
  L220, L235, L239
Shulḥan Arukh G14
Sifre Zuta F30
Simeon b. Yohai F31
Sin and punishment D80, J31, J33
Singer, Isaac Bashevis K35, M66, M138, M163
Sixtus IV O98
Sod Ha'efshar H42
Song of Songs O147
Soul(s) B24, B89, C36, C41, C60, C72, C74, D84, D86, D87, G25,
  H27, H33, J22, L115, L148, L271, O52, O60, O63, O116
  Pre-existence of B22, F32
  Revolution of N68, O5, O6, O32
Spanish Kabbalah B75, B78, B79, C49, H12, H14, H23, H29, H37,
  J35, I26
Spenser, Edmund O82, O97, O194
Spinoza, Baruch de B57, B61, C42, K20, K27, L111, O196
Star of David C75, D131, D139
Stiles, Ezra O44, O54, O138, O142, O174
Supernaturalism M58
Swedenborg, Emanuel O66, O78
Symbols and Symbolism F46

Tanya L173, L182, L191
Tarniks K24
Teraphim G32
Testament of Abraham E43, E87, E89, E91, E92

Testament of Solomon O103
Testaments of the Twelve Patriarchs E39, E41, E42
Tetragrammaton C43, D20, D148, E61, F59, O94, O190
Thenaud, Jean O98
Theodore, King of Corsica K32
Theosophy D62, O25, O27, O28, O31-O33, O35-O37, O39, O43, O48, O68, O83, O88, O203
Thirty-six just men D89, D115, M25
T'naei Nefesh LeHasagat HaHasidut L277
Toledot Yaakob Yosef L107
Torah C50, C54, C60, C74, D91-D101, E47, E54, E61, E76, E85
Tradition D95, D98, D99, D100
Tree of Life see *Etz Ḥayyim*
Tur Orah Ḥayyim G14
Tzemach Tzedek L171

Vajda, Georges H41
Vaughan, Thomas O97
Vedanta D39, D40
Vidas, Elijah ben Moses de J34
Vital, Hayyim J25, J39, J40
Viturbo, Edigio di O98
Volozhiner, Hayyim ben Isaac L276

Wallant, Edward Lewis M76
Weber, Max L166
Werbemacher, Hanna Rachel L99
Wiesel, Elie M69, M92
Wisdom literature F32, H14
Wisdom of Solomon H14
Wisdom religion O25, O35
Wolfe of Zbarazh L281
World view D72
World(s) B24, B39, B46, B66, C40, C41, C43, C60, C68, C72, C74, O60, O62, O71, O77, O85, O94, O107, O132, O167

Yaldabaoth F48, F75
Yeats, William Butler O97, O106
Yiddish L275, M56

Ẓaddik B60, D110, D114, L84, L103, L140, L155, L159, L164, L175, L190, L213, L235, L240, L246, L262, L263, L269, M64, M137, L175
Zechariah E79, E84
Zen L117, L149, L232, L243, L248, L253, L254
Zienba, Menachem L282
Zionism D46, D48, D56, D90, L99, L124, L161, L188, L197, M161
Zohar B22, B26-B28, B30, B32, B42, B43, B46-B49, B62, B64-B66, B71, B78, B79, B81, B85, B88, B89, B101, C36, C37, C39, C45, C48, C54, C55, C58, D46, D56, E56, H10, H11, H14, H23, I19-I31, M148, N56, O52, O56, O150
　　Authorship I19
　　Doctrine I27

Influence of   D156, H42, I22, I23, I29, M65, O54, O65, O66, O72,
    O90, O99, O109
  Influences on   H24, H36, I24-I26
  Interpretations   D149, I27, I28, I30, I31, O22, O186
  Origin   I19, I21
Zoroastrianism   E74
Zurath ha 'Olam   H29
Żwingli, Ulrich   O70